Footprints on the Frontier

FOOTPRINTS
ON THE
FRONTIER

A History of the Sisters of Saint Joseph
Concordia, Kansas

BY

SISTER M. EVANGELINE THOMAS, Ph.D.

Professor of History
Marymount College
Salina, Kansas

THE NEWMAN PRESS
WESTMINSTER, MARYLAND
1948

Nihil Obstat:

LEO A. CORESSEL, S.J., S.T.D.
Censor Deputatus

Imprimatur:

✠ FRANK A. THILL, D.D., Ph.D., J.C.L.
Bishop of Salina
July 15, 1948

PRINTED IN THE UNITED STATES OF AMERICA
BY GRAPHIC PRODUCTION CORP., NEW YORK

DEDICATION

*To my own mother and to all the mothers
of the Sisters of Saint Joseph of Concordia,
living or dead, this volume is lovingly and
respectfully dedicated. Without their devotion to a cause and their cooperation with the
the religious vocations of their daughters, the
work of the Sisters of Saint Joseph on the
frontiers of the Middle West would have
been impossible.*

Acknowledgments

Research necessary for a work of this scope has sent the author to archival centers throughout the country. Material has been found in out-of-the-way places as well as in prominent archival collections. Months of work in civil and ecclesiastical depositories have unearthed unexpected manuscript material which makes possible an authenticated story of the struggles and achievements of the Sisters of Saint Joseph of Concordia. History makers are seldom concerned with records; therefore, the present author feels satisfied to have located material contained herein which, although sporadic and sketchy, nevertheless, has enabled the construction of a reasonably accurate mosaic.

It would give undue length to this acknowledgment to mention the names of all who have assisted the author during the past seven years. To some, however, is owed a debt of gratitude which cannot be passed over in silence.

The author would first thank most sincerely her Community and especially three of its Mothers General, Mother Antoinette Cuff (deceased), Mother Mary Rose Waller (deceased), Mother Mary Chrysostom Wynn, and the present Generalate for encouragement and wholehearted interest in the project.

To His Excellency, the Most Reverend Frank A. Thill, Bishop of Salina, the author wishes to express gratitude for critical reading of the manuscript and for the Foreword to the volume.

To the Right Reverend Peter K. Guilday, Ph.D., dean of American Catholic historians and her former professor, whose advice has been of inestimable value during the writing of this book and who died as the book was nearing completion, the author acknowledges appreciation.

To Professor Richard J. Purcell, Ph.D., LL.B., who while on leave of absence from the Catholic University to the War Production Board, read the manuscript in its entirety and offered helpful suggestions, the author acknowledges a debt of gratitude. Doctor Purcell's interest in this work and in the writer's graduate study at Catholic University has been of great assistance.

To Reverend Mother Rose Miriam, Superior General of the Sisters of Saint Joseph of Rochester, and to Mother Alexine of the Sisters of Saint Joseph of LaGrange, is expressed appreciation for the use of manuscript materials from their archives. To the Reverend Angelus Lingenfelser, O.S.B., archivist of the Kansas Catholic Historical Archives, St. Benedict's College, Atchison, Kansas, for access to materials in that collection; to the Most Reverend Paul Schulte, Archbishop of Indianapolis, for the use of the Leavenworth Diocesan Archives; and to His Eminence Francis Cardinal Spellman for the use of the Archdiocesan Archives of New York, Dunwoodie Seminary, Yonkers, New York, the author is grateful.

A debt of gratitude is due the librarians of Catholic University, the Library of Congress, the Kansas State Historical Society, and the Harvey County, Kansas, Historical Society.

Finally, gratitude is expressed to the Reverend Leo A. Coressel, S.J., S.T.D., professor of dogmatic theology at Saint Marys College, Saint Marys, Kansas, and professor of philosophy and religion at Marymount College, Salina, Kansas, for censoring the manuscript; to the Reverend Adam C. Ellis, S.J., J.C.D., professor of canon law, Saint Mary's College, Saint Marys, Kansas, for reading of the chapter on Papal Approbation; to Sister Genevieve Hogan, head of the English department, Marymount College, for practical assistance in preparing the manuscript for the printer; and to Sister Leonida Loch of the art department, Marymount College, for art work on the cover and book jackets.

Foreword

This book is the record of a courageous and completely successful pioneering effort on the part of five Religious Sisters of the Congregation of Saint Joseph to extend the frontiers of the Kingdom of Christ from New York State into what at the time was the hinterland of Kansas. It is valuable because it affords the opportunity to study a comprehensible detail of the bewildering panorama of portraits and events connected with the settlement and development of the great plains section of our Midwest. It is one more chapter, a very worthy one, in the over-all story of our Catholic Religious Sisterhoods and their heroic contributions to the life of the Church and the history of a part of these United States.

To mitigate the possible disappointment of some readers, it should be said in the very beginning that this book, like all others, has its limitations. The author makes no effort to discuss the application of religion to the generation that discovered and more recently verified the formula $E = mc^2$. Moreover, there is in this book what Mr. Aldous Huxley calls "the unfortunate servitude to historical fact—the idolatrous preoccupation with events and things in time." The discerning reader with a trained ecclesiastical mind will look in vain for any evaluation of our Sisters of Saint Joseph of Concordia in the light of that sanctity and personal holiness of life inseparably associated in the Catholic Church with those who establish or promote great works of religion.

The answer is, of course, that the author set out to write history, not philosophy or hagiography; and that, in the measurable reality of the historical facts and events she records, there can be found material and conclusions for other writers to amplify in the future. That other writers will take off from the solid runway put down by Sister Evangeline is quite certain, for the Congregation already has eleven Sisters with doctorates in science and the liberal arts serving on the faculty of Marymount College, its noblest and proudest institution.

In the meantime, I wish to testify for the sake of the record that there is indisputable evidence of true holiness in the lives of many of the Sisters. The Congregation as a whole is noteworthy for an unusual degree of sacrificial devotion to the Church. No work of religion is foreign to these Sisters who serve as teachers in the poorest and most isolated missions of northwestern Kansas with as much zeal as they display in conducting their College. In the six hospitals they own and staff in the Diocese of Salina and elsewhere, in their home for the aged and in our diocesan orphanage, they fulfill a ministry of love that is Godlike in its care of the needy and Christlike in the redemptive way it accepts pain for the sake of alleviating the suffering of others. Such living is not compounded of wool and fudge. It is rather the painful daily effort to conform each successive act, however unimportant, small, and vulgar, to the pattern of the Gospel and the norms of Christian mysticism.

The Sisters have published this book of the history of their Congregation to commemorate the silver jubilee of the establishment of Marymount College for women in the city of Salina. They have good reason to commemorate Marymount's jubilee, for, although the College is still comely in the bloom of its youthful life of only twenty-five years, it is the oldest liberal arts college for women in the State of Kansas. It has a superb teaching staff of thirty-three faculty members, each of whom is endowed with the proper academic degree required by the North Central Association with which the College is affiliated. Its student body of three hundred women, mostly from the Midwest, but including representatives from seventeen states of the Union, from Hawaii, China, and Puerto Rico, is alert, ambitious, and vividly aware of the modern world and the opportunities it offers educated women who are willing to work intelligently and unselfishly.

For all these blessings I thank Almighty God and beg His continued providential care of Marymount College and the Congregation of the Sisters of Saint Joseph of Concordia.

Frank A. Thill

BISHOP OF SALINA

Bishop's House
Salina, Kansas
Feast of the Patronage of St. Joseph, April 14, 1948

Preface

For the past half century a number of historians have followed the Turner thesis of the influence of the frontier on American life and culture. At times the frontier thesis has been overemphasized; however, it is generally conceded that when the term *frontier* is interpreted, not so much in the narrow sense of an ever-moving fringe of civilization, but rather as a need to be faced, a challenge to be met and conquered, it holds wider significance. The frontier is a challenge; therefore, whether the culture be simple or complex, there will always be frontiers to be conquered.

Perhaps the one phase of the frontier thesis which has been most neglected is the religious phase. What has been the influence of religion on the frontier and what has been the influence of the frontier on religion? What has been the influence of the hundreds of communities of religious men and women on the various frontiers of this and of other countries? This story has never been told adequately; in fact, the story will never be told fully because of an almost innate desire of those who exercise this influence to do each day's work as well as possible without thought of human recognition. Hence, source material is often sporadic and sketchy.

The American melting pot has received representatives of European cultures and has made them as truly American as those whose cradles were in this land. The frontier has influenced them even as it in turn has been influenced by the cultures which they have transplanted in this country.

It is the purpose of this book to trace the beginnings and growth of one Motherhouse of the Sisters of Saint Joseph. There are many other foundations of this Congregation which have older and perhaps more varied histories, for in the United States alone there are over twenty-five motherhouses of the Sisters of Saint Joseph with an aggregate membership of about fifteen thousand. Further, these are but a small portion of the total number of women belonging to religious orders—all working in much the same manner, with the same zeal, and for the same ends in this mighty country of ours. Nevertheless, what is written of one unit in this body of religious women is typical of the work of all.

Footprints on the Frontier traces the history of the Sisters of Saint Joseph of Concordia, Kansas, and their work in nine states of the Middle West. No attempt is made to write the individual histories of other foundations of the Sisters of Saint Joseph in this country [1] except to follow in chronological sequence the beginnings in Le Puy, France (1650), through Saint Louis (1836) to Canandaigua, New York (1854),[2] and on to Kansas in 1883. Hence, the story of the houses in France is followed until 1836; that of Saint Louis until the opening of Canandaigua; and that of the New York foundations until the footprints are again traced westward to Kansas. At that point the detailed history of the Sisters of Saint Joseph of Concordia will be picked up.

If the term *frontier* is to be interpreted as meaning a *challenge*, it becomes necessary to describe the environments into which the various foundations entered. When a person understands the political, economic, social, and religious conditions in a region, it becomes easier to evaluate that need and how that need has been met. There will be much attention given, therefore, to historical background and little to the anecdotal and the emotional in this work.

---

[1] Appendixes contain statistical tables on the various motherhouses of the Sisters of St. Joseph in the United States.
[2] Canandaigua became the nucleus of the Buffalo and Rochester communities of the Sisters of St. Joseph.

Contents

Contents *(Continued)*

PART ONE

PART ONE

Carlson, Cincinnati
The Most Reverend Frank A. Thill, D.D., Bishop of Salina

CHAPTER I

European Background and French Foundations, 1650-1836

No period of modern history has more of the romantic, as well as more of the sordid, than that century of wars and upheaval following the Protestant revolt of the sixteenth century. European society became revolutionized during those years which witnessed epoch-making political, economic, and social changes.

Historians have come to realize that the forces which precipitated the cleavage within Christianity in the sixteenth century were not conditions which had developed rapidly and precipitately; they were a cumulative complexity, not dominantly religious, but rather the outcome of economic and social conditions. The far-reaching aftermaths of the civil and religious wars, which followed and piled up in the wake of Luther's revolt, left in their wake conditions which by the middle of the seventeenth century in Europe cried for remedy.

France during this century was not left untouched by heretical doctrines and internecine conflict. The rise of the Huguenots, the followers of Calvin, and their penetration into positions of high esteem met with the opposition of the house of Valois. Intrigue and cunning were to be found on both sides in the War of the Three Henrys, a struggle which terminated in the extinction of the house of Valois and the accession of the Bourbon dynasty to the throne of France in the person of Henry of Navarre, known as Henry IV.

Much legend and romance are interwoven with the name of Henry of Navarre. That he laid the foundation of the later greatness of the Bourbons cannot be questioned. His task was tremendous; the rejuvenation of France along political lines was minor in comparison with the problems of social and economic nature that he faced. Although not too spectacular progress was made during his reign, yet his efforts were in the right direction, as evidenced by his economic system, his spirit of religious toleration, and his ventures in the way of social amelioration. From the time of Henry IV down to the time of the "Citizen King," Louis Philippe, the several Bourbons followed more or less in the directions pointed out by Henry IV.

In 1610, upon the death of Henry IV, the throne passed to his son, Louis XIII. During his minority his mother, Marie d'Medici, another member of that influential Florentine family which had wormed its way into the French court and even into the royal family, assumed the regency. It was a period beset by corruption at court, intrigues of rival parties, and the rise of the cardinal-statesman, Armand-Jean Cardinal Richelieu.

More than any other character in modern French history, Richelieu sponsored the growth of absolutism and the dominance of France in European politics, art, literature, and culture in general. At one time he assured Louis XIII that he would make the royal power so secure that it might be "comme un ferme rocher qui brise tout ce qui le huerte."[1]

In this twofold policy, to make the king supreme in France and France supreme in Europe, lay Richelieu's course. To accomplish the former, a stringent policy was pursued in dealing with anyone or anything within the country which militated against or detracted from the power of Louis XIII. The accomplishment of his second aim necessitated the pursuit of a series of wars, now on the side of the Catholic party within the Empire and then in league with the Protestant king of Sweden against the Hapsburgs of Austria. Strategy and diplomacy rather than religion prompted the role of France in the Thirty Years' War, 1618-1648.

Thus, about the time of the death of both Richelieu and the king, in the early 1640's France had arisen from the rank of a second-rate power to that of the foremost nation in European affairs. The accession of Louis XIV, the termination of the Thirty Years' War, and the establishment of the Sisters of Saint Joseph at Le Puy, France, took place within the short space of seven years.

About the middle of the seventeenth century, the prevailing ignorance of even the better-educated Frenchmen was manifested by widespread superstition found even among the upper classes. Manners of the times kept pace with the intellectual darkness of the

---

[1] "As a firm rock which crushes all that opposes it." *Catholic Encyclopedia,* vol. XIII, p. 47.

people and highways were infested with robbers who preyed upon travelers.

Conditions were such as to try the characters of men and to bring out the deeper qualities of the human heart. Yet society was permeated by a general relaxation of morals and a libertine indifference to many of what ought to have been the most sacred ties. Such conditions precede, accompany, and follow the contempt of one man for all others.

Virtue was held at naught throughout the land, the fashion of the day being against it; and in a country where all things were fashion many a person, whom we have every right to believe actually substantially virtuous, assumed the appearance of vice for the sake of being like the rest. Suffice it to say that even the libertinism of the court of Louis XIV, great as it undoubtedly was, assumes a very mitigated appearance when compared with that of his father's.

Such was the state of affairs in France at the end of the reign of Louis XIII—everything was shaken, nothing fixed; laws and jurisdictions were unsettled and undefined; feudal rights and privileges, no longer existing as a system, disturbed that order which they had previously maintained; cities and fortresses were in the hands of individuals; governors of towns often possessed more power than the king himself; art and science were just beginning to bud forth; war was waged at every point of the frontier; ill-regulated and scanty were the finances; vehement fanaticism, a general grossness of manners, and depravity of morals pervaded the higher classes of society and seeped down to the lower ranks. Without comparing this picture with what followed, it is impossible to understand the character and the epoch of Louis XIV.[2]

Catholic Christianity had meant the civilization of the French people. The religious cleavage had been a cultural cataclysm to them, for it had unleashed passions that vented themselves first on the Church and then on the people in such fashion as to threaten the extinction of the human virtues upheld by Christianity.[3] It is stated that in one diocese alone heresy held sway in eighty towns where the

[2] George P. R. James, *The Life and Times of Louis the Fourteenth*, 2 vols. (London, 1890-1891), vol. I, pp. 28-37; vol. II, pp. 95-134.

Louis N. Prunel, *La renaissance catholique en France au XVII siècle* (Paris, 1921), *passim*.

[3] Albert S. Foley, *St. Regis: A Social Crusader* (Milwaukee, 1941), p. 67.

priests had been murdered or expelled and church property destroyed or expropriated. Many people had abandoned the faith of their fathers as a matter of policy during the Huguenot ascendancy. Others, from lack of good priests or proper training, had drifted away, and it became very difficult to reconcile these people with the Church.[4]

As Saint Ignatius Loyola revolutionized the idea of religious life for men, so did Saint Francis de Sales introduce new ideas regarding that for women. In establishing the Sisters of the Visitation in 1610, Francis de Sales realized that a great change had come over the world since the days of Saint Anthony or Saint Bernard. The holy Bishop of Geneva understood that up to that time the austerities of the religious life of women hardly allowed any except the most robust to undertake it. He believed it was possible to moderate the conditions without lowering the ideal; what would be lost in austerities would be regained by abnegation. He knew so well how to infuse into his daughters this spirit of abnegation that, with a rule notably mild, they have not ceased for more than three centuries to adorn the Church with the highest virtues. His first plan was to have a congregation without a cloister, uniting with the exercise of the contemplative life visits to the poor in their homes, whence the name *Visitation*.

Thus, a new form of religious community came into existence, although the Visitandines later became cloistered on account of the opposition of the Archbishop of Lyons. Francis de Sales acquiesced to this demand and in after years would exclaim, "I do not know why they call me the founder of the Visitation, for I have not done what I wished to do, and I have done what I did not wish to do." In establishing the cloister for his Visitandines he wrote to the superior: "If the Visitation should lead to the establishment of other Congregations of pious servants of God, even without its being itself established, it would not be less agreeable to God, for it would have less cause for self-love." This hope was fulfilled in later years in the es-

---

[4] *Ibid.*, p. 65.

[5] Louis Sempe, *St. Francis de Sales* (Milwaukee, 1933), pp. 34-35.
   Robert Ornsby, *The Life of St. Francis de Sales, Bishop and Prince* (New York, 1860), pp. 103-116.
   Marie Jean Hamon, *Vie de St. François de Sales,* 2 vols. (Paris, 1883).
   Louis-Victor-Emile Bougaud (tr.), *St. Chantal and the Foundation of the Visitation Order* (New York, 1895).
   Ferdinand Mourret, *A History of the Catholic Church,* 6 vols. (St. Louis, 1946), vol. VI, pp. 96-98.

tablishment of the Sisters of Saint Joseph at Le Puy, France.[6] The founders of that Community attributed the original idea of its establishment to Saint Francis de Sales and bid its members "cherish a very special devotion to him . . . and do all in your power to acquire the spirit he instilled into the Visitation at its institution."[7]

The origin of the Sisters of Saint Joseph took place in Puy-en-Velay, in the southern part of France. Considered one of the quaintest and most picturesque towns in France, Le Puy slumbered in unruffled security among the highlands of Massif Central. While the rest of France was convulsed in the last of the great civil and religious wars, this little city escaped actual combat. Richelieu's campaigns of aggrandizement had impoverished the people, however, for in addition to the tripling of the taxes, soldiers en route to fight in the Rhineland were quartered in Velay.[8]

The inhabitants of Le Puy lived in their memories of the past. It was a glorious past indeed, for Le Puy had been known down through the years as the City of Mary, the Loretto of the Gauls. It had been the Lourdes of the Middle Ages, and within its walls was the world-famous basilica built on the mount overlooking the city. The dearest possession of the town was the statue of the Black Virgin, which legend declared had been carved by Jeremias the Prophet, and which Saint Louis of France had borne back from his crusades and had personally donated to the shrine of Mary at Le Puy.[9]

Another glorious chapter in the history of the little town was the pilgrimage in 1095 of Pope Urban II to the shrine where he resolved to summon a council for the purpose of launching the First Crusade. This event marked the zenith of the spiritual leadership of Le Puy.[10]

Into this territory torn by the religious strife of the seventeenth

---

[6] *Gleanings in Historic Fields, 1650-1925* (Philadelphia, 1925), pp. 8-9.

[7] *Loc. cit.*

Sister M. of the Sacred Heart Dunne, *The Congregation of St. Joseph of the Diocese of Buffalo, 1854-1933* (Buffalo, 1933), p. 19.

[8] Foley, *op. cit.*, pp. 3-4.

[9] *Loc. cit.*

Catholic Encyclopedia, "Le Puy," vol. IX, pp. 185-187.

[10] Foley, *op. cit.*, pp. 4-5.

Two important congregations of men originated in Le Puy: the Brothers of the Sacred Heart, founded in 1821; and the Labourer Brothers, or Farmer Brothers of St. John Francis Regis, founded in 1850. Congregations of women which originated in the Diocese of Le Puy were: the Dominicans of Mère Agnes, 1221; the teaching Sisters of Notre Dame, 1618; the Religious of St. Charles, 1624; the Sisters of St. Joseph, 1650; the contemplative Religious of the Visitation of St. Mary, 1659; the Sisters of the Instruction of the Infant Jesus, 1667; and the Sisters of the Cross, 1673.

century came the famous Jesuit missionary, John Francis Regis. In a day when organized charity of the medieval type had fallen into desuetude and that of the modern world had not been inspired by Vincent de Paul, Regis epitomized on a small scale both the old and the new in his work in Velay.[11] A plague had savaged southern France and in its path followed seething unrest.[12] People realized that, had Richelieu so desired, the last phase of the Thirty Years' War might have been avoided; and the knowledge made them even more antagonistic to conditions as they were.

Most of Regis' social work was confined to Le Puy, where many who in the past had eked out a mere subsistence by odd jobs were now bereft of all means of livelihood by the depression of the late 1630's. Francis Regis organized bands of charitable women to work among the poor, recorded the names of the indigent in a book, and allotted a certain number to each of the ladies for her special care.[13] The paupers generally worshiped their benefactor who from the beginning of his work gave special attention to the members of the third estate.

Two contemporaries of John Francis Regis were Henry de Maupas du Tour, Bishop of Le Puy and later of Evreux, and John Paul Medaille, a zealous missionary of the Society of Jesus. To these holy founders the Sisters of Saint Joseph throughout the world owe their establishment in France in 1650.

Henry de Maupas du Tour was born in 1606 in the family Castle de Cossons, near Rheims. His parentage was of the highest order in France. His father, Charles de Maupas, Baron of Tour, was a distinguished soldier, statesman, litterateur, and counselor of state to Henry IV. His mother was Anne de Gondi, member of the illustrious family of that name to which Vincent de Paul was attached as preceptor and spiritual guide. He was the godson of Henry IV himself, after whom he was named. According to the custom of the times, at an early age he was named Abbot of Saint Denis of Rheims. However, not in keeping with the prevalent custom, he dispensed the emoluments he received from this position in charity. Later he was

---

11 *Ibid.*, p. 51.

12 *Ibid.*, pp. 30-35.

13 The arrival of a large cauldron to the home of one of these charitable ladies was an indication that Regis had chosen her for such ministrations. This was the origin of the modern soup kitchen. Foley, *op. cit.*, pp. 111-112.

Vicar General of Rheims and chaplain of Anne of Austria, wife of Louis XIII.[14]

The influence of Vincent de Paul was strongly felt by Henry de Maupas, for it was an influence which spread to "crowds of men and women, poor in spirit, clean of heart, and filled with the love of God." A lifetime friendship developed between these two men which lasted until the death of Vincent de Paul.[15]

Noted as a preacher, Henry de Maupas soon attracted the attention of dignitaries in the Church and in 1641 he was raised to the bishopric of Le Puy.[16] He was known as a man of great humility, love of retirement, and zeal for discipline. He studied the works of Saint Francis de Sales and was so imbued with admiration for him that he became his first biographer and one of the commission appointed to inquire into the cause of the Saint's beatification.[17] In 1661, he was promoted to the See of Evreux where he became famous for his work among the poor. He died in 1680.[18]

In 1649, shortly after the culmination of the Thirty Years' War in the Peace Treaty of Westphalia, a young Jesuit missionary, John Paul Medaille, gave a series of Lenten sermons in the see city of Le Puy.[19] The meeting of these holy men at that time was all in the Providence of God.

Father Medaille has been called the successor of John Francis

---

[14] Pierre Larousse, *Dictionnaire Universel* (Paris, 1873), vol. X, pp. 1357-1358.

Leon Bouchage, *Chroniques des Soeurs de St. Joseph de Chambery* (Chambery, 1911), pp. 5-6.

M. Michaud, *Biographie Universelle*, 54 vols. (Paris, 1851), vol. XXVI, p. 316.

Sister Lucida Savage, *The Congregation of St. Joseph of Carondelet* (St. Louis, 1923), p. 3.

[15] Emmanuel de Broglie, *St. Vincent de Paul* (tr. by M. Partridge), (London, 1898), p. 148.

Henry Bedford, *Life of St. Vincent de Paul* (New York, 1888), p. xix.

M. Collet, *Life of St. Vincent de Paul* (Baltimore, 1805), p. 247.

Theodore Maynard, *Apostle of Charity: Life of St. Vincent de Paul* (New York, 1939).

Bishop de Maupas pronounced the funeral eulogy of St. Vincent de Paul in the Church of San Germain L'Auxerrois (Collet, *op. cit.*, p. 247).

[16] Bouchage, *op. cit.*, p. 7.

[17] Hamon, *op. cit.*, vol. II, pp. 84.

[18] The tomb of Bishop de Maupas, in the Cathedral of Evreux, was discovered February 26, 1895, while excavations were being made for the erection of a new altar. The leaden plate on the coffin bore this inscription in French: " Henry de Maupas du Tour, Bishop of Evreux, formerly of Puy, Abbot of St. Denis of Rheims, and of the Isle of Calvara in the Diocese of Lucon, died August 12, 1680. . . . Father of the poor." Savage, *op. cit.*, pp. 5, 23 ff.

[19] *Ibid.*, pp. 6-7.

Regis in the mission field of Velay.[20] There have been some con-
tradictory statements as to the year and the place of his birth,[21] but
it has been fairly accurately established that he was born in Carcas-
sonne on January 29, 1618, and that he entered the Society of Jesus
on August 15, 1640. For a few years after the completion of his
studies, he worked in the classroom but soon was appointed to the
work of preaching which might be regarded as his lifework. He became one of the illustrious followers in the footsteps of Francis
Regis in the evangelization of Velay, Auvergne, Languedoc, and
Aveyron. His apostolic labors were attended with great and ever-
lasting fruit, because wherever he went he established fervent sodalities of men and women who by works of charity, such as instructing
children, visiting the sick, and helping the poor, perpetuated and extended the success of his labors on the missions.

These pious sodalities lacked, however, elements which Father
Medaille regarded as necessary for the stability of his work. Their
members, although devoted, were hampered in many ways and by
other ties from exercising their zeal. Father Medaille resolved, therefore, to found a congregation of sisters who would give themselves
wholly and unreservedly to spiritual and corporal works of mercy.

Having matured his plans, he laid them before Bishop de Maupas, who gave them his heartiest approval. Shortly afterward, Father
Medaille founded the Congregation of the Sisters of Saint Joseph.[22]

At the suggestion of Bishop de Maupas, Father Medaille invited
some young women whom he had been training in the virtues of the
religious life to begin to live the religious life in the home of a noble
widow, Madame de Joux (nee Lucrece de la Planche). This lady,
after the death of her husband, had been dispensing her wealth to
the poor; and when she was informed of the establishment of a

[20] Prunel, *op. cit.*, p. 186.
    Eleseban Guilhermy, *Menologue de la Compagnie de Jésus*, 2 vols. (Poitiers,
1867-1868), vol. I, p. 631.
    Ferdinand Prat, *Le Disciple de St. Jean François de Regis, notes supplementaires,*
(Paris, 1856), p. 180.

[21] Bouchage, *op. cit.*, p. 587, gives date as 1608 and Vivers as place of birth; P.
Carlos Sommervogel, *Bibliothèque de la Compagnie de Jesus*, 10 vols. (Paris, 1894),
vol. V, p. 856, gives the accepted date; while Larousse, *op. cit.*, p. 141, gives 1615.
This discrepancy was due no doubt to confusion of Father John Paul Medaille with
another Jesuit, Father Peter Medaille, who later helped establish the congregation on a
firmer basis.

[22] *Catholic Encyclopedia*, "Jean-Paul Medaille," vol. X, p. 111.
    Ludwig Koch, *Jesuiten Lexikon: Die Gesellschaft Jesu einst und jetzt* (Paderdorn,
1934), p. 1187.

congregation to work among the poor, she willingly offered the hospitality of her home to cradle the new foundation.[23]

These first six subjects received their training in the religious life under the personal direction of Father Medaille. It was during this time that the first rules were formulated, based upon the Augustinian Rule as adapted for the Visitandines by Francis de Sales, and upon the Jesuit rule, which was the rule of the founder.[24]

When the time of probation had ended, Father Medaille requested a formal reception of the habit by the new Congregation. Bishop de Maupas presided at the ceremony on the Feast of Saint Teresa of Avila, October 15, 1650.[25] An orphanage was placed under their direction at that time.[26]

The names of these first candidates received into the Community were considered lost with other important papers of the foundation during the ravages of the French Revolution. Daughters of Saint Joseph regretted this loss, but remembered that Saint Joseph was a hidden saint and that it was not amiss that such a misfortune had occurred. However, recent researches in the archives of Le Puy have brought to light much material hitherto thought to have been destroyed. Among the recovered papers were found the names of these original daughters and the dioceses from which they came. The six young women were: Françoise Eyraud, Anna Vey, and Anna Brun of the Diocese of Le Puy; Marguerite Burdier and Anna Chaleyer of the Diocese of Lyons; and Clauda Chastel of the Diocese of Meude.[27]

Careful consideration had been given to the specific works to be undertaken by the Sisters. The patron of the Congregation was Saint Joseph, this being the first time a religious group had been placed under the patronage of that great saint. The habit adopted was that

[23] Savage, *op. cit.*, pp. 7-8.

Max Heimbucher, *Die Orden und Congregationen der Katholischen Kirche*, 3 vols. (Paderdorn, 1939), vol. II, pp. 492-493.

Pierre Helyot, *Dictionnaire des Ordres Religieux* (Paris, 1847-1859), vol. II, pp. 690-693.

Charles Warren Currier, *History of Religious Orders* (New York, 1898), pp. 542-543.

Elinor Tong Dehey, *Religious Orders of Women in the United States* (Cleveland, 1930), p. 200.

[24] *Loc. cit.*

[25] The Sisters of St. Joseph have always cherished the memory of this day, celebrating with special festivities the Feast of Saint Teresa.

[26] This work—that of the care of the orphans—has remained one of the basic works of the Congregation in all parts of the world.

[27] Sister Lucida Savage (comp.), *The Century's Harvest, 1836-1936* (St. Louis, 1936), p. 9.

of poor widows of the time, and it has been altered but little through the centuries. It consisted of a robe of black serge, plaited in front and held by a cincture. Across the shoulders was worn a folded kerchief of white linen, and on the breast a small, brass crucifix. The veil worn indoors was short. For outdoor wear a longer veil was thrown over the head, falling over the shoulders and knotted on the breast.[28]

Father Medaille, busy as he was with preaching and teaching, had little leisure for writing. However, although the name of the Bishop de Maupas alone occurs on the title page of the Constitutions which were printed in Vienne in 1694, the manuscript edition, preserved at the Motherhouse in Le Puy, is in the handwriting of Father Medaille, who is therefore considered the author of them.[29]

There is also extant in the handwriting of Father Medaille a letter written to one of the first religious, no doubt to the group of six, which elaborates on his "little design" and which is quoted in full:

My very dear Daughters:

Almighty God has vouchsafed to manifest to me a perfect model for our *Little Design* in the Holy Eucharist. Jesus is there in a state of annihilation; we, likewise, my dear daughters, should labor for the establishment of an obscure Institute. In the eyes of the world let it be nothing, but before God, that which He in His infinite mercy will have it to be. Jesus, hidden in the adorable Eucharist, is totally invisible. Our little Institute will be prosperous if it maintains this obscurity in the esteem of the world, this annihilation of its members. And what comparison is there between our nothingness and the state of annihilation to which the Saviour reduces Himself in this divine Sacrament, where we find a perfect model of poverty, of chastity and obedience.

In the esteem of the world, what can be poorer than the species under which the great God veils Himself; not even as bread, only the form and appearance of it. The altar and its ornaments, the tabernacle, the sacred vessels, and all that surrounds Him in this Sacrament of His love, may be rich or poor, it matters not; whether given Him, or taken from Him, He makes no resistance; He is equally content when despoiled of all. In our poverty, we likewise should be so stripped and despoiled of all that we shall consecrate to God and to the foundation of the *Little Design*, that we shall be always equally content to have much or to have little, or to have nothing, because our *Little Design* requires this detachment.

In regard to chastity and purity, we have an admirable model in our divine Saviour. The Virgin Spouse of virgins has eyes and heart only for pure souls. In this mystery there is no use of the senses. All here is purity and for the

---

[28] Constitutions of the Sisters of St. Joseph (Vienne, 1694).
    Constitutions of the Sisters of St. Joseph (Concordia, 1944).
[29] Sommervogel, *op. cit.*, vol. V, p. 856.

purification of hearts. Should we not be happy if such were our condition; if we had neither eyes, ears, tongue, nor heart save only for the divine Lover of souls; and if all our senses tended only to purify and to the purification of hearts? This, with the aid of God, will constitute chastity in our *Little Institute*.

Is not the holy obedience of this divine Saviour miraculous? Has He ever had a thought or uttered a word to resist the will of the priest, a weak man, and often a sinner who consecrates, touches Him, and carries Him where he wills? Has He ever refused—at the will of a priest—to enter our hearts, so full of misery and so ill prepared? This thought would melt my heart, if it were not as hard as marble. Let us never lose sight, my dear daughters, of the marvelous perfection of the divine obedience. May it please the Divine Goodness that ours may resemble it, since we profess to annihilate our will in this Little Institute. May we never have a thought, a sentiment, nor utter a word, in ever so slight a degree, contrary to obedience. Let us obey, in imitation of this dear Saviour, as a child, without reasoning and without disquieting ourselves about anything; allowing Divine Providence to guide us, who, after all, absolutely governs His creatures, and provides for all according to their wants. Let us annihilate ourselves in the bosom of Divine Providence, who knows what is necessary for us. He will provide for us if we repose in Him, as a child who amorously rests on the bosom of its mother. Such ought to be the souls of our *Little Design*. O cherished and most humble obedience! which is the sure mark of solid virtue, couldst thou be always truly perfect in all the members of our new religious body, if I may be allowed to call it such, since, truly speaking, it seems to me that there is only the shadow and not the reality of a body, in as much as it is to exist in a state of annihilation.

Do we look for an example of the love of God and of charity toward the neighbor? We cannot find a better one than in the Holy Eucharist. This mystery is called the "Love of loves"; it reveals the extent, the perfection, the duration, the immutability, the grandeur of holy love. Here, my dear sisters, we shall find sufficient to imitate. Let each one endeavor to have the plenitude of this love in her heart, for the members of our little congregation make profession of the most perfect love. Moreover, this Sacrament is a mystery of perfect union, it unites the creature to God, and, by the title of communion which it bears, it unites the faithful together, by one common union, of which our Lord speaks in such ravishing terms when He asks the Father that all the faithful may be one, that they may be consummated in one, as the Father and He are one. Behold! my dear sisters, the aim of our little congregation; it tends to procure this double union of ourselves entire, with God and with our neighbor with us, but all in Jesus and in God, His Father. May it please the Divine Bounty to make us know the excellence of this aim and to assist us to become fit instruments to succeed therein. I call this union entire, because this word expresses the whole perfection which is comprised in the exercises of the love of God and of the neighbor. God is comprised in the exercise of the love of God and of the neighbor. God grant that we may contribute, in the capacity of feeble instruments, to re-establish in the Church this entire union of souls in God and with God.

In fine, our dear Institute ought to be all humility, and, in everything, to choose an end to cherish that which is most humble. The members thereof ought to be so lowly as to be annihilated by humility. They ought to be all modesty, all meekness, all candor and simplicity, wholly interior—in a word, empty of self and of all things, and all replenished with Jesus, by a plenitude which I cannot explain, but which the Divine Bounty will make you comprehend.

Are not all these virtues found, in a marvelous manner, in the Holy Eucharist? What more humble than our Divine Saviour in this mystery? What more modest, more benign and sweet, more simple and sincere, more filled with God and devoid of all besides?

Behold, my dear sisters, the model of our Institute. It seems to me that we can also find its nature and its employments in this adorable mystery, as well as the manner of living, and the dress of our Sisters, which should be extremely frugal and modest; suitable, however, to their various wants. This we remark in the species of the Holy Eucharist, which, although common, presents, nevertheless, a difference in taste and color according to the diversity of quality in the bread and wine.

The houses of our Sisters should resemble the tabernacle, which is always locked. Our Sisters, like Jesus, should leave the house only through obedience and charity, to return immediately to the hidden life in Jesus.

As the dear Saviour, in the adorable Eucharist, lives not for Himself, but for His Father's glory, and for the soul which He has redeemed with His precious blood, so, likewise, my dear daughters, our *Little Design,* and the persons who compose it, ought not to live for themselves, but be entirely immolated for God and for the neighbor, at the same time to lead the hidden life of Jesus.

May God operate these wonders in your souls, according to the measure of His good pleasure. This is the ardent desire of

Your devoted father in Christ,

J. P. MEDAILLE, S.J.
Founder of the Congregation of the Sisters of St. Joseph.[30]

The first year of the little orphanage in Le Puy was so successful that on March 10, 1651, only six months after the first reception, Bishop de Maupas gave to the Congregation his episcopal approbation. He also recommended the services of the Sisters to his fellow Bishops in neighboring dioceses. Madame de Joux, with accelerated fervor, devoted the remainder of her life to the advancement of the work of the Sisters, and before her death she saw the "Little Design" at work in schools and asylums established in Saint-Didier, Tence, Bas-en-Baset, Dunières, Saint-Paulien, and Monistrol.[31]

In 1661, when Henry de Maupas, Bishop of Le Puy, was transferred to Evreux, he was succeeeded by Ariste Armand de Bethuen,

[30] Copy of this letter was obtained from the Motherhouse in Le Puy, France.
[31] Currier, *op. cit.,* pp. 542-543.
    Catholic Encyclopedia, vol. VIII, pp. 511-512.
    Dehey, *op. cit.,* p. 200.
    Helyot, *op. cit.,* vol. II, pp. 690-691.

who had the same fatherly interest as de Maupas in the Sisters and gave his approval to the Congregation in 1665; and in order to legalize the foundation, he obtained for the Institute letters patent from the reigning king, Louis XIV, the following year.[32]

Further authorization was received in 1668 from Henry Villars, Archbishop of Vienne, into whose diocese the Sisters had been introduced that same year. Under his direction the first printed edition of the Constitutions was made, and these Constitutions governed the various houses of the Sisterhood until the time of the French Revolution and the dispersion of the Congregation.[33]

In 1693, the Congregation was laboring in the dioceses of Le Puy, Clermont, Grenoble, Embrun, Sisteron, Viviers, Usse, Gap, Vienne, and Lyons. They were successfully conducting hospitals, schools, houses of refuge, and orphanages. Many large institutions had been placed under their care, including the Hôtel-Dieu in Vienne. They visited the poor in their homes and exhorted them to patience and in some cases to penitence. They procured alms for them and maintained a pharmacy to distribute necessary drugs and medicines to them. The work they accomplished among young, unprotected girls, who were thrown into a corrupt society, was noteworthy.[34]

As the various houses were established, each was governed by its own elected superior and each established its individual novitiate. The bishops were the superiors in each diocese, and they appointed spiritual fathers, who were assigned either to one or several houses. Each house sent out from time to time new missions, which, when able to maintain themselves, became independent of the parent house, and which, in their turn, gave rise to other houses by similar sequence.[35]

At the outbreak of the French Revolution, there was at Monistrol, a little town in Haute-Loire, in the Diocese of Le Puy, a community

---

32 Sister of St. Joseph (tr.), *Mother St. John Fontbonne* (New York, 1936), pp. 7-8.

33 Savage, *The Congregation of St. Joseph of Carondolet, op. cit.*, pp. 9-10.

34 Helyot, *op. cit.*, vol. II, pp. 690-693, gives a detailed account of the works accomplished by the Sisters of St. Joseph during the one hundred and forty years before the outbreak of the French Revolution. The magnitude of the accomplishment is edifying to the reader.

35 *Ibid.*

This original idea of separate motherhouses and novitiates has persisted in many instances although central government was adopted in France during the administration of Rev. Mother St. John Fontbonne after the re-establishment of the Congregation. In America central government was established by Carondolet in 1860 at which time several of the houses remained diocesan.

of Sisters of Saint Joseph, under the direction of Mother Saint John Fontbonne, who was born at Bas, in the department of Haute Loire, March 31, 1759.[36] This fact is most important in connection with the history of the Congregation, for Mother Saint John Fontbonne was to be the second foundress of the Sisterhood at the termination of the war. Through years of trial and tribulation she was the stablizing influence which united the pre-Revolutionary Community with the post-Revolutionary one.

Her lifetime, 1759 to 1843, spanned one of the most momentous periods in European history. The peculiar conditions which in the seventeenth century had cried for a group of noble-minded women to meet the challenge and work among the poor and the ignorant, were to be found again during the reigns of Louis XV and his successor, Louis XVI. The international wars for colonial dominion culminated during the early years of her life, when France, the once-proud peer of all the nations of Europe, took a minor place in international affairs. The expense of these many wars had drained the national treasury and had added to the taxation burdens placed upon the third estate. Rumblings of discontent had been heard down through the years, and the culmination of generations of wrongs found vent in the frenzy of the French Revolution.

The complacent Bourbons were dragged from their thrones and France blazed with the outrages of fanaticism. Church property was secularized, and the clergy and religious were forced to take the oath of fidelity to the nationally established church. Many denied Roman Catholicism in taking this oath, but other and more heroic souls staunchly refused to acquiesce.

The venerable prelate of Le Puy, Bishop de Gallard, realized what the Civil Constitution of the Clergy would mean in his diocese. It separated the Church in France from the papal authority. It was

---

[36] Transcript from the Register of Births of the Commune of Bas-en-Basset, 1759: "In the year 1759 and on March 31 was born Jeanne Fontbonne, daughter of Michel Fontbonne and Benoite Theilliere, residents of Bas-en-Basset, Haute-Loire. She was baptized the aforesaid day by Father Page, parish priest; Gabriel Dupont, godfather; Jeanne Dupin, godmother; as follows from the records written in the register of births placed in the archives of the civil authority of this commune, the said record numbered and signed by Jean Baptist Callemard, Lawyer to the Parliament and Bailwick of Chauffour, in execution of the declaration of the King, April 9, 1736. This transcript given on paper, free, by us, Mayor of the Borough of Bas, guardian of the registers of births, marriages and burials of the parish of Bas. Bas-en-Basset, March 16, 1927. The Mayor, A. de Vissagnet." Sister of St. Joseph, *op. cit.*, p. 3.

no longer the Pope who appointed bishops; it was the Assembly of the Department. It was no longer the bishop who named the rectors; it was the Assembly of the District. It was no longer Rome which settled conflicts between the priests and the faithful; it was the civil authority. There was no doubt the law was schismatic.[37]

Refusing to take the oath, Bishop de Gallard was forced to abandon his diocese, and on May 19, 1791, he went into exile in Switzerland. He had the sad trial of knowing that his curé in Monistrol apostatized. It was this same Father Ollier who demanded the presence of the Sisters at his sacrilegious mass. When the soldiers called at the convent, Mother Saint John replied, "Never, never, will we consent to communicate with an apostate priest."

Upon their refusal, the Sisters were dragged by force to the church, the men beating drums and crying out, "Make way for these citizenesses whom we are leading to church." The Sisters, calm and dignified, permitted themselves to be led to the kneeling benches but refused to kneel. They stood erect during the entire service, giving no sign of participation in the sacrilegious ceremony.

Leaving the church, Mother Saint John protested aloud against the violence they had suffered. "Know well," said she, "that by force alone have we been led to the sacrilegious mass of an apostate priest. Our hearts and wills had no part therein. We remain inviolably attached and faithful to the true Catholic Church, and no violence shall ever be able to separate us from it."

Ollier was chagrined and threatened that the Sisters would not be permitted to remain in Monistrol longer. He boasted of having helped in the banishment of the Bishop.[38] On October 14, 1792, the Sisters were forced to leave the city. Most of them returned to their parents' homes.[39]

Mother Saint John, Sister Teresa, and Sister Martha remained at their convent a few days after the others had dispersed, but they, too, were forced to leave when their property was confiscated by the

---

[37] *Ibid.*, pp. 26-27.

[38] Ollier was named President of the Directory of the District after renouncing his ecclesiastical duties and was later accused of embezzlement. On June 6, 1794, he was arrested and taken to Paris. On July 16, 1794, he was condemned to death and guillotined the same day. The news of his tragic end reached the imprisoned Sisters whom he had persecuted so viciously, but like Christ they forgave him and prayed, "O God, have mercy on his soul."

[39] *Gleanings in Historic Fields, op. cit.,* p. 31.

Commune. They returned to their father's home, but a mandate of arrest was issued against them, and they were dragged through the streets to the prison of St. Didier. Not many days later another religious was admitted to the prison, and the Sisters were astonished to find that she was their aunt and former superior, Mother Saint Francis, who had been apprehended in her hiding place.

Thrown into a prison with all types of persons, the Sisters won general admiration. Their attempt to say their prayers in common, their submission to the will of God, their interest in and charity toward the other prisoners made them loved and admired. When they were commanded to work on Sundays, they refused.

Each day prisoners were led off to the guillotine, and each day the Sisters felt themselves closer to their doom. One day, the 26th of July, 1794, they were informed that they would ascend the guillotine the following morning. "Oh, then, tomorrow will be the happiest day of our lives," was their only reply.[40]

When the Sisters were making their final preparations to face death, an announcement rang throughout France: "Robespierre has fallen!" The guillotine to which he had sent so many Frenchmen had now seen the end of the tyrant. In the ways of Providence, great things are accomplished. Mother Saint John Fontbonne and her Sisters were released from St. Didier by the very blow which ended the career of Robespierre.

Although the four Sisters imprisoned at St. Didier escaped death, the Sisters of Saint Joseph claim seven martyrs to the faith during the French Revolution. It is possible that others also won the martyr's crown, but extant records indicate only the seven. Sister Saint Julien Garnier and Sister Alexis Payrard were executed in Le Puy in 1793; Sister Anne Marie Garnier and Sister Marie Aubert were guillotined in a small town of Haute-Loire on June 16, 1794; Mother St. Croix Vincent, Sister Madeleine Senovert, and Sister Marie Toussaint Dumoulin met a similar fate.[41]

[40] *Catholic Encyclopedia*, vol. VIII, pp. 511-512.
Dunne, *op. cit.*, pp. 29-31.
Gleanings in Historic Fields, *op. cit.*, pp. 25-32.
Sister of St. Joseph, *op. cit.*, pp. 27-28.
Savage, *The Congregation of St. Joseph of Carondolet*, *op. cit.*, pp. 13-15.
[41] *Ibid.*, p. 42.
Annals of the Sisters of St. Joseph of Le Puy. Cited by Abbé Rivaux, *Histoire de la Révérende Mère St. Jean Fontbonne* (Grenoble, 1885), p. 96.

Bishop Henry de Maupas
Reproduced from a painting in the Motherhouse
of the Sisters of Saint Joseph of Le Puy, France

The following official record of some of the martyrdoms bears repetition in entirety:

On the 27th prairial, in the year of the Republic II (June 15, 1794), the Central Council was informed that: "The two refractory priests of Beaune are hidden in a house there; one of them, the curé, M. Mourier, is very ill, and has received the last sacraments from his confrère. Woe to them! Woe to the house of the family of Best which has become their place of refuge!"

An armed force was sent at once to the place, and twelve residents of Beaune, with their curé, were led to the prison of Le Puy by the gendarmerie of Craponne; and on the next day, six of them mounted the scaffold. Their crime? The sheltering of priests.

Among the six persons who thus obtained the martyr's palm were two Sisters of Saint Joseph—Marie Aubert and Marie Anne Garnier. Of them only need we speak here. Marie Aubert, of Argentière, Commune of Beaune, was consecrated to God in the Institute of Saint Joseph. She was a member of the Community of St. Georges L'Agricol wherein she bore the name of Sister Alexis. She was thirty-eight years old.

Marie Anne Garnier belonged to the remarkable family, the Garniers of Lissac, which had given so many members to the Visitation, to the Trappists, and to the Carthusians. The most famous, the most widely known, is Reverend Dom Louis Garnier, who died in 1876. This pious disciple of St. Bruno ascribed his conversion, his vocation, and his entrance into the Grand Chartreuse to the merits of his martyred aunt. Her name in religion was Sister Saint Julien. She was about thirty-eight years of age.

In the list of prisoners taken to Craponne, the name of Anne Garnier does not appear, but it is on the roster of those executed. Hidden in the house of the family Best, she had fled from the investigators into the woods, where she spent the night in prayer. But at the earliest dawn, she resolved to go to the camping ground and join the other captives, longing for the joy of traveling with them the road to the guillotine, and by the guillotine to reach heaven.

But she was not allowed to journey with them, and met them again only in prison. This explains why, on some lists of the executions, her name was not found.

However, on the margin of the jail-book, beside the acts which record her as "Marie Anne Garnier, a Sister of Saint Joseph," the jailer has hurriedly inscribed the following: "In virtue of the judgment rendered by the criminal tribunal this day, the said Sister Garnier has been guillotined and put to death this 27th prairial of the year II of the French Republic, one and indivisible, or death."

Signed: CHABRIEN[42]

This and other accounts of the marytrdoms indicate the courage and steadfast faith exhibited by these women in the shadow of death. Their memory is revered by every Sister of Saint Joseph.

[42] Cited verbatim in *Gleanings in Historic Fields, op. cit.,* pp. 33-35, from A. D. de Franckieu, *Les Martyrs de l'Église de Grenoble* (Lyons, 1890).
Sister of Saint Joseph, *op. cit.,* pp. 42-73.

Not long after their release from prison, Mother Saint John Font-bonne attempted to secure rights to the property in Monistrol, but her applications were disregarded. The property had been sold by the government and the laws dispersing the Congregation were still in force, thus making it impossible to re-acquire it.[43] The Sisters lacked the finances necessary to attempt an establishment and were therefore forced to return again to the homes of their parents.

For the next twelve years Mother Saint John, Sister Teresa, and Sister Martha patiently awaited more propitious times to live again the common life, devoting themselves meanwhile to pious exercises, the instruction of the ignorant, and the care of the poor and sick, always hopeful that in His good time their previous mode of life could be resumed.

After a lapse of several years, a lengthy letter reached Mother Saint John from her friend, the exiled Bishop de Gallard, who lived in seclusion in Switzerland. His letter so full of consolation is treasured by the Congregation throughout the world. The letter is given here in full:

My beloved Daughters:

You have such sacred rights to my thoughts and affections, you have merited them on so many glorious titles—your virtues and my obligations; your tribulations and my sympathy; your hearts and mine—all speak to you of my tenderness, all warrant my lively and continual solicitude in your regard. As the eyes of the Lord are always fixed upon the just, and the ears of His mercy ever open to their prayers, so I dare also to say, my beloved children, my eyes are incessantly turned toward you, and my sorrowful heart hears, ever, the cries that proceed from yours. I remember (and how could I forget?) that you are that precious portion of my inheritance, always so dear to me and ever so worthy of my affection. You are in my eyes a chosen race, the holy people, the object of the complacency of Heaven, since in dragging you forth from your sacred retreats, impiety has not been able to rob the God of all purity of His true sanctuaries, that is, your hearts consecrated by virginity.

Up to this time, the enemy of virtue and all good has failed in his efforts to shake your constancy. Worthy spouses of Jesus Christ, like Mary you remain standing at the foot of the Cross, nor have you ever recoiled from the chalice of sorrow and opprobrium which Jesus has incessantly presented to your lips. O my beloved daughters, rejoice in the Lord and praise Him for all those sorrows which rendered you like unto your Divine Spouse, for all those triumphs by which Heaven crowns your invincible firmness!

---

[43] The laws of 1790 and 1792 had not been revoked. The law of 1790 abolished all orders requiring solemn vows; that of 1792 abolished all other congregations devoted to teaching and charity.

Jealous of your glory, dismayed at the strength of your virtues, humbled by your courage, the spirit of lies and deceit again assails you. By his efforts to annoy you and weary your patience, he believes he has almost exhausted it; and he seems to have given you over, during these times to all the sufferings and horrors of want, only to force you to bend the knee to the idol of crime and impiety, and compel you to sacrifice to him the immortal fruits of all you have had to undergo; for one cannot be deceived as to the views of the powers of darkness; they have themselves torn aside the false veil that sometimes covers their artifices.

All these means tend to but one end; it is always the same: to efface from souls every trace of virtue and religion. As the wicked can find no rest, they can give none; if they flatter, it is to destroy; if they promise, it is to deceive; if they give, it is to corrupt. Ah, could you believe that the voice of justice and humanity would be heard in those hearts hardened to every noble sentiment, as well as to remorse?

See how they have treated, how they still treat those ones of Israel, who, by degenerating from their first fervor, have had the weakness to yield to their promises or threats! What has been the result of their complaisance? They have increased the boldness and strength of impiety, brought division into the camp of Israel, and scandalized the little ones of the faith. Behold what have been the false effects of those acts, whose perfidy was concealed either by avarice or terror?

The chief pastors have constantly revealed it; and what remains of those who have preferred their own lights to those of our guides and chiefs? The bitter regret of having increased the woes of religion and their country, under the vain pretense of lightening them, and the shame of having trusted more in the lying promises of the deceiving spirit, than in the oracles of those who have received from Heaven the mission to unmask and confound him. Instructed as you are, my dear children, by these fatal examples—the subject, we doubt not, of your tears as of ours—far from me be the thought that you would allow yourselves to be deceived by the new snare which is spread before you by the enemy of your virtue and happiness! What attraction in your eyes would there be for a gift offered you by hands as perfidious as they are sacrilegious, and which you could accept only at the expense of your conscience? Who, better than you, knows what St. Paul said to the early faithful: "You cannot be partakers of the table of the Lord, and of the table of devils; you cannot drink the chalice of the Lord and of devils." The state of distress in which I see you, my dear children, pierces me to the heart, and in my personal indigence, I feel only the powerlessness in which it leaves me to succor you; but, habituated as you are to privations and sufferings of every kind, accustomed to contemplate our Divine Model who had not whereon to lay His head, penetrated with love and confidence in our heavenly Father who feeds the birds of the air, you will cast yourselves into the vast bosom of His Providence, and will expect from His infinite goodness alone the reward of sacrifices you have already made, and are still ready to make, for His great glory and the sanctity of your state.

How holy and profound, my beloved daughters, are the designs of God over us, when He permits the impious to violate the sanctuaries of virginity, and scatter their stones in the midst of a perverse world! Heaven has willed to make you a spectacle to angels and to men. You are as the seeds of flowers caught up by the wind and dropped in city, in country, even into the bosom of your own families, that you may bear everywhere the good odor of Christ.

Called to a mission so sublime, and proved so worthy of fulfilling it, can I fear from you any weakness? No, my beloved children, the true glory of virgins is "to follow the Lamb whithersoever He goeth." You have had the happiness of following Him in the path of His sorrows and humiliations; the greater number of you can, like the apostles, glory in bearing on your innocent flesh the stigmata of Jesus Christ; you all envy the blessed fate of your companions who have followed the Divine Spouse even unto Calvary, and who, after His example, have consummated thereon their sacrifice, praying for their persecutors and the executioners who murdered them. Ah, I have the firmest confidence that I shall yet share with the Spouse of your souls the inestimable consolation of having you in my crown and my glory!

Persuaded that impiety seeks only a pretext to enkindle against you the fires of another persecution, I am not affrighted at the new dangers that threaten you. There is no question of danger for you; but, while groaning in all the bitterness of my soul over the additional sufferings that may be heaped upon you, I dare to congratulate you on being always judged worthy to suffer for justice' sake, and I congratulate myself on being pastor of so many heroic souls called to the double crown of virginity and martyrdom. I unite myself, my cherished children, to your combats and to your victories, your tribulations and your favors. Let us humble ourselves beneath the Almighty hand of God, who visits us. Let us leave to Him our cares and our solicitudes and even in the midst of suffering, we shall find our surety, our protection, and our strength in the God of all grace who has called us to His eternal glory in Jesus Christ, Our Lord, Amen.

Given at the place of our exile, July 19, 1798.[44]

Napoleon I, Emperor of the French, signed the Concordat with the Papacy in 1801; six years later the uncle of Napoleon, Cardinal Joseph Fesch, Archbishop of Lyons, asked Mother Saint John Fontbonne to leave her home in Bas-en-Basset to meet with him in Saint Etienne to discuss plans for the reconstruction of the Congregation of the Sisters of Saint Joseph.

Cardinal Fesch, after his appointment to Lyons in 1802, had made earnest efforts to revive the teaching and missionary orders of men in his diocese; but, Napoleon, after his quarrel with Pope Pius VII, again declared them dissolved because he feared that attempts were being made to restore the Jesuits. The congregations of women, however, were allowed to reorganize unmolested and many of them re-established themselves at that time.[46]

[44] Sister of St. Joseph, op. cit., pp. 154-156.
[45] Abbé Lyonnet, Le Cardinal Fesch, Archévêque de Lyon (Lyons, 1841).
   Abbé J. Ricard, Le Cardinal Fesch (Paris, 1893).
[46] Sister of St. Joseph, op. cit., p. 86.

In 1805, the cardinal had appointed as his vicar general Father Claude Cholleton, a zealous and virtuous priest, who had been exiled during the upheaval in France. In order to reach the numbers who needed spiritual care, the Diocese of Lyons was divided into twenty-five sections, at the head of each of which was a superior, an assistant, several missionaries, and a layman in charge of temporal affairs.

The work of the missionaries was made easier by the auxiliary catechists, and it was to this group that Father Cholleton and Cardinal Fesch felt that the Sisters of Saint Joseph would render invaluable assistance.[47]

In the parish of Saint Etienne, at the Rue de la Bourse, Father Cholleton had gathered a group of pious women who wished to live a religious life. He instructed this group in the virtues necessary for the active life among the people and sent them out to minister to the poor, especially to the sick and dying. They were known both as the Black Daughters and as the Sisters of a Good Death. When the good vicar approached the cardinal concerning the new congregation, the latter recalled what good work had been accomplished by the Sisters of Saint Joseph before the Revolution and suggested that the Black Daughters might reap the heritage of that pre-Revolutionary period by affiliating with Mother Saint John Fontbonne and her dispersed Community.[48]

Again the Providence of God was manifested in this revival of the Congregation. The twelve Black Daughters renounced their original idea of a new foundation, and Mother Saint John acquiesced to the request that she should adopt them as true Daughters of Saint Joseph and train them in the spirit of that rule formulated over a century and a half before.[49]

For almost a year this period of probation and instruction continued; on July 14, 1808, the twelve postulants were clothed with the habit and received religious names.[50] Thus was restored the Congre-

---

[47] *Ibid.,* pp. 86-87.
[48] Konrad Hofman, *Lexikon fur Theologie und Kirche,* 10 vols. (Freiburg, 1933), vol. II, pp. 566-567.
  Heimbucher, *op. cit.,* vol. II, pp. 492-493.
  Helyot, *op. cit.,* vol. II, pp. 690-693.
[49] *Ibid.*
[50] It was at this time the cap was replaced by a veil. In 1650, widows wore a white fichu over the shoulders; the Sisters had adopted this fichu. After the Concordat the fichu was replaced by a guimpe.

gation of the Sisters of Saint Joseph of Lyons.[51] The names of these
first Sisters of the restored Congregation were:

Mother Saint John Fontbonne	Superior and foundress
Anne Matrat	Sister Saint Francis Regis
Jeanne Marie Matrat	Sister Saint Claire
Anne Marie Didier	Sister Saint Paul
Suzanne Marcoux	Sister Saint John Baptist
Jeanne Poitrasson-Gonnet	Sister Saint Francis de Sales
Philippine Menard	Sister Saint Teresa
Benoite Perrin	Sister Marie
Antoinette Monteillier	Sister Saint Michael
Marie Anne Pitiot	Sister Saint Augustine
Antoinette Cessier	Sister Marie Joseph
Marie Louise Foret	Sister Saint Madeleine
Elizabeth Placon	Sister Saint Agnes

At the time of the first reception, Father Cholleton had been replaced in Saint Etienne by Father Piron, who was delegated by the
cardinal to preside at the reception. A statement attributed to Father
Piron on this occasion is often quoted in annals of the history of the
Congregation. He said, "You are but few, my daughters; yet like a
swarm of bees shall you spread yourselves everywhere. Your number
shall be as the stars of heaven. But while increasing, preserve always
that humility and simplicity which should characterize the Daughters
of Saint Joseph."[52]

The original group was augmented within a short time when a
second group of seven from Rue Micareme begged for adoption.
They had been trained by the same director and therefore easily
adapted themselves to the rule of the Sisters of Saint Joseph. When
they asked permission of the cardinal to take the step, he said to
them, "For the children, for the mothers, for the old, and for everybody, we need apostles. The Church needs them. The number of
priests is insufficient. Enter the community of the Sisters of Saint
Joseph. You will be auxiliaries of the clergy. You will serve God and
souls."[53]

The reception of the second group took place on April 20, 1809,
at the hands of Father Piron. These Sisters, also, were important

---

[51] The word *Congregation* was avoided at that time because it would have aroused
suspicion. It was not of importance to let the public know that they were reviving the
Institute.

[52] Sister of St. Joseph, *op. cit.*, p. 97.

[53] *Ibid.*, p. 99.

enough in the newly reorganized Community to have their names
recorded for posterity:[54]

Charlotte Beneyton	Sister Saint Ursula
Marie Beneyton	Sister Saint Bernard
Etiennette Lachaux	Sister Saint Etienne
Jeanne Marie Besson	Sister Saint Pierre
Marguerite Rigaud	Sister Saint Angela
Anne Cornillon	Sister Saint Benedict
Marie Ginod	Sister Saint Louis

In less than three years, the motherhouse at Lyons had under its
jurisdiction three institutions; Saint Etienne and Monistrol confided
to the Sisters their orphanage asylums; and the schools at Valbenoite,
Saint Chamond, and Sury-le-Comtal were taught by the same Sisters.

The chronicler of this period records privations at every turn;
however, sacrifices meant little to these women who had borne so
many trials and tribuations and even the threat of death. They carried on their work with little financial assistance, in poor dilapidated
buildings, deserted chateaux, and monasteries.[55] They carried on
with a faith that moves mountains and a zeal that is without a
parallel.

On April 10, 1812, the state finally authorized the legality of the
Congregation.[56] There had been a growing feeling among the Sisters that there should be a central novitiate, in order to make for uniformity of training for the novices, and that from one central motherhouse a superior general would direct the activities of the entire
Congregation. The disadvantages of small disunited groups had been
demonstrated at the time of the French Revolution. Now it was
thought best to consider the benefits of a centralized organization. In
order to survive in the post-Revolutionary period there was even
greater need of unity of effort and of direction.[57]

The only person considered for the position of superior general
was the saintly Mother Saint John—she who was the tie which bound
the new group to that of the old tradition. Her election was approved

---

[54] *Loc. cit.*

[55] Bouchage, *op. cit.*, p. 85.

[56] Pierre F. Lebeurier, *Vie de la Révérende Mère St. Joseph* (Paris, 1869); (tr. by
a Sister of St. Joseph) (New York, 1876), p. 71.

[57] Savage, *The Congregation of St. Joseph of Carondolet, op. cit.*, p. 21.

by the ecclesiastical superiors of the diocese, and the location of the motherhouse and novitiate was designated as Lyons. There Mother Saint John purchased the Chateau Yon, which became the cradle of the Lyons foundation.[58]

In order to increase the revenues of the Congregation, the Sisters took advantage of the impetus given to the silk industry in southern France and negotiated with the factories to engage the Sisters to weave silk in their convents during their spare hours.[59]

The status of the Sisters of Saint Joseph was defined in 1822 by the new Archbishop John Paul Gaston de Pins. It was regarded as diocesan, with the Archbishop of Lyons as its spiritual head and first superior. Under him were the spiritual Father, appointed from among his vicars, and the Reverend Mother and her council, elected by vote of the Sisters of the diocese.[60] The Reverend Claude Cholleton, nephew of the former pastor of Saint Etienne, was named spiritual director. He remained in the capacity for a period of sixteen years.[61]

It must have been with regret that Mother Saint John Fontbonne realized that her beloved Le Puy would not come within the jurisdiction of the central government of Lyons. The convents there had difficulty in becoming re-established and the local Ordinary, Bishop Bonald, preferred local autonomy for the Sisters in his diocese. In spite of visitations of Mother Saint John and of Father Cholleton to Le Puy, affiliation was deemed impossible. The Le Puy foundation in turn sent out missionaries into various parts of France simultaneously with those from the establishment at Lyons.[62]

Savoy, a dependency of France until it was given to Italy by the Congress of Vienna in 1815, was the scene of a mission sent there

---

[58] Located on the "hill of Chartreux," it was formerly a dependency of the monastery, and to it were attached a court, extensive gardens, and a granary. Confiscated with the monastery in 1791, the domain passed through the hands of several owners until it became the property of Jerome Nivet and his wife, Marie Valand, from whom it was purchased on June 1, 1816.

Bouchage, *op. cit.,* p. 51.

[59] Sister of St. Joseph, *op. cit.,* p. 194.

Savage, *The Congregation of St. Joseph of Carondolet, op. cit.,* p. 23.

[60] Bouchage, *op. cit.,* p. 68.

The Constitutions were reprinted and amended to provide for the change in government.

[61] Ricard, *op. cit.,* p. 355.

[62] Savage, *The Congregation of St. Joseph of Carondolet, op. cit.,* p. 24.

Today in the United States the communities with motherhouses at St. Augustine, Fla., and Fall River, Mass., were founded from Le Puy; the community at Savannah, Ga., which later affiliated with Carondolet, also came from there.

in 1812. When Savoy was French territory, the city of Chambery was a suffragan of Lyons, but with separate national jurisdiction it was impossible to continue relations between Lyons and Chambery. Mother Saint John, therefore, consented to the erection of a novitiate and motherhouse in the latter place. This was the beginning of the Sisters of Saint Joseph of Chambery.[63]

Political conditions and the suspicion of the Italians kept the Sisters of Saint Joseph of Lyons out of Italy. The relationship of Cardinal Fesch to Napoleon I acted adversely for his fortunes and for those of the Sisters of Saint Joseph after the downfall of Napoleon. When some Sisters were ready to leave for Rome in 1824, at the request made by Pope Leo XII through his Secretary of State, Cardinal Somaglia, they were stopped on the eve of their departure by a letter from the Cardinal Secretary to Msgr. de Pins, stating that the French government "saw with uneasiness the establishment of the Sisters (in Rome) in which it discovered the hand of Cardinal Fesch," then a resident of Rome and a *persona non grata* to the civil authorities at Paris.[64]

The beginnings of the Sisters of Saint Joseph of Bourg were made in 1819, when Sisters were sent to Belley. This group also became independent, being unable to maintain itself under the jurisdiction of the Lyons motherhouse. The Bishop of Belley, Alexander Raymond Devie, also preferred local autonomy for the Sisters in his dioceses.[65]

Mother Saint John Fontbonne continued to govern the Sisters of Saint Joseph of Lyons until her retirement in 1839.[66] She had worked diligently to bring about unification and expansion within the Community. Her simplicity and piety gained the admiration and love of all. It was she who, in 1836, sent the first Sisters of Saint Joseph of Lyons to Carondolet. She lived to see the Congregation firmly established, it having grown from small beginnings to world-wide propor-

[63] The ecclesiastical superior of the Chambery Sisters, Irenaeus Yves de Solle, opposed affiliation with Lyons. The Sisters of St. Joseph of Hartford, Conn., were founded from Chambery.
Bouchage, *op. cit.*, p. 175.
[64] *Ibid.*, p. 265.
[65] Lebeurier, *op. cit.*, p. 270.
The Sisters of St. Joseph in New Orleans, La., and in Crookston, Minn., were founded from Bourg.
[66] Mother St. John Fontbonne died November 22, 1843, at the age of eighty-four, having lived sixty-three and a half years in religion. Sisters of St. Joseph throughout the world are praying for her beatification and canonization.

tions at the time of her death in 1843. Convents had been established in thirteen Departments in France—in the Departments of the Loire and the Rhone; in Corsica, Herault, La Vendée, Poiteau, Aude, the Lower Alps, Creuse, Saone-et-Loite, Isere, Côte d'Or, and Allier.[67]

The prophecy of Father Piron, at the reception of the first Sisters into the Congregation at the end of the French Revolution, when he compared them to a swarm of bees, had almost reached fulfillment. Years later, when Archbishop John Ireland of St. Paul, Minnesota, visited the motherhouse in Lyons, he said in respect to the marvelous growth of the Sisters of Saint Joseph, "Your Congregation is a Catholic congregation in the true sense of the word."

And there was counsel in that same prophecy of Father Piron, for he challenged those first Daughters of Saint Joseph to preserve always that humility and simplicity which should be their outstanding characteristics. Daughters of Saint Joseph have always gloried in these virtues.[68]

---

[67] Sister of St. Joseph, *op. cit.,* p. 197.
[68] *Ibid.*

CHAPTER II

Mississippi Valley
Early Nineteenth Century

THE settlement of the Mississippi Valley region was a part of the trans-Appalachian movement which has been called the fulfillment of our "Manifest Destiny."[1] Studied in the light of the frontier theory of American development,[2] this steady westward surge of population in search of more freedom and better economic opportunity followed the valleys of the mountain ranges running north and south and entered the Ohio Valley at an early date.

The Old Northwest and the Mississippi Valley in general produced a distinct physical and cultural type.[3] The composite civilization with its blend of ideals and the point of view of the various elements of the population was decidedly American. An outstanding writer of the region expresses it thus:

> Democracy and education and religious ideals of the austere Puritan were found in this new society, alongside the easy-going urbanity and political acumen of the Virginian and the Kentuckian, while the tolerance and the practical sense of the men from the Middle States contributed to a many-sided life. The more conservative immigrants from east of the Alleghanies toned down the impetuous and radical backwoodsmen, while the composite American civilization which these settlers founded . . . was a decided contrast to the distinctly Southern customs and institutions on the opposite bank of the Ohio.[4]

[1] Much of the material in this chapter is taken from the author's work, *Nativism in the Old Northwest* (Washington, 1936), pp. 1-62.

[2] F. J. Turner, "The Influence of the Frontier in American History," *Proceedings of the Wisconsin Historical Society* (1893); *The Rise of the New West, 1819-1829* (New York, 1906).

F. L. Paxson, *History of the American Frontier, 1763-1793* (New York,, 1924); *The Last American Frontier* (New York, 1926).

D. R. Fox (editor), *Sources of Culture in the Middle West* (New York, 1934).

[3] R. E. Chaddock, *Ohio Before 1850: A Study of the Early Influence of Pennsylvania and Southern Populations in Ohio* (New York, 1908), p. 30.

[4] B. Bond, "American Civilization Comes to the Old Northwest," *Mississippi Valley Historical Review*, vol. XIX (1932-1933), p. 4; *The Civilization of the Old Northwest* (New York, 1934), p. 508.

Before 1830 the colonization of the West was due mainly to Anglo-Saxon expansion.[5] For this migration there were many causes. The ever-present, gypsylike tendency of the American people to migrate, which at all times has been a national characteristic, was one of the factors leading to the settlement of the vast frontier region. Dissatisfaction with political, social, religious, and economic conditions in the East augmented this restlessness and its longing for the wide-open spaces. Cheap land was an inducement to people who saw no future in their present condition. The opening of the public lands at nominal prices, and the favorable reports from the West, as well as the report of Henry Clay in 1834, influenced trans-Appalachian migration from all sections. Steamboats on Western waters and the building of turnpikes facilitated travel. There were the well-known trails, such as the Lake Trail from central New York and the Wilderness Trail into Kentucky. Natural waterways connected all parts of the territory—on the north the Great Lakes, on the south the Ohio, and on the west the Mississippi with navigable streams leading into the interior.[6]

The qualities of the settlers in the region were essentially the same as those of New York and New England—"hardy, middle-class farmers, young, hopeful, ambitious, and imbued with traditions of individualism . . . cut loose from the convervative forces and set down in the midst of almost boundless natural resources."[7]

During the early period there was a close affiliation between the Mississippi Valley and the South. Frederick Jackson Turner summarized it thus: "The combination of the South, western Middle Atlantic, and the Mississippi Valley gave an ascendance to democratic ideals of the followers of Jefferson and left New England weakened and isolated for nearly half a century."[8] There was a tendency, however, even before the canal and railroad days to look longingly toward an economic affiliation with the East, a longing

[5] G. P. Garrison, *Westward Expansion, 1841-1850* (New York, 1906), p. 6.

[6] Bond, "American Civilization Comes to the Old Northwest," *op. cit.*, pp. 11-14.

[7] J. H. Lanman, *History of Michigan* (New York, 1839), pp. 295-300.

F. J. Turner, "Colonization of the West," *American Historical Review*, vol. XI (1906), pp. 304-327; "The Problem of the West," *Atlantic Monthly*, vol. LXXVIII (1891), pp. 291-293.

G. N. Fuller, *Economic and Social Beginnings of Michigan* (Lansing, 1916), p. 483.

[8] F. J. Turner, "Dominant Forces in Western Life," *Atlantic Monthly*, vol. LXXIX (1892), no. 473, p. 436.

fulfilled with the opening of new routes to the region and accelerated after a considerable representation of Easterners filtered into the Valley.[9]

The twenty-year period from 1830 to 1850 witnessed a wave of foreign immigration to our shores. This influx created a marked distinction in the social classes in the United States. These people, whose lower standards of living and unfamiliar habits repelled the native Americans, aroused another upsurge of antiforeignism. Immigrants have always been the scapegoats of religious and racial prejudices.[10] As early as 1810 there had been manifestations of suspicion of the foreign element when natives of the Mississippi Valley protested against favors to the "foreign born," especially the privilege of holding office. One editor insisted that the "Westerners were quite smugly assured that they alone held aloft the torch of freedom . . ."[11] On the other hand, immigrants were suspicious of native-born citizens. While this was especially true of the Germans, it might be stated as a generality for other nationalities.

They feared Yankee encroachments on their rights as adopted citizens.[12] There were many instances in which this suspicion was justifiable during the period of nativism which broke out about the middle of the nineteenth century.

Nevertheless, in the Middle West, in spite of mutual suspicions between native American and adopted American, there was co-operation in the upbuilding of many communities. As in the East, foreigners were at first regarded with disfavor; later the individualism prevalent on the frontier, where character and ingenuity counted for more than did social antecedents, militated against social class distinctions which continued to persist in the older sections of the country. Generalizing on the Mississippi Valley, a local historian asserted:

At first the newcomers were not looked upon with social favor, unless they spoke English and were not Catholic. The Irish were obliged to fight for recognition but, being quite ready to do that, they made their way. The Dutch

[9] For a fuller discussion of the subject, see Thomas, *op. cit.*, chaps. I-IV, pp. 1-62.

[10] F. A. Walker, *Discussion of Economics and Statistics*, 2 vols. (New York, 1897), vol. II, p. 441.

P. F. Hall, "Selection of Immigration," reprinted from *Annals of American Academy of Political and Social Science*, July, 1904.

[11] *Liberty Hall*, Nov. 15, 1809; June 27, 1810.

Bond, *The Civilization of the Old Northwest*, *op. cit.*, p. 518.

[12] E. Bruncken, "How the Germans Became Americans," *Proceedings of the Wisconsin Historical Society* (1898), p. 120.

(Germans) tended to get forward more slowly but ultimately gained a social foothold through their talent for prosperity and their ability to outskill Americans in handcraftism, to contribute to social amenities through their music, and to excel in the schools.[13]

Nationalities showed tendencies to settle in town or country with the natives. Germans and Scandinavians inclined toward agriculture, and the Irish toward employment in the cities; of native Americans one out of every six engaged in agriculture in some capacity; of Germans in the United States one out of every seven engaged in agriculture, of Scandinavians one out of every four, of Irish one out of every twelve.[14]

The earliest settlement in the Mississippi Valley was French; it was, as it were, a connecting link between the French in Canada and those in the lower Mississippi region. The so-called American bottoms was an extremely fertile tract of land of about six hundred square miles from Kaskaskia to Cahokia; it was inhabited in 1800 by approximately 1,200 French Creoles.[15] French immigration from Canada was never great, and at no time except during the years 1846-1847 was it as large as 10,000.[16] The first colonization project after 1830 was at Metamora, Woodford County, Illinois, in 1831. Another was established at Saint Marie in Jasper County, Illinois, during the 1837 panic. In the same state in the vicinity of Kankakee there was a cluster of French-Canadian settlements, chief among which was the village of Bourbonnais.[17]

A contemporary, Judge William Woodward of Michigan, characterized the French in the Valley as "habitually gay and light-hearted yet pious; honest beyond comparison; generous and hos-

[13] J. Schafer, "Immigrants and Social Amelioration," *Publications of the Norwegian-American Historical Association, Studies and Records,* vol. IV (1917), p. 58. In regard to German craftsmen, Schafer states that they established a kind of rank among the Germans. In a few years "This class of 'fine old Germans' was recognized to supplement the well-known type of 'fine old Yankee gentleman'."
J. Schafer, "Yankee and Teuton," *Wisconsin Magazine of History,* vol. VII (1908), pp. 14-15.
[14] J. R. Commons, *Report of the Industrial Commission* (Washington, 1915), vol. XV, pp. 301-302.
[15] Creoles are descendants of European parents born in America, *i.e.,* Creoles may be pure Spanish, French, or Portuguese. The idea that Creoles are a mixed race is incorrect. Place of birth determines the appellation.
R. S. Brown, *Western Gazetteer and Emigrant's Guide* (Chicago, 1817), p. 20.
J. Reynolds, *Illinois: My Own Times* (Belleville, Ill., 1855), p. 19.
[16] A. A. Young, *Report on Immigration* (New York, 1872), pp. 12-16.
[17] *Michigan Historical Collections,* vol. XXXVIII, pp. 548-549.
Detroit Free Press, Feb. 20, 1838.

pitable and often refined and with no cares from ambition or science."
Attributing the apparent lack of ambition of the French to the paternalistic regime of colonial days, he assigned that as the same reason
for their conservatism and opposition to change.[18] They recognized a
single church and, as Pooley puts it, "they were under the leadership
of the village priest who was their guide, philosopher, and friend."[19]

Among the incoming foreigners were indentured servants who
worked out their freedom in the East and then migrated to the West,
as well as recent arrivals from Europe. The early exodus was due
in part to religious unrest in Germany after the reorganization of the
Lutheran Church in the 1830's, while the later movement was stimulated by economic and political causes of which the most important
were the introduction of machine competition, the subdivision of the
land, and the crop failures of 1846-1848.[20]

Relative to foreign settlements in the Valley, an antagonistic
Congregational minister wrote to the headquarters of his church:

... Many Germans are settling here. . . . Each new family in turn brings a
circle of relatives and friends who settle around them. . . . If a farm is to be
sold in their neighborhood, a German will be likely to be the purchaser.
Americans do not like that account. Thus the effect of this immigration to
diminish our numbers, will be soon quite apparent. Their code of morals is
much the same as in Germany. . . . We can do almost nothing for them
religiously. They are slow to learn English words which convey religious
truths. If all the *immigration* be German and all our part of the *emigration* be
active religious men, it will give us but a poor chance for growth.[21]

Scandinavians played an important role in the settlement of Mid-
America, having entered the region in the early 1830's. When the
new states of the region were encouraging immigration, pamphlets
were circulated in the northern European countries, printed in the
vernacular:

Words of call came in familiar tongues, in letters from adventurers into
the new West, in interviews with prosperous immigrants who returned, in
circulars and in immigrant guide books sent out by the states, counties, railroads,
and land companies. . . . The appeal was quite as much to the imagination
as to the understanding; response was made by the sturdiest and most ambitious. . . . Thus it came about that the prospective joys of owning a farm and
of expanding its acreage with the prosperity of the years . . . made the
hardships of pioneering and the isolation of the frontier seem as very little

---

18 Fuller, *op. cit.*, p. 112.
19 W. V. Pooley, "The Settlement of Illinois from 1830-1850" (1908), reprint
from the *Bulletin of the Univ. of Wisconsin History Series*, vol. I, pp. 287-595, 316.
20 Pooley, *op. cit.*, pp. 496-497.
21 "Illinois Correspondence," *Home Missionary*, vol. XXVIII (Nov., 1854), p. 176.

things to the strong-limbed, sound-hearted, land-hungry Swedes, Norwegians, and Danes in the Middle Northwest.[22]

The Irish, who left the cities of the East for the Middle West, became day laborers upon the lines of transportation then in process of construction. For some time the Irish settlements lay close to the canals and the railroads. At times the newcomers were disillusioned when they faced stern reality after the assurance of good wages and comparatively short hours.

Many of the Irish later settled in such centers as Saint Louis; others settled on the land and changed from laborers into farmers. When the public works were discontinued for lack of funds, the workers were paid off in land script which at times was not convertible into money and was therefore redeemed with land. The contribution of Irish laborers to the growth of the Mississippi Valley might be summed up in the words of Thomas D'Arcy McGee:

The facilities of transit offered by railroads and canals leading from the old Atlantic States westward, and the adaptability of the West for agriculture attracted and made easy the progress of the Celtic multitude. If, in our own age, this young nation has been able to export its superfluous breadstuffs to the other side of the Atlantic, one of the chief causes is to be found in the constant supply of cheap Irish labor, which for fifty years has been poured along all the avenues of the West. If, moreover, Ohio, Michigan, Iowa, and Missouri have done much to increase the wealth and the glory of the Union, a great share of the historical honor is due to the Irish fugitives from British oppression and to their more fortunate sons, born as freemen.[23]

The Catholic Emigration Society of London sponsored the emigration of several parties of Catholics, and the trade unionism and Chartist failures swelled the numbers.[24]

The common opinion that the earliest settlers of the Middle West left their religion on the other side of Lake Erie is erroneous to a large degree. The absence of organized places of worship among the far-flung population makes it difficult to generalize concerning the actual religious nature of the people. However, evidence points to the fact that the settlers were moral and that they observed

---

[22] K. C. Babcock, "The Scandinavian Element in American Population," *American Historical Review*, vol. XVI (1911), pp. 301-302; "The Scandinavian Element in the United States," *Illinois Univ. Studies in Social Science*, vol. III (1914), pp. 7-49.

J. R. Reiersen, "Norwegians in the West in 1844: A Contemporary Account," (tr. and ed. by T. C. Blegan), *Publications of the Norwegian-American Historical Association, Studies and Records*, vol. I (1920-1921), pp. 110-125.

[23] T. D. McGee, *A History of the Irish Settlers in North America from the Earliest Period to the Census of 1850* (Boston, 1852), p. 179.

[24] Pooley, *op. cit.,* pp. 502-503.

Sunday as a day of rest.[25] The West exerted as vital an influence upon the religious ideals as upon political principles. There was an individualism on the frontier which gave rise to a number of independent sects. The emotional element in the Methodist, Presbyterian, and Baptist religions appealed to the frontiersmen. Representatives of the new sects traveled throughout the land preaching their doctrines and opposing tenets which they considered false. Many established periodicals to defend and propagate their doctrines.[26]

One of the significant features in the great onward movement in the American churches was the use of the press and the establishment of missionary societies which granted subsidies to be used for religious tracts which were distributed among the people.[27]

Puritan influence on legislation came early in the form of sumptuary laws and moral legislation. For example they fostered a law against "idle, vain, and obscene conversation, profane cursing and swearing," and forbade "servile labor" on the Sabbath.[28]

In spite of the fact that Catholic missionaries were the first in the Valley, the Church did not make substantial gains until near the close of the first half of the nineteenth century. Accounts of the early missionaries of the Church give credit to those "men of broad culture, refinement, and learning," who "had influence over the lives of their charges."[29] The same author, when referring to Father Gabriel Richard, the Sulpician, who was elected delegate to Congress from Michigan Territory in 1823, stated that "one of the strongest influences was Father Richard whose life was one of unselfish sacrifice in the interests of both Catholics and Protestants."[30] Another impartial observer of the missionary activities said:

---

[25] R. Payne, "Pioneer Piety," *Michigan Pioneer Collections,* vol. XIII (1888), pp. 407-408.

[26] Chaddock, *op. cit.,* pp. 111, 120.

Bond, *The Civilization of the Old Northwest, op. cit.,* pp. 465-466.

J. G. Shea, *History of the Catholic Church in the United States,* 4 vols. (New York, 1888), vol. II, pp. 481-491; vol. III, p. 334.

[27] 1803—Society for the Propagation of Christian Knowledge, first in America, within twelve years printed over 8,224 volumes and 30,000 tracts.

1807—Connecticut Religious Tract Society specialized in twenty-five tracts of which 100,000 were circulated.

1808—Vermont Religious Tract Society.

1814—New England Religious Tract Society (later called The American Tract Society of Boston) was incorporated in 1815. It was renamed in 1823. The center of activities was at Andover.

[28] *Laws Passed in the Territory of the United States North West of the River Ohio,* vol. I (1792), pp. 27-28.

[29] Fuller, *op. cit.,* p. 115.

[30] *Ibid.,* p. 115.

The earliest representatives of religion in Illinois were the Roman Catholics. The fact is not peculiar to Illinois or to any other part of our country. It has been characteristic of that church since the beginning. No body of Christians has ever shown greater missionary enterprise, zeal, heroism and self-denial in the propagation of religion. None seems to have been actuated by purer and more unselfish motives than some of those missionaries who early entered new fields. Whatever may be said in disparagement of their methods and works, it must be admitted that the world is better today because of their existence and their work.[31]

The internal improvements projects brought many laborers into the Mississippi Valley to find employment, and Catholic priests visited the construction camps and celebrated Holy Mass for the workers. Along the canals and railroads sprang up parishes which became centers of Catholic activity and the nuclei of the several dioceses which were to be created within the next few decades. With the growth of the population there was also a corresponding development in the religious life of the people.[32]

There was a great deal of proselytizing, especially among the German immigrants. A writer in the *Watchman of the Valley* stated that there were about 15,000 Germans in Cincinnati decidedly Protestant in principle, although few belonged to that faith. He continued:

. . . Germans have less affinity for Jesuitism—the controlling Romanish force here—than any other foreign Romanists . . . the paper *Wahrheit's Freund,* which is an advocate of Popery, has come to an end . . . the *German Republican,* another daily paper, recently an advocate of Romanism, has become within a few weeks an advocate of antagonistic principles, altogether more in accordance with its name. These facts show which way the current is setting in among the commercial and political portion of the Germans. Indeed interesting facts for the evangelization of the Germans. [sic][33]

Ministers of various religious sects complained that the Catholics were building spacious cathedrals and schools and "scouring to obtain Protestant children to educate."[34] These same missionaries lamented the fact that "the villages on the whole line of our railroads are beginning to be filled with Papists; and wherever they pitch their tents and gain an influence, immorality, intemperance, and crime stalk abroad unblushingly."[35]

---

[31] W. F. Short, "Early Religious Methods and Leaders in Illinois," *Illinois State Historical Society Publications,* vol. VII (1902), pp. 56-62.
[32] D. W. Rhodes, *Churches in the History of Cincinnati and Hamilton County, Ohio,* (Cincinnati, 1895), p. 195.
[33] *Presbyterian of the West,* Mar. 30, 1848.
[34] *Home Missionary,* vol. XVIII, p. 142.
[35] *Loc. cit.*

Echoes of the parochial school question, which had enkindled Protestant wrath in New York, reached the Middle West in the 1840's. From the first years of its existence, the Church in the Mississippi Valley endeavored to erect and maintain parochial schools and this was regarded by bigoted anti-Catholics as another means used by the Church to insure its control over the Mississippi Valley. As early as 1831 the *Cincinnati Journal* sounded a clarion call to Protestants:

> It is with grief and mortification that we have witnessed the facility with which Papists persuade Protestant parents to place their children in Catholic Schools and Colleges. It is a well-known fact that these schools are nothing but proselytizing schemes on the part of the Roman hierarchy.[36]

The growth of the Church in Middle America was financed to no small degree by European missionary societies whose aid, however, aroused nativistic furor when it was made known. As early as 1833, the Society for the Propagation of the Faith with headquarters at Lyons, France,[37] placed some of the dioceses on its list of beneficiaries. Similar work was done by the Leopoldine Association, founded by Bishop Frederick Résé[38] while he was Vicar General of the Diocese of Cincinnati.[39] A third society, the Ludwig-Verein of Munich, Germany, also appropriated money for the region.[40]

The nativists accused immigrants of a connection with the Austrian Metternich on the basis of the publication of the first annual report of the Leopoldine Association. Reference was made to the diplomatic terminology used in Bishop Fenwick's correspondence

---

36 *Cincinnati Journal*, May 27, 1831.

37 The annual reports of the Society for the Propagation of the Faith were called the *Annales*. Cited by J. H. Lamott, *History of the Archdiocese of Cincinnati, 1821-1921* (Cincinnati, 1921), p. 174.

R. Payne, *The Leopoldine Association and Its Work in Ohio*, M.A. thesis no. 10, Univ. of Illinois (1905), pp. 61-621.

Publication No. 10, Illinois State Historical Library (1905), p. 324.

Home Missionary, Feb., 1843.

38 Frederick Résé was born in Vinenburg, Germany, Feb. 6, 1791. He was ordained in Rome, 1822; in Diocese of Cincinnati after 1843. He was consecrated Bishop of Detroit, Oct. 6, 1833. He died Dec. 30, 1871, in Hildesheim, Germany. See sketch by Richard J. Purcell in *Dictionary of American Biography*, vol. XV, pp. 559-560.

39 Bishop Résé encountered legal restrictions in Bavaria which prevented sending funds out of the territory. This prompted his writing a pamphlet, *Abriss der Geschichte von Cincinnati in Nord-Amerika*, which inspired the establishment of the Leopoldinen Stiftung (1829), named in memory of the Archduchess Leopoldine, Empress of Brazil.

Payne, *The Leopoldine Association, op. cit., passim*.

A. J. Rezek, "Leopoldine Association," *Catholic Encyclopedia*, vol. XVI, p. 52.

T. Roemer, *The Leopoldine Society*, unpublished M.A. thesis, Catholic Univ. of America (1933).

40 Theodore Roemer, *Ten Decades of Alms* (St. Louis, 1942), pp. 47-61; 256-262.

with Prince Metternich.[41] No appropriations were made during the years 1834, 1835, and 1836. In an appealing letter written by Bishop Purcell in January, 1836, he stated that immigration was centering around the Valley and non-Catholic principal centers of immigration. He deplored the fact that calumnious writings against Catholics were distributed everywhere and that even among children religious and political tracts were broadcast, thus imbuing them with a hatred and a prejudice against the Church. The only way to counteract this was to supply Catholic schools and Catholic teachers, and that required financial support.[42]

Hitherto, Catholics had taken a retired position in regard to local politics. They belonged to the immigrant class and were poor for the most part. Circumstances compelled them to devote their time to procuring the necessities of life. When they actively entered into politics, the nativist undercurrent reached the surface.

The denunciation of the Roman Catholic Church and its designs on the Mississippi Valley in conjunction with other alien powers was first voiced in an article by the Rev. John Angel James of Birmingham, England:

> Popery has directed a longing eye to that immense tract of land and has always felt the inward heaving ambition to compensate herself for losses in the Old World by her conquests in the New. The Valley of the Mississippi has been no doubt mapped out as well as surveyed by emissaries of the Vatican; and the cardinals are exulting in the hope of enriching the Papal States by accessions from the United States.[43]

Protestant Churches appealed to their members to preserve the nation from the blight of Romanism, stating that the Valley of the Mississippi was to be a sacred depository or sepulcher of their own religious and Christian principles since both were in danger from the Roman Catholic Church.[44]

The most notable opponent to the rise of Catholicism in the West was Lyman Beecher, the crusading preacher, who removed to the West in 1832 to take charge of Lane Seminary and to influence the

---

[41] *Cincinnati Journal,* Feb. 21, 1834.
   Catholic Telegraph, Feb. 28, 1834, vol. III, pp. 14, 110.
   A. Stritch, *Nativism in Cincinnati,* M.A. thesis, Catholic Univ. (1935), p. 8.
   Cf. T. Roemer, *The Leopoldine Society, op. cit.,* Appendix, for translation of the correspondence between Fenwick and Metternich.
[42] *Berichte der Leopoldinen Stiftung* (1831-1861), (Vienna, 1861).
[43] *Cincinnati Journal,* July 21, 1832.
   Stritch, *op. cit.,* p. 7.
[44] *Cincinnati Journal,* July 25, 1833.

religious life of the West. He had toured the Atlantic seaboard warning those to whom he lectured to be alert in discovering the plans of European rulers who had civil and ecclesiastical designs on the western pioneers. "He was," to quote a historian of the Midwest, "blind both to the isomerism of the Mississippi Valley and to the adamant social crust of New England."[45]

In his *Plea for the West* (1835), he laid bare his idea of the despotic character of "Popery" in our country. He maintained that the dire plight of Americanism and Protestantism in the West was due to the Catholic Church.

It is . . . plain that the political destiny of our nation is to be decided in the West. There is the territory and there will soon be the population, the wealth, and the political power. The Atlantic commerce and manufacturers may confer always some peculiar advantage to the East. But the West is destined to be the great central power of the nation and under heaven must affect powerfully the cause of free institutions and the liberty of the world.[46]

Hopefully, he saw a spirit of distrust showing itself among the people and he continued to philosophize upon the calamities to come upon the region:

I am afraid that our ablest patriots are looking out into the deep, vexed with storms, with great foreboding and failing of heart for fear of the things that are coming upon us; and I perceive a spirit of impatience rising, and distrust in respect to the perpetuity of our republic; and I am sure that these fears are well founded, and am glad that they exist. It is the star of hope on our dark horizon. . . .

The danger from the uneducated mind is augmenting daily by the rapid influx of foreign emigrants, unacquainted with our institutions, unaccustomed to self-government, irriscessible [sic] to education, and easily acceptable to prepossession, and inveterate credulity and intrigue, and easily embodied and wielded by sinister design. In the beginning this eruption of revolutionary Europe was not anticipated, and we opened our doors wide to the influx and naturalization of foreigners. But it is becoming a terrific inundation; it has increased upon our native population 5 to 37% and is every year advancing. It seeks, of course, to settle upon the unoccupied territory of the West, and may at no distant day equal and even outnumber the native population. What is to be done to educate the millions which in twenty years Europe will pour out upon us?[47]

A controversy was precipitated when Judge James Hall, "like a lone knight championing an unpopular cause, boldly struck the sound-

---

[45] G. M. Stevenson, "Nativism in the 'Forties and 'Fifties, with special reference to the Mississippi Valley," *Mississippi Valley Historical Review*, vol. IX (1922), p. 191.
[46] L. Beecher, *A Plea for the West* (Cincinnati, 1835), pp. 11 ff.
[47] *Loc. cit.*

ing shield of the doughty crusader." The publication of *A Plea for the West* had aroused bitter feeling and is thought to have inflamed public opinion unjustly against the Catholic Church. Hall challenged the claims of Beecher's book, believing Catholics misjudged and unjustly abused. In his magazine he devoted much space to a review of the book and critically referred to it as "*A Plea for Lane Seminary and Against the Catholics.*" He published an extensive article in the May, 1835, issue devoted to the Catholic question. Other prejudiced writers, among whom was Eli Taylor, the editor of the antislavery anti-Catholic *Cincinnati Journal,* joined in the controversy. As a result Hall's subscription list suffered and he was referred to as a "Judas" and as a traitor by his own sect.[48]

Not only did ministers rant and surmise the growth of Catholic influence, but they projected a definite plan to estimate the influence of the Church and to curb it. The following editorial in the *Catholic Telegraph* expressed the Catholic attitude in the region:

> The wrath of the Presbyterians becomes more intense in proportion to the prosperity of the Catholic religion. Their Calvinistic bile is so redundant and acrimonious, that nothing short of a general conflagration of convents and Catholic institutions can act as a sedative to their spasmodic ravings against the Church of Christ. They are endeavoring to engross the whole education of the West in their own Calvinistic way; nothing can equal their cunning in seducing children into the schools but their anti-Catholic hatred and persecution. They have filled every village store with the "Key to Popery" and Fox's "Book of Martyrs" . . .[49]

Beecher, encouraged by the increased immigration of the 'Forties, became the "Americanization Worker," and in a letter to Doctor Albert Barnes on July 11, 1842, he said in part:

> The time has come in which we must unite our counsels and our forces for the West, as all we have done will be impotent to exhort the controlling influence of our Christian civilization, science and holiness over the infinitude of depraved minds here bursting forth, and rolling in from abroad upon us like a flood. . . . No human means can so certainly meet and repel this invasion of Catholic Europe as a competent ministry and revivals of religion . . . therefore the streams of Christian emigration from the East must flow again, the prayers of Christians from the West must go up day and night and the hand of benevolence must open wide. . . . The battle is begun. We give notice of it to

    [48] W. H. Venable, *Beginnings of Literary Culture in the Ohio Valley* (Cincinnati, 1891), p. 379.
    J. Hall, *The Catholic Question to which are annexed critical notices of A Plea for the West* (Cincinnati, 1838), *passim.*
    [49] *Catholic Telegraph,* Feb. 25, 1836.

our fathers and mothers and brothers and sisters in the East and call for help. Who is on the Lord's side—WHO? . . . [50]

Another factor which incited the nativists to antagonism toward the foreign element was the publication of a pamphlet in London and Dublin in 1842. It was entitled "A Proposed Plan of a General Emigration Society by a Catholic Gentleman." The object as stated in the opening paragraph was to send the Irish poor to America. Editors of the American Home Missionary Society made extensive comments in their magazine. The pamphlet contained a map to show the region it thought best to settle. The territory included Upper Canada, Wisconsin, Michigan, Indiana, Ohio, and parts of Missouri and Iowa. The desirability of the country was proven by descriptive extracts from De Tocqueville, Captain Marryatt, Harriet Martineau, and Judge Haliburton. The conclusions reached by the officials of the Protestant societies were:

1. We must expect colonization stimulated and systematized more and more.
2. The great field of conflict for religious and political supremacy will be the West.
3. NOW is the time to save the West.[51]

Scarcely a number of the *Home Missionary* appeared which did not contain some reference to the fear of a specific plan on the part of European Catholics to capture the Valley. In the 1842 *Report* of the Society was the following:

The territory of this nation is an unlimited and inviting field, to which human swarms are gathering from other lands. The crumbling dynasties of the Old World are sending hither materials to reconstruct the fabrics which are tottering to ruin. Already the foundations are laid for social institutions such as our fathers knew not. Foreign Papists are planting our fairest territories thick with their schools.

Colony after colony of men of a strange tongue and stranger associations are possessing themselves of our soil and gathering around our ballot boxes. In Missouri, Illinois, and Arkansas there are seventy-four priests with literary institutions of every grade in which, at least, a thousand youths are now training—here then the West is infected and every pulsation throws abroad a strain of influence baneful to the civil freedom and religious well-being of unnumbered thousands.[52]

[50] Lyman Beecher, *Autobiography*, 2 vols. (Cincinnati, 1864), vol. II, pp. 453-454.
[51] Illinois State Historical Society, *Publication No. 10* (1905), p. 323.
[52] *Loc. cit.*

This then was the attitude toward foreigners, and especially toward Catholic foreigners, which prevailed in the United States in general and in the Mississippi Valley in particular during the first half of the nineteenth century. It was into this region that the Sisters of Saint Joseph came to make their first foundation in the United States. Not to Philadelphia nor to New York nor to Boston did the original colony of Sisters come, but to St. Louis in the heart of America where conditions made the frontier a challenge, where there was need for the work of an active group of religious women to train the children of those frontiersmen and to save the families of the immigrant groups for the Church in the midst of a movement to "Save the West for Protestantism." It was from this heart of America, from Carondolet, the cradle of the Sisters of Saint Joseph in America, that the footprints were traced to frontiers in practically every state in the Union.

CHAPTER III

Carondolet, 1836-1854

THE story of the conquest of the Mississippi Valley by the French in the eighteenth century is a fascinating one. The *coeuer de bois* and the missionaries of the cross walked side by side to conquer the material and spiritual resources of that mighty land. Today a veritable litany of the saints attests the influence of the Church on this early frontier. It was not until about the middle of the eighteenth century that white settlers ventured to make permanent settlements on the west bank of the Mississippi. The Indian tribes, whose names are perpetuated in states and cities, such as the Omaha, the Iowa, the Kansas, and the Missouri, furnished a fertile field for missionary enterprise.

In 1784, M. Laclede Linguest, a man of noble lineage and a representative of the merchant princes of France, sought a site on the Mississippi where he might store merchandise for trade with the Indians of Missouri. He found near the junction of the Mississippi and Missouri rivers a location which he thought might become "one of the fairest cities in America," and named the city he built there Saint Louis, in honor of Louis IX, Crusader King of France.[1]

Political changes at the end of the Intercolonial Wars had their reflection in the religious complexion of the territory. Although a distinct culture area, by the Treaty of Paris in 1763 the Illinois country was transferred to England; and Louisiana, which included Saint Louis, was given to Spain. Thus, Saint Louis became an outpost of the far-off Diocese of Havana.[2] For a period of two decades this condition prevailed. In 1793 the Diocese of New Orleans, which included all of Louisiana, extended its jurisdiction to Saint Louis.[3] Ten years later,

[1] Sister Lucida Savage (comp.), *The Century's Harvest, 1836-1936* (St. Louis, 1936), p. 13.

[2] J. G. Shea, *Life and Times of the Most Rev. John Carroll* (New York, 1888), p. 570. Spain did not take formal possession until 1770, hence the jurisdiction of the Diocese of Havana dates from that date rather than from 1763.

[3] Sister Lucida Savage, *The Congregation of St. Joseph of Carondolet* (St. Louis, 1923), p. 28.

in 1803, Thomas Jefferson cast aside his strict construction theories of government and, in order to keep an enemy nation from our back door, bought the entire Louisiana country. This was the beginning of the territorial growth of the United States—the impetus which gave rise to our Manifest Destiny complex.

There is a geneological connection between the first Bishop of New Orleans and the coming of the Sisters of Saint Joseph to America. For nine years (until 1812) after the acquisition of Louisiana, the See of New Orleans remained vacant. A native of San Domingo, Valentine Du Bourg, was consecrated in Rome to fill the office. Knowing the field for missionary work in his vast diocese, the new ordinary remained in Europe for two years soliciting funds and recruits for his diocese. In Lyons, a charitable lady, Madame Petit, who later associated herself with Pauline Jaricot in establishing the Society for the Propagation of the Faith, became interested in his plea.[4] And the connection with the Sisters of Saint Joseph of Lyons was through their spiritual director, Father Cholleton, who was an active member of this new society. When Bishop Du Bourg returned to America, several Vincentian Fathers, among them Joseph Rosati, accompanied him. Therefore, Bishop Du Bourg should be remembered as a link in the chain of persons and circumstances which brought the Sisters of Saint Joseph to America. It was he who interested the future Bishop of Saint Louis in this particular community of women.

Within the next decade there was an influx of native Americans and immigrants into the vicinity of Saint Louis. In 1836 the Diocese of Saint Louis was created with the Vincentian Father, the Rev. Joseph Rosati, as the first incumbent.

The year following his consecration as Bishop of Saint Louis, Bishop Rosati wrote the following concerning the diocese:

The Diocese of Saint Louis, which includes the State of Missouri and the territory of Arkansas, is more prosperous than New Orleans, although destitute of the means necessary for the support of its priests. The Bishop as yet has no income; he has only land; but the outlay necessary to render it of value is greater than the revenue it brings in. The church is burdened with

[4] J. G. Shea, *History of the Catholic Church in the United States,* 4 vols. (New York, 1888), vol. III, p. 361.

E. J. Hickey, *The Society for the Propagation of the Faith: Its Foundation, Organization and Success, 1822-1922* (Washington, 1922), pp. 16-22.

Savage, *The Congregation of St. Joseph of Carondolet, op. cit.,* pp. 28-29.

debts contracted in building it. I have sent Father Niel to beg for help from the charitable of Europe. I trust his mission will be successful.[5]

Bishop Rosati needed priests and funds. In his necessity he appealed to Father Cholleton to act as his foreign vicar-general. His duty was to represent the interests of the diocese to the Society for the Propagation of the Faith, and to secure subjects for the missions, as appears from Father Cholleton's letter of acceptance:

It is in quality of your vicar that I shall appear at the Society of the Propagation of the Faith, and that I shall obtain from it, I hope, abundant help. I no longer doubt that Monsignor de Pins will send you subjects whom the Lord will deign to call in His mercy to the great work of the missions in Louisiana.[6]

This same priest was directed to procure subjects for convents in America by directing to these novitiates French girls who might want to devote their lives to the "salvation of poor American souls." [7]

Father Cholleton first broached the subject of sending subjects to the missions in Missouri at the time that Father Odin was in Lyons.[8] Both priests communicated with Bishop Rosati on the desirability of introducing a community of the Sisters of Saint Joseph into the diocese.

A well-known personality in aristocratic French circles and equally well-known in the traditions of the various communities of the Sisters of Saint Joseph was the Countess de la Rochejaquelin. During the first years of the publication of the *Annales de la Propagation de la Foi* many interested persons contributed money to the far-off missions. The reading of the *Annales* had revealed to the countess the great poverty of the missions along the Mississippi. Her thoughts turned to the various types of work carried on by the Sisters of Saint Joseph of Lyons and, knowing the value of religious women on such missions, she obtained the promise of Mother Saint John Fontbonne that she would give the Sisters for America, if His Lordship desired them. It was then that Madame de la Rochejaquelin suggested to Father Odin

---

[5] Letter dated Jan. 7, 1827. *Annales de la Propagation de la Foi,* vol. ii, p. 410.
See also J. Rothensteiner, *History of the Archdiocese of St. Louis,* 2 vols. (St. Louis, 1928), vol. I, *passim.*
[6] Letter from Father Cholleton to Bishop Rosati, May 27, 1837, St. Louis Archdiocesan archives.
See also Savage, *The Congregation of St. Joseph of Carondolet, op. cit.,* p. 29.
[7] Letter from Father Odin, C. M., to Father Cholleton, *Annals of the Propagation of the Faith,* Nov., 1827, vol. 36, p. 126.
[8] In note 6 reference to the Archbishop de Pins should have added that the same archbishop would encourage the Sisters of St. Joseph to espouse the cause.

to propose them in her name, saying that she would defray the expenses of the first foundation.[9]

Madame de la Comtesse de la Rochejaquelin, the wife of the great Vendean general of the same name, was born Duchesse de Duras, and became by her first marriage Princess de Talmont. She had been widowed at the age of eighteen, and her second marriage to the Count de la Rochejaquelin rendered her very obnoxious to the Revolutionary movement of 1830. She had to leave the country. Her possessions in various parts of France were confiscated, and she herself sent into exile.

. . . The heroine devoted her money, her time, her influence to endeavor to send help and comfort (to the people of La Vendée). Throughout the fifteen years of the Restoration she begged continuously for the country of her adoption.

In eloquent words Cardinal Pie describes the life of charity led by her, and of which he was an eye-witness in her later years. "It was not enough for her," he says, "to send to the poor farmers all the money she had at her disposal after her family expenses had been provided for. No, there is to such as her little merit in giving what one has. She would do more; she condemned herself to work, to incessant work. She armed herself with knitting needle and spinning wheel with an energy I should call martial. From earliest dawn till a late hour in the evening, and this for over fifty years, she could be seen preparing woolen dresses, clothes for all ages and either sex—old men, women, new-born babes. She knew by heart the facts regarding each family. The history of each generation, the names and ages of the children . . . each piece of work, therefore, had its special destination, and in spite of her cruel blindness, nothing could turn her from her occupations. While she dictated her long and charming letters, which were generally on behalf of La Vendée, her fingers were still engaged in her work. While she told her delicious stories, which kept her family enthralled, she did not neglect her knitting, or at the most, in the heat of her narrative, she would thrust her needle through her thick white hair, only to begin her work again a moment later."

"The dear lady," says the Cardinal in his beautiful funeral oration, "possessed the ancient faith, the candid simplicity of the early ages, a spirit of prayer, and habits of piety which were apparent even in her last words and moments. Her heart, open to all by her charity, was for her children and friends a treasure of tenderness and devotedness." She died Feb. 15, 1857 (born Oct. 25, 1772).[10]

[9] Sister of St. Joseph, *Mother St. John Fontbonne: A Biography* (tr. from French) (New York, 1936), pp. 334-340.

Desclée de Brouwer (ed.), *Mère St. Jean Fontbonne* (Bruges, 1929), pp. 509-518.

Savage, *The Congregation of St. Joseph of Carondolet, op. cit.*, pp. 30-31.

St. Louis Catholic News, suppl., July 3, 1936.

[10] Mary Monica Maxwell-Scott, *The Life of Madame de la Rochejaquelin* (London, 1911), pp. 220-223.

Cecil Biggane (ed.), *Memoirs of the Marquise de la Rochejaquelin* (London, 1933), *passim*.

Bishop Rosati delayed his answer, knowing that the beginning of the mission would consist of more than the transportation of the religious. The Countess herself wrote to him:

I think the excellent Father Odin and the Vicar General of Lyons have written you several times on the subject of the desire I have to send the Sisters of Saint Joseph to America. Your silence on this subject proves either that the letters did not reach you or that you are not anxious for this establishment. If, indeed, you have any objections to it, I wonder what they may be. It is not a vague idea to do a good work in America, which has made me propose them to you. Protected by Divine Providence, in a singular manner, in all the difficulties and misfortunes to which I have been exposed, I promised God, in so far as He would deign to bless this design, to send six Sisters of Saint Joseph to North America to convert the savages, to teach their children and those of Protestant families, and to convert also those to whom the missionaries, too busy or too few, are able to make but passing visits. The reading of the *Annals of the Propagation of the Faith* made me shed tears over these harvests for which there are no laborers.

These incomparable Sisters, once established, could be sent two by two into the little villages, and there prepare the way for Baptism, First Communion, and Confirmation. A settlement near the Indian territories, built on a rather wide plan, could be, after a short time, of the greatest advantage.

My Lord, perhaps you do not know the Sisters of Saint Joseph. They follow the rule of Saint Augustine[11] and make perpetual vows. Their rule obliges them to all the virtues of the cloister, joined to those which exact an ardent charity for their fellow beings. It was the first thought of Saint Francis de Sales; one which he renounced, with sorrow for his Visitation. Thus piety, interior recollection, self-denial, humility, and prayer on the one hand; and on the other a devotion, without restriction, to all works of charity.

If you had seen, as I, their spirit of poverty and humility. [sic] It is evangelical. I have known them for thirteen years. I have established several convents and contributed to the establishment of others. The East of France is alive with the activity of these Sisters. I have sent them to the West. They are not numerous enough for the demands. I have interested Father Cholleton, who would have chosen excellent subjects. Father Bochard sent them wherever they were requested, saying to them: "Go quickly." I know a foundation which began in a stable and with only six cents. God is there. From the example of the Crib, this establishment prospered, as well as others begun in a like manner.

My Lord, the spirit of the Congregation of Saint Joseph is something without precedent. It is this poverty and this lowliness which Our Lord taught, and which captures the world. It seems to me that if I succeeded in establishing the Sisters of Saint Joseph in your America, near the savages, and near so many heretics in your diocese, I shall have done, during my life, something pleasing to God to win His mercy for my sins. I know that what I have given is not enough, but I will give more. I will help; only say, My Lord, what you think is necessary for the beginning.

I pray you to answer as soon as possible. I am anxious that the work be

---

11 The Sisters of St. Joseph follow the Rule of St. Ignatius, but this rule has for its basis one of the four ancient rules recognized by the Church, that of St. Augustine. The other rules are: The Rules of St. Basil, St. Benedict, and St. Francis of Assisi.

accomplished. Be persuaded that I am altogether unwilling to impose my views on you as to the place and the best means to be taken to accomplish this end. Do what you think best. I have but one desire, namely, that they be not far from the territory of the savages and that they work for the conversion of poor Indians and poor Protestants; in fine, for all unhappy sects. I have an idea which I submit to you—that all the merits of the religious who will live in your establishments be consecrated to the souls of our erring brothers, no matter of what sect,—who, unknown to the world, have at the moment of death, submitted their minds and hearts to God and to truth; and have promised, if they lived, to seek it with all their hearts by this final act, which says in one form or another, "My Lord, I believe all that you want me to believe." Do you not think, indeed that this endowment of prayers and merits is the spirit of the great love of Our Lord for the salvation of souls, and at the same time a great consolation for Protestants? The thought of being eternally separated from their friends and neighbors holds back a great number who are drawn towards Catholicism.

I am imposing on your time which is so valuable. Permit me to ask you to remember me to Madame Henrietta Kersaint, my cousin, a Religious of the Sacred Heart in Saint Louis. I ask her prayers and yours particularly, while begging you to accept my sentiments of respectful consideration and devotion in Our Lord.

I have the honor of being your very humble and very obedient servant,

FELICITE DE DURAS, COUNTESS DE LA ROCHEJAQUELIN
Chambery, June 10, 1835.[12]

This letter was answered immediately by Bishop Rosati, who readily accepted her kind offer and requested that two more Sisters be prepared to teach the deaf and dumb.[13]

During these months of uncertainty as to whether the Bishop of Saint Louis would agree to the proposition of the generous Countess and of Father Cholleton, Mother Saint John began the preparation of the Sisters for a sacrifice which possibly was in store for them. She did not disillusion them concerning the sacrifices which would needs be met on the frontier in America. The prospect of deprivation of Holy Mass when the priest would be on trips to the far-flung mission stations, the poverty of the surroundings, and the thanklessness of the natives, all these situations furnished material for her conferences with the Sisters. Then she would emphasize the importance of the interior life, for the more they sanctified themselves the easier would be the sanctification of others.

---

[12] Sister of St. Joseph, *op. cit.*, pp. 336-338. This same letter in French is to be found in Brouwer, *op. cit.*, pp. 512-514. The original letter was presented to the Sisters of St. Joseph of Carondolet and is to be found today in the Motherhouse Archives in St. Louis.

[13] Savage, *The Congregation of St. Joseph of Carondolet, op. cit.*, pp. 30-31.

When news came that Bishop Rosati would accept the Sisters for his diocese, an appeal was made for volunteers. The Sisters were instructed to take time to consider the appeal, and to consult their spiritual directors, to pray for guidance, and, if called, to respond joyfully. Mother Saint John was surprised and pleased at the percentage of the Sisters who answered the summons. Among the first to present themselves for the missionary field were her two nieces, Sister Febronia and Sister Marie Delphine Fontbonne, daughters of her only brother, Claude Fontbonne. Surely the joy of her heart must have overcome the sadness she experienced at this time.

Seven Sisters were chosen from the group of volunteers. Six were to leave at once and the seventh was to prepare herself to instruct the mute. The pioneer band consisted of Sister Febronia Fontbonne, Sister Delphine Fontbonne, Sister Febronia Chapellon, Sister Saint Protais Deboille, Sister Philomene Vilaine, and Sister Marguerite Boute.[14] The seventh, Sister Celestine Pommerel, as well as Julie Fournier, a postulant, were sent to Saint Etienne to learn the deaf and dumb language.

Among the priests who volunteered for the American missions was the brother of the two Fontbonne sisters, Father James Fontbonne. Mother Saint John would not appoint the superior of the group, so Father Cholleton appointed Sister Febronia Fontbonne to that office. The day of departure was January 4, 1836, and much could be written on the departure ceremony. Suffice it to say that the parting was poignant both for those leaving for foreign parts and those remaining at home. The simple religious ceremony was in keeping with the spirit of the Sisters of Saint Joseph, each Sister receiving the maternal blessing of Mother Saint John.[15]

From Lyons the little band proceeded to Paris where they spent a few days with the Sisters of Saint Vincent de Paul. This first contact of the America-bound Sisters of Saint Joseph was significant. On their arrival in Saint Louis they were again taken care of by this same community. Later the pioneers to Philadelphia and to Canandaigua were received en route by these same daughters of Saint

---

[14] The Christian name of the Countess de la Rochejaquelin was added to Sister Marguerite's name. Thenceforth she was known as Sister Felicite.
  Sister of St. Joseph, *op. cit.*, pp. 338-340.
  Savage, *The Congregation of St. Joseph of Carondolet, op. cit.*, p. 31.
[15] This story loses significance when translated. For the original account in French of this departure ceremony see Brouwer, *op. cit.*, p. 518.

Vincent. This is an interesting contact since it was Bishop de Maupas, the founder of the Sisters of Saint Joseph in Le Puy in 1650, who preached the funeral sermon for his friend, Saint Vincent de Paul.[16]

At Havre, where there was a delay of some ten days, a pious woman, Madame Dodard, received the travelers into her home. This good woman was after the heart of Madame de la Rochejaquelin; she also had given her fortune to the poor and in support of the missions.

The group left Havre on January 17, 1836, on one of the well-known sea-going vessels of the early 1830's, the *Heidelberg*.[17] It is difficult for us in this day of modern conveniences to visualize the privations of those forty-nine days on the open sea over a century ago. There was the shadow of death to frighten the wayfarers—first, in the illness of the seminarian, John Escoffier, whom the Sisters nursed back to life; second, in the terrible tempest which was encountered in the Gulf of Mexico. Not unlike the sailors of the *Santa Maria* of Columbus some three and a half centuries before, the good Sisters breathed a sigh of relief and a prayer of thanksgiving when the *Heidelberg* docked at New Orleans on March the fifth.[18]

How happy they must have been when they learned that Bishop Rosati of St. Louis was in New Orleans and would receive them on the following day. During their brief stay in New Orleans, the Sisters lived with the Ursuline Sisters.

Their letters of introduction were eloquent testimonials of the Sisters' qualifications for their difficult undertaking. Archbishop de Pins of Lyons averred: "They will be excellent catechists, good infirmarians, perfect sacristans, and zealous instructors. Their services can but marvelously advance the work of God in your diocese."

The Countess wrote:

It is with greatest happiness that I write this letter which will be given to you by our dear Sisters whom you deign to receive among your flock. They are happy, I think, at the idea of suffering privations for Jesus Christ. I cannot say how I have been touched by their dispositions. I am confident that they

---

[16] The funeral took place in the Church of St. Germain L'Auxerrois. M. Collet, *Life of St. Vincent de Paul* (Baltimore, 1805), p. 247.

[17] It is interesting to note that when a colony of Sisters of St. Joseph from Moutiers, France, came to America in 1854 to work in the Vicariate of Kansas for Bishop Miege (although they did not engage in that field for certain reasons), they also sailed on a vessel called the *Heidelberg*.

[18] Brouwer, *op. cit.*, p. 521.
Savage, *The Congregation of St. Joseph of Carondolet, op. cit.*, pp. 34-35.
Sisters of St. Joseph, *op. cit.*, pp. 341-343.

Reverend Mother Saint John Fontbonne, 1759–1843

bring to America the true and admirable spirit of their congregation, and that the grain of mustard seed which is to be sown in St. Louis under your protection will become a large tree. My hope is that, with time, the fruits of the establishment of these good Sisters in America will be immense and that they will comprise all works, which charity may suggest. I am most anxious to be informed exactly of our humble beginnings and I shall aid them to the best of my ability, whenever it may be necessary.[19]

Another experience awaited the Sisters in the form of a trip up the Mississippi River on a river boat, the *Charles Collier*. This trip took ten days. An episode of their stay in New Orleans was the Sisters' first contact with the nativistic attitude of the Valley, and the precaution learned then was reapplied on the river journey. The immigrant Sisters were persuaded by the Ursulines to disguise their religious habit whenever they went abroad, donning at that time a cap and heavy veil worn by widows of the time. This crypto-Catholicism must have recalled the days of persecution in France. They wondered at this precaution, as the only obstacle they had expected to meet in this line was from the savages. Maybe the fear of the Ursulines was exaggerated for the territory of New Orleans, but it should be recalled that this same religious community of women had had their convent burned at Charlestown, Massachusetts, only two years previous to 1836. This disguise was worn on board the river boat to Saint Louis. We shall see a further use of it later.[20]

On the lovely Feast of the Annunciation, the Sisters of Saint Joseph reached their destination after a long, tiresome journey. Here the friendly daughters of Saint Vincent de Paul received them. There were at that time in Saint Louis three other communities: the Sisters of Loretto,[21] the Visitandines,[22] and the Ladies of the Sacred Heart.[23]

In a Pastoral Letter of 1839, Bishop Rosati spoke of religious communities of his diocese:

The other priests of our diocese who do not belong to any religious community have also been very active in propagating our holy religion. We are very grateful to them for having built many churches and institutions of

---

[19] These letters are to be found in the Carondolet Motherhouse Archives. See also, Sister of St. Joseph, *op. cit.*, p. 342; Brouwer, *op. cit.*, p. 522-523.

[20] Savage, *The Congregation of St. Joseph of Carondolet, op. cit.*, p. 35.

[21] These Sisters had schools at Apple Creek and New Madrid and a school and orphanage at Bethlehem near the Barrens. See A. C. Minogue, *Loretto, Annals of the Century* (New York, 1912), pp. 60-84.

[22] At Kaskaskia, the Visitandines from Georgetown were established in 1833.

[23] The Ladies of the Sacred Heart, brought from France by Bishop Du Bourg in 1818, were conducting an academy for girls in "French Town." Savage, *The Congregation of St. Joseph of Carondolet, op. cit.*, pp. 36-37.

learning. We are happy to see that the faithful have also been very zealous in seconding the efforts of their pastors.

The Madams of the Sacred Heart, the Daughters of Charity, the Sisters of Loretto and the Visitation nuns have founded boarding and day schools, orphanages and hospitals. Finally, the Sisters of St. Joseph founded three institutions, one of which is exclusively devoted to the care of the deaf and dumb.[24]

It is not easy to crowd the events of twenty years into a short discourse, especially when these twenty years pertain to beginnings. The French community adapted itself well to frontier conditions, received American subjects, was augmented by the arrival of a few more Sisters from Lyons and from Moutiers, France.

At this point it might be well to quote from *The Century's Harvest*, which in a general manner summarized the period under consideration:

The little band of six was soon broken, three of the number being sent by Bishop Rosati under the superiorship of Mother Febronia Fontbonne to Cahokia, then in the Diocese of Saint Louis, where a school was awaiting teachers. The remaining three, Mother Delphine Fontbonne, Sister Philomene Vilaine, and Sister Saint Protais Debouille, after a delay of some months went to Carondolet, to the log cabin convent intended for them but just vacated by the Sisters of Charity, who took their orphan boys to a new home in St. Louis.

Carondolet, about five and a half miles south of Saint Louis, was, prior to 1803, a Spanish town, where Spanish law and customs prevailed; but in 1836, its character was decidedly French. The fact that the settlers were less prosperous than their neighbors gave rise to the appellation, "Vide Poche" (empty pocket) by which the town was commonly known. The convent consisted of two rooms, a shed likewise of two; one on the ground floor and one in the loft. The latter was reached by a ladder on the outside. The house contained two empty bedsteads. The Sisters brought with them two empty ticks, some bedclothes, and a skillet. The skillet, according to an early annalist, was for the purpose of making omelets; but the providing of eggs was left to Divine Providence.

The new St. Joseph's bore no resemblance to the imposing Chateau Yon on the Hill of the Chartreuse in Lyons, France; but contentment reigned within its crude log walls, and God blessed the labor of its inmates. The tiny seed planted then grew into a mighty tree whose branches spread north, east, west, and south, to the extreme limits of the United States and into Canada. The first seed outside of Carondolet, it is true, was planted on thorny ground, and the fruit reaped did not, humanly speaking, justify their efforts. It was a school for free Negro girls on Third Street, St. Louis, opened by Bishop Kenrick in 1843 and closed the same year. The circumstances of its closing are thus graphically related by Sister Saint John Fournier, one of the three Sisters sent there, in a letter to her superiors in France:

[24] *Lettre Pastorale de Mgr. L'Évêque de St. Louis,* from collection of letters of Bishop Rosati (St. Louis, 1839), pp. 4-5.

We taught free Negro girls, and also prepared slaves for the reception of the Sacraments. This displeased the whites very much. They threatened to drive us out by main force. The threats came every day. One morning several persons called me out of the church and told me that the following night some one would come and drive us out of the house. I had no fear and I said nothing to the Sisters. I had great confidence in the Holy Virgin, and placed some miraculous medals at the street door and on the fence. At eleven o'clock that night a great noise awakened the Sisters suddenly. A crowd of people assembled in the street were crying out and blaspheming. We threw ourselves on our knees and commenced the Miserere and other prayers. During this time some mad men rushed against the door; all at once a patrol of armed police arrived and dispersed them. They came back three times that same night but the Holy Virgin protected us. In spite of their fury and their efforts, they were not able to attain their object and break open the door. The day after this adventure, the Mayor of Saint Louis advised Bishop Kenrick to close the school for a time, which he did.[25]

Thus ended the Sisters' first effort at expansion. Their courage was further put to test when, in the following year, 1844, the angry waters of the Mississippi submerged the small village of Cahokia, and the Sisters there, rescued from "The Abbey," as their convent was called by the villagers, returned to Carondolet. A boarding and day academy was flourishing there, where the log cabin had given place in 1841 to a three-story brick building, admirably planned and supervised by Mother Celestine Pommerel. She, with Sister Saint John Fournier, then a postulant, formed an addition in 1837 to the original band of six. In 1839 Mother Celestine Pommerel succeeded Mother Delphine as Superior.

With spirits undaunted by seeming failure and by the tempest waged against them by the elements as well as by man, a small group ventured forth in 1844, and, with Mother Delphine Fontbonne as Superior, took charge of Saint Vincent's parochial school in St. Louis. Outside the Academy in Carondolet, this, the oldest parish school in Saint Louis, was the first successful venture of the Congregation. Through all manner of vicissitudes of time and change, St. Vincent's has carried on.

During the eighteen years of the superiorship of Mother Celestine Pommerel, the Academy grew in efficiency and usefulness and the Congregation spread far and wide. In 1847, she sent a band of Sisters to Philadelphia; in 1851, to Saint Paul and to Toronto; in 1853, to Wheeling, Virginia; and in 1854 to Canandaigua, New York, in the

[25] Savage, *The Century's Harvest, 1836-1936, op. cit.,* pp. 14-18.

Diocese of Buffalo. Many times this noble superior visited these scattered mission houses under difficult circumstances and arduous modes of travel. At her death in 1857, the Carondolet Community numbered 149 religious, with foundations in Missouri, Mississippi, Minnesota, New York, Pennsylvania, Virginia, and Canada.[26]

The first foundation to be made at a distance from the motherhouse in Saint Louis was in Philadelphia, in the spring of 1847. It was at the request of Bishop Francis Patrick Kenrick that Mother Celestine Pommerel consented that the Sisters go to Philadelphia to take over an orphan asylum which previously had been conducted by the Sisters of Charity.[27] There were many needs on the Missouri frontier for the limited number of Sisters. This in addition to the perils and inconveniences of travel and communication made the granting of the request for Sisters to go to such a distance almost an unthought-of consideration.

Yet four Sisters were sent on this mission—Sister Saint John Fournier as superior and Sisters Mary Magdalen Weber, Mary Joseph Clark, and Elizabeth Kinkaid. Although Mother Saint John Fournier was recalled to work in the newer mission fields of Virginia and Minnesota, she was later returned to Philadelphia, where she became an important factor in the development of that mighty branch of the Sisters of Saint Joseph.

The diaries of the pioneer band tell of jubilation and rejoicing as they traveled East at the news recently received of the victory of General Scott at Vera Cruz. The journey, now capable of accomplishment in a day, took nearly three weeks. Again the Sisters dressed in widow's weeds in order to conceal as much as possible their religious habits. Philadelphia had been a hotbed of nativist activity and had only recently emerged from one of the worst episodes in the annals of American intolerance.[28] The Catholic population of Philadelphia was about one hundred thousand in a total population of a million. There were several parochial schools in charge of many different communities.

---

[26] At that time what is now West Virginia was still part of Virginia.

[27] When the American Sisters of Charity became affiliated with the Daughters of Vincent de Paul of France, they discontinued the orphanages in both St. Louis and Philadelphia. In both cities, therefore, the Sisters of St. Joseph replaced them.

[28] R. A. Billington, *The Protestant Crusade* (New York, 1938), has an account of this period in Philadelphia nativism. There has been a series of studies of nativism for various states and cities made at Catholic University under the direction of Prof. Richard J. Purcell.

On Chestnut Street in a large building known as the Gothic Mansion, Mother Saint John and her companions took possession of the orphanage. There were about forty boy inmates. Postulants who soon applied for admission were indeed an asset when, in addition to the orphanage, a parochial school and a hospital were opened within two years.

This was the first hospital conducted by the Sisters of Saint Joseph in the United States. It remained under their jurisdiction for a period of ten years, ministering largely to Irish immigrants who were coming into Philadelphia in large numbers, many of whom were suffering from fever.[29]

The next missionary foundation of the Sisters of Saint Joseph was made in Toronto, Canada, at the request of Bishop Armand Charbonnel. Quoting from a pamphlet written by the Sisters in Toronto: "His Lordship, on his return from Rome in the autumn of 1851, visited Bishop Kenrick in Philadelphia. While there he met Mother M. Delphine Fontbonne, whose aunt, Mother Saint John Fontbonne, had been well known to the Charbonnel family. The Bishop, esteeming the young kinswoman, a valiant woman and capable of undertaking a work which he had in mind, begged the good Bishop Kenrick to allow her, with three of her Sisters, to go to his aid in Toronto." [30] With the consent, therefore, of Bishop Kenrick, they set out for the northern mission and arrived there on October 7, 1851.[31] In a letter addressed to Father Denavit, director of the Grand Seminary of Lyons, Bishop Charbonnel said in reference to the Sisters of Saint Joseph: "I could make use of one hundred of them at once, if I had them. The Sisters are called to do immense good here. They give everything but absolution." The first work of the Sisters was in an orphan asylum known as the House of Providence. Again, the footprints met another frontier, and from this foundation several other foundations were made in Canada.[32]

In the same year that the pioneer band left Philadelphia for To-

---

[29] Savage, *The Congregation of St. Joseph of Carondolet, op. cit.,* pp. 68-73.

[30] Sisters of St. Joseph (Toronto), *Diamond Jubilee, St. Joseph's Convent* (Toronto, 1926), p. 5.

[31] Mother Delphine Fontbonne went from Toronto to Hamilton, Can., to establish a mission. Returning to Toronto to assist in caring for the victims of a typhus epidemic, she contracted the disease and died Feb. 7, 1856. Sister of St. Joseph, *op. cit.,* p. 360; Brouwer, *op. cit.,* p. 545.

[32] See appendices for statistics of various communities of Sisters of St. Joseph in the United States and Canada.

ronto, another group left Saint Louis for Minnesota Territory. These two foundations, one to British Canada and the other to the frontier of the growing United States followed parallel patterns of growth as well as hardship in rugged, ever-changing environments.

The opportunity to meet and convert savages had been uppermost in the minds of the six Sisters who crossed the ocean from France in 1836. Now, fifteen years later, that opportunity presented itself in the invitation of Bishop Joseph Cretin of Saint Paul.

Included partly in the Old Northwest, Minnesota has had a colorful and interesting history. The Church has been intimately connected with this history. The Saint Paul of the 1850's has been described as "a frontier town, where Indians in gay blankets stalked the streets and scalping was still known."[33] It is more than a coincidence that two of the four subdeacons who accompanied Bishop Loras in 1838 from France to work among the Indians were from Le Puy; in fact one of them, Father Lucien Galtier, is considered the founder of Saint Paul. This town became the nucleus of a Catholic population of French, Irish, and Swiss, and within ten years warranted the establishment of a see and the appointment of a bishop.

The expansion of the work of the Sisters of Saint Joseph was never by chance, rather it was always because of some contact with the members of the hierarchy. In the instance of Bishop Cretin, shortly after his ordination at St. Sulpice in 1823, he was sent to Ferney on the French frontier facing Geneva. Ferney was the only part of the Diocese of Belley in which Calvinism had taken a foothold. In 1824, a school was opened by the Sisters of Saint Joseph from Lyons, and for a period of fourteen years he knew the work of the European Sisters. Therefore, on his appointment to the Diocese of Saint Paul, he at once interceded with Mother Celestine Pommerel for a colony of Sisters. The Sisters chosen were: Sisters Saint John Fournier, Philomene Vilaine, Francis Joseph Ivory, and Scholastica Vasquez. At the end of a six-day boat trip to the headwaters of the Mississippi, the Sisters saw their convent—"a long shanty, one and a half stories high, facing the river."[34] One week later the first school of the Minnesota foundation was opened—this was the beginning of the splendid work of the Community in the Northwest.[35]

[33] John F. Carr, "John Ireland," *Outlook*, Apr. 24, 1908, p. 972.
[34] Savage, *The Century's Harvest, 1836-1936, op. cit.*, pp. 103-104.
[35] *Ibid.*
      Sister of St. Joseph, *op. cit.*, pp. 548-549.
      Brouwer, *op. cit.*, pp. 362-363.

Early in 1853, Bishop Whelan of Wheeling, Virginia, requested
Mother Celestine to send Sisters there to take charge of a community
hospital under Catholic auspices. A rented house, which the Bishop
had prepared, was put in readiness for the Sisters; but on the eve of
their taking possession, the owner insisted on canceling the contract
which she had made, declaring that she could not permit her house
to be used by Catholic Sisters. She had understood that the occupants
were sisters of one family and not members of a religious order.
Another temporary habitation was procured. On April 13, 1853, the
Community was installed in what was known as the Wheeling Hospital, chartered under that name by the Virginia Assembly and used
as a military base during the Civil War. The original band in Wheeling consisted of Sisters Anastasia O'Brien, Alexis Spellicy, Sebastian
Reis, and Agatha Guthrie.[36] The number was increased in May when
Mother Celestine, who had accompanied Mother Saint John Fournier
back to Philadelphia, took from there to Wheeling Sister Liguori
Leigh and Mother Agnes Spencer.[37] The latter was appointed superior
in Wheeling, and remained there until the fall of 1854, when she
returned to Carondolet.[38]

There remains only one other foundation, that of Canandaigua,
New York, before the end of the period under consideration.[39] Since
that is the direct line of geneological descent from which the Sisters
of Saint Joseph of Concordia have had their being, a full chapter of
historical background of the region and then the chapter on that
foundation from 1854 to 1883 will take up the story.

Let us summarize the work of the first twenty years of the Sisters
of Saint Joseph in America. It is well to emphasize the fact that most
people unacquainted with the history of education in this country
labor under a false impression that the public schools have been a
traditional American institution. The colonies did not have public
schools, neither did the Republic until 1840. The colonial schools, and
practically all schools until 1840, were religious schools. Thus, about

[36] Sister Agatha Guthrie later became Mother Superior of the Sisters of St. Joseph
of Carondolet. Her term was from 1872 to 1894.

[37] Mother Agnes Spencer was in Philadelphia when Mother Delphine Fontbonne
left to establish a house in Toronto in 1851. At that time the former was made
Superior. In 1854 she led the mission band to the Diocese of Buffalo to establish the
mission at Canandaigua. In 1860 she established a diocesan community in Corsica, Pa.
This was the beginning of the Erie Motherhouse.

[38] Savage, The Congregation of St. Joseph of Carondolet, op. cit., p. 74.

[39] Before 1860 there were four foundations in New York alone. These were:
Canandaigua, 1854; Buffalo, 1856; Oswego, 1858; Cahoes, 1860.

the time of the beginning of the public school system, the schools opened by the Sisters of Saint Joseph continued their traditional career.

Not only the daughters of the Catholic came to the Sisters; the convent boarding school was even then the entrepôt of culture and recognized as such by those not of the faith. Many Southern planters sent their daughters to Carondolet; many a daughter of the merchant princes of Philadelphia and environs found her way to Chestnut Hill; the Indian agents and military commanders found the schools of the Sisters of Saint Joseph in Minnesota convenient places for the education of their offspring. Hence, wherever an establishment was made, soon students came to learn to grace society as cultured women.

In the curriculum, as Americanized by Sister Mary Rose, the French language still held a prominent place. The *Method of Instruction,* printed in Lyons for the Sisters of Saint Joseph, was used by the pioneer Sisters.[40] It was a book of about three hundred pages, a model course of study with minute instructions regarding the matter to be taught and the manner of presenting each subject. There is no duty of a Catholic teacher that does not receive its share of attention in this beautifully written manual. Prepared under the direction of Bishop Devie, it was printed with his approbation. In addition to the elementary branches, with stress on religion, the Sisters included sacred and profane history, Latin, and vocal music. To these, Sister Mary Rose added a secondary course with mathematics, rhetoric, German, and the natural sciences of botany, physics, chemistry, and astronomy. The ornamental branches were not overlooked, and, besides instrumental music, including instruction on piano, harp, and guitar, were taught painting, tapestry, fancy needlework, and the old-time accomplishment of molding fruits and flowers in wax.[41]

In each foundation, the close of the academic year was similarly celebrated with exhibitions and the bestowal of honors. Plays recalled the simple and the sublime, and furnished the entertainment for the entire community.

The houses opened from Carondolet in the East and in the North gradually increased in numbers and were able to take care of their own needs.

Bishop John B. Miege, Vicar Apostolic of Indian Territory, had

---

[40] *Mèthode D'Enseignement pour les Classes des Soeurs de St. Joseph* (Lyons, 1832).
[41] Savage, *The Congregation of St. Joseph of Carondolet, op. cit.,* pp. 95-96.

a brother who was Abbé Miege in a seminary in Savoy. This Abbé was a friend of the Sisters of Saint Joseph in Moutiers. Quite an extensive correspondence took place between the missionary bishop and his brother in regard to sending Sisters of Saint Joseph to work in his territory. In 1854, in consultation with Mother Celestine of Carondolet, a plan was drawn up that the community at Moutiers would send a colony of Sisters to Carondolet to work in Kansas Indian schools.[42] The Sisters who came were Sister Euphrasia Meiller, Sister Saint John Facemaz,[43] Sister Gonzaga Grand, and Sister Leonie Martin. These Sisters sailed on the *Heidelberg*—a name which recalled to the Sisters of Carondolet the little band of six in 1836. It is interesting to note that they landed in New Orleans the same day that the colony of Sisters landed in Canandaigua, New York. Although they came to America to work in Kansas, the plan did not materialize[44] but, strange to relate, a colony of Sisters from Canandaigua foundation came to Kansas some thirty years later. Those Sisters furnish the subject of this book.

The growth of the Sisters of Saint Joseph during twenty years was prodigious: from six they had increased to thirty times that number; from a log cabin on the banks of the Mississippi they were now working in nine dioceses from the heart of America to the Gulf, to Canada and into the East and Northwest.

The challenge of the frontier had been answered. What influence would far-flung foundations have on the history of the Sisters of Saint Joseph in America? As we know, the Constitutions of 1650 were written for isolated, independent communities. After the French Revolution, the communities of the Archdiocese of Lyons formed a central government, which received a decree of commendation from Rome on May 5, 1829. This applied only to the houses in the Archdiocese of Lyons. In order to adapt themselves better to the needs of

[42] The jurisdiction of Bishop Miege extended over Kansas and Nebraska, and included all the Indian tribes west to the Rocky Mountains. He was then residing at St. Marys, Kans., in the neighborhood of the Potawatomi settlements.
Savage, *The Congregation of St. Joseph of Carondolet, op. cit.*, p. 102.
[43] Second Superior General of Carondolet, 1860-1872.
[44] Since the Sisters of St. Joseph did not go to Bishop Miege's vicariate, on the occasion of his visit to St. Louis during the Provincial Council of 1848 the superior of a colony of Sisters of Charity from Nashville, Tennessee, looking for a home in another diocese, appealed to him on the advice of the Jesuit, Father De Smet; and with the permission of Archbishop Kenrick, the community was received into the diocese.
J. Garin, *Notices Biographiques sur Mgr. J. B. Miege, Premier Vicaire Apostolique du Kansas et sur les Prêtres de la Paroisse du Chevron (Savoie)* (Moutiers, France, 1886). Copy in St. Mary College Library, Xavier, Kans.

their new country, the Sisters in America were released in 1847, with ecclesiastical approval, from their diocesan character. This severance of jurisdiction by no means affected the affectionate relations between the houses on two sides of the Atlantic.[45]

Archbishop Kenrick advised the Sisters in America to convene to draw up a form of central government in order to give stability and uniformity to the growing congregation. A General Chapter, meeting at Carondolet, drew up such a plan. Delegates came from each diocese in which the Sisters were represented, with the exception of Buffalo, Philadelphia, Brooklyn, and Wheeling. The Archbishop interpreted this absence as a rejection of central government. It was the bishops in those places who preferred diocesan status for their Sisters. Therefore, from 1861 on, those houses subject to Carondolet maintained central government, and the diocesan communities became the parent foundations of still more communities. In this way, the frontier has been widened and deepened. Many of the diocesan communities have become pontifical institutes and as such have pontifical status.

Whether provincial, pontifical, or diocesan the same spirit animates all Daughters of Saint Joseph—and the category of services might be summed up in the words of the Reverend John P. Spencer, at the Solemn Benediction at the motherhouse in Carondolet on the occasion of the centenary of the coming of the Sisters to America: "Ignorance, blindness, deafness, mute tongues, the sick, the poor, the aged, infants, needy mothers, struggling priests, and people—all have a share in the work of the Sisters of Saint Joseph."[46]

---

[45] St. Louis Catholic News, suppl., July 3, 1936, p. 2.
[46] Ibid., p. 3.

CHAPTER IV

Western New York, Middle Nineteenth Century

WESTERN New York was passed by when the first immigrant movements made their way to the Great Lakes and Ohio Valley lands. After the War of 1812, at the time Nathaniel Rochester was laying out lots in the city he was beginning to build, Catholicism had obtained hardly more than a foothold on the banks of the Hudson River within the State of New York.

In 1822, the *Catholic Almanac,* in its clergy list of the New York Diocese, named the first resident pastor of Rochester as follows: "Rev. Patrick Kelly, Auburn, Rochester, and other districts in the western parts of the State." His field of labor embraced all that constitutes the dioceses of Rochester and Buffalo today. Like his predecessor, he repeatedly advertised his ministrations in the *Cayuga Republican* for the benefit of Catholics in the vicinity. On July 25, 1821, the advertisement announced that: "The Reverend Mr. Kelly, Roman Catholic Clergyman and Pastor of the Auburn district, will officiate on Sunday next, July 29th, in the School House, alias the Academy Green, between 10 and 11 o'clock."[1] Bishop John Timon, first Ordinary of Buffalo, asserted that Father Kelly extended his territory to Buffalo: "The few Catholics of this place were visited by the Reverend Mr. Kelly of Rochester, who said Mass in St. Paul's Episcopal Church, only five Catholic families in attendance."[2]

The first Catholic Church of Rochester, begun in 1822, was listed thus in the Directory of the Village of Rochester, dated 1827, but printed in February, 1828:

---

[1] *Cayuga Republican,* July 25, 1822. Cited by F. J. Zwierlein, *Life and Letters of Bishop McQuaid,* 3 vols. (Rochester, 1925-1927), vol. I, p. 13.
[2] John Timon, *Missions in Western New York* (Buffalo, 1862), p. 211. Zwierlein, *op. cit.,* vol. I, p. 14.

THE ROMAN CATHOLIC CHAPEL

is situated on Platt Street, a few rods west of State street, in the north part of the village. It is built of stone, on elevated ground, from which a fine prospect of the village is presented.

The building is forty-two feet long and thirty-eight feet wide, with large Gothic windows. It was built in the year 1823.[3]

On the passage of the Catholic Emancipation Bill by the British Parliament in April, 1829, world-wide celebrations took place. In the Diocese of New York Bishop Dubois set aside Sunday, June 21, 1829, as a day of thanksgiving, the date coinciding with the *Te Deum* celebration. An advertisement in the local newspaper stated that the first annual festival of Saint Patrick's Church would be held. "This Festival will be celebrated in the customary style of the Natives and Friends of Ireland in Rochester and its vicinity. . . ."[4]

This occasion came at a time when Protestant papers were making violent attacks on Catholicism. Nativism was rampant, and the passage of the Emancipation Bill added fuel to the fire of anti-Catholicism. Even the Episcopalians were hounded because of their close resemblance to the Catholic Church. A pamphlet by Henry U. Onderdonck, Rector of Saint John's Church, Canandaigua, was printed in that town in 1815 under the title, *An Appeal to the Religious Public in Behalf of the Protestant Episcopalian Church against the Slanders and Sophistry Printed under the name of the Rev. W. Bacon: Together with Three Dissertations on Regeneration, The Ministry, and the Pretended Calvinism of the XXXIX Articles.* The postscript to the title added the following admonition: "It is possible that this pamphlet may find its way to the hands of some who know personally nothing of the Episcopal Church, but who hear it stigmatized as *popish:* some hear it ingeniously called the *second order of Roman Catholics!*—Let such dare to think for themselves."[5]

Catholics in Rochester were pleased to testify to the good relations existing between themselves and the Congregation of Saint Luke's Church, at the time of the departure of the Episcopalian pastor, the Rev. F. H. Cumings:

[3] Elisha Ely, *Directory of the Village of Rochester* (1828), p. 128.
    Zwierlein, *op. cit.*, vol. I, p. 14.
[4] C. G. Hebermann, "*Rt. Rev. John Dubois,*" *United States Catholic Historical Records and Studies,* vol. I, part II, Jan. 1900, p. 317.
    Zwierlein, *op. cit.*, vol. I, p. 25.
[5] *Ibid.*

Rev. and dear Sir:

The trustees of the Roman Catholic Church of Rochester, having learned your intention to resign your charge and leave the village, avail themselves of this opportunity to express their regret at the intelligence.

Freed from the thralls of bigotry and the promptings of intolerance, your mission has been characterized by a laudable liberality. You seemed to regulate your life by these principles of true charity which ennoble the man, and dignify the Christian. You cultivated those feelings so consonant with the spirit of the gospel; and while you forcibly inculcated your own tenets, you respected the conscientious opinions of others. . . .

With sentiments of sincere respect, we remain, dear sir, your obedient servants,

WILLIAM TONE, *president*
ROBERT ELLIOT, *secretary*
in behalf of the trustees[6]

The answer of the Rev. F. H. Cumings was not less cordial in tone. He wrote to Father McNamara on May 11, 1829:

Rev. and dear Sir:

I have this day received, through your hands, a letter from the Roman Catholic trustees of Rochester, informing me of a resolution they were pleased to pass in reference to my contemplated removal from this place. I beg you, my dear sir, to accept for yourself and to convey to the board whom you represent, my unfeigned thanks for the interest you have expressed in my welfare. I hope I may be permitted to say, without any affected humility, that I wish I merited the encomiums passed upon me by your board of trustees. May I ask an interest in your prayers, that I may be what your kind, but too partial, opinion of me has represented me to be . . ."

Truly yours,

F. H. CUMINGS[7]

It is noteworthy that this exchange of good will happened at a time when other denominations agitated against policies of the Church. One example was the observance of the Sabbath, which the commandments of the Church inculcated, without, however, going to the extremes of Puritanism. The Catholic Church was maligned by the Puritan element during the latter's endeavors to stop the Sunday operation of stages and canal boats, the public carriers of the time, and to abolish Sunday mails.[8]

A bitter controversy took place in the *Rochester Observer*, the policy of the paper being first to write anti-Catholic editorials and

[6] *The Truth Teller*, V, May 30, 1829.
Zwierlein, *op. cit.*, vol. I, pp. 27-28.
[7] *The Truth Teller*, *op. cit.*
Zwierlein, *op. cit.*, vol. I, p. 28.
[8] *Ibid.*, p. 29.

later to speak through an anonymous writer, "Republicus," a so-called impartial judge at the court of public opinion. Father Mc-Namara replied to this writer in the columns of the same paper.[9] The editors continued the abuses when the so-called "Republicus" refused to give his name at the request of Father McNamara. There was an element of the ridiculous in the stories printed about practices in the Church. Again, "Republicus" returned with a series of three articles, all addressed to Rev. Michael McNamara, Roman Catholic Pastor, Rochester, maintaining a more elevated tone. About that time an able and skillful writer, James Buchan, a member of Father Mc-Namara's parish, took up the challenge and protested to the editors of the Rochester Observer against these incessant attacks on his pastor and his religion.[10] A counterattack by "Republicus" was answered by Buchan in articles appearing in August issues of the Observer.[11] One article which was refused space in the Observer is preserved in the files of the United States Catholic Press.[12]

In spite of the nativistic attitude of western New York, the spring of 1834 saw the transformation of the village of Rochester into the city of Rochester, largely because of the influx of immigrants of whom a great number were of the Catholic faith. Another Catholic Church was built about this time to accommodate the newcomers.[13] Immigration into the United States had lessened immediately after the Panic of 1837, but, with the return of economic stability and the hope of prosperous times, crowds of foreigners again poured into the country. Many settled in the western part of New York. In towns such as Geneva, handsome churches like that of Saint Francis de Sales were raised by "a few industrious Irish laboring people, who may justly be called the pioneers of religion in that village, where Catholicity was scarcely known, or if spoken at all, only with vituperation and contempt. . . . "[14] The writer prophesied ". . . . there

[9] Apr. 16, 1830. See Zwierlein, op. cit., vol. I, pp. 32-34.
[10] Ibid, pp. 35-36. Reprint in the United States Catholic Press, July 30, 1831.
[11] Aug. 11, 1831. See Zwierlein, vol. I, pp. 36-40.
[12] United States Catholic Press, Sept. 24, 1831.
[13] The second Catholic Church in Rochester was St. Mary's Church. On p. 10 of the Charter and Directory of the City of Rochester by C. and M. Morse (1834) this description appeared: "This church, formerly a Methodist meeting house, is situated on St. Paul Street in the eastern part of the city. It is a neat building, 42 by 60, surmounted by an octagon cupola, and from the elevated site on which it stands, makes a handsome appearance. Pastor of both churches, Rev. B. O'Reilly; assisted by Rev. Patrick Foley." Zwierlein, op. cit., vol. I, pp. 67-68.
[14] New York Weekly Register and Catholic Diary, Nov. 8, 1834. Zwierlein, op. cit., vol. I, pp. 67-68.

will hardly be any town or village of note in the western district of the State of New York which will not be blessed with a Catholic house of worship. The chain is formed from Albany to Buffalo. . . ."[15]

In March, 1833, the Reverend John Raffeiner, then of New York City, was authorized by Bishop Dubois "to make with his compatriots in all parts of the diocese whatever arrangements he judged opportune for the foundation of missions and for the building of churches wherever needed; but in the vicinity of Buffalo, he had to obtain the consent and approval of the Reverend Mr. Mertz, the worthy pastor of Buffalo." It was Reverend Father Raffeiner and later the Redemptorist, the Reverend Father Prost,[16] who encouraged the German Catholics of Rochester to form their own church.

Conditions in Rochester were described by Father Prost when he was delayed there en route to the West:

We found a break in the canal that prevented our going further. I was obliged to land, and taking my luggage, I set out for the Catholic Church. Nearby lived the pastor, Rev. Bernard J. O'Reilly, an Irishman. I presented my letter of recommendation from Bishop Dubois, and was received with the greatest kindness and cordiality. Rev. Father O'Reilly had here a very large congregation, English-speaking mostly, but among them about seven hundred Germans, who were anxious to have a priest of their own. He earnestly besought me to remain at least over Sunday to preach to them. This I consented to do.

As soon as the news of my arrival was noised abroad, and that I was to preach to the Germans on Sunday at St. Patrick's, these poor people came in great numbers. They begged me to remain and become their pastor. I told them that for the present I could not give them any definite answer, as I must first visit my brethren in the West. I promised them, however, that on my return I would gladly take up my abode with them. I encouraged them to procure, in the meantime, a suitable place to serve as a place of worship for themselves. The following Monday, I resumed my journey on the Canal to Buffalo. Rochester, the place and the people, made a most favorable impression on me.[17]

Although this account was written twenty years after it happened, there is a letter in the archives of the Leopold Foundation written by Father Prost on November 12, 1835, which contains much the same information:

---

15 *Ibid.*
16 Landing in New York from Europe on Aug. 15, 1835, Reverend Father Prost spent two months assisting Father Raffeiner, having permission to work in the diocese from Bishop Dubois. He later worked in the Diocese of Cincinnati.
17 John F. Mullany, *Four Score Years, 1856-1916: St. Joseph's Church* (Rochester, 1916), pp. 13-14.

I left New York for the West on October 15th. On my way I met several German Catholic settlements that had no priest; in Rochester, a new city in the State of New York, there are about six hundred German Catholics. Rochester would be an excellent center from which to care for the spiritual needs of outlying German communities. I encouraged the faithful there to procure a church for themselves. It is my intention to return as soon as I possibly can to this community, and devote myself particularly to the care of the Germans, unless more imperative duties prevent me.

The English-speaking communities are not so badly off, as they generally possess at least a priest. But the Germans are poor in the goods of this world and abandoned in their spiritual necessities. As they do not know English, the English-speaking priest can be of little or no assistance to them. While we are evangelizing and converting sixty Indians, six hundred Germans are lost to the faith because they have no priests. It is indeed heart-rending to see the crying need of help on all sides, and not be able to relieve it because one cannot be everywhere at once. I am now on my way to Green Bay. I am leaving my countrymen with a sad heart for I see their great poverty and spiritual desolation.[18]

The Leopoldine Association offered monetary assistance to the thriving parishes in western New York and in the words of the same Father Prost, ". . . . in Rochester where there are four thousand Catholics and two fine churches, we would be without a church if the Leopold Foundation had not put us in a position to save both churches."[19]

During 1842 a census showed 200,000 Catholics in the State of New York with only forty priests and fifty churches.

The question of religious education in the common schools became the subject of active discussion in 1838 and the following years. William H. Seward, in his January, 1841, message as governor, urged the "education of all children of the commonwealth in morality and virtue, leaving matters of conscience where, according to the principles of civil and religious liberty established by our Constitution and laws, they rightfully belong."[20] John C. Spencer, Secretary of State, during this same period, in his report on petitions for fuller provisions in New York City for children of foreigners and Catholics, recommended the election of a board of commissioners to cooperate with existing authorities to that end; but his suggestions were not followed. Neither did the legislature accept Governor Seward's elab-

18 Ibid., p. 14.
   Zwierlein, op. cit., vol. I, pp. 71-72.
19 Mullany, op. cit., pp. 13-14.
   Zwierlein, op. cit., vol. I, pp. 74-75.
20 Horace E. Scudder (ed.), American Commonwealths, 2 vols. (New York, 1893), vol. II, p. 555.

orate argument, submitted in his next message, in favor of distribution of school moneys in New York City between Protestants and Catholics.[21]

The school controversy centering around Bishop Hughes in New York in 1841 had an echo in Rochester in the same year. On the eve of the election for state senators and assemblymen, it had been discovered that friends of the Public School Society, a private corporation in New York City, which received all public money for its schools there had pledged candidates of both parties to vote against the Catholic petition to the Legislature for a just share of the school fund (as it had formerly received under the School Act of 1812) and against the recommendation of the Secretary of the State, the Honorable John C. Spencer, to extend the state school system to New York City. To counteract a slate of men pledged against Catholic interests, Bishop Hughes proposed an independent ticket made up of unpledged candidates of both parties and some others.[22] This conduct of the Bishop caused "An Adopted Citizen" to send the following communication to the editor of the *Rochester Daily Advertiser:*

Mr. Hyatt's honorable and consistent conduct towards adopted citizens induces one of the class to request a place in the *Rochester Daily Advertiser* for the following resolutions, believing them to contain the sentiment of 99 in every 100 of the Irish adopted citizens.

At a meeting of adopted citizens in the 15th ward, New York, the following resolutions among others were passed.

"Resolved, That we, the citizens of the 15th ward, New York, have seen, with astonishment, and deep regret the recent interference of the respected and venerated Bishop Hughes in the political questions of our recent election, and the elective franchise of his Catholic brethren.

"Resolved, That, altho' we are devoted to our religion and respect its ministers, while in the pulpit, yet we can never recognize their right to interfere with the free and unshackled exercise of our duties as American citizens at the ballot box."

I am more anxious to have them published in your paper, as they confirm my own frequently expressed opinions.

Rochester, Nov. 8, 1841, An Adopted Citizen[23]

The communications did not remain unchallenged long. "Another Adopted Citizen" could not believe that the resolutions "contain the sentiments of 99 out of 100 of the Irish adopted citizens":

21 *Ibid.,* pp. 555-556.
22 Cf., "The School Question," Lawrence Kehoe (ed.), *The Complete Works of Most Rev. John Hughes, D.D.* (New York, 1866).
    Zwierlein, *op. cit.,* vol. I, p. 101.
23 *Rochester Daily Advertiser.*
    Zwierlein, *op. cit.,* vol. I, pp. 101-102.

Party politicians are too apt to view as good or evil whatever is calculated to result for or against their party; hence it is that so much assiduity has been evinced by hot-headed politicians to cast odium on the recent effort that has been made by a portion of our fellow-citizens to effect a reform in the mode of distributing the school fund.

If these people, in view of an existing, and to them a grievous monopoly, see fit to nominate such candidates as will represent their interests, which have been overlooked in the general nomination, why, I would ask in the name of justice, should they be libeled and misrepresented as they have been by individuals as well as by numerous portions of the public press? Are men to be held up as advocates of the Union of Church and State, as anxious to create sectarian divisions, because they peaceably and legally demanded redress of their grievances at the ballot box?

Bishop Hughes, that good and venerated man, is born down upon with such spleen and bitterness as every candid mind, unbiased by petty party feeling, cannot but despise. Because he was present, and took part in the proceedings of a meeting, convened in direct reference to the school questions, in which he has so long and so ardently persevered, he is represented as endeavoring to control the elective franchise of his Catholic brethren.

Faugh, nothing could be more wickedly false than this. Is Bishop Hughes or any other individual to be muzzled and kept at home, and a large body of people overlook their dearest rights and interests for the mere sake of party, but as free men, deserve the most cordial approbation of every honest man, however widely different their views may be on the school question or any other [sic].[24]

The next day the editor, Mr. Hyatt, printed a passage from the *New York Sunday Times* which zealously defended the course taken by Bishop Hughes in reference to the school question. It declared that "his only connection with the temporal affairs of this city has been involved in a claim on the portion of the school fund for the separate education of Catholic children—or the election of School Commissioners by the people, as in every county of the State except this." Mr. Hyatt, himself, supposed that "the whole matter has grown out of a belief, on the part of Catholics, that efforts were made in the schools to inculcate sectarian views, in addition to what has been designed to be taught in them. In many instances, this suspicion, no doubt, has been well founded. *We were yesterday informed of a circumstance connected with one of the schools of this city, bearing on this point, which should have subjected the teacher to instant dismissal.* Such interference with the 'modes of faith' should not be tolerated, but to divide the school money according to sects would hardly be acceded in this country." At the request of a prominent

---

[24] *Ibid.,* vol. I, pp. 102-103. Extract is given exactly as it appears in Zwierlein. *Rochester Daily Advertiser,* Nov. 12, 1841.

Catholic in Rochester, Mr. Hyatt even published the full text of Bishop Hughes' reply to the Address of Approval presented to him at Washington Hall, November 16, 1841, after the campaign by a great meeting of Catholics and others favorable to an alteration in the present public school system. Bishop Hughes in this reply plainly met the question: "What system should be deemed just by the Catholics?"

I answer, any system that will leave the various denominations each in full possession of its religious rights over the minds of its children. If the children are to be educated promiscuously as at present, let religion in every shape and form be excluded. Let not the Protestant forms of prayer, Protestant hymns, be forced on the children of Catholics, Jews, and others, as at present, in schools for the support of which their parents pay taxes as well as Presbyterians. The Public School Society have a right to teach *their own children* that Our Divine Redeemer "showed uncommon quickness of conception, soundness of judgment, and presence of mind" but I deny their right to introduce such degrading notions of His character into the Public Schools of the city, and impress them on the children of Catholic and Protestant denominations, who believe higher and holier things of the Son of God.

There is another system which Catholics would deem just and equal. It is that each denomination should prescribe the amount and quality, *for its own children,* of religious instruction which, consistently with the ends of the State in providing education, might be incorporated with it. This plan, if it were practicable, would in my opinion be much safer for the welfare and security of society. But, as it is, we hold that the establishment of religion in the Public Schools by the private authority of an irresponsible Board of Trustees, is a thing for which neither the State Legislature nor the Congress of the United States could constitutionally give them a particle of authority.

It is this private, clandestine, surreptitious "union of Church and State" against which Catholics have protested.

It is this which has driven us from the public schools. It is this for which one party of the community pays taxes; whilst for another the taxes are turned into tithes. It is this which for seventeen years has subjected Catholics to double taxation, first to support the educational sectarianism of the public school and second, their consciences. For no Catholic, who believes in the truth of his religion, can allow a child of his to frequent the public schools, as at present constituted, and according to the system which has prevailed in them, without wounding his own conscience and sinning against God; and this he is not allowed to do for the whole world.[25]

While Mr. Hyatt did not think the charge of mingling politics and religion disproved or justified by Bishop Hughes' apology for his conduct in this affair, he was anxious to do justice to Catholic grievances against the public schools, without, however, allowing separate schools to benefit from the public school fund.

[25] Kehoe, *op. cit.,* p. 293.
Zwierlein, *op. cit.,* vol. I, pp. 103-104.

But if this is not the aim of the Bishop, if he only seeks to expel sectarianism from the schools, he asks no more than should have been done on bare representation of the injustice practiced.

Newspapers do not necessarily constitute a portion of a school library; these therefore can be excluded from schools, if used there.

As to the merits of the Protestant or Catholic version of the Bible, we have nothing to say—neither of them being indispensable to the libraries of our common schools, but can be reserved for the domestic tuition which must necessarily constitute much of the knowledge acquired by the juvenile mind. Aside from this, all sects have their Sunday Schools, at which the distinctive features of their faith are more or less inculcated. There is no occasion, therefore, for anything like sectarianism in our schools—especially those schools which are sustained by the money of Jew and Gentile, Infidel and Christian.

In conclusion, we beg leave to say, that the duty is imperative on the Legislature to examine into the subject of school management in New York, and in all other places where complaints are made of sectarian influences in the supervision of schools, wherever abuse is found to exist. This the Legislature ought to do at once. Further than this "equal and exact justice" does not demand that they should go.[26]

The new Legislature did not change the public school system, but it extended the provisions of the state school law also to New York City by a special bill introduced by William B. Maclay, which was passed April 9, 1842. This soon put the Public School Society out of existence. Nothing, however, was gained for the Catholic separate or parochial schools.

Failure to obtain a share of the school fund certainly did not dampen the spirit of sacrifice demanded for the religious education of the children of western New York. This subject will be discussed fully in the following chapter.

Even with the help of an able coadjutor, Bishop Hughes began to realize the almost impossibility of coping with the problems in the remote parts of his vast diocese. He applied to the Holy See to divide the diocese and appoint his coadjutor to the new see at Albany, the capital of the state. He sent a map to Doctor Cullen on January 24, 1845, "to give a more accurate idea of its extent and increasing importance. The portion assigned to the contemplated See of Albany will still be too large; and you will observe, marked in red ink, two other future Bishoprics, one in the western portion, and the other in the northern portion, Rochester and Plattsburg. But of these, as new Bishops will have to be recommended, it is unnecessary to speak at present. The subject will be brought before the Bishops at the next Provincial Council, which will probably be the last until the division

26 *Ibid.*, vol. I, pp. 104-105.

of the Province. One Bishop residing at the extremity of the Diocese is not sufficient for the right government of all, especially with the great increase of missionaries. . . . Indeed, this ought to be divided into four dioceses: New York, Albany, Plattsburg, and Rochester— and I have marked on the map what may be their limits. . . . But at present the erection of Albany into an Episcopal See and the appointment of Doctor McCloskey will be sufficient." [27]

In 1847, Bishop Hughes was successful in his efforts to subdivide his vast diocese. Two sees were established, one at Albany and the other, not at Rochester, but at Buffalo. The Rochester Diocese was established twenty years later when the American prelates petitioned for the erection of another diocese in western New York.

About this time, the future Bishop McQuaid visited the region and commented on the conditions there:

> The first immigrants coming in large numbers were from Ireland. Of all the peoples of Europe, they were the best fitted to open the way for religion in a new country. Brave by nature, inured to poverty and hardship, just released from a struggle unto death for the faith, accustomed to the practice of religion in its simplest forms, cherishing dearly their priests, whom they learned to support directly, actively engaged in building humble chapels on the sites of ruined churches and in replacing altars, they were not appalled by the wretchedness of religious equipment and surroundings in their new homes on this side of the Atlantic. The priest was always the priest, wherever they met him, or from what country he had come; the Mass was always the Mass, no matter where it was offered up. They had lived among the bitterest foes and had never quailed nor flinched; misrepresentations and calumnies, sneers and scorn made no impression on their faithful hearts. Men who prefer death to denial of Christ are not cowards nor traitors. In such a school of discipline, they had been trained to do missionary work. They and their descendants have not, in a new hemisphere, unlearned the lessons taught at home.
>
> Quickly following the Irish came the Germans from all parts of the fatherland. They too were a sturdy race, able to hold their own. Many of them had known persecution for religion's sake; most of them numbered the stories of bloody times which had come to them among the traditions of their hearths. They were prompt to rival their Irish brethren in building churches. At home they had their old parish churches, with chants and ceremonial which lend to religion much that is consoling and instructive. The religious traditions and glories of their land they sought to emulate in this. Better than all, they have stood fast by the duty of maintaining Christian Schools for Christian children. There is much they can copy from the Irish, and much the Irish can learn from the Germans. All other nationalities of Europe can kneel at their feet and imbibe salutary and profitable lessons.[28]

[27] American Catholic Historical Society, *Records,* vol. VIII, pp. 458-466.
    Zwierlein, *op. cit.,* vol. I, pp. 115-116.
[28] *Memorial Volume of the Third Plenary Council of Baltimore* (Baltimore, 1884), pp. 63-64.
    Zwierlein, *op. cit.,* vol. I, pp. 116-117.

The Diocese of Buffalo, which Pius IX established April 23, 1847, comprised all that part of the State of New York which lies west of the eastern limits of Cayuga, Tompkins, and Tioga Counties. This included all the territory which is within the dioceses of both Buffalo and Rochester today. The Very Reverend John Timon,[29] a Visitor General of the Congregation of Missions, was consecrated as the first Bishop of Buffalo. Following the consecration which took place in the Cathedral in New York on October 17, 1847, he took possession of his see on October 22. It is noteworthy that he pontificated at Saint Patrick's Church in Rochester on the first morning he was in his new diocese.[30]

The 1848 *United States Catholic Almanac* credits the Diocese of Buffalo with eighteen priests, including the secular as well as the Redemptorist clergy in that number.[31] However, Bishop Timon wrote later that, at his advent in the diocese, he found only sixteen priests and sixteen churches and that "most of these churches might rather be called huts or shanties."[32]

Bishop Timon pointed out that Catholic education was at a lower ebb even than the number of priests available. In the whole Diocese of Buffalo "there were but four Catholic Schools, taught by seculars, and generally in a poor state; no religious Ladies or any Order or Community for instruction or charity, except one house of the Sisters of Charity, in Saint Patrick's Orphan Asylum in Rochester."[33] The *United States Catholic Almanac* states that two of these Sisters were "in charge of a Young Ladies Select School, which is very prosperous and has attained deserved popularity." It also mentions that "St. Patrick's Select School for Boys, attached to the same congregation, under the charge of two brothers, is also prosperous and is fast realizing the hopes of the friends of a sound Catholic system of education."[34] Saint Joseph's Church had a parochial school almost from the beginning of its existence. The same is true of Saint Peter's

[29] Bishop Timon, it will be remembered, was with Bishop Rosati in New Orleans when the first band of the Sisters of St. Joseph arrived there from France. His connections with the community in St. Louis led to the request for Sisters upon his appointment to the See of Buffalo; hence the Canandaigua foundation.

[30] "Diocese of Rochester," *Catholic Encyclopedia*, vol. XIII, pp. 102-104.
    Zwierlein, *op. cit.*, vol. I, p. 121.

[31] *United States Catholic Almanac* (1848), p. 189.
    Zwierlein, *op. cit.*, vol. I, p. 121.

[32] Timon, *op. cit.*, pp. 235-236.

[33] *Ibid.*

[34] *Ibid.*, p. 189.
    Zwierlein, *op. cit.*, vol. I, p. 122.

Church. All these schools were most elementary in character, but they attest an early appreciation of the need of safeguarding the faith of the little children through the agency of the parochial school. Yet, the *United States Catholic Almanac* of 1840 gives the attendance of the parish schools in Rochester as only six hundred children.[35]

Within the twenty-year period that the present Diocese of Rochester was part of the Diocese of Buffalo, many communities of religious men and women entered the territory to conduct eleemosynary and educational institutions. Each religious order of women that established itself there gave its attention to the education and training of Catholic girls. Among these Sisterhoods were the Sisters of Saint Joseph who located at Canandaigua where they established a parochial school on December 8, 1854.

The traditional nativism again asserted itself in the guise of Know-Nothingism. Absorption and assimilation became more difficult with the increasing volume of immigration about the middle of the nineteenth century. Criticism and suspicion directed against the newcomers centered largely about the tendency of new arrivals to settle together in national groups and thus to perpetuate their old-country customs, habits, and modes of thinking; the cherishing of old-country loyalties, which were generally considered incompatible with the duties and obligations of naturalized citizens; the disposition of the Irish to vote as a group; the insistence of the Germans on retaining their language in their churches and schools; and the fear that immigrants were entering the country in numbers so large as to make impossible their assimilation into the so-called native stock. The aggressive self-consciousness and political activities of the newcomers often aggravated the growing antagonism of the period.

The most elaborate arrangements and the most comprehensive plans for the adjustment of foreigners and settling them on the land came as a result of discussions at the Buffalo Convention of February, 1856. This was the climax of the Catholic immigrant colonization movement prior to 1860. The inception of this convention was fostered by Irish-Americans—clergy and lay—who were convinced that, though Know-Nothingism might wane, anti-Catholic agitation was not a passing phase of the political and social ideas of the American people. The proposed plans were not put into effect for many reasons,

---

[35] Timon, *op. cit.*, p. 214.
   Zwierlein, *op. cit.*, vol. I, p. 122.

particularly, the larger issue of a divided Union, and personal opposition on the part of members of the Eastern hierarchy.

Although the primary motive of Thomas D'Arcy McGee was the settlement of Irish immigrants in Canada and the western states, similar propaganda was used locally to play up the idea of such settlements in western New York. The Buffalo *Daily Courier* indignantly asserted: "this vacillating [sic], disturbing, uneasy and ambitious personage, Mr. McGee, ignores our Eastern and Middle States with but one single sentence of newspaper literature."[36]

Some who heartily favored the work of the Buffalo Convention favored colonization nearer the scene of their labors. Among these was Bishop Timon of Buffalo, who suggested that attention be paid to the "Near West" rather than to the "Far West." [37] As Bishop Whelan of Wheeling put it: "these lands are free from the fevers of Illinois, the savages of Kansas, and the uncertainties of California."[38]

The editor of *The American Celt* replied to Bishop Timon's proposition thus:

> If it were a matter of regulation, if any man or men, in high or humble station, could control prices of land, could create means of centralization to the extent of a congregation, could arrest midway a current of human travel and movement, we would, for our part cordially fall into, and heartily cooperate with the design of the Right Reverend writer. But we fear, not surely without cause, that the days of agricultural settlement for foreigners in the central counties of this State are out of date. Forty years ago, when the Erie Canal was being dug, or ten years ago when the Erie Railroad was surveyed this was possible. Alas!!
> "There is a tide in the affairs of men which taken at the flood leads
> on to fortune."
> But this tide was not taken at flood, or ebb, or quarter or half-quarter. The same necessities did not then exist; the same numbers to be settled were not there in those days; they are here now and they must go, not where they *would*, but where they *can*.[39]

Bishop Timon had from the beginning of his episcopate in 1847 tried to concentrate the Catholics in his diocese into compact parishes. While the agents of the Supreme Directory were endeavoring to pur-

---

36 Feb. 13, 1856. See Sister Gilbert Kelly, *Catholic Immigrant Colonization Projects in the United States, 1815-1860* (New York, 1949), p. 245 ff.
37 *The American Celt,* Mar. 8, 1856.
    Kelly, *op. cit.,* p. 245.
38 *The American Celt,* Mar. 8, 1856.
    Kelly, *op. cit.,* p. 245.
39 *The American Celt,* Apr. 5, 1856.
    Kelly, *op. cit.,* pp. 245-266.

chase a township somewhere in the West, he had advocated settlements in the "Near West," though land could not be had there at government prices. In this work of encouraging Catholics to enter his diocese, he was ably assisted by several of his priests, among them the Reverend Bernard McCabe. In a letter to the Boston Pilot,[40] which was intended as a general answer to the many letters which he had received from clergy and laity alike, he told of the discovery by some shrewd Bostonians of the real value of western New York as a farming region. He mentioned that there were farms offered for sale by people who were inflicted with "Western Fever." His account seemed to bring almost immediate results, for a month later he wrote that "all Ireland" seemed to be arriving and telling him that they had come in response to his letter in the Pilot. He added further that the Yankees were extending a hearty welcome to all who gave indication of becoming good citizens of the locality.[41]

Bishop Timon in his Diocese of Buffalo, carried out ideas similar to those of Bishop Loras of Dubuque, although frontier conditions were not quite so challenging in the former diocese. Newspaper publicity about the Buffalo project was not so widespread as that about Dubuque. According to one of Bishop Timon's letters, written in 1859, his interest in the Catholic colonies in his vast territory had led him to spend the preceding winter in visiting colonies settled by the Irish.[42]

With the growth of the Catholic population in western New York much of the attention of the Provincial Council of 1850 was devoted to the subject of education. The pastoral letter of the Council of the Archbishop and Bishops of the Province of New York stated:

Often has His Holiness, with truly paternal solicitude, urged us and you, dearly beloved, to watch over the Catholic education of youth. . . . But if sending them to schools in which the poor children will make a shipwreck of faith, early become familiar with crime, and grow up in it, they become a curse to themselves and society, will not the Eternal Judge call the parent to an account for the loss of his child? . . .

We still have to deplore that in most of the States comprised within this Ecclesiastical Province, the rights, the faith and the conscience of our children are not equally respected in the Public Schools, for the establishment and

---

40 July 25, 1857.
41 Ibid., July 18 and Aug. 15, 1857.
    Kelly, op. cit., pp. 266-267.
42 Boston Pilot, May 7, 1859; June 30, 1860.
    Kelly, op. cit., pp. 266-267.

maintenance of which we have an equal share of the burden. . . . In the meantime we exhort you, beloved brethren, as a duty which you owe to God and your children, to establish and support, wherever it may be possible, schools in which the faith and morals of your children may not be exposed to the danger of perversion. . . . We most earnestly exhort the venerable clergy not to rest satisfied with their zealous efforts to build schoolhouses and provide teachers, but frequently visit the schools in person. . . .[43]

Conditions, then, in western New York offered a frontier challenge to the Church in the 1850's. It was into this environment that the Sisters of Saint Joseph from Carondolet came in 1854. They were to augment the work so successfully carried out by the Sisters already established in the region. They were to begin a new frontier in New York—where today five communities of the Sisters of Saint Joseph labor in all parts of the state.

---

[43] *Pastoral Letter of the Archbishop and the Bishops of the Province of New York* (1861), pp. 13-15.

CHAPTER V

Canandaigua, Buffalo, and Rochester, 1854-1883

A CENTURY ago it was a long distance from Saint Louis to western New York, and the experiences of such a journey read like a romance. In 1854, Canandaigua was a part of the Diocese of Buffalo. The pastor, Rev. Edmund O'Connor, shortly after his arrival as pastor of Canandaigua, established a parochial school in September, 1851. Thomas Hynes taught the school the first year; he was succeeded by Peter Donnelly and Thomas Moran, the latter holding the position until the coming of the Sisters in 1854.[1]

When Father O'Connor considered inviting a religious community to take charge of his school, he asked the advice of Bishop John Timon, C.M. The Sisters of Saint Joseph of Carondolet were well-known to this prelate, who it will be remembered, was in New Orleans in 1836 as a companion to Bishop Rosati at the time the six pioneers from France arrived to work in the Diocese of Saint Louis. He was especially interested in the work of the Sisters for the deaf.

Mother Celestine Pommerel, then Superior General, sent the following Sisters to Canandaigua: Mother Agnes Spencer, Sisters Francis Joseph Ivory, Theodosia Hagemann, and Petronilla Roscoe. Leaving St. Louis on December 3, 1854, they traveled by boat to Alton, Illinois, the railroad being not yet completed. Sister Francis Joseph Ivory's *Notes*[2] state that they left Alton about midnight, taking seats in a "rickety railroad car." The weather was extremely cold, and they suffered much crossing the Illinois prairie. The following day

---

[1] *Sixtieth Anniversary of the Sisters of St. Joseph in Canandaigua, New York, 1854-1914* (Canandaigua, 1914), pp. 5-7.

[2] These *Notes* were written many years after Sister Francis Joseph Ivory left Canandaigua. They check very accurately with the other records at Carondolet. This information was furnished by Sister Lucida Savage of Carondolet.

they reached Chicago, where they took a conveyance to the Cathedral.[3] The Sisters of Mercy had a convent in the Cathedral parish. Mother Agnes Spencer was anxious to see Bishop O'Regan, the former President of the Carondolet Seminary, at that time Bishop of Chicago. He welcomed them heartily, made them comfortable, and served them a warm meal. Their train for Buffalo left late in the evening, reaching there on the evening of December 6.

Canandaigua is approximately seventy-five miles from Buffalo. Winters in that section of New York are severe, and the winter of 1854 was no exception. Leaving Buffalo on December 6 at seven in the evening, the Sisters were delayed in Rochester when the tracks were blocked by a heavy fall of snow. They took advantage of the delay to visit Saint Patrick's where they were received most kindly by the Sisters of Charity. Here Sister Francis Joseph met a friend of her youth, and each enjoyed inspecting the various features of the other's habit. Sister Francis Joseph remarked in her *Notes* that her funds had been depleted and the Superior of the Sisters of Charity had replenished her purse. However, she went on to say that "the money was returned in due time."

At ten o'clock on the evening of December 7, 1854, the Sisters reached their destination at Canandaigua. In Father O'Connor's absence, Mr. Cochran, a prominent Catholic layman, met them at the station and conducted them to the parochial residence. They were cordially welcomed by the pastor, of whom the diarist says, "from that day, his kindness never failed." He said Mass for them the next morning in the chapel of their new convent. They took possession of their home, a pretty white frame building, which had been a nursery and stood in the center of very pleasantly arranged grounds.

On that memorable day, all was white with drifted snow. How significant this homecoming to the little white convent which became the Convent of the Immaculate Conception! The day was memorable indeed, for at the center of Christendom a new dogma was proclaimed on the same day, the Dogma of the Immaculate Conception. To quote Bishop Timon, it was the day on which "the Christian world crowned its Mother."[4]

No local chronicle recorded the coming of the Sisters to Canan-

---

[3] Now Old St. Mary's.

[4] On this same day the Sisters of St. Joseph of Carondolet received more subjects from France—the band from Moutiers who had intended to work in the vicariate of Bishop Miege.

daigua. They had worn the garb of ordinary women on their journey from Carondolet to Canandaigua, in order to avoid any unpleasantness and undue attention which might have been accorded them if clothed in the habit in those days of bigoted excitement. They arrived in silence and soon began the work which has reaped rich harvests for time and eternity.[5]

The school for girls was opened in the convent and for boys in the basement of the church. Both prospered with cooperation of the pastor, Father O'Connor, and his unfailing kindness to both pupils and teachers. At the very beginning the Sisters were beset with many hardships and difficulties due to the smallness of the Catholic congregation and the poverty of its members.[6]

In connection with the parochial school at Canandaigua, the Sisters opened Saint Mary's Academy for Young Ladies in 1855. The *Catholic Almanac* gives the prospectus of this second school in its issue of 1856:

This institution, under the charge of the Sisters of Saint Joseph, located in one of the most healthy and beautiful parts of the state, is easy of access. The New York Central Railroad passes through here, as do also the Canandaigua and Niagara Falls, connecting with the Canada and Great Western Railroad.

The system of education embraces every useful and ornamental branch suitable to young ladies.

Terms:—Board and tuition for the scholastic year

Payable half-yearly in advance	$80.00
Washing, mending, bed, and bedding	$10.00
Each pupil will pay on entrance	$ 5.00

Music, drawing and the languages will form extra charges. Books, stationery, and postage charged to parents. No deduction will be made to any pupil leaving the institution before the expiration of the term, unless in case of sickness.

The scholastic year commences on the first Monday of September, ending on the 17th of July.

All communications to be addressed to St. Mary's Convent, Canandaigua, New York.[7]

During a visit to the convent on February 5, 1861, Bishop Timon decided "that all things must be *suspended* except the parish school in which Select and Free shall combine." Nevertheless, Bishop Timon found it necessary on November 14, 1863, to "engage the Pastor . . .

---

[5] *Sixtieth Anniversary of the Sisters of St. Joseph, 1854-1914, op. cit.,* pp. 2-4.
[6] Waldemer J. Isaac, "Centenary of St. Joseph Nuns in St. Louis Recalls Coming of First Nuns to Canandaigua," *Catholic Courier,* Mar. 19, 1936.
[7] *Catholic Almanac* (1856), pp. 137-138.

to have no Select School, but a general one for all." Even this direc-
tive was not effective, and on March 8, 1864, the Bishop again gave
orders that the two schools at Canandaigua be combined. He was
evidently working for a real parochial school system in which there
was no room for the select school.[8]

In addition to the parochial and select schools, the Sisters took
care of orphans. The institution was incorporated in 1885 as St. Mary's
Academy and Orphan Asylum, the object of which was "the care and
support of orphans and other children who need instruction and for
no other object or end whatsoever." It was established during the
pastorate of the Reverend Edmund O'Connor. Programs and manuscript which show the thoroughness of the educational program are
extant. The system was based on French methods, and students came
from the best families of western New York. Among them were
Teresa and Ellen McMahan, the latter of whom is known as the
translator of *Golden Sands*.[9] The institution was included in the list
of those to which the state at that time annually made appropriations
for the education of the orphans. The Sisters in 1871 petitioned the
New York State legislature for a special building fund, and the sum
of $5,000 was appropriated for this purpose. This, with the sale of
the old convent property, provided sufficient funds to secure the
Granger property, and the Rev. Father English made the purchase
for the Sisters. Thus began a new era in the history of the parish
school. The Granger mansion, a large and impressive building on
colonial lines, became the convent for the Sisters of Saint Joseph
about 1875. Canandaigua Catholics further provided for the growth
of their religion when they erected in 1880 what is now known as
the Old Saint Mary's School.[10]

A novitiate was established at Canandaigua and on October 15,
1856, two postulants were received. One of these Sisters—the first
to receive the habit of the Sisters of Saint Joseph in the State of
New York—was the future Mother Stanislaus Leary, later to be the
first Superior of the Rochester Community and foundress and first
Superior of the Concordia (Kansas) Community. She figures to such

---

[8] Zwierlein, *Life and Letters of Bishop McQuaid*, 3 vols. (Rochester, 1925-27).
vol. I, pp. 138-139.
[9] *Annals of the Sisters of St. Joseph of the Diocese of Rochester*, 4 vols. of unpublished material in the Archives of the Nazareth Motherhouse, Rochester, N. Y., vol. I,
pp. 15-16.
[10] *Catholic Courier*, Mar. 19, 1936.

an extent in this work that it is well to describe in full the happy day of her reception.

Miss Margaret Leary of Corning, New York, a young girl scarcely sixteen years of age, was admitted on October 15, 1856, and received the holy habit on February 14, 1857, with the name Sister Mary Stanislaus.[11] Concerning this reception, Sister Anastasia of Buffalo, the former Miss Donovan, who received the habit the same day, gave the following interesting details:

It was in Saint Mary's Church, Canandaigua, that the late Mother Stanislaus and myself were clothed in the garb of the Sisters of Saint Joseph on Sunday, the 14th day of February, 1858 [sic], by the saintly Bishop Timon. As he was instrumental in having us enter at Canandaigua, he made it a point to come there from Buffalo to invest us with the habit. A little incident in connection with our reception will amuse you. It is this: good Father Lee, who was pastor of a little village nearby, announced to his flock that the Bishop would be in Canandaigua on the day above mentioned for the purpose of giving the veil to two nuns. He told them that he would be present and added that he would like to see them present also.

He said an early Mass for his people, and just imagine them winding their way to Saint Mary's to see the sight. The consequence was a well-crowded church at the ten o'clock Mass on that memorable Sunday morning. The two prospective nuns, preceded by a procession, were a spectacle to angels and to men as they marched around the aisles, whilst the Sisters in the organ loft rendered sweetly a Litany of the Blessed Virgin.

Our reception, as far as I know, was the first held in the church. Sister Aloysius Hendrick received the habit two months later at the hands of Rev. Edmund O'Connor. The following year Sisters Nativity, Alphonsus, and Nicholas received the habit in the convent chapel. These were the last received in Canandaigua as the novitiate was removed to Buffalo.[12]

On the same day two novices made profession of vows, Sister Petronilla Roscoe, who evidently had left Carondolet as a novice, and Sister Julia Littlenecker, sent after the first band to reinforce the small community.[13]

Like a tree that flourished in rich and fertile soil, the little colony

[11] She was born in New York City on Aug. 15, 1841, the daughter of Michael and Anna O'Connor Leary.

[12] *Annals of the Sisters of St. Joseph of the Diocese of Rochester, op. cit.,* vol. I, pp. 17-18. Vol. I of the *Annals* has the dedicatory page: "Dedicated to Rev. Mother Stanislaus Leary and the pioneer Religious who worked with her and in whose footsteps their successors hope, with God's help, to walk until called to a happy reunion in heaven." The pages, written and decorated, were the work of the late Sister Berchmans Desmond of Rochester. Sister Anastasia wrote this letter in her later years; the date is incorrect: it should be Feb. 14, 1857.

[13] Sister M. of the Sacred Heart Dunne, *The Congregation of St. Joseph of Buffalo* (Buffalo, 1933), pp. 70-74.

in "Sleeping Beauty,"[14] continued to develop new branches until its shade and fragrance have spread to our own times. The property had been a nursery before the Sisters took possession of it; now, it became a nursery of religious life, for not a few zealously carried on the work in other parts of the vineyard. Among them may be mentioned Reverend Mother Mary Anne Burke, Buffalo, and Reverend Mother Stanislaus Leary, Concordia, Kansas, and La Grange, Illinois.[15]

In September, 1856, a school was opened in Rochester but was discontinued at the end of the year. According to the *Notes* of Sister Francis Joseph Ivory, they had "a good school, but after a year owing to some misunderstanding, were withdrawn to Canandaigua." They were assigned to Buffalo instead. From Buffalo a permanent foundation was made in 1864 in Rochester where according to the French version of the *Life of Mother Saint John Fontbonne:* "À Rochester même, l'institution porte le nom d'Etoile de Sainte-Marie! Cet asile a été ouvert pour les enfants des soldats tués à la guerre."[16]

Buffalo's saintly Bishop Timon applied for Sisters to open an establishment for the deaf and dumb. While negotiations for this institution were in progress, a parochial school was opened in Buffalo in the church building of Saint Mary's of the Lake, later named the Church of the Immaculate Conception. This mission was supplied by the Sisters who had been withdrawn from the Rochester school. In a short time it became one of the flourishing schools of the city.

A plot at Edward and Morgan Streets had been donated by Louis de Couteulx, a generous benefactor of the Church of Buffalo, for the purpose of erecting the Institution for the Deaf. According to the will of the donor the property was to revert to his heirs if it were not used for the specified purpose. Although the project of the institution had to be abandoned for a while, the parochial school was

---

14 There had been a Canandaigua for several centuries, the second principal town of the Six Nations. *Cf.* J. Albert Granger, *The History of Canandaigua* (centennial edition) (Canandaigua, 1876), pp. 2-4; *A History of Early Canandaigua* (Canandaigua, 1905), pp. 4-10. Called "Sleeping Beauty" in many instances, Canandaigua was "a beautiful village, the county seat of Ontario County, situated at the foot of Lake Canandaigua which is called 'the gem of the inland lakes'."
    Caroline Cowels (Richard) Clarke, *Village Life in America, 1852-1872* (New York, 1913), p. xiii.
    15 *Sixtieth Anniversary of the Sisters of St. Joseph in Canandaigua, N. Y., 1854-1914, op. cit.,* pp. 12-13.
    16 The permanent foundation in Rochester was an orphan asylum for the orphans of soldiers killed in the Civil War. Desclée de Brouwer (ed), *Mère St. Jean Fontbonne* (Bruges, 1929), p. 549, and an English translation by Sister of St. Joseph, *Mother St. John Fontbonne: A Biography* (New York, 1936), pp. 363-364.

continued, and in order to secure the property until he could build, Bishop Timon, an astute lawyer as well as a good prelate, had some temporary cottages removed from the grounds of the Sisters of Charity—used by them while their Foundling Home was being built—to the Couteulx block. Two Sisters were brought from Canandaigua, Sisters Francis Joseph Ivory and Bruno Nolan, and two from Toronto, Sisters Bernard Dinan and Philomene Sheridan.

Sister Francis Joseph Ivory says in her *Notes:*

We boarded in the parsonage and taught school in the church. I had the boys in the vestry: a curtain was put up before the sanctuary, and Sister Philomene taught the girls. When the cottages were ready, we removed thither, had a goodly number of boys and girls. We received no salary. We did some little work, and worked hard, but had not the necessaries of life. The Sisters of Charity over the way occasionally sent us some provisions. I shall never forget Sister Rosalie, the Superioress of the Foundling Home. All this time there was no deaf mute class (1857). The first pupils were a little German boy and some little girls from Canadaigua. The Bishop had a few brick buildings put up for the Deaf Mute Institute and he sent a young priest, Father Dunn, to Philadelphia to receive instructions in the sign language at Mount Airy School. He also sent several Sisters of Saint Joseph for the same purpose.[17] The best teacher trained in Philadelphia was Sister Evangelist, who died shortly after her return to Buffalo. The Bishop appointed Sister Mary Anne Burke[18] as Superior and established the Novitiate on a better basis than before. Sister Mary Rose Hines from Philadelphia was Mistress of Novices. The Bishop, Father Dunn, Mother Mary Anne, Sisters Thomas Ryan, Elizabeth Wheeler, and Mary Berchmans Desmond formed the Board of Trustees.[19]

The original motherhouse at Canandaigua received no new members after 1858; during that year the motherhouse was removed to Buffalo. Thereafter, for thirty-three years, the administration of the Community was located at the Institution for the Deaf on Edward Street. For ten years, this served as well as the motherhouse of the missions now in the two dioceses. In 1866 the novitiate was removed to a place at the corner of Main and Jefferson Streets later known as the "Villa" and forming a part of the property of Canisius College.[20]

At the earnest request of the Reverend Thomas F. Hines, Bishop Timon, in May, 1857, sent three Sisters of Saint Joseph to take charge of Saint Joseph's Orphan Asylum for Boys, located at Limestone Hill

---

[17] They lived as novices with the Sisters of St. Joseph at Chestnut Hill.
[18] She retained the position of Principal of the School until her death in Dec., 1927. She governed the Buffalo Community for over forty years.
[19] Dunne, *op. cit.,* pp. 71-74.
[20] *A Commemoration of the Seventy-Fifth Anniversary of the First Foundation of the Sisters of St. Joseph in the Diocese of Buffalo* (Buffalo, 1931), p. 18.

in the town of West Seneca, now Lackawanna. The orphanage, which arose out of conditions following the cholera epidemic of 1849, was first opened in Buffalo and later removed to Lancaster. Here the undertaking failed, was broken up for a time, and finally reorganized at Limestone Hill under the guidance of Father Hines, the pastor of Saint Patrick's Church. This institution, later made famous by the Reverend Nelson H. Baker, is still conducted by the Sisters of Saint Joseph of Buffalo.[21]

Not all Catholic orphan boys of Rochester were to be found in the distant Saint Joseph's Asylum. This fact apparently moved Father Early, who had ten years before been in charge of Saint Joseph's Asylum and was now pastor of Saint Mary's Church, Rochester, to provide for the care of Catholic orphan boys in Rochester itself. Accordingly in 1874, he purchased a three-story brick building at 3 South Street, facing Washington Square, and furnished it sufficiently to allow the opening of the institution on November 1, 1864. Three Sisters of Saint Joseph, Mother Stanislaus Leary (later General Superior of the Community), Sister Xavier Delahunty (later Superior at Saint Mary's Orphan Asylum), and Sister Clare Shea, a lay Sister, were sent by Bishop Timon at the insistence of Father Early to take charge of the institution. The first night of their arrival two little boys applied for admittance. The first year from twenty to thirty boys were received, ranging from five to ten years of age. The new asylum was incorporated almost immediately after its founding as Saint Mary's Asylum for Orphan Boys. The trustees were the Right Reverend John Timon, the Very Reverend J. M. Early, Sisters Stanislaus Leary, Patrick O'Brien, and James McRaden.[22]

Two and a half months after its opening, in January 14, 1865, a visitor to the new institution expressed his satisfaction with what he saw there:

The house, though not yet fully supplied with the furniture required, is provided with nice beds for the boys, with food and fuel for the time being, and the little fellows seemed to be very happy and comfortable. In the school room they are taught all the English studies adapted to children of their age. They sing pretty hymns and patriotic songs with an evidence of good feeling that sets the heart of the spectator aglow and makes him rejoice that so many

[21] Ibid., p. 21.
  Zwierlein, op. cit., vol. I, pp. 229-230.
[22] The building was purchased for $4,500 from Mrs. S. Hughes. Annals of the Sisters of St. Joseph of the Diocese of Rochester, op. cit., vol. I, pp. 21-23.
  Zwierlein, op. cit., vol. I, pp. 231-232.

homeless lads have been made comfortable and placed on the road of usefulness in life. This orphan asylum will continue to receive boys as they are
found neglected, and they will remain there to be instructed and when of
suitable age, they will be provided with homes where they can engage in
respectable avocations to earn their livelihood. Such an institution commends
itself to the public and bespeaks for it the attention of the benevolent and
the assistance of the public authorities.[23]

During the early days of the Asylum, a fair was scheduled for its
benefit. An article from the *Union and Advertiser* is worth quoting:

. . . Having made a call there this morning, we are able to speak understandingly of the merits of this charity. The Asylum, located on 3 South Street in a
commodious brick building, is tolerably well adapted to present wants. The
rooms are well kept, in excellent order, and every part is a pattern of neatness.

The faithful Sisters who devote themselves wholly to the task of instructing the boys and providing for their wants, are omitting nothing. . . . To
boys between five and twelve with no friends, they furnish an education and
employment. There are none more healthy and more cheerful in any school in
the city. The Sisters make the care of those unfortunate boys a sacred, a religious
duty.[24]

Before closing this discussion on the work of the Sisters of Saint
Joseph in the Saint Mary's Asylum for Orphan Boys, it might be
fitting to quote from the *West End Journal or Orphan's Advocate:*

To Sister Stanislaus great praise is due and in this short notice we should
be negligent in a most important duty, should we permit her name to pass
unnoticed. In the days of its infancy she watched over it with more than ordinary
vigilance and guarded its every interest with prudence and economy.

Her solicitude for the little orphans in attending personally (or having
it done by her co-laborers) to their every want; every day adding new comfort
for the inmates of the institution, has elevated the character of the Asylum
so that it now stands second to none in the State.[25]

When Halstead Hall in West End was purchased in 1867, the
Asylum moved to more commodious quarters. Soon one hundred
and twenty boys were gathered there under the care of the Sisters of
Saint Joseph. The property was paid for within a few years, even
though the institution received but one thousand dollars from the
state during that time.[26] The people of Rochester, however, supported this noble work of benevolence with the same generosity they

---

23 *Rochester Union and Advertiser*, Jan. 16, 1865.
  Zwierlein, op. cit., vol. I, pp. 231-232.
24 *Annals of the Sisters of St. Joseph of the Diocese of Rochester, op. cit.*, vol. I,
pp. 23-26.
25 *Ibid.*, p. 26.
26 *Rochester Union and Advertiser*, Aug. 4, 1867.
  Rochester West End Journal, June, 1870.
  Zwierlein, *op. cit.*, vol. I, p. 232.

had shown in contributing to the aid of the Saint Patrick's Orphan Asylum under the care of the Sisters of Charity.[27]

Bishop Timon, the good friend of the Sisters of Saint Joseph in Saint Louis and in western New York, had laid the foundation of the Congregation in his diocese firm and deep. About this time he made the announcement that Rochester would soon have a bishop, and become the seat of a new diocese of the Catholic Church.[28] The matter was discussed at the Second Plenary Council of Baltimore, where the name of the Reverend Bernard McQuaid was mentioned. Before the official appointment was made, Bishop Timon had gone to his reward. He died April 16, 1867.[29]

Formation of the Diocese of Rochester took place on January 24, 1868, through its separation from the See of Buffalo. The Most Reverend Bernard McQuaid was consecrated as its first bishop by Archbishop John McCloskey at the Cathedral in New York on July 12, 1868. When he reached his diocese four days later, the occasion was one of great rejoicing and appreciation for the distinguished recognition which had come to the city and the region. At that time there were only sixty churches administered by thirty-eight priests. Seven of these were Redemptorists, who served in the territory embracing Monroe, Livingston, Wayne, Ontario, Seneca, Cayuga, Yates, and Tompkins counties.

Archbishop Hughes had already worked out the pattern which Bishop McQuaid decided to follow in the new diocese. Great impetus had been given the subject of Catholic education at the Second Plenary Council of 1866. At this Council it had been urged that a nation-wide effort toward a Catholic school system be supported. Although this hope was not entirely realized, attention was called to the dangers of nonreligious education of Catholic children in public schools.[30] Within the space of a few years the Diocese of Rochester, which in 1868 was poor and lacking in educational facilities, had become notable as a center of education, supplying priests not only for the diocese but also for other communities.

Through action of the Holy Father Leo XIII the Diocese of

---

[27] Loc. cit.

[28] In a sermon preached in St. Patrick's Church on Sept. 9, 1866.

[29] Zwierlein, op. cit., vol. I, pp. 289-290.

[30] Peter K. Guilday, A History of the Councils of Baltimore (1791-1884) (New York, 1932), pp. 273-274.

Rochester was enlarged on December 10, 1896, when Steuben, Tioga, Chemung, and Schuyler counties were added to its territory.[31]

Bishop McQuaid was admirably equipped to undertake the work of building a diocese. In the autumn of 1868, he secured the separation of the Sisters of Saint Joseph of Rochester and Canandaigua from their motherhouse in Buffalo. After a close study of their rules and constitutions, Bishop McQuaid was convinced that the Sisters of Saint Joseph were especially adapted for carrying out his plans of organizing the parochial school system. The direction given to the original band in 1650 by Bishop de Maupas and Father Medaille "to obey your Bishop as your Superior," to whose paternal charity and care they were recommended, appealed strongly to the Bishop of Rochester.[32]

As mentioned before, there had been a tendency in the field of secondary education to admit only students whose parents were able to pay. Bishop McQuaid wanted a more democratic system, one in which the poor could participate as well as those with means. He began a movement for the "Christian Free Schools," advocating them in lectures which he gave in other cities as well as at home.[33]

The rapid growth of the parochial system in the diocese is a monument to the idea which Bishop McQuaid expounded on every occasion. In a letter to his friend, Archbishop M. A. Corrigan, he wrote: "I requested the removal of the Sisters of Charity from the Asylum and the Parochial School. . . . I would go through twice as much to bring about the change which has been effected. I shall now be able to have good parochial schools in the parish and in the city. A schoolhouse shall be built in this parish, another in the Immaculate Conception, and a third in Saint Bridget's this coming year. . . . The Sisters of Saint Joseph who are to be the diocesan school teachers are doing very well and promise great success in their work."[34]

At the time of the separation of the Sisters of Saint Joseph of Rochester from the Buffalo Motherhouse, the individual Sisters were

---

[31] *Catholic Encyclopedia*, vol. XIII, pp. 102-104.
[32] "The Sisters of St. Joseph," *Rochester Catholic Courier*, golden jubilee ed., Nov. 2, 1939.
[33] *Catholic Encyclopedia*, vol. XIII, p. 102-104.
[34] Letter of the Rt. Rev. Bernard McQuaid to the Rt. Rev. M. A. Corrigan, Dec. 19, 1870. Original is in the Archives of the Archdiocese of New York (Dunwoodie Seminary). From Bishops and Dignitaries to Archbishop Corrigan, C3. A photostat is in the Archives of the Nazareth Motherhouse, Concordia, Kans.

left free to remain or to return to the motherhouse at Buffalo. About twelve remained to form the nucleus of the Congregation of the Sisters of Saint Joseph of Rochester. Saint Mary's Orphan Asylum on West Avenue, Rochester, became the temporary motherhouse and novitiate, and Mother Stanislaus Leary, then Superior of the Orphan Asylum, became Mother General of the new Community with Bishop McQuaid Ecclesiastical Superior.[35]

Within the period of the administration of Mother Stanislaus Leary (1868-1882) the infant community grew steadily from a mere handful of subjects to one hundred and sixty.[36] The new motherhouse was formally opened August 15, 1871. Many parochial schools and eleemosynary institutions came into existence during those eventful years.

Bishop McQuaid's movement started with three teachers and a few hundred pupils. To each Sister of Saint Joseph he gave as many boys and girls as she could teach. It was a great work, and Bishop McQuaid is best known for the part he has taken in the agitation for religious schools. It was mainly due to his efforts in Rochester and in Rome that the old policy of the Church was revived and carried out in this country. It was commonly supposed that the movement which he had begun tended toward a demand for a share of the public money for sectarian schools. He maintained simply that it was not the business of the state to educate children whose parents were able to pay for their education. At the close of a lecture in Boston, February 3, 1876, he declared his principles to be, for a republic whose citizens are of different religious beliefs and for voters wanting knowledge intelligence: first, the non-interference of the state in religious matters, in church or in school; second, compulsory knowledge, through parochial schools, under parents' control and at their cost; third, free trade in education, or no monopoly of the teaching profession.[37]

A report sent to the Bureau of Education in Washington, in

---

35 Zwierlein, *op. cit.*, vol. II, pp. 82-85.

36 This data is contained in an address delivered in honor of the silver jubilee of Mother Stanislaus Leary in 1882. It also mentions that sixteen Sisters "have joined the Just made Perfect." Original in writing is in the Archives of the Nazareth Motherhouse, La Grange, Ill. A photostat is in the Archives of the Nazareth Motherhouse, Concordia, Kans.

37 *Catholic Courier*, golden jubilee ed., 1889-1939. Facsimile of *Rochester Catholic Journal*, Oct. 5, 1889.

December, 1876, contained information regarding Nazareth Academy which had been established a few years before:

Date of organization, 1872; value of grounds and buildings, $40,000; receipts of last year's tuition, $7,200; instructors, 5; students, 90; English course, 90; modern language, 25; Latin, 10; volumes in library, 500; annual charge per tuition, $150; number of weeks in the scholastic year, 36.[38]

In the *Annals of the Sisters of Saint Joseph of Rochester* an amusing incident is told about a German priest, Rev. D. Laurenzis, who gave a retreat to the Academy students. As he made arrangements for the daily schedule with Mother Stanislaus, he asked, "At what time, Reverend Mother, do the young ladies stand up?" Mother Stanislaus, not knowing German idioms, did not understand and asked him to repeat his question. After a third similar request he tried to clarify himself by saying, "At what time do the young ladies stand up in their beds?"[39]

The physical needs of the Sisters were met when the summer residence of Bishop McQuaid was leased for a period of ten years at a yearly rent of $1,000. An extra frame building was erected to serve as a chapel, refectory, and dormitory. The Bishop erected another place for himself and his guests. "How well," wrote one of the Sisters, "did our kind Superior understand that after the hard work of the school year, the Sisters needed more relaxation and pure air than they could command within the narrow limits of their convent walls. Oh! the grand times we enjoyed on the charming lake, in the hills and woods and fields of dear old Hemlock. We arose at six A.M., attended Mass, had breakfast, then went to the fields to pick berries, roam over the hills, read and study. There were boats and fishing enticed many. One large rowboat could accommodate about twenty passengers."[40]

Bishop McQuaid mentioned this summer residence in a letter to his friend, Archbishop Corrigan, August 16, 1877:

The Sisters will leave the lake next week. They have derived immense benefit from their stay and will return to their work full of vigor. There were twenty-seven through the vacation and thirty-eight during the retreat. Father John, the Passionist, regrets that both retreats could not be given there. It is

---

[38] *Loc. cit.*
[39] *Annals of the Sisters of St. Joseph of Rochester, op. cit.*, vol. I, pp. 125-126.
[40] Zwierlein, *op. cit.*, vol. II, p. 86.
Annals of the Sisters of St. Joseph of Rochester, op. cit., vol. I, pp. 130-132.

probable that the Sisters will put up a large addition to accommodate about seventy Sisters.[41]

In 1880, Mother Stanislaus was seriously ill; but her health returned much to the joy of the Sisters. The *Catholic Times* contained this note: "Reverend Mother Stanislaus, the respected superior of the Sisters of Saint Joseph in the Diocese of Rochester, was seriously ill last week. We are pleased to be able to state that the worthy lady is now convalescing, for her death would prove an incalculable loss to religion in this part of the vineyard." [42]

In line with his educational program, Bishop McQuaid requested that Mother Stanislaus send two Sisters to Europe to study and Sisters Seraphine and De Sales were selected. Bishop McQuaid wrote to Archbishop Corrigan from Tours, France, on November 11, 1878: ". . . Bruges; where I made arrangements to place two Sisters of Saint Joseph in a Normal School for Religious, conducted by the Sisters of Saint Andre. . . ." [43]

Sister Seraphine contracted quick consumption. Bishop McQuaid sent Mother Stanislaus Leary and Sister Berchmans Desmond to Europe to see the actual condition of the student. En route, they remained overnight with the Sisters of Saint Joseph of Brooklyn, whose Superior, Mother Baptist, was a lifelong friend of Mother Stanislaus. They sailed on the *Nederland* of the Red Star Line to Antwerp. According to Sister Berchmans, the boat had only one deck and was scarcely seaworthy. Both were sick for the entire journey. They spent the Fourth of July aboard ship, and the day was duly celebrated. The deck was decorated with Belgian and American flags; toasts were given by members of all nationalities aboard.[44]

The strange, old-fashioned customs of the French peasantry greatly amused Mother Stanislaus, who, according to Sister Berchmans, who was Belgian herself, seemed to think that all Belgians were like those in the market places and at the docks. "Poor Mother,"

[41] Letter of the Rt. Rev. Bernard McQuaid to Archbishop Corrigan, Aug. 16, 1877. Original is in the Archives of the Archdiocese of New York (Dunwoodie Seminary) From Bishops and Dignitaries to Archbishop Corrigan, C3. A photostat is in the Archives of the Nazareth Motherhouse, Concordia, Kans

[42] Zwierlein, *op cit.*, vol. II, p. 89.

[43] Letter of the Rt. Rev. Bernard McQuaid to Archbishop Corrigan, Nov. 11, 1878. It is interesting to note that in this letter Bishop McQuaid gives an account of his attendance at the funeral of Cardinal Manning.

Zwierlein, *op. cit.,* vol. II, pp. 111-112.

[44] Upon landing at Antwerp they heard of the assassination of President Garfield by the fanatic, Guiteau.

continued the diarist, "had no chance to be disabused of her error, for soon we were inside the walls of Saint Vincent's Convent," a sort of hospice where they accommodated lady boarders.

From Antwerp they continued their journey to Bruges, where they found Sister Seraphine prostrate but still sufficiently strong to undertake the voyage home. Mother Stanislaus resolved to set out immediately. They returned on the same vessel. The sea was rough, and it was dangerous to go on deck although the heat was unbearable in the cabins and the portholes had to be kept shut on account of the high seas. They almost collided with another vessel near Antwerp; one sailor fell from the mast; a child died; an engineer fell and died; and one Catholic woman died without a priest. There was one on the ship but he was unable to leave his cabin to reach steerage.[45]

Mother Stanislaus not having been expected to return so soon, the homecoming was somewhat of a surprise to everybody. They had been absent only six weeks, and in those days it was a considerable feat to cross the ocean and return in such a short time. However, hurried preparations were made at Nazareth; there was illumination, song, and other festivities to welcome the Reverend Mother and Sisters Berchmans, Seraphine, and De Sales. There was a round of visits to the various missions with a festive reception in each place. All were eager to see Mother Stanislaus and hear details of her voyage. As a great number of Sisters were still at Hemlock Lake, Reverend Mother went there also and was received with acclamations of joy and heartfelt "Welcome Home."[46]

A copy of the address of welcome delivered at Hemlock is extant and worth quoting in full:

At last it is permitted us, your loving children, to welcome home from a distant land our much revered and fondly loved *Mother!!*

Little did we think, dear Mother, when we bade you "good-bye" about six weeks ago, that we would in so short a time have the unutterable happiness of welcoming you back again to our midst. How can we ever thank Almighty God enough for protecting you from so many dangers, to which those who take such a trip are exposed; and how ungrateful we will be if ever we cease blessing Him for bringing you safe over the deep blue sea. But He is so good to us, and by the intercession of His Mother Mary who is justly styled "Star of the Sea" this great favor has been granted us. We can see this even more clearly when we reflect that when we did not know, perhaps you were being

[45] *Annals of the Sisters of St. Joseph of Rochester, op. cit.,* vol. I, pp. 168-173.
[46] *Ibid.,* vol. I, pp. 173-174.

tossed about on the deep Atlantic, we praying as fervently as we knew how for your safe passage, fearful, lest we might not be worthy of so great a favor. Scarcely had fourteen days passed ere the One who has given us so many proofs of His love, consoled us by permitting us to receive the "Joyful News" of your safe arrival in the Eastern Continent, and only a few more days passed, when we received a letter, written by our dear Mother who was then in a foreign clime. Shortly after this, we received word that she would soon embark for home. This news, dear Mother, brought to us feelings of joy and sorrow; joy that we would soon have the happiness of having you with us again; sorrow that your sojourn there would be so short, that you would not be able to see all that you have so often desired to see in that remote land. The next glad news that reached us was that you had arrived safe in New York, and the last, but not the least, that you had arrived in Rochester. It was then, dear Mother, that we fully realized all that had taken place during these six weeks and we almost envied the Sisters who were at home, and had this greatest of pleasures—to see you.

So you may imagine our feelings today, dear Mother, when we ourselves partake of the same pleasure, and see for ourselves that God has in an especial manner protected you and given us the happiness of greeting you after your safe arrival at Hemlock.

Then, dear Mother, we heartily welcome you home, and earnestly pray Almighty God, that He will spare you to us for many years to come, that you may continue to guide and lead us on safely over the thorny path of life so that we may be well prepared for eternity, and enjoy there with you the company of our Spouse, Jesus, forever.

We sincerely hope, dear Mother, that your health for the future may be better than it has been in the past few years, and that the remainder of your life may be free from sickness, crosses and trials. We are almost afraid to wish this latter, when we reflect that it is principally by means of these that Heaven is gained; but we wish it may be as nearly so as possible.

To conclude, dear Mother, we again greet you, and bid you *"A thousand welcomes."*

Your devoted Children,

Exiled at Hemlock.[47]

This heartfelt greeting reveals the love and affection of the Sisters for their Reverend Mother.

On February 13, 1882, Reverend Mother went to Canandaigua to hear Mass quietly in the same church where twenty-five years before she had received the holy habit. Reverend Father English, however, having received an intimation of Mother's intention, became very enthusiastic on the subject and the result was chronicled in the *Ontario Messenger:*

[47] "Welcome Address to Mother Stanislaus, August, 1881." Original is in the Archives of the Sisters of St. Joseph, La Grange, Ill. A photostat is in the Archives of the Nazareth Motherhouse, Concordia, Kans.

On Monday last, February 14th, the very interesting celebration of a happy religious jubilee of Reverend Mother Stanislaus took place in Canandaigua. Twenty-five years ago at the age of fifteen Mother Stanislaus entered the Sisters of Saint Joseph. Although the Church in her wisdom and economy never encourages the practice of imposing obligatory vows on minors, yet her superiors seeing her sterling worth and piety, judged her capable of bearing the burden which religious life always imposes upon members. Well and happily did they judge, since this esteemed lady has, from that moment down to the present, proved herself faithful to her high vocation, and to the confidence reposed in her, not only as a simple member of the community but as a wise and prudent Mother.

As superior for nearly all the time, she has, by her piety, prudence, and perseverance, accomplished wonders under the most trying circumstance, from the beginning even unto this hour. When she joined the order, it could count but seven members in the present Diocese of Rochester, and now there are in the same Diocese, under her care and influence, nearly two hundred members.

The congregation that gathered in St. Mary's Church to do her honor on the happy occasion was a proof of the warm place she occupies in the hearts and affections of the people. Indeed had it been known to the people of the surrounding country that such a celebration was to take place, the church could not have contained more than a fraction of the numbers that would have been present to give expression to the respect and regard which they have always held and still hold for her.

But her humility prevented this; few, if any, knew of it outside the town itself. It was concealed even from the clergy for the same reason, none of whom were apprised of it save three, and two of these were present in the sanctuary merely in time for the Mass which was sung by Reverend D. English.

After Mass the Reverend Father Morin made a few brief remarks, appropriate to the occasion, giving an outline of the valiant woman's sacrifices and success, congratulating her on both, and praying that she may live to celebrate her golden jubilee, grace and success attending her even to the end.[48]

A few months after the events chronicled above, there was general unrest in the Community when Bishop McQuaid requested the election of a new superior. In the words of the annalist, "Suffice it to say in advance that in the most trying events in the life of a religious, it were well to remember the words of the inspired prophet: 'He that watchest over Israel slumbereth not, nor sleeps'."[49]

There was the incident of Sister Herman McGuigan's visions and the refusal of the Community to allow her to make her profession. Father Saltig, C.S.S.R., pleaded for her, but she was dismissed. She left for the West and joined the Precious Blood Sisters but later severed connections with that community also.

Whether these things were connected with the subsequent dis-

---

[48] *Annals of the Sisters of St. Joseph of Rochester, op. cit.,* vol. I, pp. 186-188.
[49] *Ibid.,* vol. I, pp. 184-186.

turbance in the Community during the spring and summer of that year is hard to tell. Disturbance had found its way into the hitherto peaceful Community, and it is not improbable that among so many members were some who delighted in stirring up the fires of excitement and eagerness for change.[50]

In May, 1882, for reasons best known to himself, Bishop McQuaid resolved to make the change in the government of the Community. To effect his purpose, he addressed a copy of the following letter to each professed Sister, together with blank slips upon which she was instructed to write the names of three members of the Community whom she judged to be worthy and capable of filling the office of Superior for the ensuing term of three years:

Dear Sister:

It is now nearly fourteen years since the Community of the Sisters of Saint Joseph began its work as an independent organization in the Diocese of Rochester. During these years the Community has grown to be large and flourishing. The work accomplished by it, under the helping hand of Divine Providence, has been worthy of devout religious, whose lives are consecrated to God for the salvation of their own souls and the spiritual welfare of those entrusted to their care. Mother Stanislaus has ably and successfully managed the important and responsible task confided to her judgment and zeal. But the time has come when it seems expedient to bring the government of the Community more in harmony with the spirit and rules under which it exists. The rules prescribe that superiors shall hold office for three years, although the same superior may be re-elected or re-appointed. In the Book of Constitutions of the Sisters of Saint Joseph, it is directed that each election shall take place on the Tuesday after Ascension Thursday.

The order to be followed is this:

1. Each Sister entitled to vote shall offer up her Holy Communion on the Sunday within the Octave, and recite daily the "Veni Creator" to obtain light and grace to be guided aright in giving her vote.

2. She shall hold no communication with anyone, superior or fellow-subject, or extern, concerning her intention, nor will she permit anyone to offer her suggestions as to how she shall vote, nor disclose to anyone the names she has written on the enclosed paper.

3. On Tuesday after Ascension Thursday, after having heard Mass and receiving Holy Communion, each Sister will write the names of three Sisters best suited in her judgment and according to her conscience to fill the office of General Superior for the next three years, place the paper in the prepared envelope, seal it and deliver it to the local superior for immediate and direct transmission to the Bishop.

4. No superior has any right to ask from the Sisters under her care any information regarding the vote she may have given.

5. This vote will be given to secure for the Community the superior

50 *Loc. cit.*

best fitted to carry on the good work, to be a source of edification to her fellow-Sisters and to further the end for which the Community was instituted.

6. Local superiors will collect the sealed envelopes from the members of their houses, place them in a large envelope and without delay mail them to the Bishop.

You will readily appreciate the importance of a wise selection in effecting a change in the government of your Community. . . .

Praying that God will be with you and lead you according to His Holy Will, I am, with sincere esteem,

Yours devotedly in Christ,

BERNARD, Bishop of Rochester

Rochester, May 15, 1882.[51]

Mother Stanislaus exhorted the Sisters to submit to the Bishop's directions in all humility, assuring them of her own readiness to accept the change. The circular sent to the missions a few days after the letter of Bishop McQuaid read in full:

Nazareth Convent
Rochester, N. Y.
May 22, 1882

Dear Sisters:

As our good Bishop has thought fit to make a change in the government of the Community, it is your duty as good and obedient religious to submit in all humility and to show no opposition of any kind, as all authority comes from God.

My wish is that in returning the blanks you should act according to conscience. Do not be influenced by the natural affection you bear to anyone. Do not return the blanks unfilled, as this would give offense to the Bishop. Surely out of such a large Community, three persons can be found to fill my office. If, in your judgment, there are not three persons, then write the names of two or one.

This change will not deprive me of watching over the Community and its interests, which are the dearest objects of my life. I would be a miserable religious, indeed, if I could not bear it with resignation and conformity to God's will. I will try to make myself happy in whatever work may be assigned me. I have always tried to do my duty as well as I know how. None of us can do all things perfectly.

Now, my dear Sisters, pray that God may direct your choice. I trust that as good religious you will try to be satisfied with the one the Bishop appoints. Show the obedience and respect due to her office and love and obey your rules.

My beloved Sisters, I ask your prayers that God may give me humility and meekness.

Yours affectionately in Christ,

M. STANISLAUS.[52]

51 *Annals of the Sisters of St. Joseph of Rochester, op. cit.,* vol. I, pp. 194-196. Zwierlein, *op. cit.,* vol. II, pp. 86-87.
52 *Annals of the Sisters of St. Joseph of Rochester, op. cit.,* vol. I, pp. 197-198.

It was well understood in the Community that the Bishop intended a change in administration, and in his letter he had asked each Sister to write three names of her choice. Many of the Sisters, however, consonant with the letter of the Bishop referring to the Rule which allows a re-election of superiors, and strongly devoted to Mother Stanislaus, wrote on their ballots but one name, *Mother Stanislaus.* The Bishop, however felt it wiser to make use of his right to appoint a superior as given in the Rule and named Sister Agnes Hines[53] as Mother General with Sister Evangelist Haggerty as Assistant Superior.

The newly appointed Superior besought the Bishop not to lay the heavy burden on her; but fully cognizant of her worth, the Bishop replied, "Obedience, Sister." Placing her trust in Him who says to every leader in the House of Israel "I will never leave thee, nor forsake," she took up the burden; and her administration of thirty-nine years proved the fulfillment of this confidence in His assistance.[54]

After the installation of Mother Agnes, Mother Stanislaus, accompanied by Sister Ursula, left for an extended rest in Florida. While there she was invited by Bishop J. B. Salpointe, Vicar Apostolic of Arizona, to establish a motherhouse in that territory. Since her health was impaired, Mother Stanislaus considered the proposition seriously. An excerpt of an interesting letter from Bishop Salpointe is extant:

. . . You have not to be afraid of the climate, it is rather warm for a few months during the summer season but it is healthy in both places (Tucson and Florence). If you could come and see for yourself, it would be the best. The Sisters being here can get more help from the people in a few days than the priest in the same number of years.

Hoping to hear soon about what you determine, I remain,

Your most devoted in Xt,

J. B. SALPOINTE, Vic. Ap. of Arizona.[55]

Another letter which bears mention in regard to the western foundation is one found in the Archives of the Kansas Catholic Historical Society. This earliest communication between Mother

---

[53] She had been Assistant Superior to Mother Stanislaus before the election.
[54] *Annals of the Sisters of St. Joseph of Rochester, op. cit.,* vol. I, p. 199.
[55] Letter addressed to Sister Ursula, Jacksonville, Fla.; dated Feb. 7, 1883, at Tucson, Ariz. It is interesting that Mother Stanislaus and her pioneer companions to Kansas started out for Arizona, in fact bought their tickets for that place, but hearing of Indian troubles there accepted the invitation of Bishop Fink of Leavenworth to establish a school at Newton, Kans. The original of this letter is in the La Grange, Ill., Archives of the Sisters of St. Joseph; a photostat is in the Archives of the Nazareth Motherhouse, Concordia, Ill.

Stanislaus and Bishop Fink, O.S.B., of Leavenworth, Kansas, promised "good religious and competent and well-trained teachers to work in your vineyard." This letter, followed by others, negotiated for the expansion of the Sisters of Saint Joseph from Rochester, New York, to the frontier of Kansas.[56]

Mother Stanislaus sought and obtained from Bishop McQuaid the necessary permission to leave the Diocese of Rochester to found the new congregation. The Bishop likewise gave permission to any Sisters who wished to accompany Mother Stanislaus to her new field of labor. Among those who availed themselves of this permission were Sister Francis Joseph Leary and Sister Josephine Leary (both sisters of Mother Stanislaus), Sister Armella McGrath, Sister Domitilla Gannon, and Sister Antoinette Cuff, a novice.[57]

The departure of the Sisters was regretted by all who knew and appreciated their good qualities and especially their years of devoted and disinterested service. "All of us," wrote the late Sister Teresina, in an unpublished manuscript, "realize the sacred ties that bind us to our early associates and co-workers in religion. To rend these ties after years of intimate companionship, must have caused sorrow to those who were departing for other scenes. Only those who have experienced the strength of the bonds that unite the Sisters of the same Community can understand what such a parting means. Through the work of Mother Stanislaus and her co-workers, the work of the Sisters of Saint Joseph in the central West was greatly extended and the three large and flourishing communities of the Sisters of Saint Joseph of Concordia, Kansas, of Wichita, Kansas, and of La Grange, Illinois, owe their origin and development to her efforts."[58]

Thus, while Mother Stanislaus Leary became the organizer of a flourishing Community at Newton, Kansas (later transferring the motherhouse to Concordia), the appointment of Mother Agnes Hines as Superior of the Rochester Community gave a powerful impetus to the educational work in that region.

"True," in the words of the annalist, "many a hardship was to be encountered, many an unpleasant fact was to be chronicled, but

---

[56] Letter from Sister Ursula, Jacksonville, Fla., to the Rt. Rev. Louis M. Fink, O.S.B., Bishop of Leavenworth; no date (possibly late 1882 or early 1883). Original is in the Archives of the Kansas Catholic Historical Society; a photostat is in the files of author.
[57] Mms. of Sister Teresina.
Zwierlein, op. cit., vol. II, pp. 87-88.
Annals of the Sisters of St. Joseph of Rochester, op. cit., vol. II, pp. 11-12.
[58] Mms. of Sister Teresina, op. cit.

it is on the royal road of the Cross that noblest triumphs can be won, and with the poet we may say:

> Be still, sad heart, and cease repining:
> Behind the clouds is the sun still shining:
> Thy fate is the common fate of all;
> Into each life some rain must fall,
> Some days must be dark and dreary.
>
> *Longfellow*[59]"

Today more than sixty years after the trying year of 1882 in Rochester, there are four communities of the Sisters of Saint Joseph, in addition to the Rochester Community, to whom the name *Mother Stanislaus Leary* means much. The Sisters of Saint Joseph of Concordia, of Wichita, of La Grange, and of Orange, California, owe their existence largely to her efforts. This valiant woman was an instrument in the hand of God for the expansion of His Kingdom in the Middle and Far West.

---

[59] *Annals of the Sisters of St. Joseph of Rochester, op. cit.,* vol. II, pp. 5-6.

PART TWO

CHAPTER VI

Kansas,
Late Nineteenth Century

THE West has always been a relative term in American history. It is a condition of development, as Fredrick Jackson Turner so brilliantly pointed out, a frame of mind. The psychological outlook of the West has always been one of vigor, of youth, and of progress in spite of temporary setbacks and heartrending circumstances.

Manifest Destiny—the theory of the two oceans as the natural boundaries of the United States—furnished the emotional impetus for this ever-changing frontier. The prairies were not conquered until the 'Fifties, nor the Great Plains of Kansas and Nebraska until the 'Nineties. Yet, as each succeeding frontier took upon itself the stamp of organized society, East joined hands with West in the amalgamation of this country.[1]

The same reasons which contributed toward the settlement of the older sections of the United States played an important part in that of the Middle West. But added to these were other factors unique to the period: the free grants of land in the public domain; the growth of the railroad net which was binding the country together; propaganda in Europe sponsored largely by the individual states and by the railroads and steamship companies; the cattle boom of the Great Plains; the bad harvests in the wheat-growing sections of the world in the 'Seventies which sent many European peasants as well as Eastern farmers into the West to open new wheat lands;

---

[1] L. M. Hacker and B. B. Kendrick, *The United States Since 1865* (New York, 1940), pp. 129-131.

F. J. Turner, "The Influence of the Frontier in American History," *Proceedings of the Wisconsin Historical Society* (1893); *The Rise of the New West, 1819-1829* (vol. 14, American Nation Series) (New York, 1906).

F. L. Paxson, *History of the American Frontier* (New York, 1924); *The Last American Frontier* (New York, 1910).

D. R. Fox, ed., *Sources of Culture in the Middle West* (New York, 1934), *passim*.

and finally, the series of wars in which European nations were involved during the second half of the nineteenth century led to the heavy immigration of men weary of military service in their own lands.

No chapter in our Western annals is more sheerly spectacular than the conquest of Kansas, and many of the apparently fantastic tales current in earlier days were based on actual experiences incident to buffalo hunts, Indian attacks, droughts, grasshopper swarms, bushwhacker raids, and county seat wars. No less astonishing is the transformation accomplished by the million or so "Kansas-or-Bust" homeseekers who arrived in the decades between 1870 and 1890.[2]

It might be well to pause at this point to outline briefly the historical background of the present State of Kansas. Dyed-in-the-wool Kansans are eager to trace the history of the white man in Kansas back to the chivalric days of Coronado and his search for Quivira,[3] and the quadricentennial of this date was celebrated recently with much pomp and circumstance in various parts of the state. Whether that claim be true or wishful is not the purpose of the present author to discuss nor to attempt to prove in one way or the other. However, the first explorers were of the faith and they tried—successfully or unsuccessfully—to bring that gift to the somewhat nomadic tribes of the Great Plains. That would take us back to 1542, over two and a quarter centuries before the United States had come into existence. Proponents of this extended view point to the death of Father Padilla, the protomartyr, in the vicinity of present-day Herington, where a monument is erected in his honor. There is a claim that filibustering expeditions, led by Francisco Leyva de Bonilla (1594), Antonia Gutierrez Vaca (1634), and Don Diega Dionisic de Penalosa (1662) explored the same territory. They found wide rolling prairies and a land of rich soil watered by streams and brooks. They found the Indian and the buffalo, but they did not find rich tribes living in cities of gold. They found only the poor villages of the Indians, the first pioneers of the great American Plains. Regardless of the number or frequency of these Spanish exploratory parties, no

---

[2] Frederick Simplich, "Speaking of Kansas," National Geographic Magazine, LXXII, No. 2 (Aug. 1937), pp. 135-182.
[3] Kansas Facts, 3 vols. (Topeka, 1929), vol. I, p. 41 ff. The editor selected the history of William Connelly as authority, because Mr. Connelly, as secretary of the Kansas State Historical Society, has become the officially recognized Kansas historian and had devoted his life to the study of Kansas history (editor's note, p. 42).

claim of proprietorship was established to any part of what is now Kansas.

The French, after the discoveries of La Salle, in 1719, made an exploration into the country which became Kansas. Charles Claude Du Tisne, a French Canadian, had been commissioned by Governor Bienville to visit the tribes in the Missouri River basin. His second trip brought him further south into eastern Kansas. Five years later, in 1724, Etienne Venyard Sieur de Bourgmont penetrated into Kansas almost its entire length east to west.

This region, claimed by France until 1762, was then transferred to Spain by secret treaty which was not made known until the following year. During the French Revolution, by the Treaty of San Ildefonso concluded in October, 1800, Spain retroceded to France the Louisiana Territory.

The imperialistic plans of Napoleon Bonaparte extended into the heart of America. Having attempted to establish himself in the West Indies, his eyes looked longingly toward an empire which would shut off the youthful United States from further expansion. But his worldwide interests were beginning to meet stiff-backed opposition, and the black natives of Haiti had resisted his attempts with overwhelming success. This unexpected loss made him realize the unfeasibility of his plan regarding the Mississippi Valley; he began to make overtures to the United States that it buy at a bargain this territory which to Napoleon had become a white elephant.

Thomas Jefferson, strict constructionist that he was, saw the advantage of acquiring this territory, but he also saw the disadvantage of loss of time if another foreign country might have the same thought. Knowing that the legislative procedure, which strict construction of the Constitution would necessitate, would take time, he put his political ideas aside and negotiated with France for the purchase.

After the purchase of the Louisiana Territory, the United States made an effort to discover itself. To obtain information concerning the vast domain which had thus unexpectedly been acquired, the federal government equipped an expedition headed by two young army officers, Captain Meriwether Lewis and Captain William Clark, to explore the territory. In June, 1804, they left the mouth of the Kansas River, and on July 2nd reached Kickapoo Island, the old

French fort which was the first trading post in Kansas history. It is interesting to note that perhaps the first celebration of the Fourth of July recorded in Kansas history occurred here. It is the first official record of the region.

In 1806 Zebulon M. Pike led the second federal exploratory party to cross the state. He mentioned in his diaries various Indian villages and rivers en route. Major Stephen Long in 1819 led the third expedition which was valuable for its scientific observations; the confirmation of facts gathered by the Lewis and Clark and the Pike expeditions; and a council or peace parley with the Kansas Indians at Cow Island, at which the Indians promised to cease their depredations and hostilities toward the white men.

That romantic figure who later became a political figure also, John C. Fremont, made several trips through the state between 1841 and 1853 checking information and surveying land. On his last trip in the interests of his father-in-law, Senator Benton of Missouri, who had conceived a Pacific railroad and wanted to evaluate its possibilities, Fremont surveyed the Smoky Hill River to a point at which Hays now stands.

Another romantic and enigmatic figure stepped into Kansas history in 1854 in the person of Stephen A. Douglas who in his Kansas-Nebraska bill attempted to stem the tide of the slavery question and to inflate his stock as a politician. President Franklin Pierce signed the bill on May 30, 1854. Territorial government was set up, and from that time Kansas became identified with national issues.

The next seven years were trying in the newly organized territory. Abolitionists and slave owners rushed colonists there to gain supremacy under the doctrine of squatter sovereignty; the balance of power in the United States Senate was becoming all-important. Kansas became the battleground for the issues which had been troubling the Eastern seaboard states for some time.

January 29, 1861, after a long and sanguinary struggle as well as several constitutions promulgated as bona fide by the opposing groups, Kansas was admitted to the Union as the thirty-sixth state. The Homestead Act of the following year materially aided settlers in the state.

The State of Kansas dates from 1865. From then until the frontier line had been pushed beyond the western limits of the state, the settlers came singly, in families, and in colonies. "It was not a crusade of families, or a raid of filibusters," said one commentator, "but the measured march of earnest men and women seeking homes." [4]

It has been fairly said of Kansas historians that they are too prone to treat the state's history as a series of local annals and detached events without logical connections with national progress. The fertile field of Kansans' nationalities has not had suitable attention. [5]

Kansas pioneers came, it is true, from New England, but it is often erroneously considered the "All-American" daughter of Massachusetts—a state with little or no foreign population. Statistical tables show that Kansas became a melting pot where Irish, Germans, Bohemians, French, German-Russians of both Mennonite and Roman Catholic affiliations, Scandinavians, and Englishmen met and mingled with their pioneer co-laborers and evolved that spirit which is "Kansas." They came from all corners of this country, possessed of traits and training and prejudices; but, because of their interdependence, a relationship resulted whereby men of the Great Plains became *Kansans* in the true sense of the term.

Railroads were penetrating central Kansas and demonstrating how its future might not lie under the scalping knife of the Indians nor the hoofs of the buffalo. The Kansas Pacific Railway from Kansas City to Denver reached the latter point in 1870, passing through Abilene in March, 1867. [6]

The Cheyenne Indians under Roman Nose became the scourge of the newly settled plains. Governor S. J. Crawford addressed the following letter to Captain W. P. Peak on September 1, 1868:

Please say to the settlers of Cloud and Republic counties that I am now using every means in my power to procure cavalry armed with ammunition from the government, and that I have notified the President, that the Indians *must* and *shall* be driven out of the State and not permitted to return. Also that General Sheridan has agreed to send troops immediately to the Saline, Solomon, and Republican valleys for the purpose of protecting the settlers;

---

[4] R. S. Elliott, *Report on Industrial Resources* (Chicago, 1883), p. 25.

[5] William E. Connelly, *History of Kansas*, 5 vols. (New York, 1928), vol. I, p. v, cited by Nell Blythe Waldron, *Colonization in Kansas, 1861-1890*, Ph.D. dissertation Northwestern Univ. (1932), p. 9; manuscript in Kansas State Historical Society Library, Topeka, Kans.

John Sterling Bird, *Prairies and Pioneers* (Hays, Kans., 1931), p. 14.

[6] Henry Stuart, *Conquering Our Great American Plains* (New York, 1930), pp. 8-9.

Joseph G. McCoy, *Historic Sketches of the Cattle Trade of the West and the Southwest* (Chicago, 1874), p. 54-55; reprinted in 1932 by The Rare Book Shop, Washington, D. C.

that the people may rest assured that they will in the future be protected. If the government fails, the state will not, although I am seriously embarrassed on account of the present Indian policy.

I hope that the people will remain at their homes, and not abandon the country. No possible effort will be spared to secure protection, and to relieve the wants of those who are in a destitute and suffering condition. I shall not rest until the Indians are driven out of the state; and if they return within reach of the settlements, I trust the people will dispose of them in the most summary manner. I shall endeavor to do my duty. We have submitted to these atrocities until forbearance has ceased to be a virtue.

Yours respectfully,

S. J. CRAWFORD, Gov.[7]

It was time that the state and national governments were trying to alleviate the sufferings and worries of the frontiersmen, for some families were returning to more thickly settled and better protected parts of the Middle West.

The Eighteen Seventies were the heyday of the cow country. In 1871, the rival towns of Wichita and Abilene began sending out couriers to cattlemen in Texas to sell them the advantages of each town as cattle markets. Joseph G. McCoy, whose name is closely identified with the period, told about the search for a suitable terminus for the Chisolm trail:

. . . Junction City was visited concerning a site and a proposition made to a leading businessman to purchase from him a tract of land sufficiently large to build a stockyard . . . but an exorbitant price was asked, in fact, a flat refusal to sell at any price was the final answer of the enlightened and wideawake Junctionite . . . so by that one act of donkey stupidity and avarice Junction City drove from her a trade which soon developed into many millions. . . . Various points between Junction and Salina were inspected with regard to adaptability to a cattle business until Solomon City was reached, near which a fine site for stock yard was found; and after one or two conferences with the leading citizens it became evident that they regarded such a thing as a cattle trade with stupidity and horror and from all that can be learned through inquiry the citizens of Salina are of much the same mood. The person making such propositions was apparently regarded as a monster threatening calamity and pestilence. . . . Abilene was selected . . . a very small, dead place, consisting of about a dozen log huts, low, rude affairs, four-fifths of which were covered with dirt for roofing. Indeed there was but one single roof in the whole city. . . .[8]

[7] Noble L. Prentis, *A History of Kansas* (Topeka, 1899), p. 137 ff.
    I. O. Savage, *A History of Republic County, Kansas* (Topeka, 1883), p. 26, contains a copy of this letter.
[8] McCoy, 1932 edition, *op. cit.*, pp. 41-44.

Despite Mr. McCoy's apparent disapproval of the attitude of Junction City, Solomon, and Salina as not farsighted from the point of view of financial returns, still he admitted: "their (the cowboys) reckless conduct . . . has filled many graves with victims, bad men and good men, at Abilene, Newton, Wichita, and Ellsworth. . . . By far the larger portion . . . are of that kind which can be spared without detriment to the good morals and respectability of humanity." [9]

There were nine land districts in the state in 1883: (1) the Arkansas Valley Land District, (2) the Northern Land District, (3) the Topeka Land District, (4) the Northwestern Land District, (5) the Osage Land District, (6) the Republican Land District, (7) the Salina Land District, (8) the Western Land District, and (9) the Wichita Land District. [10] Pamphlets to encourage immigrants to the several regions were broadcast far and wide. [11]

Amusing are the extravagant claims made in these pamphlets of propaganda. "The Best Thing in the West," "The Garden of the West," "Kansas in the Centennial Year the most vigorous product of the nineteenth century." Famous men—some of whom had never stepped on Kansas soil—wrote testimonials such as "the Italy of the American Continent" (Schuyler Colfax); "I like Kansas. . . . there is no better prairie state" (Horace Greeley); ". . . . a soil of unsurpassed richness and a fascinating, undulating beauty of surface with a health-giving climate, calculated to nurture a powerful and generous people, worthy to be the central pivot of American institutions" (speech of Charles Sumner delivered in the United States Senate on May 19, 1856); and, the last but not the least glowing, Vice President Wilson's exhortation in 1875: "But to you who are young, full of vigor, life and hope and ambition, I say to go to our newer New England, the bright, broad fields of sunny Kansas." [12]

These advertisements included information concerning schools and churches as well as the availability of limestone and rock for building purposes. [13] "The inhabitants," wrote one enthusiast, "are in the main intellectual, industrious, moral, and wide awake—indeed

---

[9] *Ibid.*, p. 141.

[10] W. G. Cutler, *History of Kansas* (Chicago, 1883), p. 293; often referred to as Andreas Edition after A. T. Andreas, who was the publisher of histories of various states.

[11] *The Great Northwest!* published at Clay Center, Kans., in 1888, is an example.

[12] Pamphlet distributed by the A., T. and S. F. R. R. (Topeka, 1876) entitled *Ho! for the New Kansas! the Best Thing in the West*, p. 1.

[13] *The Great Northwest* (Clay Center, Kans., 1888), p. 40.

such a class as furnishes the best hands for vocations requiring mind as well as muscle."[14]

"Is Kansas a Garden of Eden, as some have represented it to be?" wrote someone in a pamphlet advertising Salina as a suitable place to settle. "We will answer just as frankly that since the original experiment in that direction somewhere in Asia, a number of years since, there has been no earthly paradise . . . . Kansas is a living reality, with the faults only of lusty manhood. It has been prettily described as a State four hundred miles long, two hundred miles wide, eight thousand miles thick, and reaching to the stars. It then is certainly large enough for you and yours. The motto of Kansas is 'Ad Astra per Aspera'."[15]

The amount and the type of publicity received in older settlements influences pioneer movements of people. First reports and rumors are likely to arouse only the restless and footloose to migrate, but when the tidings are of better economic conditions and opportunities, men of enterprising character who possess some property are also induced to try their fortune on the frontier.[16]

Following the Civil War, the railroad companies became zealous press agents for the state, broadcasting superlative descriptions of its resources throughout the nation and in foreign lands. Land speculators, town site promoters, and the local press added their rosy portrayals to the gallery of praise, and many cities actually subsidized publicity programs. These efforts culminated in the remarkable boom which rose and fell in the 'Eighties.[17]

The land boom hiked prices to absurd heights. Farm land near

[14] Albert Griffin (ed.), *An Illustrated Sketch Book of Riley County, Kansas—The Blue Grass County* (Manhattan, Kans., 1881).

[15] Andrews and Page (eds.), *Picturesque Salina* (Salina, 1887), pp. 28-29. It is interesting to note on page 29 a picture of the Catholic School which elsewhere (p. 3) is referred to as "the Catholic College." Pamphlet is to be found in the Library of Congress; a photostatic copy in files of the author.

[16] C. D. Clark and R. L. Roberts, *People of Kansas: A Demographic and Sociological Study* (Topeka, 1936), p. 19.

[17] *Ibid.*, p. 21.

Cutler, *op. cit.*, p. 252, contains a tabulation of railroad lands unsold in Kansas on Jan. 1, 1883, listing counties in the state, the important railroad communications through each county, and the number of acres of land still available.

The Great Northwest offered inducements in the form of excursions leaving all points as far East as Buffalo and Pittsburgh in time to reach Kansas on stated dates as "it's a good time to visit Kansas" for

> "There's a wideness of the prairies
> Like the wideness of the sea:
> There is room in Northern Kansas
> For the thousands yet to be." *Ibid.*, p. 21.

Abilene, which sold for $6.25 an acre in 1867, was sold for $270 an acre in 1887. Town lots increased tenfold in value in a few years. Railroads were now extended, not to meet legitimate needs, but as a means of increasing land values.[18]

The most disastrous effects of the boom were felt by the counties of the middle section where expansion had been most rapid and extreme. Many towns in this area lost heavily in population, and not a few were abandoned outright when railroad lines projected on paper failed to materialize. However, as one writer put it, this worked out for the good of the state for "since that time the get-rich-quick element has never been conspicuous in the Kansas population."[19]

This turbulent Kansas was not only the daughter of New England, but also the meeting place of many nationalities who in the melting pot became the real Kansans. French-Canadians seeking better economic opportunities came into the north central part of the state; Scandinavians into the south central part of the state; Irish in colonies and as individuals into various parts of Kansas; Germans, many exiled after the revolutions of 1848, came to help build the railroads and add their old cultures to the new land in practically all parts of the state, especially in the eastern and south central parts. In the 1870's there were several colonies of German-Russians established in Kansas: Mennonites in Marion and Harvey Counties, Lutherans in Russell County, and Catholics in Ellis and Rush Counties. Concerning these latter Blackmar states: "A. E. Touzaliar, general passenger agent and land commissioner of the Santa Fe, and Carl B. Schmidt, immigration agent, succeeded in attracting some of these Russian immigrants to Kansas. Mr. Schmidt conducted a part of them to Great Bend and Larned while A. Rodelheimer of the Kansas (now Union) Pacific showed them lands in Rush, Ellsworth and Ellis Counties."[20]

At this point a brief résumé of the history of the Church in Kansas until 1883 showing the *need* which was felt for the work of religious orders in the new state will be given. Emphasizing the word *frontier,* always synonymous with the word *need,* it will be an easy transition to

---

[18] Clark and Roberts, *op. cit.,* pp. 26-27.
[19] *Ibid.*
[20] F. W. Blackmar (ed.), *Kansas: Encyclopedia of State History . . . Institutions . . . Counties . . . Cities . . . Prominent Persons,* 3 vols. (Chicago, 1912), vol. I, p. 397.

the introduction of the Sisters of Saint Joseph into the State of Kansas in 1883.

Nearly every religious denomination known among civilized nations had been organized in the State of Kansas before 1890. The statistical report that only about twenty percent of the population of Kansas in 1883 was affiliated with some organized religious denomination shows clearly, however, the need for religious effort at that time.[21]

Previous to the first attempts to send Catholic missionaries to present-day Kansas, there is mention of the visit of the Reverend Charles de la Croix in 1822.[22] It was in 1825, however, that General Clark, the Indian agent, requested the Jesuits to establish a mission among the Kansas Indians. Father Charles Van Quickenborne, S.J., the founder of Saint Louis University, began his missionary tours in 1837. In 1835 he had made application to the Secretary of War, stating that he was ready to start a mission school among the Kickapoos; thereupon the Secretary of War ordered that five hundred dollars a year be paid toward its upkeep as soon as the school was built. The following year, Father Van Quickenborne, accompanied by Brothers Maxella, Bary, and Miles, arrived at the mission. The Catholic Missionary Society of Missouri furnished one thousand dollars with which the Jesuits began immediately to build the chapel.

Five years later, in 1841, a band of Religious of the Sacred Heart, under the direction of the saintly Mother Duchesne, opened a school for girls. These were the first religious women to work in the State of Kansas. The United States Government subsidized both the priests and the Sisters. Year by year the number of conversions increased,

[21] William Sims, *Kansas: Information Concerning Agriculture . . . Churches . . .* (Topeka, 1884).

Denomination	Organizations	Edifices	Members	Valuation
Presbyterian	181	82	2,826	$370,300
Congregational	121	53	4,458	256,550
Baptist	286	63	12,127	246,650
United Presbyterian	39	14	1,303	49,200
Methodist	621	96	22,696	340,400
Episcopal	34	22	1,136	173,000
Catholic	202	165	37,198	408,300
Lutheran	25	10	524	40,750
Universalist	14	4	300	28,800
Total	1,523	509	82,668	$1,913,950

[22] This fact is contested by Gilbert Garraghan, S.J., in his *Saint Ferdinand de Florissant* (Chicago, 1923), *passim,* and in *Catholic Beginnings in Kansas City* (Chicago, 1920), pp. 25-34.

and education and civilization of the Indians progressed. A number of prayer books, grammars, and dictionaries were printed and distributed to the Indians.[23]

The second school established by the Jesuits was the Osage Mission at St. Paul. The Religious of the Sacred Heart could not supply teachers for this school; therefore, the Sisters of Loretto from Kentucky entered the mission field, opening the first boarding school within the borders of the present state. Wonderful are the tales recounted concerning these pioneer sisterhoods in Kansas.[24]

In 1851, the Reverend John Baptiste Miege, S.J., was appointed Vicar Apostolic of the newly formed Vicariate of Kansas which included the Indian Territory east of the Rockies.[25] Out of the log cabin pro-cathedral of Bishop Miege at the Mission of Saint Mary's among the Pottawatomi grew the Catholic Church of Kansas.[26] In

[23] J. M. Moeder, *Early Catholicity in Kansas and History of the Diocese of Wichita* (Wichita, 1937), *passim*.
[24] *Ibid.*
Sister Mary Paul Fitzgerald, *Beacon on the Plains* (Leavenworth, 1939), pp. 33, 36, 38, 42, 241; 76-81.
[25] *Catholic Almanac* (1856), p. 60.
Richard H. Clarke, *Lives of Deceased Bishops of the Catholic Church in the United States*, 4 vols. (New York, 1888), vol. III, pp. 611-625.
Joseph B. Code, *Dictionary of the American Hierarchy* (New York, 1940), pp. 237-238.
James A. McGonigle, "Rt. Rev. John B. Miege, S.J., First Catholic Bishop of Kansas," *Kansas Historical Collections*, IX (1905-1906), pp. 153-159.
J. Garin, *Notices Biographiques sur Mgr. J. B. Miege, Premier Vicaire Apostolique du Kansas et sur Les Prêtres De La Paroisse De Chevron (Savoie)* (Moutiers, France, 1886), *passim*. The only copy known to be in the United States of this French work is in the St. Mary College Library, Xavier, Kans., where the author used the book.
Sister Paul Fitzgerald, "John Baptist Miege, S.J., 1815-1884," *Historical Records and Studies*, vol. XXIV, pp. 284-362, quoting from *Mission Chronicles*, I:27, states: "John Baptiste Miege was fitted by birth, temperament and training to be the first resident Vicar Apostolic of the Great Plains. He was a Savoyard, the twelfth of fourteen children, the son of simple farmers. . . . His education at Conflans and Moutiers was begun under the watchful eye of his older brother Urban, who was a priest. . . . At nineteen he entered the Society of Jesus and was ordained in Rome in 1847. . . . He cherished a desire to do missionary work among the Indians of North America. . . . He was one of the five Jesuits who left Marseilles (driven out by the Revolution of 1848) for the Missouri Province. . . . Two years later he received the Brief of Pius IX appointing him Bishop of Messenia *in partibus infidelium* and Vicar Apostolic of Indian Territory. His arrival, May 31, 1851, at his see, the Mission of St. Mary's of the Pottawatomi, marked the beginning of twenty-three years of arduous responsibility as a missionary bishop in the territory lying east of the Rocky Mountains and not included within the limits of the present states of Arkansas, Missouri, Iowa and Minnesota. . . ." This quotation was reprinted in footnote on pp. 171-172 of Sister Mary Paul Fitzgerald's *Beacon on the Plains*.
Peter Beckman, *The Catholic Church on the Kansas Frontier, 1850-1877* (Washington, 1943).
[26] In 1940 the Kansas State Historical Society erected a monumental marker at the site of the first cathedral in Kansas. The speaker on that occasion was Roy Bailey of Salina whose daughter Royana unveiled the marker. Royana Bailey was at that time a student at Marymount College, Salina.

1855, there was in the Kansas Territory one bishop, seven hundred Catholics (many of whom were Indians), six completed churches and three others in process of construction, eleven mission stations, and eight priests.

When Kansas had begun its existence as a territory of the United States the year before in 1854, among the settlers who flocked to the territory were scattered Catholics to whom the missionaries on the far-flung frontier began to minister. In thirteen counties mission stations were established for this purpose. Most of these stations were in Irish and German communities although a few were among the French settlers. As the communities grew, the mission stations grew into churches. This era of self-sacrifice on the part of the priests and people is a glorious chapter in the history of Catholicism in Kansas.[27]

The Benedictine Fathers came to Kansas in 1856 under the leadership of the Reverend Augustine Wirth, O.S.B., and established a priory at Atchison. A short time later the Benedictine Sisters came to the same town to establish what is known today as Mount Saint Scholastica. In 1858, a foundation of the Sisters of Charity, under the superiorship of Mother Xavier Ross, came from Nashville, Tennessee (the foundation was a branch of the Kentucky Sisters of Charity), and established their motherhouse at Leavenworth. These religious communities which ministered to the educational and humanitarian needs of the expanding frontier are still a vital factor in Catholicism in the state.

The extensive span of land under the Vicar Apostolic, Bishop Miege, was decreased in 1858 when the Vicariate of Nebraska—under the jurisdiction of the Right Reverend James M. O'Gorman—was created, leaving only Kansas Territory to the former.[28]

Priests ordained in those early days faced a broad horizon of missionary endeavor. Fathers Anthony Kuhls, John F. Cunningham, later a dominant factor in the religious upbuilding of the Church in Kansas, and Francis J. Wattron were sent out to comb the prairies to reclaim those who had fallen away from the Church and were willing to reassume their status in the Mystical Body of Christ, and to carry their momentous message to those who had not yet heard

[27] Moeder, op. cit., passim.
[28] Catholic Encyclopedia, vol. IX, pp. 102-104.
    Moeder, op. cit., passim.
    Fitzgerald, Beacon on the Plains, op. cit., p. 172. (Cf. R. H. Clarke, op. cit., vol. III, pp. 626-636, for account of O'Gorman; Code, op. cit., pp. 267-268.)

the words of eternal salvation. The well-known Father Paul Mary Ponziglione, the apostle of Kansas, was relieved of some of his vast territory only when settled conditions facilitated the appointment of resident pastors in such places as Fort Scott and Wichita.[29]

During this period the Civil War was raging even within the borders of Kansas. At the close of the conflict, there came a period of expansion in which new settlements of Catholics appeared, while the Indian population was largely moved into Oklahoma after having sold their reservation back to the Government. The Carmelite Fathers came into Leavenworth about the end of the Civil War and have added much to the religious vitality of the region.

The desire of Bishop Miege to return to the common life of the Jesuits met with opposition from his ecclesiastical superiors; however, in 1871, he was granted a coadjutor in the person of the Reverend Louis Mary Fink, O.S.B., who was consecrated titular Bishop of Eucarpia.[30] The petition of Bishop Miege to resign was not accepted until 1874 at which time Bishop Fink assumed jurisdiction. According to available statistics there were in Kansas in that year sixty-five priests, eighty-eight churches, three colleges, four academies, one hospital, one orphan asylum, and thirteen parish schools with seventeen hundred pupils. Communities of Benedictine, Jesuit, and Carmelite priests, Religious of the Sacred Heart, Sisters of Saint Benedict, Sisters of Charity, and Sisters of Loretto worked among the Catholic population of nearly 25,000.[31] Therefore, at the three-quarter mark in the nineteenth century one can find a steady growth of the Church.

About this time, as part of the threefold immigration of German-Russians into Kansas, the Catholic group settled in Herzog, Hays, Munjor, Catherine, Pfeifer, Schoenchen, and other nearby places.[32]

[29] Fitzgerald, *Beacon on the Plains, op. cit.*, has devoted chap. 11, pp. 171-190, to the life and activities of Father Ponziglione. This is without doubt one of the best evaluations available of this worker for Christ.

[30] A sketch of the life of the Rt. Rev. Louis Mary Fink, O.S.B., will be found in Code, *op. cit.*, pp. 106-107.

[31] J. A. Shorter, "Diocese of Leavenworth," *Catholic Encyclopedia*, vol. IX, pp. 102-104.

[32] "Rev. Valentine Sommereisen, Pioneer Priest of the West," *Central-Blatt and Social Justice*, vol. XXIX (1936-1937), pp. 242-243.

F. S. Laing, "German-Russian Settlements in Ellis County, Kansas," *Kansas Historical Collections*, vol. XI (1907-1908), pp. 1-40.

Capuchin Fathers, *Some Early History of the Pioneer Catholic Settlers and Parishes of Northwestern Kansas* (Herndon, Kans., 1913), *passim.*

Sister Eloise Johannes, C.S.J., *A Study of the Russian-German Settlements in Ellis County, Kansas* (Washington, 1946), *passim.*

The Sisters of Saint Agnes of Fond du Lac, Wisconsin, and the Capuchin Fathers from Pittsburgh, Pennsylvania, have been closely identified with these groups.

The diocese of Bishop Fink, embracing as it did the entire State of Kansas, was constantly in need of funds from outside sources. In a letter written to his friend the Right Reverend M. A. Corrigan, Bishop of Newark, New Jersey, Bishop Fink said in part:

. . . Allow me to express to you my most sincere gratitude for the great kindness shown by your Grace to my poor Father Cunningham (later the Bishop of Concordia) at present in your diocese. I feel your kindness so much the more gratefully as it renews my attachment to Newark and its venerable and worthy bishop—as in days gone by I was myself a subject of the Bishop of Newark as a member of the religious clergy of the diocese. Our poor Vicariate has been tried very severely for the last two or three years—and I offer up my poor prayers for our benefactors, who gave us a helping hand— and I shall ever be mindful of your Lordship's kindness to us. . . .[33]

The *Catholic Almanac* of 1878 listed clergy who might be contacted by prospective immigrants to Kansas. This interesting list included the Reverend Louis Mollier of Shirley, the Reverend John Pichler of Hanover, the Reverend H. Temphaus of Beloit, and the Reverend F. M. Hayden of Solomon.[34] These priests conducted missions among the French, Irish, and Germans in the central part of Kansas, the section which was especially affected by the influx of settlers in the late 'Seventies and early 'Eighties.

The Reverend John F. O'Leary, pastor of Solomon City in Dickinson County, organized a local immigration board to buy up farms and unoccupied lands for immigrants. However, it is recorded that Father O'Leary remarked that the documents which he sent out had been issued too late and therefore brought only a few families to his parish.[35]

In Ellsworth, near Fort Harker, the Reverend J. F. Kelley, who ministered to the Catholics in Lincoln County and a part of Saline County, wrote that in 1883 there were about 40,000 acres of unoccupied land in his missionary district. The Irish were in the

---

[33] Original letter of the Rt. Rev. Louis Marie Fink, O.S.B., to the Rt. Rev. M. A. Corrigan, Bishop of Newark, N. J., Sept. 22, 1875. Original is in the Dunwoodie Seminary Archives of the Archdiocese of New York—classified as C2. The author was graciously allowed the use of the material at Dunwoodie and has had the letters photostated for her own files.

[34] *Catholic Almanac* (1878), p. 293.

[35] *Monthly Visitor*, Aug. 15, 1883. File is to be found in Kansas State Historical Library, Topeka, Kans.

majority in this region, with large groups of Germans and Bohemians.[36]

The twin questions of nationality and national antipathies appeared at this time in the region of Ellsworth and Wilson. The following letter is self-explanatory:

> St. John Nepomuk Church
> St. Louis, Missouri
> February 19, 1883

Rev. J. F. Kelley
Ellsworth, Kansas
Rev. and dear Sir:

On request of the Bohemian Catholics in Ellsworth County, I write you these lines in order to explain to you the opinion of the Bohemians in regard to building the new church. I write this letter because the Bohemian folks at Wilson say that they are not able to speak the English language and so make themselves clear to you. The Bohemians will be understood, they do not refuse to join themselves with the Irish and German Catholics in Wilson to erect a Catholic Church. But they only wish to have some guarantee that their nationality shall be regarded in the congregation and that sometimes the Bohemian priest shall be called to them to hear their confessions and to preach to them in their national language.

And in case they would build a proper church only for the Bohemian nationality they do not refuse to give the deed for the church property to the bishop. They will never resist the regulations of the diocese. These are the sentiments of the Bohemians in Wilson, explained to your reverence and to the Right Reverend Bishop to whom I wrote a letter yesterday and from whom I received a reply just today.

The Bishop wishes that I should mediate between the Bohemians in Wilson and the ecclesiastical authorities as he heard that the Bohemians will not submit to the laws of the diocese deferring to the Bohemian priest in Saint Louis who visited them last year. This is an unfair misunderstanding.

First, I have never been in Wilson and secondly, I never provoked the Bohemians in Wilson to resistance against the rules of the diocese. On the contrary I induced them to obey the Bishop's regulations; otherwise they would not be considered as Catholics. That's the truth in the affair. I shall be very happy if the Bohemians in Wilson will get along on the path of the holy Faith and keep good order as Catholic Christians.

Recommending you to the protection of God, I remain,

> Yours respectfully,
>
> JOSEPH FLESSOUN[37]

In Sedgwick County, at Saint Marks, Father B. Schmiehausen publicized Sedgwick and Kingman counties. "The land," wrote he, "is adapted to farming, also to stock raising. The Catholic population

---

[36] *Loc. cit.*
[37] Original letter in the Kansas Catholic Historical Society Archives at St. Benedict's College, Atchison; photostatic copy in files of the author.

in some congregations is German, in others Irish and German. A Catholic school is attached to Saint Mark's Church.[38] In Kingman County alone there are over 400,000 acres of unoccupied land—the half of which is government and homestead land. . . . How many families could be put in Kingman County alone at 320 acres to the family? See on how grand a scale God has provided for his children."[39]

An interesting pamphlet was published in France concerning Catholicism in Kansas in 1880, the purpose of which was to encourage immigration.[40] The religious appeal was stressed strongly to encourage colonies of various nationalities to migrate.

One of the most interesting projectors of emigrant aid was Bryan Mullanphy, son of John Mullanphy, "the noblest Catholic St. Louis has ever known."[41] His son established the so-called Mullanphy Fund in his will: "one equal and undivided third of my property, real, personal and mixed, I leave to the city of St. Louis . . . in trust to be and constitute a fund to furnish relief to all poor emigrants and travelers coming to St. Louis on their way, bona fide, to settle in the West."[42] Many migrants to the plains of Kansas blessed the Mullanphy Fund for tiding them over on their trip.

Later identified with the establishment of the pioneer community of the Sisters of Saint Joseph in Newton, Kansas, and one of the prime promoters of the Catholic colonization movement to Kansas, Father Felix P. Swemberg wrote the following letter to the editor of the *Catholic Review* shortly before the convocation of the National Colonization Convention in Chicago on March 17, 1879:

---

[38] This school was one of the first taken over by the Sisters of St. Joseph after their arrival in Newton in 1883.

[39] *Monthly Visitor,* Aug. 15, 1883.

[40] "Les populations du Kansas sont très pieuses, tous les cultes y sont representés et chacun suit avec beaucoup d'assiduité le culte auquel ils appartient. La religion romaine possède un évêque à Leavenworth et une cathédrale qui a coutée plus de deux millions de la monnaie française: les cultes les plus repandus avec le catholicisme sont ceux des Méthodistes, des Anabaptistes, des Presbytériens, des Congrégationalistes, et des Épisco-paliens. . . . L'État reconnait tous les cultes. . . . Il y a douze ans, un mais áprès l'établissement de la premier colonie qu'ait possédé l'État, à Lawrence, un service regulier etait établi; j'ai vu souvent à la frontière le service divin célèbré sous des tentes." Georges de Pardonnet (special agent of immigration to Kansas), *Émigration au Kansas —Conseils Pratiques aux Émigrants* (Mont-belierd, 1880), p. 34.

[41] J. P. O'Hanlon, *Life and Scenery in Missouri: Reminiscenses of a Missionary* (Dublin, 1890). Sister Evangela Henthorne, *The Irish Catholic Colonization Association of the United States* (Champaign, 1932), p. 22.

[42] Thomas F. Meehan, "The Unbreakable Grip of a Dead Hand," *America* (Sept. 8, 1928), cited by Henthorne, *op. cit.,* f.n., p. 22.

Newton, Harvey County, Kansas
February 22, 1879

To the Editor of the *Catholic Review:*

"The world is moving West!" "They are coming, Father Abraham, a hundred thousand strong." "Still they come." Such are the enthusiastic phrases which welcome to the Western Territories the thousands that are moving from the overcrowded East to our fertile prairies. And truly, as by magic, the lonely desert is changing into a beehive of industry; the steamboat and railroad coaches are loaded down with innumerable immigrants and the white-covered prairie schooners are everywhere seen to wend their way on our wagon roads. Whence do they come? From every state in the Union and from Europe. Whither do they go? To the hospitable soil, that like another land of promise, opens its arms to receive them. And the majority are bound for Kansas.

What is the motive which presses forward this surging wave of humanity? It is not—as it was of old, when our ancestors fled in dismay from the European shore—religious or civil persecution; nor is it the spirit of adventure which once directed gallant knights to rush to unknown lands in defense of a threatened principle; or latterly caused the seekers of gold to fight their way through the murderous wilderness to a new Eldorado; it may be the stagnation of business, or any other cause. I feel not at liberty to determine now; but certain it is, the wave rolls on—the movement has become general. It is a complete exodus.

In the midst of this universal move, what are our Catholic brethren doing? They are not idle. The question of immigration is receiving due attention at the hands of the most interested in the welfare of their fellow-brethren. Hence the National Colonization Convention at Chicago, on March 17.

A rich vein has been struck here. A really grand and Catholic idea has entered into the heads of truly benevolent, philanthropic, and I might say, in the language of the Church of God, charitable friends of the human race. I have little to say, nor is it my place to commend it to the attention for all who have a heart to feel for their brethren in the East, and I am satisfied that, once understood, it will be duly considered. The right chord has been touched; let it give out the true note.

In view of the unprecedented flow of immigrants to the West, the National Colonization Convention, if properly managed, is destined to act a prominent part in the work of the amelioration of the working class now-a-days. The air is wild with the cries of the rights and wrongs of labor; one of the remedies, if not the only one, is reached here. The effects of the Convention, materially, morally and religiously, will be felt for untold and as yet unborn generations. Much that needs light on the question will be cleared up, and the way of the colonist will be made bright and easy. I hope fathers of this Convention will not be satisfied with poetical descriptions and speculative doctrines, which may be good in their place, but [instead] will deal mainly with figures and facts. It will be no harm to make it a question of dollars and cents. I hope they will call out the practical element and discuss at will the advantages of colonization over what I would style single-handed or individual emigration. I hope in fact that they will do much and everything to promote the good work already begun, having no other motive than the welfare of their fellow-beings. It must not only be a question of "Where to go," but above all and especially of "How to go" and "How to succeed once settled."

Let no "sectionalism" swallow up the main object, viz., the welfare, temporal and spiritual, of our people. "Our Kansas" is good enough, but I would rather see it unpeopled than that their welfare should be endangered. There is enough now to suit all tastes and inclinations.

The lands of the I.C.B.U. of Right Reverend Bishop Ireland, and of the St. Louis, New York, and Chicago boards of colonization, are all so many different ways of obtaining the same purposes, namely to achieve the independence of the working class and to secure unto them the benefits of Christian Catholic colonization.

It is perhaps "out of order" for me to write thus on a subject where others may be more experienced; but I feel as though a great work was being done, and everyone called upon to contribute their mite.

Not many miles from where I am now writing, the work of colonization is being pushed on both by German and Irish Catholics. The result is most gratifying and I doubt not but that my brethren in other parts can corroborate my testimony. In one of these colonies, less than two years ago, the congregation was limited to four or five families, which have now increased to over one hundred. Then the Holy Sacrifice of the Mass was offered up in a cabin, or, rather, "dug-out," of one of the earlier settlers; now there are two commodious churches within six miles, with prospects of another soon some eight miles distant. The "dug-outs" have become replenished cellars for beautiful farm residences, and the early "adobes" have been replaced by elegant cottages; then the settlers felt as the Hebrew captives, strangers in a foreign land; now they enjoy the fruits of independence and the joys of home.

Besides the Minnesota, Cincinnati, Tennessee, Illinois, and Austrian-German colonies which have been established in Kansas of late years, the St. Louis Irish colony in Pottawatomie County has done much to prove the success of the colonization plan. Another Society under the name of St. Dominic's Colony from New York has now purchased a large tract of land in Rice County.

It may not be out of place to give a brief sketch of their lands. It has been my privilege to traverse this country in missionary pursuits for years; and I will be easily pardoned if I digress somewhat from my original subject as stated in the beginning of this communication. . . .

It was my fortune to accompany to the lands of the colony a committee of gentlemen appointed by the society for the purpose of reporting on the quality of the land heretofore selected. The committee consisted of Messrs. J. P. O'Hanlon, President; T. Brennan and Thomas Bannon, all of New York; and James Gibbons of Albany, N. Y. The party started out in company with Col. Edward Haren, one of the agents of the Atchison, Topeka and Santa Fe R. R., as a guide. I am free to state here that in all things the committee acted with perfect freedom. Their deliberations were untrammelled, the railroad agent himself in question not even having alluded once to the advantages of the land. Justice to whom it is due.

The starting point was Ellinwood in Barton County, some eleven miles from the colony lands. As we rode northward, the fertile farms of our German Catholics, mostly from Illinois, displayed at every step the fertility of the soil and the thrift of the tillers. Many were the exclamations of surprise from our New Yorkers many of whom had never beheld such an ocean of verdure; for hundreds of acres could be seen on either side of the road covered with a luxuriant growth of wheat. Many farmers were at work in their fields slowly turning up the soft mellow soil and losing no time in the preparation of their lands for spring crops. The enthusiasm was at its height when we reached the beautiful section of country which borders Cow Creek. There on the left, in the midst of a gently rolling prairie, shadowing its tiny steeple against the blue sky, the humble chapel, surmounted by the holy sign of our redemption, told again of the faith of these tillers of the soil, while on the right stretched the chequered valley that was to be reported on. Nothing was left undone by the party to satisfy their employers: old and experienced farmers were consulted; a veritable examination and cross-examination was made; the "New Ireland" was minutely, scrupulously gone over; every forty acre lot was the subject of their deliberations; as they would phrase it in Rome, there was no one to act the part of God; but everyone was there to play the role of the devil and the work of criticism was thoroughly performed not without an abundance of wit for which the Irish race is so proverbial.

But what of the land? It is black limestone loam from two to five feet in depth with a very light touch of sandy matter, pre-eminently adapted to cultivation, and is watered by a stream of living water called Cow Creek. Of timber there is none, but fuel is cheap and the lumber sells at about the same price as it does in Pottawatomie County. Not a quarter section in the entire body of land but can be used to advantage. It is but fair to say that the best of inducements have been given by the A. T. and S. F. R. R. Co.

But I have not begun this communication to describe the land; at another time a description will answer better and I will refrain for the present from any further comment.

May God bless the endeavors of all who have at heart the welfare of their fellow-Catholics and engage so earnestly in the work of colonization as do my New York friends. It is not always a grateful work, and often a thankless one, but it contains a principle, and has a worthy and soul-saving aim: in the end it must triumph.

Yours truly in Christ,

FELIX P. SWEMBERG[43]

The Convention mentioned in Father Swemberg's letter met on March 7, 1879, in Chicago. Chief among those present were the Reverend Felix Swemberg and the Reverend Stephen Byrne, O.P. The former in his capacity of founder of colonies was peculiarly fitted to pass judgment on the new project. He laid stress (as he did in the letter quoted *in toto* above) on the need of placing the enterprise on a business basis. Father Byrne became a member of the Board of Directors and continued to be active in the cause.

For many years the secular press had published accounts of colonization schemes, and speculators and land agents manifested considerable interest in this development. For the most part this interest was friendly, and it was enhanced when the colonization plans as proposed by Archbishop Ireland were adopted. Bishop Fink of

[43] This letter was written four years before Mother Stanislaus Leary and her five companions settled in Newton and thus introduced the Sisters of St. Joseph to the Kansas frontier. Father Swemberg was pastor at that time.
Catholic Review (of which Villanova College has a file), vol. XV, p. 167.

Leavenworth was a member of the board of seven bishops.[44] The Eastern bishops, with the exception of the Bishop McQuaid of Rochester, were convinced of the wisdom of the project. The opposition has gone on record, but it is uncertain whether it was active or not. The press of the period does not mention the fact, nor is it to be found in the writings of Bishop Spalding. The authority of the supposition is one of the letters of Bishop McQuaid himself.[45]

When there are several pet theories put forth at any gathering, there are usually accusations of misrepresentation made against some of the delegates. Reference was made to "A Kansas clergyman [Father Swemberg] who, in a New York lecture, took for his main argument in favor of his State what he imagined and perhaps believed were the adverse climatic conditions of Minnesota. We write now," continued the *Chronicle,* "as giving caution to our friends in the work of colonization for the future, rather than as making a reproach for the past. The representatives of Kansas and Western Missouri are the only ones so far, fortunately, who have sinned in this regard." [46]

As President of the Saint Dominic Colonization Society, Father Swemberg wrote a pamphlet in 1880 which will be quoted at length on account of its bearing on the study in hand:

Right Reverend Louis M. Fink, O.S.B., Bishop of Leavenworth, Kansas, whose courtesy we have had often occasion to test for our welfare, is the custodian of the land fund for the colonization society. He has expressed himself as in thorough sympathy with this movement and has said that anything that he or his good priests could do to further the interests of the colonies would gladly be done. Rev. Felix P. Swemberg, Newton, Kansas, is the general President. He has spent a long number of years on the plains as a missionary and is credited with knowing more about southern and southwestern Kansas than any living white man.

Colonel A. F. Johnson, the land commissioner, of the Atchison, Topeka and Santa Fe Railroads, has been very lenient in dealings with the colonies and in a great measure their success can be attributed to his patience and endurance. He is a native of Kansas and was the first white person born in that state. He has the habits and instincts of a gentleman with thorough business qualities and is known all over Kansas as one of those whose word is as good as their

44 Henthorne, *op. cit.,* pp. 38-40.
  Northwestern Chronicle, Mar. 29, 1879.
  "Catholic Colonization as Actually Established," *Catholic World,* vol. XXIX (1879), pp. 120-126.
  Other articles pertinent to this subject are "The European Exodus," *Catholic World,* vol. XXV (1877), pp. 433-443, 677-678; and "The German Element in the United States," *Catholic World,* vol. XXVI (1877), pp. 372-382.
  45 Frederick J. Zwierlein, *Life and Letters of Bishop McQuaid,* 3 vols. (Rochester, 1925-1927), vol. II, p. 66.
  46 *Northwestern Chronicle,* Oct. 4, 1879.
  Henthorne, *op. cit.,* p. 66.

bond. In the spirit of enlightened-liberality he is ready to aid and urge by every means in his power Catholic immigration to the lands which he controls.

The various agents of the A. T. and S. F. R. R. in the East have rendered the members of the colonies many services and are always willing and ready to assist intending immigrants. How can one become a member of St. Dominic's Colonization Society and what are the advantages of members over any individual purchasing direct from the railroad company? The constitutions and by-laws as printed in this pamphlet furnish an explanation to this question. Lands are chosen by personal inspection of the colony land and from the descriptive maps in the hands of the secretary or again through the general president of the Society, who, however, prefers any other course. Not less than 40 nor more than 160 acres can be purchased by any one member. The reason is obvious as any other course would pave the way to speculation, which it is the intention of the Society to discard by all means.

The advantages of colonization are as follows: 1. To secure good land at low prices and yet have neighbors. 2. The land will increase in value the moment the colony is started. 3. You can have schools, churches, stores, post offices, etc., and good society without having to wait for the slow settlement of the whole country. 4. While you are improving your home, your neighbors are improving theirs which never fails to advance the value of property.

A member of the St. Dominic Colonization Society obtains advantages over any other individual purchasing property direct from the railroad company in that, on account of the large tracts of land preserves the society can give a rebate from the ordinary prices and reductions on the railroad, the terms being the same. . . .

What is the best time to come to Kansas? There are many differences of opinion as to this. But we think the early spring, about as good a time as any, say from February 15 to April 15. How to come? Many persons in the Eastern states have an impression that Kansas is a great distance off, yet the Arkansas Valley can be reached in three days and a half, from any part of New England, in three days from New York, in two days and a half from Buffalo and Pittsburgh, and in 36 hours from Chicago, 24 hours from St. Louis, and at greatly reduced rates, either single or round trip, the latter good for forty days and freight rates can be had on all the principal railroad stations on through lines, or by applying to the nearest general agent in the list given below producing your certificate of membership in St. Dominic's Colonization Society. Has Kansas any disadvantages as well as advantages? It has disadvantages as well as advantages, want of timber and occasional high winds which without ever being injurious is [sic] somewhat disagreeable. The country like other parts of the west and northwest has also been visited by the grasshopper, but it is not known that they have ever injured to any extent the wheat crop which is our staple product. As for the want of timber, the reader has seen what we think about it on another page. What is the necessary amount of capital required to succeed on the colony land? This is the most important of all questions we have had to deal with so far, and consequently the most uncertain and difficult to answer. No two men see it alike. The price is also often different from the theory. Where a man with a thousand dollars or more cash in hand may fail, another with no means at all will prosper. So much is owing to the character of the family, the economy, energy and perseverance of the farmer. The climate, caprices of the seasons and other causes are beyond the control of the colony that [sic] no facts and figures can be deemed reliable. While a great deal depends on the industry and the energy of the man and his willingness to endure hardships . . . no conclusion can be reached. . . .

Conclusion: The foregoing pages honestly and truthfully state the advantages to be derived from the settlement of the West. . . . We have no desire to interfere with other societies. . . . Make up your mind and wait no longer. Let not the golden opportunity slip through your fingers.

We call attention to the fact that no member of the Society is responsible for any but himself and that we guarantee to all members the absolute right and privilege in handling and disposing of his own fund individually and without the intervention of the colony as a body as soon as the first payment has been made on the land. We are honest in our purposes and seek no profit . . . and under the guidance of God and with the determination to build up an independent home in the West we enter on the march that thousands may follow us. May God bless our work.[47]

Governor Glick of the State of Kansas was interested in these projects which were dear to the heart of Bishop Fink. In a letter to the latter May 7, 1883, he said in part: "I see there is to be quite a heavy immigration from Ireland to this country. I would like to get as many of these immigrants to come to this State as possible. Can you aid me in this matter and put me in the right way to success on our part of it?"[48] The answer of the Bishop has not been located, but in yet another letter the Governor thanked him for his of the 24th of May, stating that he was glad to have the friendly interest of the Bishop on the subject of immigration and adding, ". . . . Of course we have no funds with which to operate, a matter that I very much regret. . . . I am now corresponding with Colonel Jackson, the superintendent of immigration at Castle Garden, New York, who promises to aid me all he can in the matter. I will forward him . . . a large number of documents. . . . The pamphlet is printed in English, German and Swedish."[49]

There was an extended correspondence between the civil and ecclesiastical heads of Kansas during that summer and fall of 1883. The former told Bishop Fink that at Castle Garden the Irish immigrant agent was Mr. William Connelly and the German one M. L. P. Reichard, stating that it might be well for the Bishop to correspond with these two gentlemen.[50] A short time later Mr. Connelly wrote

[47] As far as can be determined there is only one copy of this pamphlet extant and that is to be found in the Diocesan Archives of Kansas City-in-Kansas, where with the permission of the Most Rev. Paul Schulte, the Bishop of Leavenworth, the author used it. Another pamphlet, *Progress*, by Father Swemberg could not be located.

[48] Original letter of G. W. Glick, Governor of Kansas, to the Most Rev. Louis M. Fink, O.S.B., Bishop of Leavenworth, May 7, 1883, in the Archives of Kansas Catholic Historical Society collection. Atchison, Kans.; a photostat in possession of author.

[49] Letter of G. W. Glick, Governor of Kansas, to the Most Rev. Louis M. Fink, O.S.B., Bishop of Leavenworth, May 29, 1883, in the Archives of Kansas Catholic Historical Society collection; a photostat in possession of author.

in answer to Bishop Fink assuring him that he would be happy to cooperate with him in his colonization plan. He mentioned that the people, especially the Irish, needed to be backed up by friends, because most of those who reached the New York port undetermined as to where they would locate were needy and anxious for employment wherever it might be procured.[51]

That this combined effort was effective is apparent in further correspondence between Governor Glick and Bishop Fink: "I am glad," wrote the former, "that you are assisting and desire to thank you for the interest you have taken in this matter. It has already had an effect upon our State and the value of real estate is increasing. A good many settlers are coming to the State this year and next year we will have an immigration running from one hundred to one hundred and fifty thousand people with the fine crops that we have this year placing our State in the first rank as an agricultural state. It will not be many years until we will number two million of souls."[52]

It is natural to conclude that this influx of Catholics into the State of Kansas created a problem for the Bishop of Leavenworth. There were the closely related questions of supplying priests for the scattered settlements, of financing the ever-growing needs, and of Christian education for the children of the settlers. The Society for the Propagation of the Faith in Paris contributed substantial sums to the diocese yearly. However, according to records, in 1884 money began to go out of the diocese to the treasury of the Society, so that it is a strange coincidence to find a letter answering a request for an appropriation written at approximately the same time as another letter acknowledging the receipt of the diocesan contribution. Suffice it to say that the sum flowing *from* Paris far surpassed the sum flowing *to* Paris.[53]

[50] Letter of G. W. Glick to the Most Rev. Louis M. Fink, O.S.B., June 13, 1883, in Archives of Kansas Catholic Historical Society. A letter from James F. Fitzgerald of New York inquiring about Kansas was forwarded to Bishop Fink by W. J. Onahan, the Catholic layman who did so much for colonization of Nebraska. Dated Aug. 11, 1883, the original is in the Archives of Kansas Catholic Historical Society.

[51] Letter of William Connolly to the Most Rev. Louis M. Fink, O.S.B., Aug. 24, 1883, in Archives of Kansas Catholic Historical Society.

[52] Letter of G. W. Glick to the Most Rev. Louis M. Fink, O.S.B., Sept. 17, 1883, in Archives of Kansas Catholic Historical Society.

[53] Letters from the Society for the Propagation of the Faith to the Most Rev. Louis M. Fink, O. S. B.: July 1878—74,000 francs; and July, 1882—160,000 francs to be used in the Diocese of Leavenworth. Originals are in Archives of Kansas Catholic Historical Society; photostats in files of the author.

Letter from the Society of the Propagation of the Faith to the Most Rev. Louis M. Fink, O.S.B., acknowledging receipt of 3,840 francs as contribution from Diocese of Leavenworth, Oct. 17, 1884. Original is in Archives of Kansas Catholic Historical Society; a photostat in files of the author.

From Washington, D. C., Ellen Ewing Sherman, wife of General Sherman, wrote that she would do everything in her power in behalf of Christian education.[54]

Summarizing the condition of Catholicism in Kansas in 1883, the year in which the Sisters of Saint Joseph from Rochester, New York, arrived to begin their work in the state, the *Catholic Directory* for that year gives the following statistics:

RELIGIOUS COMMUNITIES WORKING IN KANSAS IN 1883:

Jesuits—St. Mary's College, 250 pupils; also Osage Indian Mission
Benedictines—St. Benedict's College, 22 preparatory, 66 classical and commercial, and 15 ecclesiastical pupils
Carmelites—Leavenworth and Anderson County
Precious Blood Fathers—Beloit
Capuchins—Victoria
Franciscans—Emporia
Sisters of Charity—Leavenworth, 152 Sisters
Benedictine Sisters—Atchison, 20 Sisters at Academy
Sisters of Loretto—Osage Mission, 17 Sisters
Sisters of St. Agnes—Victoria
Franciscan Sisters—Emporia, hospital in process of construction

RECAPITULATION

Bishop	1	Colleges	3
Priests—secular and religious	94	Academies	3
Ecclesiastical students	17	Parochial schools	35
Churches and chapels	152	Number of pupils	3,500
Churches finished since last report	6	Orphanage	1
Churches under construction	5	Hospital	1

Catholic population ....about 80,000[55]

From the statistics quoted it is evident that there was a frontier for that band of religious women who had left the amenities of western New York and had cast their lot with the future of Kansas. Theirs was to be a hard road with privations and hardships; but they came with a determination to work for God and souls in this missionary country and that determination was blessed in the years to come. Kansas needed women whose lives were dedicated to the cause of humanity and of Christian education. It needed more laborers in the vineyard and again, under the hand of God, the Sisters of Saint Joseph came to another frontier to meet that *need,* that *challenge,* which their predecessors had before them met on the frontiers of France, Carondolet, and Canandaigua.

[54] Letter of Ellen Ewing Sherman to the Most Rev. Louis M. Fink, O.S.B., Feb. 10, 1883. Original is in Archives of Kansas Catholic Historical Society.
[55] *Sadlier's Catholic Directory* (New York, 1883), pp. 353-366.

CHAPTER VII

Administration:
Reverend Mother Stanislaus Leary
Part 1: Newton and Concordia, 1883-7

THE frontier in Kansas had been open to the Sisters of Saint Joseph some thirty-five years before Mother Stanislaus Leary and her companions began their work there. It is recorded in the writings of John Baptiste Miege, first Vicar Apostolic of Indian Territory (which embraced the future State of Kansas), that he had intentions of establishing a colony of Sisters from Moutiers in France in his vicariate.[1] In 1850 the community at Moutiers thought of sending Sisters to Kansas as Lyons had a few years before sent them to Carondolet. When Father Miege came to America, he promised the Sisters at Moutiers that he would take up the matter with several bishops in America.

He later wrote to them, however, that he had spoken of the project to the Bishops of three or four dioceses; but, although they would be happy to receive religious into their dioceses, their means were limited so that financial assistance was out of the question.

Later, upon his arrival in his own vicariate, Bishop Miege wrote his brother regarding the Sisters:

> The difficulties in which I saw them taking this trip made me feel sorry for them, but I did not have the necessary means to help them. Later on I shall help them all I can. . . . I shall try to soften for those good Sisters the hardships which are nearly always experienced when one arrives in a new country. I am convinced that they shall be well received by the Sisters of Saint Louis and that their crosses will not be half as heavy as I made them believe they would be; but I purposely made them believe that their crosses would

---

[1] Moutiers, France, was the site of a diocesan seminary where Bishop Miege pursued his ecclesiastical studies. The brother of Bishop Miege was a teacher in that seminary.

be numerous in order that they might have nothing with which to reproach me in such a hazardous undertaking. . . .[2]

Comforted by the wise advice of the prelate, several Sisters of Saint Joseph of Moutiers embarked for the United States at the end of July, 1854, and arrived in St. Louis, having come by way of New Orleans. The superior of the little group wrote to Father Miege of their joy and happiness at being in St. Louis in an exemplary house where the rules of the order were admirably kept and where they were the object of every charitable care.[3]

It is interesting to note that these Sisters from Moutiers, by a strange coincidence, sailed from Havre on the *Heidelberg* on which the Sisters came to Carondolet in 1836. They landed at New Orleans on December 7, 1854, the same date on which that other band from St. Louis arrived in Canandaigua.[4]

Thus, we have an interesting parallel between the desire of Bishop Miege to have the Sisters of Saint Joseph enter the missionary field of his vicariate and the coming of the Sisters from Moutiers on the same date that Canandaigua was established. It is true that during the administration of Bishop Miege the Sisters of Saint Joseph did not enter his diocese;[5] it wasn't until twenty-nine years later that this wish of Bishop Miege was fulfilled. Fortunately, all worked to the best advantage. From the frontier in the Middle West a courageous band went to a frontier in western New York and then returned to the frontier of Kansas within a period of thirty years. Four flourishing communities were working on four frontiers within that space of time.[6]

Mother Stanislaus and her co-laborers, courageous and self-

[2] J. Garin, *Notices Biographiques sur Mgr. J. B. Miege, Premier Vicaire Apostolique de Kansas et sur les Prêtres de la Paroisse de Chevron (Savoie)*, (Moutiers, France, 1866), *passim.*

[3] Leon Bouchage, *Chroniques des Soeurs de St. Joseph de Chambery* (Chambery, 1911), p. 295. They left Moutiers on Sept. 3, 1854.

Sister Lucida Savage, *The Congregation of St. Joseph of Carondolet* (St. Louis, 1923), pp. 101-103.

[4] Garin, *op. cit., passim.*

[5] On the occasion of Bishop Miege's visit to St. Louis during the Provincial Council of 1858, the superior of a colony of Sisters of Charity from Nashville, Tenn., looking for a home in another diocese, appealed to him on the advice of the Jesuit missionary Father De Smet, and, with the permission of Archbishop Kenrick, was received with her community under his jurisdiction.

It is interesting to note that Bishop Miege died in July 21, 1884, thus living to see the Sisters whom he wanted in his vicariate at that time established at Newton.

Savage, *op. cit.*, f.n., p. 103.

[6] Carondolet, Canandaigua (nucleus of Buffalo and Rochester Communities), and Newton (later Concordia).

sacrificing women, were typical of the frontier woman who has been extolled in song and in story. These women were on the frontier of human endeavor applying what was old and accepted to conditions which were new and untried. They adjusted themselves and the culture and customs which they cherished fondly and which were deeply embedded in their lives to a new, to a more challenging environment, where somewhat different circumstances were bound to influence their outlook.

Carl Becker, in his excellent essay on Kansas, writes understandingly and truly on this subject:

... the men who make the world's frontiers, whether in religion or politics ... have certain essential and distinguishing qualities. They are primarily men of faith. Having faith in themselves, they are individualists. They are idealists because they have faith in the universe, being confident that somehow everything is right at the center of things; they give hostage to the future, are ever . . . transforming the world into their ideal of it. They have faith in humanity, and in the perfectability of man, and are likely, therefore, to be believers in equality, reformers . . . always aiming to level others to their own high vantage. . . . The frontier develops strong individuals. . . . The individualism of the frontier is one of achievement, not of eccentricity, an individualism of fact rising from a sense of power to overcome obstacles. . . . The frontiersman is a man of faith . . . this gives a tremendous power of initiative. . . . Those who remained in Kansas from 1875 to 1895 must have originally possessed staying qualities of no ordinary sort, qualities which the experiences of those years could only accentuate. And as success has at last rewarded their efforts, there has come too, a certain pride, an exuberance, a feeling of superiority that accompany a victory long delayed and hardly won. The result has been to give a peculiar flavor to Kansan spirit of individualism. With Kansas history back of him, the true Kansan feels that nothing is *too much* for him. . . . To venture into the wilderness, one must see it, not as it is, but as it will be. . . . The secret of the enthusiasm of the Kansan is that he lives in the great country of some day. Such are Kansans. Like Saint Augustine, they have their City of God, the idealized Kansas of someday. It is only necessary to have faith in order to possess it. . . . The Kansas spirit is the American spirit doubly distilled. . . . Kansas is America in microcosm. . . . The devotion of the State is to an ideal, not to a territory, and man can say "Dear Old Kansas" because the name symbolizes for them what the motto of the State so well expresses, "Ad Astra per Aspera."[7]

These were sentiments of that intrepid group which wended its way to the plains of Kansas in 1883. Ten years before its arrival in Newton, a missionary wrote of conditions at that place:

I passed the warmest days of the last summer west of the 96th meridian about 150 miles distant from this mission. That country is no longer a desert,

---

[7] Carl L. Becker, *Everyman His Own Historian: Essays on History and Politics* (New York, 1935), pp. 1-28.

for except in some localities, you meet everywhere with the industrious and patient settler trying to make himself a home. I visited several stations of the A. T. and S. F. seeing to the building of two small churches, the one in Marion Center and the other in Wichita. I also established two missionary stations, one at Sedgwick and the other at Hutchinson.

The settlers everywhere received me kindly and I found them all eager to attend to their Christian duties. Generally speaking, these people are pious and well disposed; many of them are very poor and most of them live in barracks or shanties, while some, unable to find either planks or logs, dig for themselves habitations in the ground and cover them over with sods. Though some of our Catholics are fervent, still others are deplorably negligent, and the spirit of indifferentism so widely spread over this country is heart-rending. Unfortunately, morality is frequently a desideratum in many of our new towns and no wonder for the full measure of iniquity seems to pour in on us from the oldest and most substantial cities of this great continent. To give you an idea of this I shall simply state that I was told in Newton last summer that of thirty-six persons buried in the cemetery of the place only one had had a natural death. Such is the field in which we are working. . . .[8]

Beginnings are usually painful, and the above and similar accounts given by the pioneer Sisters illustrate what a particularly hard beginning must have been that of the Newton foundation. But the Sisters did not complain.

In 1882, during Mother Stanislaus' sojourn in Florida after being relieved of her duties as Mother General of the Rochester Community, Bishop Fink reiterated a request he had made for Sisters while Mother Stanislaus was still in Rochester. Sister Ursula, her companion on this trip, answered in Mother Stanislaus' behalf, promising to try to send "good religious and competent and well-trained teachers . . . to work in a little corner of your vineyard."[9]

Bishop Salpointe, Vicar Apostolic of Arizona, also made a plea for Mother Stanislaus to make a foundation in his vast territory, stressing the healthful climate and the help they would get from the local people.[10]

Source material other than these letters is not available, but we know from the *Diary* of Mother Stanislaus that she and her two

---

[8] Cited from a letter written by Father Paul Mary Ponziglione, Dec. 31, 1872. Sister Paul Fitzgerald, *Beacon on the Plains* (Leavenworth, 1939), p. 182.

[9] *Annals of the Sisters of St. Joseph of Rochester*, vol. I, p. 199.
Letter from Sister Ursula, Jacksonville, Fla., to the Rt. Rev. Louis M. Fink, O.S.B., Bishop of Leavenworth; no date (possibly late 1882 or early 1883). Original is in the Archives of Kansas Catholic Historical Society; a photostat in files of author.

[10] Letter from the Rt. Rev. J. B. Salpointe, Tucson, Ariz., to Sister Ursula, Jacksonville, Fla., Feb. 7, 1883. Original is in the Archives of Sisters of St. Joseph, La Grange, Ill.; a photostat in files of the author. Only page two of this letter is extant.

sisters, Sister Josephine Leary and Sister Francis Joseph Leary, received their obedience from Bishop McQuaid of Rochester and offered their services to Bishop Salpointe of Arizona.[11] They set out for Florence, Arizona, to open a school. "We purchased our tickets at Chicago for that place," wrote she, "but when we arrived at Kansas City, learning of the Indian troubles there, we were afraid to continue our journey. We then offered our services to the Bishop of Leavenworth, Kansas, and he kindly accepted us and appointed us to Newton, Harvey County, Kansas."[12]

Bishop Fink was interested in the project from the beginning, and his fatherly care of the new foundation was evident on numerous occasions. With the creation of the two new dioceses of Concordia and Wichita in 1887, the Sisters were placed under the jurisdiction of the Ordinary of Concordia (with the motherhouse located there). However, not wishing to lose the Community entirely to his diocese, Bishop Fink did everything in his power to have the motherhouse transferred to Abilene. This account will be given later.

No doubt when the first four Sisters visited Bishop Fink in Leavenworth in June, 1883, they were received hospitably by the Sisters of Charity whose motherhouse was located there. There is no reference to such a visit either in the records of the Sisters of Charity[13] or in those of the Sisters of Saint Joseph. There has been a close friendship between these two communities down the years, and it would be pleasant to think of its inception in June, 1883, when the pioneering group on its way to Arizona stopped over and was persuaded to stay in Kansas.

To continue the account as written by our foundress: "A good

---

[11] There was a Sister Joseph Teresa who came in the original group, but, according to the *Diary*, she lost her mind on Aug. 17, 1883, and Mother Stanislaus was obliged to take her to St. Louis and place her in an institution there. Later Sister Joseph Teresa recovered sanity and was discharged from the institution. She was not received into the community, and it cannot be determined what course she pursued.

Sister Teresina, *Sister of St. Joseph in the Diocese of Rochester, 1878-1897*, unpublished manuscript in Archives of Nazareth Motherhouse, Rochester, N. Y.

Zwierlein, *op. cit.*, vol. II, pp. 87-88.

Annals of the Sisters of St. Joseph of Rochester, op. cit., vol. II, pp. 11-12.

[12] Mother Stanislaus Leary, *Diary and Book of Records*, written by hand. Original is in the Archives of the Nazareth Motherhouse, Concordia, Kans., a photostat in files of author.

[13] According to information furnished by Sister Leo Gonzaga of the Sisters of Charity of Leavenworth, apparently the annals of that community before 1890 were destroyed when the first history of the Sisters of Charity of Leavenworth was written. In the case of the Sisters of St. Joseph, although Mother Stanislaus left a record, it is brief and sketchy, outlining the coming of the Sisters in large measure with few details.

Catholic man of Newton, Mr. Wiener, gave us without rent a cottage until the priest, the Reverend Felix Swemberg, was able to purchase a house for us. A purchase of two houses which connected together by an addition was effected in September. The property cost $3,000."[14]

Good fortune has preserved two letters written on the same day in mid-June from Newton, the one from the superior of the little band of Sisters of Saint Joseph and the other from the pastor of the place. These letters, the earliest correspondence extant about the project, are well worth quoting. The letter written by Mother Stanislaus Leary was short and to the point:

> We are very much pleased with Newton and would like to locate here if such is pleasing to your Lordship. I will visit Hanover very soon and from there will go to see you and bring you a copy of our rules. Commending myself and companions to your fatherly solicitude, I remain, Right Reverend Father, your Lordship's most humble and obedient servant. . . .[15]

And Father Swemberg wrote more lengthily:

> The Sisters arrived here safely and have decided to stay. I was given at once a house free of rent for them by a member of the congregation, a committee of our Catholic ladies are collecting among our own people to furnish the house properly, and another committee (Catholics and Protestants) are interviewing the businessmen to still further help the Sisters out.
>
> I am very thankful to you for thinking of Newton in this matter. I know the Sisters will succeed.
>
> I will want some instructions from you in regard to the acquiring of property for them, etc. Your plans as suggested in your letter strike me the best; yet I will want to see you and, if you kindly would tell me when I can better come up to Leavenworth to find you, I will come and see you about these matters.[16]

In the meantime the little missionary group was augmented by the arrival from Rochester of Sister Antoinette Cuff on August 18, 1883, and of Sister Armella McGrath on September 28, 1883.

It might be well to become acquainted with the pioneer Sisters of Saint Joseph in Kansas. The first postulant to receive the habit of that Community in the State of New York was Sister Stanislaus

[14] Leary, *Diary and Book of Records, op. cit.*

[15] Letter of Mother Stanislaus Leary to Bishop Louis M. Fink, Leavenworth, June 17, 1883. Original is in the Archives of Kansas Catholic Historical Society; a photostat in files of the author.

[16] Letter of Father Felix Swemberg, Newton, Kans., to Louis M. Fink, Bishop of Leavenworth, June 17, 1883. Original is in the Archives of Kansas Catholic Historical Society; a photostat in files of the author.

Reverend Mother Stanislaus Leary, First Mother General
of the Sisters of Saint Joseph of Concordia, 1883–1899

Leary. An autobiographical sketch written by Mother Stanislaus is extant:

It is a painful exercise to recall the particulars of a lifetime marked by sufferings neither few nor small—the loss of one dear relative after another and all my fortune, and the mental struggles that have filled up each sad interval. It is moreover an undertaking of no small difficulty to one unused to composition to prepare a work for the press; nor is it without extreme reluctance that I can bring myself to make reference to those whom during a long period of years I have been on the most friendly terms and received unvarying kindness.

I (Margaret Leary) was born in New York City, August 15, 1843. My parents were Irish. My father was a merchant. When I was seven years old circumstances caused our removal to western New York, an event which was followed shortly after by the death of my father. This was the first trial of my life. About this time I was placed at a Protestant academy in charge of the Thomson sisters. I made my First Holy Communion under the direction of the Reverend Thomas Cunningham of the Diocese of Buffalo October, 1856; with the advice of the late Bishop Timon of Buffalo, I entered the convent of the Sisters of Saint Joseph at Canadaigua but was removed to Buffalo in 1868.[17]

The two sisters of Mother Stanislaus, Sister Josephine Leary and Sister Francis Joseph Leary, were born in Corning, New York. After the division of the territory of western New York into the dioceses of Buffalo and Rochester, at the first reception held in Rochester on January 1, 1869, Nellie Leary of Corning, New York, received the name of Sister Josephine. She made her profession in Saint Patrick's Chapel on January 5, 1871.[18]

December 31, 1869, the second sister of Mother Stanislaus, Bridget Leary, received the habit. In 1870, when the Sisters of Charity of Emmitsburg withdrew from the Saint Patrick's Orphanage in Rochester and the institution was taken over by the Sisters of Saint Joseph, Sister Frances Joseph was one of the first to teach there. She made her religious profession on January 1, 1872, the first time the chapel at the new motherhouse had been used for these ceremonies.[19]

Sister Armella McGrath and Sister Domitilla Gannon,[20] also among the pioneers who came from Rochester, were younger than

[17] Mother Stanislaus Leary's autobiographical sketch in her own handwriting is in the Archives of the Nazareth Motherhouse, Concordia, Kans.; a photostat in files of author.

[18] *Annals of the Sisters of St. Joseph of Rochester, op. cit.,* vol. I, pp. 42, 47.

[19] *Ibid.,* vol. I, pp. 43, 46, 47.

[20] Through some mistake the name of Sister Domitilla Gannon was omitted from the list of Sisters who made the foundation, as left in the handwriting of Mother Stanislaus. Mother Antoinette Cuff in an interview assured the author that Sister Domitilla was one of the original band.

the Leary sisters. Sister Domitilla Gannon received the habit July 14, 1874, and made her profession August 22, 1876.[21]

The youngest member of the group and one who was to make a significant contribution to the history of Catholicism in Kansas, was Sister Antoinette Cuff. Miss Margaret Cuff, daughter of Mr. and Mrs. George Cuff, was born in Killala, County Mayo, Ireland, on July 28, 1861. Her father, seeking better economic opportunity, came to America while North and South were locked in the horrors of the War between the States. He sent for his family which at that time consisted of his wife, Bridget Caviston Cuff, two daughters, and a son. Accompanied by Eliza Caviston, sister of Mrs. Cuff, they arrived in New York in 1865 just at the close of the war. They settled in Carbondale, Pennsylvania, from which place Margaret Cuff entered the Sisters of Saint Joseph at Rochester where on October 16, 1880, she received the habit of the order.[22] We shall hear much more of Sister Antoinette Cuff, who became second Mother General of the Concordia Community and who, until her death, July 27, 1947, was active in the affairs of the large, flourishing group of religious women who have done splendid work in Kansas. She had seen the early hardships; she had seen the Community which numbered six become a Community which numbers six hundred; and she had been largely responsible for this remarkable growth during sixty-five years in Kansas.

Of Mother Stanislaus, Sister Antoinette wrote: "She was a woman of strong character, and great suavity of manner, whose confidence in God and filial reliance on the paternal care of Saint Joseph for his religious daughters was an inspiration to all whom she met. She was largely instrumental in attracting the friendship and support of Bishop Fink, then Bishop of the entire State of Kansas."[23]

"We suffered much from poverty," wrote Mother Stanislaus, "until the school opened; the necessities of life we often needed. Our beds were poor, thin straw pallets and our pillows shavings and straw."[24] The first mention of the Sisters in Newton appeared in the

21 *Annals of the Sisters of St. Joseph of Rochester, op. cit.*, vol. I, p. 103.
22 *Idem.*
23 Mother Antoinette Cuff, *Historical Reminiscence of the Sisters of St. Joseph and Their Early History in Kansas.* Original in handwriting of Mother Antoinette is in files of the author.
     In an interview with Mother Antoinette, July 2, 1946, the author asked her why she had come to Kansas. She replied that it was the hand of God and the inspiration of the Holy Ghost, for many others in the Rochester Community had the same desire but did not carry it out.
24 Leary, *Diary and Book of Records, op. cit.*

weekly newspaper, *The Newton Democrat,* under the caption of "Valuable Improvements." It stated in part that Father Swemberg as pastor of Newton was displaying an indomitable energy which, "of course, insures the benefit of the city. He has secured the location of a parochial or convent school and already six Sister teachers have arrived and will make this place their home and two more are expected soon."[25] The article continued that Father Swemberg had purchased the Green and Starr properties adjoining his property on the east and that soon the erection of a large building to be used as a convent and select boarding school would begin. The Chamber of Commerce instinct was present even at this early date and manifested itself in the editor's remark: "It will, no doubt, be a credit to the city and cannot fail to be a pecuniary benefit as many students will be in attendance from a distance." Besides this, the article continued: "There is also a strong possibility of the establishment in this place of a classical seminary for the education of young men to the priesthood."[26]

During the summer months when the sting of hunger and privation was at its highest, Bishop Fink wrote to the Sisters advising them to open a school at Hanover, Washington County, Kansas. Although the number of Sisters available at that time would hardly be sufficient to staff two schools, Mother Stanislaus hastened to comply with the request of the ordinary of the diocese. "We went there," she wrote, "July 13, 1883, to see the place . . . our traveling expenses to Hanover and back were $16.00."[27]

But, something, yet to be determined, had made Bishop Fink change his mind and give the school in Hanover to the Benedictine Sisters of Atchison. On July 13, 1883, the same day when the Newton Sisters went to Hanover, Father J. Pichler of Hanover wrote two letters to his Bishop. In the first, he thanked Bishop Fink for sending him the Sisters at last: "Those from Newton, I mean. They came last night and like the place so well on account of the new schoolhouse (which is a daisy) and church that they at once made up their minds this would be their headquarters. I expect to come to Leavenworth about next Tuesday or Wednesday to consult with your Lord-

---

[25] *Newton Democrat,* Aug. 10, 1883. Original is in Kansas State Historical Library; a photostat in files of the author.

[26] A few months later a letter was sent out to all pastors of the diocese encouraging the establishment of a seminary within the diocese in which to educate young men for the priesthood.

[27] Leary, *Diary and Book of Records, op. cit.*

ship about future arrangements. I believe and hope that these Sisters will fill the bill. Immigration matters are prospering. . . ."[28]

That same evening a letter from the Bishop forced Father Pichler to write again under the same date:

I received your kind letter tonight and after I communicated its contents to the Sisters they were quite consternated [sic], as they had already laid their plans for the future and liked the place very much and the buildings so well. I also got a letter from the Mother Superior in Atchison letting me know that she would send me Sisters (3) about August 16th to take charge of my school entirely. Well, that is all very good, I suppose one order will do as well as another. . . .[29]

No doubt there was disappointment among the little band of Sisters, and surely the sixteen dollars which they paid as train fare meant a great deal to them at that time. Although Father Pichler offered to pay the expenses connected with the trip, it was never refunded and Mother Stanislaus refers to it in her *Diary*.[30]

Speaking of Father Swemberg, the foundress gave another insight into the conditions in Newton: "The priest, Father Swemberg, has shown marked unkindness toward us. We were not even allowed to arrange our house to our own liking without his dictation. One act of kindness from him we have not received." In her charity, however, she continued: "Still he is a good pious man but has been so long used to roughing it among the Indians no doubt that he has lost all feeling for kindness. In our isolated and unprotected position we feel this very much. I write this so as to let our Sisters see how much the foundation suffered. We often became discouraged enough to break up the mission, but when we considered the wants of the poor children here and how much they would lose we cheered up and continued the good work."[31]

Meanwhile, the Newton newspapers and the *Kansas Catholic*[32] carried items regarding the new school under construction. As the time approached for the opening of the school the people of Newton were invited to call on or to address the Mother Superior to secure

[28]Letter of Father J. Pichler, Hanover, Kans., to Louis M. Fink, Bishop of Leavenworth, July 13, 1883. Original is in Archives of Kansas Catholic Historical Society; a photostat in files of author.

[29] Second letter of Father Pichler to Bishop Fink written the same day. Original is in Archives of Kansas Catholic Historical Society; a photostat in files of author.

[30] Leary, *Diary and Book of Records*, *op. cit.*

[31] *Loc. cit.*

[32] This newspaper, published by John O'Flanagan of Leavenworth, appeared weekly during the 1880's. An almost complete file is to be found in the Kansas State Historical Library in Topeka where the author found many pertinent facts for this book.

information. It was announced that the German language would be taught by one of the Sisters.[33] The select school was to be a separate school from the parochial school and "they will admit all well recommended pupils," according to *Newton Democrat*.[34]

Finally on October 2, 1883, the school was ready to operate. It was a gala day for the pioneer Sisters of Saint Joseph. The people of Newton considered it a landmark in Newton history, and it gained the appreciation of the non-Catholics of the town as well as the support of the Catholics. Surely, Mother Stanislaus and her Sisters must have rejoiced that day and felt grateful that those few months of discouragement had not dampened their enthusiasm and forced them to turn their attention elsewhere. How gratefully must they have poured over the account which the little weekly newspaper gave that memorable day in 1883:

The Catholic school opened on Tuesday of last week, with an attendance of over one hundred pupils, at eight o'clock. Such of the pupils as are Catholics repaired to the church and assisted at the High Mass celebrated by Rev. Father Swemberg, invoking the blessing of God on the undertaking. The services were the most impressive character. The pupils under the direction of Sister Josephine did ample credit to their new teacher. The attendance was quite large as a number of parents had come with the children to witness the opening of the school. After Mass, Reverend Father Swemberg delivered a short but feeling sermon especially addressed to the children, but in which he briefly referred to the parents in connection with the school. He said in substance that today was the feast of the Holy Angels. It was a very appropriate time to open the school. "Children are God's favorites. When the disciples asked the Savior, 'Who thinkest Thou is the greatest in the kingdom of heaven?' He called unto Him a little child and set him in the midst of them and saith, 'Amen, I say unto you, unless you become converted and become as little children you shall not enter the kingdom of heaven. Whoever, therefore, shall humble himself as this little child, he is the greatest in the kingdom of heaven.' So great was the Savior's estimate of children that He made man's salvation dependent on his becoming like a little child. That was an honor for little children. The Savior places them higher in His estimation for in another passage He compares them to the very angels and says, 'Suffer little children to come unto Me for theirs is the kingdom of heaven.' Children, you are God's angels on earth. The Savior has made you even His representatives on earth for has He not also said, 'He that shall receive one such little child in My name, receiveth Me.' and again, 'Take heed that you despise not one of these little ones for I say

---

[33] According to the *Diary and Book of Records, op. cit.,* a German novice from the Notre Dame Community, Rochester, was received on Sept. 15, 1883. Her name was Agnes Groser. This reference to a German teacher must have meant that she would teach that subject.

[34] *Newton Kansan,* Aug. 30 and Sept. 6, 1883.
   Newton Democrat, Sept. 7 and 31, 1883.
   Monthly Visitor, Oct. 1, 1883.

unto you that their angels in heaven always see the face of My Father Who is in heaven.' Be then, oh children, our earthly angels to God. Be then worthy of your vocation, and as for the parents let them not hinder the words of God in the education of their children. Let them remember the solemn curse of the Savior for those who scandalize little ones. 'He that shall scandalize one of these little ones that believe in Me, it were better he were drowned in the depths of the ocean.' Parents cooperate with the teachers. Harmonize with them. Let home education be hand in hand with school education. You have found in the good Sisters guardian angels to protect the tottering footsteps of your children. May God bless the work." After the sermon the pupils were assigned to their different classes.[35]

And the blessing of God was on the work. From the first day in Newton until the present time, the Sisters of Saint Joseph have earned the reputation of splendid school teachers. According to Mother Stanislaus' *Diary* and corroborated by Mother Antoinette's recollections, there were sixty little children enrolled in the "old school" and about one hundred in the "new school house"; half of those children were Protestant. The following year the attendance was about the same, with Sister Francis Joseph in charge of the large school and Sister Antoinette in charge of the small one. The priest instructed the children every Friday.[36] The tuition was a dollar a month.[37]

Among the first pupils to attend the school were Maude Winnie Olinger, Rebecca Gerson, Elizabeth McGenney, Margaret Kelley, La Vanta Fisher, Philip Anderson, John Earley, John Landon, and Pat McGenney. Among the boarders were Mary Furstenberg (later Sister Aloysius), Gertrude Fisher (later Sister Regina), and Rose Shaffer.[38]

Philip M. Anderson, a non-Catholic, who as a child attended the school, recently wrote his recollections of the early days:

In the fall of 1884, I attended the Sisters' School on East 6th Street in Newton. At that time, the school was in two sections. One section was a large, square frame building at the rear of the church property on Oak and 6th Streets, the second section was conducted in a large frame building which had been a

---

[35] *Newton Democrat*, Oct. 12, 1883.

[36] Leary, *Diary and Book of Records, op. cit.*

[37] This information was secured from a receipt made out Oct. 31, 1883, for tuition for that first month of school. The author has a receipt which was printed by Bargar, Job Printer, Newton, for that purpose. This particular receipt was signed by "Sister Stanislaus."

[38] Evidently these were the first boarders taught by the Kansas Community. The author wrote to the Harvey County Historical Society in an effort to secure information from the files there and to try to locate a picture of this first building. The President of the Society, John C. Nicholson, referred the request to May Harrison, who, although she was unable to locate a picture of the school, did succeed in obtaining valuable information. It was she who supplied these names of the first students. She interviewed Philip Anderson and was responsible for the information which he furnished.

hotel, and sat about one hundred feet east of the old stone church and just north of the old frame Santa Fe freight depot.

The school in this building was in the higher classes and specialized in music, and if I remember right, was divided in two rooms. Most of the children were from twelve to fifteen years of age and for all I was only seven years old, I was taken into this school in the first grade.

I can still remember Sister Francis, a very kindly lady who gave me my lessons. The priest to whom I paid the $1.50 per month tuition, I think, was Father Swemberg, and I remember him giving me a present of a large marble when I paid him the tuition one month.

This school was quite prosperous and there must have been 25 or 30 students [sic.] among whom I remember some of the following names: Maud Winnie Olinger, Rebecca Gerson, John Landon, and Maud Snyder. The school was mostly girls. . . .

I remember quite well the Christmas play, or entertainment, that they put on at the old Wright's Rink, which was Newton's auditorium in 1884. I know this school continued through 1884 and 1885. I do not know just what date it was discontinued. I attended from September, 1884, to January, 1888.

It is my remembrance that very few of the children, if any, were Catholics. It seems to me that the Catholic children were taken care of in the old square building on Oak Street.[39]

The report cards were issued monthly. Subjects listed were reading, spelling, penmanship, arithmetic, Christian doctrine, geography, grammar, composition, drawing, Bible history, United States history, civil government, bookkeeping, algebra, vocal music, French, and German. Included in the general average also were application, attendance, and conduct.[40]

Apparently entertainments and programs were offered at an early date. On the feast day of Saint Stanislaus in 1883, a program was given in honor of the venerable Superior of Newton. Beginning with an entrance march and ending with an address to the Reverend Mother, the agenda included a hymn to the saint, vocal duo, instrumental duo, dialogues, and chorus. These were interspersed with tableaux depicting the life of Saint Stanislaus—"Baby Stanislaus at Prayer," "The Voice of Stanislaus," "Evening Prayer at School," and "The Death of Stanislaus." [41]

Another program in May, 1884, consisted of musical and dramatic entertainment as furnished by Rebecca Gerson, Miss Reighter, and Julia Perry (later Sister Madeleine). The performance closed with the operetta *Twin Sisters* in which all the juveniles appeared in the

---

[39] Recollections of Philip M. Anderson of Anderson's Book Store, Newton, Kans.
[40] Original of this in *Scrap Book*, vol. II, p. 45, of Mother Stanislaus Leary, Archives of the Sisters of St. Joseph, La Grange, Ill.
[41] *Ibid.*, undated, p. 115.

cast. According to the newspaper writeup, "the audience was delighted."[42]

Thus it is evident that there was a cultural repercussion felt in
the little town of Newton almost immediately after the opening of
the school.

From her friends in the East, Mother Stanislaus received encouragement to go on with her noble work. Father James J. Leary wrote:

> I am very pleased that you have established a religious community of the
> Sisters of Saint Joseph in the State of Kansas. . . . Undoubtedly, as the pioneer
> of your community in a young and rapidly growing State, you will have many
> heavy labors and many trials to bear. But the heavier the burden, the more
> brilliant the crown is a truth that cheers the fainting heart. There is no reason
> why, with God's blessing, your undertaking should not succeed, for, with
> your experience and zeal, you will leave no stone unturned in laying the
> foundation in a substantial and durable manner. You will probably meet with
> many obstacles but you have met such before and were not discouraged by
> them, but bravely overcame them as many lasting monuments of your energy
> and zeal proclaim in the city of Rochester. I shall pray to God to bless you and
> aid you. . . .[43]

Nor was Bishop Fink unmindful of his little community in central
Kansas. Both he and his Vicar General, the Reverend John F. Cunningham, wrote paternal letters of encouragement. On April 15,
1884, Bishop Fink appointed as spiritual director of the Sisters of
Newton Father Dominic Meier, O.S.F., of Emporia whom he described in a letter to the community: "He is," wrote Bishop Fink,
"a very kind priest and I hope his appointment will prove a great help
to your Sisters. As he is very busy about his parish etc., you will see
that he be not troubled unnecessarily to make trips to Newton, but
whenever his advice or action is required you will apply to him without any scruple. I do advise you, however, to pay his traveling
expenses whenever his personal presence will be required."[44]

Father Dominic Meier, O.S.F., therefore, became an important
factor in the spiritual advancement of the Sisterhood. When the
Franciscan Fathers were given charge of the Emporia parish in 1880,
Father Dominic had been named as pastor of that place. He was

---

[42] *Newton Democrat*, May 16, 1884.

[43] Letter of Father James J. Leary, Honeoye Falls, N. Y., to Mother Stanislaus Leary,
Newton, Kans., Feb. 11, 1884. Original is in *Scrap Book, op. cit.*, vol. II, p. 9; a photostat in files of author.

[44] Letter of the Bishop Louis M. Fink, Leavenworth, Kans., to Mother Stanislaus
Leary, Apr. 15, 1884, *Scrap Book, op. cit.*, vol. II, p. 128; a photostat in files of author.

transferred to another house of his order in 1885,[45] but during these first few years, his guiding hand was ever ready to assist in all matters which pertained to the community. He was faithful about giving retreats to the Sisters, and wrote the Bishop concerning visitation which, according to canon law, should be made annually by the bishop of the diocese.[46]

The first person to receive the habit of the Sisters of Saint Joseph in Kansas was Miss Julia Perry, a former student at Nazareth Academy in Rochester, New York. Miss Perry was an accomplished musician, and her name appears frequently in the *Annals* of the Rochester Sisters as a pianist, a reader, or a member of an instrumental quartette.[47] Quoting from the *Annals:* "On the feast of Saint Joseph, March 19, 1879, at five P.M., the Father George J. Osborne (himself a convert) administered the Sacrament of Baptism to Julia Hastings Seymour Perry, one of the boarders."[48]

The irresistible personality of Mother Stanislaus was a magnetic urge to Julia Perry to cast her lot with the Sisters in Kansas.

Father Dominic mentioned the reception in two separate letters to the Bishop.[49] A short descriptive account of the reception is to be found in the *Monthly Visitor:*

> On Friday, August 15th [1884], Reverend Father Dominic, O.S.F., Superior of the Franciscan convent in Emporia, visited Newton and gave the habit of the Sisters of Saint Joseph to Miss Julia Perry, in religion, Sister Madeleine de Pazzi. The ceremony took place after the Gospel at High Mass which was sung by Rev. Father Dominic assisted by the pastor, the Reverend Father Schmiehausen. The novice was dressed in bridal costume and a procession formed at the Sisters' residence and from there to the church. The altar was beautifully decorated by the Sisters and members of the Altar Society.[50]

From the time of the first reception, candidates began to come

---

[45] *Kansas City Catholic Register,* June 12, 1924, article on the golden jubilee of the parish of Emporia mentions this data on Father Dominic Meier, O.S.F.

[46] Letter of Father Dominic Meier, O.S.F., to the Rt. Rev. Louis M. Fink, O.S.B., July 22, 1884. Original is in Archives of Kansas Catholic Historical Society; a photostat in files of author.

[47] *Annals of Sisters of St. Joseph of Rochester, op. cit.,* vol. I, p. 133.

[48] *Ibid,* vol. I, p. 146.

Sister Teresina, *op cit.,* mentions the same fact and adds further information about Miss Perry joining the Sisters of St. Joseph in Kansas.

[49] Aug. 12 and Aug. 19, 1884. Originals are in Archives of Kansas Catholic Historical Society; photostats in files of the author.

[50] *Monthly Visitor,* Aug. 28, 1884.

Sister Madeleine Perry, Act of Reception, Aug. 15, 1884, and Act of Profession, Sept. 1, 1886. *Reception and Profession Books,* book I (1883-1896), vol. I, pp. 10-11. Original is in Archives of the Nazareth Motherhouse, Concordia, Kans.; a photostat in files of the author.

from distant places to join the Sisters of Saint Joseph. With more Sisters available for missionary work, the expansion program began.

In the north central part of the state, in Cloud County, there was a large settlement of French Canadians who had come to Kansas from Kankakee, Illinois, and from Canada about 1870. This migration of French Canadians from Illinois was a result of the Chiniquy schism, detailed treatment of which will be given in a later chapter when the mission of Saint George, Illinois, is discussed. Father Louis Mollier was assigned to Saint Joseph's in the eastern part of Cloud County in 1873. Having the care of many counties of northwestern Kansas, Father Mollier was able to pay only infrequent visits to Concordia, where he said Mass in private homes.

In 1877, at a meeting of the parishioners, it was decided that they build a church; a site was acquired almost immediately and construction was begun. Father Joseph Perrier [51] received the appointment as first resident pastor of Concordia on July 2, 1880. Two years later the first parish school, taught by lay teachers, was opened in the basement of the rectory. [52]

Father Perrier's interest in securing Sisters to teach in this school was indicated in an article which appeared about this time. It stated that a schoolhouse had been erected during the past year at a cost of $3,000, and that a fine location next to the church had been reserved for a home for the Sisters as soon as they could be secured. "There are," it continued, "about fifty pupils already attending the parish school, and the number would be increased to one hundred on the arrival of the Sisters. Both English and French branches are taught and at the exhibition given lately in the city hall, the pupils acquitted themselves very creditably in readings and recitations in both languages." [53]

---

51 Born in Savoy, France, in 1839, Father Perrier was graduated at the College of St. Pierre-Albigny in 1857, and received a degree as professor of languages at the University of Chambery in 1862. He entered the priesthood the following year, and came to Kansas as a missionary in 1866, becoming a teacher in the Catholic Seminary at Topeka the following year. Later he organized forty missions in a circuit four hundred miles long and one hundred miles wide. He was with General Sheridan when he routed the Indians from the frontier, and ministered to the sick and wounded soldiers. He also ministered to the railroad forces from 1868 to 1875. In these frontier services he suffered many hardships; there were few railroads and scarcely any wagon roads over some of his district. His missionary work in Kansas lasted from 1866 to 1911. He became vicar general in Concordia, 1888, and domestic prelate in 1911. He retired to La Grange, Illinois, in 1913, and died in Los Angeles, Calif., Dec. 30, 1917.

52 "Original Catholics in Concordia were French," *Northwestern Kansas Register,* Nov. 20, 1938 (special edition dedicated to the Most Rev. Frank A. Thill on the occasion of his installation as Bishop of Concordia), section 2, p. 3.

53 *Monthly Visitor,* May 15, 1883.

That the financial conditions of his parish were not good is evident in the report Father Perrier wrote to Bishop Fink late in 1883:

I came here three years ago. I was then proprietor of a house, I had a little money, two horses and a buggy. Now my house is gone, I had to sell my horses and buggy, my organ and all that I had. We spent in Concordia for improvements $5,600 of which I personally contributed $1,400, a free gift in cash and the other by loan, (one half a free gift and the other a loan besides one half of school support for two years.) My traveling expenses amount to $200 a year. I never had full salary. I had to help small missions, very poor, so I am almost played out financially.[54]

It was in that memorable year of 1884 that the Third Plenary Council was held at Baltimore, Maryland. That meeting was of extreme importance in many respects, but primarily in regard to its promulgations on Christian education. At just about the time that the Sisters of Saint Joseph in the United States were preparing to enter a new field of work, there was the happy coincidence of a hierarchical statement on parochial school education. In the Provincial Council of 1833, three years before Carondolet was established, a committee of three college presidents was appointed for the purpose of revising non-Catholic textbooks for use in our schools. In 1852, two years before the mission at Canandaigua was launched, the First Plenary Council adopted a decree exhorting the bishops, in view of the very grave evils arising from the defective spiritual education given in the common schools, to establish Catholic schools in connection with all the parishes of their dioceses, and to provide for their support from the revenues of the churches. In 1866, the year before the establishment of the Diocese of Rochester, and also the year before Mother Stanislaus assumed superiorship of that community, the movement toward parochial school education received its greatest impetus from the Second Plenary Council of Baltimore. And finally, in 1884, the year of the establishment of the school in Concordia, the final and insistent promulgation of the Third Plenary Council came.[55]

The Council of 1884 surpassed all preceding councils in the number, importance, and cogency of its regulations on the subject of education; and the general law was binding on the clergy and laity to establish schools when possible. "God grant our fondly cher-

[54] Letter of Father Joseph Perrier, Concordia, Kans., to Louis M. Fink, Bishop of Leavenworth, Dec. 7, 1883. Original is in the Archives of Kansas Catholic Historical Society.
[55] Peter K. Guilday, *A History of the Councils of Baltimore, 1791-1884* (New York, 1932), pp. 273-274.

ished hope," the prelate wrote, "of seeing matters so arranged that these desires may be fully accomplished by facilitating the advancement of Catholic children by regular ascent from the elementary to the superior Catholic schools."[56]

At this same time in the Diocese of Leavenworth, there was a movement to centralize supervision of the parochial schools by establishing a Diocesan School Board:

> . . .To our judgment it seems that one of its most important duties will be the selection of teachers. The holding of periodic examinations is very necessary and an excellent means of testing the management of the schools, and the presence of a member of the school board will add character and importance to such occasions. But as they take place at the end of the season when the good or bad management of that year is a thing of the past, the public examination can only show the result, it cannot change it. And if the examination should show bad management, the only way the difficulty could be mended would be a substitution of teacher for the next year.
>
> Good schools depend upon good teachers, and by a good teacher we mean something more than one who possesses a competent knowledge of the subjects intended to be taught. That every teacher must possess this qualification passes without argument but that alone does not make a good teacher—everyone has not a talent for imparting to others what he himself possesses—but apart from this the advancement of the pupils largely depends upon the discipline of the schools.
>
> So a talent for teaching combined with the ability to conduct a school orderly and systematically are the distinguishing characteristics of a good teacher.
>
> In advocating the importance of paying a due regard to the selection of teachers, we are not thinking of examining teachers—the public school system of propounding to teachers a set of questions, we believe to be utterly useless. There are more effectual and private means of ascertaining the fitness of teachers.
>
> Supposing that an applicant possesses the necessary requirements for the position and has some talent for teaching . . . the important question then arises—can this person control himself—if he cannot, he is unfit for the position, although he be the wisest man in the State. A teacher who will fly into a fit of passion with his pupils for some breach of rules is incapable of managing children and should be sent first to learn self-control. Such a person will lose the respect of pupils, which would end all hope of a profitable year.
>
> It may be said that this question belongs properly to the pastor under whose immediate direction the school is conducted. . . .[57]

With this national and diocesan background, it is clear why, even though the picture looked dark to the good missionary, Father Perrier began negotiations with Mother Stanislaus Leary early in 1884 for the opening of a school in Concordia. There must have been some con-

[56] *Ibid.*, pp. 237-239.
[57] Editorial in the *Monthly Visitor*, July 31, 1884.

sideration of the project earlier than May, 1884, but the first source
found by the author was a mention in the *Monthly Visitor* of the fact
that in Concordia a new two-story school house was being built and
that the Sisters were expected soon.[58] The next reference is in a
letter from Bishop Fink to Mother Stanislaus: " . . . . If you can take
Concordia as Father Perrier suggested, I will be pleased, but there
must be at least one French teacher at Rev. Perrier's school. I
would also be glad if you could take Rev. Mollier's school,[59] near
Concordia, the same qualifications of teachers would be required
for the latter place . . ." [60]

In June of the same year, construction was well under way, and
at that time Father Perrier in a letter to Mother Stanislaus drew a
floor plan, labeling the different rooms and giving their dimensions.
Interestingly, it is possible to identify in this "first Nazareth," built
according to Father Perrier's plan, the old part of the present Saint
Joseph's Hospital. In addition to the drawing he stated:

> Ad majorem Dei gloriam!! We commenced to haul rocks and sand for the
> foundation. We have got a plan as you told us.[61] A good contractor, McGuire,
> offers to put up everything for $3,800.00 or $4,000. . . . Three stories with one
> French roof with five windows and a little cupola, a porch like mine or better
> and a veranda on the second story. I send you a sketch of the plan and if you
> have anything to change, let us know. If you tell me also how much money
> you can spare for the building, or what you can reasonably hope to send,[62] we
> can have something better still. We find lumber and stone very cheap so you
> will have a fine building. . . .[63]

Father Perrier sent receipts for money received from Mother

[58] *Monthly Visitor*, May 29, 1884.

E. F. Hollibaugh, *Biographical History of Cloud County, Kansas* (Concordia,
1903), pp. 200-202. At a church meeting held in 1884, it was resolved to build a
convent and academy, provided the Sisters of St. Joseph would pay half the expenses.
The convent was begun directly afterward on the ground secured by their pastor and
later deeded to the Sisters of St. Joseph by Father Perrier. The original cost of the
building was six thousand dollars.

[59] The Sisters of St. Joseph did open this school in St. Joseph, Kans., in 1885. In
the meantime several French candidates had entered the Community.

[60] Letter of the Rt. Rev. Louis M. Fink to Mother Stanislaus Leary, Newton, Kans.,
June 14, 1884. Original is in Archives of Kansas Catholic Historical Society; a photostat
in files of the author.

[61] This would indicate that Mother Stanislaus had been in Concordia to look over
the possibilities before she began definite plans.

[62] Bishop Fink, in his letter of June 14, 1884, granted permission for two Sisters
to collect in the East for the new house, adding, "I grant this with great pleasure and
I hope you will be successful." He also mentioned that, if Mother Stanislaus would
send him the names of the two Sisters destined for the collecting tour, he would
furnish them with the proper papers giving their names.

[63] Letter from Father Joseph Perrier, Concordia, Kans., to Mother Stanislaus Leary,
Newton, Kans., June 30, 1884. Original is in Archives of Kansas Catholic Historical
Society; a photostat in files of the author.

Stanislaus to the amount of fourteen hundred and nine dollars, paid in two installments during that summer before the Sisters came to Concordia.[64]

It is evident that Father Dominic Meier, O.S.F., the spiritual director of the Sisters at Newton, feared that, once a parochial school was opened in Concordia, there would be difficulty in persuading the Sisters to maintain their motherhouse in the former place. He wrote Bishop Fink concerning this matter:

> . . . In regard to moving the Motherhouse from Newton to Concordia, I will speak to the Vicar General; it will take much time to write it all and he can tell your Lordship. When I was giving the retreat at Newton, several called upon me concerning that point and it appears that there is a great deal of dissatisfaction about the matter. I think, Bishop, if it comes once that far, that the people of Newton will give still better inducements than Concordia. Certainly I am very much in favor of the Sisters going to Concordia to teach the school, but in regard to the Motherhouse I don't think I would favor it now. . . .[65]

And Father Dominic was reluctant to see Mother Stanislaus go to Concordia herself the first year, knowing full well that with her would go the motherhouse as well. "Do you think, Bishop," he wrote, "it prudent and advisable that Mother Stanislaus should go to Concordia the very first year? She wrote to me some time ago of leaving Newton in charge of Sister Francis Joseph. If it cannot be helped, very well; otherwise, I am not in favor that the Sisters by blood have charge of everything. I fear very much that the people of Newton will be very much dissatisfied if the best Sisters are taken away. I do not think it would be prudent to do anything against Newton that would create any dissatisfaction whatever. Please let me know what you wish to have done. Please address the letter to Newton for I will leave Thursday, otherwise I would not have it in time . . . ."[66]

That the Sisters themselves wished to have Mother Stanislaus move to the new mission is evidenced in a letter which was written to Bishop Fink unknown to the Superior:

[64] Receipts, dated July 15 and Aug. 1, 1884, for money received by Father Joseph Perrier from Mother Stanislaus Leary to be used for the building in Concordia. Originals are in Archives of Kansas Catholic Historical Society, photostats in files of author.

[65] Letter of Father Dominic Meier, Emporia, Kans., to the Rt. Rev. Louis M. Fink, July 22, 1884. The original is in Archives of Kansas Catholic Historical Society; a photostat is in the files of author.

[66] Letters of Father Dominic Meier, Emporia, Kans., to the Rt. Rev. Louis M. Fink, Aug. 12 and 19, 1884. The originals are in Archives of Kansas Catholic Historical Society; photostats are in the files of the author.

In the name of the community I am called upon to address you and beg your fatherly decision in our present unsettled state of affairs.

It has been indirectly conveyed to our Reverend Mother that it is your Lordship's wish to have our Reverend Superior remain for the present in Newton. She has not expressed to the Sisters her decision, still we have reason to think that in consideration of your Lordship's wish she has decided to remain here. Now, Right Reverend Bishop, after prayerful consideration, we see no other way out of the difficulty but a direct appeal to your Lordship, stating our objections and then remaining perfectly satisfied with your conclusions.

Our Reverend Mother's health at best is poor. Last winter she suffered extremely from colds. One cold after another settled on her lungs and there was a great deal of anxiety for her health entertained by the community.

The Sisters, knowing what she has suffered in the past and seeing that she is likely to suffer still more in the coming winter, feel bound in conscience to do something for her if she won't do it for herself.

We have learned from the Reverend Pastor that the house in Concordia is very warm and that there is to be a chapel in the house. For that reason we thought if Reverend Mother located at Concordia until some accommodations were made here for the opening of a novitiate it would be a better plan. When things were in working order in Concordia, and if Newton still appeared the place for the Motherhouse, why it would be the easiest thing in the world for Reverend Mother to come and establish here.

So as to give satisfaction to the Newton people it would not be necessary to tell them that Reverend Mother contemplated remaining any great length of time at Concordia. That if the prospects were favorable she would be back in the spring to establish the novitiate. . . . Reverend Mother knows nothing of our writing this letter and we ask your Lordship the favor of not acquainting her of it. Nothing but the tenderest regard for her welfare has prompted the sentiments expressed. . . .[67]

Three postulants from Montreal, Canada, entered at Newton and were invested with the habit of the order on September 25, 1884. They were Misses Sophia Rioux, Elizabeth Saint Denis, and Clara Taillefer who were known in religion as Sisters Dominic, Cecelia, and Avila.[68] Therefore, with some French teachers at her disposal, Mother Stanislaus was ready to open the Concordia mission and at least to begin to plan the opening of the mission at Saint Joseph, Kansas.

With Sister Francis as Superior and teacher of the upper grades and Sister Antoinette as teacher of the lower grades, the Newton mission was carried on when Mother Stanislaus left for Concordia in the fall of 1884. Since then the Motherhouse has had its head-

---

[67] Letter signed "Sisters of St. Joseph, Newton, Kans." to Louis M. Fink, Bishop of Leavenworth, Aug. 23, 1884. The original is in Archives of Kansas Catholic Historical Society; a photostat is in the files of the author.

[68] Reception and Profession Books, book I (1883-1896), vol. I, pp. 12-18.

quarters at Concordia. Sisters Josephine and Madeleine and a postulant, Mary Cuff, of Carbondale, Pennsylvania (sister of Sister Antoinette) completed the group which remained in Newton. Mother Stanislaus took with her Sisters Armella, Domitilla, Avila, Cecelia, and Dominic.

Concordia definitely was a frontier in 1884. Settled only twenty-four years before, the Republican Valley quickly assumed the appearance of a typical Kansas community. From a hunter's paradise in 1860 when bison grazed on the surrounding hills, Concordia outstripped Clyde in an effort to become the county seat, thus attracting even more settlers. The rapidity of the area's development is exemplified by the growth of the railroads linking it with its neighbors: in 1876 there were no railroads in Cloud County; in 1888 the county boasted nine railroad lines, the most complete network in any county of the state.[69]

In the year the Sisters of Saint Joseph entered the missionary field in Concordia, J. M. Hageman, one of the founders of the city and the editor of its paper, published a historical summary of Cloud County. Very aptly, he explained the attitude of pioneers: "We look upon scenes of today with cold indifference that a generation hence will ransack the records to find the smallest information concerning. So when the stirring scenes of this border were being enacted, when the buffalo covered every hill and valley, the brutal savage with tomahawk and scalping knife menaced the few and scattered settlers, many things happened which were deemed by them of but passing moment, that would be read by strangers hence with quickening interest. . . . Of the present he [the frontiersman] cares little; of the future nothing. . . . Frontiersmen are not egoists and will not therefore speak."[70]

Mr. Hageman's analysis is especially applicable to the pioneer Sisters and their work. It is difficult at times to make scattered statements (never written for publication) into a mosaic which will portray, though inadequately, what noble work, what almost insurmountable difficulties, and what unexpected accomplishments were theirs.

There were two Catholic churches in Cloud County in 1884, with a valuation of about $5,000 and a combined membership of some 1,600 persons. It was a vital minority group, however, with a broad

69 *Concordia Blade Annual* (1884), pp. 1-24, 31.
70 *Loc. cit.*
The Great Northwest (Clay Center, Kansas, 1888), p. 24.

outlook toward the future: they planned schools for their children and by this time had the one in Concordia almost completed.

In an account of the visitation to the Concordia parish by Bishop Fink in September, 1884, there was reference to the church and the school:

.... The Catholics of Concordia have also a church that can compare favorably with any, both in architectural structure and decoration. In the near future, however, it will have to be enlarged to meet the growing demands of the parish. The efficient pastor, the Rev. Joseph Perrier, has just completed a large three-story school house and on the first of next November the Sisters of Saint Joseph will take charge of the education of the children. In time they will also establish an academy here. The people irrespective of creed and nationality have contributed generously to the erection of the edifice. The advent of the Sisters will be hailed with joy by the Protestants as well as the Catholics. The French Canadians under the leadership of their zealous pastor are an honor to the Catholic Church and by the number of persons who sought the Confessional and approached Holy Communion they proved that amidst the prairies of Kansas they have not forgotten the lessons learned at home.[71]

It is interesting to note the closing sentence of the above quotation because of the religious conditions in Concordia in the 'Eighties. Freethinking was rampant in the Middle West, and the editor of the *Concordia Blade* was an acknowledged freethinker and atheist. The newspaper, which was almost an official organ for the promulgation of antireligious, anti-Christian articles, was nevertheless not critical of the new school nor of its religious teachers. Since the press is always an index to prevalent public opinion, there seems to be a contradiction in the statement that the Protestants were as happy about the new venture as were the Catholics and that they contributed considerably toward the erection of the school. Contrast this with the claims and boasts of the *Blade*:

.... Infidels settled this county . . . organized the government of this county; an infidel was the first person to propose and lead in the building of the first schoolhouse; infidels were the first to move for the building of this city; infidels made the first survey and filed the first plot; an infidel first spoke the name "Concordia"; infidels were the first and foremost in an effort to build this [the public] school building. . . .[72]

And again:

.... The first purely secular and freethought paper established in Kansas.
.... The first paper in the State to assert rights of the press to live and labor absolutely independent of the priesthood, and free from their contaminating touch. It views with alarm the tyranizing influence of the clergy over the great medium of conveying thought in America, the press. . . .

[71] *Monthly Visitor*, Sept. 18, 1884.
[72] *Concordia Blade*, Aug. 28, 1885. The files of the *Blade* were used.

.... The *Blade* is independent alike of churches and saloons, holding that if the former should rule, we would all be slaves; and if the latter be our rulers, we would all be paupers.

.... The *Blade* wants no God or Gods in our national or any other Constitution....

.... The *Blade* wants all property taxed including church property....

.... It wants chaplains in the legislatures . . . in the prisons, in the schools, in the army, in all public places abolished.

.... We want better homes and happier homes. Fewer children and better ones.

....We want less religion and more humanitarianism. More science and less superstition.[73]

Shortly after her arrival in Concordia, Mother Stanislaus indicated that the steps toward incorporation had been undertaken.[74] A legal statement was drawn up, signed by the Sisters, and passed upon by the bishop of the diocese. This legalization and incorporation gave stability and assurance to the members of the congregation.[75]

In November, Father Dominic Meier, O.S.F. (who no doubt had by that time become perfectly resigned to the transfer of the motherhouse to Concordia), wrote to Mother Stanislaus concerning the blessing and dedication of the new convent:

Do not hurry the house through on account of the blessing. If necessary, you can live in the house several months before it is blessed. Let the workingmen take their time and make a good job and let the paint be perfectly dry before you occupy it. If you cannot have the blessing in December, we will have it in January—and the first of January would be a suitable day as it is no holiday of obligation in the West. As soon as you are ready you can write me and then we will agree on the day. . . . Will not the postulant you have in Newton be long enough in the congregation in order to receive the habit when we have the blessing? In case there are some more in Concordia we could have a reception at the same time.

Hoping that you will have God's blessing on your new convent. . . .[76]

The dedication and reception did not take place until March 19, 1885. Postulants were received for the first time on the Feast of Saint Joseph, a custom which has persisted in the community ever since:

[73] *Concordia Blade Annual* (1884), back cover. It is at Kansas State Historical Society, Topeka, Kans.

[74] Mother Stanislaus Leary, Concordia, Kans., to the Rt. Rev. Louis M. Fink, Oct. 3, 1884. The original is in the Archives of Kansas Catholic Historical Society; a photostat is in the files of the author.

[75] Legal statement of the Sisters of St. Joseph of Concordia, Kans. The original is in handwriting and with signatures of the individual Sisters in La Grange Archives, vol. I, pp. 34-35; a photostat in files of the author.

Solemn Contract and Agreement of 1885 of the Sisters of St. Joseph of Concordia, Kans. Written in long hand by Mother Stanislaus Leary, and with addenda and signature of Bishop Fink, the original is in Diocesan Archives of Kansas City-in-Kansas, Kansas City, Kans.; a photostat in files of the author.

[76] Letter of Father Dominic Meier, Emporia, Kans., to Mother Stanislaus Leary, Concordia, Kans., Nov. 23, 1884. Original is in the Archives of the Nazareth Motherhouse, La Grange, Ill.; a photostat in files of the author.

At ten o'clock in the morning six young ladies were invested with the veil and habit of the Sisters of Saint Joseph. Their names are as follows: Miss Mary Schuchof, Celina, Ohio, (Sister Helena); Miss Eugenia Perrier, Savoy, France, (Sister Mary Joseph); Miss Mary Cuff, Carbondale, Pennsylvania, (Sister Mary Clare); Miss Mary Furstenberg, Chicago, Illinois, (Sister Aloysius); Misses Melissa and Lucy Costello, St. Mary's, Kansas, (Sisters Teresa and Angela). The ceremonies of reception were performed by the Very Reverend Father Dominic assisted by Father Perrier and Father LaSage. At four P.M. the new convent and the stations of the cross were blessed. The discourse made by the Very Rev. Father Dominic was so clear, distinct and simple that everyone in church was affected and penetrated with the necessity of saving one's soul. A large number of Protestants were present and very much edified.[77]

In Concordia, as in Newton, there was from the first a select school and a parish school.[78] The former enrolled principally Protestants from the better families of Concordia and its environs. A Bible controversy was waged in Concordia in 1885, and the attention of the entire state was centered on this matter. At a meeting of the school board in August of that year, it was voted that the use of the Bible be prohibited in the public schools of Concordia.[79] Commenting on this action, *The Topeka Baptist* stated that dissatisfaction was strong among the better class of citizens who accordingly circulated a petition requesting the school board to call a special session to reconsider the matter.[80] The special session, however, merely reiterated the original decision. But so firm was the association in the minds of many Concordians between morality and a religious education for their children, that a number of non-Catholic children were sent to the parochial and select schools conducted by the Sisters of Saint Joseph. The establishment, therefore, of the Catholic parochial school in Concordia was appreciated by the Christian Protestant element in the city.

Whether the editor of the *Blade* realized it or not, the philosophy which permeated the teachings of the Sisters of Saint Joseph met the spiritual needs of these people, regardless of the fact that the Bible, as such, was not read in the parochial school.[81]

In the fall of 1885, the hopes of Bishop Fink were realized when the Sisters from Concordia opened a mission school at Saint Joseph,

[77] *Monthly Visitor,* Apr. 2, 1885.
[78] In the lists of receipts there were always separate references to the select school as distinct from the parish school. Leary, *Diary and Book of Records, op. cit., passim.*
[79] *Concordia Blade,* Aug. 14, 1885.
[80] *Monthly Visitor,* Nov. 26, 1885; Mar. 11, 1886.
[81] *Concordia Blade,* Sept. 25, 1885, stated: ". . . . At the Catholic school here the Bible is not read and therein the managers show better sense than those who urge the reading of the Bible in the public schools."

Kansas. Sister Francis Joseph Leary, the former superior at Newton, assumed charge of the new school. She was ably assisted by Sisters Avila Taillefer, Cecelia St. Denis, and Dominic Rioux. Saint Joseph in those days was a prosperous French Canadian settlement, and Father Louis Mollier, the saddleback itinerant missionary of Northwestern Kansas, was the pastor.[82]

A letter to the editor of the *Monthly Visitor* described parish activities in the 'Eighties:

> Perhaps a few items from this locality would find space in your valuable paper. St. Joseph's is about the fourth parish in size in the State of Kansas although being a young parish of a few years where the Rev. Louis Mollier resided since 1872. Since then a church 104 feet by 40 feet was built with a 1,100 pound bell in the belfry which could be heard six miles, at the cost of $10,000; a fine parsonage costing $4,000 and also a large convent costing $5,000 where nearly two hundred children are receiving a first class education under the direction of the Sisters of Saint Joseph Congregation. Sister Francis Joseph as Mother Superior is doing all that is in her power to have everything satisfactory to all.[83]

And again:

> The Sisters have labored hard, night and day, to teach so many children— 180 scholars. They have taught English, French, Needlework, and Music to the very best success. In fact they have done so well that it is impossible for me to keep silence. They have worked for a whole year for the benefit of the children of the parents who work hard to keep their children at school. The school will be out soon and everybody will have an opportunity to see for themselves what the children have learned during the past year's term.
>
> The examination of the scholars will take place on June first and second and the Sisters will give a picnic for the children. On the 12th about 55 will make their First Holy Communion. On the 13th there will be a great exhibition given by the children of St. Joseph's Convent and I also hear they will go down to Clyde on the 16th and it is to be hoped that they will go as there are a good many from Clyde who cannot attend and the children will be trained . . . it is to be hoped that the people will turn out en masse as it would give the Sisters great encouragement. . . .[84]

Within a period of three years after the pioneers' arrival, there were three houses: Newton, Saint Joseph, and the motherhouse in Concordia. Bishop Fink, ever the faithful friend of the infant establishment, wrote encouraging letters: "I am so glad you are getting on so well—have had hard enough time in the beginning— tell me all you wish me to know and what advice or direction I can

[82] Father Mollier was born in Chambery, France, Oct. 29, 1846. He came to Kansas in 1869 and settled in Topeka to devote himself to missionary work, and began the construction of the St. Joseph and Concordia churches simultaneously. He is considered the pioneer priest of northwestern Kansas.

[83] *Monthly Visitor*, Mar. 31, 1887.

[84] *Ibid.*, June 2, 1887.

give you, I will."[85] He arranged that the Sisters receive Holy Communion at a convenient hour rather than waiting for the later Masses on Sunday, and that the novices be given religious instructions by Father Perrier. Such acts showed clearly his paternal attitude.[86]

More candidates were received periodically. Mention shall be made of early receptions because of the extreme importance of these Sisters as contributors to the advancement of the Church on the plains of Kansas and elsewhere.

On July 18, 1885, two new members, Miss Rose Picard of St. Paul, Canada, and Miss Kathryn Cuff of Carbondale, Pennsylvania, became Sisters Mary Ann and Mary Louise, respectively.[87] The following January, Miss Mary Frances Kielty of St. Louis and Miss Mary Agnes Gosselin of Concordia received the names of Sisters Mary Ursula and Mary Alexine.[88] Others received during the year 1886 and early 1887 were Misses Jane Devine (Sister Patrick), Carbondale, Pennsylvania; Eugenie Lucier (Sister Bernadette), Concordia, Kansas; Mary Caron (Sister Borgia), Bourbonnais, Illinois; Gertrude Fisher (Sister Regina), Newton, Kansas; Mary Cayer (Sister Aurelia), Aurora, Kansas; Mary Ann Collins (Sister Sebastian), Carbondale, Pennsylvania; Ethel Fitzgibbon (Sister Amelia), Pekin, Illinois; and Lucy Gaynor (Sister Francis Xavier), Auburn, New York.[89]

The Academy in Concordia was well publicized locally and throughout the state.[90]

[85] Letter of the Rt. Rev. Louis M. Fink, Leavenworth, to Mother Stanislaus Leary, Concordia, Kans., Dec. 14, 1885. Original is in Archives of the Nazareth Motherhouse, La Grange, Ill., vol. II, p. 129; a photostat in files of the author.

[86] Letters of the Rt. Rev. Louis M. Fink, Leavenworth, to Mother Stanislaus Leary, Concordia, Dec. 22, 1885, and Aug. 11 and 14, 1886. Originals are in Archives of the Nazareth Motherhouse, La Grange, Ill., vol. II, pp. 128, 134, 136; photostats in files of the author.

[87] Reception and Profession Books, book I (1883-1896), pp. 32-33, 34-35.

[88] Ibid., pp. 36-37, 38-39.

[89] Ibid., pp. 42-43, 44-45, 46-47, 48-49, 50-51, 52-53, 54-55, 56-57.
Monthly Visitor, May 13, 1886; Oct. 7, 1886; July 28, 1887.
Clipping from Kankakee, Ill. paper—unnamed and undated, but pertaining to the reception of Sister Bernadette. Mother Stanislaus Leary, Diary and Book of Records, vol. III, p. 31.

[90] The first advertisement of the school which the author was able to locate was one which appeared in the Kansas Catholic of June 17, 1886. This same advertisement continued to run in this paper for several years. File in Kansas State Historical Library, Topeka; a photostat in files of the author.
There were several references in the writings of Mother Stanislaus Leary to amounts paid to the Kansas Catholic for these ads: "Drew a draft for advertisement for the year in the Kansas Catholic to J. O'Flannagan—$10.00." Diary and Book of Records, vol. III, Jan. 28, 1889. This Diary is in the files of the author.
"Advertisement in the paper for our school commences today, pre-paid one year in advance of $5.00. Will be due this day in 1890." Ibid., Feb. 15, 1889.

The town of Concordia seemed appreciative of the cultural bene
fits derived from the Academy. It is not out of order to cite in it
entirety one of the references to the final program given at the school

The commencement exercises of Nazareth Academy held at Concordi,
Kansas, Tuesday the 26th, 1885, were well attended. The program as carrie
out shows that Concordia's Catholic school is one of the most thorough in i
training, broad in scope, and ranks among the finest and best schools in th
land. From the beginning to the close of the exercises everything move
smoothly and in harmony, not a break nor halt was made. So well did eac
one of the pupils perform his different parts that it would be unjust to mak
special mention of any particular one. The music furnished was especially fin
and the playing and chorus of four young ladies on pianos on opposite sides ¢
the stage keeping perfect time shows that that branch of education is as car
fully looked after as any other. In the awarding of prizes in which Moth€
Superior presented many beautiful and valuable presents, the pupils all showe
a respectful appreciation and were cheered by the audience.

In conclusion, we wish to say that Concordia has reason to be proud ¢
her Catholic School. The following was the program:

PART I

Philomel—	Kunkel
Misses L. Green, N. Lyon, H. Marcotte, E. Martin	
Address—	French
Miss Laure Demers	
Birds of Notre Dame—	Clapisson
Miss Josie Marmont	
Essay—Is Life Worth Living	
Miss Gertrude Fisher	
Trio—Mermaid's Evening	Glover
Song—	
Misses E. Ames, L. Green, B. Marcotte, M. L'Ecuyer, E. Martin,	
E. L'Ecuyer	
Morceau Par Coeur—La Jeune Fille Malade et Sa Mère	
Miss E. L'Ecuyer	
French Dialogues—La Laterie De Francdort, en L'Occasion Fait Le L'arron	
Misses Ida L'Ecuyer, E. Martin, H. Theriault, J. Lannone,	
Eva L'Ecuyer	
Gallop—	Ludovic
Misses L. Mayo, R. Schafer, B. Marcotte	

PART II

Chorus—"Chime Again Beautiful Bells"	Bishop
Recitation—"The Burning Ship"	
Miss May Kelly	
The Housekeeper's Complaint—	Robinson
Miss Ida L'Ecuyer	
The Young May Queen—	Meyer
Misses A. Polley, D. Carpenter, J. Marmont, M. Kelly	

Operetta

Twin Sisters—	Saroni
Misérère—Trovatore—	Bellak
Misses S. Herwick, G. Fisher	
Address—	English
Miss Effie Stimmel	
Fascination—Grand Gallop—	Perring
Misses G. Golby, S. Herwick, G. Fisher, E. Stimmel	

Awarding of Honors, Distribution of Prizes, etc.

The Rev. Gentlemen from other towns who attended were Rev. Fr. O'Leary of Solomon City, Kansas; Rev. Fr. Carius, Ellsworth, Kansas; Rev. Fr. Mollier, St. Joseph, Kansas; Rev. Fr. Fortier, St. Peters, Kansas; Rev. Fr. Leaher, Argentine, Kansas; Rev. Fr. Leonard, Clyde, Kansas; and Rev. Fr. Perrier of this city. The house was crowded to its utmost. It is a great credit to the Catholics of this part of the state. The young ladies who took part in it have only been at this academy from 6 to 9 months; it is great indeed to see how much they have accomplished in such a short term of school. It certainly must have been gratifying to the good Mother Superior as it was creditable to the pupils and it certainly will be gratifying to their parents to know that they acquitted themselves so superbly.

Wednesday morning was a busy time at the Convent as a large number of the pupils were soon ready for their vacation, and what with adieus and good-bys and parting, all was bustle as about 60 of the pupils left on various trains for their homes.[91]

On another occasion the editor of the *Concordia Times* commented in a communication to the Catholic paper of the state:

Editor of the *Kansas Catholic:*

By request of many of the readers of the *Kansas Catholic,* I send to you the comments of the press on the Commencement Exercises of the Catholic school and academy of Concordia. It was held at the Opera House on the 22nd of June in the presence of most of the parents of the pupils, several of the clergy of the vicinity, and the best society of Concordia.

What is still more gratifying for the pastor is the exemplary conduct of 65 young ladies, Children of Mary, who are monthly communicants, some even weekly. Before the school was over they all signed a beautiful address to the Holy Father on account of his Golden Jubilee.

The following are the comments of the press: "The Commencement Exercises held at the Opera House by the Nazareth Convent exceeded the expectations of all. The program was made up of songs, instrumental music, recitations, solos, dialogues, choruses, duets, etc., both in French and English. The crowded house that greeted them was enthusiastic and very attentive. Every thing passed off smoothly and pleasantly."

It was all so excellent that we cannot very well make special mention of any for it seemed all very special. Many were in attendance from neighboring

---

[91] *Monthly Visitor,* July 8, 1885. Another similar account was found in the same paper on June 30, 1887.

cities, some coming as far as Atchison. The exercises were highly creditable to the Academy and speak as thousands for its advancement and standing of work. We are sorry that we have not more time for extended mention.[92]

We have traced the influence of the pioneer Sisters of Saint Joseph in Kansas, working in these first four years in Harvey and Cloud counties. It was a difficult, disheartening venture; but with the faith of the Church, the hope of Kansas, and the charity of these courageous women, the foundation was laid deep and solid—the foundation which in the following years their successors were to expand and deepen in Newton, which continued to be affiliated with the Concordia motherhouse until 1893; in Saint Joseph, the early pride and joy of the community; and in Concordia, the seat of the motherhouse. These three names are dear to every Sister of Saint Joseph of Concordia. The next chapters will trace the raising of Concordia to a bishopric and the detailed history of the Sisters as it parallels that of the diocese.

[92] This article was addressed to the editor of the *Kansas Catholic,* where the article appeared in the July 7, 1887, issue.

Administration:
Reverend Mother Stanislaus Leary
Part II: 1887-1899

THE unforeseen growth of the Catholic Church in Kansas in the 1870's and 1880's made it necessary to think in terms of the establishment of two new dioceses in that state. Bishop Fink found it impossible to cope with the needs of the vast territory which had been his diocese for ten years. According to the *Catholic Directory* of 1886, the Church now had:

Secular priests	74
Religious priests	49
Ecclesiastical students	25
Churches and chapels	200
Churches finished since last report	19
Churches under construction	13
Colleges	3
Academies	4
Parochial schools about	57
Pupils about	5,000
Orphanages	2
Hospitals	2
Catholic population, approximately	90,000[1]

The first indication in print that such an expansion was afoot appeared in an article in the *Monthly Visitor* early in 1886:

From a reliable source the *Catholic* is enabled to inform its readers that the formation of two new dioceses in this State will probably be certain in the near future. A number of the clergy of the diocese will meet at the Bishop's residence on the Wednesday after Easter, the 28th, for a discussion of this subject and whatever the result may be will be reported to the Bishops of the Province with the request that they take action on it at their next meeting which will occur sometime in June. The new dioceses will take up the terri-

---

[1] *Sadlier's Catholic Directory* (New York, 1886), p. 243.

tory comprising two-thirds of the present diocese between them. The propos
district of one of them has now about twenty priests and about thirty church
and the other has about twelve priests with nearly as many churches and th
prospects of building new churches and congregations are equally good in bo
the dioceses.[2]

Bishop Fink made his visitation to the French parishes in Clou
County and, whatever their motives, the citizens of Concordia ma
a special effort to show him every mark of respect. "We note here (
Concordia) that Bishop Fink thinks a good deal of Concordia ar
always helps our worthy pastor in all his labors. . . . Our mayor
the head of the procession started from the B. and M. depot, parad
through Washington and Ninth Streets to Father Perrier's residenc
The Concordia band was willing to help a good cause and gave
some fine music. A great number of our citizens joined the processio
perhaps the greatest majority would have done so if they had be
notified of such a demonstration but the time was too short." The
the correspondent prophetically (perhaps knowingly) stated that
a short time Concordia would have "our Bishop," for the citize
would do all in their power to secure the bishopric for that place

Concordia was chosen for the location of the see in Northweste
Kansas early in May. There were more priests, more churches, a
more religious orders represented in the proposed Diocese of Co
cordia than there were in that of Wichita.[4]

Through the efforts of the Reverend Joseph Perrier the Sist
of Saint Joseph had established their headquarters in Concord
Through the efforts of this same man, the city of Concordia receiv
the honor of being chosen the seat of the new diocese. There is
letter extant in which Father Perrier enclosed a clipping from
Concordia newspaper concerning a citizens' meeting at which reso
tions were passed as follows:

Whereas, The Catholic Bishop of the great State of Kansas, as well
those who with him, have charge of the widely diversified interests of t
church have been looking with watchful interest over the Middle and Nor
western portion of this State for a suitable place for the center of one or m
dioceses, have been attracted to the beautiful city of Concordia which
nestled in a rich valley, almost surrounded with picturesque hills, for
proper location of a college, cathedral, hospital or any other edifice needed
round out the most extensive See, and

Whereas, The city not only possesses a varied scenery, and a health
location, with superior natural resources to sustain a large population, but

[2] *Monthly Visitor,* Apr. 15, 1886.
[3] *Ibid.,* May 13, 1886.
[4] *Loc. cit.*

location and concentration of railroads, indicate it a natural gateway in every direction, East, West, North, and Northwest, and

Whereas, It seems entirely proper that our people should give some suitable and substantial expression of their kindly feeling and cheerful good will in aiding in laying preliminary foundation of a new Diocese if it be located here in our midst, therefore,

Resolved, That the Mayor and the City Council of Concordia, be requested and authorized to take immediate steps to raise the sum of $5,500 to enable Father Perrier and the trustees of the Catholic Church of Notre Dame of Concordia, Kansas, to purchase an eligible and suitable spot for college and cathedral grounds for said church.

Resolved, That it is the sense of this meeting that if need be and to expedite prompt action in this matter, that the city council be authorized and requested to borrow said amount of $5,500 from the waterworks fund as soon as said bonds be cashed.[5]

Mr. L. J. Crans, an attorney and United States Commissioner, was the liaison officer between the citizens of Concordia and the Bishop. He wrote several letters pertinent to the meeting and explanatory of the attitude of the residents of Concordia in general. Referring to the articles which had appeared in the two Concordia papers and which indicated that there was considerable opposition to the proposition, he pointed out that although the *Blade* until recently had been published as a liberal or atheistic paper, the editor was willing to contribute to the subscription. The article in the *Empire* expressed only the attitude of its editor. "We have determined to obtain for you the most sightly and desirable location in our city and one which we understand had met with your approbation. There are enough public-spirited men here who will see that sufficient means are raised."[6]

Although the official bull creating the new dioceses of Kansas was not received until August 2, 1886, a dispatch was received in Saint Louis on July 8, stating that four new dioceses had been created in the western part of the United States and naming the ordinaries for

[5] *Concordia Blade,* May 18, 1886. The committee appointed was F. Sturges Houston, Sr., L. J. Crans, F. LaRocque, and S. Demers.

Letter of Father Joseph Perrier, Concordia, to the Rt. Rev. Louis M. Fink, Leavenworth, May 20, 1886. Original is in the Archives of the Kansas Catholic Historical Society; a photostat is in the files of the author.

[6] Letters of L. J. Crans, Concordia, to the Rt. Rev. Louis M. Fink, Leavenworth, May 31, June 2, and June 15, 1886. In the letter of June 2 he mentions enclosing a clipping from the *Blade* which showed a changed attitude. Original letters are in Archives of the Kansas Catholic Historical Society; photostats in files of the author.

Concordia Blade, May and June, 1886.

Concordia Empire, May and June, 1886.

Letter of Father Joseph Perrier, Concordia, to the Rt. Rev. Louis M. Fink, Leavenworth, June 2, 1886. Original is in Archives of the Kansas Catholic Historical Society; a photostat in files of the author.

them: Wichita, Kansas, with the Reverend James O'Reilly as Bishop; Concordia, Kansas, with the Reverend Richard Scannell as Bishop; Lincoln, Nebraska, with the Reverend Thomas Bonacum as Bishop; and Cheyenne, Wyoming, with the Reverend Maurice Burke, as Bishop.

The Catholic paper of the state wrote on this occasion:

We congratulate the State, Catholics and non-Catholics, upon the final erection into episcopal seats of the two young and flourishing cities of Wichita and Concordia as each of these two cities will then become centers of educational, charitable and religious institutions that will be the highest value to them in their civic as well as religious bearing. We congratulate the Catholics of the State upon the division of this large and growing State into three dioceses by which the religious needs of every part of it can be well and fully attended to. We congratulate also our Right Reverend Bishop upon the lifting of responsibilities and the placing of a portion of them upon younger shoulders, now that under his supervision the Church has so marvelously grown that this has become a necessity. For the new Bishops themselves, our duty is to unite in prayer to the great throne of grace for them and during this month devoted to the Most Sacred Blood of Christ pray to God to grant them the grace and spiritual strength necessary for the high station to which He has raised them in the government of His Church.[7]

The newly appointed Bishop of Concordia was to become a staunch friend and adviser of the Sisters of Saint Joseph. He found in them a spirit of wholehearted cooperation and Christlike charity in the missionary diocese entrusted to his care. At the time of his appointment, Bishop Scannell was the Vicar General of the Diocese of Nashville. A native of Cork, Ireland, he had studied at All Hallows College, near Dublin, where he was ordained in 1871. He came to Nashville that same year.[8]

Bishop Scannell was a happy selection, for the new Ordinary was a student of languages, speaking French as fluently as English and, in addition, being well versed in German and Italian. His appointment was to be comparatively short-lived, however, for this scholarly

    [7] *Monthly Visitor*, July 14, 1886.
    [8] "Biographies of the Bishops of Concordia Given," *Northwestern Kansas Register*, special edition, Nov. 20, 1938.
    E. F. Hollibaugh, *Biographical History of Cloud County, Kansas* (Concordia, Kans., 1903), pp. 200-203.
    Kansas City Catholic Register, May 6, 1937; May 20, 1937.
    Salina Journal, May 13, 1937.
    Concordia Blade-Empire, May 24, 1937.
    Kansas Knight, Dec. 1930; Dec. 1935.
    Wichita Catholic Advance, June 15, 1929.
    Catholic Encyclopedia, vol. IV, pp. 206-207.
    Nashville Daily American, Dec. 1, 1886.
    Joseph B. Code, *Dictionary of the American Hierarchy* (New York, 1940), p. 314.

gentleman found little to build upon in Kansas except hope. There was one crop failure after another while he was in charge of the diocese and the boom, which was at its peak when he arrived, collapsed almost overnight. Three years later, Bishop Scannell was transferred to Omaha, and Bishop John Hennessy of Wichita became Administrator of the Concordia Diocese until 1897.

The new diocese created in 1886 embraced twenty-six counties in the northwestern part of the state—a territory which was soon to be dotted with the parochial schools conducted by the Sisters of Saint Joseph—being bounded on the east by the east line of Republic, Cloud, Ottawa, and Saline Counties, thence taking the southern boundary of Saline and Ellsworth Counties, thence north to the southeast corner of Russell County, thence westward to the Colorado line. It was composed of fifty-eight missions and twenty-three priests.[9]

On the 30th of November, in the Church of Saint Joseph in Nashville, the church for whose building he was so largely responsible, Bishop Scannell, was consecrated first Bishop of Concordia, by Archbishop Feehan of Chicago.[10] Father Perrier, as representative of the Concordia Diocese, read to the new Ordinary the resolution passed by the city council:

Whereas, Concordia has been honored by the preference of the Catholic Church, by being selected as the headquarters of the Diocese of Northwestern Kansas; and,

Whereas, as the result of such a selection, the Right Reverend Richard Scannell has been elected, ordained, and consecrated Bishop of Concordia; and,

Whereas, the Bishop is about to arrive in our city, therefore,

Be it Resolved, that we, the Mayor and Councilmen of the city of Concordia, in a special session assembled, believing it fitting that the arrival of such a personage should be marked by some fitting demonstration, do hereby extend to Bishop Scannell a hearty welcome to our city, and further, we do recommend that a committee be appointed by the Mayor to greet the Bishop upon his arrival with proper ceremony, and that a copy of these resolutions be drafted by the City Clerk and handed to the Very Reverend Joseph Perrier, Administrator of the Concordia Diocese.   Passed November 22, 1887

Attest: WM. M. PECK, *Clerk*[11]   J. GREENE, *Mayor*

[9] *Kansas Catholic,* Jan. 5, 1887.
     Papal Bull, Aug. 2, 1887.
[10] Assisting Archbishop Feehan were Archbishop Elder of Cincinnati, Bishops Rademacher of Nashville, Maes of Covington, O'Sullivan of Mobile, Dwenger of Fort Wayne, and McCloskey of Louisville as well as Fathers Gleason of Nashville, Beil of Memphis, Walsh of Chattanooga, Perrier of Concordia, and Gill of Chicago. *Nashville Daily American,* Dec. 1, 1887.
     Monthly Visitor, Dec. 8, 1887.
[11] *Nashville Daily American,* Dec. 1, 1887.
     Monthly Visitor, Dec. 8, 1887.

On December 9, Bishop Scannell, accompanied by his friend, Father
Gill of Chicago, arrived in Concordia, where he was met at the
station by Father Perrier, almost the entire Catholic congregation,
and a large portion of the non-Catholic population of the city. Thence
the procession moved to the Opera House where Bishop Scannell was
officially welcomed to the city. At the conclusion of a greeting song
by the children of the parochial school, Father Perrier introduced
the mayor, who welcomed the prelate in an appropriate address. He
assured him that Concordia was proud to welcome him and that its
citizens were interested in the material growth of his church as a
part of the growth of the city. The Bishop responded thanking all
the little children especially for the splendid program and the people
for the support promised him.[12]

Prior to these events, Mother Stanislaus Leary had been asked to
open a parochial school at Abilene, perhaps one of the most enterprising towns in central Kansas in the 'Eighties. The cattle trade had
made the town prosperous in 1886. Abilene seemed a promising location for another foundation of the Sisters of St. Joseph and Father
John Leary, pastor of Saint Andrew's church, was interested in building for the future.[13]

Early in September, 1886, Mother Stanislaus and a companion
went to Leavenworth to discuss the matter with the Bishop of that
place.[14] There are references in the *Diaries* of Mother Stanislaus to
two trips to Abilene, one in March, 1887, and the other in August of
that same year.[15] These early negotiations, begun at about the time
that Bishop Fink was thinking in terms of a division of the Diocese
of Leavenworth, are extremely important because of future developments. They show the desire of Bishop Fink to keep the motherhouse
of the Sisters of Saint Joseph in his own diocese. Knowing that Concordia was a likely site for the location of one new diocesan see, he
thought that with a school opened in Abilene (which he felt would be
within his jurisdiction) he would find it an easy matter to have Mother

---

12 *Kansas Catholic*, Dec. 15, 1887.
13 Father Leary succeeded Father Carius as pastor of Abilene. Father Carius, chaplain
in the Confederate army and confessor of Maximilian before the latter's untimely end in
Mexico, was a colorful frontier missionary in the Diocese of Concordia. Father Leary,
also a brave soldier, a church builder, and pioneer priest, is considered the founder of
the Sisters of St. Joseph of Wichita.
14 Mother Stanislaus, *Diary*, vol. I, p. 49, lists this expense as $12.30. The original
is in Archives of Nazareth Motherhouse, Concordia, Kans.; a photostat is in the files
of the author.
15 *Ibid.*, Mar. 22, 1887—expenses $7.00; Aug. 2—expenses $13.00. This latter trip
was for the laying of the cornerstone at Mount St. Joseph's.

Stanislaus keep Concordia as a mission and make Abilene the headquarters. Father Leary and his parish agreed to erect a building in Abilene to be used as a "college" and academy for young ladies and as a motherhouse for the Sisters. A plot of two hundred and forty acres of land to the north of the city was purchased, and a building was begun. A contemporary account of the projected building is interesting:

. . . But more especially is the attention of the reader of the *Catholic* called to the magnificent progress made by the comparatively few Catholics who laid the foundation of the church and convent which will endure for years as a testimony of their zeal for the faith when more transitory affairs will have long been forgotten. Through the combined exertions of the pastor, Father O'Leary [sic], Messrs. Berry Brothers, Kirby and others, a tract of land containing one hundred and sixty acres has been platted and the sale forms the basis of a fund to be used in erecting a convent and the necessary outbuildings. The location of this tract is unsurpassed, occupying as it does a commanding position on the elevated plateau north of the city. The tract has very appropriately been called "Kirby's Addition to the City of Abilene" in honor of Mr. Thomas Kirby, the well-known banker, and one of Abilene's most time honored and respected citizens. An inspection of the front elevation drawn by Krueger and Hagan, architects of Salina, reveals the magnificent building with a total length of one hundred and twenty feet, an average height of fifty feet and a central dome surmounted by a cross, stretching to an elevation of seventy-six feet. The basement will be constructed of stone, the first and second stories of brick, ending in a mansard roof ornamented with dormer windows. The plan is a skillful combination of taste, elegance and adaption to the purposes intended. When completed, the building will not only be a credit to the city but a lasting monument to the Catholics of Abilene. The title adopted is Mount Saint Joseph's Convent and will be in charge of the Sisters of Saint Joseph. This is simply another evidence of the untiring zeal which has ever characterized or rather an expression of the spirit which is ever animated by Catholics as a body in behalf of true Christian education. The progress of the Church in this country can best be estimated by counting the spires of churches and educational institutions which point heavenward in all the cities and hamlets in the land.[16]

This same train of thought permeated the "promotion literature" distributed to Catholics who wished to settle in Abilene: "Between the college and the city of Abilene already two hundred and sixty-five lots have been sold in the Addition for the Catholic College of the Sisters of Saint Joseph and the parochial school. . . ."[17]

A parochial school had been established in Abilene a year before the Sisters of Saint Joseph arrived there. This school was taught by Miss Elizabeth Haston and was conducted first in the church rectory

16 *Monthly Visitor*, May 5, 1887.
17 *Monthly Visitor*, June 2, 1887.

and later in a small frame house near-by.[18] In September, 1888, the first Sisters arrived to teach this parochial school. Sister Francis Joseph Leary was appointed superior of the new mission but declined because of ill-health, and Sister Bernard Sheridan was then made superior of the little group who composed the original Sisters in Abilene.[19] Her companions were Sisters Angela Costello, Amelia Fitzgibbon, Domitilla Gannon, Armella McGrath, and Sebastian Collins.

The cornerstone of the new building was laid August 4, 1887. An account of the ceremonies appeared in the *Monthly Visitor* a few days later:

> The blessing of the cornerstone of the new Mount Saint Joseph's Academy at Abilene by the Rt. Rev. Louis M. Fink, O.S.B., took place Monday. Rev. J. F. O'Leary [sic], by his untiring zeal and through the cooperation of his people, will have it ready soon to receive pupils. And the Reverend Father means that it shall be the stateliest educational institution in the western part of the diocese. In fact, Father O'Leary [sic], Mr. Kirby, the Berry brothers with others of that congregation take the greatest pride in pushing the work to completion, and we look to them to soon have this as another gem amongst their other good works for the good of religion in this part of the State and they certainly deserve every encouragement from all friends of religion and its handmaiden, education. The Academy will be placed in charge of the Sisters of Saint Joseph. Quite a number of clergy besides Father O'Leary [sic] assisted at the blessing. The Rev. E. J. Gleason, S.J., of Saint Marys delivered a splendid oration on Christian education. The citizens of Abilene, irrespective of creed, seem to appreciate the work that is being done, as they showed by the great turnout, for it appeared as if the whole of Abilene had turned out at Mount Saint Joseph's. The *Catholic* bids God's speed to the good work and desires that all praise be given to the generosity of the non-Catholics of that place who have exhibited so good and generous a spirit.[20]

It was shortly after this event that the cattle and land boom of the 'Eighties collapsed, leaving the minutely laid plans in a precarious position.

With the coming of Bishop Scannell, there were negotiations between the two Bishops and with Mother Stanislaus on whether or not the Abilene mission should remain a separate foundation. A number of letters from His Excellency, Bishop Fink, to Mother Stanislaus are extant, and they give a clear picture of the attitude of the

[18] *Wichita Catholic Advance*, June 22, 1929.

[19] Sister Bernard Sheridan came to Kansas in 1886 from Erie, Pa., and offered her services to Mother Stanislaus Leary. She received the habit on Oct. 16, 1877, and made her profession Mar. 27, 1880, at Erie. She was a native of County Roscommon, Ireland. This information was furnished by the Sisters of St. Joseph, Villa Marie, Erie, Pa.

[20] *Monthly Visitor*, Aug. 4, 1887.

former regarding this matter. Bishop Fink had one desire, namely, to keep the motherhouse within his diocese; still he wanted Mother Stanislaus herself to be the superior. However, he realized that if Bishop Scannell was opposed to that settlement, he would have to be resigned. As early as November, 1887, he advised Mother Stanislaus to go to Abilene to investigate conditions there and then on to Leavenworth to discuss the matter with him.[21]

Even before the completion of Mount Saint Joseph's, Bishop Fink advised the Sisters to take "the road of humility: the Sisters to stay at the *brick mansion* (farmer's house)[22] and to get the lower story put in repair—that is to say: plaster it, or as much of it as will be fit for day-scholars to teach the classes; the balance to be done as money will become available. . . . All I want is good religious and good teachers. . . . I would like you to be superior there; but if you do not *want to come* or your good Bishop does not wish you to leave, I must have one as Superior, who has the proper religious and financial qualifications. I expect you to find your way there as soon as you may go out of office in the near future. However, I leave everything to God's ruling. . . ."[23]

The final separation came in March, 1888. A few days earlier, Bishop Fink wrote a last entreaty to Mother Stanislaus:

. . . For certain reasons of my own, I would like to have you as superior there yourself, for a good deal of experience is required to get out all right. However, if good Bishop Scannell would not wish to let you go—some other reliable and good Sister should be appointed, who would have some experience in governing and managing temporal affairs. . . . The Sisters will have a good chance to do good and I will not interfere with Concordia; there is no academy between Leavenworth, Wichita and Concordia so that each will have a large territory tributary to the houses now existing.

Now in case you could not get away from Concordia—whatever be the reasons—then the one intended for Superior should meet Father Cunningham at Abilene—accompanied by you, as you are aware of the proceedings there heretofore. The deed should be made out for three or four Sisters, who would also sign the mortgage for the $5,000 [sic] as it may take some time till the incorporation papers can be got ready; but as soon as those papers will be all in order, then the Sisters in question transfer the title to the corporation. In

[21] Letter of the Most Rev. Louis M. Fink, Leavenworth, to Mother Stanislaus Leary, Nov. 16, 1888. The original is in Archives of Nazareth Motherhouse, La Grange, Ill., book II, p. 5; a photostat is in the files of the author.
[22] It was known as "Buckeye" and is still used as part of the St. Joseph Home property.
[23] A letter of the Most Rev. Louis M. Fink, Leavenworth, to Mother Stanislaus Leary, Feb. 22, 1888. The original is in Archives of Nazareth Motherhouse, La Grange, Ill., book II, p. 9; a photostat is in the files of the author.

the meantime each of these Sisters has to make her will conveying her property to those of her companions that may survive her; all of which to be kept by the Superior, or by myself in the Diocesan archives. By next fall the Sisters must hold a fair, if times turn out as we expect they will—God willing—I have not the least doubt, but that the proceeds of the fair will be sufficient to pay the installment of the amount payable next October, which will then reduce the $7,000 mortgage.

2. As good Bishop Scannell seems to have been under the impression that Concordia would be involved—I told him that Concordia was not expected to burden itself with the Abilene business; please tell him so again; for which reason I want matters tended to as set forth above.

3. Bishop Scannell seems to object to the two houses having but one novitiate for four or five years as the enclosed request of the Sisters shows; if the Bishop has any objection and desires a separation, his wish must be respected. It will come out all right at the latter end, although it may be a little more difficult for some time.[24]

The directions given above were carried out when Father Cunningham and Mother Stanislaus met at Abilene within the week.[25] The Sisters were given a choice of returning to the Concordia Motherhouse or remaining in Abilene to establish a motherhouse in the Diocese of Leavenworth. Sisters Bernard Sheridan, Domitilla Gannon, Armella McGrath, and Sebastian Collins, a novice, remained in Abilene; and Sisters Angela Costello and Amelia Fitzgibbon returned to Concordia.

The Abilene community thus established soon began to receive subjects from the vicinity of Abilene.[26]

Thus is reached another landmark in the expansion of the Church and the establishment of new dioceses influencing the growth and expansion of the Sisters of Saint Joseph. When the Rochester Diocese was created in 1868, two branches of the Sisters of Saint Joseph instead of one resulted, with motherhouses at Buffalo and Rochester. Again, in Kansas in 1887, circumstances made the two branches—those of Concordia and Leavenworth (now Wichita) — separate partly due to the original idea of the community to remain diocesan

24 Two letters written on the same day from the Rt. Rev. Louis M. Fink, Leavenworth, to Mother Stanislaus Leary, Concordia, Mar. 8, 1888. The originals are in Archives of Nazareth Motherhouse, La Grange, Ill., book II, pp. 3 and 9; photostats are in the files of the author.

25 Letter of the Rt. Rev. Louis M. Fink, Leavenworth, to Mother Stanislaus Leary, Mar. 16, 1888. The original is in Archives of Nazareth Motherhouse, La Grange, Ill., book II, p. 3; a photostat is in the files of the author.

26 *Kansas Catholic*, Sept. 6, 1888.
    Sister Sebastian Collins made her profession on Sept. 6, 1888, and at the same time five young candidates were received—Miss Mary Sinners (Sister Mary Rosa), Miss Annie Kennedy (Sister Mary Louise), Miss Rose Casper (Sister Mary Joseph), Miss Nora McMillen (Sister Mary Patricia), and Miss Mollie McInerney (Sister Mary Agnes). Sister Sebastian died the following year.

and partly due to the desire of Bishop Fink to retain jurisdiction over the Sisters. The hand of God is seen in these situations and the spread of the kingdom of God is often accomplished through trying times.

This division came early in the history of the Kansas foundation. The parent branch was just beginning to sink roots deeper into the soil of Kansas. It could ill afford to lose any members from that little band upon whom so many obligations and demands had been placed. However, with the perspective of time the matter may be seen objectively as in the Divine Plan.

The opening of the Abilene mission had been a financial drain on Concordia, as itemized statements of monetary outlay made in its interest attest. There is a record of a one hundred and twenty-five dollar expense for the opening of the mission in September, 1887.[27] There were furniture expenses of several hundred dollars as well as blankets, quilts, pianos, and similar items.[28] This of course was a financial loss when the separation was effected.

In March, 1896, Bishop Fink informed Mother Bernard Sheridan that there was to be a further divisioning of the state because of unequal territory and opportunities for the dioceses afforded by the 1887 arrangement. He conjectured that Abilene would fall into the Concordia Diocese, and that it would be best to move the motherhouse to Parsons, which he felt sure would remain under his jurisdiction. Again, he was mistaken, for Parsons was to be within the Diocese of Wichita. Hence, after much maneuvering, Bishop Fink lost the Sisters of Saint Joseph entirely when this second group became the Sisters of Saint Joseph of Wichita.[29] Abilene remained a mission of the Wichita Community until 1914 when the Bishop of Concordia purchased the building and grounds for twenty-five thousand dollars. After extensive improvements had been made, the Sisters of Saint Joseph of Concordia again assumed charge of the place which has been used since then as a diocesan orphanage.[30]

The enrollment of the Academy in Concordia did not suffer from

---

27 Leary, *Diary and Book of Records, op. cit.*, book I, p. 73 (Sept. 17, 1887). The original is in the Archives of the Nazareth Motherhouse, La Grange, Ill.; a photostat is in the files of the author.

28 *Ibid.*, p. 81 (Jan. 11, 1888): furniture—$45.90 and $155.00, pillows and feathers—$34.60; p. 85 (Mar. 4, 1888): piano for Abilene—$342.00.

29 An article on the Sisters of St. Joseph of Wichita written by Sister Victoria, *Wichita Eagle*, Oct. 17, 1937.

Hoffman's Catholic Directory (New York, 1896), p. 346; (New York, 1897), p. 301.

30 The story of Abilene will be taken up in a later chapter from the time it was again under the jurisdiction of the Sisters of St. Joseph of Concordia.

the establishment of another boarding school in Abilene. In a historical volume on Kansas in 1890 is the following story of the Concordia institution:

Convent of Nazareth and Academy of Concordia—The best educators are drawn to this State by its delightful climate and other advantages and they infuse into our schools the life that has made them so remarkable for the efficiency of their work. The Convent and Academy of Nazareth, although only five years old, have taken a place in the rank of our institutions of learning. The Lady Superior, Sister Stanislaus, is one of the cultured ladies the State of New York sends us. She presides over the "Motherhouse," the Convent of Nazareth. She has the assistance of twenty-four sisters. One of the finest musicians in the West gives instructions in that department. All higher branches are taught. That there are pupils in attendance from all parts of the country is evidence of the rank this institution holds. There are about fifty pupils boarding and about forty day pupils in the Academy, while in a separate building there are from one hundred seventy-five to two hundred pupils, constituting a day school. In the convent is a chapel and all the conveniences necessary to make it a first-class school. Young ladies go from here prepared to enter and adorn society.[31]

Mother Stanislaus appreciated the finer things of life and wanted her Sisters, who were to become the teachers of the community, to have every advantage to acquire them also. She employed an art teacher, a Miss Heen, to instruct the Sisters.[32] A dancing teacher taught in the school as early as 1889.[33] The students had retreats annually conducted for the most part by the Jesuits from Saint Mary's College.[34] The commencement exercises were held during these years at the Opera House, and expenses always included the moving of pianos to that place.[35]

It seems as if the Hand of God directed subjects to Concordia from all parts of the United States, Canada, and Europe. In 1888, seven were received: Misses Bertilda Beaufort (Sister Edmund), St. Cyrille, Canada; Frances Gray (Sister Berchmans), Coatbridge, Scotland; Isala Griffin (Sister St. Charles), Kenney, Illinois; Marie Savoie (Sister Agnes), Saint Anne's, Illinois; Mary Ryan (Sister Constance), Auburn, New York; Armaline Belanger (Sister Eulalia), St. Joseph, Kansas; and Josephine Caron (Sister Euphrasia),

---

[31] John Letham, *Historical and Descriptive Review of Kansas*, 2 vols. (Topeka, 1890), vol. I, pp. 188-189. This book contains a picture of the old Academy, a photostat of which is in the files of the author.

[32] Leary, *Diary and Book of Records, op. cit.*, book I, p. 47 (Aug. 4): Miss Heen —$80.00, art materials—$45.00; p. 49 (Sept. 23): Miss Heen—$10.00, art materials— $7.50; p. 53 (Nov. 3): Miss Heen—$45.00.

[33] *Ibid.*, book II, p. 59 (Oct. 18, 1889).

[34] *Ibid.*, book II, pp. 24-25 (Apr. 17 and 22, 1889).

[35] *Ibid.*, book II, p. 32 (June 21, 1889).

Bourbonnais, Illinois.[36] The following March, 1889, three subjects from Italy, one from Germany, and one each from Illinois and Tennessee were admitted.[37] And during the course of that same year, 1889, one each from Missouri, New York, and France, and five from Canada arrived to work on the Kansas frontier.[38] The community was from the beginning a melting pot, a cosmopolitan group, a truly American religious order.[39]

Mother Stanislaus was encouraged by the number of subjects who had asked for admission into the congregation. There were calls from far and wide for Sisters to staff schools which as a result of the legislation of the Third Plenary Council of Baltimore (1884) had been springing into existence throughout the country. During the remainder of her administration she opened twenty-seven schools in eight different states. Some of these schools were in operation a very few years and for various reasons then had to be discontinued; many

[36] *Reception and Profession Books*, book I (1883-1896), pp. 58-71.

[37] *Ibid.*, pp. 74-85. Those from Italy were Ermelinde Ceshi (Sister Mechtilde), Milan; Peppina Golinelli (Sister Margaret Mary), Modena; and Guisippina Incerti (Sister Mary Leo), Carpieti. Frances Ebner (Sister Seraphica), Baden, Germany; and Bridget Corgan (Sister Alphonsus), Nashville, Tenn., completed the group.

[38] *Ibid.*, pp. 72-98. Those received were: Misses Mary Sontag (Sister Albina), St. Louis, Mo.; Hannah Long (Sister Julia), Florence, N. Y.; Marie Prive (Sister Columba), Auzandelys, Fr.; Marie Moreau (Sister Veronica), St. Malo, Can.; Albina Merson (Sister Gabriel), L'Epphanie, Can.; Lea Beaudoin (Sister Michael), Nichel, Can.; Marie Gregory (Sister Mary Fidelis), Montreal, Can.

[39] *Ibid.*, pp. 99-123. Those received in 1890 were: Misses Anna Schwenzer (Sister Regis), Webster, N. Y.; Martine Lemieux (Sister Delphine), Quebec, Can.; Marie Louise Painchaud (Sister Blanche), St. John Chrysostom, Can.; Emilia Rheaume (Sister Irene), San Francisco, Calif.; Philomene Christin (Sister Mary Martha), Assumption, Can.; Theresa Trondle (Sister Fredoline), Kiesendach, Ger.; Amelia Bachle (Sister Boniface), Bogern, Ger.; Regina Wehrle (Sister Celestine), Bogern, Ger.; Aglae Belair (Sister Monica), St. Adel, Can.; Mary Norton (Sister Seraphine), S. Wallingford, Vt.; Rosa Kunz (Sister Stephanie), Fremont, Ohio; Minnie LeCuyer (Sister Paul), St. Georgia, Can.; Magdalen Bonnifield (Sister Evangelist), St. George, W. Va.

Ibid., pp. 124-141. Those received in 1891 were: Misses Charlotte St. Onge (Sister Armand), Chicago, Ill.; Agnes Arpin (Sister Flavian), Bourbonnais, Ill.; Marie Lebonte (Sister Jerome), Martintown, Ill.; Mary McPhillips (Sister Ambrosia), Batavia, N. Y.; Rose McPhillips (Sister Katherine), Batavia, N. Y.; Elizabeth L'Allier (Sister Marcelline), Des Mont, Can.; Salima Deslauriers (Sister Augusta), St. George, Ill.; Genevieve Green (Sister Gertrude), Xenia, Ohio; Rosa Benoit (Sister Georgia), Kankakee, Ill.; Mary Jane Burns (Sister Isidore), Auburn, N. Y.; Johanna Gunther (Sister Barbara), Bernstadt, Ger.; and Eva Waller (Sister Mary Rose), Springfield, Ill.

Ibid., pp. 152-180. Those received in 1892 were: Misses Margaret Vail (Sister Bernardine), Union Springs, N. Y.; Isabel Stenger (Sister Alcantara), Cuba, Kans.; Marie Theresa Kuebler (Sister Mary John), Alsace, Ger.; Emma Belisle (Sister Justina), Stillwater, Minn.; Corinne Pouliot (Sister Petronilla), Quebec, Can.; Cordilla Roy (Sister Anastasia), Ottawa, Can.; Anna Seymour (Sister Genevieve), Renfrew, Can.; Louise Grison (Sister Adrian), St. Joseph, Can.; Natalie Gladu (Sister Benedicta), St. George, Ill.; Emma Hoffman (Sister Christina), Schwarzenburg, Swtz.; Marie Delvina Gosselin (Sister Loretta), Aurora, Ill.; Ella Marinier (Sister Scholastica), Chicago, Ill.; and Hedwige Martin (Sister Simplicia), St. Michael, Can.

have remained under the care of the Sisters of Saint Joseph of Concordia until the present day. It will be necessary to give data on each mission even when the Sisters spent but one year there; each has left an indelible mark and influence on the history of the order. These accounts will vary in importance and in length depending on time or other extenuating circumstances which would influence the history of the mission.

The Society for the Propagation of the Faith which had helped Bishop Fink in an earlier decade came to the rescue of the Diocese of Concordia by sending the sum of $37,160.00 during the period between 1887 and 1901. During that same period the sum of $8,362.10 was collected within the diocese for the same society.[40] It is likely that some of the towns which established parochial schools during this period may have received some financial assistance through the Bishop from this fund.

In the vicinity of Saint Joseph, a score or so of miles from Concordia, was another French-Canadian settlement. The little town of Clyde, settled in the 1860's but growing slowly until 1884, began to feel the surge of immigration in the middle 'Eighties.[41] Mass was celebrated in Clyde in private homes until the erection of the church in 1880. The first resident priest, the Reverend Father Rivieres, came in 1883; however, he also attended the Catholics in such far-flung places as Zurich, Jamestown, and Palmer, thus being away from Clyde a great part of the time. He was succeeded in May, 1885, by Father Joseph Leonard, a man whose memory is still revered in the parish.[42] Father Leonard believed that Clyde needed a parochial school and, because the parish could not afford to erect such a building, he proceeded to do so out of his own purse with the understanding that the parish would sometime pay him back a minor share of it. As far as can be ascertained he was never reimbursed for this investment.[43]

In a letter to the editor of the *Kansas Catholic,* one of the parish-

[40] Joseph Freri, *The Society for the Propagation of the Faith and the Catholic Missions* (New York, 1912), p. 25.

[41] J. M. Hageman, "History of Cloud County," *Concordia Blade Annual* (1884), pp. 21-22.

[42] Hollibaugh, *op. cit.,* pp. 415-416.
Pamphlet issued in honor of the silver jubilee of the Rev. H. A. R. Spoorenberg, July 12, 1933.
Kansas Knight, Oct. 3, 1930.

[43] There were some difficulties between the parish and the heirs of the priest after his death. However, the civil court gave a decision favorable to the parish.

oners at Clyde spoke of the need of a parochial school two and a half years before the Sisters were brought there:

. . . . Whatever Father Leonard wants to do in this parish he is sure of success, for the whole parish forms only one heart and so it will be when arrangements can be completed for the building of the Catholic school here. Many poor Catholic children are dragging along at these public schools to learn what?— to swear, curse, and steal. The Father will commence as soon as possible to get the subscriptions. . . .[44]

Later there was mention of a fair in Clyde for the benefit of the new convent which they intended to build the next spring.[45] The cornerstone was laid about the middle of October.

. . . At three o'clock over eight hundred persons congregated on the Catholic Church grounds near the foundation of the Catholic Convent of the City of Clyde. It was the blessing of the cornerstone of the said Convent by His Lordship, the Right Reverend Bishop Scannell of Concordia. The ceremony was soon performed and His Lordship, assisted by the Reverend Leonard and the Reverend Fortier, turned towards the multitude and with a voice as persuasive as the language of logic and orthodoxy proved beyond reasonable doubt that the Catholic schools cultivate the intellect and the will.[46]

Clyde was encouraging immigrants by emphasizing that the town had never had a "boom" but that its growth had been normal, steady, and substantial.[47] In January the school was finished and ready for occupancy.[48]

Very briefly but to the point, Mother Stanislaus recorded the opening of this new mission:

February 4: Went to Clyde with Miss Rouse and then to Saint Joseph. Father Leonard hired the carriage.

February 8: Visit from Father Leonard. Purchased the bed clothing for Clyde.

February 14: Opened the convent school at Clyde, Kansas, with Sisters Avilla [sic], Aloysius and Berchmans. Sister Avilla [sic] is superior and Miss Long (later Sister Julia) is cook. We were received at the convent by the ladies of the congregation with an address of welcome. Supper was supplied by these ladies. Gave Sister Avilla [sic] in money $50.00. Traveling expenses and other expenses $10.00.

February 23: Gave Sister Avilla [sic] for her piano in Clyde for the first payment $10.00.[49]

[44] *Monthly Visitor*, Oct. 21, 1886.
[45] *Ibid.*, Dec. 2, 1886.
[46] *Ibid.*, Oct. 25, 1888.
[47] *Great Northwest! Most Successful Farming Region in Kansas—Clay Center* (Clay Center, Kans., 1888), p. 23.
[48] *Monthly Visitor*, Jan. 4, 1889.
[49] *Loc. cit.*, p. 3.

The local correspondent for the *Monthly Visitor* recorded the opening of the Clyde parochial school:

> Times are hard with us out here in this western country, but nevertheless we rejoice once in a great while as we did yesterday. The convent school of the parish of Saint John the Baptist is completed and it is one of the finest buildings of its kind in western Kansas. Rev. Father Leonard, our parish priest, announced to the congregation that the Rev. Sisters of Saint Joseph Congregation would come down from Concordia by the four o'clock train and invited all the ladies of the parish to be present to give the good Sisters a grand reception and most of them had a nice present to offer the Sisters upon their arrival. Each one of the ladies was then introduced to the Sisters. Soon after Benediction of the Most Blessed Sacrament was given by the Vicar General, the Most Reverend Joseph Perrier, in the Convent Chapel after which the good Sisters were taken through the Convent by the Rev. Leonard and Mother Superior Stanislaus of Concordia who came down with Mother Superior Avila, Sisters Aloysius and Berchmans for the Clyde Convent where they will teach English, French, and the common branches of studies and music also. The school will commence on Monday, February 18, and it is hoped that Christian parents will make it their duty to send their children to that holy institution. Fathers and mothers, don't be afraid to send your children to a good Catholic school. The good Sisters will take good care of them all. No boy will be allowed to have a revolver about his person as done in the public school of this city where two boys by the names of Davis and Miller fired pistols when school was dismissed for recess among three hundred youngsters, but fortunately no one was hurt. Dear parents, you have reason to say times are hard, I cannot send my children to school, but remember this where there is a will there is a way. The Sisters are more than pleased with the ladies of the parish of St. John the Baptist of Clyde. It was a grateful sight to see the amount of presents given to the Sisters. The house looked like a store of general merchandise.[50]

The school has continued since that time with the exception of a period from 1904 until 1910 when it was conducted by lay teachers.[51] Clyde was used as an orphanage for the Concordia Diocese as well as a parochial school. There were about ten or twelve orphans there at one time. This combination orphanage and parochial school persisted until the opening of the Diocesan Orphanage at Saint Joseph's Home in Abilene in 1915.

[50] *Monthly Visitor,* Feb. 21, 1889.
   Northwestern Kansas Register, Oct. 30, 1938. On Oct. 16, 1938, the parish of Clyde celebrated the golden anniversary of the parochial school. There was a plate dinner and a reunion of the original class of 1889 which consisted of Sister Paul (Minnie LeCuyer) of Concordia, Mrs. Belanger, Charles Lafond, Eli Balthasar, and E. E. Murphy. This celebration was ill-timed because according to the sources available the school wasn't opened until the following February.
   [51] Since the parish was unable to pay the salary of the Sisters, Father Mollier gave a two hundred and eighty acre farm to the Sisters of St. Joseph of Concordia shortly before his death in 1911 with the agreement that the community would furnish two Sisters salary-free and that, if a third or fourth teacher were needed, the parish would pay their salaries.

A high school was opened in Clyde in the fall of 1919 and lasted four years, taking one class through high school. It had to be closed in 1923, due to lack of teachers to staff the high schools conducted by the Community. In 1947, the grade school, which continued after the closing of the high school, had a staff of five teachers and sixty-nine children enrolled.[52]

Another school, opened in 1889, is still thriving—the parochial school in Beloit, Kansas. The first settlement in Beloit was made in 1868 by a Mr. A. A. Bell at a place in Mitchell County which he called Willow Springs. Immigrants came in large numbers within the next few years and in 1873, when the name was changed to Beloit, it was considered the county seat and a third-class city. It is interesting to read that as each building in the town was completed it was used first for a dance and then for a religious meeting before being turned over to the owner.[53]

During the year 1873, Father Mollier, previously mentioned in connection with the Saint Joseph, Concordia, and Clyde missions, ventured into present-day Mitchell County. It is recorded that Holy Mass was first said there in that year. From 1873 to 1877 the Church of Saint John was attended from Saint Joseph as a mission, Father Mollier coming on weekdays every three months. He said Mass in the hall of the Finnigan and Williams store. On Sundays the congregation met in this same place to recite the rosary, sing hymns, and, when possible, to hear Mass.

In 1877 Father Henry Temphaus organized the parish. This same priest served missions in Cawker City and Stockton. Father Temphaus was not only pastor; he was land agent as well and advertised in the German papers in this country and abroad. Within a year or two between thirty-five and forty families settled around Beloit, where land was selling at $600 to $800 a quarter.[54] Father Temphaus was far-sighted and saw possibilities for this north central Kansas location.

This same priest erected in 1878 the first church in Beloit. It measured 84 by 42 feet and was of natural limestone quarried in the vicinity. From 1878 to 1890 the Precious Blood Fathers had charge

[52] *Kenedy's Catholic Directory* (New York, 1947), p. 694. Sister Euphrasia Barth was in charge.

[53] F. W. Blackmar (editor) *Kansas: Encyclopedia of State History ... Institutions ... Counties ... Cities ... Prominent Persons*, 3 vols. (Chicago, 1912), vol. I, p. 171. vol. I, p. 171.

[54] William G. Cutler, *History of Kansas* (Chicago, 1883), p. 1024. Since the publisher of a series of state histories was Mr. A. T. Andreas, this history is often referred to as the *Andreas History of Kansas*.

of Beloit, Osborne, Tipton, Cawker City, and western missions including New Almelo. The first priest of the Precious Blood to work
in this region was the Rev. Frederick Schalk.[55] These priests were
replaced in the diocese in 1890 by secular priests after a misunderstanding about the deeding of church property to the order instead of
to the bishop as provided by Kansas law. Father E. Keiffer, a native
of Strassburg, Germany, who then took charge of the parish, opened
the school taught by the Sisters of Saint Joseph. This was not the first
parochial school in Beloit, however, because as early as 1878 a school
was conducted for fifteen scholars by Mr. R. Hune. In 1883 the
Fathers of the Precious Blood sent for the Sisters of the Precious
Blood of St. Louis who took charge of the school from that time
until the spring of 1889. It was in the fall of that year that Bishop
Scannell replaced them by the Concordia Sisters who have since that
time conducted the parochial grade and later high school.[56]

On August 26, 1889, the *Diary* of Mother Stanislaus Leary contained the following entry: "Sisters Aloysius, Angela, and Madeleine
left for Beloit to take charge of the school."[57] Beloit was destined
to become one of the important missions conducted by the Community. The forty original students were distributed throughout the
grades.

From the time that the Reverend Henry Heitz[58] was sent to
Beloit, the parish began to thrive. This builder's monumental work
was based on his idea of wholehearted cooperation. The farmers were
set to work quarrying stone and in 1901, three years after the coming
of Father Heitz, the foundation of the church was built around the
old foundation. The stone from the old church was used in the walls
of the new one. In 1904 the church, built of native stone and unique
in that it is one of a very few buildings in the United States with
flying buttresses and an entire stone ceiling throughout, was completed. The Sisters' home was built at a cost of $12,000 in 1911. One
of the Sisters recorded this event as follows: "In 1911, while Sister

[55] *Monthly Visitor*, Aug. 15, 1883.
  Kansas Knight, Oct., 1930.
  Northwestern Kansas Register, Nov. 20, 1939.
[56] *Loc. cit.*
[57] *Loc. cit.*
  The *Kansas Catholic* of Sept. 12, 1889, marked the event thus: "Sisters of Nazaret
Convent have taken charge of the school at Beloit, Kansas."
[58] He was born Mar. 16, 1856, died Feb. 7, 1941, and was instrumental in buildin
the group of five buildings.

Regis was attending Institute in Concordia, and some of us were keeping up the music class in Beloit, we had the happy privilege of moving out of the poor little house into what we called 'the little castle' which is now inhabited by our good Sisters. Sister Constantia was most interested in the change."[59] And another Sister wrote: "During my stay in Beloit, the Sisters' Convent was built and four years later the school (1914). The full cooperation of the Altar Society was given in moving from the old convent to the new and they gave us valuable aid in furnishing the convent."[60]

The new school, valued at $20,000, replaced the old one.[61] A high school was opened in 1920; it was accredited in 1925, when four students were graduated.[62] Today the school consists of two hundred and twenty-seven pupils, taught by ten teachers, two of whom are music teachers.[63]

The first mission conducted by the Sisters of Saint Joseph of Concordia outside the State of Kansas was among the French Canadians in the Kankakee Valley of Illinois.[64] At a time when distance meant much and transportation haphazard, it was a courageous venture on the part of the infant organization. There certainly was a frontier in Illinois among the French Canadians of the little hamlet of Saint George, for it was in this very same valley that the great schism of the nineteenth century had taken place when the infamous Chiniquy had flaunted the authority of the Bishop of Chicago and had led thousands of his fellow countrymen out of the Church. This had happened some thirty years before so that when the Sisters of Saint Joseph began their missionary work in St. George there was another generation of French Canadians, some of whom had been permanently weaned away from Catholicism and others whose allegiance to the Church was tinged with pro-Chiniquy sentiments. Ap-

[59] Sister Isabelle Poisson's questionnaire. The author sent detailed questionnaires to the 600 living members of her Community. Much material used in this book is derived from the answers. The questionnaires and replies are in the author's files.

[60] Sister Cornelius Perrault's questionnaire.

[61] *Northwestern Kansas Register,* Nov. 20, 1938.

[62] Sister DePazzi Wynn's questionnaire.

[63] *Kenedy's Catholic Directory* (New York, 1947), p. 695.

[64] Burt. E. Burroughs, *Legends and Tales of Homeland on the Kankakee* (Chicago, 1923), *passim.*

   Diary of Bishop Quarter, First Bishop of the Catholic Church in Chicago as cited by J. J. McGovern in *The Catholic Church in Chicago* (Chicago, 1890), pp. 77, 84, 112, 177.

   Illinois: A Guide, Federal Writers Project (Chicago, 1939), pp. 62, 422.

   New World, Sept. 6, 1940.

parently it was a nationalistic movement which within a short time reached extensive proportions. Such mass movements are largely emotional and spontaneous without much thought or reason. A strong leader makes his cause appear to justify his actions; and, if he has the support of a number of people of standing, he has little difficulty in enlarging his following so that the movement becomes ever greater and the cause a symbol of persecution. It was thus with the ex-priest, Chiniquy. Born in Kamouraska, Canada, July 30, 1809, Charles Paschal Telesphore Chiniquy became a linguist and a mathematician, and later a promoter of the temperance movement in Canada. He had practically the same ideas as the great Irish leader, Father Mathew. Later he was chosen to lead a new and important movement of French Canadians into the Mississippi Valley. There, after having surveyed the land and selected the territory suitable for this immigration, he returned to Canada to lead some 5,000 people to the vicinity of St. Anne, Kankakee, Illinois.

There was considerable communication between Bishop O'Regan and Chiniquy. Rumors spread among the people that they should guard against the perfidious designs of the Irish bishops of Chicago who wanted to discourage and destroy the prosperous French colony. A stern determination was aroused in the people to resist apparent ecclesiastical encroachment. Practically the entire colony of several parishes followed the apostate. Even the pleas of Bishop Duggan, who went there in 1858 only to have the people laugh at him, went unanswered. He pleaded: "My dear French-Canadian friends: I ask you in the name of Jesus Christ, your Savior and mine; in the name of your desolated mothers, fathers and friends who are weeping along the banks of the Saint Lawrence River; I ask it in the name of your beloved Canada . . . ."[65]

It was to Saint George that Sisters Josephine Leary, Antoinette Cuff, and Aurelia Cayer were sent on August 29, 1889.[66] Since only

[65] Charles P. T. Chiniquy, *The Priest, the Woman and the Confessional* (Chicago, 1880), pp. 5-17. A biased account of the movement by its author.

According to the *Catholic Almanac* (New York, 1856), pp. 266 and 306, Chiniquy was pastor of St. Anne's Church and attended Aroma and Momence. Other books by this apostate were *Fifty Years in the Church of Rome and Forty Years in the Church of Christ* (Chicago, 1900). Another book, *Papal Idolatry* (Chicago, 1889), was dedicated to Cardinal Gibbons with the hope that "by its perusal God might enlighten your mind and change your heart."

[66] Leary, *Diary and Book of Records, op. cit.*, book II, p. 114 (Aug. 29, 1889).

Kansas Catholic, Sept. 12, 1889, stated: "A colony of Sisters from Nazareth Convent have gone to the diocese of Chicago to take charge of the St. George French School."

Sister Aurelia was able to teach French, Sister Euphrasia Caron was sent there later to assist in the school.[67] There is a copy extant of the county certificate of Sister Antoinette Cuff which entitled her to teach in the schools of Illinois. As far as can be determined this is the first out-of-state certificate obtained by the Sisters of Saint Joseph of Concordia.[68] The following year there was a reference to the school in a volume published in the Archdiocese of Chicago.[69] The pastor was the Father Joseph LaSage, the priest who was later responsible for the establishment of another mission of Sisters in the Archdiocese of Chicago.

This school in St. George has remained one of the outposts of the Community. In 1913 a high school was opened.[70] In 1921 recognition of the State Board was sought; this recognition was achieved two years later. The district then erected a school building in which was housed the high school and the four upper grades. The lower grades continued to be taught in the convent by a teacher supplied free by the Community.[71] Today the enrollment in the school at Saint George is forty-two, taught by four teachers.[72]

Two other missions were opened in Kansas in the same year as were Clyde and Saint George. Zurich, a small village in Rooks County, was a French-Canadian community settled by migrants from Clyde (who incidentally had come from the Kankakee settlement in Illinois—hence there is an intimate connection between the Illinois and the Cloud and Rooks County, Kansas, missions).[73] Sisters Avila Taillefer and Eulalia Belanger and a postulant, Miss Belere, were assigned to the mission.[74] Father Guillame was pastor; there were about fifty pupils enrolled in a small school. The priest lived in a sod house, and the Sisters had a poor frame house. Due to financial

---

[67] Interview with Mother Antoinette Cuff, July 12, 1947.

[68] Dated Kankakee, Ill., Sept. 9, 1889. It was good for two years and was signed by Fayette S. Hatch, County Superintendent of Schools. A photostat is in the files of the author.

[69] James J. McGovern, *The Catholic Church in Chicago* (Chicago, 1890). A souvenir volume dedicated to Archbishop Feehan in 1890 lists the attendance as: boys, 75; girls, 45.

[70] Questionnaire of Sister Adolphus Maloney.

[71] Questionnaire of Sister Helena Marie Hebert.

[72] *Kenedy's Catholic Directory* (New York, 1947), p. 58.

[73] The names Thibault, Odette, Dandurand, Betourney, Letourneau, Baltazar, Goyette, Custeneau, and Deschon were common to St. George, Aurora, Clyde, St. Joseph, Zurich, and Damar. All these places were "Little Canadas."

[74] Leary, *Diary and Book of Records, op. cit.,* book II, p. 51, Oct. 2, 1889. "Sent Sisters Avila and Eulalia with Mme. Belere [later known as Sister Monica] to open the Zurich school. Went with them as far as Beloit. Expense $15.00."

conditions, the mission was short-lived, closing at the end of the first year of its existence.[75]

Toward the end of 1889, Sisters were sent to Tipton, Mitchell County, Kansas. Settled by a dominantly German group, Tipton became a center in north central Kansas for both Lutheran and Catholic missionary activity. It is interesting to note that this was the first mission (except Abilene) opened since the Sisters of Saint Joseph made their first establishment in Newton, Kansas, which was not to French-speaking peoples. There had been a steady flow of postulants to the Concordia Community from Canada and central Illinois, and naturally there had been more opportunities to open schools in parishes where French-speaking Sisters were needed. However, a number of German Sisters had entered the Community in the late 'Eighties; therefore, when a call came from Tipton, the request was granted. Sister Antoinette Cuff was recalled from St. George to become superior of the new mission. This was the first time Sister Antoinette assumed the responsibility which was to grow with the years—in fact at no time for the next fifty-three years was she without the responsibility of office. Accompanying her were Sisters Alphonsus Corgan, Albina Sontag, and Celestine Wehrle.[76] The pastor was Father J. Abel. The school, named in honor of Saint Boniface, was attended by forty pupils the first year of its existence. The mission was closed from 1892 until 1900 during which time lay teachers were employed to teach the school. Since that time it has been a progressive mission housed in a school building built by the Father Charles Menig and valued at $75,000. The high school is fully accredited by the State Board of Education. In 1947 the two hundred and five students enrolled were taught by six teachers.[77]

In the Diocese of Wichita, another school was opened in 1890. The Newton school was still functioning under the direction of the Concordia Sisters. Two Sisters were sent to Danville, Sisters Angela Costello and Berchmans Gray. The school was closed at the end of four years, primarily because of loss in Catholic population of the town. In addition, the Sisters were needed for other missions which

75 Ibid.
   Sadlier's Catholic Directory (New York, 1890), p. 205.
76 Questionnaire of Mother Antoinette Cuff.
   Kansas Knight, Oct., 1930.
77 Kenedy's Catholic Directory (New York, 1947), p. 696.

were opening at that time.[78] The pastor was Father William Bitter.[79]

On January 29, 1891, Concordia was saddened by the news of the appointment of Bishop Scannell to a broader field of usefulness when Rome transferred him to the vacant See of Omaha. The sentiments of the Daughters of Saint Joseph, who had grown to know and revere him as philosopher, guide, and friend, were well expressed in the words of the Vicar General, the Reverend Joseph Perrier, at the farewell banquet:

... On the eve of your departure from us to a more important field of labor in God's vineyard, we, the priests of the Concordia Diocese, while we must congratulate Your Lordship on your well-earned promotion, respectfully beg to express the deep sorrow with which the separation fills us. During your episcopate among us we have always found you the mild director, the prudent counselor, the untiring cooperator, the faithful friend—in a word the ideal bishop.

You have won the confidence of your priests because you have ever been true to them, as their cares and concerns you have made your own, and you have won the veneration and the gratitude of the faithful committed to your charge by your zeal and care in providing for their wants.

The many church buildings erected and the many congregations organized within the last years in Northwestern Kansas, in all of which work your co-operation and counsel were leading factors, are abundant evidence of the efficiency of your short episcopate.

But Reverend Bishop, we feel your separation from us most of all because of the cordial and happy relations that have uninterruptedly existed between your lordship and every one of us.

In our needs, in our trials and doubts, we could always turn in confidence to our good Bishop, and we found you always accessible and always ready to lend a willing hand.[80]

The policies of the Sisters of Saint Joseph have always had the support of the bishops in whose dioceses the Community has conducted institutions and schools. Bishop Fink tried by every means to maintain the motherhouse of the Sisters in his diocese. Bishop Scannell had much the same attitude. His paternalistic solicitude was shown in letters to Mother Stanislaus Leary while he was Bishop of Concordia,[81] and later when he was Bishop of Omaha to the same

---

[78] Leary, *Diary and Book of Records, op. cit.,* book II, p. 119 (Oct. 1890). Questionnaires of Sisters Eulalia Belanger and Flavian Arpin.

[79] *Hoffman's Catholic Directory* (New York, 1890), pp. 430-431.

[80] *Omaha Bee,* Apr. 10, 1891. The Bishop left Concordia on Apr. 19 and was installed in Omaha on the 11th. *Omaha Bee,* Apr. 11, 12, and 13, also carried articles. *Omaha World-Herald,* Apr. 11 and 13, 1891. Code, *op. cit.,* p. 314.

[81] Letter of the Most. Rev. Richard Scannell, Omaha, to Mother Stanislaus Leary, Oct. 22, 1890. The original is in the Archives of the Nazareth Motherhouse, La Grange, Ill., book II, p. 143; a photostat is in the files of the author.

superior and to her successor, Mother Antoinette Cuff. He arranged to return to Concordia for the reception and profession two months after his removal to Omaha.[82]

As the years passed, his interest in the Community did not diminish although opportunities to visit his old friends were few. In a letter to Mother Antoinette some eighteen or twenty years later, he remarked: ". . . . I hope yourself and the Community are all well and happy. I saw a picture of your new convent and it is really fine. I suppose I should no doubt find many interesting things were I to visit Concordia now, could I only pay it a visit. But I am getting rather old for visits and I travel when I must . . ."[83] And again: "Whoever forgets me, you do not; and there are no friends whom we ought to prize more than the old friends. . . . I hope that you and all the Concordia Sisters are well; and you cannot be better than I wish you to be. . . ."[84]

Another kind friend became associated with the little Community when Bishop Hennessy of Wichita was appointed Administrator of the Diocese of Concordia during the interim between Bishop Scannell's transfer and the appointment of his successor.[85] Due to the unfortunate and untimely death of the Reverend Thaddeus Butler, the day before his consecration as Bishop of Concordia,[86] the interim lasted until the consecration of Bishop John F. Cunningham in 1898. This was a trying period in Kansas history and especially in the history of the Diocese of Concordia. The diocese was on the verge of utter collapse, and many petitions were sent to Rome by the citizens of Concordia and environs praying for the appointment of a bishop. Notwithstanding the advice of the pastor, one hundred and seventy-four families moved from Concordia parish during the bad years occasioned by repeated crop failures. It is estimated that over

[82] Letter of the Most Rev. Richard Scannell, Omaha, to Mother Stanislaus Leary, June 12, 1891. The original is in the Archives of the Nazareth Motherhouse, La Grange, Ill., book II, p. 143; a photostat is in the files of the author.

[83] Letter of the Most Rev. Richard Scannell, Omaha, to Mother Antoinette Cuff, Dec. 22, 1909. The original is in the files of the author.

[84] Letter of the Most Rev. Richard Scannell, Omaha, to Mother Antoinette Cuff, Jan. 2, 1911. The original is in the files of the author.

[85] Code, op. cit., p. 155.

It was through the interest and direction of Bishop Hennessy that his ward, Eva Waller, the future Rev. Mother Mary Rose, third Superior General of the Community, became a candidate in 1891.

[86] "Biographies of the Bishops of Concordia Given," Northwestern Kansas Register, Nov. 20, 1938.

eight thousand people left the diocese which comprised thirty-one counties.[87]

Bishop Hennessy, in spite of the broad expanse of territory under his juridiction, took an interest in the affairs of the Sisters of Saint Joseph of Concordia. He wrote concerning the reception of subjects when he himself could not be present.[88] And in a *Pastoral Letter* he had the Concordia Diocese as much at heart as he did his own Diocese of Wichita. This letter is well worth quoting as it, better than any other description available, explains conditions in Kansas in 1893:

John Joseph, by the grace of God and the Apostolic See, Bishop of Wichita and Administrator of the Diocese of Concordia . . . To the Clergy and Laity of these Dioceses:

. . . We realize the sacrifices you are often obliged to make in this new and sparsely settled country in order to bring the consolations of our holy religion to our people. . . . We take this occasion to express our gratification at the material as well as the spiritual progress which has characterized your work in Western Kansas. . . . Our times are not favorable to a healthy and hearty appreciation of the self-sacrifice and self-restraint which the yoke of Christ demands of those whose happiness it is to bear it. We are surrounded with an atmosphere tainted with the blighting influences of the worst and lowest forms of infidelity and irreligion. Materialism, utilitarianism, and rationalism are the false deities to whom many men offer the homage of their intelligence. . . . Our State of Kansas seems to be prolific of such societies, hence our anxiety to give our people warning not to hastily enter them. The Church does not condemn them by name, and a Catholic finding himself a member of such benevolent organizations is not, on that account, cut off from the Church. . . . Owing to the sparsely settled condition of a large district comprised within our jurisdiction, it is extremely difficult if not impossible to provide for our youth the inestimable privileges of a parochial school. Where the number of Catholics will justify, we look upon the parochial school as an adjunct to the parish church. It is deplorable to witness the defections of our young people whose religious training has been neglected. We cannot impress too strongly upon Catholic parents the conscientious duty of teaching their children the principal doctrines as well as the usual prayers of the Church. The moments they spend in this blessed practice will be the most cherished in their lives. . . . The question of a school to which the child with safety might be sent is the next matter for the consideration of the parents. Naturally if there be a school in charge of conscientious religious teachers there is no reason for anxiety. The parochial school satisfies all the requirements of a conscientious Catholic parent. Such a parent appreciates his obligations to God and His Church and will not hesitate a moment as to what he should do. Where he has no parish school he should select the best that he has, but his own responsibility for the religious educa-

---

[87] Leary, *Diary and Book of Records, op. cit.,* book II, p. 150.
[88] Letter of the Rt. Rev. John J. Hennessy, Wichita, to Mother Stanislaus Leary, Aug. 13, 1891. The original is in the Archives of the Nazareth Motherhouse, La Grange, Ill., book II, p. 144; a photostat is in the files of the author.

tion of his child becomes the graver. No parent, with a right conscience, can but be convinced that his own salvation is bound up with that of his child. The purely secular instruction which is imparted in our State schools will never direct—nor is it intended to direct—any child towards heaven. When a child is deprived by necessity of religious instruction the parent is obliged under pain of sin to supply the defect. . . .

February 11, 1893.   JOHN JOSEPH HENNESSY
                          Bishop of Wichita and Administrator of Concordia [89]

An important and interesting school conducted by the Sisters of Saint Joseph of Concordia was begun in 1891 at Brighton Park, a suburb of Chicago. French Canadians were the first to explore the vicinity of Chicago and to settle it later. As the city grew in the second half of the nineteenth century, many of the French Canadians moved to the outskirts and suburbs of the city, particularly to the village of Brighton Park. Desiring a church of their own, they sought the approbation of Archbishop Patrick A. Feehan. In the fall of 1889 he granted their request. Father Joseph LaSage was appointed pastor of Saint Joseph Church; it was he who had been instrumental in procuring the Sisters of Saint Joseph to conduct the school in Saint George, Illinois, two years earlier. He immediately began to arrange for the same Community to take over the projected parochial school in his new parish. The generosity of his parishoners encouraged Father LaSage in his efforts to organize a complete parochial unit. Convinced of the need for a new school he converted the first church and rectory into a school building and residence for the Sisters. [90]

After the temporary church had been remodeled, Father LaSage invited the Concordia Sisters of Saint Joseph to assume charge of the school. His plans were outlined in a letter which was written in the spring of 1891 to Mother Stanislaus Leary:

> I have received your letter and am pleased with the answer. For the first year I need two Sisters for the teaching, one musician and one for housekeeping as you may choose. This number will not certainly be sufficient for the following years. The Sisters must speak and be able to teach both languages, French and English. They will not receive anything from the board of education; but I guarantee that they shall get as much, *if not more,* as you required for the Sisters at Saint George. In the course of time they shall receive much more. The musician, *if good,* shall certainly get as many pupils as may be desired. You may feel positive that I shall spare nothing to assure the success

[89] Pastoral Letter of John Joseph Hennessey, Bishop of Wichita and Administrator of Concordia, to the Clergy and Laity of these Dioceses.

[90] *Golden Jubilee of St. Joseph and St. Anne Church, 1889-1939,* a commemorative volume (Chicago, 1939), pp. 9-15.

of the Sisters and as you know yourself that the future success of the school depends greatly, if not entirely, on the good foundation of the same, you will give me your very best. There is certainly a bright future for your Community in Chicago and its neighborhood. You have lost your good Bishop but remember that our Archbishop is his best friend. He is well disposed towards your Community and so am I. There I shall make it a duty and a pride for me to help it. Please do not restrain your ambition within the limits of Kansas. The Sisters shall have to be here in the latter part of August to begin school on the first of September. I shall rely on your word, shall I not? For you see there are two other communities that I promised I would give them an answer in the first part of May. We began today the work on the new school. I hope the Sisters in St. George are well and well disposed and presume that the news of this new foundation here in Brighton Park will be agreeable to them.[91]

Again in August he wrote to assure the Sisters that he was expecting them toward the end of the month and asked for definite information as to the date and time of arrival.[92]

The five sisters assigned to Brighton Park were all French-speaking Sisters. The superior was Sister Avila Taillefer and her companions were Sisters Fidelis Gregory, Columba Prive, Jerome Lebonte, and Raphael Cardinal. Father LaSage was later transferred to Aurora, Illinois, and was replaced by Father C. A. Poisson, who continued the improvement of the parish buildings and instituted the devotion to Saint Anne in the parish. In 1908 Father Poisson left to assume the pastorship of Saint George and was replaced by Father LaMarre who, mindful of the sacrifices and inconveniences of the Sisters, purchased the building adjoining the school to serve as a convent. It was remodeled and made ready for the Sisters at the beginning of the school term in 1917. A new school building and an annex have been completed since that time, due largely to the efforts and untiring zeal of the present pastor, Father Louis F. DeCelle.

This parish is widely known as an important shrine of Saint Anne in this country. Several relics of the saint are enshrined in the church. One of these, a piece of the shin bone of Saint Anne, is the largest single relic of the Saint in the United States. It was presented to the shrine by Bishop L'Enfant of the Diocese of Avignon, France.[93]

---

[91] Letter of Father J. C. LaSage to Mother Stanislaus Leary, Apr. 23, 1891. The original is in the Archives of the Nazareth Motherhouse, La Grange, Ill., book II, p. 151; a photostat is in the files of author.

[92] Letter of Father J. C. LaSage to Mother Stanislaus Leary, Aug. 8, 1891. The original is in the Archives of the Nazareth Motherhouse, La Grange, Ill., book II, p. 151; a photostat is in the files of the author.

[93] *Golden Jubilee of St. Joseph and St. Anne Church, Chicago, 1889-1939, op. cit.,* p. 27.

The mission school in Brighton Park, Chicago, has prospered an‹ grown apace down the years. Today with a staff of eighteen Sister there are five hundred and nine students enrolled in the grade an‹ two-year commercial course.[94]

Two other schools were opened that same year in the North, on‹ at Somerset, Wisconsin, and the other at Escanaba, Michigan. Some‹ set is a French-Canadian town in the Diocese of LaCrosse. Fathe‹ J. Riviere was the pastor the first year of its existence during whic‹ seventy-six pupils were enrolled. The first Sisters were Sister Mar‹ Joseph Perrier, superior, and Sisters Evangelist Bonnifield and Agne‹ Savoie.[95] Somerset furnished many vocations to the Sisterhood whil‹ the mission was operated from Concordia. It was impossible to retai‹ the mission later on account of distance; therefore, it was discontinue‹ in 1905.[96]

Escanaba, in the Diocese of Marquette, is in the center of th‹ copper country in the Upper Peninsula of Michigan. It has bee‹ called the "Iron Port of the World." Today it is cosmopolitan i‹ population—Belgians, Germans, Scandinavians, French, Irish, Eng‹ lish, Russians, Austrians, Scotch, and Italians are living side by side— but in 1890 the two dominant groups were the English-speaking an‹ the French-speaking, each of which had its own church. In 1888 th‹ French church, Saint Anne's, was built by Father J. E. Martel.[97] H‹ asked for the Sisters to teach in his school; however, his untimel‹ death two years later left most of associations of the Sisters with hi‹ two successors, Father Peter Menard and Father Jacques. Accordin‹ to the *Catholic Directory* there were three hundred pupils enrolle‹ the first year of the school's existence.[98] Sister Francis Borgia was th‹ first superior and her co-laborers were Sisters Aurelia Cayer, Eulali‹ Belanger, Euphrasia Caron, and Paul Le Cuyer.[99] Escanaba had ‹ thriving population and the school expanded and prospered. In 1922 the Sisters were recalled to Concordia at the request of the Bisho‹ of that place, who wished to use them to more advantage in his ow‹

---

[94] *Kenedy's Catholic Directory* (New York, 1947), p. 51.
[95] Questionnaires of Sisters Evangelist Bonnifield and Agnes Savoie.
[96] *Wiltzius' Catholic Directory* (New York, 1906), p. 591.
[97] Alvah L. Sawyer, *A History of the Northern Peninsula of Michigan and I‹ People*, 3 vols. (Chicago, 1911), vol. I, p. 371.
    Walter R. Nursery, *The City of Escanaba, Michigan* (Escanaba, 1890), pp. 2‹ 33-35.
[98] *Sadlier's Catholic Directory* (New York, 1892), pp. 327-328.
[99] Questionnaires of Sisters Aurelia Cayer and Eulalia Belanger.

diocese.[100] It is interesting to note that at the time she became Mother General of the Community, Sister Antoinette Cuff was superior at Escanaba.[101]

Another school was opened in 1891 in North Platte, Nebraska, a town in Lincoln County in the Diocese of Omaha, situated at the forks of the North and South Platte Rivers.[102] North Platte was the home of the famous Colonel William Cody, otherwise known as "Buffalo Bill." His daughter, Irma Cody, was a student at the Sisters' school.[103] The first Sisters were Sisters Francis Joseph Leary, superior, Alphonsus Corgan, Madeleine Perry, and Antoinette Cuff.[104] The Reverend Michael O'Toole was pastor.

A series of articles in the local paper showed the community interest in the new school. The following article was written by one of the pupils in the second year of the school's existence:

September 8, 1891, saw our school first opened, and the Feast of the Blessed Virgin Mary occuring [sic] on this day, it was named "Nativity Convent School."

The Sisters of Saint Joseph who have charge of it were sent to us from Concordia, Kansas, at the request of our Right Reverend Bishop. The school building is situated on Fourth Street in the eastern part of the city on North Platte. It has a very pleasant location, being east of the church and west of the Sisters' residence. There are two school rooms in the old church building and one adjoining the convent. The primary department is presided over by Sister Mary Alphonsus, the secondary by Sister Katherine, and the seniors in the room adjoining the convent by Sister Superior Antoinette. There are about one hundred and twenty pupils in our school. We have a library filled with a choice collection of very interesting and instructive books as well as maps, blackboards and everything requisite to make the time spent here very pleasant. Our composition class is made up of several very lovely girls; our instructress, Sister Madeleine, is also in charge of the music class, consisting of about forty pupils. Friday afternoon we have a class meeting for the purpose of being instructed

---

100 *Kenedy's Catholic Directory* (New York, 1922), p. 459, lists the enrollment in 1921-22 as 370 pupils.

101 Questionnaire of Mother Antoinette Cuff.

102 *Nebraska: A Guide*, Federal Writers' Project (Lincoln, 1939), pp. 211-216.

Archibald R. Adamson, *North Platte and Its Associations* (Lincoln, 1910), pp. 76-77.

Ira L. Bare and William H. McDonald (eds.), *An Illustrated History of Lincoln County, Nebraska, and Her People*, 2 vols. (Chicago, 1920), vol. I, pp. 151-152, 209-260.

103 Wilhelm Stolley, *Geschicte der Ersten Ansiedlung von Hall County im Nebraska von 1859 mit Anhang bis zum Jahre 1907* (Omaha, 1907), p. 5. About this time it was suggested that the national capital be moved to the central part of the United States. North Platte was considered as a likely site.

104 Sister Antoinette Cuff joined the group in November, 1891. She became local superior the following year and remained there until 1895 when she was sent to Monett, Mo., to open the first foundation of the Sisterhood there.

Questionnaire of Mother Antoinette Cuff.

in the theory of music. Twice a week we have drawing and on the same days our pastor, Father O'Toole, teaches us Latin.[105]

No tribute paid to the Sisters of Saint Joseph was more sincere or more complimentary than the one which the editor of the local newspaper paid in June, 1892, after he had witnessed the first closing exercises:

> On June 8 in the Keith Opera House at North Platte, Nebraska, the children of the Nativity School gave us an intellectual treat, the like of which one can seldom have the pleasure of enjoying. The audience was large and its almost continuous applause was a certificate of success to the performers, and a thorough endorsement of the efficiency of the zealous Sisters who had charge of the school for the past ten months.
>
> When you stand before a well-formed statue, or beautiful painting, there will, perhaps, arise in your mind a grand association of ideas. You can turn from the statue to the quarry and see the shapeless block, just hewn rough from the rock. But gradually the skilled sculptor plies the mallet and chisel until the statue comes forth in all its beauty and perfection. So, too, you can conceive the various paints and the canvas resting in a kind of chaos until the trained artistic mind orders the parts and guides the graceful pencil—and the picture is produced.
>
> A very analogous association of ideas arose in my mind while I gladly enjoyed the sayings and doings, yea, the every movement of the above-mentioned children on the stage. From the beautiful picture before me my mind was carried back to one year ago, when these same children, in part, on a certain occasion caused much pain by their wildwest rudeness. A grand material for zeal and efficiency to work upon!! But is it possible that such a change has come over these children? YES!! The Sisters of Saint Joseph became the sculptors of their hearts, the artists of their characters, and the pleasure which they afforded by their closing exercises cast a pall of oblivion over the past and bids their friends rejoice and wish them continued success; for all was creditable beyond expectation, praiseworthy beyond limit. Their successful closing exercises have concluded a successful year; and may a pleasant vacation be the lot of those good Sisters whose untiring zeal has made the Nativity School at North Platte second to none of its kind in the State of Nebraska.[106]

This commendation, beautifully couched, could well repay any inconvenience which attended the labors of the Sisters. Here is a concrete instance of a *frontier* where there was a *need* and how within a short year the cultural acquisition displayed by the pupils met with general acclaim. This may serve as an example of the expansion of the frontier of culture and correct living carried on by the Sisters from the northern climes of Michigan, through Illinois, Nebraska, and Kansas in 1891. At a later date, the local paper again marked the presentation of another program by the pupils at the close of which

[105] *North Platte News*, undated.
[106] *Ibid.*, June, 1892.

Colonel Cody arose and congratulated the pupils and the Sisters on their work.[107]

Four years after the arrival of the Sisters in North Platte, six young ladies were graduated from the high school.[108]

There was a misunderstanding in 1902 concerning the salaries of the Sisters and the Motherhouse of Concordia recalled them to be used elsewhere. The situation was lamented. When a new pastor was appointed to North Platte, he requested the return of the Sisters on a salary rather than on a tuition basis. However, in the meantime, other missions had been opened leaving no Sisters available for the mission which had recently been closed. It is regrettable that this successful school was discontinued.[109]

One of the most picturesque ventures of the Community occurred in 1891 when, at the request of Mother Katherine Drexel, the Sisters of Saint Joseph of Concordia took charge of the Indian Mission at St. Stephens, Wyoming.

Bishop James O'Connor, Vicar Apostolic of Nebraska, in the jurisdiction of which Wyoming was included, had been instrumental in re-establishing the Jesuits in the missions among the Arapho and the Shoshoni Indians in Fremont County, Wyoming. The authorities of the Jesuit Order had then sent Father Paul Ponziglione, whose work among the Osages of Kansas has been touched upon, to take over these Indian missions in June, 1886. Father Ponziglione shortly after his arrival began to build a large brick house to be used as a convent for the education of Indian girls. In September, 1886, Father Ponziglione had been replaced by Father Francis Kuppens in order that the former might return to Kansas on account of his health. It became necessary to raze the building intended for a convent because the location chosen was sandy and insecure. It had been at this time that Katherine Drexel of Philadelphia became markedly interested in the Indian and Negro missions, and St. Stephen's was one of the first projects she sponsored. In January, 1889, the Sisters of Charity of Leavenworth had taken charge of the school only to withdraw in 1890.[110] The next pastor, Father Ignatius Panken, invited the Sisters of Saint Joseph to replace them.

107 *Ibid.*, Jan., 1893.
108 *Ibid.*, June, 1895. Among the students were William Jeffers, later president or the Union Pacific Railroad, and his wife, Lena Schutz Jeffers.
109 Questionnaire of and interview with Mother Antoinette Cuff, Aug. 1942.
110 Gilbert J. Garraghan, *The Jesuits in Middle United States,* 3 vols. (New York, 1938), vol. III, pp. 512-516.

On February 12, 1891, Katherine Drexel had forsaken the world and pronounced her vows, dedicating not only her wealth but also herself to the sacred cause of Christian education. She founded the Sisters of the Blessed Sacrament whose work was to be among the Indians and Negroes. Mother Katherine was interested in the mission of St. Stephen's but she had no Sisters prepared to take charge at this time as her first Sisters had just been received. Therefore, she began a correspondence with Mother Stanislaus Leary relative to this project. Mother Katherine visited the Sisters in Concordia and spent several days there making arrangements whereby she would pay the salaries of the Concordia Sisters of Saint Joseph if they would teach the school until such time as she was able to furnish teachers herself.[111]

Bishop Scannell, shortly after his transfer to Omaha, referred to the matter:

. . . about the Indian Mission. After you have a talk with Mother Katherine and have learned more about the circumstances you will be better able to decide what to do. I really know so little about the matter that I feel I ought not to give any advice. . . .[112]

In a letter written a short time after Mother Katherine's visit to the Motherhouse in Concordia, Father Panken said in part:

I have just received a letter from Mother Katherine Drexel, giving particulars about your Sisters taking the Mission of St. Stephen's. We are gathering in the crops—alfalfa hay is being cut—oats is [sic] nearly ripe. Over 500 bushels of potatoes, beets, onions, salad, and tomatoes—well, about 800 head of cabbages and turnips also—thirty head of cattle are around the mission, the rest on the prairies have to be brought in here. The Indians are well disposed towards the Sisters. I trust you have gotten my letter explaining the manner of traveling. . . . The house is fifty by fifty-five, three stories high—a substantial building in brick, rock foundation. Mother Katherine has explained how many Sisters can be usefully employed here. The priest's house is half a mile away from the Convent, but Mother Katherine will build a new one. Please let us know soon the day of starting and by what route. . . .[113]

The government had set aside a reservation in St. Stephens, or Lander as it was also called, which contained a depot of supplies

---

111 Interview with Mother Antoinette Cuff, Aug. 1942.

112 Letter of the Most Rev. Richard Scannell, Omaha, to Mother Stanislaus Leary, July 31, 1891. The original is in the Archives of the Nazareth Motherhouse, La Grange, Ill., book II, p. 141; a photostat is in the files of the author.

113 Letter of Father Ignatius Panken, S.J., to Mother Stanislaus Leary, Aug. 4, 1891. The original is in the Archives of the Nazareth Motherhouse, La Grange, Ill., book I, p. 72; a photostat is in the files of the author.

for the Indians, a church, a general trading store, a post office, and a school for the Indian children.[114]

Bishop Maurice F. Burke was the ordinary of the newly created Diocese of Cheyenne.[115] There was a difference between St. Stephen's Indian School, conducted by the Sisters of Saint Francis, and St. Stephen's Boarding School for Indians, conducted by the Sisters of Saint Joseph of Concordia.[116] Sisters Teresa Costello, superior, Angela Costello, Julia Long, and Appolonia Rogan were the original band of Sisters to work among the Indians.[117]

An undated letter from Mother Katherine Drexel gives information concerning the hardships and details about the arrangement with Mother Stanislaus:

> It is a comfort to know that your Sisters have succeeded in inducing the greater portion of the Indian children to return to school.
> I would have enclosed at least a partial payment of the Sisters' salaries, but on looking over the account I find I have only entered the sum previously paid, the terms of the agreement, rate of salary and number of Sisters—I neglected to enter and in consequence have forgotten what I promised last summer. Will you be kind enough to let me know as soon as possible? Do you think they will need more Sisters for St. Stephen's? As the pupils still are coming I thought perhaps they might be a great source of anxiety to you.
> Trusting everything will work together for the great glory of God, I am....[118]

It appears that Mother Stanislaus Leary did worry about the welfare of the Sisters to such an extent that in a few years she closed the agreement with Mother Katherine Drexel. About the same time the Sisters of Concordia were in correspondence with Father William Ketcham, Muskegee, Indian Territory, concerning the possibility of working among the Quapaws on a reservation there. These missions were also financed by Mother Katherine Drexel. Nothing came of

---

[114] J. T. Norton, *The Resources of Fremont County, Wyoming* (Lander, Wyo., 1891), pp. 3, 18. Two works of this same region which are worth reading are Frank R. Hebard, *Wasakie: An Account of the Indian Resistance to the Covered Wagon and the Union Pacific Invasions of Their Territory* (Chicago, 1885) ; Leroy Hafen and F. M. Young, *Fort Laramie and the Pageant of the West* (Glendale, Calif., 1938), p. 313.

[115] This diocese and Concordia were created in 1887.

[116] *Sadlier's Catholic Directory* (New York, 1892), p. 216; (1893), pp. 222, 544; (1894), p. 233.

[117] Interview with Mother Antoinette Cuff, Aug. 1942.

[118] Letter of Mother Katherine Drexel, Torresdale, Pa., to Mother Stanislaus Leary, undated (from all indications sometime in the summer of 1892). The original is in the Archives of the Nazareth Motherhouse, La Grange, Ill., book II, p. 143; a photostat is in the files of the author.

the correspondence as far as the establishment of missions there was concerned.[119]

Herndon, a small parish in northwestern Kansas, was settled by Catholics of Hungarian descent. Early in its history there was a division in the parish and, finally in 1892, after much controversy concerning the location of the church, Father Bitter was sent by order of the Administrator of the Diocese, Bishop Hennessy, to take charge of the congregations. He consolidated the so-called west and town congregations into one parish; and, in order that no further strife occur, he removed the northwest church to Herndon and converted it into a Catholic school. He later built a convent and invited the Sisters of Saint Joseph to take charge. Sisters Aurelia Cayer and Mary John Kuebler were the first Sisters to work in Herndon. From January, 1895, until September, 1897, the Sisters did not conduct the school; during this interim Father Heiman, the pastor, Miss Mary Scheitz, Miss Rosa Heiman, and the Precious Blood Sisters from Ruma, Illinois, taught the school. In 1897, Sisters Boniface Bachle and Alcantara Stenger reassumed charge. Again, from 1904 until 1908 the Sisters gave up the school. In the latter year when it reopened, Sisters Celestine Wehrle, Annunciata Steichen, Vincent Breth, and Scholastica Marinier were missioned there.[120]

Today different nationalities besides the original Hungarian comprise the parish school at Herndon. There are children of German, Irish, and Bohemian descent as well attending the school. The sixty-nine pupils are taught by three teachers.[121]

Also in 1892 another far northern mission opened at New Richmond, Wisconsin. Father Walter Fardy was pastor and Sister Josephine Leary superior. Sisters Louise Cuff, Berchmans Gray, Constance Ryan, and Amelia Fitzgibbon were co-workers. One hundred and eighty pupils enrolled in the school in its first year; however, on account of distance and of inconveniences of travel routes, the mission was closed in 1895.[122]

The following year, the Community saw fit to discontinue the

119 Letter of Father W. H. Ketcham, Muskegee, I.T., to Mother Stanislaus Leary, Jan. 13, 1893. The original is in the Archives of the Nazareth Motherhouse, La Grange, Ill., book II, p. 7; a photostat is in the files of the author.

120 Capuchin Fathers, *Some Early History of the Pioneer Catholic Settlers and Parishes of Northwestern Kansas*, souvenir booklet (Herndon, 1913), *passim*.

121 *Kenedy's Catholic Directory* (New York, 1947), p. 695.

122 *Sadlier's Catholic Directory* (New York, 1892), p. 302; (1893), p. 316; (1895), p. 324.

mission at Newton in the Diocese of Wichita, which was later re-opened by the Sisters of Saint Joseph of Wichita. The beginnings of the Sisters of Saint Joseph have been traced to their humble cottage in Newton and from thence throughout the Middle West, and the Concordia Sisters remember with regret the withdrawal from New-ton, the cradle of the Community in Kansas; however, they are thankful that the Sisters of the Wichita Community are in charge of the school.

Grand Island, Nebraska, has been another important frontier post of the Sisters of Saint Joseph of Concordia. The field was cul-tivated by the famous Father DeSmet, S.J., who ministered to the Indians of the Platte and Upper Missouri regions. The original set-tlers of Hall County were Irish—Pat and Alex Moore, who were later joined by their brother-in-law, a Mr. O'Brien. A large number of Irish settled in the region and seemed to have prospered from the beginning. Soon Germans moved into the vicinity, and they too found Nebraska to their liking and economic advancement.[123]

The city of Grand Island was within the jurisdiction of the Dio-cese of Omaha in 1893 and again it was the good friend of the Sisters, Bishop Scannell, who was instrumental in introducing them into this promising location. The pastor, Father W. Wolf, whose name is indelibly associated with the growth of the parish and es-pecially of the school, wrote to Mother Stanislaus for Sisters.

The first letters are missing, but one written just before school opened is interesting:

Since the public schools of our town will open on September 11th, I thought that it would be the best way for us to commence on the same day. Besides, this is Reunion Week [Soldiers' Reunion] and our ladies are running a dining hall on the Reunion grounds and the cleaning of the house and school and the furnishing of the same had to be somewhat neglected and delayed so that we could not be ready before the 11th. You may send the Sisters most any time when suitable to you and they will find accommodations even if the house should not be entirely in order. Of course they should arrive at least two or three days before the eleventh. We will find a young lady for housework alright.[124]

[123] A. F. Buechler and R. J. Barr, History of Hall County, Nebraska (Lincoln, 1920), p. 14.
    Nebraska: A Guide, Federal Writer's Project (Lincoln, 1939), pp. 114, 162-166. In 1859 a gold hunter from Colorado passing through set fire to the grass because he hated the Germans. All houses but one burned. Omaha citizens raised money to help rebuild Grand Island. It was named after the French "La Grande Ile."
    [124] Letter of Father W. Wolf, Grand Island, Nebr., to Mother Stanislaus Leary, Aug. 29, 1893. The original is in the Archives of the Nazareth Motherhouse, La Grange, Ill., book II, p. 12; a photostat is in the files of the author.

And again a few weeks later:

I have visited the school in North Platte several times and I have always admired the system and success of your Sisters in that school.

I shall help the Sisters here all I can but I shall leave to them—and to you as you advise them—the complete control of the school. I prefer the "graded system" too.[125]

Four Sisters were sent from Concordia with Sister Eugenie Gravelle as superior. One hundred and eighteen pupils were enrolled.[126] Grand Island became a stopping-over place for the Sisters bound for the other Nebraska missions, when they could not reach their destinations in one day due to train inconveniences.[127]

A standard high school was added in 1908, making the parochial unit one of the most up to date and progressive in that part of the state.[128] The creation of the Diocese of Grand Island in 1917 raised the school to the dignity of a cathedral school. Today there are four hundred and thirty-four enrolled in the school taught by thirteen Sisters.[129]

A strong German settlement in Sedgwick County extended almost fifty miles from the location of the original settlement, St. Marks. This happened in a peculiar way and the manner of its extension was unique. The original settlers bought nearby land for their children as they grew up or as their friends and relatives came from the old country. It was only a question of time before the two colonies became united by crowding out in-between settlers, and the entire territory was one dominated by German influence. "You can tell the strides taken in the progress of the colony by the churches built."[130] Sisters Aurelia Cayer and Amelia Fitzgibbon were sent to Saint Marks in 1893.[131] The Reverend B. Schmiehausen was the pastor. The mission closed in 1897.

Again Bishop Scannell interceded for the Sisters to work in his diocese:

Father Müller, who met your Sisters at the depot here a few days ago,

---

[125] Letter of Father W. Wolf to Mother Stanislaus Leary, Sept. 2, 1893. The original is in the Archives of the Nazareth Motherhouse, La Grange, Ill., book II, p. 15; a photostat is in the files of the author.
[126] *Sadlier's Catholic Directory* (New York, 1894), p. 376.
[127] Questionnaire of Sister Isabelle Poisson.
[128] Questionnaire of Sister Lucy LaSage.
[129] *Kenedy's Catholic Directory* (New York, 1947), p. 468.
[130] "Big Western Kansas Land," *Kansas City Star*, Nov. 19, 1904.
    Wichita Daily Eagle, Aug., 1904.
[131] Questionnaire of Sister Aurelia Cayer.

asks me to write to you on his behalf. He has built a new school, but now he cannot find any Sisters to take charge. The congregation is entirely German. It is an important one, though the settlement is quite new, and I think it will soon be one of the most important in the diocese. He agrees, I believe, to pay the regular salary besides what the Sisters may get from boarding some of the children. I shall be glad if you can come to his relief.[132]

Then later:

Father Müller is becoming uneasy about his school. I hope you will manage to take that school next September. Send him one German-speaking and two English. I think you will do well in accepting as he will pay the Sisters a regular salary, and as there is a good future before that part of Nebraska. Please let me know what you decide to do.[133]

The school mentioned was in Petersburg (Raeville P.O.), Boone County, Nebraska. In reference to the qualifying examinations necessary before a teacher could teach in the Omaha Diocese, Bishop Scannell wrote Mother Stanislaus:

The examiners of the School Board of the Diocese cannot very conveniently go to Concordia at present. They will however send, in a day or two, a list of questions to Father Perrier with a request that he propose them to those Sisters who may need certificates. They will answer all the questions in writing and then give their papers properly signed to Father Perrier who will send them to Omaha. The Sisters need not worry about the examination.[134]

The original Sisters included: Sisters Josephine Leary, superior, Berchmans Gray, Amelia Fitzgibbon, and Celestine Wehrle. One hundred and twenty children were enrolled that year. This mission was a little longer-lived then some of the others of the period. It was closed in 1907.[135]

Two missions opened for a few months each were Hammond, Wisconsin, from January until June in 1894, and Sandusky, Ohio, a short time also. Sisters Francis Joseph Leary, Amelia Fitzgibbon, and Isidore Burns were the only Sisters who worked on the frontier of Hammond. In Sandusky, conditions were anti-Catholic and inadequate for the simple needs of the Sisters. Sisters Angela Costello, Barbara Gunther, and Innocentia Brennan took charge.

[132] Letter of the Rt. Rev. Richard Scannell, Omaha, to Mother Stanislaus Leary, June 20, 1893. The original is in the Archives of the Nazareth Motherhouse, La Grange, Ill., book II, p. 19; a photostat is in the files of the author.
[133] Letter of the Rt. Rev. Richard Scannell, Omaha, to Mother Stanislaus Leary, July 18, 1893. The original is in the Archives of the Nazareth Motherhouse, La Grange, Ill., book II, p. 13; a photostat is in the files of the author.
[134] Letter of the Rt. Rev. Richard Scannell, Omaha, to Mother Stanislaus Leary, Aug. 21, 1893. The original is in the Archives of the Nazareth Motherhouse, La Grange, Ill., book II, p. 14; a photostat is in the files of the author.
[135] Questionnaires of Sisters Evangelist Bonnifield, Raymond Wagner, Mechtildis Yoos, Lawrence Trudell, Juliana Yoos, Cornelius Perrault, and Anacletus Wenk.

At the junction of the Saint Louis and Texas Railroad with the Frisco, is Monett, Barry County, Missouri. Originally it was named Billings, later Plymouth, and finally Monett.[136] Monett, therefore, was a railroad center settled largely by Irish Catholics. The first resident pastor was Father Bernard Zell, O.S.B., from New Subiaco Abbey in Arkansas. Father Zell was responsible for the beginning of the school. In August, 1894, he bought lots adjoining the church property and arranged to build a school, believing that a parish without a school is like a home without a mother. In September, 1895, he opened the school with the Sisters of Saint Joseph of Concordia as teachers. The first Superior was Sister Antoinette Cuff, who was assisted in teaching the school by Sisters Regis Schwenzer, Raphael Cardinal, and Justina Belisle.[137] One hundred pupils were enrolled.[138] The school is still taught by the Sisters of Saint Joseph.

An undated newspaper carried an article on the school in its first year:

The building accommodates over one hundred pupils and is always full to its utmost capacity. The school is in charge of the Sisters of Saint Joseph of Concordia, Kansas, and its remarkable success is almost entirely due to their ability as educators and the earnest effort employed in their work.

The superior is Venerable Sister Mary Antoinette, first teacher, while Venerable Sister Mary Regis is second teacher. Besides, there are Sister Mary Justina, assistant teacher and Sister Raphael, who teaches music exclusively, including organ and piano. All Monett is proud of the existence of this grand institution and a great deal of good followed immediately in the wake of its founding.

The school besides being an excellent educational institution looks carefully to see the eternal welfare of its pupils and morally it has been of incalculable value to Monett. Our people regardless of religious creeds unite in wishing this school continued prosperity and the noble ones who have it in charge abundant success in their good work.

Each and all extend to the Sisters our heartfelt thanks for the good they have wrought during their short stay among us and may God always bless their efforts in the future as He has done in the past is the prayer of all.[139]

A new residence for the Sisters was built in 1913. A high school, established during the pastorate of the Father P. J. Kilkenney, was discontinued in 1929 when the enrollment did not justify the expense

---

[136] *History of Newton, Lawrence, Barry . . . Counties, Missouri* (Chicago, 1888), pp. 691-692.
[137] Questionnaire of Mother Antoinette Cuff.
[138] *Hoffman's Catholic Directory* (New York, 1896), p. 349.
  "Local Hospital Chaplain Founded Monett Parish," *Kansas City Catholic Register,* Aug. 6, 1925.
[139] *Monett Times,* May, 1896.

and number of teachers necessary to enable the school to uphold the former standards. The grade school still continues however, and there are now sixty-four students enrolled, taught by four Sisters.[140] In 1939, the old school house in which the pioneer band of Sisters taught was torn down, and a residence was remodeled for the school. The convent was renovated in 1940 through the efforts of the pastor, Father D. T. Murphy.[141]

The first venture into the Southwest was also short-lived. Sisters were sent to Paris, Texas, in 1895. Sisters Josephine Leary, Florence Sullivan, Bernardine Vail, and Edmund Beaufort comprised the mission band. There was a devastating fire in Paris that year, and the Sisters' school and residence burned. They were obliged to live with seculars for two weeks. There was no insurance on the parish buildings and no thought of rebuilding; therefore, the Sisters were withdrawn.[142]

Some of the same Sisters were then transferred to another Texas town, Gainesville, which move also was short-lived. Sister Francis Joseph Leary was in charge, assisted by Sisters Bernardine Vail, Florence Sullivan, Edmund Beaufort, and Robertine Byrne.[143]

Clay Center, Clay County, was considered the "Banner Country" of the Golden Belt region of Kansas. A railroad center, it promised a bright future. The first Catholic Church was established there in 1877 by Father J. Pichler.[144] Almost twenty years later, in the fall of 1896, the Sisters went there with Sister Aurelia Cayer as superior, Father Power as pastor. Six years later the mission was closed due to some misunderstanding concerning salaries.[145]

[140] *Kenedy's Catholic Directory* (New York, 1947), p. 518.

[141] Questionnaires of Mother Antoinette Cuff, Sisters Regis Schwenzer, Isabelle Poisson, Joseph Marie Viau, Joseph Patricia Hagan, and Christopher Reiter.

[142] Questionnaire of Sister Bernardine Vail. There was an entry in the *Diary* of Mother Stanislaus Leary, book II, July 10, 1896, p. 180, which stated that the note made by the Sisters who borrowed money from the National Bank of Paris, Texas, to the amount of $124.00 had been paid in full. No doubt this money was borrowed after the fire.

[143] Questionnaire of Sister Bernardine Vail.
      There is a picture extant of the pupils of Gainesville with their teachers, Sisters Bernardine, Edmund, and Florence.

[144] Cutler, *op. cit.*, p. 1314.
      Good description of Clay Center in *The Great Northwest: Most Successful Farming Region in Kansas—Clay Center*, (Clay Center, Kans., 1888), p. 22.

[145] Questionnaires of Sisters Aurelia Cayer and Bernardine Vail. It is interesting to note that Sister Mary Rose Waller, later third Mother General of the Community, spent her only years of missionary life at Clay Center. She was music teacher in the Academy until the time of her election as Mother Superior.

Two northern missions, Norway and Lake Linden, Michigan, began their work in parochial education in 1896. Norway was under the spiritual jurisdiction of the Diocese of Marquette with the Reverend Charles Langner as pastor. Sisters Ursula Kielty, superior, Delphine Lemieux, Blanche Painchaud, Gertrude Green, and Mary John Kuebler were the pioneer Sisters in Norway. In February, 1900, the mission closed.

The mission, opened at Lake Linden in the Upper Peninsula of Michigan in 1896, is still under the direction of the Sisters of Saint Joseph. Situated in Houghton County in the heart of the Copper Country, Lake Linden has had a picturesque and varied history. The settlement was organized in 1868, the year following the opening of the first Calumet and Hecla Stamp Mill. The first organized church, named in honor of Saint Joseph, was that established by the French Canadians in 1871.[146]

Early in the history of the parish, there was interest in providing a parochial school. The first parochial school was opened in improvised quarters in 1881 with seventy pupils enrolled in charge of Madame (Adeline Gareau) Pierre Pichette. The following year the attendance almost doubled. In 1885, a real school was erected and the Sisters of the Holy Cross from Notre Dame, Indiana, took charge. In 1889, they gave up the school which was then taught by five lay teachers until the religious community of the Sisters of Jesus and Mary from Montreal accepted it for a period of two years when there was a change in administration.

In 1896, the Sisters of Saint Joseph of Concordia took charge and, as the jubilee book of the parish proclaims, "a new era began."[147] The Reverend Paul Datin was instrumental in procuring the Sisters who were already well known in the Upper Peninsula because of the successful schools then in operation elsewhere. Sister Mary Anne Picard was appointed superior.[148] There were several sisters selected for this mission, most of whom were of French descent: Sisters Flavian Arpin, Justina Belisle, Edmund Beaufort, Mary Martha Christin, Lorretta Gosselin, Evarista Lapine, Anastasia Roy, and Ger-

---

[146] Alvah L. Sawyer, *A History of the Northern Peninsula of Michigan and Its People*, 3 vols. (Chicago, 1911), vol. III, pp. 488-489.

[147] *Noces d'Or de la Paroisse Saint Joseph, Lake Linden, Michigan, 1871-1921*, (Lake Linden, Mich., 1921), jubilee pamphlet.

[148] Questionnaires of Sisters Flavian Arpin, Evarista Lapine, Anastasia Roy, Armand St. Onge, and Concordia Dumas.

maine Fournier (a postulant).[149] In 1930, the convent and school burned, and a new combination of school-convent was erected, which is an outstanding example of the latest architectural and educational developments.[150]

A unique experience was that of Saint Anne's School in 1935-36 when it was made a public school. An Associated Press article concerning this test case before the Michigan Legislature is worth quoting:

LANSING, January 17.—A proposal to extend primary school fund aid to parochial, denominational and private schools is included in a bill submitted today to the lower house of the Michigan legislature by Representative Drystra.

Representative Drystra said the depression has brought about a crisis in many parochial schools which will have to close unless state aid is extended. If they should close, he pointed out, the expense of public school education would be increased substantially. Public school boards, he explained, would have to erect more school buildings. The alternative, he argued, is to contribute to the maintenance of the parochial and private schools.

Representative Drystra believes that the bill will stand a constitutional test, citing as authority an opinion of the Illinois Supreme Court which holds that when state moneys are expended for educational purposes in less amount than actual costs of education, the state is benefited to such an extent as to deny any charge of expenditures for religious education solely.

The Drystra Bill provided that the aid extended shall not exceed one-sixth of the school's total financial requirements.

Representative Drystra is not a Catholic.[151]

A fuller history of this test case was given in Catholic newspapers throughout the country:

LAKE LINDEN, Michigan—(NC).—As a consequence of the economic depression the pastor of St. Joseph's parish here found himself on the verge of closing his parochial school. When matters were at their worst, in the summer of 1935, he appealed to the local school board for aid, saying that, if help were not given, the parochial school would be closed and his 250 pupils would have to be cared for by the local public school system.

It happened that the school board was not in a position to accommodate the children in their schools. As a result they came to an understanding with the pastor. The parochial school would be taken over by the school board for use but the Sisters would be retained as teachers. The school board would pay the salaries, would furnish heat, electric light, books, etc., as was provided in the regular public schools. To satisfy the State Department of Education, religious instruction would be taught outside of regular school hours.

As an emergency measure, the pastor received permission from the Most

---

149 *Noces d'Or de la Paroisse Saint Joseph, Lake Linden, Michigan, 1871-1921,* op. cit., p. 21.
150 Questionnaire of Sister Eveline Fraser.
151 Questionnaire of Sister Frances Clare Garvey.
Kansas City Star, Jan. 17, 1935.

Reverend Joseph C. Plagens, Bishop of Marquette, to accept this arrangement. It was accepted later by the two neighboring parishes which found themselves in the same predicament.

After a year's experiment the plan, it was stated, seems to have worked to the advantage of all. Financially the school was saved. The school board met all of the expenses, which amounted to almost $5000. The pastor, being saved from this burden, was able to pay off a debt on fuel for the school which was due from the previous year. He had his regular catechetical instructions immediately after Mass before the opening of school but was free to visit the school for additional instruction at any time. It is true that the crucifixes were taken down from the walls but religious pictures, considered as works of art, took their place and standing crucifixes were provided for each Sister's desk.

There was no interference on the part of the school board as regards discipline or curriculum of studies. Only the pastor's own pupils frequented the school. The superintendent visited the school at intervals during the year and his representative occasionally examined the children. The only change in the staff of teachers at the end of the year was the removal of those Sisters who did not have the qualifications required by the State.

The present ordinary has given his approval to the continuance of the arrangement which in the present instance causes no grave compromise and gives the people a share in the education funds raised by their taxes. In his opinion "the Catholic school has a right in justice to receive state financial aid which is raised by taxes. . . . Where such aid is offered and there is no interference in religious matter by the state school authorities it should be accepted." [152]

Lake Linden is a thriving school today with one hundred and sixty-four pupils taught by eleven Sisters. [153]

A school was opened in 1896, in Saint Libory, Nebraska, a village not far from Grand Island. Sister Stephanie Kunz and Sister Helen Zimmerman were the pioneer Sisters in Saint Libory. There is a record in the *Diary* of Mother Stanislaus concerning these Sisters. [154] During the first of its two-year existence there were seventy pupils in attendance. [155] However, the influence exercised on a frontier must not be judged by the length of time a school remained in operation.

In 1898, Sisters Angela Costello, superior, Helen Zimmerman, and Alcantara Stenger went to Olyen, Colfax County, Nebraska, in the Diocese of Omaha to conduct a school. The following year the school was closed due to the inability of the Community to supply an organist as was requested by the pastor, Father V. End. This matter was the occasion for a letter from Bishop Scannell to the new Mother General in the fall of 1899 when he thanked her for supply-

152 *New World*, Jan. 24, 1935.
153 *Kenedy's Catholic Directory* (New York, 1947), p. 562.
154 *Loc. cit.*, Aug. 27, 1896.
155 Questionnaire of Sister Walburga Wuerth, Superior when it closed. Questionnaire of Sister Helen Zimmerman.

ing an organist for that year and stated that the pastor would provide one for the following year. When none was provided, the Sisters were withdrawn.[156]

Two missions in Illinois, one in L'Erable and the other at Saint John the Baptist parish in Chicago, were supplied wtih Sisters in 1898 and 1899, respectively. L'Erable was a French Canadian parish, one of the numerous offshoots of Kankakee. Father J. E. B. Levasseur, pastor, requested a colony of French-speaking Sisters. Sister Mary Joseph Perrier was appointed superior, assisted by Sister Petronilla Pouliot. There were ninety pupils enrolled. For undetermined reasons this mission was closed in 1901.[157]

Saint John the Baptist School in Chicago was staffed by Sisters in 1899. At this time the health of Mother Stanislaus was breaking, and it was found advisable to effect a change in administration. A new ordinary for the Diocese of Concordia had been chosen at last— the Vicar General of the Diocese of Leavenworth, the Right Reverend John Francis Cunningham. When Bishop Hennessy of Wichita gave over the jurisdiction of the diocese to Bishop Cunningham, he suggested that a change in government among the Sisters of Saint Joseph was necessary.[158] Therefore, in July, 1899, Sister Antoinette Cuff was summoned from Escanaba, Michigan, where she was superior, to take over the responsibilities of the new and growing Community. Mother Stanislaus Leary, accompanied by Sister Alexine Gosselin, went to Chicago to consult a specialist about her health and after some time at St. Joseph's Hospital, Chicago, and at a sanitorium at Lake Geneva, Wisconsin, she became local superior at Saint John the Baptist Convent in Chicago.[159] When Father Ulric Martel, pastor of La Grange, requested her to go to his residence and open a mission, stating that he would leave the residence furnished for her and her companions and that he would board elsewhere, she accepted his offer. She and Sister Alexine Gosselin were joined by Sisters

---

[156] Letter of the Rt. Rev. Richard Scannell, Omaha, to Mother Antoinette Cuff, Oct. 11, 1899. The original is in the files of the author.

[157] Questionnaires of Sisters Petronilla Pouliot, Marie Noel Cyrier, and Sebastian Allard.

Hoffman's Catholic Directory (New York, 1899), p. 419.

Wiltzius' Catholic Directory (New York, 1900), p. 432; (New York, 1901), p. 440.

[158] Letter of the Rt. Rev. John J. Hennessy, Wichita, to the Rt. Rev. John F. Cunningham, Concordia, Aug. 23, 1898. The original is in the Archives of the Kansas Catholic Historical Society; a photostat is in the files of the author.

[159] Interview with Mother Alexine Gosselin, Sept. 10, 1939.

Francis Joseph Leary, Josephine Leary, Constance Ryan, and Berchmans Gray.[160]

In the meantime, arrangements were in progress to establish a separate motherhouse in La Grange. When the authorities at Concordia realized that there was an undercurrent operating at Saint John the Baptist mission in Chicago, Sister Mary Anne Picard was sent there by Bishop Cunningham and Mother Antoinette to assume charge as local superior. After some disagreeable misunderstandings, some of the Sisters went to La Grange to establish a separate community. Mother Stanislaus was dying at that time, and in February of the following year she passed to her well-earned reward, separated from the Community which she had founded in Kansas but with plans laid for another in Illinois.[161] She instructed Sister Alexine Gosselin to carry on her work there. The latter wavered and considered returning to Concordia but, when asked by Archbishop Feehan to continue, she acquiesced. Sisters Josephine Leary, Francis Joseph Leary, Constance Ryan, and Berchmans Gray did not want to remain with Mother Alexine and attempted to establish a third motherhouse at Belvidere, Illinois. This venture was not successful; therefore, after a few years, they begged the Concordia Community to allow them to reaffiliate with it.[162] They were accepted.

The new Superior General, Reverend Mother Antoinette Cuff, brought order and stability into the Community after a period of unrest which had shaken its foundations. A new day had dawned. Horizons stretched forth far and wide. There was much work to be done on the frontier of the Middle West.

---

[160] These Sisters, other than Mother Stanislaus and Sister Alexine, went to Chicago from their missions when school closed in 1899 instead of to the Motherhouse in Concordia.

[161] On Feb. 14, 1900, Mother Stanislaus Leary died. She is buried in Calvary Cemetery, Chicago, Ill.

[162] Interview with Mother Antoinette Cuff, July 2, 1946.

CHAPTER IX

Administration: Reverend Mother Antoinette Cuff Part I: 1899-1914

THE frontier in Kansas at the *fin de siècle* was considerably different from that of 1883 when the Sisters of Saint Joseph first located in Newton. Sixteen years is a long time in a new country where the process of change and the impact of civilization and culture are at work. Kansas was considered young in 1883, but by 1899 it had amalgamated the characteristics of the East with the challenge of the frontier to produce a new, distinct type, "the Kansan." Much has been written about the cow country with its picturesque Chisolm Trail and the romance of the cattle trade. The new Kansas of the twentieth century became the center of the great breadbasket of America, the wheat and corn country. The change from the romantic cowboy to the steady-going, persevering, God-trusting tiller of the soil was one, not only of pursuit, but also one of general outlook on life. A different psychology had become prevalent among the people of the state, one in which stability was an outstanding characteristic.

Some sociologists maintain that the closer a man is to the soil, the closer he is to God. Anyone who observes nature at its source is bound to think more of the Creator. Too, when a man becomes dependent on God for the fruit of his labors in the form of good crops, he hearkens more often to the voice that is within him which reiterates: *"There is a God."*

There was, therefore, in Kansas at the turn of the century, a growth in religious endeavor. Comparing the condition of the Catholic Church in Kansas at this time with the period when Mother Stanislaus established her Community there bears out this statement.

According to the *Catholic Directory* of 1883 there were:

Bishop	1	Churches under construction	5
Priests—secular		Colleges	3
and religious	94	Academies	3
Ecclesiastical students	17	Parochial schools	35
Churches and chapels	152	Number of pupils	3,500
Churches finished		Orphanage	1
since last report	6	Hospital	1

Catholic population......about 80,000[1]

In the course of the years three dioceses were created from the territory included in the above-mentioned statistics. The Concordia Diocese was the least populous in 1899; hence, the statistics enumerated below are less than one-third of the combined statistics of the entire state:

Bishop	1	Chapels	2
Priests—secular		Ecclesiastical students	5
and religious	35	Academies	2
Churches with resident		Pupils	172
pastor	28	Parishes with parochial	
Missions with churches	50	schools	15
Total churches	78	Pupils	1,788
Stations	15	Catholic population......about 18,000[2]	

The Concordia Diocese had received money from the Society for the Propagation of the Faith during the period 1887 to 1901 to the amount of $37,160, while during that same period the diocese contributed $8,362.10 to the missionary cause.[3] Many of the mission stations and new churches were financed by the Society, much as the Extension Society contributes to poor dioceses and churches today. The Diocese of Concordia was sustained by the Society for a longer period than was the Diocese of Wichita, for the reason given by Roemer: "If this diocese [Concordia] was sustained for a somewhat longer period than the sister diocese in the same state and if the alms were much larger, we may find the reason in an intensification [in Concordia Diocese] of the needy conditions found in Wichita.

[1] *Sadlier's Catholic Directory* (New York, 1883), p. 353, p. 366.
[2] *Hoffman's Catholic Directory* (New York, 1899), p. 233.
[3] Joseph Freri, *Society for the Propagation of the Faith and Catholic Missions* (New York, 1912), p. 25.

Although the pioneers helped their priests as much as they could, it did not seem enough for the many problems that had to be solved."[4]

According to the *Diary* of Mother Antoinette Cuff, conditions were adverse for the struggling young community from 1883 until 1899. It was during this period that the local ordinary, Bishop Scannell, was transferred to the Diocese of Omaha. As previously stated, Rome did not appoint a successor to Bishop Scannell for seven years, placing the diocese instead under the jurisdiction of Bishop Hennessy of Wichita. It was an epoch of hard times, and many of the settlers moved back to the more favorably disposed East. Perhaps the process of the "selection of the fittest" was at work. Those who braved the vicissitudes of failure and hardship became all the sturdier because of their experiences, and the frontier profited by their determination of character and their perseverance.

A parallel might be drawn between the activities of the Sisters of Saint Joseph of Concordia and the growth in importance of the State of Kansas. The administration of Mother Stanislaus Leary was a pioneering one, in which the band of six noble women faced the conditions of a new land with the faith of a Boniface or a Patrick. They might well be compared to the traditional pioneer women whose memory survives in song and sculpture. More were added to that original group until at the end of the century the number had increased to eighty.[5]

The new administration of Mother Antoinette Cuff paralleled the stabilization period of Kansas history. Between 1899 and 1922 footholds were strengthened and deepened, and previous foundations of precarious financial standing took upon themselves the stamp of permanence. While Mother Stanislaus Leary was known as a foundress, Mother Antoinette Cuff might be known as a consolidator.

In the spring of 1899, as will be recalled, Mother Stanislaus Leary went to Chicago. Shortly afterward, Bishop Cunningham summoned Sister Antoinette to return to Concordia to assume leadership of the Community. She was at that time in charge of the school in Escanaba, Michigan.[6]

The telegram which recalled her from a well-earned vacation at

---

4 Theodore Roemer, *Ten Decades of Alms* (St. Louis, 1942), pp. 188-197.
5 *Wiltzius' Catholic Directory* (New York, 1900), p. 243.
6 Mother Antoinette Cuff, *Diary*. The original is in the files of the author. Interviews with Mother Antoinette Cuff at various times.

Lake Linden, Michigan, contained an important message. We have the words of Mother Antoinette regarding those important days:

> When the school year was finished in June, 1899, Sister Antoinette went to Lake Linden, Michigan, for her vacation. She intended to remain there all summer. However, she received a telegram to return to the Motherhouse in Concordia. She arrived home on July 25th, and on the next morning after Holy Mass, Right Reverend John Francis Cunningham, Bishop of Concordia, announced that Sister Antoinette was to be the Superior of the Community. She received this news with surprise and sorrow. . . . The Bishop being new and the Sisters strangers to him, except a few, it was difficult to make the choice. He therefore consulted with Bishop Scannell, who knew most of the Sisters and with his advice chose the one he thought would best carry on the work of the Community. . . .[7]

It must have been a challenge indeed to the young religious who was barely thirty-eight years of age; and her meeting and conquering that challenge reads like a book of romance. The courage and faith requisite for the accomplishment of so many things in such a successful manner calls forth admiring emulation. The work of God was to advance by leaps and bounds on the Midwest frontier in these years of the first quarter of the twentieth century.

Mother Antoinette tells in her own simple way how she felt and how she reacted to the new responsibility placed upon her:

> It was a trying time for Sister Antoinette, more so than anyone knew, but since she was chosen, she had to make the best of it and she did. At the time, the Community was composed of about eighty Sisters and the resources were anything but good. The foundation of the new Motherhouse had been started, but Mother Stanislaus Leary had been forced to abandon it for lack of funds. The old Motherhouse was badly in need of repairs. All in all, things were not the brightest for the young Superior but Sister Antoinette, although new at such things, started with a good will to do her best. . . .[8]

The *Catholic Directory* for 1900 listed the Nazareth Academy, with an enrollment of about forty pupils, as a boarding school in connection with the Convent in Concordia and offering courses for "the practical education of young ladies and a preparatory department and kindergarten for little girls."[9]

The same source listed the parochial schools in operation in the Diocese of Concordia:

---

[7] Autobiographical data compiled by Mother Antoinette Cuff. The original in the handwriting of Mother Antoinette is in the files of the author.

[8] *Loc. cit.*

[9] *Wiltzius' Catholic Directory* (New York, 1900), p. 243.

PAROCHIAL SCHOOLS[10]

School	Teachers	Pupils	Superior	Pastor
Beloit	5 Srs. of St. Joseph (Concordia)	140	Sr. Regis	Fr. Heitz
Clay Center	2 " "	60	Sr. Celestine	Fr. Browne
Clyde	4 " "	75	Sr. Angela	Fr. John Maher
Concordia	3 " "	95		Fr. Perrier
Herndon	3 " "	30		Fr. Wenzel
Junction City	lay teacher	60		Fr. Hurley (S.J.)
Saint Joseph	5 Srs. of St. Joseph (Concordia)	185	Sr. Michael	Fr. Mollier
Salina	4 Srs. of Charity (Leavenworth)	150		Fr. Maurer
Tipton	lay teacher	66		

Missions conducted outside of the Diocese of Concordia by the Sisters of Saint Joseph at the time of the change in administrations were: Monett, Missouri; Grand Island, North Platte, Saint Libory, Petersburg, and Olyen, Nebraska; St. George, and two schools in Chicago—St. John the Baptist and Brighton Park—in Illinois; Somerset, Wisconsin; Escanaba, Norway, and Lake Linden, Michigan. An impressive array of schools when one considers the age and size of the community! The problem of staffing the various schools and meeting educational requirements was one to vex the new administration.

One of the most flourishing schools in the Diocese of Concordia today is that of the Sacred Heart, Salina. The opening of this school, formerly taught by the Sisters of Charity, was the first project in the expansion program of Mother Antoinette Cuff.

The history of the Sisters of Saint Joseph of Concordia in Salina is of such importance that it is imperative that extensive attention be given to that city. Since December 24, 1944, Salina has been the episcopal see of the territory formerly included in the Diocese of Concordia. It is also the home of three of the largest institutions conducted by the Community.

Established along the main line of the Kansas Pacific (now the Union Pacific Railroad), Salina early became the entrepôt of the region.[11] The town was founded by Colonel William Phillips, a native of Scotland, sent to Kansas by Horace Greeley and Charles

[10] *Ibid.*, pp. 241-243.
[11] Frank W. Blackmar (ed.), *Kansas: Encyclopedia of State History . . . Institutions . . . Counties . . . Cities . . . Prominent Persons,* 3 vols. (Chicago, 1912), vol. II, pp. 663-635.

Dana as a correspondent of the *New York Tribune,* to obtain first-hand information regarding the Kansas troubles and their implication in national affairs during the pre-Civil War period.[12] It was while in Kansas on this mission that on an exploratory trip to the Saline Valley, he decided to establish a city devoted to the interests of the free North. In 1859, the townsite was chosen. Strategically located, Salina promised a great future.

Salina lacked the enthusiasm to profit by the lucrative cattle trade. The city authorities knew that economic gain is secondary to the by-products of such a trade. Disreputable characters and a disregard for morals are natural by-products of a transient civilization, and Salina was wise in declining the tempting offers to commercialize.[13]

The geographical area now comprised in the city of Salina and the nearby towns was first served by the Jesuit Fathers from the Saint Mary's Indian Mission at Saint Marys, Kansas. Records of the missionaries show that in 1859 Salina became a mission station under the spiritual jurisdiction of Father Louis Dumortier, S.J. A room was always reserved in the home of A. M. Campbell, a non-Catholic, one of the founders of Salina, for this zealous missionary.[14]

During the pastorate of Father Adolph Wibbert the first parochial school was opened in Salina. Miss Kate Cantwell was the first teacher and Professor Darliendon was employed as instructor in music. The Sisters of Charity of Leavenworth took charge of the school the following year and continued to work successfully and untiringly until 1900 when the Sisters of Saint Joseph of Concordia replaced them as the parochial teachers.[15]

The Catholic newspaper of the State of Kansas in the 1880's periodically referred briefly to the school:

---

[12] *Loc. cit.*
   Marion Klema, "Salina Founded by Colonel Phillips, New York Journalist, March, 1858," *Northwestern Kansas Register,* spec. ed., May 21, 1939.
   [13] Joseph G. McCoy, *Historic Sketches of the Cattle Trade of the West and Southwest* (Chicago, 1874), pp. 41-44, 141.
   [14] Father Dumortier was a victim of cholera when it was raging among the pioneer groups of the Kansas plains in 1867. He determinedly returned to Fort Harker, a military post (now Kanopolis), about four miles east of Ellsworth, to be with his boys who were plague-stricken. He contracted the plague and died in a box car on July 26, 1867. His remains were sent back to St. Mary's and interred in a cemetery belonging to the Indians, which was close to the spot where Loyola Hall now stands.
   "Jesuits First Served Needs of Faithful Around Salina," *Northwestern Kansas Register,* spec. ed., Nov. 20, 1938.
   [15] *Loc. cit.*

Salina is the possessor of a fine church attended by the Reverend Maurer. There are four Sisters. The number of pupils is about one hundred.[16]

And again:

There are seventy-seven pupils attending the Sisters' School and over one hundred would attend were the building larger.[17]

Then in 1884 an article written by Father Maurer himself gives a rather comprehensive picture of the parish:

The population of Saline County is about 16,000 and that of the county seat of Salina about 4,500. The Catholic population of the county is about 2,000 and that of Salina 1,000. There are two other Catholic parishes in Saline County, viz., one at Brookville about fifteen miles west of here and one at Solomon City. Solomon City is in Dickinson County but most of the congregation live in Saline County and attend the Solomon City church.

The Salina Catholic congregation owns about $15,000 worth of property. This property consists of the following: one moderately sized church building, a parsonage, and a cemetery. This property except the cemetery is located in the most beautiful part of the city.

The Catholic school in Salina is in charge of the Sisters of Charity from Leavenworth. There are now four sisters here and owing to the rapid growth of our congregation and especially of the children in numbers, we are compelled to have another teacher next year. There are at present attending our school in the neighborhood of eighty children and being at the present very discommoded for want of room. We have concluded to and are making arrangements to build a two-story addition to our present parsonage and turning it into a school and living house for the Sisters.[18]

The following exaggerated statement appeared in a promotion pamphlet put out by the city:

. . . Situated in the central part of the city on Iron Avenue, is the Catholic School Building, a handsome three-story structure, ample for the accommodation of several hundred pupils. . . .[19]

They also referred to the school as the "Catholic College" in the pamphlet.[20]

In 1900, when the Concordia Sisters replaced the Sisters of Charity from Leavenworth, Sisters Ambrosia McPhillips, Angela Costello, and Cyril Schumacher, were the original Sisters.[21] In 1902

---

[16] Monthly Visitor, Oct., 1882.

[17] Ibid., Feb., 1883.

[18] Rev. Prosper Maurer, "The Catholic Church and Schools of Salina County." Filed as 1Sa 3, Clippings 1, in Kansas State Historical Society Library, Topeka, Kans. March 3, 1884.

[19] Andrews & Page (eds.), Picturesque Salina (Salina, Kans., 1887), p. 29. The original is in Library of Congress; a photostatic copy is in the files of the author. There is a picture of the parochial school building in this pamphlet.

[20] Ibid., p. 29.

[21] Questionnaire of Sister Philip Giersch, who was the first postulant received from the Sacred Heart Parish.

om F. L. Bond the property which had been
hillips. This served as a convent and school
e of the dedication of the present grade school
.... eight Sisters teaching in the school. That same
year a high school was opened in the parish,[22] beginning a new
era in the history of Catholic education in the city of Salina. Teaching
in the basement of the church while waiting for the completion of the
new grade school building in 1908-1909 were Sisters Loyola Powers,
Bernard Toomey, Rosella Raymond, and Mary Chrysostom Wynn.
The latter was the first high school principal in the parish. In 1916,
the James Mason High School was erected through the generosity of
James Mason, retired Salina businessman. In 1923, accreditment by
the North Central Association was secured. The association advised
a building program in 1936; the outcome of which was the $30,000
addition completed in 1938. Extensive improvements were made in
1947. The school has had an outstanding scholastic and athletic
record. The Ladies' Guild of the parish has sponsored every activity
proposed by the teaching faculty.

Today the Salina parochial school system stands as a monument
to the late Right Reverend John Maher, who for nearly forty years
administered to the needs of the parish. It was Monsignor Maher who
was later responsible for the expansion program of the Sisters of
Saint Joseph of Concordia in Salina. To him the Community owes a
debt of filial gratitude for the interest he showed in the Institute from
his early contacts with it in Clyde until his death in 1940.

Monsignor Richard Daly, V.G., successor to Monsignor Maher,
maintained the same fatherly interest in the school and in the
Sisters. His death on June 28, 1946, was a loss to the Church and
to the civic life of Salina.[23] Of the appointment of the Right Reverend
John A. Duskie, as Vicar General of the diocese and rector of its
cathedral, Bishop Thill wrote: "Long and tested faithfulness to duty,
combined with loyal devotion to the Church at the price of personal

---

[22] Sacred Heart Academy High School, Manhattan, opened the same year as did
Sacred Heart High School, Salina. There has always been a dispute between the two
schools as to which one actually opened first. The dates have not been "historically
established." Since this is an important step in Catholic education in the Diocese of
Concordia, joint credit should be given to the parishes of Salina and Manhattan. Information for the above from the questionnaire of Rev. Mother Mary Chrysostom Wynn.
[23] *Salina Journal*, June 29, 1946; July 1-2, 1946.
Salina Advertiser-Sun, July 3, 1946.
Northwestern Kansas Register, July 3, 1946.

sacrifice, prompts this appointment." Monsignor Duskie, as rector of the Cathedral of the Sacred Heart, manifests untiring zeal in the promotion of Sacred Heart Cathedral grade and high schools.[24]

The necessity of reorganizing the Corporation was felt early in the new administration; therefore, a meeting was called. Since the Community was to be legally represented under that Corporation for the next hundred years, the minutes of the first meeting will be quoted *in toto:*

NAZARETH CONVENT AND ACADEMY, CONCORDIA, KANSAS

January 8, 1900

On the second Monday of January, 1900, at ten a.m. the first meeting of the Corporation of the Nazareth Convent and Academy, Concordia, was held. The charter which was obtained by the Sisters of Saint Joseph, Nazareth Convent and Academy, Concordia, Kansas, in October, 1884, having become null the same institute has obtained a new charter for one hundred years. The first meeting of the Corporation having been held at ten o'clock in the morning on the second Monday of January, 1900, in the above named institution for the purpose of electing five trustees. Fourteen members of the order were represented. The meeting of the Corporation of Nazareth Convent and Academy took place in the principal room and votes were cast for five trustees of said Corporation as follows: Mother Antoinette Cuff, 58; Sister Aurelia Cayer, 46; Sister Julia Long, 57; Sister Regina Fisher, 53; Sister Aloysius Furstenberg, 39; Sister Mary Rose Waller, 23; Sister Raphael Cardinal, 23; Sister Louise Cuff, 25; Sister Gonzaga de St. Aubin, 15; Sister Loretta Gosselin, 15; Sister Michael Beaudoin, 8. Reverend Mother and Sisters Regina, Julia, Aurelia, and Aloysius, receiving the highest number of votes were, accordingly, elected trustees of the corporation for one year.

The meeting adjourned at 10:23 A.M.

SISTER ALOYSIUS FURSTENBERG
Secretary[25]

It was not long before the project for the new Motherhouse was again brought to the attention of the Sisters. The site had been purchased by Mother Stanislaus Leary with the first deed dated June 30, 1892.[26] The foundation was begun in 1898, but for the space of

---

[24] *Northwestern Kansas Register,* Aug. 11, 1946.

Today twenty teachers instruct five hundred and sixty-two students in this school. *Kenedy's Catholic Directory* (New York, 1947), p. 694.

[25] The minutes were in error that the charter of 1884 was null. The fact is that the Corporation of the Nazareth Convent and Academy is still functioning under the Charter of 1884, with the addition of two amendments, one permitting the Sisters to operate hospitals and the other to conduct colleges and grant degrees. *Minutes of the Meetings of the Corporation of the Sisters of St. Joseph of Concordia, Kansas,* vol. II, (1900-1939), pp. 53-54. The original is in the Archives of the Nazareth Motherhouse, Concordia, Kans.; a photostat is in the files of the author.

[26] Deed for the same in the Archives of the Nazareth Motherhouse, Concordia, Kans.

one and a half years the project was discontinued. The cost of the completed building was $90,000, a part of which was from the Community savings and the rest a loan.[27] Mother Antoinette spoke of this in her *Diary:*

At the time the improvements were in progress on the old Motherhouse, we were trying to borrow money to continue the convent on the hill. At last, in 1901, we succeeded in getting a loan of $40,000 from the Saint Joseph's Missionary Society of London, England. The building was started now for good. . . .[28]

The cornerstone of the new Nazareth Convent was laid on May 15, 1902. An editorial appeared in the local newspaper concerning the event, illustrating the opinion the residents of Concordia had of the Sisters:

The Sisters at the Academy can always be depended upon to do the correct thing in the way of etiquette. They issued very neat invitations, in as fine a manner as would be issued to the most swell wedding, to their friends to attend the ceremonies incident to the laying of the cornerstone of the new convent, which ceremony takes place this evening. Twenty years from now, when the new site of the Academy will be covered with a quarter of a million dollars worth of buildings devoted to the educational interests of the society, persons will be proud to say that they were invited guests to the laying of the cornerstone for the first building of the group.[29]

The account of the ceremonies follows:

The ceremonies attendant on the laying of the cornerstone at the new convent of the Sisters of Nazareth occurred at 6:30 last evening, though owing to some mistake on the part of the railroad the stone had miscarried and a temporary stone had to be used. There was an immense crowd in attendance, made up of people of all denominations, showing the great public interest in the magnificent structure, that, after much delay, is being pushed rapidly toward completion. Bishop Cunningham officiated at the ceremony, blessing the stone and the building, upon which he sprinkled holy water, as preceding the choir and a procession of priests and altar boys while the choir chanted the psalm, "Miserere Mei," a march was made about the walls [sic.] Afterwards the choir sang the "Veni Creator."

The address, or lecture, was delivered by Father Maher, of Salina, and his subject was that of monastic institutions. It was a masterpiece of logic, delivered in an eloquent and scholarly manner and replete with happily drawn similes and a convincing argument to show what the Catholic Church, the priesthood, and the sisterhood had done for the welfare of humanity, for the advance of civilization, for the sciences, the arts and the general progress of the world in all those things which have made life today worth living. His defense of the monks from the ignorant belief which holds them up as objects

[27] Cuff, *Diary, op. cit.* The original is in the files of the author.
[28] *Loc. cit.*
[29] *Concordia Blade,* May 14, 1902.

of contempt was very able and he quoted from history the names of many of these holy men whose industry and forethought have preserved to posterity the history of the early ages and whose contribution to literature, music, science and all the higher arts have been so valuable as aids in the advance of all these branches.

Father Maher has an excellent voice, his delivery is fine and his language, at all times good, was at times most eloquent. . . .[30]

The building, built of red brick with limestone trimming, was an outstanding piece of architectural work for its time and seemed ample for the needs of the growing Community.[31] Beginning with 1905 additional land purchases were made.[32]

Mother Antoinette will always be remembered for her great devotion to her patron saint, Saint Anthony of Padua. In the undertakings of the Community she trusted in his aid. In her *Diary* she mentioned that fact on several occasions. In connection with the financing of the new Nazareth Motherhouse, she said in part:

While the building was going up, Mother tried in every way and every place to obtain donations. She had great devotion to Saint Anthony, and she put the building into his hands and told him that she looked to him for success. He did not fail her. The building was ready in June, 1903. The Sisters had their first meal in the new building on June 23, 1903, and the next morning, the feast of Saint John the Baptist, the patronal feast of the local Ordinary, saw the celebration of the first Mass in the new Motherhouse.[33]

This Motherhouse, with improvements and additions, is still the headquarters of the Sisters of Saint Joseph of Concordia. The older Sisters who still remember "dear *old* Nazareth" tell of the hardships and the happiness found there. The now old, still new, Nazareth is dear to the living Community.

Two short-lived undertakings on widely separated frontiers were those of Laramie, Wyoming, and Parkston, South Dakota. The former was in operation only one year and the latter two years.

Laramie, the county seat of Albany County, Wyoming, situated on the Laramie River,[34] is historically known as an entrepôt on the Overland Trail and later was on the Pony Express Route. Located in

---

[30] *Ibid.*, May 16, 1902.

[31] Information furnished by Mother Antoinette, July 2, 1946.

[32] Feb. 1, 1905; May 15, 1905; Sept. 1, 1909; Sept. 28, 1909; Sept. 16, 1911; Apr. 22, 1921; Oct. 4, 1921; June 21, 1928. Deeds for the same in the Archives of the Nazareth Motherhouse, Concordia, Kans.

[33] Cuff, *Diary, op. cit.*

[34] Named for Jacques de La Ramie, a French fur trader in the region (1821).
  Encyclopedia Americana, vol. XVI, pp. 745-746.
  Encyclopedia Britannica, vol. XIII, p. 720.
  J. H. Triggs, *History and Directory of Laramie City, Wyoming Territory* (Laramie, Wyoming, 1875), p. 25.

the midst of cattle and mining industries, the prospect of a parochial
school seemed encouraging. The first Sisters sent there in 1902 were
Sisters Isidore Burns, superior, Cyprian McHale, Gregory Raboin,
Amelia Fitzgibbon, Martha Christin, and Juliana Yoos. There was
an orphanage in connection with the school which had about one
hundred pupils enrolled. Father Hugh Cummiskey was pastor.
Because of the lack of financial stability, the Sisters were not returned
in the fall of 1903.[35] Many schools opened and closed after a short
period during these first twenty years following 1884. This phe-
nomenon had deeper significance than appears at first glance. The
Plenary Council of 1884 emphasized a school near every church.
Parishes tried to carry out this injunction, but many were not financially able to do so. Many early missions of the Sisters of Saint Joseph
of Concordia fall into this category.

Parkston, Hutchinson County, South Dakota, is in the Diocese of
Sioux Falls. Father J. J. Reiland was pastor at the time the Concordia
Sisters conducted the school.[36] Sister Celestine Wehrle, superior, was
assisted by Sisters Clotilda Fraser, Cyril Schumacher, and Francis
Costello. The distance to be traveled was great, and there was a
scarcity of Sisters for the nearer missions which were to be opened
within the next few years. Therefore, since the conditions were inadequate in Parkston, the Community saw fit to terminate its work there
in the spring of 1905.

The new administration sponsored the conversion of the old
Motherhouse into a hospital. This, the first venture of the Sisters of
Saint Joseph into the field of nursing, was an important step because
of the future hospital work of the Sisters of Saint Joseph.

In September, 1903, the Saint Joseph Hospital, Concordia, was
opened. The institution was placed under the care of Sister Clare Cuff,
a sister of Mother Antoinette. Her co-laborers were Sisters Boniface
Bachle, Zita Martel, Irene Rheaume, Philomene Belisle.[37]

The *Concordia Kansan* early in the following spring spoke of
the hospital:

35 *Wiltzius' Catholic Directory* (New York, 1903). p. 239; (1904), p. 240.

Questionnaires of Sisters Gregory Raboin, Cyprian McHale, and Juliana Yoos.
36 *Wiltzius Catholic Directory* (New York, 1903), p. 545; (1904), p. 559. The
school was omitted from the 1905 report.

Questionnaires of Sisters Clotilda Fraser and Francis Costello.
37 Information secured from Sister Philomene Belisle, second Superior of the hospital,
and from the records in the hospital furnished by Sister Francis Joanne Bonfield.

Reverend Mother Antoinette Cuff, Second Mother
General of the Sisters of Saint Joseph of Concordia,
1899–1922

Last Friday the editor of this paper visited Saint Joseph's Hospital and was surprised at the improvements that have been made there during the past few months. There is nothing on the townsite that has brought so much notice to Concordia, or impressed the importance of the town on the people in every town of the northwest part of the State, as has this fine Concordia institution. It has been a dream of the people of the town for years, and especially of the Sisters of Saint Joseph of Nazareth to have a fine hospital here. The dream has been realized, it is now a demonstrated fact.

There is no finer, though there may be larger, institution of this character in any city west of Chicago or Saint Louis.

It is, as we have said, a great thing for Concordia. It is of much more value to the unfortunate people of the whole northwest who require the services of skilled physicians and surgeons and the latest and most modern hospital service.

When the new academy was established and the school moved thereto, it was decided to remodel the old academy building for the uses of a hospital.

Sister Clare, a blood sister of the Mother Superior, came here from Michigan and took complete charge of the work of establishing the hospital. She brought with her a fund of experience in such work, and a rare genius as an executive in business affairs, and best of all, determination to found a hospital second to none in every appointment suggested by modern medical science—and she has succeeded beyond the expectation of her most optimistic friends, and she has many. The hospital was opened to the public in September, 1903, and from that day to this has grown in usefulness and benefit to the unfortunate. Patients who would be required to go to Kansas City or Saint Joseph, Missouri, were it not for the establishment of Saint Joseph's at this place, are now saved the expense and physical injury such a long trip would entail; they are now brought here and get the best treatment that it is possible to secure anywhere.

The place is a model of systematized cleanliness and home-like perfection. It is a pleasure to visit the place — the reception of visitors is so cordial and hearty and the environment so cheerful. At the right of the hall is the reception parlor, where all visitors are received, and off from this room is a fine office of the superintendent.

The second floor is given up to rooms for the patients — all nicely furnished, well lighted, and cheerful.

The operating department is in the top story and is the marvel of all the physicians and surgeons who have visited it. They all say there is not a finer operating department in any of the big hospitals in Kansas City. Attached thereto is the sterilizing room for the proper sterilization of every appliance used in a surgical operation. Nearby is the surgeons' room, devoted exclusively to the use of the operating surgeons preparatory to operations and where they retire to complete their toilet when their work is over.

Every precaution and appliance is used to secure absolute freedom from septic conditions. It has been the privilege of the editor of the *Kansan* to visit several well-known hospitals and operating rooms for surgeons. We state frankly that we have not seen the one at Saint Joseph's, Concordia, excelled and rarely equalled.

There is at present accommodation for forty patients and no doubt the time is not far-distant when more room will be required. There is at least $40,000 invested in the property at this time and it is a fine monument to the energy of the Superintendent, Sister M. Clare. Bishop Cunningham is a warm friend of the hospital and has been a liberal supporter since the work began. The medical staff is especially strong and bears the names of many of the leading physicians, not only of Concordia, but of other towns in this part of the State, which is as follows: Dr. W. R. Priest, Dr. Caton, Drs. Coffey, Marcotte, Weaver, Sawhill, Raines, Zimmerman and Pigman of Concordia; Drs. Hartwell, Jamestown; Brierley and Newton, Glasco; Daily, Beloit; Eckblad, Scandia; Beach and Sexton, Clyde; Hall and Farr, Miltonvale; McDonald, Aurora; Gardener, Greenleaf; Toley, Washington; Hawley, Burr Oak; Appleton, Delphos.

The charges for care of the patients at the hospital are very reasonable and within the reach of people of moderate means. Sister Clare has for her assistants several Sisters of Saint Joseph and it is a fine sight to witness these good women religiously, yet cheerfully, performing their work of charity and mercy in nursing the sick back to health and worldly usefulness.

Since the opening of the hospital nearly two hundred cases have accepted the benefits of this hospital at Concordia. It is pleasing to note that Concordians are all friends to the institution, as they may well be.[38]

The field of nursing was a new endeavor for the Sisters of Saint Joseph of Concordia; the mother institute at Rochester had not launched out into that type of work at the time of the separation in 1883. In northwestern Kansas there was a need for this kind of service and the challenge of the care of the sick presented a new frontier which was to serve as an impetus to the Congregation and send it on to new heights and endeavors.

The hospital was placed under the protection of the patron saint of the Community, Saint Joseph. The surgeon in charge was Doctor W. R. Priest, who became a life-long friend and benefactor of the institution. His co-workers on the staff were Doctors Caton, Doty, Coffey, Weaver, and Raines.[39] Since none of the original band of Sisters were registered nurses, Anna Ford, R.N., of Elmira, New York, worked at the hospital until some of the Sisters became registered. There were few patients in the beginning, but each year has meant an increase in numbers and equipment.

In 1916, it was necessary to build a $65,000 fireproof addition and to install more modern equipment.[40] The present hospital is a

[38] *Concordian Kansan*, Sept. 6, 1903.

Gomer Davies was the editor then and for many years. He always showed interest in the Nazareth Convent and Academy.

[39] *Loc. cit.*

Information secured from Sister Philomene Belisle, second Superior of the hospital and from the records furnished by Sister Francis Joanne Bonfield.

[40] *Minutes of the Meetings of the Corporation of the Nazareth Convent and Academy, 1900-1939*, vol. I, pp. 38-39 (June 9, 1916).

Ibid., p. 41 (Jan. 1, 1917).

completely modern three-story brick building with fully equipped laboratories, operating rooms, X-ray, and dietary departments. Two large homes have been purchased for the use of student nurses, one the old Caldwell mansion,[41] purchased in 1934, and the other the Bedor home purchased in 1944.[42]

Property was acquired in 1930 in the west part of Concordia for the new Saint Joseph's Hospital, plans for which are completed at the present writing.[43]

Saint Joseph's Hospital in Concordia has always been an asset to north central Kansas. It serves the surrounding territory and has won a reputation for self-sacrifice, efficiency, and devotion to the sick. The project has been blessed in manifold ways and with its success the Congregation has been encouraged to extend this same type of service to other frontiers.

There are twenty-seven Sisters and sixty student nurses at the hospital at present with 2,633 in-patients and 3,114 out-patients during 1947.[44]

A second hospital project materialized the same year as the opening of the Concordia hospital. It will be remembered that when Mother Stanislaus Leary died in LaGrange, Illinois, in 1900, Archbishop Feehan of Chicago appointed Sister Alexine Gosselin as the Superior of the newly-established Community there. When Mother Stanislaus Leary died, that group consisted of Sisters Josephine Leary, Amelia Fitzgibbon, Francis Joseph Leary, Alexine Gosselin, Constance Ryan, Berchmans Gray, Liguori McDonnell, and a postulant.[45] All except Sisters Alexine and Liguori and the postulant left La Grange to establish a third motherhouse at Belvidere, Illinois.[46]

Belvidere, county seat of Boone County, Illinois, is about seventy-

---

[41] *Ibid.*, pp. 145-146 (Jan. 23, 1934).

   Minutes of the Councillors of the Sisters of St. Joseph of Concordia, 1925-1940, pp. 63-64 (Jan. 23, 1934).

   Concordia Blade-Empire, Jan. 23, 1934.

[42] *Northwestern Kansas Register,* July 2, 1944.

[43] Fontbonne Hall, acquired in the spring of 1945, will become part of the hospital property. This home was the former residence of the Bishop of Concordia, who, when the diocesan see moved to Salina, sold it to the Community. *Minutes of the Meetings of the Corporation of the Nazareth Convent and Academy, 1900-1939,* vol. I, pp. 118-119 (Jan. 1, 1930); pp. 141-143 (Aug. 31, 1939).

[44] *Kenedy's Catholic Directory* (New York, 1947), p. 697.

[45] Sister Liguori and the postulant later affiliated with the Wichita Community.

[46] *Diary* of Mother Alexine Gosselin. A typewritten copy is in the files of the author; an interview of the author with Mother Alexine Gosselin, Sept. 11-12, 1939.

eight miles northwest of Chicago in an important agricultural section of the state.[47] It is in the Diocese of Rockford.

In October, 1900, the original band lived in a private residenc while waiting to open their hospital to receive its first patients th following March. Sister Josephine Leary was the superior. The hos pital was erected at the cost of $30,000, and no attempt was made t conduct schools or teach music classes. Several postulants were re ceived within the next three years. At the end of that time, the grou realized that, financially, the work was failing and the stability o the Community was endangered. Fearing extinction, they appeale to Mother Antoinette Cuff and her Council and begged permissio of the Most Reverend John F. Cunningham of Concordia to reaffiliate In a few months the five Sisters who had formerly belonged to Con cordia and six Sisters who had been received at Belvidere wer formally readmitted with the permission of the Concordia Ordinary The new sisters were Sisters Catherine Beck, Mary Agnes Beck, Mar garet Mary Cox, Joseph Theresa Owens, Mary Joseph O'Brien, an Anthony Callaghan.[48]

Saint Joseph's Hospital, Belvidere, has always had a difficult ex istence. However, within the past decade or two it has come to th front as one of the important institutions conducted by the Concordi Community. At one time a change in policy was contemplated: th hospital was to be converted into a sanatorium for tubercular patient This was thought to be a solution to the financial problem. Howeve there was a clause in the original contract restricting the use of th building for contagious cases and for that reason the change wa not made.[49]

Today there are twenty Sisters administering to the needs of ap proximately two thousand patients.[50] Located in a healthful part o Illinois, with extensive and beautiful grounds, the hospital bids fo a favorable and opportune future.

Five schools were opened in 1904—Aurora, Illinois; Angelus Schoenchen, Pfeifer, and Saint Peter, Kansas. The Community ha

[47] *Encyclopedia Americana*, vol. III, pp. 495-496.
Encyclopedia Britannica, vol. III, pp. 390-391.
Illinois: A Guide (Federal Writer's Project) (Chicago, 1939), p. 521.
[48] Interview with Sisters Catherine Beck and Mary Agnes Beck, two of the sister received in Belvidere and later affiliated with the Concordia Community, June 28, 194
[49] *Belvidere Times*, Aug. 17, 1912.
[50] *Kenedy's Catholic Directory* (New York, 1947), p. 671.

rown in numbers since the turn of the century, and there are now
recruits to staff new schools.

Aurora, Kane County, Illinois, is an enterprising city, rather cosmopolitan in composition. Located about thirty-eight miles west of
hicago, the city has had an interesting history as a trading and mill
te.[51] As far back as 1849 the place was of interest to the Catholic
ierarchy in Chicago. Bishop James Oliver Van de Velde, second
ishop of Chicago, made mention of it in his *Diary:*

> . . On the 13th of September, he left for Aurora, a thriving town on the
> ox River, in Kane County, which had never yet been visited by a Bishop.
> urora and its vicinity contains about 700 Catholics, nearly all Canadians,
> ho have been occasionally visited by the Reverend R. T. Courjault of Bour-
> onnais Grove. This Reverend Gentleman has spent several days among them
> prepare the Canadian children for confirmation whilst the Reverend George
> amilton of Joliet has instructed the English portion of them. . . . The largest
> ll of the principal hotel has been rented and appropriately decorated for the
> erformance of Divine Service on Sunday . . . a meeting was held to adopt
> easures for building a Catholic Church in Aurora. . . . It is the Bishop's
> tention to have several free schools, a hospital and a Church for French-
> anadians. . . .[52]

Although the French obviously preferred city life and were essen-
ally city dwellers, many moved into the Middle West. The Sacred
eart Church in Aurora was built in 1866. A school was built in
880 which was placed under the direction of the Congregation of
otre Dame.[53]

The mission in St. George, Illinois, was opened by Father Joseph
a Sage. Two years later this same priest, having been transferred to
hicago, asked for the school in his parish in Brighton Park to be
affed by the Concordia Sisters. Again, in 1904, Sacred Heart Church,
urora, Illinois, was his pastorate, and he contacted the authorities in
oncordia for Sisters. Forced to resign the parish on account of poor
ealth, he was succeeded by Father J. C. Simard (resigned in 1946)
der whose fatherly kindness the school attained its present success.

Sisters Victorine Allard, Eulalia Belanger, Eveline Fraser, Pauline
elisle, and Mary Agnes Beck were the first Sisters missioned in

[51] *Encyclopedia Britannica*, vol. II, p. 696.
 Rudolphus W. Joslyn, and Frank W. Joslyn, *History of Kane County, Illinois,*
vols. (Chicago, 1908), vol. I, p. 540.
[52] *Diary of the Rt. Rev. James Oliver Van de Velde, second Bishop of Chicago* as
ed by James J. McGovern, *The Catholic Church in Chicago* (Chicago, 1890), pp. 115,
8-129, 144, 184.
[53] Joslyn and Joslyn, *op. cit.*, vol. I, p. 606.
 Biographical and Historical Record of Kane County, Illinois (Chicago, 1898),
. 954-955.

Aurora.[54] Today there are five teachers with one hundred and fifty five students enrolled.[55] The mission is now in the Diocese of Rock ford.[56]

Angelus, Sheridan County, Kansas, was opened in 1904, and wa the westernmost mission in the state. Settled by migrants from the Walker-Herzog section of Kansas and Germans from Missouri and Illinois, this small community was staunchly Catholic and early rea lized the benefits to be derived from establishing a parochial school in its midst. At the request of the pastor, Father Martin J. Schmitt three Sisters of Saint Joseph of Concordia were sent to Angelus in the fall of 1904. The first Sisters were Sisters Stephanie Kunz, superior Aloysius Furstenberg, and Celestine Wehrle. The latter was replaced later in the fall by Sister Lucy LaSage when the mission of Saint Peter needed a German Sister.[57]

Angelus remained under the direction of the Sisters from Con cordia until 1912 when crop failures throughout that part of the state made it financially impossible to maintain the parochial school.[5] However, the school continued under the direction of lay teacher until the fall of 1915 when the Precious Blood Sisters assumed charge.[59] Today the school, staffed by five sisters, instructs abou ninety pupils.[60]

We shall digress to give a short summary of the Russian-German immigration to central and western Kansas, because the Sisters of Saint Joseph later conducted other schools among these people.

Movements of groups are always interesting. When individual or single families move from country to country or within the same country, it speaks of enthusiasm, initiative, and manly courage. When whole colonies transplant themselves elsewhere, it speaks of those same qualities with the important addition of an *esprit de corps*, spirit of cooperation, which is truly admirable. That *esprit de corp* was prevalent among those sturdy Germans who, wishing to improve

---

[54] Questionnaires of Sisters Pauline Belisle, Mary Agnes Beck, and Eveline Fraser. *Wiltzius' Catholic Directory* (New York, 1905), p. 527.

[55] *Kenedy's Catholic Directory* (New York, 1947), p. 664.

[56] The Diocese of Rockford was created Sept. 23, 1908. *Kenedy's Catholic Director* (New York, 1946), p. 660.

[57] St. Peter was one of the Russian-German settlements which are to be discusse below. Three of these schools were opened the same year as was the school in Angelu It is interesting to note that Sister Celestine Wehrle's name appears often among th first Sisters on many missions. Her knowledge of German may account for this fact.

[58] Questionnaire of Sister Philip Giersch, Superior at the time of the closing in 191

[59] *Wiltzius' Catholic Directory* (New York, 1916), p. 334.

[60] *Kenedy's Catholic Directory* (New York, 1947), p. 694.

economic conditions, hearkened to the invitation of Catherine the Great of Russia. Catherine issued a "Manifesto"[61] in which she guaranteed to all foreigners who would form colonies in hitherto unsettled districts of Russia free exercise of religion, freedom from taxes, levies, and land service for thirty years, and exemption from military duty for an indefinite period.[62]

For over a hundred years the arrangement was successful, but new generations of these Russian-Germans found the original promises forgotten. The military service exacted by the Russians in their new hunger for conquest was especially obnoxious to Catholics who were deprived of religious ministration during long years of service in the army and in addition were denied official rank in the army unless they professed the Orthodox religion.[63]

Scouts were sent to Brazil and the United States, but the latter seemed preferable from the beginning. They returned to Russia with a favorable report which gave impetus to the emigration. Promotional literature in various languages put out by the railroad companies was responsible for much mass immigration. America was not totally unknown to these colonists.

Considerable material has been written in scattered places on this transplanted Catholic Russian-German colony on the plains of western Kansas.[64] The new settlers were a curiosity to the people already established there. Their manners, customs, and interests were foreign and created a cultural conflict in the first generation. Americanization has removed this cultural conflict.

The five original Russian-German settlements in Ellis County

[61] A preliminary summary invitation of this nature was issued Dec. 4, 1762. On July 22, 1783, a more detailed statement followed. It was Article 6, section 1, of this latter so-called "Manifesto" which made the above-mentioned guarantees.

[62] The expression used to designate the exemption from military service was "na vyak," which had several meanings. It was variously interpreted as an indefinite time, as one hundred years, five hundred years, or as forever; traditionally it meant one hundred years.

Francis S. Laing, O. M. Cap., *German-Russian Settlements in Ellis County, Kansas, Kansas Historical Collections*, vol. XI (1909-1910), pp. 489-528.

[63] Laing, *op. cit.*, p. 491.

[64] The Laing pamphlet mentioned in note 62 is authoritative and informative. There are several manuscript accounts of the emigration and the several settlements still extant. Periodically the story is reprinted in such newspapers as the *Kansas City Star*, Dec. 13, 1911; *Kansas City Times*, July 25, 1938; *Kansas City Catholic Register*, Sept. 2, 1926; and *Northwestern Kansas Register*, Nov. 20, 1938. The most recent and by far the most scientific study is by Sister Eloise Johannes (Concordia), *A Study of the Russian-German Settlements in Ellis County, Kansas* (Washington, 1946). This study was in partial fulfillment of the doctor's degree in the Department of Sociology at the Catholic University of America. Much of the information herein has been taken from Sister Eloise's work and notes.

were Herzog (now known as Victoria), Munjor, Catherine, Pfeifer, and Schoenchen. Gorham in Russell County, St. Peter in Graham County, Emmeram, Walker, Antonino, and Vincent in Ellis County were established from these parent colonies. The schools in these settlements, with the exceptions of Victoria, Munjor, and Catherine, are now or have at one time been conducted by the Sisters of Saint Joseph of Concordia. These missions will be treated in chronological order. In 1904 three of these schools (Pfeifer, Schoenchen, and Saint Peter) were opened.

The town of Pfeifer is located twenty miles southeast of Hays in Ellis County on the south bank of the Smoky Hill River. Pfeifer, one of the five original Russian-German settlements, has had a typical development as a rural, inland village. The inhabitants were from the towns of Pfeifer, Kamenka, Semenoka, and Rothamel, Russia.[65] Dominantly religious in tone, the village was served during the first year by Father Valentine Sommereisen[66] until the Capuchin Fathers assumed charge in 1878.[67]

In 1877, Stephen Appelhans, who had taught school in Russia, offered his services as a teacher and his home as a school. The teaching was in German and the school term short. In 1895, the first school in Pfeifer was built, and in 1897 the present four-room structure was erected. It is interesting to note that the school was parochial from the beginning even before 1904, when the Sisters of Saint Joseph of Concordia took charge.[68]

The first mission group to work in Pfeifer were Sisters Helen Zimmerman, superior, Cyril Schumacher, Anacletus Wenk, and Hildegarde McAndrew.[69] The pastor at the time of the coming of the Sisters was Father Joseph, O.M.Cap. There were one hundred and forty pupils enrolled.[70]

Because additional farms were no longer to be had, many of the

[65] The Golden Jubilee of the German-Russian Settlements of Ellis and Rush Counties, Kansas, jubilee pamphlet (Hays, Kans., 1926), pp. 69-72. The jubilee was held Aug. 21-Sept. 2, 1926.

Johannes, op. cit., p. 21.

[66] Ibid., p. 64.

John M. Lenhart, "Reverend Valentine Sommereisen, Pioneer Priest of the West," Central-Blatt and Social Justice, vol. XXIX (1936-37).

[67] The Capuchin Fathers have done noble work among the Russian-Germans in Kansas. Through their efforts the religious life of the colonies has shown little influence from the surrounding indifferentism.

[68] Johannes, op. cit., pp. 89-90.

[69] Questionnaires of Sisters Helen Zimmerman, Anacletus Wenk, and Hildegarde McAndrew. Sister Mildred Huber replaced Sister Anacletus in the middle of the year.

[70] Wiltzius' Catholic Directory (New York, 1905), p. 275.

ounger generation tended to seek livelihood elsewhere, thus leaving he growth of the parish at a standstill. In 1947 four Sisters of Saint 'oseph taught the school in which seventy-six pupils were enrolled.[71]

The second Russian-German school, opened in 1904, was Schoen-hen, another of the five original settlements in Ellis County. Located leven miles south of Hays on the main highway between Hays and .a Crosse, on the south bank of the Smoky, Schoenchen was composed •f immigrants from Liebenthal in Rush County, who in turn had nigrated from New-Obermunjor and Schoenchen, Russia. Originally he village was called San Antonio, but after some disagreement •etween those from the two places in Russia, it was decided to name he town Schoenchen and the church Saint Anthony in honor of the hurch patron in New-Obermunjor. The parish was under the direc-ion of the secular clergy, but the Capuchin Fathers succeeded them n 1877.

A beginning in the field of education was made in the home of ohn Dreher in Schoenchen. Since the teacher himself knew practically o English, the common branches were taught in a German dialect. 3efore there was a formal organization of a school district, a school vas built and maintained.[72]

The Sisters of Saint Joseph sent three Sisters to Schoenchen in the all of 1904 to open the parochial school. The convent was built that ame year. Sister Alphonsus Corgan, superior, was assisted by Sisters Iildred Huber and Modesta Arnoldy.[73] Later in the year, Sister Iildred was replaced by Sister Anacletus Wenk. Father Michael Jeff, O.M.Cap., was instrumental in the beginning of parochial edu-ation in the parish. The Sisters were withdrawn for a few years and eturned in the fall of 1917 to teach in the newly constructed native-one school.[74] The first Sisters on the reopened mission were Sisters •orgia Moritz, superior, Romanus Deneke, Mary John Kuebler, and Iary Nicholas Arnoldy.[75]

In 1940, the school was changed from parochial to public school

[71] *Kenedy's Catholic Directory* (New York, 1947), p. 696.
[72] Laing, *op. cit.*, pp. 27-28.
  Johannes, *op. cit.*, pp. 22, 90-91.
  The Golden Jubilee of the German-Russian Settlements in Ellis and Rush ounties, Kansas, pp. 65-68.
[73] Questionnaire of Sister Mildred Huber and interview with Sister Cleophas Arnoldy.
[74] *Golden Jubilee of the German-Russian Sesttlements in Ellis and Rush Counties, ansas, op. cit.*, pp. 65-68.
  Johannes, *op. cit.*, pp. 90-91.
[75] Questionnaires of Sisters Mary Nicholas Arnoldy, Borgia Moritz, and Romanus eneke.

status. From 1921 to 1926, two years of high school were taught b the Sisters. The scarcity of high school teachers obliged the Com munity to turn over the high school to lay teachers at that time.[7] At present there are five Sisters in Schoenchen with seventy-five pupi enrolled in the grade school.[77]

The influence of the frontier may be seen in the extension of th Russian-German settlements into parts of Kansas farther west. was a normal frontier movement similar to those of the early settle in this country. When an immigrant family staked farm land an reared a large family, it often became necessary for the younger son to push on to new frontiers availing themselves of new country an greater economic opportunity.

Saint Peter, Graham County, several miles off the highway an the Union Pacific Railroad, was known as Hoganville. It was Russian-German settlement established by Ellis County families i 1894.[78] From small beginnings, the village has had a normal agricu tural growth with a church and school among the first consideration of the colonists.

In 1904, the same year as the opening of schools in the two old settlements of Pfeifer and Schoenchen, the Sisters of Saint Joseph (Concordia, at the request of the pastor of Saint Peter, Father Charl Weber, took charge of that parochial school. The school building wa completed the following year. Sisters Innocentia Brennan, superic Ildephonse Winkler, and Lucy LaSage were the first Sisters to I missioned there.[79] About eighty children enrolled that first year.

For a period of three years (1908-1911) the school was staffed I lay teachers, but the Sisters of Saint Joseph reassumed control aga in the fall of 1911. Sisters Canisius Meier, superior, Christina Ho man, Prudentia Corpstein, Mariana Burke, and Purificata O'Conn composed this second "first" group.[81] The school today enrolls in th vicinity of one hundred pupils with three teachers in charge.[82]

The developments so far described in this chapter were the resu

---

[76] Johannes, *op. cit.*, pp. 90-91.

[77] *Kenedy's Catholic Directory* (New York, 1947), p. 696.

[78] *Golden Jubilee of the German-Russian Settlements of Ellis and Rush Counti Kansas*, *op. cit.*, p. 89.

[79] Mission list of 1904. It is in the Archives of the Nazareth Motherhouse, Conc dia, Kans.

It will be remembered that in this same year Sister Lucy was replaced by Sis Celestine Wehrle because of the language requirement necessary for this school.

[80] *Wiltzius' Catholic Directory* (New York, 1905), p. 206.

[81] Questionnaire of and interview with Sister Prudentia Corpstein.

[82] *Kenedy's Catholic Directory* (New York, 1947), p. 696.

of five years of the administration of Mother Antoinette Cuff. In 1905, Mother Antoinette observed the twenty-fifth anniversary of her entrance into religion and the Community celebrated the event with special festivities. Therefore, it is a strategic time and place to evaluate the work thus far accomplished and look toward the rest of her term as Superior of the Congregation.

Note has been taken of the renovation work on the old Mother-house, the building of the new Nazareth, the conversion of the former Motherhouse into Saint Joseph's Hospital, and the reaffiliation of the group which had established a hospital and Motherhouse at Belvi-dere, Illinois. Many parochial schools opened during these years, among which were Sacred Heart School, Salina; Laramie, Wyoming; Parkston, South Dakota; Aurora, Illinois; and Angelus, Pfeifer, Schoenchen, and Saint Peter, Kansas. The jubilee year was to see the added schools at Aurora, Damar, and Gorham, Kansas. Another building project was formulating in the minds of the young Superior and her Council, namely, the Music Hall wing and the Chapel at the Motherhouse. Between 1906 and 1922 the Congregation was to open ten more schools in Kansas, one in Nebraska, one in Michigan, and three in Missouri. In addition the Community was to build another splendid hospital in Salina, an addition to the Concordia hospital, accept as a gift the Sabetha Hospital, and open the orphanage at Abilene. The crowning endeavor of Mother Antoinette's administra-tion was monumental Marymount, built in Salina. It is a marvel to all to find such an institution on the plains of Kansas.

It was appropriate that the Sisters honored Mother Antoinette on the occasion of her silver jubilee. Qualities of leadership and initia-tive make themselves known; and the Concordia Sisters early realized the Hand of God in the choice of their Superior in 1899. It has been mentioned that Mother Antoinette may be remembered in history as the consolidator and expansionist. It must always be remembered that the General Council and the Community as a whole gave approval and wholehearted support to these projects. It should be emphasized also that expansion should not be measured only in the material sense. The spiritual progress made by the members of the Community was remarkable and commented upon from many and widely scattered places. It was truly a period of stabilization.

At a special celebration on August 2, 1905, priests and Sisters assembled for the Jubilee Mass celebrated by Father John Maher of

Salina, administrator of the diocese in the absence in Europe or Bishop Cunningham. Sisters from Kansas, Nebraska, Missouri, Michigan, Illinois, and Wisconsin were home for the celebration. It was the first time in the history of the Community that all the Sisters met at the Motherhouse and the reason was twofold: to attend the silver jubilee anniversary of the Mother General, and to see the new Motherhouse.[83]

The Community had grown in numbers. According to the statistics of 1905 there were one hundred professed Sisters, forty-six novices, and four postulants, making a total of one hundred and fifty.[84] The Nazareth Academy was at that time a boarding school[85] with about fifty pupils.

In the fall of 1905, the following article appeared in a Concordia newspaper:

Forty-seven of the Sisters of Saint Joseph of Nazareth went away this morning. They had a chartered special car over the Burlington, direct to Chicago. From there they will go in parties to the various missions to which they have been assigned. Many will go to points in Michigan and others to various cities and missions in Illinois. The Mother General went with them as far as Wymore and will return this evening. . . . They have been here a month or more, and now after their retreat they again take up their work to which they have dedicated their lives. It is a fine sight to see such a large party of fine women going out into the world again to lift up fallen humanity, to direct the young into paths of usefulness and righteousness, to nurse the sick and cheer the disconsolate, to perform their duty in the light that is given them through their order and the great Church under whose teachings they labor. Churchman and he of no church can well afford to wish these noble Sisters well and Godspeed on their missions.[86]

This excerpt portrays in well-couched words the esteem of the people of Concordia for the work carried on in their midst. Concordia was a hotbed of freethought when the Sisters first arrived there in 1884. Nevertheless, references to the Sisters were highly laudatory.

Aurora, settled by French-Canadians from the vicinity of Bourbonnais, Illinois, is near Clyde and Saint Joseph. An interesting account in the *Kansas City Star* referred to Aurora as "Frenchy." Although French manners and customs have shaped the habits of the people, Aurora has become thoroughly Yankee in every respect except in a tenacious adherence to the French language. For a period after

83 *Concordia Blade,* Aug. 1, 3, 1905.
84 *Wiltzius' Catholic Directory* (New York, 1905), p. 277.
85 *Loc. cit.*
86 *Concordia Blade,* Aug. 17, 1905.

these colonists came to Kansas, poverty was rampant and they considered returning to "God's country in Illinois." Some did return but the majority remained, and, like the Bohemians, they kept the land they originally bought and added to it.[87]

The parochial school in Aurora was opened in 1905 under the direction of Sisters Evangelist Bonnifield, superior, Catherine Beck, Alberta Savoie, and Cornelius Perrault. The latter was replaced the following month by Sister Flavian Arpin.[88] Father P. Fortier was pastor. One hundred pupils enrolled.[89] The school, under the direction of the Sisters of Saint Joseph since its inception, continues to exert an important influence on the community. In 1916, during the pastorate of Father G. Lecoutre, a high school was opened with Sister Bertille Bridgeman as teacher. In 1919, it was accredited. Today there are fifty-one students in the grades and thirty-three in high school. There are six Sisters of Saint Joseph on the mission.[90]

Another school at Damar, Rooks County, Kansas, among the French-Canadians, was established in 1904. As Aurora, Saint Joseph, and Clyde were frontier foundations from the Illinois colonies, so Zurich and Damar in western Kansas were colonies from the older Kansas settlements. The same family names persist from one locality to the other. Like a typical European village with the church large and impressive around which the few buildings which make up the town cluster, Damar was described thus in 1910:

. . . Five years ago there were less than a half dozen buildings on the Damar townsite. Today it has a thrifty population of about three hundred; it has two general stores, a lumber yard, a bank, and two elevators . . . a Catholic Church and a convent. . . .[91]

When the first Sisters arrived, their home was still unfinished and they had to live under trying circumstances. There were in this original group Sisters Michael Beaudoin, superior, Assumption Martin, Victorine Allard, and Cyprian McHale.[92]

The mission was closed from the spring of 1909 until the fall of 1917. When it reopened, it was in charge of Sisters Philomene Belisle,

[87] *Kansas City Star,* Dec. 10, 1911.
[88] Questionnaires of Sisters Evangelist Bonnifield, Catherine Beck, and Alberta Savoie.
[89] *Wiltzius' Catholic Directory* (New York, 1906), p. 274.
[90] *Kenedy's Catholic Directory* (New York, 1947), p. 695.
[91] *Topeka State Journal,* July 27, 1910.
    Blackmar, *op. cit.,* vol. I, p. 491.
[92] Questionnaire of Sister Cyprian McHale and interview with Sister Edmund Simoneau, a native of Damar.

Adolphus Maloney, Mariana Burke, Josina Wynn, and Anita Marie Caron.[93] The high school has been under the direction of the Sisters with the exception of a few years. There are now six Sisters on the mission with about one hundred and forty-five students enrolled.[94]

One of the first divisions of the Russian-Germans in the Victoria parish was made in 1893 when several families sponsored the building of a new church in Gorham, seven miles east of Victoria on the Union Pacific Railroad. In those days of mud roads, it was deemed advisable to establish another congregation.[95] The parish has remained small, but since the discovery of oil in the vicinity it has become an active center of that industry.

Sisters of Saint Joseph were invited to teach in the parochial school in Gorham, and, they opened the school in the fall of 1905. Sister Katherine McPhillips was the Superior, with Sisters Helen Zimmerman and Dolorosa Golden as co-laborers.[96] Father Peter Hoeller was pastor at that time, and there were about sixty pupils in attendance.[97] In 1922-1923, a six-room school was built; a parochial high school was opened in 1926. In 1940 the town voted for a public high school, and the Sisters withdrew, confining their teaching to the parochial school.[98] There are now three Sisters in Gorham with about seventy pupils enrolled.[99]

One of the most important schools under the direction of the Community is Saint Xavier in Junction City, Kansas. The city is located on the Union Pacific Railroad and on the principal east-west highway in the state. Junction City has an interesting history as far as Catholic beginnings are concerned. The first authentic record of a service held there is contained in an item in the *Junction City Weekly Union,* June, 1861: "Father Dumortier organized the Catholic Church June 4, 1861."[100] It is not known where the first services were held. Father Dumortier traveled through Salina and other points along the Union Pacific during this formative period. Junction City was settled largely by the Irish. Later other nationalities moved in.

[93] Questionnaires of Sisters Philomene Belisle, Adolphus Maloney, Mariana Burke, Josina Wynn, and Anita Marie Caron.
[94] *Kenedy's Catholic Directory* (New York, 1947), p. 695.
[95] *Golden Jubilee of the German-Russian Settlements in Ellis and Rush Counties, Kansas, op. cit.,* pp. 87-88.
[96] Questionnaires of Sisters Katherine McPhillips, Helen Zimmerman, and Dolorosa Golden.
[97] *Wiltzius' Catholic Directory* (New York, 1906), p. 275.
[98] Questionnaires of Sister Lorena Heidrick and Francis Ellen Riordan.
[99] *Kenedy's Catholic Directory* (New York, 1947), p. 695.
[100] *Loc. cit.*

The school was opened in 1906 during the pastorate of Father John O'Brien, who was instrumental in encouraging the authorities in Concordia to send Sisters to take charge of his school. Since the turn of the century the parish had operated a school on a parochial basis taught by lay teachers.[101] Sisters Alphonsus Corgan, superior, Carmel Deiss, Armella Penegor, and Dolorosa Golden comprised the first group of Sisters.[102] Sister Dolorosa was replaced by Sister Vincent Breth later in that year. There were ninety-five pupils enrolled.[103]

In 1918, with the city and parish increasing in numbers, Father O'Brien seized the opportunity to build an up-to-date school building. The people became enthusiastic as the plans were laid before them, and the community as a whole generously supported the project. The high school building was completed in 1920. Four years later a large, comfortable residence near the school was purchased for the Sisters. The school has grown and is recognized for its high scholastic standards. Under the direction of Father James Bradley it is prospering and is training future leaders for the faith.[104] The total enrollment is now two hundred and thirty-seven, taught by eight Sisters of Saint Joseph.[105]

The steady growth of the Community made it necessary to build an addition to the Motherhouse in Concordia. In 1906, the Music Hall wing was erected which also served as living quarters for the Sisters.[106] Since the chapel had become inadequate for the accommodation of Sisters and boarders, a fund was accumulated for an addition. Begun in 1907, the chapel wing was completed and ready for dedication the following May. A separate laundry and power-house were built at the same time.[107]

Elaborate dedication ceremonies were held on May 8, 1908, with the local newspapers carrying accounts before and after the event.

[101] "First Record of Beginning of Kansas Church Dated June, 1861," *Northwestern Kansas Register*, spec. ed., Nov. 20, 1938.

Kansas City Catholic Register, July 5, 1934; July 15, 1937.

William G. Cutler. *History of Kansas* (Chicago, 1883), p. 1008.

[102] Questionnaires of Sisters Carmel Deiss, Armella Penegor, and Dolorosa Golden.

[103] Questionnaire of and interview with Sister Vincent Breth.

Wiltzius' Catholic Directory (New York, 1907), p. 292.

[104] *Northwestern Kansas Register*, spec. ed., Nov. 21, 1938.

[105] *Kenedy's Catholic Directory* (New York, 1947), p. 696.

[106] Cuff, *Diary*. Cost of this wing was $30,000.

[107] *Ibid.* The special meeting to decide on the building was called July 1, 1907; the contract was let to S. J. Hayden of Kansas City, July 2, 1907; work commenced July 8, 1907; first spade of dirt turned by the Most Rev. John Cunningham, July 15, 1907. Cost with furnishings was $90,000.

Concordia always showed appreciation for the building projects sponsored by the Sisters of Saint Joseph. One editor wrote as follows:

A notable event in religious circles here today was the dedication of the new Chapel of the Sacred Heart at the Convent of the Sisters of Saint Joseph — an event which gave pleasure not only to the townspeople but also to a large number of visitors as well. This beautiful new House of God, one of the most beautiful in the west, and built and furnished at a cost of nearly $100,000, is a grand addition to the church property of Concordia. . . . Fourteen young women received the habit of the Sisterhood at the conclusion of the dedication of the Chapel. . . .[108]

And to conclude the article he said:

. . . Thus concluded the services of the day and it was a fitting close to an occasion which marks a red-letter day in the holy Sisterhood through whose untiring efforts there is being built up in Concordia a Community of which we are all proud — Protestant and Catholic alike. . . .[109]

And in the same issue it was stated:

. . . In walking over the grounds and buildings at Nazareth Academy you can hardly realize that it was only five short years ago that the Sisters of Saint Joseph took up their home there, for the place now looks like a small town.[110]

Walker, Kansas, on the Union Pacific between Victoria and Gorham, was settled from the Victoria colony of Russian-Germans. The first school building, erected in 1893, was used later for a church. The Sisters of Saint Agnes from Fond du Lac, Wisconsin, conducted the school before the advent of the Sisters of Saint Joseph; and when the school was discontinued under the direction of the latter, it was resumed by the former.

In the fall of 1908, Sisters Sylvester Moritz, Anacletus Wenk, and Ephrem Fortier were sent to Walker to conduct the mission.[111] The pastor at that time was Father Sylvester, O.M.Cap. There were sixty pupils enrolled.[112] The present parochial school, begun in 1924, was ready for occupancy in 1925. The school passed from the jurisdiction of the Sisters of Saint Joseph to that of the Sisters of St. Agnes in 1923.[113]

---

[108] The following Sisters received the habit on that day: Sisters William Zimmerman, Praxades Hamil, Wilfred Jacobs, Geraldine Boudreau, Cecelia Cloutier, Cortona Robben, Leander Mayer, Alexius Gignac, Dositheus St. Aubin, Chrysostom Wynn (now the fourth Mother General of the Congregation), Scholastica Kennedy, Coletta Rupp, Charles Wolsieffer, and Claude Koerner.

[109] *Concordia Blade,* May 6, 1908.

[110] *Loc. cit.*

[111] Questionnaire of and interview with Sister Anacletus Wenk.

[112] *Wiltzius' Catholic Directory* (New York, 1908), p. 295.

[113] Questionnaires of Sisters Sylvester Moritz, Borgia Moritz, and Joan of Arc Letourneau.

Another city in Kansas to become a center of activity for the Sisters of Saint Joseph was Manhattan in Riley County. Organized as a town and first given the name of Boston by a group of New England settlers in 1855, the colony was augmented by settlers from the vicinity of Cincinnati within a short time. The population was for the most part American stock of Methodist affiliation.[114]

Served by the famous Jesuit, Father Louis Dumortier of Saint Mary's Mission, the early group of Catholics was insignificant as far as numbers were concerned but it demonstrated the faith zealously to those who surrounded it. The first church was the old Methodist Church purchased in the summer of 1880 by Father McCune.[115]

In the promotional literature are found such references as:

Last summer the Catholics purchased the stone church formerly used by the Methodists. It is 32 x 55 feet, has been thoroughly repaired, will seat about 250 persons, and is valued at $2000. Rev. McCune is resident pastor and holds services two Sundays in each month.[116]

During the pastorate of Father J. M. J. Reade, a consciousness of need for Catholic education for the children of the parish led to the establishment of a school conducted by the Sisters of Saint Joseph. His courage and vision were shown in the purchase of the Colonel Anderson property in June, 1903, for parochial school purposes. Thus began the history of the Sacred Heart Academy. Since that time, it has become one of the outstanding grade and high schools conducted by the Sisters.[117]

Sacred Heart Academy was opened in September, 1908, with the following Sisters in charge: Sister Louise Cuff, superior, Sisters Aquinas Fenton, Geraldine Boudreau, Cornelius Perrault, Rita Rivard, and Mildred Huber.[118] The Academy offered the complete grade and high school education from the beginning, and Manhattan claims the distinction of operating the first Catholic high school in the Dio-

114 Northwestern Kansas Register, spec. ed., Nov. 20, 1938.
    Seven Dolors Parish, Manhattan, Kansas (Manhattan, n.d.), passim.
    L. R. Elliott (ed.), The Blue Valley in Kansas—Marshall, Nemaha, Riley and Washington Counties (Manhattan, Kans., 1888), p. 7.
115 Cutler, op. cit., p. 307.
116 Alfred Griffin (ed.), An Illustrated Sketch of Riley County, Kansas—The Blue Grass Country (Manhattan, Kans., 1881), pp. 34-35.
117 Northwestern Kansas Register, Nov. 20, 1938.
    Seven Dolors Parish, Manhattan, Kansas, op. cit., passim.
118 Questionnaires of Sisters Mildred Huber, Aquinas Fenton, Rita Rivard, Cornelius Perrault, and Geraldine Boudreau.
    Seven Dolors Parish, Manhattan, Kansas, op. cit., passim.

cese of Salina.[119] The course was accredited in 1916. The enrollment the first year was 102 pupils.[120]

In 1938, crowded conditions necessitated expansion. A Methodist building was purchased and remodeled into the Sacred Heart Academy Grade School.[121] Much of the educational progress of Sacred Heart Academy is due to the interest of the scholarly Monsignor A. J. Luckey, present pastor of the parish. Today nine Sisters conduct the school in which two hundred and ten pupils are enrolled.[122]

Rulo, Richardson County, Nebraska, is in the Diocese of Lincoln. During the administration of Mother Stanislaus Leary, the Concordia Sisters were asked to conduct the school. No correspondence between the Sisters and the pastor in Rulo, Father John J. Hoffman, is extant. However, a letter from the latter to Bishop Thomas Bonacum of Lincoln shows this intention.[123]

Finally, in the fall of 1909, Sisters Isidore Burns, superior, Jerome Bombardier, and Clementine McGuigan were sent there only to be recalled the following spring. Conditions made it necessary for four religious communities ultimately to withdraw their Sisters. Today there is no school in the parish.[124]

The history of Park, Gove County, Kansas, is interesting. The settlers first called the town Buffalo,[125] later Buffalo Park,[126] and finally Park.[127] The original Catholic population of Park consisted of various nationalities: Irish, English, German, and Russian-German from the Volga and Odessa regions, as well as settlers from Illinois and the Victoria section of Kansas.[128]

Enterprising Catholic settlers tried to establish a dominantly Catholic colony in Park and to that end sent out advertisements to

119 Cf. f.n. 22, p. 206, of this work.
120 *Wiltzius' Catholic Directory* (New York, 1909), p. 297.
121 *Northwestern Kansas Register,* July 31, 1938.
122 *Kenedy's Catholic Directory* (New York, 1947), p. 696.
123 Sister Bernadette Reiffert, O.S.U., *Origins of Catholicity in Richardson County, Nebraska,* Creighton Univ. thesis, 1934. Manuscript in the Archives of the Kansas Catholic Historical Society; references to the letters in the Archives of the Diocese of Lincoln; affidavit of Rulo Parishioners, April 9, 1894.
   Letters of John J. Hoffman to Bishop Bonacum, July 31, 1895; Nov. 27, 1899.
124 Reiffert, *op. cit.,* p. 81.
125 K. W. Weston, *Guide to the Kansas Pacific Railroad for 1872* (Chicago, 1872).
126 Since this location was the center of their range, buffaloes were found here in greater numbers than elsewhere. Charles A. Sternbert, noted Kansas fossil hunter, in his account of a trip to this place in 1876 referred to it as "Buffalo Park."
127 In 1898 the U. S. Post Office changed the name to Park and the church established that same year used that name.
128 Peter L. Burkhart, *History of Sacred Heart Church, Park, Kansas* (Park, Kans., 1938), pp. 1-19.

encourage families to migrate there. The following is a translation of a German advertisement:

German Catholic Settlement in Western Kansas. This settlement, Buffalo Park, is in the process of development and is located on the main line of the Union Pacific Railroad, 350 miles west of Kansas City and 290 miles east of Denver, Colorado. Consists of level, rich land, fertile and crop bearing. The Church itself is 350 feet square and borders on fifteen acres of land also the property of the Church. The Church is nearly completed. The price of land is cheap at five or six dollars an acre, with one-fourth down payment and the balance payable in six years at seven percent interest. A discount is allowed for cash. For detailed information write to B. Albers, Angelus, Kansas, or to P. Schamber, Buffalo Park, Kansas. Information can also be had from Rev. P. Paul, O.M.Cap., of Hays, Kansas, from which place the parish of Park is attended.[129]

The Capuchin Fathers first ministered to the mission, but in 1901 the secular clergy took charge. Father Peter Hoeller introduced the Sisters of Saint Joseph to Park. In 1909, a Sisters' residence was built in order to secure Sisters to teach in the district school. The move gave the district school a permanent Catholic character. Although the grade and high school are public, the Sisters conduct them.[130]

Park holds the honor of having built the first school in Gove County. Since 1909 the Sisters have taught in the school. The original band consisted of Sisters Cleophas Arnoldy, superior, Visitation Nolan, and Albina Holmes. [131] The school term lasted nine months for the upper grades and six months for the lower grades. The other three months German and religion were taught to those who wished those subjects and the school was referred to as a parochial school. The school opened with about eighty pupils.[132]

In 1916, a rural high school was inaugurated, with Sister Virginia Burke as the teacher. The present high school building, erected in 1936, is the pride of the town. At present six Sisters of Saint Joseph teach one hundred and ten pupils.[133]

Antonino is a small village nine miles southwest of Hays inland from highway and railroad connections. Founded in 1906, it is a branch of the Munjor Russian-German colony, about seven miles west of the Munjor settlement.[134] During the pastorate of Father

---

129 *Ibid.*, pp. 15-16.
130 *Ibid.*, pp. 15-16.
131 Questionnaires of and interviews with Sisters Cleophas Arnoldy and Visitation Nolan.
132 *Wiltzius' Catholic Directory* (New York, 1910), p. 304.
133 *Kenedy's Catholic Directory* (New York, 1947), p. 696.
134 *The Golden Jubilee of the German-Russian Settlements in Ellis and Rush Counties, Kansas* (Hays, Kans., 1926), p. 100.

Anthony Basil, O.M.Cap., the Sisters of Saint Joseph of Concordia were invited to establish a small school there. Sisters Ildephonse Winkler, Frederica Brungardt, and Ethel Bresnahan composed the pioneer group. There were seventy pupils enrolled that year.[135]

The parish has not grown since that time. In fact, as was the case with most of the inland rural villages, the population has either remained static or has decreased. Today there are three teachers on the mission with about sixty-eight pupils enrolled in the school.[136]

Leoville, Decatur County, in the northwestern part of Kansas, is a German Catholic settlement. It was founded by three young men who migrated from Iowa in 1885, took out claims, built a sod church, and named it for the reigning pope, Leo XIII. Surrounded by a rich agricultural countryside, Leoville consists of a few houses, a village store, a large church, and a modern school.[137] The Precious Blood Fathers ministered to the needs of the parish until they were replaced by the diocesan clergy.

A priest influenced the early work of the Sisters of Saint Joseph in this community. As in the case of the location of the Sisters in three schools in Illinois,[138] so in the three missions of New Almelo, Park, and Leoville we can trace the influence of a priest. Father Martin J. Schmitt, after his transfer from New Almelo to Leoville, erected the convent so that the Sisters of Saint Joseph might be prevailed upon to teach in the public school.[139]

The first Sisters who went to Leoville in the fall of 1910 were Sisters Euphrasia Caron, Henry Healey, and Liguori Roth.[140] Catholic laymen and laywomen had been teaching in the public school. On June 22, 1910, after legal notice had been given, a vote was taken to make U. G. 1 a graded school and to employ two Sisters of Saint Joseph from Concordia. The vote carried and the school became graded, supported by seventeen and a fourth sections of land. The first year the enrollment was eighty pupils.[141]

In 1911 the present grade school was erected, and from 1913 to

[135] Questionnaires of Sisters Frederica Brungardt and Ethel Bresnahan.
[136] *Wiltzius' Catholic Directory* (New York, 1911), p. 320.
Kenedy's Catholic Directory (New York, 1947), p. 694.
1939), p. 448.
[137] *Kansas: A Guide to the Sunflower State*, Federal Writers Project (New York,
[138] The priest referred to here is the Rev. Joseph LaSage who was instrumental in locating the Sisters at St. George, Brighton Park, Chicago, and Aurora, Ill.
[139] *Oberlin Herald*, undated, 1939.
[140] Questionnaires of Sisters Henry Healey and Liguori Roth.
[141] *Wiltzius' Catholic Directory* (New York, 1911), p. 320.

1918 a two-year high school course was offered in connection with the grade instruction. Credit is due to Sister Aloysius Furstenberg for her zeal in teaching secondary education in this rural district. Her policy was to educate farm boys to love rural life, to see its advantages, and to encourage them to remain in a rural community.

The high school building was organized as a separate unit and received the approval of the State Board of Education in 1918. A new building, erected in the winter of 1925, was accredited as a four-year high school the following spring. It continues to train leaders in this rural settlement and has been commended for scholarship.[142] Today there are six Sisters of Saint Joseph teaching in the two departments with a total enrollment of one hundred and thirty pupils.[143]

Vincent, Ellis County, Kansas, was established as a branch of the Victoria parish. In 1907 a group of families who desired a church nearer than the Victoria church favored a movement to separate. At first twenty-two families were interested. Actually, only seven families participated and built the church.[144]

When the Sisters of Saint Joseph were invited by Father Pancratius, O.M.Cap., to take charge of the school, Mother Antoinette sent Sisters Sylvester Moritz and Borgia Moritz.[145] Seventy-five pupils enrolled that first year, 1911-1912.[146] The present enrollment is twenty-nine pupils with two teachers.[147]

Plainville, Rooks County, is about twenty-five miles north of Hays. Irish settlers first settled Plainville but were soon joined by immigrants of several other nationalities. As described by a pamphlet:

. . . Settled by active, energetic people from the eastern states . . . who brought with them the religious and educational tone of their old home but left its vices behind. . . . One fourth are from Iowa, one fifth from Missouri and Illinois and the rest from Nebraska, Pennsylvania, Indiana, and Ohio. The foreign nations in the order of their presence in the vicinity are Canada, Bohemia, England, Holland, Germany, Denmark, Sweden, France, and Scotland.[148]

---

142 *Oberlin Herald*, undated: "It is an interesting note that this community has the splendid record of having employed Catholic teachers at all times since its organization as a frontier rural school."
  Questionnaire of Sister DePazzi Wynn.
143 *Kenedy's Catholic Directory* (New York, 1947), p. 696.
144 *Golden Jubilee of the German-Russian Settlements of Ellis and Rush Counties, Kansas, op. cit.*, p. 99.
145 Questionnaires of Sisters Sylvester Moritz and Borgia Moritz.
146 *Wiltzius' Catholic Directory* (New York, 1912), p. 334.
147 *Kenedy's Catholic Directory* (New York, 1947), p. 696.
148 *Cheap Homes for Everybody in Northwest Kansas, Rooks County* (Stockton, Kans., 1887), *passim*. The information quoted applies to the entire county.

Plainville was served by several of the diocesan clergy after 1894, including the pioneer itinerant priest, Father J. B. Vornholt, and the late Father Joseph Perrier.[149] It is to be remembered that Father Perrier was mainly responsible for the location of the Motherhouse of the Congregation of the Sisters of Saint Joseph in Concordia.

Recognizing the need for Catholic education among the youth of the parish, Father Henry Baumstimler requested that his school, which had been in charge of lay teachers the year before, be placed under the jurisdiction of the Concordia Sisters. Mother Antoinette sent Sisters Carmel Deiss, superior, Cortona Robben, DePazzi Wynn, and Felix McCarthy[150] to open the school in the fall of 1911. There were seventy-five pupils enrolled that fall.[151]

The mixed character of the congregation has made the school cosmopolitan. From its inception, the pupils have always been a credit to their teachers. There are now three teachers and eighty-three pupils enrolled.[152]

Another school opened in 1911 was at Nevada, Missouri. Situated in Vernon County about ninety miles southeast of Kansas City, Nevada is in the coal region with iron works and flour milling the chief industries. Sisters Celestine Wehrle, superior, Joanna Rutledge, Constance Mullen, and Laurentia Wynn went there in 1911.[153] Father Boniface Spanke, O.S.B., was the pastor.[154] The Sisters of Saint Joseph from Wichita had preceded the Concordia Sisters as teachers in the school.[155] Sixty pupils enrolled the first year.[156] When the Sisters were withdrawn in the spring of 1917, the number had fallen considerably.[157] In railroad centers the fluctuating population influences the enrollment in parochial schools.

Emmeram, Kansas, opened in 1912, was another short-lived mission. Several of the parishioners of Saint Fidelis Parish in Victoria

149 *Kansas City Catholic Register*, July 15, 1937.

150 Questionnaires of and interviews with Sisters Carmel Deiss, Cortona Robben, and DePazzi Wynn.

151 *Wiltzius' Catholic Directory* (New York, 1912), p. 333.

152 *Kenedy's Catholic Directory* (New York, 1947), p. 696.

153 Questionnaires of and interviews with Sisters Joanna Rutledge and Laurentia Wynn.

154 One of the later pastors while the Sisters of St. Joseph of Concordia conducted the school was the Reverend M. F. X. Jennings, who was instrumental in procuring the Sisters for Boonville, Mo., in 1923.

155 *Wiltzius' Catholic Directory* (New York, 1906-1911), listed the school under the Diocese of Kansas City, Mo.

156 *Ibid.* (1912), p. 469.

157 *Ibid.* (1917), p. 458.

petitioned Bishop Cunningham to establish a new parish six miles north of Victoria. The permission was granted in 1899, and a church and school were established.[158] In the fall of 1912, Sisters Anacletus Wenk, Victoria Flannigan, Mary Nicholas Arnoldy, and Felix McCarthy were sent there.[159] Father Basil, O.M.Cap., was the pastor when the school was opened with an enrollment of ninety-five.[160] Lay teachers had preceded the Sisters; and, when in 1916 the Sisters were withdrawn, they were succeeded by lay teachers again.[161] The parish school has not been conducted by religious teachers since.

Clinton, Henry County, Missouri, is in the Diocese of Kansas City. A trading center for the surrounding prairie and stock-raising country, Clinton is near the Kansas City markets, eighty-seven miles to the northwest.[162]

There were enough Catholics in Clinton in 1875 for the congregation to erect the first church. Clinton was originally served by the Precious Blood Fathers from Montrose, a thriving German-Catholic settlement. Later it was taken over by secular clergy when the railroad center was established there and brought many Catholic families to the town. One of the early priests in the parish was Father John Hennessy, later the Administrator of the Diocese of Concordia and a staunch friend of the Sisters of Saint Joseph in that diocese.

Father Edward Fitzgerald, realizing the importance of the parochial school as a vitalizing force in every parish, made a petition to Concordia for Sisters to conduct his school. He had purchased the old Clinton Business College and converted it into Holy Rosary Academy the year before the Sisters were procured.[163]

Sister Ambrosia McPhillips, superior, was assisted ably that first year by Sisters Walburga Wuerth, Martina Heidrick, Rosella Raymond, Fabian Mulhearn, Assisium Guinan, Borromeo Bouchard, Vin-

---

[158] *Golden Jubilee of the German-Russian Settlements of Ellis and Rush Counties, Kansas, op. cit.,* pp. 90-91.

[159] Questionnaires of and interviews with Sisters Anacletus Wenk and Mary Nicholas Arnoldy.

[160] *Wiltzius' Catholic Directory* (New York, 1913), p. 344.

[161] *Ibid.* (1912), p. 332; (1917), p. 317.

[162] *Encyclopedia Britannica,* vol. V, p. 830.

Alfred E. Woods (ed.), *History of Henry and St. Clair Counties, Missouri* (Kansas City, 1883), p. 27. This promotional pamphlet is interesting especially in that it contained a picture of the Clinton Business College which was later to become Holy Rosary Academy under the direction of the Sisters of St. Joseph of Concordia.

[163] Sister Evangeline Thomas, "Court House Scene of First Mass in Clinton, Missouri," *Kansas City Catholic Register,* Apr. 14, 1925.

cent Marie Martin, and Purificata O'Connell.[164] From its inception, the school was a boarding and parochial day school. The number of Catholics was never very large and, that number dwindling down through the years, the student body became largely Protestant. A high school and commercial department were always highly regarded by the local citizenry. Amicable arrangements between the authorities of the Clinton Public High School and Holy Rosary Academy enabled students of the public high school to enroll for certain subjects at Holy Rosary.

The Community of the Sisters of Saint Joseph felt that splendid opportunity was offered in Clinton to work for souls. However, when there was a scarcity of Sisters to staff the missions, the authorities in Concordia felt that Catholic students had first claim to the ministrations of the Sisters. Therefore, the school was closed in the spring of 1925.[165]

A third school was opened on the northern peninsula of Michigan in the fall of 1912. The Community conducted two other schools in this vicinity. Gladstone, Delta County, is in the Diocese of Marquette. A terminus for the export and distribution of wheat brought from Minneapolis and the Northwest, Gladstone became an active and thriving city soon after its establishment. The population is cosmopolitan, with Scandinavians in the majority. A Catholic Church was erected in 1889.[166]

The parochial school, All Saints' School, has been large and prosperous from the beginning. Father Owen Bennett, pastor, knowing the Sisters of Saint Joseph from the splendid work accomplished in the near-by parishes of Escanaba and Lake Linden, appealed to Mother Antoinette for her Sisters to take charge of Gladstone.

Sisters Florence Sullivan, superior, Armand St. Onge, Loretta Gosselin, Pauline Belisle, Joanna Rutledge, Adelaide Parnell, Clementine McGuigan, and Assumption Martin went to the new mission

---

[164] Questionnaires of and interviews with Sisters Walburga Wuerth, Rosella Raymond, Assisium Guinan, and Borromeo Bouchard.

[165] *Kenedy's Catholic Directory* (New York, 1913), p. 492, mentions that there were eighty-seven enrolled in Holy Rosary Academy the first year it was conducted and in 1925, p. 456, there were one hundred and two enrolled. The first figures were larger in Catholic students while the latter were dominantly Protestant.

[166] Sawyer, *op. cit.*, vol. I, pp. 374-375.
A. I. Rezek, *History of the Diocese of Sault Ste. Marie and Marquette*, 2 vols. (Houghton, Mich., 1906-1907), *passim*.

in August, 1912. It was Father Bennett's intention to add a year of high school each year until he had a completed high school. In 1913, the ninth grade was added with Sister Bertille Bridgeman as teacher. The high school continued until the spring of 1916, when the pastor decided it was a financial burden on the parish. Sister Evarista Lapine taught the high school during 1915-1916.[167] There were three hundred and ten pupils enrolled that first term.[168] Today there are six Sisters teaching two hundred and thirty-eight pupils.[169]

California, Moniteau County, Missouri, was the only new mission added in 1913. Boasting a long Catholic life, the town of California has had a Catholic Church since 1859. The town had been officially named Boonesborough, but confusion with Boonville made a change of name expedient.[170]

Father P. Rosch, pastor of California, had a parochial school conducted by lay teachers for two years before the advent of the Sisters of Saint Joseph.[171] In the fall of 1913, Sisters Isidore Burns, superior, Madeleine Perry, Herman Joseph Schroll, and Vincentia Pfeifer took charge of the school which had forty-two pupils enrolled. When the parish fund was unable to support a group of teaching Sisters, they were recalled to Concordia in 1917, to be used on other missions conducted by the Community.[172]

Although the school in Cawker City, Kansas, was not opened until two years later than the school in California, Missouri, it will be considered in this chapter because it was the last parochial school opened during the administration of Mother Antoinette Cuff. The remaining years of her administration (1914-1922) were devoted to building projects which will be treated as a unit in the following chapter.

Cawker City was settled in 1870 by migrants from Towanda,

---

[167] Questionnaires of and interviews with Sisters Adelaide Parnell, Pauline Belisle, and Joanna Rutledge.

[168] *Kenedy's Catholic Directory* (New York, 1913), p. 545.

[169] *Ibid.* (1947), p. 562.

[170] James E. Ford, *A History of Moniteau County, Missouri* (California, Mo., 1936), p. 249.

[171] *Wiltzius' Catholic Directory* (New York, 1912), p. 469.
Kenedy's Catholic Directory (New York, 1913), p. 497.
"Young People Don't Leave California, Missouri, Parish," *Kansas City Catholic Register*, Jan. 15, 1925.

[172] Questionnaires of Sisters Herman Joseph Schroll and Vincentia Pfeifer.
Kenedy's Catholic Directory (New York, 1914), p. 503.
Kansas City Catholic Register, Jan. 15, 1925.

Pennsylvania, among whom was a man by the name of E. H. Cawker for whom the town was named.[173] Nine years later a Catholic Church was erected by Father Clemens, a Precious Blood Father.[174] In 1883, property and a residence were purchased with the idea of converting it into a parochial school and "this is the first step toward making Cawker the school town of the State."[175] Plans miscarried, and it was not until the fall of 1915 that Sisters were secured to teach in the parochial school.[176] Father Louis E. Wahlmeier invited the Sisters of Saint Joseph to teach in the school, and Sisters Carmel Deiss, superior, Romanus Deneke, Martin Killeen, and DePazzi Wynn comprised the pioneer group.[177] There were boarders from the beginning, and in that first year, thirty pupils were enrolled.[178] Today the enrollment is forty-four with two Sisters in charge.[179]

Considering 1914 as the logical date at which to make a division in the administration of Mother Antoinette Cuff, we shall glance at the accomplishments of the fifteen years of her administration thus far discussed.

In 1900 the *Catholic Directory* lists the following institutions in the Diocese of Concordia under the jurisdiction of the Sisters:

Nazareth Academy, Concordia	40 (boarders)
Cathedral School, Concordia	95
Beloit	140
Clay Center	60
Clyde	51
Herndon	30
Saint Joseph	185
Total in Concordia Diocese	601 pupils[180]

In comparison to the above statistics, we shall quote those of 1914 which will show the progress during those years:

---

[173] Blackmar, *op. cit.*, vol. I, pp. 300-301.

[174] Cutler, *op. cit.*, p. 1027.

[175] *Monthly Visitor*, Feb., 1883; Apr., 1884.

[176] The building now known as St. Teresa's Academy was the first public school in Cawker City. When the town built away from the school, other schools were erected for the public school system and the original building was purchased by the parish.

[177] Questionnaires of Sisters Carmel Deiss, Romanus Deneke, and DePazzi Wynn.

[178] *Kenedy's Catholic Directory* (New York, 1916), p .334.

[179] *Ibid.* (New York, 1947), p. 695.

[180] *Wiltzius' Catholic Directory* (New York, 1900), pp. 241-243.

Nazareth Academy, Concordia	80 (boarders)
St. Joseph's Hospital, Concordia	100 (patients)
Clyde	72
Cathedral School, Concordia	105
Antonino	78
Aurora, Kansas	100
Beloit	145
Dresden (Leoville)	94
Emmeram	75
Gorham	81
Herndon	76
Junction City	175
Manhattan	102
Park	92
Pfeifer	101
Plainville	105
Saint Joseph	65
Saint Peter	80
Salina	285
Tipton	150
Vincent	60
Walker	80
Total in Concordia Diocese	2,201 pupils[181]

This indicates almost a fourfold multiplication of opportunity within the Diocese of Concordia alone. Similar statistics for the missions in dioceses in several states of the Midwest would impress the fact even more indelibly upon our minds.[182]

Whereas there were eighty Sisters in the Community in 1900, there were two hundred thirty-two professed Sisters, thirty-four novices, and twelve postulants in 1914.[183] This showed a gain of almost unbelievable proportions. Spiritually, there was progress in the annual retreats conducted at the Motherhouse for those within reasonable distance and at a central place in the North for those who could not return annually to the Motherhouse. There was spiritual direction by the chaplain at the Motherhouse and regular conferences for the novices on the religious life by Mother Antoinette herself who each Sunday devoted a part of the day to this instruction.

---

[181] *Ibid.* (New York, 1914), pp. 352-354.

[182] This latter number is listed at 3,565 as a grand total for the entire school system conducted by the Sisters of St. Joseph of Concordia in 1914. *Wiltzius' Catholic Directory* (New York, 1914), p. 907.

[183] *Ibid.*, p. 907.

The Community was homologous with the frontiers on which the Sisters were working. There were additions from Ireland, France, Italy, and Germany but the American frontier stock became numerically predominant. Although there were calls for the various nationalities to work among their own, Sisters who were unfamiliar with the language were sent into missions to perform work which was difficult but which did much toward meeting the challenge of Americanizing the peoples among whom they worked. Thus we see the frontiers opening, the challenges being met, and the work of the Sisters of Saint Joseph of Concordia stretching out to conquer new frontiers for God and country.

CHAPTER X

Administration:
Reverend Mother Antoinette Cuff
Part II: 1914-1922

IN 1650, in the parish church in Le Puy, France, the Bishop Henry de Maupas du Tour handed the daughters of France a cross with the admonition: "Wear it openly, bear it bravely just as Christ did up anguished heights." The Daughters of Saint Joseph heeded the advice of their founder and friend, and down through the years they exemplified that spirit which identifies the Sisters of Saint Joseph throughout the world.

"Carry it," said he, "down the ways of pain into homes of fever, into the warrens of the poor; bear it to far-off lands. Be it your oriflame to light you on to victory. When in death you resign it, let other hands and hearts like to yours in consecration take up the burden, preserving it ever in their and your society's keeping through the onrolling centuries."

Let us stop at this point in the history of the trek across land and sea, in the meeting of the challenge of the frontiers in widely scattered lands, and see how the spirit in the minds of the founders has permeated the thoughts and actions of those who followed.

The Kansas foundation was not one of the easiest by any means. There was *annihilation of self,* a carrying out of the parallel which the venerated Father Medaille drew between the animating spirit of the *Little Design* and the poverty, chastity, humility, and charity of Our Lord Jesus in the Holy Sacrament of the Altar. There was *poverty,* whereby the poverty of Christ in the Blessed Sacrament might have been emulated. There was *faith* and *hope* that the efforts to meet the challenges which confronted them might be supplied by that same

239

Father who always knows what is best for the Community. There was *charity* in their dealings with others, in their assistance to the sick and the needy and to the needs of the children placed under their care. There was *humility* in its various degrees in all types of work. There was the fulfillment of the purpose of the *Little Design* and those who composed it, to live not for self, but to be wholly lost and annihilated in God and for God; to be everything for the dear neighbor, nothing for self.

The preceding pages show how this spirit has crossed the frontiers with their challenges to take Christ to souls. In the present chapter, we shall continue to describe the work of the Congregation accomplished during the last eight years of the twenty-three-year administration of Mother Antoinette Cuff. This period under her courageous leadership was one in which one institution after another was raised up for God's work among men, for the accomplishment in a greater, broader, and more efficient way of the aims of the Congregation in this particular portion of the vineyard.

The Motherhouse, finished in 1903, had been augmented by the addition of a Music Hall and Chapel. The total cost, assumed and entirely paid for between 1902 and 1912, of $208,802.32 [1] was in addition to the expenses incurred in the conversion of the old Motherhouse into a hospital and the expenses of the Belvidere institution. The cemetery to the south of the Motherhouse had been laid out and beautified. The local editor spoke of some of the improvements in the following manner:

Those who have not lately been out to Nazareth Academy will be greatly surprised the next time they visit that part of the city at the great amount of work that has been done to improve and beautify the grounds in front of the academy. The land has all been leveled off to a grade, 8,000 feet of cement walks have been laid, a summer rest house of beautiful design has been erected near the main entrance to the convent, trees have been set out along the driveways and walks, and bluegrass has been sown on the broad lawns. A decorative stone wall is to be built along the whole front of the grounds, with artistic entrances, gate, etc. A great deal of work has been done and much money spent in carrying out this broad plan of improvement.[2]

As will be seen from the following excerpt, the city cooperated with the improvement program in many ways:

Mayor Short told the council that Mother Superior, who is at the head of the Nazareth Academy, was contemplating building about 8,000 square feet

---

[1] Statement of the Costs of the Buildings and Improvements of Nazareth Convent and Academy From 1902-1912.
[2] *Concordia Blade*, undated.

of cement sidewalk in and along the Academy yard. Upon her request he suggested that the council grant water free of charge for the mixing of the cement. Upon a motion the request was granted. Mother Superior also has another request to make of the city. In the year 1903 she gave the city about thirty feet of land of the frontage of the academy ground to be used as a street; in consideration of this deed the city agreed to furnish $50.00 worth of water each year to the academy for ten years free. The ten years were up last January and she requests that she be allowed $50.00 worth of water each year for the next ten years.

The discussion brought out the fact that the churches of the city were not paying water rent, but that the schools were, and inasmuch as the convent is a school and church combined and that the convent is the largest water consumer in town, using in the neighborhood of $200.00 worth a year, Councilman McConahey made a motion the request be granted.[3]

There was always expressions such as "Deo Gratias" and "The Lord be praised for all He has done for us" in mention of payment of loans for the various institutions. The following entry was made on March 26, 1912:

Today Sister Mary Rose and myself went down to the Farmer's Bank and paid the interest on $5,000 for six months at 5% which was $125.00. We also paid the principal $5,000 which is the last payment on all the money borrowed. At present we owe no one except for the monthly expenses. All we have is paid for. We can indeed say "The Lord is good." We called upon the Bishop [Cunningham] and told him the good news. He is going to say Mass tomorrow in thanksgiving and we will offer our Holy Communion for the same intention.[4]

As soon as one building project had been completed, paid for, and a sizeable sum accumulated, there would be a trip to the home of Bishop Cunningham to secure the permission to begin another enterprise. There was a courageous trust in God who blessed each new undertaking with unlimited success.

The city of Salina is favorably situated for parochial and hospital work. Through the influence of the late Monsignor John Maher, the Sisters of Saint Joseph were established in the parochial life of the city in 1900. Their contribution to the educational and religious life of Salina was soon manifest even to those not of the faith. When, in 1912 and 1913, there was local concern for hospitalization needs, the citizens of Salina were ready to consider the Sisters of Saint Joseph to fill that need. Father Maher, who was well thought of by his parishioners and by the citizens of Salina as a whole, suggested that he invite the Sisters to undertake another building project.

---

[3] *Ibid.*, undated but apparently in the spring of 1913.
[4] Cuff, *Diary*. The original is in the files of the author.

On July 11, 1912, Mother Antoinette, as president of the Corporation of the Nazareth Convent and Academy, called a meeting of the trustees. It was announced that the Bishop was anxious to have the Congregation build a hospital in Salina. Bishop Cunningham promised to give his share of a tract of land, and the parish of Sacred Heart Church would give its share of the same tract of land on North Penn Street to the Corporation for that purpose.[5] The remaining share belonging to Mrs. Katherine Baier was purchased.[6]

Early in January, 1913, sixteen building contractors from various parts of the State met with trustees of the Corporation of the Nazareth Convent and Academy at Concordia and submitted bids for the new hospital. The contract was let to the Nelson Building Company of Salina and the Salina Plumbing Company. C. A. Smith was the architect.[7]

Father Maher offered, on behalf of his parish, to furnish one-fourth of the $100,000 original figure for the building. In a short time, he had received pledges for $25,000.[8]

The *Salina Union* recorded the turning of the first spadeful of soil:

The first spadeful of soil for the new Saint John's Hospital to be erected on East Ash Street was turned yesterday evening by Bishop Cunningham of the Concordia diocese. The ceremony of thus starting out the work on the

[5] *Minutes of the Meetings of the Corporation of the Nazareth Convent and Academy, 1901-1939,* vol. I, p. 30. This transaction took place on Mar. 17, 1913. The deed is in the Archives of the Nazareth Motherhouse, Concordia, Kans.

[6] *Loc. cit.* The site, acquired on Mar. 17, 1913, is legally described as all of block eleven in the Riverside Park addition of the city of Salina. The deed is in the Archives of the Nazareth Motherhouse, Concordia, Kans.

[7] *Minutes of the Meetings of the Corporation of the Nazareth Convent and Academy, 1901-1939,* vol. I, pp. 32-33. Further references in this source are vol. I, pp. 35, 38, 44.

This same information was contained in articles in the Salina and Uniform Contract, May 2, 1913, in the Archives of the Nazareth Motherhouse, Concordia, Kans.

Salina Journal, May 2, 1913.

[8] The names of twenty-one donors of large sums may be seen on the slabs in the hospital vestibule. They were:

James Mason	$1500	Patrick Donohue, Niles	$3000
Hugh Carlin	1000	Mrs. F. K. Baier	1000
D. D. McAuliffe	1000	Salina Deanery	1000
Edward Carlin	1000	Ladies Guild	1000
J. A. Skelley	1000	William Sullivan	1000
John J. Geis	1000	Mrs. Clara Schippel	1000
Edwin J. Kaffer	1000	Wm. Wessling Family	1000
Charles L. Schwartz	1000	H. D. Lee	1000
Mrs. Julia Martin	1000	Weber and Co., Wilson	1000
Cunningham Brothers	1000	T. T. Sullivan	4000
Frederick and Elizabeth Hinnenkamp	1000	Helen O'Reilly	1000

Northwestern Kansas Register, July 2, 1939.

Nazareth Motherhouse, Concordia, Kansas

Saint Joseph's Hospital, Concordia, Kansas

Saint Joseph's Hospital, Belvidere, Illinois

Saint John's Hospital, Salina, Kansas

Saint Joseph's Home, Abilene, Kansas

Saint Anthony Murdock Memorial Hospital, Sabetha, Kansas

Seneca Hospital, Seneca, Kansas

hospital building was attended by the Mother Superior and her Council of the Sisters of Saint Joseph and by the Reverend Father Maher of Sacred Heart Church. The site for the new building was also located by the Bishop and the Sisters from Concordia. The hospital will be in the center of the block between Ash and Johnstown and will face the east on Penn Avenue. It will be east of the ravine on the block but the building may eventually be extended back over this.

The work on the new hospital will start in a short time....[9]

On June 28, 1914, the hospital was dedicated to the service of God and suffering humanity. More than 3,000 people attended the ceremonies which included the dedication of the chapel as "the house of God" and the hospital as "the house of man." The dedicatory address was given by Father A. J. Kuhlman, S.J., noted retreat master, of Saint Mary's College, St. Marys, Kansas. He said in part:

Today is a great day for Salina. Something is being done here that calls out the citizens of all classes to this event. It is something in which we are all interested. It is not for one; not for a few; not for one body only but for all. It is something permanent. The walls are firm but the institution is firmer.

This represents something that is a benefit; something that is good. It is true it has been built and is being dedicated by one form of religion alone. But its charity is for all. All will find an equal welcome here. Wide indeed it is opened for all. All that are human can find an entrance here. This is a work in which we all have an interest. Some have a special interest. We come here not only to witness a dedication but also to give honor to whom honor is due. All who have in any way done anything are given acknowledgment. There are those who have given time, work, energy. And since this is public it is right to give a special mention to all who have given. Not to do it would detract. But there is something more and that is true charity. That is known in the inspection of Almighty God, Who knows what work was done and what time spent in this great work. Human words cannot rightly reward them. It is a great thing to take stone and brick and make them into a fit habitation. [Here he paused to read the list of donors. See footnote 8.]

The walls are high and the roof is on but the work is not yet done. They look to you yet. Out-pouring, large numbers and good words are all good but there are other things that are essential. There must be those who by the sweat of their brow have accumulated of this world's goods who will give to those who conduct something like this. If money is given freely, then a great work is done. Look to this building today and you will see that is being given for a great cause....

And then the Sisters behind the walls are back to their work. It is the beginning of a great labor for them. These women whose services could not be bought are giving themselves. They are giving to Salina generation after generation of Sisters. They are to live and die here and others will be called to take their place. [Then a well-deserved tribute was paid to Monsignor Maher through whose efforts the work had been projected.]

Why are you interested? Why are you here? Why are the Sisters here?

[9] *Salina Daily Union,* May 2, 1913.

It is because of the common bond of human suffering that brings us closer together. It is the sight of suffering. Every one who has had a share in this building can thank God when a sick and suffering person receives comfort here. . . .

We have immortal souls. But as we are all mortal spirits they are encased in bodies and these bodies need hospitals. The Sisters who will work here will show equal love to all. The life to which she is dedicated is not carnal and prevents her love for one more than another. It is a spiritual life. The hospital and its work will make a better education for this town and this nation. We need more than schools and the preaching of the Word of God. We need the example such as women of this kind can give. The Sisters do not want money for themselves when they ask for money in the building of a hospital. A Sister comes here and stays fifty years and when she leaves it, she leaves as she came— without a cent. The nation needs a lesson in the use of money. These Sisters have given up all. Home ties are broken for those who enter here. There can be no cry of mother love, no love as a wife, but only a spiritual love for all who enter here. This is a free nation and always will be free but the real champions of liberty are those who chain themselves in the service of others.[10]

Shortly after the dedication of the hospital, it opened to the public with the following Sisters in charge: Sister Clare Cuff, who had opened the Saint Joseph's Hospital in Concordia in 1903, superior, with Sisters Mechtildis Yoos, Mildred Huber, Henry Healey, Leonard Millette, Felicitas McAuliffe, Praxades Hamil, Marcella Glynn, Hubert Rajewski, Prosper Marqueling, and Cordelia Svec.[11]

Saint John's was referred to at that time as ". . . . Salina's first $100,000 building." [12] The total cost of the building with the furnishings was set at $136,600.[13] The *Catholic Directory* lists the institution in its first year as having ministered to the needs of over four hundred patients.[14]

When the Saint John's Hospital in Salina celebrated its silver jubilee in 1939, the following tribute by His Excellency, the Most Reverend Frank A. Thill of Concordia, expressed in graphic words the contribution a hospital staffed by a Catholic Sisterhood makes to the environment in which it labors:

In the name of the Church I bless the Sister-nurses and physicians of Saint John's Hospital on the occasion of the silver jubilee of their institution.
Possibly no science in modern times has extended its boundaries as widely

10 *Salina Journal*, June 29, 1914.
11 Questionnaires of Sisters Mechtildis Yoos, Mildred Huber, Henry Healey, Leonard Millette, Felicitas McAuliffe, Praxades Hamil, Marcella Glynn, Hubert Rajewski, Prosper Marqueling, and Cordelia Svec.
12 *Salina Journal*, Jan. 1, 1914.
13 Cuff, *Diary, op. cit.*
    Year Book, Concordia Community, 1914-15, p. 476.
14 *Wiltzius' Catholic Directory* (New York, 1915), p. 349.

as the science of medicine; no art has reached out as far into other fields as the art of healing. I congratulate all who have served so valiently for a quarter of a century in Salina to conquer disintegration, to forestall decay, and to challenge death. I stand in admiration at the courage with which you have sought to touch, not only the palpitating walls of flesh, but to lay your hands, for healing, on the impalpable substance of the mind.

May the Divine Physician, Our Lord Jesus Christ, be your ideal and guide in the coming years as He has been in the past. He is greater than Galen or Hippocrates, greater than Osler or Mayo, because He cleansed lepers without serums, restored sight without surgery, needed neither pills nor potions, but only a word to bring dead men back to life.

May you be always loyal to Him, for, in His name, it has been said that, although we are subject to the humiliations of decay and death, nevertheless, one day even this corruption shall put on incorruption, and this mortal put on immortality.[15]

Saint John's Hospital has increased its facilities and staff until today it is on a par with the best in the state. A word of gratitude is in order to those modern Oslers and Mayos of the staff who by their devotion to humanity and to the work carried on by the Sisters of Saint Joseph in Salina, as elsewhere, have merited the eternal gratitude of Church and state. The graduates of the hospital training school are to be found in important positions serving as they learned so well to serve under the direction of the Sister nurses.

During the year 1947, twenty-one Sisters and thirty-two student nurses administered to the needs of 2,675 patients[16]—a six-fold increase since the first year. Again, the frontier has been cultivated to a remarkable degree and the work for humanity has long been blessed even in a material manner.

In the youthful days of the Concordia Diocese attention was not needed for many of the complexities of a larger population. However, the need for hospitals was felt early and was met by the establishment of Saint Joseph's Hospital in Concordia in 1903, and Saint John's Hospital in Salina in 1913. Special institutions for the orphan and the aged were not considered seriously until about 1910 when the Sisters of Saint Joseph began to care for the orphans of the diocese at Saint Ann's Academy in Clyde. The school, in operation since 1888, was considered adequate in accommodations for the few children who needed such care.[17] Sister Evangelist Bonnifield and Sister

15 *Northwestern Kansas Register,* July 2, 1939.

16 *Kenedy's Catholic Directory* (New York, 1947), p. 697.

17 *Salina Journal,* Oct. 14, 1914.
   Souvenir of the Silver Jubilee of Rev. H. A. R. Spoorenberg, St. John the Baptist Church, Clyde, Kansas (Concordia, Kans., 1933), July 12, 1933.

Blanche Bueche were among the Sisters who cared for the little one of the diocese when they were housed in Clyde.[18]

The problem of a diocesan institution with ample accommodation and suitable location for the proper care and training of dependen and neglected children was one of major importance. Foster home were not readily available except through systematized institutiona placement. After much thought and consideration on the part o Bishop Cunningham and those interested in establishing a wel equipped charitable institution, it was decided that overtures woulc be made to the Sisters of Saint Joseph of Wichita to purchase propert from them to the north of the city of Abilene.

One of the first missions opened in the present diocese of Salin. had been in Abilene in 1887 when Mother Stanislaus Leary sent few Sisters to that flourishing cattle town to open a school and pos sibly with the intention of later moving the headquarters of the Concordia Community to that place. We have traced the vicissitude of the early days of Abilene, its separation from the mother stem, anc the establishment of the separate Community of the Sisters of Sain Joseph of Wichita. It was considered wishful thinking on the part of the Concordia Sisters to hope that one day the institution would be placed under their care again.

The Sisters of Saint Joseph of Wichita had discontinued the Academy two years before the purchase of the institution and ground by the Diocese of Concordia. During that time, the faithful veteran John Nicholson, had kept watch and ward over the forlorn institu tion. The negotiations completed in October, 1914, transferred pos session for the sum of $25,000.[19] The improvements carried out b Bishop Cunningham doubled the cost of the venture.[20]

On September 1, 1915, the Sisters from Concordia took charge ol Saint Joseph's Home under the leadership of Sister Regis Schwenzer Her co-laborers in the work were Sisters Fabian Mulhearn, Constanti Colehan, Xavier Cunningham, Edward Brungardt, Flavian Arpin

---

[18] Questionnaires of Sisters Evangelist Bonnifield and Blanche Bueche.
    Rev. Joseph J. Conway, *Memoirs of Rev. Joseph J. Conway of St. Joseph's Home Abilene, Kansas;* manuscript in the files of the author.
  [19] Conway, *op. cit.,* p. 1.
    Wichita Catholic Advance, June 22, 1929.
    Salina Journal, Oct. 14, 1914.
    Abilene Reflector, Oct. 10, 1914.
  [20] Conway, *op. cit.,* pp. 1-2.

DeChantal Norton, and Purificata O'Connell. In October, Sister Loretta Gosselin was added to this group.[21]

Father Joseph Conway, first resident chaplain at the orphanage, has described the first two years of its existence. In one place he refers to the visitors:

... Other visitors always cheerful and leaving cheer behind were Sisters from the neighboring missions. Best of all was the Reverend Mother. Mother acted like King Clovis in the Rheims Cathedral as she crossed the threshold of the Home. Of course the large hall floor was shining like a mirror and the beautiful statue of the Sacred Heart beamed with tender majesty upon its donor. Reverend Mother needs every cent because of the debt on the Salina Hospital and projected improvements yet she has been profusedly generous to the orphanage....[22]

The formal dedication was held on December 8, 1915, with Bishop Cunningham officiating. Again Father Conway described the occasion:

The Feast of the Immaculate Conception was a beautiful day. It broke clear and balmy, with not a tinge of crispness in the air. At the Mass the children united with the Sisters in offering the Holy Sacrifice for my dear mother's happy repose. Our Lady's altar was richly decorated, so too the main altar, with chrysanthemums and narcissus, Mrs. Sullivan's gift. The children sang beautifully.... His Lordship arrived for dinner. Soon came Mother Antoinette, Sisters Mary Rose and Louise who came with Mrs. Priest and Michael. They had come by auto straight from Concordia. Then came the autos and carriages— nearly a hundred of them. It was a big day and a big turnout. We were ten priests and then there was the Bishop. His Lordship bore himself through the long ceremony of blessing the bell without seeming fatigue. Father Maher gave a grand address forgetting nothing and nobody. His talk bore early fruit for useful gifts began coming in the very next day. Father Horgan chanted like a two-year old. Father Fleming scrubbed the bell like a graduate laundry worker....[23]

There were fifty-eight persons in all residing at the Home in February of that year. This number included the chaplain, the Sisters, some half dozen or so aged persons and about forty children.[24] Among the early visitors was Doctor William Turner, professor of philosophy at the Catholic University, who was visiting his friends in Concordia in June, 1916.[25]

The orphanage and home for the aged in one building was never satisfactory, and as early as October, 1916, when visiting in Abilene,

[21] Questionnaires of Sisters Regis Schwenzer, Xavier Cunningham, Flavian Arpin, DeChantal Norton, and Purificata O'Connell.

[22] Conway, op. cit., passim.

[23] Ibid., pp. 5-6.

[24] Kenedy's Catholic Directory (New York, 1916), p. 336.

[25] Conway, op. cit., pp. 15-16.

Bishop Cunningham spoke of building a separate old people's home in Abilene or elsewhere.[26]

The annalist closed his two-year summary with the following:

> . . . There is a real improvement in the deportment of our children over their conduct a year ago, a sure sign that the Sisters have done their work well. Our old people have diminished in number, three having answered the last call. Who are left ought to be satisfied for they are treated with great consideration and kindness. Our children have escaped illness since January.
>
> Thus, we all felt grateful to God when we sang the *Te Deum* December 31, and we enter the New Year with a humble prayer for the blessings of the Sacred Heart and of our Blessed Mother and Saint Joseph on the Home through 1917.[27]

The material progress during the thirty years of the existence of the orphanage has been great. The spiritual progress and the educational and cultural contribution has benefited Abilene, the surrounding territory, and society in general.

The youths at the institution are active members of 4-H clubs and meet periodically to discuss projects in operation at the Home. Guest speakers, educators from Kansas State College, Manhattan, and county home demonstration agents, bring messages of progressive living and opportunity to the orphans.[28]

Early in the history of the orphanage, a herd of Holsteins of fine stock was developed at St. Joseph's Home. By the end of the 1930's, the herd had won state and national recognition. This project, in addition to supplying the institution with an abundance of milk, butter, and meat, serves an important role in directing the energies and recreational activities of the boys into constructive, educational channels. In well-equipped quarters, a herd of 140 prize animals is cared for with the most modern methods by the boys at St. Joseph's.

At a time when the leading social workers of the country are concerned with the problem of juvenile delinquency, it is a happy event to find a group of boys learning and enjoying themselves and taking pride in such projects as are carried on at the Home.

Annual exhibitions at the local, regional, and state fairs require weeks of careful preparation. Each boy takes pride in the animals which are given to his care. In order to hold the record from year to

---

[26] *Ibid.*, p. 17.
[27] *Ibid.*, p. 23.
[28] *Northwestern Kansas Register*, Dec. 1, 1940, Aug. 3, 1941.

year, the animals require special feeding, hair clipping, currying, and training.[29]

Blue ribbon awards, medals, cups, and other prizes in the showcases at the Home bear testimony to the teaching of the Sisters. Best known of all is Sister Xavier Cunningham who has trained a generation of boys to judge animals. An excerpt from the *Holstein Friesian World,* the national Holstein breed magazine published in Lacona, New York illustrates this point:

> Sitting at the ringside at the St. Joseph's Home classification at Abilene, Kansas, one could not help but be impressed that something important was taking place there. As each cow came into the ring, which was surrounded by breeders from all over the state, awaiting the rating of Professor Atkinson, she was followed by several solemn-faced boys. When the decision was announced, it was always relayed back to the boys working in the barn. To say that the boys were the most interested is not literally true, because back of everything there has been the guiding mind and hand of Sister Xavier.
>
> Sister Xavier is not only admired and respected by every dairyman in Kansas because of her success in dairy farm management, but because of the contribution she has made in the training and development of the scores of boys who have come under her care in the close to three decades since her outdoor program was forced upon her by her health. . . .[30]

Farm pasture experimental work on the property of the Home is conducted by some of the boys who, after finishing their grade school work there, continued to live at the Home and to attend public high school in Abilene. Later many of them, some on scholarships, majored in agriculture at the Kansas State College in Manhattan.[31]

Annual Christmas plays are always well received by the citizens of Abilene, and on one occasion as many as 1,200 attended. The boys and girls who attend the public high school have done creditable work and have participated in choral societies, clubs, student government. In fact, one boy was the president of the student board.[32]

One instance of an orphan from the Home awarded a scholarship to Kansas State College was reported in the *Abilene Reflector* and later in the *Northwestern Kansas Register:*

> [Omer] was one of fifteen Kansas boys to be awarded a Sears Agricultural Foundation scholarship of $150. This award brings honor to Abilene and to

[29] *Ibid.,* Sept. 25, 1938.
[30] *Holstein Friesian World,* July 8, 1929.
    Northwestern Kansas Register, Sept. 25, 1938; May 14, 1939; July 23, 1939; July 28, 1940; Sept. 29, 1940; Aug. 17, 1941; Aug. 24, 1941; Sept. 6, 1942 are samples of articles on this subject.
[31] *Ibid.,* Apr. 5, 1942; Dec. 25, 1938; Dec. 24, 1939.
[32] *Ibid.,* Nov. 12, 1939.

Saint Joseph's Home. The scholarship aids boys to attend Kansas State College. F. W. Costello, county agent, and Fred Allison, vocational agricultural instructor in the high school, nominated Omer for the award. Omer spent eleven years at the orphanage and finished his high school work last spring. He was a member of the high school live stock judging team that won first place in the State two years ago. Besides being an outstanding agricultural student, Omer is also active in dramatics, was president of the student council and made an average grade of nearly ninety-four in his four years of high school work.[33]

Another instance reports the winner (another boy from the Home) in Holstein division of the statewide essay contest sponsored by the Purebred Dairy Cattle Association of America in cooperation with the *Kansas Farmer's* magazine of Topeka.[34]

There has been much local pride in Abilene since the inception of the Home. Leading citizens have given their time and money to sponsor activities for the orphans. The Chamber of Commerce and the Knights of Columbus[35] have encouraged the work of the band. For nearly twelve years Mr. Clem Pleiser of St. Andrew's parish, Abilene, made weekly visits, gave music instruction to the children, and repaired and loaned instruments. When he was unable to work up a band for the annual orphan's Christmas program, he selected his talent from Abilene musicians to furnish the music.[36]

The spiritual activities of the Home are organized under the diocesan Catholic Youth of Salina. There has been a close correlation between the 4-H and the CYS. The spiritual assets of the CYS implement the 4-H ideals.[37] Spiritual retreats are held just as in the ordinary grade and high schools of the diocese.[38] And in traditional manner, a May Queen is crowned in the grotto on the grounds of the orphanage.[39]

Since 1915, the Home has been a real home to boys and girls who are either orphans or dependent. When the silver jubilee of the institution was celebrated in the fall of 1940, about 1,000 children had spent from one to fifteen years with the Sisters of Saint Joseph. Today we can find these citizens of the new generation living in various parts of the country and engaging in many types of endeavor.[40]

---

[33] *Ibid.*, Nov. 12, 1939.
[34] *Ibid.*, Aug. 17, 1941.
[35] Questionnaire of Sister Cornelius Perrault who was in Abilene from 1922-1926.
[36] *Northwestern Kansas Register*, Dec. 15, 1940.
[37] *Ibid.*, Jan. 26, 1941, and Feb. 23, 1941, are good examples of this correlation.
[38] *Ibid.*, Dec. 8, 1940.
[39] *Ibid.*, May 28, 1939.
[40] *Ibid.*, Sept. 4, 1938; Oct. 19, 1941.

Saint Joseph's has served well in the Diocese of Salina. Today there are twenty-one Sisters with approximately fifty orphans for most of the year.[41]

Institutional expansion seems to have been the dominant interest of the Sisters of Saint Joseph during the second part of the administration of Mother Antoinette Cuff. Between the opening of St. John's Hospital, Salina, and the orphanage in Abilene, there was a period of four or five years in which institutions in operation were expanded. The new wing on Saint Joseph's Hospital, Concordia, was added. The cemetery and Lourdes Park at the Motherhouse greatly enhanced the value of the property, and several additions of land in the vicinity of the Motherhouse were made. A new project was being planned, and a fund was growing for that purpose. In the meantime, there was an unanticipated demand for the labors of the Sisters when the Sabetha Hospital, Nehema County, Kansas, was taken over by the Community.

Sabetha, an agricultural trading point, according to legend was named by a pious Biblical scholar who reached this point in the 1850's on his way to California. One of his oxen died on a day he calculated to be the Hebrew Sabbath—so he named his camp Sabetha.

Albany Hill, established in 1857 by pioneers from Castle Creek, New York, who named it for the capital of their state, antedated Sabetha. Albany Hill was two miles north of Camp Sabetha. When a railroad was built through the country in 1871 and a station erected on the old camp site, Albany Hill's inhabitants moved to Sabetha. It was here, at an important station on the Underground Railroad, that John Brown, ardent abolitionist, was said to have spent his last night.[42]

The need for a hospital in northeastern Kansas and southern Nebraska urged Dr. Samuel Murdock, in 1900, to establish a rudimentary hospital; and in 1904, he augmented his nursing staff by starting a nurses' training school. The hospital prospered, and the fame of Dr. Murdock as a surgeon spread. In 1910, he felt it necessary to build a thirty-bed brick hospital which he operated until 1920.[43] Needing an adequate staff that would allow him to devote

[41] *Kenedy's Catholic Directory* (New York, 1947), p. 697.

[42] *Kansas: A Guide to the Sunflower State,* Federal Writers' Project (New York, 1939), p. 313.

Dr. Samuel Murdock, Sr., had established in Sabetha and was later associated with his son, although it was the son who originally built the hospital in 1900.

[43] *Northwestern Kansas Register,* Mar. 4, 1945.

his time to surgery, Dr. Murdock approached the Sisters of Saint Joseph of Concordia to purchase for half price his hospital, valued at about $100,000. When they replied that at that time such a purchase was impossible since the plans for a new educational institution were in the making, Dr. Murdock generously offered the hospital and its contents to the Community.[44]

Dr. Murdock wrote to the authorities in Concordia that the hospital was in good financial standing, that the highest ideals were maintained, that all bills were paid, that the people of the vicinity were educated to the proper care of the sick, and that they had an appreciation of the work done by the Sabetha Hospital for the past sixteen years.[45]

At a special meeting of the trustees of the corporation of the Nazareth Convent and Academy, November 1, 1920, the offer of the hospital was accepted.[46] A week later, Mother Antoinette and Sister Mary Rose went to Sabetha to visit the hospital and received the deed.[47] In consideration of the gift, the Corporation agreed to give the control of the medical and surgical staff to Dr. Murdock.[48]

The transfer of the hospital from Dr. Murdock to the Sisters of Saint Joseph was not made without unpleasantness. An article by Father James J. Kehoe in a two-volume work on the Leavenworth Diocese shows many people in Sabetha resented the gift:

> Doctor S. Murdock donated his institution to the Sisters of Saint Joseph of Concordia, Kansas. When this became known in the vicinity, the people were incensed over the thought that the hospital was going to be under the auspices of Catholic Sisters. Even to the day the contract was signed and put into effect there was a meeting held in the town trying to persuade the Doctor to sell it to the Methodists. They offered $75,000 but he refused. The Sisters took over on November 22, 1920, and strange to relate those who were responsible for the meeting to prevent their coming to Sabetha turned out to become their very best friends.[49]

[44] The educational project was the new boarding school in Salina which today is known as Marymount College.

[45] Letter of Dr. Samuel Murdock, Jr., to Mother Antoinette Cuff, Oct. 8, 1920. The original is in the Archives of the Nazareth Motherhouse, Concordia, Kan.

[46] *Minutes of the Meetings of the Corporation of Nazareth Convent and Academy, 1901-1939*, vol. I, p. 65.

[47] *Loc. cit.*, dated Nov. 2, 1920. Legal description of land—plot in Sec. II to 2514 in Nemaha County, Kans.—approximately 10 acres. *Hiawatha World*, Nov. 1, 1920; *Concordia Blade*, Nov. 1, 1920; *Salina Journal*, Nov. 4, 1920; *Falls City Journal*, Oct., 1920; and the *Sabetha Herald*, Oct. 30, 1920 (these latter references seem to be the first public announcement of the transfer contemplated).

[48] *Minutes of the Meetings of the Corporation of Nazareth Convent and Academy, 1901-1939*, vol. I, pp. 65-67.

[49] *Loc. cit.* The volumes are to be found in the Kansas State Historical Library in Topeka, under Sabetha — alphabetically filed clippings.

The institution was renamed the Saint Anthony Murdock Memorial Hospital. The original Sisters were Sisters Philomene Belisle, superior, James Bombardier, Winifred Hinrich, Victoria Flannigan, Charles Wolsieffer, and Victorina Barrins.[50]

When the Sisters of Saint Joseph took charge of the hospital in Sabetha, there was no resident Catholic priest there. The Sisters had to travel to Fidelity to attend Mass. Father A. J. Dixon went to Sabetha occasionally to conduct services in the bungalow on the grounds of the hospital. In May, 1921, Father J. S. Moriority became resident chaplain and remained there until July. He was succeeded by Father J. A. Wasinger who erected the church in Sabetha during his time as pastor.[51]

The nurses' home, a frame building to the north of the hospital, and the Sisters' residence, to the south, were purchased a short time after the Sisters established themselves in Sabetha.[52] Realizing that the parish was small and unable to buy a home for the priest, the Community decided in 1928 to purchase a home for the priest who would also be chaplain at the hospital.[53] In 1922, there were twelve Sisters, eight student nurses, and two hundred fifty patients cared for at the hospital.[54]

The need for expansion was felt from the beginning, but it was several years before the Community felt financially able to build an addition to the Saint Anthony Murdock Memorial Hospital. However, in the late 'twenties that need became more pressing than ever. Therefore, the local superior, Sister Regis Schwenzer, also a member of the General Council, proposed at the regular meeting of the Board of Trustees of the Nazareth Convent and Academy that the Community build an addition of at least thirty rooms to the hospital. The questions of cost and the procurement of funds were discussed at length, the cost being approximated by Mr. Brinkmeier, Emporia architect, at $80,000. It was agreed to borrow $50,000 at five and a half percent interest, Dr. Murdock pledging himself to pay the interest on

[50] Questionnaires of Sisters Philomene Belisle, James Bombardier, Winifred Hinrich, Victoria Flannigan, Charles Wolsieffer, and Victorina Barrins.

[51] Article by the Rev. J. J. Kehoe, cf. f.n. 49.

[52] *Minutes of the Meetings of the Corporation of the Nazareth Convent and Academy, 1901-1939*, vol. I, pp. 69-70.

[53] *Ibid.*, vol. I, p. 97.

[54] *Kenedy's Catholic Directory* (New York, 1922), p. 436.

the loan. Friends of the Sisters of Saint Joseph would come to their assistance with donations for the project.[55]

Fifty thousand dollars was borrowed from the Massachussets Life Insurance Company on a note which matured on October 1, 1939.[56] Dr. Murdock fulfilled his part of the contract by sponsoring clinics. The following undated clipping illustrates this point:

> Physicians who attended the clinic at the Murdock Memorial Tuesday this week pronounce it an even equal in importance to notable clinics they have seen. Physicians were present from Nemeha County and surrounding counties in Kansas and Nebraska. Doctor Murdock, Jr., who performed the operations, worked laboriously from ten o'clock in the morning until after two in the afternoon. Surgical science as it is known and practiced today was employed in usual and rare major operations.[57]

In the same clipping, Dr. Murdock referred to a contemplated expansion program which would accommodate more patients. He said that the hospital would always operate as a standard hospital; that is, that a complete history and diagnosis would be made in each case, that a written record would remain on file of every operation and all treatments administered in the hospital. Every member of the staff signed the pledge of honorable practice at the hospital.[58]

At the thirty-first annual meeting of the Corporation of the Nazareth Convent and Academy held on the first Monday of January, 1930, Sister Regis gave an account of the work done on the new addition. She reported that $10,000 at six percent interest had been borrowed from the bank in Sabetha, that $3,000 raised by holding clinics had been given by Dr. Samuel Murdock, about $5,000 had been given by friends, and that $2,500 had been borrowed from Miss Pearl Wilson, one of the nurses at the hospital.[59]

The addition, erected at a cost of more than $80,000,[60] was opened and dedicated on November 20, 1930,[61] during the administration of Reverend Mother Mary Rose Waller. Laboratory and

---

[55] *Minutes of the Meetings of the Corporation of Nazareth Convent and Academy, 1901-1939*, vol. I, pp. 112-113, dated July 1, 1929. First mention of the addition was in the *Sabetha Herald*, Jan. 4, 1929.

[56] *Minutes of the Meetings of the Corporation of Nazareth Convent and Academy, 1901-1939*, vol. I, p. 110.

[57] *Hiawatha World*, undated but possibly in 1929.

[58] *Loc. cit.*

[59] *Minutes of the Meetings of the Corporation of Nazareth Convent and Academy, 1901-1939*, vol. I, pp. 117-118; pp. 160-161.
Minutes of the Meetings of the Councillors of the Sisters of St. Joseph of Concordia, Kansas, June, 1925-July, 1940, pp. 11-12.

[60] Abstract, Seneca, Kans., Oct. 17, 1929; General Contract, Sept. 4, 1929.

[61] Questionnaire of Sister Martina Heidrick.

other equipment have been improved until today the Saint Anthony Murdock Memorial Hospital in Sabetha is known as one of the best-equipped hospitals in northeastern Kansas.

A newspaper item concerning the death of the noted surgeon and benefactor of the Sisters of Saint Joseph, Doctor Murdock, on February 28, 1945, described conditions as they were at that time. The hospital was staffed by twenty-two Sisters and approximately thirty-six student nurses.[62] Statistics showed 1,600 patients cared for in 1946, and one year later 1,800 patients were cared for.

Again we have witnessed the challenge of a frontier in northeastern Kansas met and conquered. Saint Anthony's Hospital today exemplifies the Community's success.[63]

The growth of both the Community and Nazareth Academy during the first two decades of the twentieth century made necessary an expansion program which began in 1913 and ended in 1922. Concordia had been by-passed by the important railroads and highways, and earlier expectations for its development as an important center in northwestern Kansas were not realized. Although Concordia is still very dear to the Community of the Sisters of Saint Joseph as the seat of the Motherhouse, it was thought best to build the new school elsewhere. Therefore, about the time that plans were in the making for Saint John's Hospital, Salina, the Sisters of Saint Joseph were investigating other towns in the Diocese of Concordia as a location for the new academy and college.

Residents of Junction City, Manhattan, and Salina wanted to attract the Sisters. A Manhattan editor remarked:

It became known today that Manhattan stands a fair chance of being chosen as the location for the new Catholic seminary for girls that the Sisters of Saint Joseph of Concordia are planning on building in the near future.

Three towns are making efforts to land the big school. They are Manhattan, Junction City, and Salina. In speaking of the matter today, J. B. Floersch stated that it was his opinion that the matter rested between Manhattan and Salina. He said he knows that Manhattan stands a better chance of getting it than Junction City. Manhattan is urging its railway facilities covering the northern part of the diocese of Concordia and no doubt is going to be an exceptionally strong competitor. The location of the school here would add much to the school facilities already afforded by Manhattan and would tend to make it an even stronger educational center than it is now.

With Salina and Manhattan as the strongest competitors, it would seem

[62] *Northwestern Kansas Register*, Mar. 4, 1945.
[63] *Kenedy's Catholic Directory* (New York, 1946), p. 542; (1947), p. 542.

that Manhattan would stand the best chance, as Salina has just been chosen as the location of a large $100,000 Catholic hospital.

It is rather difficult to get a line on the exact situation here on account of the recent death of Father J. M. J. Reade. His successor, Rev. A. J. Luckey, arrived here today from Ellsworth.[64]

Salina would not be outdone in hoping for the location. Commenting on the above article, the editor of one of the Salina newspapers said:

... While it is said that no particular location in Salina has been decided upon, Salina is still considered the first choice for the location of the seminary, provided that a proper location could be secured. It is said that negotiations were started at one time to secure a tract of ground, but that the price asked was too high for the Sisters to consider its purchase. . . . Many citizens are interested in holding the school here if possible and are anxious that nothing be done that would interfere with its going elsewhere [sic] . . .[65]

Salina made a greater effort to secure the school than the other two towns. Early in 1913, the Chamber of Commerce and the Retail Merchants' Association appointed a committee to investigate the matter.[66] Some sites previously considered were not available because the owners, hearing of the plan, raised the price beyond reason. The committee, with Fred H. Quincy, chairman, secured an option for thirty days on sixteen and a half acres of the D. A. Van Trine property, east of Deer Park on East Iron Avenue.[67] Mr. Quincy contacted several businessmen of Salina and before the meeting of the Chamber of Commerce was held, he had over half of the purchase price in subscriptions. The property was to be purchased, if acceptable to the Sisters, and donated to them.[68]

The next day the press announced the completion of the canvass. Everywhere the project had been given a favorable reception and everyone had subscribed with the firm belief that the proposition was a good one. The list of subscribers contained names of people who had given generous support to Kansas Wesleyan University (Methodist), and to Saint John's Military School (Episcopalian), when they established or expanded their institutions in Salina.[69]

[64] *Manhattan Mercury,* Jan. 14, 1913.

[65] *Salina Journal,* Jan. 16, 1913.

[66] *Ibid.,* Feb. 12, 1913.

[67] Legal description of the tract of land: 16½ acres in NE ¼ of Sec. 18 T. 14: R.2 west of 6th Principal Meridian, Saline County, Kansas.

[68] *Minutes of the Salina Chamber of Commerce,* Feb. 12, 1913. *Salina Journal,* Feb. 13, 1913.

[69] *Salina Journal,* Feb. 14, 1913. (Footnote continued on next page.)

Father Maher, pastor of the Church of the Sacred Heart, who was largely responsible for the establishment of both the hospital and the college in Salina, was authorized by the committee of the Chamber of Commerce to offer the site to the Sisters of Saint Joseph at once. The next day Bishop Cunningham, Mother Antoinette Cuff, and members of the Council arrived in Salina to inspect the site.[70] They were shown other sites but were delighted with the one offered by Salina. Mother Antoinette was quoted in the *Salina Journal* as remarking that "the location is one of the most beautiful I have ever seen." The Sisters were pleased with the beautiful view of the winding Smoky Hill River and the valleys which surrounded it.[71] That same afternoon the agreement was signed, with the city promising to donate the site and the Sisters promising to erect a building valued at $100,000. Work was to begin within the two years fol-

---

[69] (continued)

The honor roll of subscribers was as follows:

H. D. Lee	$1,000
Farmers National Bank	350
Traders State Bank	350
Planters State Bank	250
National Bank of America	250
Cravens Mortgage Company	100
C. Eberhardt Lumber Company	100
L. S. Rosenwald	100
Stevenson Clothing Company	100
P. L. Gebhardt and Son	100
J. C. Wilson	100
Putnam Investment Company	100
C. A. Smith	100
Stroup Lumber Company	100
Sudendorf Brothers	100
W. W. Watson	100
Shellabarger Mill and Elevator Company	200
J. Duncan	100
Ledigh and Havens	100
Steifel Brothers and Company	100
L. A. Will	50
T. W. Roach	50
M. B. Palmer	50
Salina Produce Company	50
Salina Candy Company	50
Lynn and Wakenhut	50
Z. C. Millikin	50

[70] *Ibid.*, Mar. 5, 1913.

It is interesting to note that the sum of over $4,000 was pledged within less than a day and a half and that after the canvass had closed two substantial donations were received.

An offer by the Salina Vitrified Brick Co. of $100 in cash was changed to that same amount in brick. The Salina Steam Laundry made a similar offer donating the amount of $100 in laundry at the opening of the new institution.

[71] *Ibid.*, Mar. 6, 1913.

lowing January 1, 1913.[72] Because of financial burdens incident to the uncompleted Saint John's Hospital in Salina,[73] construction could not begin immediately.

The people of Salina evidenced a spirit of cooperation and civic-minded goodwill which might well be emulated elsewhere. It may have had another motive: the betterment of business enterprise in the city. Whatever the reasons were, this spirit has continued and the Sisters of Saint Joseph are grateful to the original benefactors of Marymount College.

Considerable publicity was given to the proposed agreement by the local press and the Associated Press.[74] Since this was the first attempt in the State of Kansas to establish a four-year college for women, the project received attention from Catholics and educators. By the time the two years had expired, war in Europe made prices for building materials and labor too high to launch any extensive plans.

In 1916 Bishop Cunningham advised Mother Antoinette Cuff and her council to consult an architect for an estimate of the cost of the building. Mr. C. A. Smith, Salina, was chosen to draw up plans. The $100,000 building originally contemplated now became a $450,000 venture. Before a loan could be negotiated, our country became involved in the war and work was abandoned.[75]

In the fall of 1918, when the war was over, Bishop Cunningham encouraged the Community to make another attempt to build. Facilities at Nazareth Academy were taxed to capacity. The steady growth of the Sisterhood convinced authorities in Concordia of the need for a school which would in the summertime minister to the educational needs of the Sisters. In view of this need, and with their character-

---

[72] Warranty Deed from Ina S. Van Trine and D. A. Van Trine to Nazareth Convent and Academy, A Corporation. The deed is in the Archives of the Nazareth Motherhouse, Concordia, Kans.

   Proposition and Agreement to Build, Feb. 12, 1913. The Archives of the Nazareth Motherhouse, Concordia, Kans.

[73] *Minutes of the Meetings of the Corporation of the Nazareth Convent and Academy, 1901-1939,* vol. I, pp. 44-46.

   Salina Journal, Feb. 12, 1913.

[74] *Ibid.,* Feb. 13, 1913.

   Salina Daily Union, Feb. 15, 1913.

   Kansas City Star, Feb. 13, 1913.

[75] *Minutes of the Meetings of the Corporation of the Nazareth Convent and Academy, 1901-1939,* vol. I, pp. 46-54.

istic dauntless courage, the Congregation met the challenge and reassumed interest in the building program.[76]

In February, 1919, Mother Antoinette recorded in her *Diary* that the Congregation had asked permission of the local Ordinary to secure a loan. Permission was granted[77] and negotiations were reopened with the Chamber of Commerce in Salina and soon definite plans for the erection of the building were made. One of the first benefactors to the cause was Bishop Cunningham, whose inspiration and encouragement during these trying years meant a great deal to Mother Antoinette and her Sisters. On February 21, 1919, he donated $25,000 to the building fund. This and other promises served as an impetus to the work.[78]

Knowing the interest Father Maher had always taken in the Sisters of Saint Joseph, the Bishop advised them to ask his assistance in the project. Father Maher gave generously and should be given much of the credit for the enlargement in the plans of the institution and in its successful accomplishments during the years which followed.[79]

On February 18, 1919, Father Maher outlined a proposition to a group of bankers and businessmen, guests at a dinner given at the Salina Country Club by J. F. Merrill, president of the Farmers National Bank.

In substance the plan was this: a building costing more than $300,000 would be erected instead of the $100,000 building originally promised if the city of Salina would donate the sum of $50,000 toward the enterprise. The presidents of each of the five banks were named as a committee to devise plans for raising the money. It was the unanimous opinion of those present that the $300,000 building should be built speedily.[80] "No promises," wrote the local editor, "were made, other than those outlined, but it is apparent from the history of other enterprises, that if Salina is successful in this achieve-

[76] *Ibid.*, pp. 46-54.

[77] *Minutes of the Meetings of the Corporation of the Nazareth Convent and Academy, 1901-1939*, vol. I, pp. 46-54.

[78] *Ibid.*, pp. 46-54.

[79] *Ibid.*, pp. 46-54.

[80] *Salina Journal*, Feb. 19, 1919.

Minutes of the Meetings of the Corporation of the Nazareth Convent and Academy, 1901-1939, vol. I, pp. 46-53.

ment, it would eventually make Salina the bishop's residence, the principal institutions of the diocese being located here. Salina would thus become the center of the diocese, which extends from Manhattan west to Colorado and north to the Nebraska state line."[81]

If the plan was successful, work on the building would start in the spring. However, if the $50,000 could not be raised, the $100,000 building would be erected and part of the boarding school, the secondary school, would have to be maintained in Concordia, and the entire Salina institution used for work on the college level.[82]

The next evening a mass meeting was held. This followed the meeting of the Board of Directors of the Chamber of Commerce, the Municipal Improvements Committee, and the Rotary Club, which approved the proposition. Mr. D. J. Hanna was elected chairman of the mass meeting and he called upon Father Maher to present the case. Father Maher said in part:

. . . I am not bringing this matter to the attention of the citizens of Salina from a sectarian standpoint, but in the way of a general business proposition of interest to the city. Our parochial school, church and other buildings are matters for our parish to take care of. We built them without outside help. This is a different matter. I have no control over this school. I am interested in having it come here as a citizen of Salina is interested in anything that is for the good of the city. Our plan is to bring here a great institution. The school at Concordia now has more than one hundred boarding students. These will come here. Remember these students do not come from Salina. Our institutions of this kind are not local but they are statewide, and national. . . . I cannot say what the Sisters charge, but I know what the Fathers charge at St. Mary's and the charges, I understand, are about the same. It was the school that made St. Marys—understand, also, these schools are not sectarian. . . .

Our institutions always grow. We do not go back. Now we are concerned only with the beautiful $300,000 building we propose to erect on the hill. The Catholic institutions are noted for their artistic design and I assure you that the building which will go up on the hill, if you wish it to go up, will be something to which this whole community can point with pride.

You men of the Country Club have kindly given permission for our students to wander about your grounds for recreation. I am authorized by the Sisters to tell you that when you take your wives to the club you can take them to the school where they will be made at home. There will be paintings, the finest of lace work and genial hospitality for them.

I am not a dreamer of dreams. I am not a prophet. Yet I see six great buildings on that hill. I do not care to go into the future, yet I can say that

---

[81] *Salina Journal,* Feb. 20, 1919. This was almost a prediction for in March, 1945, the diocesan see was removed from Concordia to Salina when His Excellency, the Most Rev. Frank A. Thill, moved to Country Club Heights to make his residence and the Church of the Sacred Heart was designated the Cathedral of the Sacred Heart.

[82] *Salina Daily Union,* Feb. 20, 1919.

most of you will have few additional grey hairs until these other buildings are realized....[83]

Then Mr. J. R. Geis, prominent Catholic banker of Salina and friend of the Sisters of Saint Joseph for many years, outlined a plan for selling building lots to realize part of the sum asked from the city. He stated that the option held by a Wichita company on the Highland Court addition, the old Wallerius estate, had been taken over temporarily by Father Maher. The plan was to sell these lots. One-fourth of the money raised would go to the school fund. He pointed out that this had been done when the Wesleyan addition lots had been sold.[84]

When it was suggested that $12,500 be the assessment of Sacred Heart parish, Father Maher questioned the fairness of the suggestion. At that point, Mr. T. D. Fitzpatrick, a non-Catholic businessman, suggested: "There is only one thing to do. We built the Wesleyan by the sale of lots; we built the Normal by the sale of lots; we built Saint John's Military School by the sale of lots; we will build this school the same way." He moved that the meeting cooperate in everyway in raising the money.[85]

Mr. Fred H. Quincy, chairman of the Chamber of Commerce, proposed a Committee of Forty with D. J. Hanna as chairman.[86] This committee at its meeting the next night adopted as its slogan "Salina must have this school!!!" That was the spirit which permeated the atmosphere of the meeting. Mention was made of the big arch which confronts people entering the town with the words: "Salina Your Opportunity." The Sisters of Saint Joseph in Salina would add another moral and intellectual force to the town besides adding to its commercial growth and wealth. The drive for subscriptions was set for Tuesday, March 4, with a detail committee con-

---

[83] *Salina Journal,* Feb. 20, 1919.
  Salina Daily Union, Feb. 20, 1919.
[84] *Ibid.,* Feb. 20, 1919.
[85] *Ibid.,* Feb. 20, 1919.
  Salina Journal, Feb. 20, 1919.
[86] This Committee of Forty was really one composed of forty-one: D. J. Hanna, chairman, Fred Quincy, J. J. Eberhardt, F. C. Bulkley, C. P. Coffey, L. S. Rosenwald, R. P. Cravens, L. G. Gottschick, Frank Hageman, Henry Eberhardt, T. D. Fitzpatrick, J. L. Brady, R. F. Bailey, J. R. Geis, Charles Schwartz, Charles Lee, Fred Abel, George Watson, P. C. Remler, C. A. Morrison, J. B. Smith, Hugh Pitzer, John Schumacher, Arthur White, C. H. Gawthrop, B. I. Litowich, Earl McChesney, John Weber, E. J. Guilbert, Frank Bangs, Ernest Putnam, Ben Gurley, Mac Stevenson, Ray Eghart, Tom Vallette, Frank Eberhardt, Ralph Anderson, E. P. Quillen, C. B. Dodge, B. A. Mason, and Reverend John Maher. With the exception of four this entire committee was non-Catholic.

sisting of Charles Schwartz, chairman, F. C. Bulkley, Jesse Smith, J. J. Eberhardt, F. H. Quincy, L. G. Gottschick, and C. H. Gawthrop.[87]

It was announced that the college would be named Marymount.[88] It was to be modeled after the memorial building being built at Catholic University in Washington, D. C., in honor of Cardinal Gibbons.[89] It was to be one of the finest institutions west of Chicago. The original plans were expanded and at the outset of the drive for the city's contribution hopes of the authorities in the Congregation of the Sisters of Saint Joseph ran high.

Salina began to show its old enthusiasm and its confidence in its ability to reach whatever goal it chose. The first contribution to the fund was the Salina Light, Power, and Gas Company's donation of $1,000,[90] and it gave impetus to the campaign.

The night before the drive began, the Committee of Forty met again to check final plans for the "cleanup" the next day. At that time between $8,000 and $10,000 had been subscribed.[91] $25,000 was realized on the first day in spite of inclement weather and the fact that several businessmen were out of town.[92]

Father Maher issued a statement making it clear that with such a start the building was assured to the city. In his statement he said:

... As head of the parish committee and the representative of the Catholic people of the community, I want to say that the members of the parish have been very generous. The weather yesterday was very inclement and it was not possible to see everyone, but judging from the subscriptions I have received, there is not the slightest doubt that our quota will be obtained. ... In addition let me say that the results of the businessmen's campaign yesterday and the subscriptions received not only make me feel extremely grateful, but I firmly believe that no other town in Kansas could duplicate the enthusiasm and the spirit of fraternal cooperation between Catholics and Protestants, manifested in this campaign, and which has made this drive a success....[93]

And Chairman Hanna praised the "old Salina spirit which you can't beat. There's nothing like it, not even the Liberty Loan campaign that received the spontaneous response from the businessmen. . . .

---

[87] *Salina Daily Union,* Feb. 20, 1919.
[88] The name "Marymount" was chosen because of the location of the institution on a high elevation. Interview with Mother Antoinette Cuff, Dec. 28, 1936.
    Salina Daily Union, Feb. 27, 1919.
[89] *Loc. cit.*
[90] *Salina Journal,* Feb. 28, 1919.
[91] *Ibid.,* Mar. 3, 1919.
[92] *Ibid.,* Mar. 4, 1919.
    Salina Daily Union, Mar. 4, 1919.
[93] *Ibid.,* Mar. 5, 1919.

And don't forget the physicians and surgeons of Salina who have gone over one hundred percent in this drive, every one of the twenty-two doctors of the town giving $100 each. That's the kind of spirit that helps Salina accomplish whatever she undertakes."[94] The next day the fund had soared to $40,000,[95] and before the campaign closed it had passed the $42,000 mark with enough promises to make the drive go over the top.[96]

A loan secured from the Massachusetts Life Insurance Company, Springfield, Massachusetts, donations, and the Community savings made the building possible, the size and cost having soared far beyond expectations.[97]

On June 23, 1919, at the time when his assistance was of greatest value, Bishop Cunningham was called to his reward. From that time until its completion the responsibility of Marymount College rested on the shoulders of Father Maher.[98] Such trials were difficult for Mother Antoinette and her Sisters to bear when they were showing magnificent courage in building for the future of the Community and the Church in Kansas. But with the courage of frontierswomen, they looked ahead and envisioned Marymount on the plains of Kansas. Their faith and courage were recognized. The editor of the *Salina Daily Union* in an editorial, "The Right Spirit," said:

> The bids for the construction of the Marymount school in Salina were opened and proved a great disappointment. They were expected to be high but not so high as they actually were. Did this daunt the Mother Superior? Hardly. It caused her good heart to flutter but her resolution quickened. "We will build the school," she declared. Yesterday the contract was let. There was some more figuring, some changes made but the school will be built as originally planned.
>
> The spirit which actuated the Mother Superior was the spirit of leadership. She could not bring herself to abandon the school or even hold in abeyance

---

[94] *Ibid.*, Mar. 5, 1919.

[95] *Ibid.*, Mar. 6, 1919.

[96] *Ibid.*, Mar. 7, 1919. The large contributors included: Most Reverend John F. Cunningham, Mrs. William Priest, James Mason, John Weber, Godfrey Swenson, Dr. S. Murdock, Schipple Bros., Lee Institutions, H. D. Lee, Salina Vitrified Brick Co., Farmers National Bank, D. D. McAuliffe, T. W. Carlin, Hugh Carlin, Edward Carlin, Salina L. P. & G. Co., Wm. Wessling family, Ben Gehlenberg, C. A. Smith, Mrs. Mary Commerford, J. A. Skelley.

[97] Agreement between the Massachusetts Life Insurance Co., Springfield, Mass., and the Nazareth Convent and Academy, A Corporation (August 16, 1919). The original is in the Archives of the Nazareth Motherhouse, Concordia, Kans. Interview of the author with Mother Antoinette Cuff, Dec. 28, 1936.

[98] A series of articles ran in the Concordia and Salina papers following the death of Bishop Cunningham, June 23, 1919. His passing was a great loss to the civic and ecclesiastical world.

her plans. The school was needed and must be built. That was all there was to it. The *Union* congratulates the Catholic Church on having such a woman in this responsible place, and congratulates Salina for the same reason. The school means much to the Church but it means just as much to the city.[99]

And another Salina editor said in like vein:

. . . However this stout-hearted woman took courage and declared that, if the bids were the best the contractors could make, it meant they were the best that could be secured and she expressed a willingness to go through. She declared that some paring might be done to advantage but that the school must be built. That is the kind of spirit that wins and the kind of spirit the nation must have. The Catholics will provide the money because they have been educated to give and have learned that it is a privilege rather than a burden. But the main thing is the fine exhibition of courage shown by the Mother Superior at Concordia when the bids disclosed that her worst fears had been realized.[100]

The bids were finally let on August 7, 1919, with the Swenson Building Company, Kansas City, Missouri, awarded the general contract on a straight bid.[101] Other contracts were let later.[102]

Another donation by Bishop Cunningham, the result of his lifetime private savings and investments, was a last indication of his fatherly interest in the Sisters of Saint Joseph. The Immaculate Conception Chapel at Marymount College was erected to his memory.

So the dream became a reality and the townsfolk wondered when they saw the immensity of the foundation. Built like the Church on a rock, Marymount was to stand there amid the stress and storm of the succeeding years as a monument to Christian education, a monument to the courage of the frontierswomen who had come to Kansas less than forty years ago. Built of Pennsylvania crystal brick with Bedford stone trim, Marymount stands as a beacon light on the plains and is a symbol of education in the heart of America. It cost over a million dollars—a fit monument to Christian education.

Bishop Thomas Shahan of the Catholic University of America visited his friends in Concordia and Salina while the building was

---

99 *Salina Daily Union*, Aug. 7, 1919.

100 *Salina Journal*, Aug. 7, 1919.

101 Uniform Contract between the Swenson Building Co., Kansas City, Mo., and the Nazareth Convent and Academy, Concordia, Kans., dated Aug. 31, 1919. A copy of the contract was sent to Rev. John Maher, Administrator of the Diocese of Concordia, and another to Rev. Mother Antoinette Cuff, president of the Corporation. The original is in the Archives of the Nazareth Motherhouse, Concordia, Kans.

102 Contract for plumbing and draining awarded to James P. Graham, Kansas City, Mo., on April 16, 1920. The original is in the Archives of the Nazareth Motherhouse, Concordia, Kans. Contract for plumbing and heating, ventilation and electric wiring awarded to Salina Plumbing Co., Salina, Kans., on April 16, 1920. The original is in the Archives of the Nazareth Motherhouse, Concordia, Kans.

in process of construction. Looking over the site and the expansive view, he blessed it and prayed that its future would meet the fairest expectations of the Church.[103]

Bill Whelan, of Tipperary, Ireland, in Salina in the interests of Irish freedom, was so impressed with the building that he remarked: "I think it [Marymount] will be a landmark in Salina. There is no city in the State, and I will include Kansas City, that has anything better."[104]

Father Maher, as administrator of the diocese, presided at the laying of the cornerstone. Father Damian, president of Saint Benedict's College, Atchison, Kansas, was the speaker for the occasion. After the blessing of the cornerstone and the completion of the rites, there was placed in the receptacle of the cornerstone a copy of the *Salina Daily Union,* the *Salina Journal,* a Kansas City paper, medals, coins, and a record containing the names of the Pope, president, governor, and mayor, and a record of the proceedings of the day. This latter was read by Father Maher before it was sealed in the cornerstone:

... Education must help mould character, develop the mental, the moral, and the physical. . . . This is a memorable day for all of us irrespective of creed. This building, laid on a solid foundation, rearing its wall up into the pure air, speaks to us of something out of the ordinary. We are gathered here to witness this laying of a foundation stone for higher education. All that the ages have said, all that they can ever say, can never overshadow the beauty of that one word, *education.* In the dim ages, education was spoken of with awe; now it has caught a new meaning; education is the power that rules the world. . . . Unless education tells the man what is right and what is wrong, there is something lacking in it. Mental education is necessary but it cannot go deeper than knowledge. It tells us that two and two make four, but it does not reach down into the soul. Citizenship and character are built on more than knowledge; without moral training the superstructure must necessarily fall. This glorious institution rears itself under the Stars and Stripes and there will issue from it young women who will wear the glowing image of the Cross, teaching the value of true morality, of true light and true justice. . . .[105]

He noted that the Sisters who were to take charge of the college were making a noble sacrifice, doing a noble work for the sake of Christ and His Church. In closing he glowingly referred to the power for good that is to be found in such institutions.[106]

---

103 *Salina Daily Union,* June 30, 1920.
104 *Ibid.,* undated.
105 *Ibid.,* June 20, 1920.
106 *Loc. cit.*

The dedication of Marymount College was a gala occasion. The million-dollar structure, the largest of its kind in this country at the time of its erection, was blessed and consecrated by the Most Reverend Francis J. Tief,[107] newly appointed Bishop of Concordia, in the presence of more than one hundred Sisters, many priests, and about five hundred of the laity.[108] Erected in Tudor Gothic style with a total frontage of 325 feet, with north and south wings 147 feet wide and a center wing housing the Immaculate Conception Chapel 155 feet wide, the building was ready for inspection by the general public that day.[109] It was a remarkable feat for the Sisters of Saint Joseph who had been in Kansas for only thirty-nine years to have built such an institution.

In his sermon on this occasion, Bishop Tief congratulated the Sisters and encouraged the priests and the laity of the diocese to support the institution:

We are assembled here this morning in order to assist at the solemn blessing of this new and magnificent edifice which is dedicated to the great cause of education. It will, we hope, last for ages as a memorial to the zeal and the sacrifice and to the perseverance of the Sisters of Saint Joseph of the Diocese of Concordia. It is a living proof of their desire to cooperate with and to help the priests and the bishop in carrying out the commission which they received from the Divine Master, Jesus Christ, when He said, "Go ye forth and teach all nations."

Proud indeed and filled with joy and gladness must be the hearts of these good Sisters today when they witness the completion of the task to which they have set their efforts for many years and the completion of the task which has been the burden of their fondest hopes and prayers. Today, while they have the great material difficulties and financial burden, they realize that they enjoy the good will and I hope the generous support of the priests and the laity of the Diocese of Concordia and of their numerous friends outside.

This building, magnificent as it is, is material and like all things that come from the hands of man it will crumble and decay with the ravages of time but the cause for which it is built will last forever. "Teach me, O Lord, goodness, discipline and knowledge." These words embody the principles which underlie Catholic education. Today, great attention is given to education. Representatives of our convents and colleges attend conventions in order that they may

[107] He was born on Mar. 7, 1881, Greenwich, Conn.; was educated at Niagara Univ., Niagara, N. Y., and St. Bonaventure's College, Allegheny, N. Y. He was ordained on June 13, 1908; engaged in pastoral life in the Archdiocese of New York and the Diocese of Kansas City; was vicar general of the Diocese of Kansas City, 1916-1920; was consecrated Bishop of Concordia, Mar. 30, 1921; retired, and appointed titular Bishop of Nisa on June 11, 1938.

[108] *Kansas City Catholic Register,* spec. ed., dedicated to Marymount College, June 8, 1922.

Salina Daily Union, spec. ed., dedicated to Marymount College, June 4, 1922.

[109] Both of the editions mentioned in note 108 contained various items regarding type of brick, amount used, special features of the building, etc.

better the existing system. We must be abreast of the times. We must follow
in the march. Today there is a great and increasing demand in every walk of
life for the best educated and trained men and women. We must be ready and
willing to give many years of training to our mental faculties. But in training
ourselves mentally we must not forget we have other faculties and that all our
faculties come from God. To be a learned man is a noble thing but to be a
learned Christian man is far nobler in the sight of God and of the world.
Place education and the influence of education in the hands of a man who does
not know God and who does not know how to control education and you have
a dangerous man. The Catholic Church has always endeavored to give a Christian education to its children in its own institutions not only in secular knowledge but also in the knowledge of God. Catholic people realize that this is the
only education which is proper for their children. Throughout our land you
will find numerous academies and universities dedicated to this purpose. You
will find in Salina a magnificent edifice, a monument to the Sisters of Saint
Joseph and to the persons who are willing to support Christian education.

My friends, we are only too often sadly misunderstood. Others cannot
understand why Catholic people will make such great sacrifice for principle
when we have in our midst magnificent institutions under public control. It is
believed by some that the Catholics are opposed to the public schools and state
institutions and as a consequence we build our own Catholic schools and
colleges. Catholic Sisters constantly remind their children to have respect for
authority. They teach obedience to the law of the land. When we respect
authority, we must respect the institutions of the land. The Catholic people
love the public schools and for that reason they support them. But the Catholic
people believe that the public schools may not train children to know God
and to love Him. For that reason they build and support their own parochial
schools. . . . On occasions such as this, these questions are brought to light
and explained. It is a proof of the divinity of Christ when these Sisters give
up everything to devote their lives to fulfill the words of Holy Scripture:
"Blessed are they that instruct others unto justice." Christian education is
carried on by sacrifice of these women and it is through their efforts that
Catholic educational institutions are built and maintained. The Sisters of Saint
Joseph of Concordia deserve our praise. They came into the State of Kansas
and into the Diocese of Concordia thirty-eight years ago. They came to the
city of Concordia thirty-eight years ago. They came to the city of Concordia
with very little of the world's goods. They scarcely had enough to eat. There
were many days when they felt the pangs of hunger but they placed their
trust in God and He did not desert them. Through trial, through sacrifice,
through hard labor they acquired their Motherhouse in Concordia of which
the beautiful Marymount College of Salina is an outgrowth. They have taught
the little ones of the diocese; they have nursed the sick back to health and
they are trying to supply a mother's love to the little orphans in Abilene.

They labored long at Nazareth Academy teaching the young ladies in the
higher branches of education. This institution grew to such proportions that
the old home at Nazareth was no longer adequate. A few years ago they turned
their gaze southward to the beautiful city of Salina. These good Sisters have
come to you citizens of Salina, not in the throes of poverty, but they come
to your city bringing this magnificent institution. They are here to serve you
and to serve God. The citizens of Salina ought to be proud of this building.
No other institution will come to you for many years that will mean as much

to you as Marymount College. I ask you, therefore, for hearty cooperation. These Sisters are yet laboring under a great burden, heavily in debt, because of the great cost of this building. I, the Bishop of Concordia, am very much interested in the debt on this institution and I do hope the people of the town will do what they can to relieve the Sisters of their responsibility. The teachers that will teach here are the very best that can be had. The Sisters who will constitute the teaching staff of Marymount College are holders of degrees of Bachelor of Arts, Master of Arts, and Doctor of Philosophy obtained after years of study in the great universities of our country. They are prepared to train the young women who will come to Marymount for a college education.

In conclusion, I wish to congratulate the Sisters of Saint Joseph on the splendid institution which they have erected. I wish to congratulate you also in the name of the priests who are assisting me in your beautiful sanctuary. Do not be discouraged. God will be with you. You have made great sacrifices in the past and you will be asked to make sacrifices in the future. May God bless you. May God prosper you. May God reward you.[110]

W. A. Layton, City Manager of Salina, extended the welcome of the city to Marymount:

The citizens of Salina have a just reason for feeling proud of the splendid building to our east and strangers as they come and go shall in years to come point to this magnificence itself in the building of this most beautiful structure. The true worth of the structure will not come from its beauty without and within but the greatest results therefrom will be the fine and beautiful womanhood that shall come from it resultant from the teachings that they may receive therefrom.

After all, the greatest asset of our city is the fine character of citizenship which we may build; character, mature, resultant from the functions of the fine churches and schools and their advantages extended to the young manhood and womanhood of our city and its progressive citizenship.

We welcome as a city every institution that may come to us and establish itself among us that will build for better manhood and womanhood.

The measure of sacrifice that has been on the part of those connected with the building of Marymount College, which is the pride of Salina, will never be known but the measure of benefit resultant from the sacrifice that has been made will be.

The City of Salina and her people extend a glad hand of welcome to all those who are directly connected with Marymount College and feel that we have gained and profited much by acquiring an institution of its kind to locate among us, and trust that the citizens of Salina will continue to promote the ideals for which it stands.[111]

Before this account of the building and dedication of Marymount College is completed, an editorial in the *Kansas City Catholic Register* entitled "Mother Antoinette" must be given in full:

"Magnificent."

This one word seemed to be universally used by all who viewed the new

110 *Kansas City Catholic Register,* June 8, 1922.
111 *Salina Daily Union,* June 4, 1922.

Marymount College and Academy dedicated and formally opened to the public at Salina, Kansas, last Sunday.

But in all that vast throng scarcely a one gave thought or expression to the wonderful woman who conceived and carried to a successful completion the gigantic task of building the finest and largest single unit educational structure in the entire United States. Our nuns are appreciated, of course, but one should not forget that they are human the same as the rest of us and while they get their greatest pleasure in their thought that all their work is done for God, nevertheless, a kindly word of encouragement will bring a sweet smile to their eyes.

From a small diocesan order of a few members in 1899, when Mother Antoinette was appointed superior by the late Bishop Cunningham, to one of the finest teaching and nursing orders in the country with a membership of over four hundred — that alone has shown the wonderful directing ability of Mother Antoinette. But to take the same order, situated in what was but a few years ago considered a missionary country diocese and produce the finest educational building of its kind in America, either Catholic or non-Catholic—that gives but a faint idea of the homage the entire State of Kansas owes this woman.

Her community is also entitled to a mede of praise, for it was through the humble cooperation and hearty encouragement of its members that Mother Antoinette received her greatest encouragement in the many months of heart-rending work in the financing, the planning, and the buying of the materials in the completed structure.

We sincerely hope that our people will appreciate what our own good nuns are doing at our very doors and instead of sending their children to far away schools, that they will send them to schools in their own district—this will be our nuns' greatest reward on this earth.[112]

Nazareth Academy had served steadily and well between 1884 and 1922. Students went away from Nazareth richer in knowledge and experience to take their places in the world. Educational standards were kept high until the school closed in the spring of 1922. The building was converted into a Motherhouse and Novitiate for the growing Community. When classes opened in the fall, there was not the usual trek back to Nazareth but rather back to a new, larger, and better Nazareth—to Marymount College and Academy in Salina. Nazareth had played its role successfully. It became an inspiration of the Sisters of Saint Joseph, and from that firm basis rose Marymount to augment and to expand the influence of Nazareth on the frontier of the Mid West.

The death of Bishop Cunningham in June, 1919, removed another member of the hierarchy who had taken a deep interest in the activities of the Sisters of Saint Joseph of Concordia. They were

112 *Ibid.*, June 8, 1922.

fortunate in the choice of the Most Reverend Francis J. Tief, Vicar General of the Diocese of Kansas City, as successor to Bishop Cunningham. From his coming to Concordia in 1921 until his resignation in 1938, Bishop Tief manifested the same interest in the Community as had his predecessors, Bishops Fink, Scannell, Hennessy, and Cunningham. The support of the hierarchy means much to a congregation of religious teachers, and their effectiveness as diocesan teachers can be attributed in large part to its loyal cooperation.

With the completion of the building of Marymount College, there was a change in the administration of the Community. Mother Antoinette had borne the burden for twenty-three intensely active years. Much has been said of the material prosperity of the Sisters of Saint Joseph during these years. The spiritual growth kept pace with the material; annually there were the community retreats which brought Sisters from far and near to the Motherhouse for a spiritual rejuvenation before beginning new work in the fall. The numbers had increased by leaps and bounds, and the stability of the Community was beyond question.

A circular letter to the Sisters at the opening of the school year in 1919 expressed faith and trust in God:

Another year with its ups and downs has passed and gone from us, and although we have had many blessings during it, still, death has claimed some of our dear ones; and while they have departed from us we feel that they have swollen the ranks of our dear friends in heaven where they will do more for us than they could ever have done here. These thoughts cheer us on, and again we start another year with fresh energy to work more faithfully for God and for souls. Some of us may have to go into new fields where we will meet strange faces and scenes, but these are not going to daunt us for our motto is "To do and to dare; to live and to die provided God's will be done and souls saved." Vacation is now passed. It has been a time of rest and recuperation, still most of it has been spent in hard study, but it has prepared you better for your coming school year; and with your good retreat, we feel the work done by you last year will be done better this coming year. More knowledge and more experience makes you fitter in many ways for the noble work which God has entrusted to you. Dear Sisters, our good wishes and our prayers go with you, for we know how difficult the work is which God has appointed you to do. But with His grace and your good-will it will be accomplished. Wishing you God-speed and God's blessing on this year's work, we are,

Your sincere and devoted

SISTERS IN CHRIST
The Council of 1919[118]

[118] Letter of Mother Antoinette Cuff (in name of the Council of 1919) to the Missionaries of the School Year, 1919. Aug. 16, 1919. A copy is in the files of the author.

On July 19, 1922, a General Chapter was held at the Nazareth Motherhouse, Concordia, at which Mother Antoinette Cuff was succeeded in office by Mother Mary Rose Waller. Her close association with Mother Antoinette for many years as secretary and member of the General Council of the Congregation made for a continuance of policy during her administration which was to last for nineteen years. A unity of purpose can be seen in the consolidation and solidification of the aims and objectives of the Sisters of Saint Joseph of Concordia in the various works they sponsor in the several dioceses of the Midwest.

CHAPTER XI

Administration:
Reverend Mother Mary Rose Waller
1922-1941

With Reverend Mother Mary Rose as Superior General, another milestone in the history of the Sisters of Saint Joseph of Concordia had appeared. The next nineteen years would bring abundant opportunities for further missionary work in the Midwest.

In the last chapter we discussed the dream which launched Marymount College. This chapter will bring the story of Marymount up to date.

In an article published in June, 1922, at the time of the dedication of Marymount College, the educational aims of the College were enumerated:

. . . Marymount takes as a working basis the definition of education attributed to the Most Reverend John Lancaster Spalding: "The soul's response to God's appeal to make itself like unto Him—self-active, knowing, wise, strong, loving and fair." It stands for the highest development of mind and heart, and aims to make its students women of ideas rather than women of mere accomplishment; to bring them into personal relation with wider worlds, larger life, by placing before them truth as far as it may be comprehended, truth in its various aspects—literature, history, science and art. In its training of the intellect, Marymount distinguishes between the cultural and the vocational in education. Education is to prepare the student for life but this is to be taken in its larger sense. The years spent at school cannot give both a cultural and professional training. Within limits, election is allowed, and this choice directs the teacher's effort toward developing skill and inculcating appreciation in the student.

Believing that "character is higher than intellect," Marymount attaches a special value to many things that are not in the curriculum—a sense of honor, self-respect, courtesy, gentleness, reverence, right values, recognition of personal duty; in a word, "the art of living and the science of conduct." All this presupposes a certain discipline, and to the Catholic school there is

272

no problem regarding the relations that should exist between the instructor and the students. The restraint which makes for true freedom rests upon a clear understanding of personal obligation to self and to others and on trust in those who guide rather than govern. This understanding and this trust added to spiritual motives born of religion insure right moral growth and give dignity and worth to discipline.

That law and order are necessary in these, our days, is granted by all; and that religious training brings about the only order compatible with right reason and self-respect should be obvious. The discipline of love will alone save the young from the discipline of pain, and it is this discipline which makes the difference between coming up and being brought up.

It is this emphasis placed by Marymount on character and religious principles that best meets the conditions of the times. Marymount endeavors to make practical in the training of her students the theories advanced above and to this end conscientious effort is put forth to insure competent teaching and thorough equipment, while every advantage is taken of the educative force of environment, which is made to appeal on all sides to the growing minds, hearts, and souls of the students. Marymount's endowments are a boundless sympathy with its students, their love and respect, the devotion of its alumnae, the consecrated lives of its teachers, the encouragement of the Church, the blessing of God.[1]

Educational objectives such as these will bring blessings to Church and state. Not only Catholic parents appreciated such an idea of education but, as at Nazareth, there was a large percentage of non-Catholics enrolled from its first year.

Marymount admitted students on the secondary and the college levels on September 8, 1922. The first superior of Marymount was the one who had planned its erection, had watched its progress from the first blasting of the rock on the hill overlooking Salina and had, after its dedication, relinquished the office of Mother Superior. Those acquainted with her accomplishments rejoiced when Mother Antoinette Cuff became Superior of the College. Sister Louise Cuff,[2] a pioneer educator of the Community, was appointed dean of studies. She was succeeded the following year by Sister Chrysostom Wynn who was dean until her election as Mother Superior of the Community in 1941. During the first year, there were forty students in

---

[1] Sister Louise Cuff, "Educational Aims of the New College," *Salina Daily Union,* June 4, 1922; *Kansas City Catholic Register,* June 8, 1922.

[2] Sister Louise Cuff entered the Community in 1885 and from that time until 1922 was identified with the progress of Nazareth Academy in Concordia. She was one of the first Sisters to attend Sisters' College, Washington, D. C., receiving her first degree there. In 1920, Sister Louise received her degree of Doctor of Philosophy at the Catholic University, one of the first women in its history to receive such a degree. She taught in the winter and summer sessions of the University several years. When she died in 1932, she was vice president of the College and head of the education department.

the College and one hundred in the academy.[3] Teachers were selected who could meet the challenge of higher education in the diocese.[4]

Late in October, Bishop Tief visited the college. He was given a reception by the student body and faculty.[5] Later Justin Casey, the editor of the *Kansas City Catholic Register,* and life-time friend of the Community, wrote his reactions to the "homey" atmosphere of the institution:

> With its formal opening dress discarded and with its working clothes broken in, Marymount College is now even more impressive to visitors than ever. The reporters for the *Register* who visited there last Saturday afternoon looked in vain for the big hotel-like structure which was dedicated by Bishop Tief last summer. After six months of occupation by the Sisters and four by the 130 students, it can now well be called a home. Massive as it is, the residents know every nook and corner, and have short cuts between the various sections that serve to eliminate that first impression of bigness. . . . The three dioceses of Kansas and the Kansas City diocese are well represented among the student body of the institution. . . . The work on the grounds around the college has been going on ever since the building was finished and already the surroundings are of nearly the shipshape appearance that prevails inside the big building.
>
> The stone walks and drives in front on the west side are now nearing completion and are available to visitors. . . . Still further west the property is fenced and playgrounds for the little girls and cool study nooks for the older girls are being prepared against the coming of warm spring weather. . . . The stained glass windows for the chapel arrived last Friday. . . .[6]

Marymount College sought educational recognition early in its career. Regardless of faculty qualifications, recognition by the state university, the State Department of Education, and national associations (Catholic and secular), is necessary before a student can have the assurance of par value for credits earned at a given institution. Therefore, during its first year, Marymount sought and obtained the approval of the University of Kansas for freshman and sophomore work.[7] Naturally, this first step toward recognition

---

[3] *Kenedy's Catholic Directory* (New York, 1923), p. 304.

[4] The names of the first Sisters to be missioned at Marymount were: Mother Antoinette Cuff, Superior, Sisters Louise Cuff, Evangelist Bonnifield, Marcelline L'Allier, Gabriel Merson, Walburga Wuerth, Elizabeth Belisle, Gregory Raboin, Thomas Halle, Rita Rivard, Aquinas Fenton, Presentation Houston, Pius Bechard, Geraldine Boudreau, Charles Wolsieffer, Blanche Bueche, Genevieve Hogan, Vincent Marie Martin, Calasanctius Flannigan, Dionysia Winkler, Mary Grace Waring, Beatrice Cyr, Marie Eleanor Kelly, Immaculate Flannigan, Marie Antoinette Martin, Jane Frances Haynes, Rosarii Hamil, Antoinella Thibault.

[5] *Kansas City Catholic Register,* Nov. 18, 1922. The day was proclaimed "Bishop Tief Day."

[6] *Ibid.,* Jan. 3, 1923.

[7] Recognition was granted by the Senate of the State University.

Marymount College, Salina, Kansas

Reverend Mother Mary Rose Waller, Third Mother
General of the Sisters of Saint Joseph of Concordia,
1922–1941

Home of the Little Flower, Concordia, Kansas

Fontbonne Hall, Concordia, Kansas

Campus, Saint Mary's Academy, Silver City, New Mexico

Saint Joseph's Sanatorium, El Paso, Texas

was a landmark in the development of Marymount College.

In the charter of the corporation of the Nazareth Convent and Academy no mention was made of conducting colleges. It became necessary in January, 1924, to amend the charter in order to include Marymount College in the corporation. The revised charter recorded its purposes as follows:

. . . To establish, support, conduct, maintain and control convents, colleges, academies, hospitals, and orphanages in the city of Concordia, Cloud County, Kansas, and other places in said State and other States and territories in the United States; to prescribe courses of study and standards of excellence in accordance with the laws of the State of Kansas and the rules and regulations promulgated by the State Board of Education of said State, as now existing or may be hereafter enacted and adopted; to confer degrees and issue certificates under the supervision of the State Board of Education; to purchase, own, control, lease and otherwise use real, personal, and mixed property for the accomplishment of such purposes and to do all other things requisite and proper for the purpose of carrying into effect the foregoing powers. . . .[8]

Under the authority of the amendments and with the full recognition of the University of Kansas (1923), Marymount was empowered to confer degrees on the class of 1926. These were the first commencement exercises of any senior college for women under Catholic auspices in the State of Kansas. This fact was impressed upon the seven graduates[9] and their friends when Bishop Tief of Concordia paid his tribute to Marymount. He compared the class to the first-born of the family. He painted the picture of a young mother gazing with happiness on her first child, caring for it, working for it, and praying for it.

Bishop Tief traced the progress of the Sisters of Saint Joseph since they had come into the diocese. Showing that after nineteen years the faith of the Sisters was rewarded with the erection of the new Motherhouse and Academy in Concordia, and that after another nineteen years Marymount College was erected, he continued:

. . . I want to say a word here as to the teaching ability of the Sisters. They are untiring in their efforts to give every educational advantage. They attend

---

[8] *Charter of the Corporation of the Nazareth Convent and Academy, Concordia, Kansas.* Amendment as to aims and purposes. Jan. 11, 1924.

Minutes of the Meetings of the Corporation of the Nazareth Convent and Academy, 1901-1939, vol. I, pp. 74-77.

Letter of Attorney Charles L. Hunt, lawyer for the corporation, Concordia, Kans., relative to the by-laws to be found in the *Minutes,* vol. I, p. 100.

[9] First graduates were Estelle Kyne, Marie Finan, Mildred Ludes Habiger, Maurine McCullough Egenberger, Emma Weber Schwarz, Theresa Layden Oderman, and Stella Murphy Barrett.

College and they fit themselves to meet every requirement of the State of Kansas and the educational requirements of the State of Kansas are on a higher plane, I believe, than most of the other States. It is the untiring zeal of these Sisters that has made maintenance of these schools and colleges possible. We could build them but we could not maintain them without the Sisters. For themselves, they are paid nothing. Their only compensation is the reward of work well done and the satisfaction that they have given the best that is in them. . . .[10]

According to information furnished by Reverend Mother Chrysostom Wynn, before the College made application to the State Department of Education for accreditment, a request was made to the Rector of Saint Mary's College, St. Marys, Kansas, for advice as to equipment, college organization, and faculty competence. The rector, Father B. Rodman, S. J., sent Father J. A. Herbers, S. J., to give advice. Here began an interest of the Jesuit Fathers which has lasted through the years.

The College was recognized for the granting of one hundred and twenty hour life certificates by the State Board of Education of the State of Kansas, November 15, 1927.[11] The first summer school session in 1927 was attended largely by the Sisters of the Community. The summer school has been a great asset to the Sisters and has reached widely scattered communities in various parts of the country. Secular enrollment has also shown marked increase. In 1947 the enrollment was two hundred and eighty-seven.

Recognition by the National Catholic Educational Association was granted and admission to full membership accorded the College after it was examined by Father Bonaventure Schmitz, O.S.B., an inspector of the NCEA.[12]

In 1930, in the presence of the bishop, twenty-five members of the clergy, Reverend Mother Mary Rose Waller, and hundreds of Sisters and friends among the laity, Mother Antoinette Cuff, former Mother General of the Sisters of Saint Joseph of Concordia and then superior at Marymount College, observed her golden jubilee as a religious. The editor of the *Kansas City Catholic Register* remarked:

[10] *Salina Journal,* June 2, 1926.
[11] *Ibid.,* Nov. 16, 1927.
   Catholic Daily Tribune (Dubuque, Ia.), Nov. 19, 1927. Questionnaire of Sister Chrysostom Wynn, dean of Marymount College, 1923-1941; now Superior General of the Community and, as such, *ex officio* president of the College.
   Nov. 15 has been celebrated as traditional "Marymount Day" since that time. In the first years its celebration consisted in a holiday. Later the crowning of "Miss Marymount" became one of the highlights of the social year.
[12] June 27, 1929. Questionnaire of Sister Chrysostom Wynn.

. . . The occasion was possessed of all the solemnity that the Church can give to such an affair and was also marked by the personal touches usually associated with a private anniversary celebration, the combined features being typical of the life and career of Mother Antoinette, who is known in Kansas as a pioneer nun, a remarkable leader with vision, and a thoroughly human person, a lovable Mother to the Sisters under her charge, and a kindly friend to nearly everyone she has ever met. . . . It was typical of Mother Antoinette and of Marymount that the bishop, priests, sisters and laity were all served together in the one large dining room. . . .[13]

Accreditment is the stamp of approval of the regional accrediting association. And the requirements of the North Central Association are exceptionally high.

On application by Marymount College in 1932, the Association took steps to determine the qualifications of the college. In a letter to the missions of the Community, Reverend Mother Mary Rose Waller spoke of this step in the educational development of the Community:

. . . At last the North Central Association has decided to send an examiner to Marymount College. He will arrive on February 28. This year's report has been accepted by the Secretary of the North Central and the visit by an examiner ordered. The examiner will report his findings to the committee next month and the final decision will then be made. So much depends on the visit and the report of the examiner!! We feel that we are ready for him, as certainly every effort has been made this year to meet all stringent requirements. For the rest we must depend on prayer. . . .[14]

Within a few weeks, Mother Mary Rose could write to the missionaries concerning the visit of the official examiner:

. . . Reverend Father Schwitalla, S.J., the examiner, sent out by the association, visited Marymount and was well pleased with the organization and equipment of the College. He expressed great approval of the library, the science laboratories and other parts of the building. He said that Marymount is certainly a monument to Catholic education. Our dear Lord has certainly blessed the Sisters' efforts and I feel that their earnestness to promote God's honor and glory will be generously rewarded. Your cooperation, spiritually and financially, is making Marymount possible. Father Schwitalla's report together with the Dean's report, will be placed before the reviewing board of the North Central in Chicago some day next week. It will be this committee that will make the recommendation for the acceptance of Marymount. I know that you are praying that the final decision will be favorable. We are having Masses said for that intention. Keep on praying much, please. . . .[15]

[13] *Kansas City Catholic Register,* June 5, 1930.
[14] Letter of Rev. Mother Mary Rose Waller to the Community, Feb. 14, 1932. The original is in the files of the author.
[15] Letter of Rev. Mother Mary Rose Waller to the Community, Mar. 10, 1932. The original is in the files of the author.

The hopeful expectations materialized when the Associated Press announced the list of colleges accredited at the meeting, March 17, 1932.[16] The following article appeared in several newspapers of the region:

... Acceptance of Marymount College of Salina into membership in the North Central Association of Colleges and Secondary Schools, at a convention of the Association in Chicago last week, crowned ten years of achievement for the Sisters of Saint Joseph, Catholic religious order, in charge of the college. The college was founded in 1922 and was the first four-year college exclusively for women and sponsored by Catholic Sisters in the State. Although now there are three other schools of the same type in Kansas, Marymount is the first to receive an accredited rating. . . .[17]

In 1939, the College was affiliated with the Catholic University in accordance with requirements of its Board of Trustees.[18] The College is also a member of the Association of American Colleges,[19] the American Council on Education,[20] and the American Library Association. These affiliations contributed to the effectiveness and stability of the institution.

Soon after his arrival in the Diocese of Concordia, Bishop Thill[21] showed an interest in the College and proposed sending members of the science faculty to Cincinnati, Ohio, to participate in the research program of the Institutum Divi Thomae.[22]

The Institutum is a graduate school of scientific research under the direction of Doctor George Speri Sperti, famous biochemist and member of the Pontifical Academy of Sciences. The Institutum was founded in 1935 by the Most Reverend John T. McNicholas, O.P., S.T.D., Archbishop of Cincinnati. A limited number of research workers are trained to direct and carry on experiments in the units established by the Institutum.

Preparatory to the establishment of a unit at Marymount College, Doctor Elton S. Cook, professor of biochemistry in the cancer research department at the Institutum, visited the College on December

---

16 *Concordia Blade-Empire*, Mar. 17, 1932, Mar. 22, 1932.
Salina Journal, Mar. 18, 1932.
17 *Kansas City Times*, Mar. 24, 1932.
18 Questionnaire of Sister Chrysostom Wynn.
19 Dec. 2, 1939.
20 Apr. 30, 1942.
21 Appointed to the See of Concordia, Aug. 24, 1938; consecrated Oct. 28, 1938.
22 Late in 1939.

2, 1939. Plans were made for a unit to be established in the near future.[23]

The diocesan paper recorded this meeting and inspection:

. . Final arrangements for the establishment of a department for advanced scientific research in a newly equipped laboratory at Marymount College were made last week when the Most Reverend Frank A. Thill, Mother Mary Rose, superior of the Sisters of Saint Joseph, Sister Mary Grace, head of the science department at the College, and Dr. Elton S. Cook, professor of biochemistry of the Institutum Divi Thomae, Cincinnati, Ohio, met at the Episcopal Residence.

The new research unit, which will operate under the direction of Dr. George Speri Sperti, nationally known for his discoveries in the field of biochemistry and light irradiation, will be headed by Sister Mary Grace, who has been making notable progress in research problems in the highly efficient Cincinnati institution.

A great amount of new equipment is being purchased by the College in order to make the course available for the girls who attend Marymount. A laboratory that will be separate from the physics and chemistry laboratories will be designed for this particular department, and every effort will be made to encourage young women to qualify themselves for work in this highly specialized phase of advanced scientific work.[24]

In an announcement sent out from the Institutum, the type of work planned for the sixth unit of the Institutum was explained:

. . The new laboratory will cooperate indirectly with the Cancer Research Foundation's attack on cancer. The foundation, an educational and fund-raising auxiliary of the Institutum, is supporting the basic cancer investigation of Dr. Sperti and his staff. Research conducted at Marymount will be correlated with clinical investigation now under way at St. Francis Hospital, Cincinnati. St. Francis was equipped recently as one of the finest cancer research hospitals in the United States. . . . The Cancer Research Foundation, headed by Mr. Charles F. Williams, maintains the hospital.[25]

The dedication of the laboratories took place on April 16, 1940. The new unit was named the Rose Waller Research Laboratories in honor of Reverend Mother Mary Rose Waller. The event was looked upon with interest in scientific circles of the state and invita-

[23] *Northwestern Kansas Register*, Dec. 24, 1939.
[24] *Ibid.*, Dec. 31, 1939.
    Cincinnati Telegraph-Register, Dec. 28, 1939.
    Denver Catholic Register, Dec. 27, 1939.
[25] The announcement appeared in the *Northwestern Kansas Register*, Mar. 31, 1940; *Cincinnati Telegraph-Register*, Mar. 30, 1940; *Cincinnati Times-Star*, Mar. 31, 1940; *Catholic Daily Tribune*, Apr. 2, 1940.
    Other syndicated articles appeared during the interim in the *Cincinnati Post*, Apr. 11, 1940; *Salina Journal*, Apr. 10, 1940; Apr. 16, 1940; *Salina Advertiser-Sun*, Apr. 11, 1940; *New York Times*, Apr. 14, 1940; *Northwestern Kansas Register*, Apr. 4, 1940.

tions were issued to leading scientists, presidents of the various institutions of learning, the governor, and physicians of Salina and
surrounding towns. The local editor reported the event:

. . . Bishop Frank A. Thill, head of the Concordia diocese of the Roman
Catholic Church, attended and spoke briefly to the public, when he paid tribute
to the Sisters of Saint Joseph who conduct Marymount College and whose
"daring, spirit of pioneering, accomplishments and devotion to learning," he
commended. . . .
The evening revealed that Bishop Thill was responsible for establishment
of the research unit here and for the affiliation with the Institutum, which he
knew well by reason of his long residence in Cincinnati. He remarked on the
surprising development in education he found in the Concordia diocese and
on the accomplishments of the Sisters of Saint Joseph, both the diocese and
the order of nuns being only fifty years old. . . .[26]

The diocesan paper praised the College for "completing a step in
the field of scientific research which gives this institution particular
qualifications for teaching science that are not to be had by any other
college west of the Mississippi."[27]

The address of Dr. Sperti was well received by those present.
He cited personal experiences in working with women in scientific
research to prove that they were becoming highly efficient in this
work. He stressed that there was no cause to worry about a conflict
between the Church and science and that many of the important
discoveries were coming from small units such as the one at Marymount.[28]

Research at the new Marymount unit would be devoted largely
to investigations of cancer, particularly the chemistry of substances
which have already been shown to have value in the treatment of the
disease in laboratory mice. The unit as well was assigned the study of
problems in agricultural chemistry, in particular the process of
photo-synthesis.[29]

When the United States entered World War II, a new field of
endeavor was opened to the Rose Waller Research laboratories.

26 Salina Journal, Apr. 17, 1940.
27 Northwestern Kansas Register, Apr. 21, 1940. Although Marymount College was
the sixth unit established with affiliation with the Institutum Divi Thomae, the other
five units were all east of the Mississippi River. Hence Marymount holds the distinction
of being the first west of the Mississippi. The other units were St. Francis Hospital,
Cincinnati, Ohio; Good Samaritan Hospital, Dayton, Ohio; Siena Heights College,
Adrian, Mich.; Rosary College, River Forest, Ill., and temporarily, Rosarium Academy,
West Palm Beach, Fla.
28 Salina Journal, Apr. 17, 1940.
29 Northwestern Kansas Register, Apr. 21, 1940.

Father Cornelius H. Jansen, assistant director of the Institutum Divi Thomae, visited the laboratory late in 1942 and launched the war research program. "Marymount's laboratory," he said, "is very well equipped to carry on organic research assigned to it, and there is a great deal of enthusiasm and some very interesting results in the growth-promoting fractions have been gathered from irradiated yeast and algae, which are part of the cancer program of the unit."[30] This unpublicized contribution of the unit to the war effort is significant.

One of the projects dear to the heart of Bishop Thill is the CYS, the Catholic Youth of Salina. Organized into grade, secondary, and college units, the organization has permeated the youth activities of the diocese.[31] At Marymount College, the CYS has undertaken several worth-while projects such as the work of the mission committee among the Mexican people of Salina. Weekly, students instruct the children of Mexiville in catechism and visit their homes to encourage Americanization. Baskets of food are contributed by the girls, and collections of clothes are made for the same purpose.[32] This work over a period of years has blessed the students who have participated.

Another project of the CYS is the work of the altar linen committee which has made and distributed to needy churches vestments and small linens for ecclesiastical service. The training of leaders to teach in the religious summer schools of the diocese is also a noteworthy activity. Building up Catholic leadership in the college will add to the glory of the Church in the Middle West and wherever these young women locate in the future.

A CYS project with far-reaching results and publicity is the work of the correspondence committee, approved by the bishop, to instruct children of Catholic families handicapped in the practice and knowledge of their religion. About a hundred children take the course of instruction annually. Reports from parishes where the correspondence committee has students are gratifying and indicate that much influence is exerted for the good of souls.[33] All in all, the CYS at Marymount College has been an asset. One of the latest projects was the

[30] Ibid., Dec. 20, 1942.

[31] First proposed at a meeting of Bishop Thill and the priests of the diocese held at the episcopal residence in Concordia, June 20, 1939. It was launched as a diocesan project, Oct. 19, 1939. Ibid., Oct. 15, 22, 29 and Nov. 5, 12, 1939.

[32] Ibid., Dec. 21, 1941; Dec. 20, 1942.

[33] Ibid., Nov. 29, 1942.

accumulation of the sum during the school year of 1944-45 presented
to Bishop Thill as a contribution toward the education of a priest.[34]

During World War II, Marymount showed its initiative and
spirit of cooperation with city, state, and national projects. The curriculum was enriched with courses in first aid, nutrition, home nursing, canteen, and air raid warden training. Members of the faculty
gave instruction in first aid and air raid precautions.[35] The greatest
contribution, and it is one which is so intangible that it is difficult to
evaluate, is the philosophy of life which a Catholic college instills in
its graduates. If there is a correct philosophy of life, an understanding of the value of a human soul, the appreciation of the rights and
privileges of others, there will be no greater defense against false
philosophies and ideologies which in turn make for war. Therefore,
we may say that *the* greatest contribution any Catholic college can
make to a defense program is to develop these qualities in the students
it gives to society.

The various departments became defense-conscious: the history
department organized an international club; the modern language
departments emphasized inter-Americanism; the economics and commerce departments helped the civilian and military in times of need;
the art, the music, and the drama departments shared in entertainment and art work; the science department carried on war research;
the home economics department gave training in food preparation
and sewing. Each department of the college contributed something.[36]

Among the students, a spirit of cooperation manifested itself.
Contributions were made toward the Pearl Harbor Scholarship Fund:

> As a project of post-war preparedness, girls at Marymount College are
> contributing their single stamps to a "Pearl Harbor Scholarship Fund," thus
> making provision for the Catholic college education of some war hero's daugh-
> ter. Many of the students are aiming to secure defense bonds for themselves
> but those who buy only occasional stamps are contributing these to the fund.[37]

[34] *Ibid.*, May 10, 1945.
     During the scholastic year, 1945-46, a traditional Christmas party for under-
privileged children of Salina and the Abilene orphanage, irrespective of race or creed,
was sponsored for the first time by the CYS. A fund is now being accumulated as a gift
of Marymount students toward the new cathedral to be built in Salina.
[35] *Ibid.*, July 7, 1942.
     Salina Journal, July 4, 1942.
     Salina Advertiser-Sun, July 6, 1942.
[36] *Ibid.*, Jan. 29, 1942.
     Northwestern Kansas Register, Mar. 16, 1941, Aug. 31, 1941, Feb. 1, 1942,
Apr. 5, 1942.
[37] *Salina Advertiser-Sun*, Feb. 12, 1942.

And that spring the student body cancelled the annual spring formal and contributed the sum they would have spent on that affair as another scholarship fund, the "Junior Prom Scholarship." [38]

Although there was a measure of recompense in the social activities sponsored for servicemen in the area, the same zeal and enthusiasm was manifested. Groups from Fort Riley and Camp Funston were entertained in cooperation with the Salina Military Hospitality Committee of the Chamber of Commerce. These affairs were given the wholehearted cooperation of the local committee and families of the city. [39] After the establishment of the camps near Salina, week-end informal dances and other means of recreation were arranged. Groups worked in conjunction with the Red Cross in entertaining convalescent soldiers and in inviting them as guests of the college to concerts and plays. Special choirs were supplied for solemn religious services.

The Victory Commission of the National Federation of Catholic College Students did creditable work in selling bonds during the war and worked with the Red Cross in soliciting funds. These facts indicate the vast scope of war work activity sponsored by the College.

Traditions have become part of the College with "Marymount Day" and the crowning of the representative girl as queen; "May Day" and its honor to the May Queen and Mary, Queen of Marymount; the usual "Education Week" programs; and numerous activities which distinguish Marymount from other colleges.

The annual Nazareth Educational Conferences of the Sisters of Saint Joseph are held at Marymount College during the summer session. Founded in 1923, in Concordia, with Sister Chrysostom Wynn as president, the organization was known as the Community Board of Educational Administration. Since then, twenty-five meetings have taken place. These meetings give impetus to the work of the coming year and serve as a medium for the exchange of ideas in the departments and the various levels of education. [40]

When Marymount opened its doors for the twenty-first year, the entire building was turned over to education on the college level. Part of the building had been set off for the use of the Academy, but

[38] *Salina Journal,* Apr. 20, 1942.
    Ibid., Feb. 6, 1942, Feb. 9, 1942.
[39] *Salina Advertiser-Sun,* Feb. 5, 1942, Feb. 12, 1942.
    Northwestern Kansas Register, Feb. 8, 1942.
[40] *Ibid.,* July 20, 27, 1941.

in 1942 the Academy was closed to allow room for expansion of the College.[41]

The first state meeting of the Kansas State Sodality Union,[42] the second diocesan meeting of the CYS,[43] the Central Student Peace Federation,[44] the state convention of the International Federation of Catholic Alumnae,[45] the Midwest Regional Conference of the Catholic Library Association,[46] the meeting of the Classical Association of Kansas and Western Missouri,[47] the first state convention of the National Catholic Music Educators Association,[48] the first state convention of the National Federation of Catholic College Students in the Central Midwest Region,[49] and the regional meeting of the North Central Association were held at Marymount.[50] Most of these conventions were sponsored when a faculty member at Marymount was president or chairman of the particular association. In each instance the local Chamber of Commerce cooperated in welcoming the delegates to the city.[51]

Faculty competence is exemplified, not only in the classroom, but also in active participation in learned societies and in productive writings.[52] Advanced degrees have been achieved, and the College has won recognition for the type of work offered.[53] To date approximately five hundred and fifty young women have received degrees in sixteen major departments, many of whom have pursued higher studies at outstanding universities. All in all, Marymount has met a need in the field of Catholic education and has shown in its twenty-five-year existence that the challenge has been faced and met.

---

[41] *Ibid.*, Aug. 30, 1942.
    Salina Advertiser-Sun, Aug. 27, 1942.
[42] *Wichita Catholic Advance-Register* (then *Wichita Catholic Advance*), spring of 1932.
[43] *Northwestern Kansas Register*, Oct. 20, 1940.
[44] *Ibid.*, Mar. 27, 1938; Apr. 3, 1938.
    Salina Journal, Mar. 28, 1938.
[45] *Ibid.*, Nov. 30, 1941.
[46] *Northwestern Kansas Register*, Oct. 22, 1939.
[47] *Ibid.*, Feb. 18, 1945.
[48] *Ibid.*, Feb. 18, 1945.
[49] *Ibid.*, Apr. 16, 1944; Apr. 23, 1944.
[50] *Ibid.*, Oct. 27, 1946.
[51] An example of this cooperation is evidenced in a letter from Charles Bren, secretary of the Chamber of Commerce, Salina, Kans., to Mother Antoinette, Superior of Marymount College, in which he speaks of the letters of greeting to 420 guests expected for the meeting of the Catholic Library Association. The letter is dated Oct. 2, 1939.
[52] A résumé of the educational activities of the faculty for the year 1941-1942 appeared in the *Northwestern Kansas Register*, Aug. 9, 1942.
[53] All major departments are headed by Sisters holding doctors' degrees assisted by those holding masters' degrees.

This brief résumé of the history of Marymount College from its opening in 1922 to the present recounts one of the larger developments during the administration of Reverend Mother Mary Rose Waller. Interest in parochial school development during these same years was shown in the establishment of schools in New Almelo, Herington, and Collyer, Kansas.[54]

New Almelo, Norton County, Kansas, was an early entrepôt for Catholic missionaries in the northwestern part of the state. The earliest work in that territory was in charge of the Precious Blood Fathers, and the name of Father Augustine Reichert is held in veneration by the Catholics of the region.

Catholicism in Norton County was organized as early as 1878 when Father Reichert located in New Almelo to minister to the area north and west of Beloit. He took a homestead and built a sod church and dwelling combined. New Almelo, therefore, became the center of Catholic activity for a decade, until Norton outstripped it in population and communication.

One of the pioneer priests of the diocese, Monsignor John B. Vornholt,[55] took charge of New Almelo in 1904. In 1922 his request that the Sisters of Saint Joseph staff his parochial school was granted. The school had been in operation for many years under the supervision of lay teachers.[56] September, 1922, Sisters Bernadette Gladu, superior, Marietta Egle, and Veronica Marie Brinkmeier opened the school with sixty-three pupils enrolled.[57] The school has not grown to any extent due to the static population of the agricultural town. Today there are three Sisters on the mission with sixty-two pupils enrolled.[58]

Boonville, Cooper Couny, Missouri, southeast of Kansas City, has a long, interesting history. Named for the trail-blazer, Daniel Boone, the town first boasted a Catholic church in 1859. A school

---

[54] It is necessary that detailed attention be given to Marymount College, as this institution is the core of the educational system of the Community.

[55] "Monsignor Vornholt, Pioneer, Served as Administrator," *Northwestern Kansas Register,* Nov. 20, 1938.

[56] Information furnished by Msgr. J. B. Vornholt, New Almelo, Kans.

[57] Questionnaires of Sisters Marietta Egle and Veronica Marie Brinkmeier.

[58] *Kenedy's Catholic Directory* (New York, 1923), pp. 301-303; (1947), p. 696.

This New Almelo school made an important change in the fall of 1945, when through the efforts of the pastor, Father J. Sander, advantage was taken of new state rulings on re-districting and the enrollment was thereby greatly increased, necessitating the services of another teacher.

was erected later and taught by lay teachers.[59] Until the close of the term in 1920, the Sisters of Saint Francis conducted the school. For two years after that it was again taught by lay teachers; and in 1923, Father M. F. X. Jennings sought teachers from the Sisters of Saint Joseph of Concordia. That autumn, Sisters Lawrence Trudell, superior, Dolorosa Golden, and Veronica Marie Brinkmeier undertook the supervision of the parochial grade school.[60] There were eighty-three pupils enrolled.[61] The first two years the Sisters lived in the old schoolhouse, and the third year they lived with the Benedictine Sisters at Saint Joseph's Hospital until Christmas when they moved into their own home.[62]

In a chapter entitled "Catholics Carry Education Burden," in his study of Cooper County, Missouri, a recent author remarks:

... The Boonville church supports a parish school that saves the public treasury $12,000 annually because members maintain the Saints Peter and Paul School. It was erected in 1924 and is a credit to any city. If at any time it were to close there would have to be an increase of teachers and funds in order to maintain the public schools. ... It is staffed by the Sisters of Saint Joseph of Concordia, Kansas, who reside in a convenient dwelling on the school campus. That is a labor of love rather than for financial advancement because most of their monetary reward goes back into further educational preparation.[63]

And again the same author in referring to the Catholic schools explained:

... Four Catholic churches in the county at Boonville, Pilot Grove, Martinsville, and Clear Creek, maintain parochial schools providing religious as well as scholastic training for children of parishoners ... exert a daily influence. ... The need of more consistent training along religious and moral lines is felt so keenly today that some leading public school executives are including religious training and study of the Bible from a non-sectarian point of view. ... The Boonville Catholic High School is a magnificent building, has fine equipment and its courses are approved by the North Central Association which rates it. ...[64]

When the residence and the school were completed in 1925, the first Catholic High School was opened in Boonville.[65] The enroll-

---

[59] History of Howard and Cooper Counties, Missouri (St. Louis, 1883), p. 828.

[60] Questionnaires of Sisters Lawrence Trudell, Dolorosa Golden, and Veronica Marie Brinkmeier.

[61] Kenedy's Catholic Directory (New York, 1924), p. 452.

[62] Questionnaire of Sister Isabelle Marie Finn.

[63] Elston J. Melton, History of Cooper County, Missouri (Columbia, 1937), pp. 357-358.

[64] Ibid., pp. 175-176.

[65] Questionnaires of Sisters Etta Louise Knaup and Francis de Sales Stritchfield.

ment has steadily increased until in 1947 there were ten Sisters teaching two hundred and seven students.[66]

The Home of the Little Flower, a diocesan institution for the aged located in Concordia, was built in 1923 and opened as a mission of the Sisters of Saint Joseph at the beginning of 1924. The property on which the Home was built is located in the old courthouse square at Tenth and Kansas Avenues.[67] It was purchased by Bishop Tief, who enlarged and improved it. The Home of the Little Flower was blessed on January 17, 1924.[68]

Previous to this time the aged of the diocese had been cared for at Saint Joseph's Orphanage in Abilene, but new state regulations made it necessary to care for the aged at a different location.[69] The pioneer Sisters were Sisters Magdalen Filiatreault, superior, Conception Breen, Imelda Hilpert, and Leonard Millette.[70] There were eighteen inmates during the first year of the existence of the Home.[71]

The Home has been a haven of rest and security to many aged people of the diocese and of other dioceses; in fact, there are also non-Catholics among the inmates. In one account of activities at the Home the writer said:

. . . When Mrs. Ida Fiffe of Aurora came to live at the Home of the Little Flower, she became the eighty-eighth person to register at the institution since its foundation in 1924. . . . Two of the inmates, William Dunlop, 85, and Joseph Hefflinger, 84, have been resident since it was founded. Mr. Dunlop, a former Texas cowboy, still recalls many adventures that he had while working in the Lone Star State. While the average age of the inmates is 81 years, two are already in their 90's, one being 94 and another 96.

The Sisters of Saint Joseph, who conduct the Home, try to make it not an institution but a true home for old people. . . . It is interesting to drop in any time of the day to notice what each one is doing. One old man will be reading a German newspaper, another will be saying a litany from a French prayerbook, one old lady will be doing her favorite fancywork, one listening to her radio serial, and often someone else will have fallen asleep in her rocker on the veranda. Truly these people find life very kind to them, and, even if they

---

[66] Kenedy's Catholic Directory (New York, 1947), p. 517.
[67] Northwestern Kansas Register, Nov. 20, 1938; Dec. 26, 1937. On Dec. 17, 1945, the property was deeded to the Community of the Sisters of St. Joseph, in an agreement between the Ordinary and the Sisters. The latter agreed to convert the present St. Joseph's Hospital, Concordia, into a home for the aged of the diocese, upon the completion of the new St. Joseph's Hospital.
[68] Ibid., Nov. 20, 1938.
[69] Loc. cit.
[70] Questionnaires of Sisters Magdalen Filiatreault, Imelda Hilpert, and Leonard Millette.
[71] Kenedy's Catholic Directory (New York, 1924), p. 316.
Questionnaires of Sisters Magdalen Filiatreault, Imelda Hilpert, and Leonard Millette.

do have anxieties there is always someone ready to listen to them and sympathize with them. . . .[72]

Today thirty aged are cared for by six Sisters.[73]

Foundations made from the Concordia Motherhouse [Wichita, Kansas (1888), and La Grange, Illinois (1899)] have been discussed. The affiliation of the Community of the Sisters of Saint Joseph of Silver City, New Mexico, with the Community of the Sisters of Saint Joseph of Concordia will now be considered.

Silver City, in the foothills of a branch of the Rocky Mountains, holds an interesting note for the historian. New Mexico was early explored and settled by the Spanish from old Mexico. The Catholic Church is everywhere evident with its fine church buildings and its religious institutions of learning and of charity. Many of the old mission buildings, some of which antedate the California missons by more than a century, are still in use and form one of the state's many attractions to tourists. The cross-crowned wayside chapels are an attractive feature of the country districts.[74]

Grant County, in the southwestern part of New Mexico, has great possibilities for agriculture, stock-raising, and mining. This is the center of mineral deposits of gold, silver, copper, and lead known in song and story. Silver City has an elevation of over 6,000 feet. One writer referring to the large proportion of sunshiny days declared "this is a silver city with a golden climate." The climate attracts health-seekers from all parts of the country. Unlike most towns of the Southwest, Silver City is an American town with a Mexican quarter.[75]

The Sisters of Saint Joseph from Tipton, Indiana, opened an institution in Silver City in 1915 which was known as Saint Joseph's Hospital and Sanatorium. There were seven Sisters on the mission with Sister Magdalen Thomas, superior. At the same time the Sisters of Mercy conducted an academy with one hundred pupils enrolled.[76]

Sister Magdalen Thomas had come from mission work in the Diocese of Boise, where she was in charge of Saint Joseph's Academy

[72] Northwestern Kansas Register, July 13, 1941; Dec. 26, 1937; Jan. 3, 1943.
[73] Kenedy's Catholic Directory (New York, 1947), p. 697.
[74] Santa Fé, New Mexico, Publicity Bureau, A Guide to New Mexico for the Homeseeker, Investor, Tourist, Sportsman, Healthseeker. (Santa Fé, New Mexico, 1917), p. 3.
[75] New Mexico Health Resorts, Atchison, Topeka, and Santa Fé Railroad (Topeka, 1899), pp. 53-55.
[76] Kenedy's Catholic Directory (New York, 1916), p. 388.

for Indians and whites at Lapwai (Slickpoo P.O.).[77] The year after the mission in Silver City was established from Tipton, there was a separation from the Indiana Motherhouse and Mother Magdalen became superior of the school opened when the Sisters of Mercy withdrew. The small Community continued to maintain the sanatorium in addition to Our Lady of Lourdes Academy.[78] The Sisters of Saint Joseph of Silver City were incorporated August 26, 1915.[79]

The little group encountered hardships and difficulties in every shape and form. In 1917 it listed seven Sisters and two novices;[80] in 1918 and 1919 the same information was given;[81] in 1920 it listed four Sisters and two novices;[82]; in 1923 twenty-one Sisters;[83] and then a drop to thirteen Sisters in 1924.[84] Financial difficulties faced the struggling group at every turn. A group of postulants from Ireland temporarily bolstered the hopes of the group but failed to ensure the stability which the Community needed.

Mother Magdalen Thomas realized in 1925 that steps must be taken for affiliation with some other community of Sisters of Saint Joseph to ward off the dissolution of the little band in Silver City. She had worked hard and prayed hard but adverse circumstances left her with a tremendous debt and little in the way of courage to try again and again. She, therefore, chose to write to the Sisters of Saint Joseph in Concordia to see if arrangements could be made for the amalgamation of her small group with a large, well-established community. Although hesitant about the proposal's advisability at first, the authorities in Concordia were most cordial and invited Mother Magdalen to visit the Motherhouse to discuss the proposition in person with the Superior General and her Council.[85] This visit resulted in a return visit to Silver City by Bishop Tief, Mother Mary Rose Waller, Mother Antoinette Cuff, and Sister Regis Schwenzer. The report of this visit was recorded in the minutes of a meeting held after their return:

[77] *Ibid.*, (1911), p. 265; (1912), p. 276; (1913), p. 285; (1914), p. 291.

[78] *Ibid.*, 1917), p. 369. The sanatorium was discontinued in 1919.

[79] Articles of Incorporation for the Sisters of St. Joseph of Silver City, New Mexico. Aug. 26, 1915.

[80] *Kenedy's Catholic Directory* (New York, 1917), p. 369.

[81] *Ibid.*, (1918), p. 371; (1919), p. 374.

[82] *Ibid.*, (1920), p. 329.

[83] *Ibid.*, (1923), p. 350. The group from Ireland accounted for this increase.

[84] *Ibid.*, (1924), p. 364.

[85] Information furnished by Sister Bertille Bridgeman, July 22, 1945. Sister Bertille was Secretary.

. . . At nine o'clock on the morning of January 29, 1926, the Feast of Saint Francis de Sales, the councillors held a meeting for the purpose of considering the Silver City, New Mexico, proposition. His Lordship, Right Reverend Bishop Tief, honored the meeting by his presence. Those present were: Mother Mary Rose, Superior General, Sister Cleophas, Mother Antoinette, Sister Regis, and Sister Ambrosia, councillors, and the Mistress of Novices, Sister Isabelle. . . . The visit (to Silver City) had been made at the urgent invitation of Mother Magdalen, the Superior of the Sisters of Saint Joseph of Silver City, it being the wish of Mother Magdalen to affiliate with our Community. Right Reverend Bishop Schuler of El Paso was consulted and it was found that he fully approved of the affiliation.

Mother Mary Rose further stated that the property of the Sisters was investigated and that everything was beyond what they had expected to find from the report of Mother Magdalen on her recent visit to Concordia; that there were advantages for both Communities as it would be an excellent place for the members of our Community who needed such a climate and that it would insure the future of the Silver City Community.

Quite a detailed account of the trip to Silver City was given by Right Reverend Bishop Tief. He spoke of his first interview with Mother Magdalen. . . . He took special care to consult the Bishop of El Paso, Bishop Schuler, as to the spiritual care of the Sisters in Silver City and had received the assurance that such care would be provided.

The question of whether the Silver City Community be accepted or not was then voted on by a secret ballot . . . the result was unanimous in favor of the affiliation. . . . The appointment of a superior was considered. . . . Sister Innocentia was chosen for superior of the new mission. By a secret and unanimous vote, it was decided that Mother Magdalen retain the title of Mother from regard for the years of strenuous endeavor to bring to so successful a condition the holding of the Silver City Community. . . .[86]

There was a considerable debt on the affiliated Community.[87] However, the Sisters of Saint Joseph of Concordia saw a new frontier, a new field of endeavor, and they again met the challenge regardless of liabilities. The vocations of the Sisters in Silver City were at stake and monetary consideration is as naught when something of greater value is in jeopardy. That God had blessed this project has been evidenced many times since the affiliation took place in 1926.

The agreement entered into was a legal contract which is herein quoted in part:

This Agreement, made and entered into this 26th day of January, 1926, by and between the Sisters of St. Joseph of Silver City, a corporation, the party of the first part, and the Sisters of St. Joseph of Concordia, the party of the second part:

[86] *Minutes of the Meetings of the Councillors of the Sisters of St. Joseph, Concordia, Kansas,* vol. II, Jan. 29, 1926.
[87] *Minutes of the Meetings of the Nazareth Convent and Academy, a Kansas Corporation, Feb. 17, 1926,* lists the debt as $93,000. The trustees approved the assumption of this indebtedness and authorized the paying off of these notes and bills.

Witnesseth: Whereas, the party of the first part is desirous of conveying and assigning to the party of the second part its property of any kind whatsoever situated either in Grant County, New Mexico, or in the State of Texas, and of merging with the party of the second part as a religious organization, and the party of the second part has agreed thereto, and in consideration therefor has undertaken to assume all the debts and obligations of the party of the first part, and to continue the religious work of the party of the first part at Silver City, Grant County, New Mexico, under the control of the Mother General and her council of the Sisters of St. Joseph of Concordia, Kansas. . . .[88]

The heartfelt gratitude of Bishop Schuler of El Paso, in whose diocese Silver City is located, was expressed at this time and on many occasions throughout his life. His interest in the Sisters of Saint Joseph of Concordia never lessened. In fact, it was through his influence that the following year another institution was opened in the El Paso diocese. At the conclusion of the negotiations mentioned in detail above, Bishop Schuler wrote to Mother Mary Rose:

... Your generous favor of the 30th just received [referring to a check to cover amounts advanced to Mother Magdalen when she was in stress financially] ... I cannot thank you and yours sufficiently and particularly for the fine spirit of charity and zeal you all have evidenced in coming into my diocese to work— as you so well know how—for the glory of God. . . . Our dear Lord will repay you and will bless you—as I ask Him—a hundredfold. What little I can do to help, encourage or inspire will always be cheerfully and cordially done. It will be my way of reciprocating the kindnesses you have showered on me during these last three months. . . .[89]

The property was deeded to the Concordia Community.[90] The Sisters from Concordia assumed the debt and paid it. The amalgamation was so complete that within a few months it was barely perceptible which Sisters had originally belonged to which Community.

February 24, 1926, the first group of Sisters left for the Southwest. Sister Innocentia Brennan was chosen superior; she was assisted by Sisters Angelicia Guinan, Christina Hoffman, Nazarius Poisson, Beatrice Cyr, Florentia Murphy, and Frances Eileen Healey. Mother Magdalen became assistant to Sister Innocentia. Sister Angelicia was appointed directress of Saint Mary's Academy and secretary-treasurer

[88] *Agreement between the Sisters of St. Joseph, Silver City, New Mexico, and the Sisters of St. Joseph, Concordia, Kans., Jan. 26, 1926.* It was signed by Mother Magdalen, Sister Dolores of the Silver City Community, Mother Mary Rose and Sister Bertille of the Concordia Community, and was approved by Bishops A. J. Schuler and F. J. Tief.

[89] Letter of the Most Rev. Anthony J. Schuler, Bishop of El Paso, to Mother Mary Rose Waller, Apr. 9, 1926. The original is in the Archives of the Nazareth Motherhouse, Concordia, Kans.

[90] Property in Silver City known as St. Mary's Academy was deeded to the Nazareth Convent and Academy, a Kansas corporation, on Mar. 10, 1928.

of the mission. Later the number was augmented by the arrival of other Sisters from Concordia.[91]

During the term of superiorship of Sister Louis Letourneau, successor of Sister Innocentia in 1930, the new auditorium was built and St. Mary's High School was accredited by the State of New Mexico. This latter achievement may be credited to the interest and forethought of Sister Angelicia Guinan. An addition to the school building enlarged the high school and enabled the institution to accommodate more pupils and, therefore, to extend its influence more widely throughout the Southwest.[92] Today eighteen Sisters care for an enrollment of two hundred and eight students.[93]

In September, 1926, Sisters were sent to Collyer, Trego County, Kansas, to conduct the parochial school. The history of the little town dates to 1878 when Colonel C. N. Pratt originated the Soldiers', Sailors', and Citizens' Colony. The name "Collyer" was taken from the name of the Reverend R. Collyer, a Protestant minister of Chicago. Later a new Collyer was located east of this settlement on the Kansas Pacific Railroad.[94] The prevailing nationalities in the settlement were German and Irish.

An interest in a parochial school had been manifested several years before the school was finally opened; in fact the parish had erected a building awaiting the coming of the Sisters. The first Sisters were Sisters Geraldine Boudreau, Angela Doyle, and Alvarita Rajewski.[95] There were ninety-five pupils enrolled the first year.[96] The original plan was to have the Sisters occupy the upper story of the school building, but failing to secure Sisters under these conditions, the parish erected a modern residence. When the Sisters arrived in 1926, the residence was complete except for a few

[91] Notes of Sister Bertille Bridgeman.

Names of the Sisters who arrived in Silver City in September were: Sisters Cyril Schumacher, Ermelina Wasinger, and Mary Ellen Cunningham.

[92] *Diocese of El Paso—Texas Centennial Celebration, 1536-1936.* (El Paso, 1936). Article on institutions conducted by the Sisters of St. Joseph of Concordia.

Silver City and Southwest New Mexico—Home of the World's Finest Climate (issued by the Junior Chamber of Commerce), no date.

[93] *Kenedy's Catholic Directory* (New York, 1947), p. 433.

[94] William G. Cutler, *History of Kansas* (Chicago, 1883), p. 1926.

Western Kansas World, Dec. 27, 1879.

[95] Questionnaires of Sisters Geraldine Boudreau, Angela Doyle, and Alvarita Rajewski.

[96] *Kenedy's Catholic Directory* (New York, 1926), p. 327.

details.[97] Father Peter Schaefer was pastor when the school opened. Today the enrollment is forty-seven.[98]

A third school was opened in 1926 in Herington, Kansas. The boast has been made on many occasions that the first Mass within the confines of the present State of Kansas was offered by the proto-martyr, Father Juan de Padilla, in the vicinity of Herington. Father Padilla, sent out by Charles I of Spain to accompany the Coronado expedition, is said to have celebrated that Mass with only the open spaces for a church and a ledge for an altar stone. A monument was erected in Herington several years ago to commemorate this event.[99]

The town of Herington was established in 1881. A man by the name of Herington imported laborers and, by careful business meth-ods, changed his ranch into a prospective town, encouraging the authorities planning the route of the Missouri Pacific to build its tracks that way. Thus, Herington, the rancher, became the father of the town which grew along the route of the Missouri Pacific.

Through the courtesy of a non-Catholic benefactor, B. L. Thomp-son, a prominent businessman, a block of ground upon which the church, the residence, and the school were erected, was donated to the parish.

With the passing of time, as the parish continued to grow, the people conceived the plan of completing the parish unit by building a parish school. The school, erected and equipped at a cost of $60,000, was dedicated and ready for classes in September, 1926.[100] Sisters Immaculata Hopkins, superior, Ann Joseph Mulvihill, Cortona Marie Dome, Georgina Maher, Mary Josephine Young, and Francis Inez Grabbe were the first Sisters to work in Herington.[101] There were one hundred and twenty-five enrolled, with forty Mexican children included in that number.[102] A goodly percentage of Mexican chil-

97 Questionnaire of Sister Alvarita Rajewski.

98 *Kenedy's Catholic Directory* (New York, 1947), p. 695.

99 Historians are not in agreement as to the location of Quivira. Most of them insist that Coronado never reached Kansas. The question remains unsolved: "Where was Coronado when he thought he was in Quivira?" Many historians believe he was not in Kansas, but in the Texas Panhandle. Be that as it may, Kansans claim Quivira and consequently the ministrations of Father Padilla.

100 *Kansas City Catholic Register*, Sept. 2, 1926.

Northwestern Kansas Register, May 11, 1941.

101 Questionnaires of Sisters Immaculata Hopkins, Ann Joseph Mulvihill, Cortona Marie Dome, Georgina Maher, Mary Josephine Young, and Francis Inez Grabbe.

102 *Loc. cit.*

dren attend the school, since Herington as a railroad center attracts Mexican families. The school today is conducted by four teachers with sixty pupils enrolled.[103]

A year after the affiliation of the Silver City Community, another request was made to send Sisters into the Southwest, again into Bishop Schuler's Diocese of El Paso. The fascination of the historic Southwest has been a favorite subject of dramatist and novelist. Texas, settled by the Spaniards about the middle of the sixteenth century, was successively under the sway of Mexico, the Republic of Texas, and the United States.[104] The Diocese of El Paso comprises an area of 62,394 square miles, including the section of Texas surrounding El Paso and several counties in southern New Mexico.[105] Silver City, Grant County, was included in this jurisdiction.

On May 21, 1927, the Councillors met at Marymount College, Salina, to consider the proposal made to Mother Mary Rose Waller of taking over a sanatorium in El Paso. Present at the meeting were Bishop Tief, Mother Mary Rose, Mother Antoinette, Sisters Cleophas and Regis. Bishop A. J. Schuler of El Paso and his chancellor, Rev. Robert O'Laughran, had interviewed and corresponded with Mother Mary Rose; Dr. Orville Egbert of El Paso, together with his associates, had presented a plan for the establishment of the sanatorium. They proposed to draw up a contract if the Sisters of Saint Joseph of Concordia decided to send Sisters to El Paso.[106]

Two months later another meeting of the Council was called to consider the letters and contract submitted by Dr. Egbert and his associates.[107] The lawyer for the Nazareth Convent and Academy, a Kansas corporation, Mr. C. A. Hunt[108] had been consulted. In the event that the institution be accepted, the Council appointed Sister Ursula Kielty as superior. The Council suggested that Dr. Egbert and his lawyer be invited to visit Concordia.

The proposition was accepted and on July 29, 1927, Sisters Ursula Kielty and Hildegarde McAndrew left for El Paso. They stayed with the Sisters of Loretto for three weeks, and then were joined on

---

[103] *Kenedy's Catholic Directory* (New York, 1947), p. 695.
[104] Carlos Castaneda, *Our Catholic Heritage in Texas, 1519-1936,* 5 vols. (Austin, 1936).
[105] *Catholic Encyclopedic Dictionary,* p. 329.
[106] *Minutes of the Meetings of the Councillors of the Sisters of St. Joseph, Concordia, Kansas, June, 1925-July, 1940,* vol. II, pp. 9-10.
[107] *Ibid.,* pp. 10-11.
[108] Letter of Dr. Orville Egbert to Rev. Mother Mary Rose Waller, dated July 22, 1927. The original is in the Archives of the Nazareth Motherhouse, Concordia, Kans.

August 20 by Sisters Praxades Hamil, Alexis Gignac, and Leonarda O'Donohue. That same day Bishop Schuler blessed the sanatorium which was to be known as Saint Joseph's Sanatorium. After the services, Father Leo McIntyre was appointed chaplain.[109] There were thirty-two patients that first year.[110]

The contract with Bishop Schuler was to expire five years from the date of its signing, with the Congregation given an option to renew the contract. At the time of the expiration, rather than buy the sanatorium, the Community offered to renew the contract for another five years.[111] This period was later reduced to three years.[112]

The depression which swept the land was felt for several years. The Community met the problem by offering to send a dietitian salary-free to cut down expenses.[113] Later the cooperation of the three Doctors Homan of the Homan Tubercular Sanatorium gave more stability to the institution.[114] It is now in splendid condition; a new laboratory was equipped in 1940; a new X-ray department was opened in 1941; and several other important improvements have been made.[115]

The agreement between the Bishop of El Paso and the Sisters of Saint Joseph of Concordia provided that the Sisters' salaries were to be paid one half in cash and the other half in notes signed by the Bishop of El Paso. These notes were held at the Motherhouse in Concordia until the final purchase was made in 1945. That amount has made possible the acquisition of the property as a part of the holdings of the Sisters of Saint Joseph.[116] Today there are thirteen Sisters working in the Saint Joseph's Sanatorium caring for two hundred two tubercular patients, who, under pleasant conditions, are seeking to regain their health in the "nation's only eighty per cent sunshine belt."[117]

The election of Reverend Mother Mary Rose as Superior General

[109] Questionnaire of Sister Hildegarde McAndrew.
[110] Questionnaires of Sisters Hildegarde McAndrew, Alexis Gignac, Praxades Hamil, and Leonarda O'Donohue.
    Kenedy's Catholic Directory (New York, 1928), p. 329.
[111] *Minutes of the Meetings of the Councillors of the Sisters of St. Joseph, Concordia, Kansas, June, 1925-July, 1940*, vol. II, pp. 38-39, 46-47.
[112] *Ibid.*, pp. 51-52.
[113] *Ibid.*, pp. 58-59.
[114] *Ibid.*, pp. 75-76.
[115] Questionnaire of Sister Felicitas McAuliffe.
[116] *Minutes of the Meetings of the Councillors of the Sisters of St. Joseph*, vol. III, p. 61. Final transfer of ownership to the Sisters of St. Joseph of Concordia, Sept. 28, 1945.
[117] *Kenedy's Catholic Directory* (New York, 1947), p. 432.

for a second term took place at a General Chapter—the first General Chapter held by the Congregation—June 11-12, 1930. It was composed of eighty delegates who represented the Sisters as a whole.[118]

Through the consideration of the Cunningham family, friends of the Sisters, property west of Abilene was given to the Community upon which were built two modern buildings known as Villa Maria. A part of this property not covered by the Cunningham donation was purchased by St. Joseph's Home later.[119] The Villa has become a favorite rest and vacation spot for the Sisters.

Under the discussion of Saint Anthony's Hospital, Sabetha, the building of the addition to that institution was mentioned. Credit for this splendid work is due Mother Mary Rose Waller, during whose administration the project was undertaken. Built at a cost of $80,000, the addition of thirty rooms and a chapel almost doubled its capacity.[120] Today, Saint Anthony Murdock Memorial Hospital in Sabetha, well established and well known in northeastern Kansas, is staffed by twenty Sisters and during the past year cared for eighteen hundred patients.[121]

The celebration of the silver jubilee of the priesthood of Bishop Tief, May 15, 1933, serves as a milestone in evaluating the work of the Church in the Diocese of Concordia. Practically every parish in the diocese had made material gains in the form of church buildings, rectories, convents, parochial schools, and other improvements.[122] The spiritual growth was manifested in an increase in the number of parishes and of vocations to the religious life. Many young women had cast their lot with that of the Sisters of Saint Joseph of Concordia.[123] Represented in the choir which sang the jubilee Mass on the campus of Marymount College were students

---

[118] By the time of the General Chapter in 1936, the Community had adopted at a General Chapter in 1933 the revised Constitution, which provided that all professed Sisters were members of the General Chapter. When the Constitutions were approved in Rome in 1940, the Holy See made the change to the delegate system.

[119] *Minutes of the Meetings of the Councillors of the Sisters of St. Joseph, Concordia, Kansas, June, 1925-July, 1940*, vol. II, pp. 49-50.

[120] *Sabetha Herald*, Nov. 20, 1930.

[121] *Kenedy's Catholic Directory* (New York, 1947), p. 542.

[122] *Kansas City Catholic Register*, May 11, 1933.

[123] A series of articles appeared in the *Kansas City Catholic Register* for several weeks prior to the jubilee in which religious vocations from the various parishes of the diocese were listed. The completed list contained names of 627 men and women of the diocese who had entered the religious life during a period of 52 years. The Sisters of St. Joseph of Concordia received 228 nuns from 43 parishes of the diocese. *Kansas City Catholic Register*, Dec. 29, 1932.

from parochial, grade, and high schools, and from Marymount College.[124] The Sisters of Saint Joseph paid due homage to the Bishop of Concordia, who at all times had shown a paternal interest in the work of the Community.[125]

If the coming to Newton was considered the important date in the history of the Community, the golden jubilee should have been held in June, 1933. However, since, a year after the settling in Newton, the foundation was made permanently in Concordia and the Motherhouse moved there, the 1884 date has taken on more meaning to the Sisters of Saint Joseph. The jubilee was delayed another year; on June 18, 1935, the celebration actually took place.

In the early part of 1934 an historical article appeared in the Wichita Catholic paper which reviewed the accomplishments of fifty years. At that time the Community was credited with the management of one fully accredited college, three academies, fourteen high schools, thirty-two grade schools, four hospitals, a tubercular sanatorium, a home for the aged, and an orphanage.[126]

The first official notice of the approaching celebration was in a letter to the missions written by the Superior General, Mother Mary Rose Waller:

... October, 1934, is the fiftieth anniversary of the establishment of our Community in Concordia. 1934-35 will, therefore, be our jubilee year; we have decided to have the celebration in June. We wish it to be a spiritual occasion and will leave to each mission the decision as to what prayers will be offered. The children's spiritual bouquet may be included in the Sisters' bouquet or may be sent in separately. . . . Let each superior have a little meeting of the Sisters and plan what is convenient and allowable. . . .[127]

And again in the spring, before the Sisters had left their missions, Mother Mary Rose wrote:

... The Golden Jubilee of our Community will be observed on June 18. Kindly let me know when your schools will close. Then we can arrange for the number of Sisters that will come home for the jubilee. For those schools whose closing date is late, arrangements might be made with the pastors for a date which will permit the Sisters to come home for the jubilee. This is a

124 Ibid., May 11, 1933.
    Wichita Catholic Advance-Register, May 11, May 18, 1933.
125 Letter of Mother Mary Rose Waller to the Community, Apr. 10, 1933.
    Letter of Sister Bertille Bridgeman (chairman of the program committee) to the Community, Apr. 12, 1933.
126 Wichita Catholic Advance-Register, Feb. 17, 1934.
127 Letter of Mother Mary Rose Waller to the Community, Oct. 12, 1934. The original is in the files of the author.

great event in our Community and out of consideration, the pastors might be willing to close school a week earlier. . . .[128]

History becomes more vital when a panorama in broad outline sketches achievements of an era. The era of the first half century in the Midwest was reviewed in the golden jubilee ceremonies held in Concordia in mid-June, 1935.

Pope Pius XI sent greetings and his apostolic blessing to the Sisters of Saint Joseph of Concordia on the occasion of their golden jubilee celebration last week. Bishop Francis J. Tief, who received the letter on the jubilee day, conveyed the message to the Community.[129] Thus, with the blessing of His Holiness, the two days of jubilation began with a Solemn Pontifical Mass, celebrated by Bishop Tief. Present in the sanctuary were three members of the hierarchy who had always shown an interest in the work of the Sisters: the former Bishop of Lincoln, Bishop J. Henry Tihen; Bishop Stanislaus Bona, of Grand Island; and the friend and advocate for papal approbation, Abbot Martin Veth, O.S.B., of Atchison, Kansas. The first day of festivity was set aside exclusively for the clergy and religious. Officers of the Mass were chosen from among the relatives of the Sisters of the Community. Fifty members of the clergy attended. More than three hundred seventy Sisters at home for the celebration represented all the missions conducted by the Sisters. Four other Motherhouses, St. Louis, LaGrange, Wichita, and Orange, of the Sisters of Saint Joseph, were represented as were the Benedictine Sisters, Atchison, the Sisters of Charity, Leavenworth, and the Sisters of Saint Agnes, Fond du Lac.[130]

For the benefit of the Sisters unable to attend the jubilee in person, Mother Mary Rose wrote a detailed account:

. . . . Words fail to describe the glorious event. We feel that it was the happiest and most spiritual celebration that has occurred since the establishment of our Congregation. Well may we rejoice for I feel certain that God bestowed many blessings upon us, blessings which will benefit us during the days which lie ahead of us. . . . There were about 370 of our Sisters here for the jubilee days; some that could not come on the 18th were here on the 19th. We owe our Bishop a debt of gratitude for the interest he took in our celebration. First of all, in an announcement that he sent to all of the clergy of the diocese, he

[128] Letter of Mother Mary Rose Waller to the Community, Apr. 17, 1935. The original is in the files of the author.

[129] A copy is in the files of the author. The original is in the Archives of the Nazareth Motherhouse, Concordia, Kans.

Kansas City Catholic Register, June 22, 1935.

[130] Ibid., June 22, 1935.

praised the work of the Sisters in his diocese, and asked each priest to offer a Mass for our Community. Many of these Masses were High Masses.

His Excellency pontificated and preached on the 18th and gave a short talk at the entertainment on Tuesday. He said the Community Mass and presided at the Solemn High Mass and preached on Wednesday; and also at the luncheon he welcomed the guests in the name of the Sisters. The visiting Sisters were deeply impressed with his Excellency's wholehearted devotion to the Community. . . .

All enjoyed the wonderful talk that dear Mother Antoinette gave on Tuesday and especially appreciated the tribute that Mother paid to the four Bishops she has known so well—Bishops Fink, Scannell, Cunningham, and Tief.

We received telegrams and letters of congratulation and commendation from all over the country. They expressed the appreciation of our friends and praised the Sisters for the great good they are doing for God and for souls. . . . We did not forget the dear departed members of our Community and I feel certain that they were present with us for the jubilee.

We had a Mass offered for dear Mother Stanislaus on June 25. A Requiem High Mass was offered for all deceased Sisters on June 26. Thus we were all united together in the Communion of Saints. We are now beginning to look forward to the next fiftieth milestone, and trusting in Divine Providence, our Congregation will continue to accomplish much for God's honor and glory. . . .[131]

In the course of his sermon, Bishop Tief referred to a petition sent from the Community to the Holy See asking that the status of the Sisters of Saint Joseph of Concordia be raised from diocesan to pontifical.[132] The subject of papal approbation, which was achieved[133] in 1940 not long before the death of Mother Mary Rose Waller, will be treated in full in the following chapter.

In accordance with the spirit of canon law regarding the third term for a Superior General, at the General Chapter held in June, 1936, the name of Mother Mary Rose was not considered at first; however, a vote was made to postulate to Rome. Rome acceded to the postulation, and again the Community was under the direction of Mother Mary Rose Waller.[134]

[131] Letter of Mother Mary Rose Waller to the Community, June 28, 1935. A copy is in the files of the author.

[132] Kansas City Catholic Register, June 22, 1935.

[133] Decree issued from the office of the Sacred Congregation for Religious, July 7, 1940. Degree N. 3988. C. 110. The original is in the Vatican Archives. A copy is in the Archives of the Nazareth Motherhouse, Concordia, Kans.

[134] Document N. 4734-36, July 2, 1936. The original is in the Vatican Archives. A copy is in the Archives of the Nazareth Motherhouse, Concordia, Kans.

Cablegram from the Sacred Congregation of Religious to the Most Rev. Amleto Giovanni Cicognani, July 2, 1936.

Telegram of the Most Rev. Amleto Giovanni Cicognani to the Most Rev. Francis J. Tief, July 3, 1936.

Telegram of the Most Rev. Francis J. Tief to Rev. Mother Mary Rose Waller, July 3, 1936.

Letter of Mother Mary Rose Waller to Community, July 12, 1936. Photostats of the above are in the files of the author.

One of the primary activities of the Sisters of Saint Joseph of Concordia is the care of the sick in hospitals. This work began in 1903 when Saint Joseph's Hospital, Concordia, and St. Joseph's Hospital, Belvidere, Illinois, were opened. In 1915 St. John's Hospital, Salina, received its first patients. Five years later, Dr. Samuel Murdock, Jr., of Sabetha, benefactor of the Community, turned over his well-established institution, now known as St. Anthony Murdock Memorial Hospital, to the Sisters. The next institution of the same nature, Saint Joseph's Sanatorium, was opened in El Paso in 1927. Negotiations took place with the Charlotte Swift Memorial Hospital, Manhattan, in 1936.

Dr. Charles F. Little and his daughter, Dr. Belle Little, established the Charlotte Swift Memorial Hospital in 1915.[135] At an early date, Dr. Belle Little realized the advantageous location of her hospital in the vicinity of Kansas State College and made arrangements for supplementary courses in chemistry to be given to the student nurses. In cooperation with President Jardine of the college a five-year course was worked out as early as 1921, making the Charlotte Swift one of the first hospitals in the state to offer such possibilities.[136]

In October, 1936, Dr. Belle Little found it necessary to borrow money to maintain some other property and her health prevented her continuing to practice medicine. She had previously asserted that at her death the hospital in Manhattan was to be given to the Sisters of Saint Joseph of Concordia.[137]

Dr. Belle Little asked Monsignor A. J. Luckey, Manhattan, to ask the authorities in Concordia if they would consider taking over the hospital immediately for the sum of $15,000. At that time the Community was considering an addition to the hospital in Belvidere and thought best not to incur further expense. However, early in October, 1936, word was received in Concordia that negotiations were practically closed for selling the hospital to parties not countenanced within the medical profession. When Mother Mary Rose interviewed Dr. Belle Little, the latter stated that this concern had offered her $25,000 but that she would prefer the Sisters to get it

135 Named for the wife of Dr. Charles Little.
136 Material furnished by The St. Mary Hospital, Manhattan, to Sister Evangeline Thomas to be used in an article which was incorporated into a book on nursing history and hospitals of Kansas.
137 Several years before the purchase of the hospital, Dr. Belle Little had conveyed this information to Msgr. Luckey.

and would compromise on $20,000. After the hospital had been visited and inspected by the councillors, a special meeting was held in the presence of Bishop Tief and it was voted that the Community accept the hospital proposition.[138] The arrangements were completed and the Sisters took possession on December 1, 1936.[139] Sister Frederica Brungardt was appointed superior.[140]

The local press in Manhattan recorded the transfer:

Purchase of the Charlotte Swift Memorial Hospital, 400 North Eleventh Street, by the Sisters of Saint Joseph, an order of Catholic nuns, was announced today by Monsignor A. J. Luckey, pastor of the local church, after the contract had been signed in Concordia, where the order has its Motherhouse. The Sisters of Saint Joseph will take over the institution on December 1st. The organization of the hospital will remain much the same as at present, but improvements inside the building and the addition of equipment are planned. The school of nurses is to remain as it now is conducted. The change in the hospital management meets with the full approval of the Riley County Medical Society, according to the president, Dr. Darrell L. Evans. . . . The Sisters of Saint Joseph agreed to take over the hospital, at the urging of Monsignor Luckey, who felt that it would be in accord with the order's ideals of service and would offer a field for expansion and development. . . .[141]

A circular letter to the missionary Sisters, written on the day of the opening of the hospital, gave details not recorded in the minutes or by the press:

. . . On the eighth (December 8) his Excellency will bless the hospital, and there will be a meeting of the doctors. Since the Sisters will not be prepared for the opening, this ceremony will be private. The opening to the public will take place later. The name of the hospital is The Saint Mary Hospital. This morning, at the Motherhouse, we had Mass and Holy Communion for its success. Please pray that God's blessing will guide and direct all concerned. . . .[142]

Assisting Sister Frederica Brungardt were Sisters Adelaide Parnell, Hubert Rajewski, Edith Charbonneau, Lawrence Trudell, and Alicia Arsenault.[143] Later the group was augmented by the arrival of Sis-

[138] *Minutes of the Meetings of the Councillors of the Sisters of St. Joseph, Concordia, Kans., June, 1925- July, 1940,* vol. II, pp. 79-82.

[139] At a special meeting of the trustees of the Corporation on Nov. 3, 1936, it was moved and seconded that the contract be approved by the Board of Trustees. The contract provided that the hospital and all its equipment would be purchased for the sum of $20,000. Of this amount $10,000 was paid at the time of the contract; $5,000 on Jan. 1, 1937; and $5,000 on July 1, 1937. *Minutes of the Meetings of the Corporation of Nazareth Convent and Academy, 1901-1939,* vol. I, pp. 181-182.

[140] *Minutes of the Meetings of the Councillors of the Sisters of St. Joseph, Concordia, Kans., June, 1925- July, 1940,* vol. II, pp. 82-83. (This special meeting was held on Nov. 7-8, 1936.)

[141] *Manhattan Mercury,* Oct. 28, 1936.
Manhattan Chronicle, Oct. 29, 1936.

[142] Letter of Mother Mary Rose Waller to the Community, Dec. 1, 1936.

[143] Questionnaires of Sisters Adelaide Parnell, Frederica Brungardt, Hubert Rajewski, Edith Charbonneau, Lawrence Trudell, and Alicia Arsenault.

ters Palma Dumas, Mary Luke Bowker, De Chantal Norton, Alfreda Kruse, Rose Irma Morin, Rose Alma Newell, and Harriet Baldwin.[144]

A month later, it was found necessary to buy a home in the vicinity for the student nurses. At meetings of the councillors and of the trustees of the Corporation on January 4, 1937, it was decided that the Fairman estate near the hospital be purchased.[145] This and further improvements added to the effectiveness of the hospital.[146]

The formal opening of The Saint Mary Hospital took place the first Sunday in May, 1937. The opening gave the people of Manhattan and its environs an opportunity to see the hospital arrangements and equipment and to meet the staff and the Sisters:

. . . Much time and expense have been used in renovating and improving the hospital since the Sisters of Saint Joseph took charge on December 1st. A new laboratory is in charge of a technician, Sister Alicia. An elevator and ambulance entrance, decoration of the entire interior, six hundred yards of linoleum laid, much new equipment, a children's ward are a few of the interesting things that pleased the visitors. The lobby of the hospital was decorated with cut flowers and plants. Members of the hospital staff and women of the city met visitors, then former and present members of the nurses' training school escorted the guests through the hospital, returning to the lobby for tea. The tea service was under the direction of Sister Adolphus [Maloney], head of the home econompartment at Marymount College, Salina. She was assisted by five seniors in her department. . . .[147]

Many other improvements have been made in the ten years the hospital has been Community property.[148]

From the beginning the institution has been filled to capacity. Soon mention was made of further expansion. Much of the development of the hospital and its prodigious progress is due to the guiding policies of Sister Frederica Brungardt. In 1940 at the silver jubilee convention of the Catholic Hospital Association in St. Louis, Sister Frederica was awarded one of the distinguished service crosses bestowed upon individuals of various nursing orders in recognition of service in the hospital field within the past twenty-five years.[149]

[144] Questionnaires of Sisters Palma Dumas, Mary Luke Bowker, De Chantal Norton, Alfreda Kruse, Rose Irma Morin, Rose Alma Newell, and Harriet Baldwin.
[145] *Minutes of the Councillors of the Sisters of St. Joseph, Concordia, Kans., June, 1925-July, 1940,* vol. II, pp. 86-87.
[146] *Ibid.,* pp. 86-87.
[147] *Kansas City Catholic Register,* May 6, 1937.
Northwestern Kansas Register, May 6, 1937.
[148] *Ibid.,* Dec. 5, 1937; Apr. 24, 1938; Jan. 21, 1940; Feb. 2, 1941; Feb. 8, 1942.
[149] This recognition was in the name of the Sisters of St. Joseph of Concordia. *Ibid.,* July 7, 1940.

An article sent to the *Register* from the Motherhouse in June, 1941, launched the expansion project of The Saint Mary Hospital. The work was begun before the death of Mother Mary Rose. The article read as follows:

... A forty-room addition to The Saint Mary Hospital in Manhattan is now a well-assured improvement. In compliance with the requirements of the newly approved constitutions, the Sisters of Saint Joseph of Concordia, applied to the Holy See for permission to build. On May 10, permission was transmitted through the Apostolic Delegate in Washington, D. C., to the Most Reverend Frank A. Thill, Bishop of Concordia. On May 15, Bishop Thill's approval was given to the project. F. O. Wolfenbarger, Manhattan architect, has already submitted sketches for the addition and has now been authorized by the Sisters to complete the blue prints as soon as possible.

The enlargement of the Manhattan hospital is the last Community improvement to receive the recommendation of the late Mother Mary Rose. The decision to apply to Rome for the necessary permission was made at a meeting which Mother Mary Rose held for her Council on February 3, 1941. Since the death of the Mother General, Sister Cleophas Arnoldy and the Council have gone forward with the necessary plans. . . .[150]

And the following spring contracts were let and all was in readiness for construction:

... Building contracts, which are to make the present St. Mary Hospital, Manhattan, a five story edifice, were let Friday, April 3, by the Sisters of Saint Joseph of the Nazareth Convent, Concordia. The total cost of building is approximately $223,000, and covers general construction, heating, plumbing, and electrical work. . . . Work is expected to start as soon as priority ratings shall have been established for the hospital under the existing emergency. A service building, to be a separate unit for the housing of the power plant and the laundry, will be built first. . . . The chapel will be a separate wing of the building, and will harmonize with the general modernistic design of the new addition to the hospital. It is worthy of note that this will be the first church edifice in the Diocese of Concordia to be built in modernistic . . . style. A substantial contribution by an anonymous donor, to be used in the erection of the chapel, has made possible the building of a separate wing which was not included in the original plans. . . .[151]

It was impossible to secure adequate building materials; and although the contracts had been let, the building was postponed until the end of the war.[152]

In 1937, the Diocese of Concordia celebrated its golden anniversary in three cities of the diocese—St. Joseph's Military College,

150 *Ibid.*, June 8, 1941.
151 *Ibid.*, Apr. 12, 1942.
152 *Minutes of the Meetings of the Councillors of the Sisters of St. Joseph of Concordia, Kans.*, vol. II, Nov. 2, 1941, p. 44; Nov. 24, 1941, pp. 46-47; May 27, 1942, pp. 64-65; June 15, 1942, p. 67; Oct. 21, 1942, p. 81; Jan. 4, 1943, p. 85.

Hays, May 11, 1937; Marymount College, Salina, May 13; and the Cathedral of Our Lady of Perpetual Help, Concordia, May 25.[153] Progress of the diocese during the half-century of its jurisdiction formed the topics of sermons preached on these occasions. One article written by the diocesan superintendent of schools made several interesting observations on the growth of education in the diocese:

... The diocese offers educational opportunities in two institutions of higher learning, besides maintaining thirteen parish high schools and thirty parish elementary schools. There is one institutional elementary school for the children of St. Joseph's Home, Abilene. This year the parish high schools have enrolled 336 boys and 356 girls. The largest parish secondary school in the diocese, Sacred Heart, Salina, has an enrollment of 191, the largest number in its history. Several other high schools are virtually filled to capacity. Children attending the elementary schools make up an enrollment of 2,163 boys and 2,061 girls. . . . Comparing the enrollment status of the schools with that of previous decades, it is found that the general enrollment has not increased appreciably since 1930. A total of 4,986 pupils make up the composite enrollment of our elementary and secondary schools. In 1930 the figure for this enrollment was 4,557. In 1910, the parish schools had an enrollment of 3,304 pupils. . . . In 1900, the parish schools of the diocese had an enrollment of 1,850. The diocese then had only 16 elementary schools. The first parish high schools were organized some years later. . . .[154]

In June, 1938, Bishop Tief resigned his office and left for the East to regain his health. His going was regretted by the Sisters of Saint Joseph; he had shown interest and solicitude in every undertaking sponsored by the Community. Bishop Tief had come into the Diocese of Concordia as Marymount College was nearing completion, and he had continued the noble work of his predecessor, Bishop Cunningham. He so successfully emphasized the need of attendance of Catholic children in parochial schools, that, in spite of the fact that the diocese is rural and the Catholic population a scattered one, more than one-half the children of the diocese were in parochial schools. A pioneer in the religious vacation schools movement, Bishop Tief opened two such schools in 1927. Six years later there were more than thirty such schools within the confines of the diocese, with an enrollment of approximately 3,000 pupils.

Another undertaking of Bishop Tief was the promotion of Gregorian chant in accordance with the *Motu Propria* of Pope

[153] *Kansas City Catholic Register,* May 6, 1937; May 20, 1937.
     Salina Journal, May 13, 1937.
[154] *Northwestern Kansas Register,* Nov. 21, 1937.

Pius X.[155] For the Sisters of the diocese, he insisted that in every convent there be erected a chapel so that even on the poorest missions the Sisters have the wonderful privilege of the Blessed Sacrament under their roofs. For all of these things and especially for the great blessing of papal approbation, which had his support, the Community of the Sisters of Saint Joseph of Concordia is indebted to Bishop Tief.

Following the resignation of Bishop Tief in June, 1938, the Most Reverend Frank A. Thill, former chancellor of the Archdiocese of Cincinnati,[156] was appointed the new Bishop of Concordia. Again the Sisters of Saint Joseph were fortunate in the choice of the new bishop. Primarily a teaching order, the Community appreciated the choice of one of the great youth leaders of the country as Bishop of Concordia.

In a testimonial ceremony honoring Monsignor Thill, held by the Cincinnati Catholic Student Mission Crusade in 1929, the toastmaster, Thomas P. Hart, editor of the *Cincinnati Telegraph,* referred to him as "a Castle Builder—not a castle built in air of stone and mortar but rather a castle of ideals built in the hearts of Catholic men and women throughout the length and breadth of the land. . . ." As organizer of the CSMC, Msgr. Thill was "without a parallel in achievements within the clergy of the United States. . . ."[157]

The news of the appointment of Msgr. Thill to the Diocese of Concordia was heralded far and wide.[158] The consecration took place in Cincinnati, October 28,[159] and the installation in Con-

[155] *Kansas City Catholic Register,* May 11, 1933.
    Wichita Catholic Advance, May 13, 1933.
[156] He was born in Dayton, Ohio, Oct. 12, 1893; was ordained Feb. 28, 1920; was invested as Very Reverend Monsignor, Feb. 28, 1939; was made chancellor of the Archdiocese of Cincinnati, Dec. 6, 1935; was made domestic prelate, Dec. 14, 1937. Appointed Bishop of Concordia, Aug. 24, 1938, he was consecrated at the Cathedral of St. Monica, Cincinnati, Oct. 28, 1938, and was installed in the Cathedral of Our Lady of Perpetual Help, Concordia, Nov. 15, 1938. *Northwestern Kansas Register,* Nov. 20, 1938.
    Joseph B. Code, *Dictionary of the American Hierarchy* (New York, 1940), pp. 337-338.
[157] *Cincinnati Enquirer,* Mar. 1, 1929; Mar. 13, 1929.
[158] *Ibid.,* Aug. 27, 1938; Aug. 28, 1938.
    Concordia Blade-Empire, Aug. 27, 1938.
    Wichita Catholic Advance-Register, Sept. 3, 1938.
    Northwestern Kansas Register, Sept. 4, 1938; Oct. 9, 1938; Oct. 16, 1938; Oct. 23, 1938.
    Denver Catholic Register, Oct. 13, 1938.
[159] *Kansas City Catholic Register,* Nov. 3, 1938.
    Cincinnati Enquirer, Oct. 28, 1938; Oct. 29, 1938.

cordia, November 15.[160] A special edition of the diocesan paper reviewed the notable history of the diocese and the new bishop.[161]

Monsignor Francis A. O'Brien, of Fairbury, Nebraska, was desirous of securing the Sisters of Saint Joseph of Concordia to teach his parochial school. Early in 1939, he contacted Mother Mary Rose to ask for Sisters for the coming September.

Fairbury, county seat of Jefferson County, was built by ranchers and traders who took advantage of the Homestead Act of 1862. When lean years came, these sturdy pioneers weathered the depressions and became the backbone of the vicinity. In the 'Seventies a wave of prosperity established the earliest settlers as independent farmers and owners and tillers of the soil.[162] The Russian-German immigrants who settled in Fairbury in the 1870's[163] were, for the most part, of the Mennonite persuasion rather than Roman Catholic as were the Russian-Germans of Ellis County, Kansas. Both, however, had the same motives for seeking better economic opportunity in mid-America.

The Catholics of Fairbury received their first religious ministrations in 1873, and from that time the fortunes of the Catholics of Hebron and Fairbury were linked together. A parochial school was opened in September, 1924, with the Sisters of the Holy Cross, Notre Dame, as teachers. These Sisters conducted the school until 1939 when they were recalled to their Motherhouse, South Bend, Indiana.[164] At that time overtures were made to the Concordia Sisters to continue the school which was in thriving condition.

According to the Minutes of the Meetings of the Councillors the Fairbury school proposition was as follows:

> On February 13, 1939, Rev. Mother Mary Rose called together the councillors, Sister Cleophas and Sister Bertille, to make a final decision concerning our Congregation accepting the elementary parochial school in Fairbury, Nebraska. Rev. Francis A. O'Brien, pastor of Saint Michael's Church, had requested our Sisters several months ago. The Sisters of the Holy Cross, Notre Dame, Indiana, who now teach the school, are desirous of giving it up because it is too far removed from the Motherhouse. Rev. Mother spoke to

160 *Ibid.*, Nov. 13, 1938; Nov. 20, 1938; Nov. 27, 1938.
  Concordia Blade-Empire, Nov. 17, 1938.
161 *Ibid.*, Nov. 20, 1938.
162 Charles Dawson, *Pioneer Tales of the Oregon Trail and of Jefferson County, Nebraska* (Topeka, 1912), *passim.*
163 *Nebraska: A Guide*, Federal Writers' Project (New York, 1939), pp. 375-376.
164 *Denver Catholic Register*, July 16, 1931.

The Saint Mary Hospital, Manhattan, Kansas

The Saint Mary Hospital—Parkview Annex, Manhattan, Kansas

Pietro Cardinal Fumasoni-Biondi, Cardinal Protector of the
Congregation of the Sisters of Saint Joseph of Concordia

his excellency, Bishop Thill, who raised no specific objection to our accepting the school if we desire to do so. Mother Mary Rose had communicated with Mother Antoinette on the question. Mother Antoinette favored accepting the school but expressed the desire that it would not interfere with our educating more Sisters for Marymount College. Sister Regis told Mother that she was 100% in favor of accepting the school. It was voted that we accept the school for September, 1939. The decision was sent to Rev. Father O'Brien. A prayer was said for the success of the new school. We shall need four grade teachers, a music teacher, and a housekeeper. . . .[165]

When the school opened, Sisters Josina Wynn, superior, Emily Curry, Mary Jude Gudenkauf, Mary Leo Zeman, Mary Louise Bruns, and Mary Anthony Keller comprised the group.[166] Today there are four Sisters teaching one hundred and six pupils.[167]

On February 13, 1941, Mother Mary Rose wrote a circular letter to the missions in which she spoke extensively of the Lenten fast, the health of the Sisters, the retreat scheduled for the next month, and some points in the constitutions. Mention was also made of the proposed addition to the Manhattan hospital, and at the end of the letter she concluded:

. . . I have been in the hospital now for a month, and really feel greatly improved. When Doctor Haughey examined me this week, he found my physical condition must better. I feel well enough now to return to the Motherhouse; but the Sisters think it better for me to remain in the hospital for at least two more weeks. Although I am satisfied here, I am looking forward to returning to the Motherhouse. The Sisters here at the hospital are extremely kind to me and I have been very contented to be here with them. . . .[168]

Mother Mary Rose's condition did not improve, however, although on March 5 she did return to the Motherhouse. Her determination to make the retreat preceding the feast of Saint Joseph was most admirable. At the completion of the retreat her physical strength was depleted. Sister Cleophas, Assistant Superior, wrote to the missionary Sisters on March 20:

. . . We know you are waiting for another report on the condition of Reverend Mother Mary Rose. She came home from the hospital two weeks ago yesterday. Mother seemed to feel fairly well, although weaker. When the retreat started, she was able to go to the chapel for Holy Mass and Communion. We know

[165] *Minutes of the Meetings of the Councillors of the Sisters of St. Joseph, Concordia, Kans., June, 1925-July, 1940*, vol. II, pp. 106-107.
[166] *Northwestern Kansas Register*, Aug. 27, 1939.
    Questionnaires of Sisters Josina Wynn, Emily Curry, Mary Jude Gudenkauf, Mary Leo Zeman, Mary Louise Bruns, and Mary Anthony Keller.
[167] *Kenedy's Catholic Directory* (New York, 1947), p. 544.
[168] Letter of Mother Mary Rose Waller to the Community, Feb. 12, 1941. A copy is in the files of the author. This letter was the last written by Mother Mary Rose to her Community.

Mother Mary Rose is getting weaker each day; and in fact we have noticed a decided change the last three days. Mother was not able to see the Sisters who came to the Motherhouse yesterday for the reception. Today she is taking a complete rest. She says she has no pain, not even a headache, but she feels extremely exhausted. . . .[169]

That same evening witnessed the death of Mother Mary Rose Waller. Surrounded by her Sisters, having received the last Sacraments administered by the chaplain, Father Emil Duchene, she peacefully went to her Maker.

The passing of this splendid woman, this gentle superior, who had governed the Sisters of Saint Joseph for many years, was regretted far and near. The Community, which had postulated Rome to retain her as their Mother, felt the loss keenly. Masses, flowers, telegrams, condolences of all kind found their way to the Motherhouse during those days when her body lay in state.

In articles appearing in newspapers in the various dioceses in which the Community works, her administration was summarized:

. . . During the administration of Rev. Mother Mary Rose, the Community has grown from 400 to 600 members. This increase in numbers has made possible a parallel expansion in missionary endeavor. Marymount College and Academy in Salina opened its doors to students for the first time in the fall after she assumed office. The Home of the Little Flower, Concordia, a diocesan institution for the aged, was opened in 1924. Early in 1926, a Community of Sisters of Saint Joseph in Silver City, New Mexico, was accepted by affiliation into the Congregation, thus extending the work of the Concordia Sisters into the Southwest. Within a year, the El Paso Sanatorium was instituted. The addition to the Saint Anthony Murdock Memorial Hospital in Sabetha was built during her administration. In 1936, The Saint Mary Hospital, Manhattan, began its ministrations to that city. One of the last official acts of Mother Mary Rose was the endorsement of the proposed addition to that institution. Parochial schools opened during the period are: New Almelo (1922); Boonville, Missouri (1923); Collyer (1926); Herington (1926); and Fairbury, Nebraska (1939). . . . The interest of Mother Mary Rose was not only in the material growth of the Community but in the spiritual advancement of the Community as a whole and of each Sister in particular. This interest was especially noticeable in her cooperation with the Ordinaries with whom she had worked in providing Sister-teachers and nurses and in the Religious Vacation School movement and in emphasis on the teaching of Gregorian chant and liturgical music in the schools. Signal recognition came on July 7, 1940, when the institute was elevated to the status of a papal institute. . . .[170]

169 Letter of Sister Cleophas Arnoldy to the Community, Mar. 20, 1941. That same evening Mother Mary Rose died.

170 Sister Evangeline Thomas, "Mother Mary Rose Waller Dies in Concordia," *Northwestern Kansas Register*, Mar. 21, 1941; Mar. 30, 1941; *Salina Advertiser-Sun*, Mar. 27, 1941; *Eastern Kansas Register*, Mar. 21, 1941; *Salina Journal*, Mar. 21, 1941; *Wichita Catholic Advance-Register*, Mar. 28, 1941; *Fairbury News*, Mar. 27, 1941; *Western American*, Apr. 5, 1941; *Concordia Kansan*, Mar. 27, 1941.

Among the accomplishments of the administration of Reverend Mother Mary Rose Waller were the educational progress of the Congregation and the paying of a large part of the debt on Marymount College, Salina. The opening of a four-year college in 1922 presented a challenge to the authorities in the Community to staff that institution with faculty members who would meet all the requirements of the regional and national accrediting agencies. In 1922 there was one Doctor of Philosophy among the Sisters, and in 1941 there were nine; in 1922 there were three who held the Master's degree, and in 1941 that number had increased to eighteen; in 1922 eleven held the Bachelor's degree, and in 1941 the number had increased to seventy-five.[171]

The total indebtedness of the Congregation in 1922 was approximately $500,000 and that amount had been reduced to less than $100,000 at the time of the death of Mother Mary Rose in 1941.[172]

Mention has been made of the revision of the Constitutions in 1933. There had been an earlier effort in 1924, when Mother Mary Rose and her Councillors, with the encouragement of Bishop F. J. Tief, had enlisted the assistance of Father Charles Augustine, O.S.B., D.D. The revision was completed in 1924, printed, and given to the Congregation. In 1924 a Community Directory was printed, and in 1928 a Book of Customs was also made available for Community use.[173]

In his sermon at the funeral Mass, Bishop Thill said in part:

. . . So death comes even to those who are the chosen children of God, those who are the favored of God. Mother Mary Rose for whom we have offered the Holy Mass was one of the chosen souls. Her life was a full life even when measured in the terms of the world. Not too many women have been given the spiritual and even temporal experiences through a long, through a glorious life. She was a success as the world measures success, she had a share—a grand share—in building the kingdom of God on the plains of Northwestern Kansas. . . . In our Commonwealth of Kansas, because of her careful and talented administration, the Sisters of Saint Joseph have no problems to vex them. . . . I have had chance during the last three months since she received her death sentence from her physician to see the glorious

---

[171] It was also during these years that the requirements for high school teachers were raised and had to be met with the life certificate. It should be noted here too that Marymount College assisted in this increase in the number of Sisters qualified to teach in Kansas and other States. This information was furnished by Sister Bertille Bridgeman, Secretary General.

[172] Interest on this amount was extremely high—$28,000 a year.

[173] The Congregation had hitherto used the English translation of the French original of the Constitutions which had been "given to the public" in 1827.

manner, the heroic manner, the true Christ-like manner with which she looked forward to death. . . . Mother Mary Rose in her consecrated virginity was fruitful unto God. Her good work for the Church in this diocese and in other dioceses was glorious. . . .[174]

These forceful and beautiful words of eulogy touched a responsive chord in the hearts of all who knew Mother Mary Rose. Her administration closed gloriously, as Bishop Thill emphasized. Her role on the frontier of the Church was one to be emulated.

[174] Sermon preached by the Most Reverend Frank A. Thill at the funeral services of Mother Mary Rose Waller, Mar. 23, 1941.

CHAPTER XII

Papal Approbation, 1933-1941

THE Congregation of the Sisters of Saint Joseph of Concordia, nearing its golden jubilee on the frontiers of the Midwest, began to think in terms of Roman approbation. Originally, the founders of the Le Puy Congregation, Bishop de Maupas and Father Medaille, S.J., had no thought other than to establish diocesan congregations, which, as they spread to other parts, would establish new motherhouses directly under the supervision of the local ordinaries. Thus, in France, in 1836, there were several motherhouses of the Community, all of which owed their primary allegiance to the bishop of the diocese in which they had located. However, all felt closely affiliated with the other motherhouses by the common bond of their foundress, Mother Saint John Fontbonne, and the early trials and tribulations, especially the horrors of the Reign of Terror, which left the Congregation prostrate. Then, too, there were the common way of life, the rules, the customs, and traditions which also tended to bind the various units of the body together.

In America, it was not long before foundations were scattered from Canada to the Atlantic coast, from western New York and Virginia to Minnesota. Many had severed their allegiance to Carondolet and had become diocesan institutes. At the time of the movement for general government and Papal Approbation under Carondolet, it was the privilege of the houses which so desired to remain outside the jurisdiction of the Saint Louis Motherhouse and to remain diocesan in character. Thus, Rochester, the cradle of the Concordia foundation, is still diocesan, because most of the houses of that institute are centrally located in the Diocese of Rochester.

A short survey of the growth of the movement among religious communities toward papal approbation is not out of place here.

According to canon law, bishops can establish religious congregations; but they must not establish them nor permit them to be established without consulting the Holy See.[1] Action by ecclesiastical authority has always been necessary for the development of an order or a religious congregation. From the thirteenth century, the sovereign pontiffs have reserved to themselves the right to authorize these foundations. While opposed to the excessive multiplication of new forms of religious congregations, the Holy See tolerated, especially since the eighteenth century, congregations to be founded with the approbation of the bishops only. However, the earlier interpretation of the right of the Holy See has been expressly recognized once more. On July 16, 1906, Pope Pius X, by his *Motu Propria Dei Providentia* made the exercise of this right dependent on the consent of the Holy See. The Code confirms this legislation.[2]

The decree of November 30, 1922, directed that all ordinaries ascertain that diocesan institutes whose motherhouses were in their dioceses possess a formal decree of erection. Where that decree was wanting, the local ordinary should see that it was provided unless he judged it preferable to suppress the institute. The same decree stated that, if the institute had spread to other dioceses, the decree of erection could not be issued by the ordinary except with the consent of the ordinaries of those dioceses.[3]

Letters from Bishop Louis M. Fink, O.S.B., of Leavenworth, to Reverend Mother Stanislaus Leary clearly indicated the existence of a decree of erection. But, although the documents of incorporation as well as an early testimonial of the Sisters of the original band point in the same direction, search of the archives of the diocese and those of the Motherhouse failed to produce the formal decree. Therefore, on April 12, 1928, that decree was issued by Bishop Francis J. Tief, of Concordia, Kansas. It read as follows:

DECREE OF FORMAL APPROVAL

FOR THE SISTERS OF SAINT JOSEPH OF CONCORDIA, KANSAS

Whereas, by decree of the Sacred Congregation of Religious of November 30, 1922, the Holy See has commanded the ordinaries to issue a formal decree of approval by them; and

Whereas, the documents reserved in our diocesan archives or in the archives

---

[1] Canon 492, p. 1.
Joseph Creusen (translated by Adam Ellis, S. J.), *Religious Men and Women in the Code* (Milwaukee, 1940), pp. 21-23.
[2] Creusen, *op. cit.*, p. 21.
[3] *Ibid.*, p. 23.

of the Sisters of Saint Joseph of Concordia, Kansas, show no proof that said decree ever had been formally issued; and

Whereas, religious professions have been made in said Institute of the Sisters of Saint Joseph of Concordia, Kansas, and canonical visits have been held, and their Constitutions have been recognized by our predecessor and by us; and

Whereas, said Institute of the Sisters of Saint Joseph of Concordia, Kansas, had been in existence and was producing rich fruits of Christian piety and charity in our diocese before the issuance of the *Motu Propria Dei Providentia* in 1906;

Therefore, in compliance with said decree and of the Sacred Congregation of Religious mentioned above, and with the understanding of the ordinaries in whose dioceses said Sisters of Saint Joseph of Concordia, Kansas, have located either schools or local houses, We hereby formally recognize said INSTITUTE OF THE SISTERS OF SAINT JOSEPH OF CONCORDIA, KANSAS, and do declare it erected as a *diocesan Institute,* and also approve of their Constitutions as far as the Code of Canon Law permits us to approve them and what is herein contained in accordance with said Canon Law.

Notwithstanding to the contrary.

Given at our episcopal residence this 12th day of April, 1928, A.D.

FRANCIS J. TIEF, Bishop of Concordia [4]

Two years after this formal decree had been issued, the Diocese of Concordia was honored to entertain an illustrious guest, His Excellency, the Most Reverend Pietro Fumasoni-Biondi, Apostolic Delegate to the United States. Pope Pius XI had arranged for a general visitation of all of the dioceses of the United States by the Apostolic Delegate. This work had been begun by the late Cardinal Bonzano and was being continued by Cardinal Fumasoni-Biondi. At the time of this visitation to the Diocese of Concordia about eighty percent of the dioceses had been visited.[5] He spent some time at Marymount College, Salina, where the student body entertained him and where he visited the Sisters. In Concordia he was the guest of the Bishop. After visiting the Motherhouse of the Sisters of Saint Joseph, he inquired concerning the ecclesiastical status of the Congregation. Upon discovering that it was diocesan, he encouraged Bishop Tief and the Generalate to apply for Roman approval, there being no reason why a stable, flourishing Community operating houses in many dioceses should have difficulty transferring from

---

[4] Formal Decree of Diocesan Approval by the Most Rev. Francis J. Tief, Bishop of Concordia. The original is in the Archives of the Nazareth Motherhouse, Concordia, Kans.; copies are in the archives of Concordia, Leavenworth, Kansas City, Grand Island, El Paso, Chicago, Marquette, Rockford. A photostat is in the files of the author.

[5] *Wichita Catholic Advance-Register,* May 10, 1930.

diocesan to pontifical status. The wholehearted cooperation of Bishop Tief was extended to the Sisters of Saint Joseph in this new venture as in all which had preceded it.

The matter of papal approbation was touched upon briefly at the General Chapter of 1930.[6] It was next brought to the attention of the Sisters in the spring of 1931 by Mother Mary Rose Waller:

Last summer the question of applying to Rome for approbation was brought before the General Chapter and briefly discussed. As those who were there will recall it was our Right Reverend Bishop who proposed the question for our consideration. Since that time his Excellency has considered the method of obtaining the preference of the Sisters, and it was decided it would be best to submit the question to the vote of the perpetually professed Sisters of our Community.

Before we send out the request for a vote on the question, we believe it will be well to acquaint the Sisters with arguments *for* and *against* the approbation by Rome.

The following are arguments in favor of approbation:

1. When the Apostolic Delegate was here, his Excellency spoke favorably of approbation and said he did not see why we were not approved. He brought up the subject a second time and said that he favored it; but that the request would need to be made through the Right Reverend Bishop.

2. Our Right Reverend Bishop has proposed it to the Community so he must be in favor of it.

3. It would give our Congregation a better and a safer standing— more prestige. To be approved by Rome certainly means a great deal; otherwise, why do the strongest and oldest communities seek approbation?

4. We should get more subjects and hence our Congregation would grow. Spiritual directors, and Jesuits in particular, admit that when asked to recommend a community, they recommend one that is approved. They feel safer by doing this; hence why should we not be safer?

5. One of our diocesan priests recently sent two young ladies to an approved community saying, "Concordia is all right now, but will it always be?"

6. Dispensations would have to be obtained from Rome.

7. Decisions regarding our habits and so on would continue to be made by the General Chapter.

8. As the years go by and our Community, God willing, continues to grow and expand, the members will have greater respect for their Congregation and greater confidence in all regulations and decisions, and in our Constitutions. Our Directory of Prayers and Constitutions would have to be reaffirmed by Rome.

9. Father Jacobmeyer, S. J., said: "The Community has everything to gain and nothing to lose by becoming a Pontifical Congregation."

10. It would be fine if we might receive the pontifical approbation by the time of the golden jubilee of the Community in 1934.

[6] *Minutes of the General Chapter, 1930*, pp. 4-5.

She proceeded to state that the principal argument against approbation was the fact that the Sisters of Saint Joseph were established as a diocesan institute.[7] The Sisters were to vote after a ten-day period of prayer and deliberation.

The voting took place at assemblies called by the superiors of each house before the Sisters left the missions in the spring. The vote, according to directions received from the Bishop, was secret. Votes were sealed in small envelopes by the Sisters and then sent in a large envelope to the Motherhouse.[8]

On June 17, in the presence of the Mother General and the Councillors of the Community, the Bishop counted the votes: 330 Sisters voted in favor of approbation and 47 against it. The Bishop sought formal approbation for the Sisters of Saint Joseph of Concordia in the fall of 1931.[9]

The next step in the proceedings was the choice of a canonist to direct and forward the cause before the Sacred Congregation of Religious. Within a convenient distance from Concordia was one whose experience and erudition recommended him: the Right Reverend Abbot Martin Veth, O.S.B., of Saint Benedict's Abbey, Atchison, Kansas.

Abbot Veth had recently carried through the approbation of certain Benedictine Sisterhoods with marked success and well understood the mind of Rome in regard to religious congregations.[10] Bishop Tief visited Abbot Veth at Atchison on November 1-2, 1932, conferring with him concerning the proceedings for papal approbation and informing him of the aspirations of the Sisters of Saint Joseph. The Abbot consented to carry on the work, and the Bishop and the authorities of the Community approved. Thus, the work was put into the hands of the scholarly Benedictine abbot, who immediately manifested a fatherly interest in the Community.[11]

Upon his return from the conference with the Abbot, Bishop Tief explained to the Sisters that Rome acts slowly and that it might take seven years or longer to obtain a hearing on the matter. He

[7] Letter of Mother Mary Rose Waller to the Community, Apr. 25, 1936. The original is in the files of the author.

[8] Letter of Mother Mary Rose Waller to the Community, Apr. 29, 1931.

[9] Letter of Mother Mary Rose Waller to the Community, Aug. 15, 1931.

[10] Letter of Mother Mary Rose Waller to the Community, July 26, 1933.

[11] *Minutes of the Meetings of the Councillors of the Sisters of St. Joseph, Concordia, Kans.*, Nov. 17, 1932, vol. II, p. 37.

further advised that changes would be the normal course so that the Constitutions, when returned, would need revision. He was given copies of the Constitutions, the Directory, the Custom Book, and letters which were on file in the Community archives. These letters were for the most part testimonial letters from the ordinaries in whose dioceses the Community had houses. A copy of the Decree of Formal Approval was also sent to Abbot Veth.[12]

The choice of a canonist was announced to the Sisters:

His Excellency is not forgetting to take care of the approbation and has chosen the Right Reverend Martin Veth, Father Abbot of Atchison, for the work. Abbot Veth has just begun the preparatory work and it may take considerable time to complete it. As progress is made we will keep you informed.[13]

Many conferences were held with the Abbot during the first months of work. It was deemed advisable to call a General Chapter composed of all professed Sisters of the Congregation to discuss general points, with as many as possible present in person and those unable to be present to be represented by proxy. The Chapter was to be held at Marymount College, Salina, Kansas, August 16-19, 1933.[14]

The meeting, presided over by Abbot Veth, was fruitful. Point by point the revised Constitutions received consideration. The meetings became informal, deliberative bodies—the type in which much can be accomplished within a short time. Impetus was given to the movement by the enthusiastic support evidenced by all concerned. A resolution was passed by the General Chapter petitioning His Excellency to "Grant us his approbation for the immediate adoption and observance of our new Constitutions, pending their approval by the Holy See."[15]

This matter was called to the attention of Bishop Tief at a special meeting with the Mother General and the Councillors on August 27, 1933, at which time His Excellency graciously approved the new Constitutions and further promised to secure approval from the other

---

[12] *Ibid.*, Nov. 17, 1932, vol. II, p. 37.
  The Constitutions were translated into Latin according to the directions of the Sacred Congregation of Religious for such procedure.
[13] Letter of Mother Mary Rose Waller to the Community, Dec. 20, 1932.
[14] Letter of Abbot Martin Veth, O.S.B., to Mother Mary Rose Waller, Nov. 23, 1932. Letter of Mother Mary Rose Waller to the Community, July 26, 1933.
[15] *Minutes of the General Chapter of the Sisters of St. Joseph, Marymount College, Salina, Kans.*, Aug. 16-19, 1933.

ordinaries in whose dioceses the Congregation had foundations.[16] The following letter was sent to them:

The Congregation of the Sisters of Saint Joseph of Concordia, Kansas, is taking the preliminary steps necessary for applying to the Holy See for papal approbation. They are doing this with my approval; and at my request the Right Reverend Abbot Martin Veth, O. S. B., of Atchison, Kansas, is directing the Sisters in the preparation that must be made.

The Sisters have accordingly held a General Chapter in Marymount College, Salina, Kansas, on August 16-19, 1933. This Chapter was presided over by Father Abbot, as my delegate. In this Chapter a revision of their Constitutions was adopted and approved by a vote of the General Chapter.

The Sisters will as soon as possible send a formal petition to the Holy See for recognition. However, it may be years before this matter may be acted upon by Rome.

In their General Chapter, the Sisters voted to petition for permission to adopt and observe immediately the new Constitutions. This permission I granted readily.

It is also necessary to have permission of all Ordinaries in whose dioceses these Sisters have foundations. Therefore, I am writing to request your Excellency to grant these Sisters your permission to adopt and observe immediately the new Constitutions, pending their approval by the Holy See. These Sisters conduct in your diocese schools in ...., ..., and ....[17]

These form letters were sent to Bishop S. V. Bona of Grand Island, Bishop E. F. Hoban of Rockford, Bishop F. J. Johannes of Leavenworth, Bishop T. F. Lillis of Kansas City, His Eminence George Cardinal Mundelein of Chicago, Bishop P. J. Nussbaum of Marquette, and Bishop A. J. Schuler of El Paso. Within the course of a week this request was granted by these ordinaries.[18]

Illustrative of the good will of the ordinaries mentioned above and of the type of testimonial letter they sent to Rome to support the petition of the Sisters of Saint Joseph of Concordia, is the following quotation from a letter sent to Bishop Tief at the same time the form letters were returned:

[16] *Minutes of the Meetings of the Councillors of the Sisters of St. Joseph, Concordia, Kans.*, vol. II, pp. 48-50.
Letter of Mother Mary Rose Waller to the Community, Sept. 1, 1933.
[17] Letter of the Most Rev. Francis J. Tief, Bishop of Concordia, to the Bishops mentioned above, Aug. 30, 1933. The original is in the Archives of the Nazareth Motherhouse, Concordia, Kans.; a photostat is in the files of the author.
[18] Original letters are in the Archives of the Nazareth Motherhouse, Concordia, Kans.: Bishop S. V. Bona, Sept. 2, 1933; Bishop E. F. Hoban, Sept. 2, 1933; Bishop F. J. Johannes, Sept. 2, 1933; Bishop T. F. Lillis, Sept. 2, 1933; His Eminence George Cardinal Mundelein, Sept. 4, 1933; Bishop P. J. Nussbaum, Sept. 4, 1933; Bishop A. J. Schuler, Sept. 2, 1933. Photostats are in the files of the author.

I was pleased to receive your communication . . . with reference to the Sisters of Saint Joseph. I believe that the Community will have greater opportunity for development after they receive papal recognition. The Sisters do very good work at both missions in our diocese. . . .[19]

The petition, according to form, was duly drawn up by the authorities in Concordia and forwarded to the Holy Father soon after the General Chapter had adjourned. Written in Latin, it was signed by the Mother General and her Councillors. To it the seal of the corporation was affixed. It read:

Beatissime Pater:

Sorores S. Joseph de Concordia, Kansas, U. S. A., in Capitulo Generali in civitate Salina, Kansas, diebus 16-19 Augusti, 1933, habito congregatae ad pedes Sanctitatis Vestrae prostratae precantur, ut Constitutiones omnium in illo Capitulo praesentium consensu acceptae et ab Ordinariis, in quorum diocesibus variis officiis Sorores funguntur, iam approbatae nunc a Sanctitate Vestra saltem experimenti causa approbentur.
Subscr.

> Sister M. Bertille Bridgeman
> *Secretaris Generalis Capituli*
> Mother Mary Rose Waller
> *Mater Generalis*
> Sister M. Cleophas Arnoldy
> *Soror Assistens*
> *(Consiliaria prima)*
> Mother M. Antoinette Cuff
> *Consiliaria secunda*
> Sister M. Regis Schwenzer
> *Consiliaria tertia*[20]

Thus the die was cast; preliminary steps neared completion; initial steps had been taken. The Community must now wait and pray for a favorable reaction on the part of the authorities in Rome.

Three steps lead to final papal approbation of an institute: (1) the Decree of Praise, (2) the approval of the institute, and (3) the approval of the Constitutions of the institute.[21] Canon Law

---

[19] Letter of the Bishop Edward F. Hoban of Rockford to Bishop Francis J. Tief of Concordia, Sept. 2, 1933. The missions referred to were Belvidere and Aurora, Ill.

[20] Petition of the Sisters of St. Joseph of Concordia, Kans., to the Holy Father, Pius XI, Begging Papal Approbation on Their Institute. Copies are in the Archives of the Nazareth Motherhouse, Concordia, Kans., and in the files of the author.

[21] *Normae*, 1921, nos. 9-22.

Ferdinand Schoensteiner, *Grundriss des Ordensrechte* (Wien, 1930), p. 56.

Timotheus F. Schaefer, O.M. Cap., *De Religiosis ad norman Juris canonici* (Munster, 1931), no. 74.

Fintan Geser, O.S.B., *The Canon Law Governing Communities of Sisters* (St. Louis, 1938), pp. 46-47.

states that a diocesan institute may make application for the Decree of Praise when, afer a sufficient lapse of time, it has satisfactorily spread and has shown itself fruitful in piety, religious observance, and spiritual advancement. This is to be learned from the testimonial letters of the ordinary or ordinaries in whose diocese or dioceses the institute has a house or several houses.[22]

To obtain a Decree of Praise the following documents are to be sent to the Sacred Congregation of Religious:

1. A petition to the Supreme Pontiff, signed by the Superior General and her assistants or councillors.

2. The testimonial letters of the ordinaries mentioned above, which letters should be sealed and sent as confidential correspondence.

3. An account, in writing, by the Superior General and her councillors, and vouched for as authentic and genuine by the Bishop of the place where the principal house of the institute is located. This account shall include a report concerning the origin of the institute, together with the name and special qualities of its founder; also a statement of the personal, disciplinary, material, and economic status; and, in addition, a report on the novitiate and of the number and training of the novices and postulants.

4. The Constitutions (previously examined and approved by the bishop) written and printed in Latin, Italian, or French.[23]

The Quinquennial Report, an obligation imposed on institutes with papal approbation, is also obligatory for institutes seeking that privilege. Accordingly, the Relatio A Die 1 Jan. 1924 Usque Ad Diem 1 Jan. 1934 was submitted to the Sacred Congregation according to stipulation. This report answered one hundred and five questions on the spiritual and temporal status of the community. It, too, was signed by the Mother General and the Councillors.[24]

Work on the revised Constitutions progressed steadily and copies were distributed early in 1934.[25] A few months later the missions

---

[22] *Normae*, 1921, no. 7.
    Schoensteiner, *op. cit.*, p. 57.
    Geser, *op. cit.*, p. 47.
[23] *Normae*, 1921, no. 8.
    Schoensteiner, *op. cit.*, p. 57.
    Geser, *op. cit.*, p. 48.
[24] Quinquennial Report of the Sisters of St. Joseph, Concordia, Kans. Submitted to the Holy See, Mar. 14, 1934. The original is in the Archives of the Nazareth Mother-house, Concordia, Kans.; a photostat is in the files of the author. This is the third such report submitted by the Concordia Congregation (first covered years 1884-1924; second, 1924-1929) but according to Canon Law such a report must be sent in every five years.
[25] Letter of Mother Mary Rose Waller to the Community, Mar. 25, 1934. The new Constitutions were to be put into effect on Easter Sunday, 1934.

were presented with copies of the new Directory and Book of Customs.[26]

The golden jubilee of the Sisters of Saint Joseph in Kansas took place in the spring of 1933; however, the Community celebration was postponed for two years, perhaps with the hope that within that time sanction of the Holy See would have been bestowed upon the Institute. A two-day celebration took place on June 18-19, 1935, with the greetings and apostolic blessing of His Holiness, Pope Pius XI, conveyed to the Sisters through the local ordinary.

Amid jubilation and rejoicing, the first announcement to the laity was made concerning the dignity sought by the Community. Bishop Tief, toward the end of an address sketching the growth of the Community from its small beginning to its membership of over five hundred working in eight dioceses and seven states, said:

. . . But enough of past history. What has the future in store? There is a happy announcement which I wish to make.

For fifty years the Sisters of Saint Joseph of Concordia have served faithfully as a diocesan community. During all these years, the most amicable relations have existed between the Sisters and my illustrious predecessors, now of happy memory; also between the priests of the diocese and the Sisters. These happy relations continue under my unworthy regime and are most evident today. The Sisters were willing and satisfied to remain in their present status as a diocesan community, but I have given the matter careful and prayerful consideration. Acting on the suggestion of the former Apostolic Delegate and reflecting on the marvelous growth of the community, the wonderful accomplishments in every field of labor, and its splendid spirit of organization, I have, with the consent of the Sisters, and through the proper channels, postulated the Holy See to elevate this community of the Sisters of Saint Joseph of Concordia to the status of a Pontifical Institute.

Recently we have received word from Rome that our petition is being favorably considered and that by next Easter the Constitutions will be approved.

This does not mean that the bishop and the priests of the diocese will be less interested in the Community than before. But it does mean that the bishop and priests of the diocese wish to show their full approbation and appreciation of all that the Sisters have done for the welfare of this diocese. . . .[27]

The golden jubilee celebration culminated in expressions of good will on the part of the clergy and the laity alike as recorded in a letter which Mother Mary Rose Waller wrote to the Sisters

---

[26] Letter of Mother Mary Rose Waller to the Community, Oct. 11, 1934. The new Directory and Book of Customs was to be put into effect on Oct. 15, 1934. Oct. 15th is an important date in the annals of the Sisters of St. Joseph, for it was on that day in 1650 that the Congregation was established in Le Puy, France.

[27] *Kansas City Catholic Register*, June 22, 1935.

summarizing the glorious event in the annals of the Community.[28]

Eagerly and expectantly Mother Mary Rose anticipated the news promised at Easter. Papal approbation was her constant hope and prayer. Shortly before Easter she wrote to the Sisters, mentioning that she had written to Father Abbot who had informed her that he had again importuned Rome. "No doubt," she wrote, "he will soon be favored with a reply. How happy we should be if this privilege would come to us on Easter. Include this intention in your prayers."[29]

Another reason, and a weighty one it was, for Mother Mary Rose's fervent prayers for approbation in 1936, was that on April 15 the Sisters of Saint Joseph of Carondolet were to celebrate the one hundredth anniversary of their establishment in this country. Mother Mary Rose wrote to the Concordia Sisters of this approaching centenary:

All Sisters of Saint Joseph in this country should celebrate in spirit. Let me suggest that all our Sisters offer their Mass and Holy Communion for these Sisters and for all Sisters of Saint Joseph throughout the world. In addition to this, let us offer all our community prayers on that day, and if possible the stations and one hundred ejaculatory prayers. The Motherhouse will make the offering for several special Masses.[30]

Mother Mary Rose and Mother Antoinette represented the Sisters of Saint Joseph of Concordia at the Saint Louis celebration. There, at the fountainhead of all the various branches of the Congregation in this country and in Canada, these two lovers of the Community and of all that it holds dear in rule and tradition, met and mingled with the representatives of the other Communities from far and near. There, at Carondolet they pondered the great blessings God had bestowed on the daughters of Saint Joseph, and they conversed together of His special protection to their own Concordia Congregation. How much nearer to Mother Saint John Fontbonne all Sisters of Saint Joseph felt that day. What a spiritual strength permeated the entire organism congregated there to help the parent stem celebrate a century's harvest. How much greater became the longing in the hearts of those two leaders of the Concordia Congregation, that longing to see the Decree of Praise granted to it by the Holy See.[31]

[28] Letter of Mother Mary Rose Waller to the Community, June 28, 1935.
[29] Letter of Mother Mary Rose Waller to the Community, Apr. 6, 1936.
[30] *Loc. cit.*
[31] *Loc. cit.*

Articles on the centenary were published in various magazines and diocesan newspapers. Each branch of the Sisters of Saint Joseph became history-conscious and some enterprising members, through sheer love or perhaps through obedience, dug into archival material and published an article or a brochure about the local Community. All were proud of the centenary held at Carondolet. Among the articles was one from Rochester, New York, relating how the Sisters from Carondolet eighty-two years before had arrived in Canandaigua; how Mother Stanislaus Leary was the first Sister of Saint Joseph to receive the habit of the Order in the State of New York; how this same Mother Stanislaus became the first Mother General of the Rochester Community when the new Diocese of Rochester was carved out of that of Buffalo.[32]

This and similar articles served as a bond to unite the Sisters in various parts of the country in feeling and in aim. It was a consolation to Concordia to know that it now stood on the threshold awaiting papal approbation when few of the other, older branches of the Order had ventured to take such a step.

The time had come for the calling of the General Chapter to vote for a Superior General; the second term of Mother Mary Rose Waller was at an end. Sentiment in the Community favored postulation for a third term, but this trend met staunch opposition from both Mother Mary Rose and from His Excellency, Bishop Tief.[33]

In her letter announcing the General Chapter, Mother Mary Rose expressed herself on the subject:

. . . As the present Superior of the Community, I feel bound in conscience to tell our dear Sisters that a third term is contrary to Rome's wishes. I feel that in following the laws of the Church, I am fostering the best interests of the Community. I have opened my heart to our dear Bishop, and have obtained his Excellency's consent. . . . Pray earnestly that the Holy Ghost will preside over the election. . . . In writing to the Sisters, I have never referred to anything that they had written concerning their sentiments about the election. You know that I have always appreciated your loving kindness and support.[34]

In response to a special request made by Bishop Tief, Abbot Martin Veth consented to be present for the General Chapter. The

[32] *Rochester Courier,* June 14, 1936.
[33] Letters of Mother Mary Rose Waller to the Community, Ascension Thursday, 1936; May 2, 1936.
[34] *Loc. cit.,* Ascension Thursday, 1936.

presence of Abbot Veth was welcome since it was in his hands that the application proceedings had been placed.[35]

Abbot Veth informed the General Chapter that Canon Law does not permit a third term for a Mother General. However, it does leave the way open for a third term by permitting postulation to the Holy See. Father Abbot fully explained to the electors the reasons for and against postulation; that the electors do not have the power to elect for a third term, but if two-thirds of the electors vote for postulation, his Excellency, Bishop Tief, could and would submit the wish of the Chapter to Rome.[36]

The Chapter voted for postulation. The request was sent to Rome and in July the confirmation was received.[37] The fact that the question of papal approbation for the Community was pending did not seem to affect the request.

Many obstacles seemed to impede progress of the cause of papal approbation. The Benedictine Vice Rector, the Reverend Peter Bastien, working on the matter in Rome, was forced to discontinue because of ill health and the work was turned over to the Reverend George Bartsch, O.S.B., of the Collegio S. Anselmo, Rome.

---

[35] *Minutes of the General Chapter of the Sisters of St. Joseph, Concordia, Kans.,* 1936. A copy is in the files of the author.

[36] *Loc. cit.,* p. 7.

[37] N. 4734/36

F. 34—bis.

Beatissime Pater:

Vocales Sororem a Scto. Josepho, dioec. Concordian in Amerika, ea qua par est reverentia, S.V. exponunt se ad munus Superiorissae Generalis 273 ex 346 suffragiis postulasse tertiam sexemium Sororem Rosam. Quare ad pedes Sanctitatis Vestrae humilime provolutae implorant praefatae postulationis benignan admissionem. Et Deus, etc.

Vigore specialium facultatum a SSmo Dno Nostro consessarum, Sacra Congregation Negotiis Religiosorum Sodalium praeposita, audito voto Excmi Ord. Concordien in Amerika. Eidem benigne commissit ut enunciatam Sororem ad Superiorissae Generalis munus praefati Instituti ad tertium sexemium pro suo arbitrio et conscientia admittat et confirmet, ita tamen ut eadem peractae suae administrationis rationem prius reddat. Contrariis quibuscumque non obstantibus.

Datum Romae, die 11 Julii, 1936.

fr. D. L. H. PASETTO, Secr.

Cablegram from the Sacred Congregation of Religious to the Most Reverend Amleto Cicognani, July 2, 1936.

Telegram of Most Reverend Amleto Giovanni Cicognani to the Most Reverend Francis Joseph Tief, July 3, 1936.

Telegram of the Most Reverend Francis Joseph Tief to Mother Mary Rose Waller, July 3, 1936.

Photostats of the above are in the files of the author.

Letter of Mother Mary Rose Waller to the Community, July 12, 1936.

At the General Chapter in 1936, Father Abbot announced that he had heard from Father Peter Bastien who stated that the Constitutions were on their way from Rome and that they had been recast. As soon as they arrived, Father Abbot promised to return to Concordia to present them to the Sisters for the purpose of giving the Community an opportunity to discuss the revised Constitutions and of suggesting any changes that they considered to the best interest of the Sisters. Father Bastien had requested that the Constitutions be returned to Rome by July 1. That date could not be considered due to delay in transit.[38] The conference actually took place on January 2, 1937, with the Mother General and her Councillors present. The Constitutions prepared in Rome had incorporated almost all of the rules and regulations as submitted by the General Chapter.[39]

War came to Europe and, eventually, to the world. The Sisters of Saint Joseph of Concordia again felt that the possibility of the decree's reaching them was small. A spirit of resignation to the Will of God was promptly rewarded when suddenly word reached Concordia that the Decree of Praise had been issued. Long years of waiting were amply repaid when in 1940 that treasured document at last found its way to the archives of the Motherhouse.

A translation of the Decree of Praise will be given in the body of this work and photographic plates of the Latin copy will be included:

N. 3988. C. 110

DECREE OF PRAISE

In the year 1884 the Most Reverend Ordinary of the place erected the Institute of the Sisters of Saint Joseph in the city of Concordia in America, which was the work of the Sisters originating under the same title, from the religious house of the Diocese of Rochester, of the Archdiocese of New York.

It is now evident from the commendatory letters of the Bishops of the places in which the houses of the Institute exist, that the Institute is diffused in the United States of America, and that its members work for the welfare of Christian society.

The general purpose of the Sisters of Saint Joseph of Concordia is the sanctification of its members through the observance, in perfectly practised common life, of the three simple vows of obedience, chastity, and poverty according to their own Constitutions.

---

[38] *Minutes of the General Chapter of the Sisters of St. Joseph, Concordia, Kans., June 13, 1936.* A copy is in the files of the author.

[39] *Minutes of the Meetings of the Councillors of the Sisters of St. Joseph, Concordia, Kans., vol. III, pp. 85-86.*

Their special purpose consists in the education of youth, and in the nursing of the sick, provided that there is a sufficiently large number of Sisters.

Having sent a copy of their Constitutions, the Mother General of the aforementioned Institute and her Councillors, most humbly besought our Most Holy Father, Pius XII, Pope by Divine Providence, supported by the recommendations of the Bishops, that the Institute be recognized by some particular favor, and that he deign to approve their Constitutions with Apostolic Authority.

In the audience granted on July 7, 1940, to the Most Reverend D. L. H. Pasetto, Secretary of the Sacred Congregation charged with the affairs of Religious, His Holiness, after having perused the commendatory letters of the Bishops, as above mentioned, and after having heard the recommendations of the Most Eminent and Reverend Cardinals of the Holy Roman Church who preside over the same Sacred Congregation of Religious, who had maturely weighed the question in Plenary Session in the Vatican held on the fifth day of the same month, most graciously deigned to praise and commend in a most laudatory manner the aforementioned Institute as a Congregation of simple vows under the government of a Mother General who is to be elected every six years.

His Holiness also deigned to approve and confirm, for a period of seven years and as a trial, the Constitutions drawn up in the Latin language, as contained in the present copy, whose original is preserved in the archives of the Sacred Congregation. By this decree the Institute itself is praised and commended, and its Constitutions are approved, the jurisdiction of the Ordinaries of the places remaining intact, in conformity with the Sacred Canons.

All things to the contrary notwithstanding.

Given at Rome, from the office of the Secretary of the Sacred Congregation of Religious, on the day, month, and year as above indicated [that is, July 7, 1940].

[signature] VINC. CARD. LA PUMA
Prefect

D. L. H. PASETTO
Secretary[40]

SEAL

Concerning the Decree of Praise, Father George Bartsch, O.S.B., wrote immediately to the Sisters. His fears were warranted by war conditions:

Roma, Collegio S. Anselmo
August 9, 1940

Rev. and dear Mother General:

Today on the vigil of the feast of Saint Lawrence, the great Martyr of Rome, I am very glad to bring you good news. This morning I was called to the S. Congregation of Religious and the Secretary presented me the approved copy of your Constitutions.

The date of the approval is 7 July 1940, the number of the document is: N. 3988. C. 110. But now comes a difficulty, a practical difficulty to me,

---

[40] Translation of the Decree of Praise issued from the office of the Sacred Congregation of Religious, July 7, 1940.

how to forward to you the bound copy of your Constitutions. I made for this purpose also inquiries at the Vatican itself. But I was advised not to send you during the present wartime the so important document, for the risk was too great. In case I find someone, on whom I can absolutely rely, and who is going to the United States, I shall give him your Constitutions and he will send them from America to you. And I hope to have good reason not to make you wait too long for the document. . . . As soon as I know that someone is leaving for U. S. A. I send you at once note . . . will send you the Constitutions. Ever ready for further services. . . .

Fr. GEORGE BARTSCH, O. S. B.[41]

What happiness must have filled the heart of Mother Mary Rose Waller when on the feast day of her patroness, Saint Rose de Lima, she was privileged to inform the Community of pontifical status of the Congregation. It was fortunate that the news came when it did. Had it been delayed another year, Mother Mary Rose would not have been living to receive it. She wrote to the Sisters:

I know you will be happy to receive the information which came to us on August 20th. We have a letter from Father George Bartsch, O. S. B., in Rome, stating that the Secretary of the Sacred Congregation has presented him with the approved copy of our Constitutions. The date of approval was July 7, 1940.

We are indeed grateful to Our Dear Lord for bestowing this blessing on our Congregation. We have had a Mass offered in thanksgiving.

His Excellency, Bishop Thill, is pleased to learn that we have received the assurance of Papal Approbation. His Excellency says that the proper procedure would be for him to wait until we receive the Decree of Approbation, either directly from Rome or through the Apostolic Delegate in Washington, before he makes official and public announcement of the event. When the Decree arrives, His Excellency will appoint a day for special observance. His Excellency advises that in the meantime, all of the Sisters should be informed of the blessing that has come to us. On account of war conditions and danger to mail, Father George has been advised to wait until he can entrust the Constitutions to someone coming to this country. . . .[42]

Perhaps no one outside of the Congregation of the Sisters of Saint Joseph of Concordia rejoiced over the important news as did their scholarly, fatherly friend, the Abbot of the Benedictines at Atchison, the Right Reverend Martin Veth, O.S.B. His congratulations were forwarded to the Sisters:

God be praised for having brought our project to a happy close! I have been worrying about it of late, and feared it might be delayed because of the war.

Please accept my most sincere congratulations for yourself and community in that you are now an Institute of Pontifical Right. May this new status insure

[41] Letter of Father George Bartsch, O.S.B., to Mother Mary Rose Waller, Aug. 9, 1940.
[42] Letter of Mother Mary Rose Waller to the Community, Aug. 30, 1940.

and strengthen your house materially and spiritually, and introduce a new flourishing period of prosperity and usefulness for the glory of God and the welfare of Holy Church! Your future is now established on a safe basis.

With the assurance of the Papal Approbation in hand, you can well afford to wait for the arrival of the official document, though I do not think it will be long before Father George will find a safe way of sending it. . . .[43]

The Congregation could indeed well afford to wait for the arrival of the official document, knowing that the venture was an accomplished fact. Yet how welcome was another letter from the Reverend George Bartsch written September 9, 1940, announcing Papal Approbation. He told the Sisters that the coveted document was en route to the Motherhouse by special consideration of the Vatican:

Today a month ago I had the pleasure to give you the good news, that your Constitutions had been approved by the Holy See. Today a month later I am glad to be able to announce you that I succeeded to forward you your approved Constitutions via Vatican. I asked again the Secretary of the Segreteria de Stato di Sua Santita for the favor to send the copy to His Excellency the Apostolic Delegate in Washington. And my petition has been granted. Thus after some time you will get your Constitutions forwarded to you by the Apostolic Delegate in Washington. That's the surest way I could select under the present circumstances. . . .[44]

The document had been entrusted to Bishop Joseph P. Hurley, newly consecrated Ordinary of Saint Augustine, returning from Rome where he had served as attaché to the Papal Secretariate of State. The formal announcement of the advanced status was made by His Excellency, the Most Reverend Frank A. Thill, Bishop of Concordia, as soon as he had received the communication from the Apostolic Delegate:

The official act of the Sovereign Pontiff and the Sacred Congregation of Religious advances the Sisters from the juridical status of a diocesan institute to that of a Roman congregation with a Cardinal Protector at the Vatican to look after the best interests of the Sisters at the center of the Church's life. The Bishop of the diocese, priests, religious, and faithful unite in congratulating Mother Mary Rose, superior general, and her Sisters on the receipt of this great honor from the Holy Father. It has been well merited by more than fifty years of faithful service in the missions and hospitals of the Concordia diocese and other places where the Sisters have their missions. A solemn Te Deum of Thanksgiving in the Cathedral at Concordia to commemorate the Roman Approval of the Sisters will be announced later.[45]

[43] Letter of Abbot Martin Veth, O.S.B., to Mother Mary Rose Waller, Aug. 21, 1940. A copy of this letter was sent to all the houses of the Congregation.

[44] Letter of Father George Bartsch, O.S.B., to Mother Mary Rose Waller, Sept. 9, 1940. The original is in the Archives of Nazareth Motherhouse, Concordia, Kans.; a photostat is in the files of the author.

[45] Northwestern Kansas Register, Nov. 17, 1940.

"When the Decree of Praise is obtained, the Institute becomes an Institute approved by the Holy See and from that moment no article of the Constitutions can be modified without the consent of the Holy See."[46]

Not long after, the Congregation mourned the loss, on March 20, 1941, of Mother Mary Rose Waller. Sister Cleophas Arnoldy, Assistant, became Superior of the Community during the interim until the convening of the General Chapter for the election of a new Mother General. At the election, the government of the Community was placed in the hands of the former dean of Marymount College, Sister Mary Chrysostom Wynn, who became fourth Superior General of the Congregation. Mother Mary Chrysostom began the task with the cooperation and support of the Community. She continued the policies of Mother Mary Rose, and it was she who petitioned the Holy See to appoint a Cardinal Protector for the Community.

Any approved Congregation may ask for a Cardinal Protector. This request should be made by the Superior General to the Cardinal Secretary of State. The name of the Cardinal desired may be indicated, and it may be added that the Cardinal is prepared to accept if that be the case. The Secretariate of State gives notification if the favor is granted, and instructs the Department of Briefs to draw up the brief of nomination. The next step is to send a fee proportionate to the expenses incurred in the drawing up of the brief. As this fee is very high, poor institutes may ask for a reduction before making the deposit. Once the money is received, the Secretariate draws up and presents the brief. In case the Congregation has no house in Rome, the business is transacted through a Roman agent. The agent of the bishop of the diocese in which the motherhouse is located is usually the agent recommended.

The Cardinal Protector of an institute possesses no jurisdiction over the institute or over any of its members; his only concern is to promote the good of the institute by his counsel and his patronage (Canon 499, 2).[47]

The Most Reverend Pietro Fumasoni-Biondi, while Apostolic Delegate to the United States, having proposed Papal Approbation to the Congregation of the Sisters of Saint Joseph of Concordia, the

[46] Creusen, *op. cit.*, pp. 23-24.
[47] *Ibid.*, p. 39.
    Geser, *op. cit.*, p. 62.

Sisters' choice as Cardinal Protector was this saintly friend of the Congregation. Mother Mary Chrysostom wrote to the Cardinal asking his consent. The Sacred Congregation of Religious with the approval of His Holiness, Pope Pius XII, approved the request.

The Vatican issued the decree of appointment on April 16, 1942:

Segreteria De Stato   Dal Vaticano, 16 Aprile, 1942
        Di
Sua Santita

No. 47673

La Santita Di Nostra Signore si e benignamente degnata de nominare l'E, mo e Rev. mo Signor Cardinale

PIETRO FUMASONI-BIONDI

Protectore dell'Instituto delle Suore di S. Guiseppe di Concordia (Kansas, U. S. A.).

Tanto si partecipa alla Superiora Generale del suddetto Instituto per sua intelligenza e norma, avvertendola in pari tempo che sono stati impartiti alla Cancelleria dei Brevi Apostolici gli ordini opportuni per la spedizione del relativo Breve da ritirarsi nei modo d'uso.

L. CARDINAL MAGLIONE

Rev. de Superiora Generale
dell'Instituto delle Suore di S. Guiseppe
Concordia, Kansas, U. S. A.[48]

The Most Reverend Pietro Fumasoni-Biondi received the appointment in another document which is translated herein:

HOLY FATHER PIUS XII

Our Dearly Beloved Son, Greetings and Apostolic Blessing:

Since the Institute of the Sisters of Saint Joseph of Concordia, Kansas, within the confines of North America, is at present time without a Patron at the Roman Court, We, in order that We may provide for the good of those same Sisters in the Lord, assign to You, Our Beloved Son, this requested office, from whose assiduous care We trust the aforesaid religious Family will receive the greatest advantage and benefit, and so of Our own accord, with sure knowledge and mature deliberation, by these Apostolic Letters and Our Authority, mindful of the Institute at Concordia and of its houses and all its religious without exception, do make, and declare You, Our Beloved Son, with Us and at this Apostolic See, the *Patron* or *Protector* for life, with all the honors, privileges, prerogatives, rights, faculties, and the usual customary duties. Accordingly, We command all, both individual superiors and religious of the said Institute, to accept you as their Patron and to perform respectfully all things expected of them; all things to the contrary notwithstanding. Given at Rome at Saint Peter's, under the Seal of the Fisherman, on the seventeenth

[48] Original is in the Archives of the Nazareth Motherhouse, Concordia, Kans.; a photostat is in the files of the author.

day of the month of April, in the year of Our Lord, nineteen hundred and forty two and in the fourth year of Our Pontificate.

CARDINAL MAGLIONE
Papal Secretary of State

To Our Beloved Son,
Fumasoni-Biondi, Cardinal Priest of the Holy Roman Church
Assigned to the Church of the Holy Cross in Jerusalem[49]

Several communications between the Cardinal Protector and the Congregation took place within the next few weeks. Cardinal Fumasoni-Biondi wrote immediately to the Sisters:

I assure you that it is a pleasure to become your Cardinal Protector, and whatever or whenever you need help, do not hesitate to write. From my diary I note that in your convents at Salina [Marymount] and at Concordia I enjoyed the hospitality of your Sisters, back in 1930 when I was making the Apostolic Visitation of the Diocese of Concordia.

Please have the kindness to communicate to my good friend, His Excellency, Bishop Thill, the news of my nomination as Cardinal Protector, and present to him my greetings.

Asking a remembrance in the prayers of the Community, and with my blessings to you, dear Mother, and all the Sisters. . . .[50]

Cardinal Fumasoni-Biondi delegated his brother, Commendatore Dr. Guilio Fumasoni-Biondi, as agent for the Congregation for the drawing up of the Brief.[51] The latter wrote as follows:

I have the honor of sending herewith enclosed the Apostolic Brief naming my brother, His Eminence Cardinal Fumasoni-Biondi, Protector of your Institute. The total expenses amount to 77 dollars. . . . It gives me great pleasure to perform this first act of service for you in my capacity as ecclesiastical agent, and I wish to assure you that in the future if you have need of anything here in Rome I shall deem it a privilege to expedite the matter.[52]

The official Vatican newspaper *l'Osservatore* of April 27 carried the article announcing the appointment of the Cardinal Protector.[53] The diocesan paper of May 24 carried the following article:

[49] Translation of the Brief Appointing Pietro Fumasoni-Biondi Cardinal Protector of the Sisters of St. Joseph of Concordia, Apr. 17, 1942. A Latin copy is in the Archives of the Nazareth Motherhouse, Concordia, Kans.; a photographic copy is in the files of the author. Photographic plates are included in this work.
[50] Letter of the Most Rev. Pietro Cardinal Fumasoni-Biondi, Cardinal Protector, to Mother Mary Chrysostom Wynn, Apr. 19, 1942.
[51] *Loc. cit.,* Apr. 19, 1942.
[52] Letter of Commendatore Dr. Guilio Fumasoni-Biondi to Mother Mary Chrysostom Wynn, Apr. 19, 1942. The original is in the Archives of the Nazareth Motherhouse, Concordia, Kans.; a photostat is in the files of the author.
[53] *L'Osservatore Romano,* Apr. 27, 1942.
Letter of the Most Rev. Pietro Fumasoni-Biondi, Cardinal Protector, to Mother Mary Chrysostom Wynn, Apr. 28, 1942. The original is in the Archives of the Nazareth Motherhouse, Concordia, Kans.; a photostat is in the files of the author.

In a communication from Vatican City received through the Apostolic Delegation in Washington, D. C., His Eminence, Cardinal Pietro Fumasoni-Biondi has been chosen Cardinal Protector of the Sisters of Saint Joseph. The communication informed Mother Mary Chrysostom, Superior General of the Sisters of Saint Joseph, that the Apostolic Brief confirming the appointment will be forwarded in the near future.[54]

The effects of Papal Approbation may be summarized briefly:

1. A nonexempt institute can anywhere in the world, except in localities subject to the Sacred Congregation for the Propagation of the Faith, erect new convents with the sole consent of the ordinary in whose diocese the convent is to be established. (Code 497)

2. Neither the ordinary in whose diocese the convent is to be established nor the Chapter of the Papal Institute may change a rule or constitutions. (Canon 618)

3. The right of erection, division, new circumspection, and suppression of provinces belongs solely to the Holy See. (Canon 484)

4. A convent belonging to a Papal Institute (nonexempt) can be suppressed by the superior general of the institute, if the consent of the local ordinary has been obtained. (Canon 498)

5. The superior general of the institute, with the consent of her council, expressed by secret vote, can dismiss a religious with temporary vows. (Canon 647)

6. The ordinary of the place cannot interfere with the internal government and discipline of the institute, except in cases specified by Canon Law. (Canon 618, 2;533-535) [55]

A new era had dawned for the Sisters of Saint Joseph of Concordia, an era under the patronage of the Seal of the Fisherman. The affirmation of the Holy See and its stamp of approval on the Institute, on its members, and on its work, gives an assurance of stability. The footprints have been traced from one frontier to another since 1650. In the 1930's the challenge and need felt on the frontiers of the Middle West in the work of the Sisters in dioceses in seven states was a challenge to appeal to Rome for the status of a Papal Institute. That appeal was answered favorably, and with new horizons ahead the Community felt ready to march on to new and more difficult frontiers of endeavor for God and man.

[54] *Northwestern Kansas Register*, May 24, 1942.
[55] Schaefer, *op. cit.*, no. 88a.
    Geser, *op. cit.*, p. 51.

CHAPTER XIII

Administration:
Rev. Mother Mary Chrysostom Wynn
1941-

THE death of the third Mother General of the Congregation of the Sisters of Saint Joseph of Concordia, occurring at the time that the Institute had assumed pontifical status, marked another milestone in the history of the Congregation. The passing of Reverend Mother Mary Rose Waller, a pioneer religious and administrator, left the government of the Community in the hands of the Mother Assistant, Sister Cleophas Arnoldy.[1]

At the time of the election of Mother Mary Rose Waller in 1922, Sister Cleophas was elected Mother Assistant and remained in that position during the entire administration. These two women governed the Community for nineteen years. Upon the death of Mother Mary Rose, Sister Cleophas was able to carry on.

Writing to the Sisters on the missions April 16, 1941, Sister Cleophas said in part:

> Holy Week and Easter Sunday have passed and I am certain that all of us prayed for our many intentions, and especially for the happy repose of the soul of our dear Reverend Mother Mary Rose. May God rest her soul. We miss Mother Mary Rose so much here at the Motherhouse and I know that the Sisters on the missions are lonely too. We have the comfort of knowing that Reverend Mother and the Sisters whom God has called to their reward are our friends and intercessors with God. . . .[2]

[1] Born in Tipton, Kans., she entered on May 10, 1904; received her habit Aug. 15, 1904; professed on Aug. 15, 1906; became first superior in Pfeifer, Kans., and remained there from 1905-1909. She was also the first superior in Park, Kans., 1909-1922. From 1922-1941 she was in the Nazareth Motherhouse, Concordia, Kans., as Mother Assistant of the Congregation; 1942-1946 was a member of the General Council and assistant superior, Marymount College, Salina, Kans., and died June 30, 1946.

[2] Letter of Sister Cleophas Arnoldy, acting Superior of the Sisters of St. Joseph of Concordia, to the Community, Apr. 16, 1941.

Sister Cleophas announced the calling of a General Chapter for the purpose of electing the new Mother General. The delegate system, as outlined in the Constitutions, would be used in the selection of the members of the General Chapter. Sister Cleophas asked that special prayers be said on the missions to beg the blessing of God upon the Chapter.[3]

Preceded by a six-day retreat, conducted by Father Bernard Sause, O.S.B., who had recently translated the Latin version of the rules into English, the General Chapter convened at the Motherhouse, on June 14, 1941. The Most Reverend Frank A. Thill, Bishop of Concordia, delegated Monsignor John A. Duskie to preside at the Chapter. Present as chaplain at the Motherhouse was the Reverend Emil Duchene.[4]

Fifty-six eligible delegates assembled and cast their votes. On the first ballot Sister Mary Chrysostom Wynn was elected Mother General.[5] Monsignor Duskie, after determining that all details of canon law had been satisfied, administered the oath of office to the newly elected Mother Superior. He informed Bishop Thill of the outcome of the election,[6] and the latter graciously consented to be present at the Benediction of the Blessed Sacrament at which the solemn Te Deum would be sung and to announce to the assembled Sisters the name of the fourth Mother General of the Congregation.[7]

Reverend Mother Mary Chrysostom Wynn is well known in educational circles, having served as dean of Marymount College for eighteen years; it was largely through her organizational ability and efforts that the college has grown to the proportions which it has achieved.[8] As dean of the college she had been closely associated with the deceased Mother Mary Rose, especially in educational mat-

[3] *Loc. cit.*

[4] *Minutes of the General Chapters of the Sisters of St. Joseph, Concordia, Kans.,* vol. I, pt. 2, June 14, 1941, pp. 41 ff.

Northwestern Kansas Register, June 15, 1941.

[5] *Ibid.,* p. 48.

[6] *Ibid.,* p. 49.

[7] *Ibid.,* p. 50.

[8] Born in Juniata, Nebr., 1886, she is the daughter of Mrs. and the late Mr. Thomas Wynn, Hastings, Nebr. All five daughters of this family entered the Congregation of the Sisters of St. Joseph of Concordia. Mother Mary Chrysostom entered May 6, 1908, and was professed on Aug. 15, 1910; a graduate of Creighton University, A.B., M.A., and having done further graduate work at the University of Notre Dame, and Catholic University; she was one of the first high school teachers in Sacred Heart High School, Salina, Kans., 1908-1923. She was dean of Marymount College, Salina, 1923-1941.

Northwestern Kansas Register, June 22, 1941.

ters; and she was in a position to carry on the same traditions and policies in Community affairs.

The election of the other members of the Generalate took place on the same day under the presidency of Mother Mary Chrysostom. The delegates elected Sister Helena Robben as first Councillor and Mother Assistant,[9] Sister Cleophas Arnoldly as second Councillor,[10] Sister Frederica Brungardt as third Councillor,[11] Sister Bertille Bridgeman as fourth Councillor and Secretary General[12] and Sister Louis Letourneau as Bursar General.[13]

In her first letter to the Sisters, Mother Chrysostom challenged them to better and higher things:

In the infinite plan of Divine Providence, we are being privileged to undertake another year of work for Christ, our King and Leader. Each of us has accepted the assignment given us by obedience as coming from Him; to Him we shall be asked to make our final report for the year.

We would remind you to check frequently on the good resolutions made during the annual retreat. Make much of your monthly day of recollection. *Work together, play together, pray together.* . . . Keep in mind the function of the teaching Sisterhoods of the Church—handmaids of the Church—hence, *helpers* in furthering the work of Christ in whatever place we have been assigned. Strive to build up in the minds of the children the love and esteem that they should have for the priesthood, the obligation of love and devotion to the Ordinary of the diocese, and to our Holy Father, the vicar of Christ upon earth. . . .[14]

At the time of the death of Mother Mary Rose, plans were in progress for the proposed addition to The Saint Mary Hospital, Manhattan.[15] During the interim between the death of Mother Mary Rose and the election of Mother Chrysostom Wynn, at a meeting of the General Council, it was decided to proceed with the plans which had been inaugurated.[16] These negotiations continued for a

[9] Entered from Angelus, Kans., Aug. 13, 1910, and professed on Mar. 19, 1913. At the time of the election, she was Superior of St. Mary's Cathedral High School Mission in Grand Island, Nebr.

[10] Cf. footnote 1.

[11] Entered from Victoria, Kans., Sept. 3, 1906, and professed on Aug. 15, 1909. At the time of the election she was superior of The St. Mary Hospital, Manhattan, Kans.

[12] Entered from Salina, Kans., Nov. 25, 1910, and professed on Aug. 15, 1913. At the time of the election she was Councillor and General Secretary, having been at the Motherhouse since 1924.

[13] Entered from Aurora, Kans., June 29, 1898, and professed on Dec. 28, 1900. At the time of the election she was at Motherhouse, having been there since 1933.

[14] Letter of Mother Mary Chrysostom Wynn to the Community, Sept. 2, 1941.

[15] At a meeting of the General Council attended by Bishop Thill, Jan. 15, 1941, the first official mention was made of this need of The St. Mary Hospital. It was decided to appeal to Rome for permission to assume this obligation. *Minutes of the Meetings of the Councillors of the Sisters of St. Joseph of Concordia, Kans.,* vol. II, pp. 7, 8, 9.

[16] *Ibid.,* pp. 10-12. This meeting was held at the Motherhouse, Apr. 14, 1941.

period and there was hope of securing a federal grant under the Lenham Act.[17] Permission to build had been secured from the Holy See;[18] the contracts were let;[19] and the urgent need in Manhattan encouraged the Community to make every effort to go ahead with plans in spite of difficulties. However, priorities were exceedingly difficult to secure and, finally, upon the advice of the contractors, the project was abandoned for the duration of the war.[20]

Although the addition to The Saint Mary Hospital was not possible, another opportunity presented itself in the spring of 1944 when the Parkview Hospital in Manhattan was for sale. This hospital, within a block of The Saint Mary Hospital, had been operated privately for eighteen years. The matter was discussed at a meeting of the Generalate May 5, 1944.[21]

A special meeting was called in Manhattan, June 16, at which time members of the Council met with the Committee of Seven, to discuss the problem of more hospital facilities for the city. Since the closing of the Parkview Hospital, the city realized that too heavy a burden had been placed upon the facilities of the hospital operated by the Sisters. When approached by the city, the owners of the Parkview Hospital replied that though the hospital would not be leased, the building and its equipment could be purchased for $30,000. It was decided that the only way to solve the problem would be for the city to buy the Parkview Hospital and then turn it over to some organization to manage. The consensus among the members of the Committee was that, if the hospital were purchased by voluntary contributions, it should be offered to the Sisters. However, the Community insisted that, in the event the Sisters were given management of the hospital, they were to be given freedom in its affairs. The Sisters would contribute $5,000 toward the subscription

---

[17] *Ibid.*, June 16, 1941, pp. 17-18; July 17, 1941, pp. 25; Aug. 9, 1941, pp. 34-35; Oct. 9, 1941, pp. 41-42; Nov. 24, 1941, pp. 46-49; Dec. 28, 1941, pp. 51-52; Feb. 6, 1942, p. 53; Apr. 2, 1942, pp. 59-61; May 5, 1942, p. 63; May 27, 1942, pp. 63-65.

[18] This permission had been received during the interim. Reference to it is to be found in the *Minutes of the Meetings of the Councillors of the Sisters of St. Joseph of Concordia, Kans.*, vol. II, Jan. 15, 1941, pp. 7-8; Feb. 3, 1941, p. 9; Apr. 14, 1941, p. 11; and on June 16, 1941, pp. 17-18, reference is made to this permission as an accomplished fact.

[19] Contracts were let on Apr. 2, 1942, to Mont Green, general contractor, for general construction work at $155,000, for heating and plumbing to the M. W. Stevens Co. for $55,000, for electrical work to the Hotte Electric Co. for $13,000. *Northwestern Kansas Register*, Apr. 2, 1942.

[20] *Minutes of the Meetings of the Councillors of the Sisters of St. Joseph of Concordia, Kans.*, May 27, 1942, pp. 63-65.

[21] *Ibid.*, May 5, 1944, pp. 139-140.

cost and make at least a $10,000 investment in further equipment.

The proposition did not materialize at that time in spite of the fact that, in general, the citizens of Manhattan favored it. Another private concern entered into negotiations with the original owners, and the institution changed hands in the fall of 1944. Thus, another plan for expansion in Manhattan failed, and the Sisters of Saint Joseph turned elsewhere until the original plan of building the $225,000 addition could be reconsidered.[22]

In the meantime, a fund having been started for this building project, it was thought best to apply it toward outstanding loans on institutions belonging to the Community. Among these loans was one which encumbered Marymount College; it was paid in full before January 1, 1943.[23]

The number of college students enrolling at Marymount College had increased until it was decided to discontinue the Academy, which had opened in the fall of 1922, to accommodate collegiate demands. The Marymount Academy was an outgrowth of the Nazareth Academy, Concordia. Thus, over a period of sixty years the Academy had served a particular need which in 1942 the Community felt had passed. The needs of the College far outstripped those of the Academy, and the entire building was thereafter utilized for college purposes.[24]

In the preceding chapter, an account was given of the attainment of pontifical status and the designation of His Eminence, the Most Reverend Pietro Fumasoni-Biondi as Cardinal Protector of the Congregation. This latter negotiation was transacted during the administration of Mother Chrysostom Wynn.[25]

One of the oldest and most influential pioneer families in Con-

---

[22] *Ibid.,* June 16, 1944, pp. 140-142; June 19, 1944, pp. 144-145; July 3, 1944, p. 147; July 15, 1944, p. 150.

This apparently checked expansion in Manhattan. However, two years later Parkview Hospital closed and after further negotiations the Sisters of St. Joseph accepted the offer of the city to assume control. This will be discussed later in this chapter.

[23] *Ibid.,* Nov. 2, 1941; p. 44; Nov. 24, 1941, pp. 46-47; May 27, 1942, pp. 64-65; June 15, 1942, p. 67; Oct. 21, 1942, p. 81; January 4, 1943, p. 85.

[24] *Northwestern Kansas Register,* Jan. 11, 1942.

Minutes of the Meetings of the Councillors of the Sisters of St. Joseph of Concordia, Kans., vol. II, Nov. 24, 1941, pp. 46-47, contained the first official action taken in the matter when Mother Mary Chrysostom explained the position of the faculties of the College and Academy at Marymount and advised the Council that proper notification would be necessary to the accrediting agencies.

[25] *Ibid.,* Nov. 2, 1941, p. 43; Nov. 24, 1941, p. 45; May 27, 1942, p. 65.

cordia was the N. B. Brown family, who owned the old Grand Theater. Upon the death of Mrs. Kate Brown in 1942, it was learned that Brownstone Hall, the pretentious residence of the family, had been willed to the Sisters of Saint Joseph. Mrs. Brown, who had always manifested a deep interest in the work of the Community, directed that her home be used as a place of relaxation for the Sisters. However, the will contained various specifications which made the acceptance of the bequest almost impossible to a religious Community. But after much deliberation and consideration, with legal and ecclesiastical advice, the Sisters accepted Brownstone Hall, which is again in condition for occupancy.[26]

At a meeting of the Generalate, February 19, 1943, specifications and proposal for redecorating the Sacred Heart Chapel at the Motherhouse were offered and discussed. It was voted to accept the terms of Griewe, Inc., Cincinnati, with work to begin at an early date.

The diocesan paper made mention of the redecoration of the chapel early in May:

Sacred Heart Chapel at Nazareth Convent in Concordia was completely renovated for the first services of the month on Holy Thursday morning. The work was started March 22 by four workmen from Greiwe, Inc., ecclesiastical designers and decorators of Cincinnati, Ohio, and was under the personal supervision of Gene J. Griewe, a member of the firm. The color scheme, tiffany ceiling and walls of modulated green-blue-white was chosen by Mother Mary Chrysostom and her Council because of the beautifully designed stained glass windows that occupy practically all of the wall space of the chapel. The frames of the stations of the cross were changed to an antique gold, harmonizing with the light onyx on the altar and in the altar railing. The walls of the sanctuary were stenciled with a silver-white pattern with the monogram of Christ worked into the design. The adoring angels, formerly at the sides of the main altar, were not returned to the sanctuary, and in their places were put white alabaster vases of elaborate design. The chapel, which was built in 1907 when Mother Antoinette was superior of the order, is Romanesque in style and combines the Corinthian pilasters with the accompanying and proper cornice, frieze, and architrave. It had last been decorated in 1923, when Mother Mary Rose was

[26] *Minutes of the Meetings of the Councillors of the Sisters of St. Joseph of Concordia, Kans.*, vol. II, Sept. 7, 1942, p. 76; Oct. 21, 1942, p. 79; July 10, 1943, p. 106; Aug. 1-2, 1943, p. 107; Aug. 13-14, 1943, pp. 109-110; Nov. 3, 1943, p. 120; and Dec. 1, 1943, pp. 127-128.

Letters of Mother Mary Chrysostom Wynn to the Community, Nov. 2, 1942, and Mar. 29, 1945. In the last one it was stated that by decree of the court the Sisters of St. Joseph were granted the property free of all restrictions of the will; and under those conditions it was accepted.

[27] *Ibid.*, Feb. 19, 1943, p. 91, and entry of May 10, 1943, pp. 98-99, record the contracting with the Holstein Rubber Co., for tiling for chapel sanctuary and floors.

Mother General, by the Conrad Schmidt studios of Milwaukee, Wisconsin. . . .[28]

In Damar, Rooks County, Kansas, the Sisters had conducted the public grade school since 1904 and for a period had taught in the high school. However, a scarcity of high school teachers made it necessary to discontinue the latter. In May, 1943, at the annual meeting of the patrons of the Damar school district, it was decided by a vote of 33 to 3 to turn the high school over to the Sisters.[29] The Sisters accepted the request and a contract was signed to furnish three high school and three grade teachers for the following year.[30]

Seneca, Nemaha County, is a small town in northeastern Kansas, not far from Sabetha, where the Sisters of Saint Joseph have operated Saint Anthony Murdock Memorial Hospital since 1922. The town was settled in pre-Civil War days on the banks of the sluggish Nemaha River as a rival of Richmond, a feeder for the Oregon-California Trail. The rivalry between these two towns was keen and legend has it that some boosters of Seneca in an effort to outwit Richmond planted oats in a section of the Trail and detoured it through their town. When the oats came up with the first spring grasses, the old trail had the appearance of having been abandoned. Thus, immigrant traffic was brought to Seneca. A few years later, when the Pony Express station was established there and when, still later, this became an overland stage depot, people from Richmond moved into Seneca.[31]

Enterprising citizens of Seneca, realizing the need of hospital facilities for its inhabitants and those of the surrounding countryside, began to consider a local hospital. The government at this time endeavored to alleviate national unemployment problems by sponsoring works which would be of benefit to the communities to which

[28] *Northwestern Kansas Register*, May 2, 1943.
    Letter of Mother Mary Chrysostom to the Community, Apr. 19, 1943.
    [29] Cf. Chap. IX, pp. 223-224, for account of the opening and history of the Damar mission.
    [30] *Minutes of the Meetings of the Councillors of the Sisters of St. Joseph of Concordia, Kans.*, vol. II, Apr. 12, 1943, pp. 96-97; May 10, 1943, pp. 98-99.
    Contract between the Damar School District 71, and the Sisters of St. Joseph, Concordia, Kans., May 21, 1943.
    [31] *Kansas: A Guide to the Sunflower State*, Federal Writers' Project (New York, 1939), pp. 313-314.

PIVS PP. XII

Dilecte Fili Noster; salutem et apostolicam benedictionem

cum Sororum Sancti Ioseph Institutum, cujus domus principes in dioecesi Concordiensi America Septentrionalis intra fines extat, non Ill. trium vir apud Romanam Curiam caret, Nos, ut earundem Sororum bono in Domino prospiciamus, Tibi, Dilecte Fili Noster, e cujus multa tuteta praestabis religiosam Familiam, plurimum utilitatis ornamentique suscepturam fore confidimus, id munus demandare dum voluerimus. Itaque mota proprio, certa scientia ac matura deliberatione Nostris Te, Dilecte Fili Noster, hisce Litteris Apostolicis atque auctoritate Nostra, memorati Concordiensis Instituti Sororum utriusque diversorum ac religiosarum provinciam gubernationemque sub Nostri et hanc Apostolicam Sedem Patronum, seu Protectorem, quoad videat, cum omnibus honoribus, privilegiis, praerogativis, juribus, facultatibus atque omnibus aliis et concessis legitimis facimus ac renuntiamus. Omnibus protecta et erigenda sint. Instituti Moderatricibus ac religiosi ejusdemque personae mandamus ut Te, in unum Patronum et agnant, et ea, quae debent reverentia prosequantur, contrariis non obstantibus quibuslibet. Datum Romae apud Sanctum Petrum, sub anulo Piscatoris, die XVIII m. Aprilis an. MCMXXXII, Pontificatus Nostri quarto.

Dilecto Filio Nostro

S.R.E. Presbytero Cardinali Fumasoni Biondi
Civitate Sanctae Crucis in Hierusalem

Mgr. [signature]
[signature]

Document Appointing Cardinal Fumasoni-Biondi, Cardinal Protector of the Congregation of the Sisters of Saint Joseph of Concordia

Reverend Mother Mary Chrysostom Wynn, Fourth
Mother General of the Sisters of Saint Joseph of
Concordia, 1941 –

funds were allotted. Therefore, as a cooperative project a hospital was built at a cost of $95,000, half of which was contributed by the city itself and $20,000 by the WPA.[32]

As the building neared completion, another and perhaps a more serious problem confronted the citizens of the town: it was necessary to place the management of the institution in the hands of a competent organization. The first unofficial request for the Sisters of Saint Joseph of Concordia to take charge of the hospital came during the interim between the death of Mother Mary Rose Waller and the election of Mother Mary Chrysostom Wynn. Although the Sisters realized that the correspondence was not an official invitation to accept the management of the Seneca Hospital, references were made to it at several meetings of the Generalate although no action was taken.[33]

The first invitation to assume control of the hospital was made May 10, 1941, when John D. Cunningham, a lawyer and member of the Board of Trustees of the Seneca Hospital, wrote to Concordia in regard to the hospital then in process of construction. He explained details of the plan of construction and begged the Sisters to consider taking charge of it upon its completion.[34] Seneca's proximity to Sabetha was one reason why the Concordia Community considered this hospital at a time when several other offers of similar nature were rejected due to the scarcity of hospital Sisters.[35]

From the first correspondence in 1941 there was a steady interchange of ideas on the part of the Community and of the trustees of the hospital,[36] until the definite request was made June 19, 1942.[37] Since Seneca is in the Diocese of Leavenworth (now Kansas City-in-Kansas), the Most Reverend Paul Schulte, then Bishop of Leavenworth, was consulted. Bishop Schulte graciously consented, stating

[32] The Sisters of St. Joseph later contributed $25,000 or the balance of the amount. *Seneca Courier-Tribune*, May 1, 1944.

[33] *Minutes of the Meetings of the Councillors of the Sisters of St. Joseph of Concordia, Kans.*, vol. II, Apr. 14, 1941, pp. 10-12. Letters had been dated Mar. 30, 1941; Apr. 11, 1941; and May 6, 1941.

[34] Letter of John D. Cunningham to Sister Cleophas Arnoldy, May 10, 1941.

[35] *Minutes of the Meetings of the Councillors of the Sisters of St. Joseph, Concordia, Kans.*, vol. II, Apr. 14, 1941, pp. 11-12.

[36] *Ibid.*, June 27, 1941, pp. 21-22.

[37] *Loc. cit.*

he was happy to hear the Sisters of Saint Joseph of Concordia were to be in charge and asking God's blessing upon the work.

The contract was certified March 13, 1943.[39] Shortly after the signing of the contract, the Ordinary of the Diocese of Leavenworth again expressed his appreciation to the Sisters for the further work they would execute in his diocese.[40] The Most Reverend Frank A. Thill, Bishop of Concordia, who approved the taking over of the Seneca Hospital, also congratulated the Sisters on this new project.[41]

At a meeting of the Generalate before the formal opening of the hospital, it was announced that the Community would not have the privilege of selecting a name for the hospital as the city wished it called The Seneca Hospital. At that time it was moved that the institution would, nevertheless, be placed under the patronage of Saint Rose of Lima, in memory of Reverend Mother Mary Rose.[42]

As has been mentioned above, the Sisters of Saint Joseph contributed approximately $25,000 to the hospital, mostly in movable equipment.[43]

The local newspaper carried weekly news items concerning the progress of the plans for the opening of the hospital.[44] Patients were first received in September, 1943. Sister Ferdinand Giersch, superior, was assisted by Sisters Virgilia Barrins, Rose Catherine Brungardt, Alvera Burghart, and Rose Irene Gibbs.[45]

[38] Letter of Mother Mary Chrysostom Wynn to the Most Rev. Paul Schulte, the Bishop of Leavenworth, Feb. 24, 1943.

Letter of the Most Rev. Paul Schulte, then Bishop of Leavenworth, to Mother Mary Chrysostom Wynn, Feb. 25, 1943.

Minutes of the Meetings of the Councillors of the Sisters of St. Joseph of Concordia, Kans., vol. II, Apr. 12, 1943, p. 96.

[39] Ordinance No. 542: an ordinance providing for the leasing of the hospital building, premises, and equipment by the city of Seneca, Kans., to the Nazareth Convent and Academy, a religious, educational, and charitable corporation. A certified copy is in the Archives of the Nazareth Motherhouse, Concordia, Kans., signed by Mother Mary Chrysostom Wynn, president of the Nazareth Convent and Academy Corporation, and by the mayor of Seneca, Mr. J. R. Houston.

Seneca Courier-Tribune, Mar. 15, 1943.

[40] Letter of the Most Rev. Paul Schulte to Mother Mary Chrysostom Wynn, Mar. 23, 1943.

[41] *Minutes of the Meeting of the Councillors of the Sisters of St. Joseph of Concordia, Kans.,* vol. II, Apr. 14, 1941, pp. 13-14; Apr. 12, 1943, pp. 97-98.

[42] *Ibid.,* Apr. 12, 1943.

[43] *Ibid.,* May 10, 1943, p. 99; June 19, 1943, pp. 101-103; Mar. 10, 1944, p. 133 mentioned a complete report on the amount the Community had spent to date on equipment, given as $24,736.19. The questions of reimbursement by the city of Seneca and the maintenance and insurance items were discussed.

[44] *Seneca Courier-Tribune,* Mar. 15, 1943; June 7, 1943; June 28, 1943; May 1, 1944; May 8, 1944; May 15, 1944.

[45] *Ibid.,* May 15, 1944.

Minutes of the Meetings of the Councillors of the Sisters of St. Joseph of Concordia, Kans., vol. II, June 19, 1943, pp. 101-103; July 4, 1943, p. 105.

Open house was held May 14, 1944, at which time eight counties, and eleven states other than Kansas, were represented among the five hundred who inspected the building. Nine Sisters on the mission in 1947 ministered to the needs of eight hundred and fifty-two patients.[46]

Simultaneously with the plans for the opening of the Seneca Hospital, the Sisters of Saint Joseph were considering the opening of a parochial grade school in Silver City, New Mexico, and of a high school in the Cathedral parish in Concordia. Both projects were considered favorably because of special needs in these parishes.

The interest of the Congregation in the Southwest began in 1926, when a community of Sisters of Saint Joseph with Motherhouse in Silver City, New Mexico, became affiliated with the Concordia Motherhouse. As we have seen, Saint Mary's Academy, Silver City, is today one of the outstanding institutions under the direction of the Sisters. The large Mexican population of Silver City challenged the crowded accommodations of the Academy, but even most urgent efforts to enroll a relative number of them proved unsuccessful. The only solution to the problem of providing these Spanish-American children with a Catholic education was to establish a parochial school near the church.

In the first correspondence concerning the proposed St. Vincent de Paul parochial school in Silver City between Father John P. Linnane and authorities in the Congregation, Father mentioned the possibility of having some of the Sisters who lived at St. Mary's Academy teach the school:

I have hopes of starting a parochial school here in the parish of St. Vincent de Paul next September. I have a building made of brick and concrete which will require considerable modification before it can be utilized for teaching purposes. I hope to get started on this work as soon as possible.

Due to the proximity of St. Mary's Academy I thought it might be possible for the Sisters to come from that institution to teach during the day and return in the afternoon. Needless to say we need a parochial school here. Due to absence of religious education indifference is increasing and is widespread. It is my firm conviction that a school staffed by the Sisters will be the salvation of this parish. . . .[47]

In her reply Mother Chrysostom congratulated the pastor in this

[46] *Kenedy's Catholic Directory* (New York, 1947), p. 542.
    An interesting article, "The Best Thing in Town," by Grace Alexandra Young, appeared in the *Saturday Evening Post*, Sept. 14, 1946, about the Seneca Hospital. The author explained the asset such a hospital is to a community such as Seneca.
[47] Letter of Father John P. Linnane to Mother Mary Chrysostom Wynn, Feb. 25, 1943.

work of zeal, assuring him that the Sisters of Saint Joseph of
Concordia would be happy to cooperate with him in this undertaking
in whatever manner he suggested. "It is surely a worthy cause,"
wrote she, "and one which should mean much for the furtherance
of Catholic education in that community." This encouragement of
the Sisters assured the pastor that their interest in the Mexican
children was sincere and all-embracing.[48]

Mother Chrysostom announced the proposition to the members
of her Council who agreed that the parish of Silver City furnished
a fertile field for good.[49] Since the Community does not maintain
a foreign mission, it was felt that the work in Silver City would
approach the mission field better than in any other school under the
auspices of the Congregation.

The Council advised Mother Chrysostom to make arrangements
as to the number of Sisters needed, the salary of the Sisters, and
requirements for grade teachers in the State of New Mexico. Permission would have to be obtained from the Most Reverend Frank
A. Thill, Bishop of Concordia, and from the Most Reverend Sidney
M. Metzger, Bishop of El Paso, in whose diocese Silver City is
located.[50]

In his answer on April 13, 1943[51] to the letter of Mother Chrysostom, Bishop Metzger said in part:

. . . I am aware that Father Linnane wants to open a parochial school in
Silver City, and if you can comply with his request to furnish Sisters, I will
be greatly pleased. Your acceptance, therefore, of this new school in the Diocese
will be certainly agreeable to me. . . . I feel sure that, if you can furnish
teachers for the Silver City parochial school, their work will come up to your
usual fine standards. . . .[52]

The State Department of Education's requirements for a parochial grade school in the city were the same as for the private grade
school connected with the Academy.[53]

Further correspondence between the pastor of Silver City and the
Sisters continued throughout the summer, but in August it was

[48] Letter of Mother Chrysostom Wynn to Father John P. Linnane, Mar. 3, 1943.
[49] *Minutes of the Meetings of the Councillors of the Sisters of St. Joseph of Concordia, Kans.*, vol. II, Mar. 8, 1943, p. 94; Mar. 12, 1943, p. 95.
[50] *Ibid.*, Apr. 12, 1943, p. 97.
[51] Letter of Mother Mary Chrysostom Wynn to the Most Rev. Sidney M. Metzger,
Apr. 13, 1943.
[52] Letter of the Most Rev. Sidney M. Metzger to Mother Mary Chrysostom Wynn,
Apr. 17, 1943.
[53] Letter of Mrs. Georgia L. Lusk, Superintendent of Public Instruction, State of
New Mexico, to Mother Mary Chrysostom Wynn, Apr. 15, 1943.

thought best to postpone the opening of school for another year since wartime restrictions made improvements almost impossible.[54]

The matter rested until March, 1944, when a letter from Father Linnane assured the Community that, building repairs advancing rapidly, he was confident the school could be opened in September. He asked consideration of a plan to reconvert a building near the school into a residence for the Sisters, stating that there would be definite advantages in having the Sisters close to the school and church: "They would be of inestimable value in the organizing of the Children of Mary Sodality and the supervision of the children in church. Then, if any of the Sisters could organize a choir, a special Mass could be celebrated each Sunday for the parish children. . . ."

The contract was signed June 1, 1944, by the Bishop of El Paso, the pastor of Silver City, and the Mother General of the Sisters.[56] Sister Myra Joseph McConn was appointed superior and Sisters Fulgentius Burkhart, Ann Louis Kongo, and Stanislaus Porter were her co-workers.[57] One hundred and twenty-three Mexican children were enrolled in September, 1944,[58] and in 1947 there were one hundred and thirty-nine.[59]

The parochial school in Concordia had been in existence since 1884 but, except for an unsuccessful attempt to establish a high school in 1922, there had been no opportunity for Catholic children

---

[54] Letters of Mother Mary Chrysostom Wynn to Father John P. Linnane, Apr. 13, 1943; May 11, 1943; June 22, 1943.

Letters of Father John P. Linnane to Mother Mary Chrysostom Wynn, May 5, 1943; May 18, 1943; June 28, 1943.

Telegram of Mother Mary Chrysostom Wynn to Father John P. Linnane, Aug. 3, 1943.

Telegram of Mother Mary Chrysostom Wynn to Father John P. Linnane, Aug. 3, 1943.

Minutes of the Meetings of the Sisters of St. Joseph of Concordia, Kans., vol. II, May 10, 1943, p. 99; May 24, 1943, p. 100.

[55] *Ibid.,* Apr. 16, 1944, p. 136.

Letters of Father John P. Linnane to Mother Mary Chrysostom Wynn, Mar. 8, 1944; Apr. 7, 1944; June 1, 1944.

Letter of Mother Mary Chrysostom Wynn to Father John P. Linnane, Apr. 21, 1944.

[56] Letter of Father John P. Linnane to Mother Mary Chrysostom Wynn, June 1, 1944.

Form of Contract for Parochial Schools, June 1, 1944.

[57] *Northwestern Kansas Register,* Aug. 27, 1944.

[58] *Kenedy's Catholic Directory* (New York, 1945), p. 411.

[59] *Ibid.* (1947), p. 431.

Interview with Sister Myra Joseph McConn, June 27, 1946. The new school building opened Apr. 13, 1946. It was the gift of philanthropist Mr. Harry Wright, Mexico City, D. F.

to secure a secondary education under Catholic auspices. This condition was brought to the attention of the Congregation in 1944 when a request was made to staff a parochial high school.

The opening of a parochial high school in Concordia had been considered sometime before any definite record was made. In the Minutes of the July 4, 1943, meeting of the Councillors of the Sisters of Saint Joseph, it was first suggested the Community would probably be asked to supply teachers for the proposed school.[60] Brownstone Hall was considered for the housing of the high school.[61]

However, the parish opportunely purchased the former Concordia Normal and Business College, a building readily reconvertible into a high school. A newspaper account stated:

. . . The structure is conveniently located in the eastern section of the city, at the end of Seventh Street and about six blocks east and south of the Cathedral. Approximately three-fourths of the members of the Cathedral parish reside in that vicinity. The school grounds embrace three acres and are sufficient for all outdoors sports. According to reliable estimates, the building and grounds are valued at $25,000.

Used for twenty-six years as an accredited normal and business college, the edifice is sufficiently spacious for a parish high school department. It is in excellent condition, and the county, during the few years the building was in its possession, spent considerable sums of money for improvements.

In connection with the building is a gym, which will serve for intramural athletics and as a parish center. The school was constructed in 1905 and was for many years under the presidency of A. B. Carney. . . . The parish high school department will be staffed by the Concordia Sisters of Saint Joseph. . . .[62]

The acceptance of the school as a community project was announced formally to the Sisters later in the fall.[63] It was hoped that the parish would be able to purchase a home midway between the grade school and the high school buildings so that the Sisters could live in the parish rather than at the Nazareth Motherhouse and Saint Joseph's Hospital as formerly. The pastor assured them that he would make every effort to find such a location.[64]

Considerable renovation on the school building took place the following year, and in August, 1944, it was ready for occupancy.[65] Sister Agnes Clare Sheridan was appointed principal with Sisters

60 *Minutes of the Meetings of the Councillors of the Sisters of St. Joseph of Concordia, Kans.,* vol. II, July 4, 1943, p. 105.
61 *Ibid.,* July 10, 1943, p. 106.
62 *Northwestern Kansas Register,* Oct. 17, 1943.
63 Letter of Mother Mary Chrysostom Wynn to the Community, Oct. 21, 1943.
64 *Minutes of the Meetings of the Councillors of the Sisters of St. Joseph, Concordia, Kans.,* vol. II, Apr. 16, 1944, p. 137.
65 *Northwestern Kansas Register,* Aug. 27, 1944.
Concordia Blade-Empire, Aug. 17, 1944.

REVEREND MOTHER MARY CHYRSOSTOM WYNN, 1941–   345

Eugenia Teahan, Miriam Uhler, Athanasia Weber, and Father John Poell completing the faculty.[66] The formal opening took place September 5, at a Mass celebrated by Bishop Thill. Forty-five students were enrolled;[67] the 1947 statistics show seventy-two in attendance.[68] The school was known as the Cathedral Catholic High School; however, when the seat of the diocese was transferred to Salina, December 24, 1944, the name was changed to the Concordia Catholic High School.

Within a year after its establishment, the Concordia Catholic High School had won two state recognitions. At a meeting of the State Board of Education, May 28, 1945, the school was recognized as a fully accredited four-year high school, having met, under the direction of Monsignor James McErlean, all requirements for the complete organization of a four-year course of study. The library, the science laboratory, and the school organization were fully approved. About the same time, the Kansas State High School Activities Association approved the athletic program of the high school.[69] The future of the Concordia Catholic High School seems assured in educational circles.

Three important properties were acquired during the fall of 1945, adding to the Community holdings of the Sisters of Saint Joseph. Soon after Bishop Schuler of El Paso had been succeeded by Bishop Metzger,[70] the Saint Joseph Sanatorium, El Paso, Texas, was acquired by the Sisters after twenty years' administration of that diocesan institution.[71]

The original plan when the Sisters took over management of the Sanatorium was that eventually the Community would assume ownership. The Sisters were to be compensated, half by cash to be taken from the earnings of the Sanatorium and half by notes payable from the net assets of the institution. These notes had accumulated against the diocese to the amount of $66,726.66 at the beginning of the fiscal year of 1945.[72] It was believed at that time

[66] Loc. cit.
[67] Kenedy's Catholic Directory (New York, 1945), p. 678.
[68] Ibid. (1947), p. 695.
[69] Northwestern Kansas Register, Oct. 28, 1945.
[70] The Most Rev. Sidney M. Metzger, appointed Titular Bishop of Birta and Auxiliary of Santa Fe, Jan. 5, 1940; was consecrated on Apr. 10, 1940; was appointed Coadjutator Bishop of El Paso, Dec. 26, 1941; and succeeded to the See of El Paso on Nov. 23, 1942. The Most Rev. Anthony J. Schuler died June 3, 1944.
[71] Cf. Chapter XII, pp. 294-295.
[72] Letter of the Most Rev. Sidney M. Metzger to Mother Mary Chrysostom Wynn, July 27, 1945.

that the value of the Saint Joseph Sanatorium, including buildings, grounds, and equipment, was between $75,000 and $100,000. Through a series of negotiations between the interested parties, an agreement was reached whereby the ownership of the institution passed from the hands of the Diocese of El Paso into those of the Sisters of Saint Joseph of Concordia.[73]

Salina, the largest city in the Diocese of Concordia, had been considered for many years the best location for the cathedral and residence of the bishop. During the administration of Bishop Cunningham, consideration had been given to the transfer of the seat of the diocese and Bishop Tief purchased lots in Salina for that purpose. At the time of the visit of the Apostolic Delegate, Cardinal Fumasoni-Biondi, in 1930, the proposal was made a matter of record.[74] Bishop Thill was interested in the transfer and, after negotiations with the Holy See, it was effected December 23, 1944.[75] The announcement of this episcopal transfer was made on March 12, 1945.[76]

Within ten days after the announcement of the removal of the episcopal see to Salina, Mother Mary Chrysostom and the Councillors met in conference with Bishop Thill, who informed them that he was willing to sell his Concordia residence to the Sisters.[77] The following day, the Councillors voted to purchase the residence, the resolution being passed also by the Board of Trustees of the Nazareth Convent and Academy.[78]

It was thought best to have the building occupied pending per-

[73] Loc. cit.
Letter of Mother Mary Chrysostom Wynn to the Most Rev. Sidney M. Metzger, Aug. 22, 1945.
El Paso Times, Oct. 27, 1945.
Letters of the Most Rev. Sidney M. Metzger to Mother Mary Chrysostom Wynn, Nov. 6, 1945; Dec. 28, 1945.
Warranty Deed 66303 signed Sept. 28, 1945; filed for record Oct. 18, 1945; and recorded Oct. 26, 1945. The Most Rev. Sidney M. Metzger, as Roman Catholic Bishop of the Diocese of El Paso, Texas, to The Nazareth Convent and Academy.
Minutes of the Meetings of the Councillors of the Sisters of St. Joseph of Concordia, Kans., vol. III, p. 61. Aug. 29, 1945—resolution passed by Councillors to purchase St. Joseph's Sanatorium, El Paso.
[74] Ibid., vol. II, Mar. 10, 1944, p. 133; Apr. 16, 1944, p. 136.
[75] Northwestern Kansas Register, Mar. 18, 1945.
[76] Concordia Blade-Empire, Mar. 12, 1945.
Northwestern Kansas Register, Mar. 18, 1945.
[77] Minutes of the Meetings of the Councillors of the Sisters of St. Joseph of Concordia, Kans., vol. III, Mar. 20, 1945, p. 31.
[78] Loc. cit.

mission from Rome to sell the property; therefore, Bishop Thill requested that a group of Sisters take up residence there when he moved to Salina. The Council appointed Sister Xavier Cunningham superior.[79] In August the Holy See granted permission for the sale, and the property was deeded to the Sisters of Saint Joseph.[80]

The addition of this beautiful residence and grounds to Community property was a decided asset. The land intended for the new Saint Joseph's Hospital in Concordia was sold, the newly acquired property being already landscaped and beautified, whereas the former would have demanded further investment in grading and landscaping.[81] Thus, the purchase of the former episcopal residence became closer identified with the new hospital project since the building could be used as a residence for nurses and Sisters when the hospital would be erected.[82]

The Generalate named the place "Fontbonne Hall" in memory of Reverend Mother Saint John Fontbonne who re-established the Community in France after the depredations of the French Revolution and who was later responsible for the sending of the first Sisters of Saint Joseph to the United States.[83]

Closely associated with the acquisition of Fontbonne Hall by the Sisters were two other projects which followed these negotiations. Bishop Thill, in a letter to Mother Mary Chrysostom, asked that ownership of the Home of the Little Flower, Concordia, pass from diocesan to Community ownership on condition that the Sisters convert the present buildings of Saint Joseph's Hospital, Concordia, into a home for the aged as soon as the new hospital was completed. In other words, His Excellency requested that the Sisters accept the ownership as well as administration of the Home of the Little Flower.[84]

The diocesan Consultors, after thorough discussion,[85] agreed unanimously to having the institution and cash balance turned over

---

[79] *Ibid.*, vol. III, Mar. 21, 1945, p. 42.
[80] *Ibid.*, vol. III, Aug. 29, 1945, p. 59.
[81] *Ibid.*, vol. II, Mar. 10, 1944, p. 133.
[82] *Loc. cit.*
[83] *Ibid.*, vol. III, May 11, 1945, p. 43.
[84] Letter of the Most Rev. Frank A. Thill to Mother Mary Chrysostom Wynn, Sept. 26, 1945.
    Minutes of the Meetings of the Councillors of the Sisters of St. Joseph of Concordia, Kans., vol. III, Oct., 1945, p. 67.
[85] *Ibid.*, vol. III, Oct. 16, 1945, pp. 69-70.

to the Sisters in consideration of the assumption of their responsibility to maintain a home for the aged in the diocese.[86]

The chaplain's residence at St. John's Hospital, Salina, was ready for occupancy in September, 1945. Formerly the chaplain at the hospital had had a suite of rooms in the hospital but crowded conditions made it imperative to erect a separate building. In the basement, a soundproofed classroom and demonstration room was equipped for the class work of the student nurses.[87]

While waiting for a more favorable time to begin construction in Manhattan, the room previously used for a chapel was converted into rooms for patients. Therefore, a $10,000 chapel was built on the grounds and solemnly dedicated.[88]

Parkview Hospital, Manhattan, had functioned for two years after the new management took over in 1944. However, it was announced in July, 1946, that the hospital was forced to close its doors on August 1 for lack of funds. Again, a critical problem confronted the city of Manhattan: The Saint Mary Hospital, crowded to capacity, could not assume additional responsibility for the care of the sick. The Chamber of Commerce appointed a Hospital Study Commission to investigate ways and means of meeting the new emergency.

The Commission's report was explained to the Generalate of the Sisters of Saint Joseph of Concordia by representatives of the Chamber of Commerce. A request was made that the Sisters accept the former Parkview Hospital on condition that the city raise $25,000 to be used in the purchase of the institution. This gift would demonstrate to the Sisters the good will of the city and would impress upon them the appreciation of the citizens of Manhattan of the work of The Saint Mary Hospital.

An agreement being reached, the Chamber of Commerce organized a highly successful drive under a Council of Service Clubs, which was completed during the latter part of August. It assured Manhattan of doubled service by the Sisters of Saint Joseph. The

86 *Ibid.,* vol. III, Nov. 5, 1945, pp. 73-74.
   Letters of Mother Mary Chrysostom Wynn to the Community, Nov. 12, 1945; Dec. 17, 1945.
87 *Northwestern Kansas Register,* Sept. 23, 1945.
88 *Ibid.,* Dec. 16, 1945.
   Minutes of the Meetings of the Councillors of the Sisters of St. Joseph of Concordia, Kans., vol. II, Nov. 27, 1945, p. 78.

second hospital is known as The Saint Mary Hospital—Parkview Annex.[89]

Saint Joseph's Hospital, Concordia, purchased a second residence for nurses when the cadet program sponsored by the United States government went into effect. All of the hospitals staffed by the Sisters of Saint Joseph which had training schools were accepted under the cadet program and quarters for the nurses became a problem, not only in Concordia, but also in Salina, Manhattan, and Sabetha.[90] In Concordia the Bedor residence, east of the hospital, became a new investment in July, 1944.[91]

Mention has been made of the steadily increasing clientele of Saint Joseph's Hospital, Concordia, which serves, not only the city of Concordia and Cloud County in general, but is patronized by a large territory extending into Nebraska. To meet the expanding service demanded of the local hospital, in August, 1945, the Mother General and the Councillors voted to erect a hospital of 125-150 beds at a cost of from $500,000 to $750,000. The site chosen was that of the former residence of the Bishop of Salina.[92] The contracts were let to Carroll and Dean, architects, Kansas City, Missouri.[93] The building will be constructed of light-colored brick and will face northeast toward the plaza. Construction has not been begun at the writing, but as soon as materials are available work will begin immediately.[94]

The plans for this new hospital mark another step in the growth of the work of the Sisters of Saint Joseph of Concordia. The Community now conducts six hospitals and a sanatorium for tubercular

[89] *Northwestern Kansas Register,* Aug. 11, 1946; Aug. 18, 1946.
Manhattan Mercury, Aug., 1946, issues.
Manhattan Chronicle, Aug., 1946, issues.

[90] *Northwestern Kansas Register,* Jan. 23, 1944 (approval of The St. Mary Hospital, Manhattan); Feb. 6, 1944 (approval of St. Anthony Murdock Memorial Hospital, Sabetha); Apr. 23, 1944 (approval of St. Joseph's Hospital, Concordia); Apr. 15, 1945 (approval of St. John's Hospital, Salina).

[91] *Minutes of the Meetings of the Councillors of the Sisters of St. Joseph of Concordia, Kans.,* vol. II, Apr. 2, 1942, p. 62; vol. III, June 19, 1944, p. 144; June 23, 1944, p. 145; July 3, 1944, p. 146-147.

Deed signed by Mrs. Zelia Bedor to the Sisters of St. Joseph of Concordia, July 1, 1944. The purchase price was $4,500.
Northwestern Kansas Register, July 2, 1944.

[92] *Ibid.,* Sept. 30, 1945.
Minutes of the Meetings of the Councillors of the Sisters of St. Joseph of Concordia, Kans., vol. III, Aug. 29, 1945, p. 63.

[93] *Ibid.,* vol. III, Aug. 29, 1945, p. 63.
Northwestern Kansas Register, Sept. 30, 1945.

[94] At the time of writing this cost is estimated at over a million.

patients as well as an orphanage and a home for the aged. There are thirty-three grade schools, sixteen high schools, and one college under the direction of the Congregation. These houses are located in seven states of the Midwest and Southwest—in Kansas, Nebraska, Missouri, New Mexico, Texas, Illinois, and Michigan. Ecclesiastically, these institutions are within the jurisdiction of the Ordinaries of the Archdiocese of Chicago, and of the Dioceses of Salina, Kansas City-in-Kansas, Kansas City, Lincoln, Grand Island, El Paso, Rockford, and Marquette.[95]

The six-year term of Reverend Mother Mary Chrysostom Wynn expired in June, 1947. In December, 1946, a circular letter was sent to the missions conducted by the Sisters, announcing the convening of the General Chapter. Special prayers were designated to be said each day "to implore the blessing of God upon the Chapter—so that all may proceed according to the Holy Will of God for the praise and honor of His Majesty, and for the welfare of the Congregation."[96]

The General Chapter began its deliberations June 13, 1947. Sixty-two delegates answered roll call.[97] A report of the six-year administration since the last General Chapter was read. On July 14th, Reverend Mother Mary Chrysostom Wynn was re-elected on the first ballot. Mother Chrysostom's highly satisfactory work as Mother General was reflected in the vote of confidence given her. Sister Helena Robben was elected first councillor and Mother Assistant; Sisters Frederica Brungardt, Bertille Bridgeman, and Wilhelmina Heidrick were elected councillors, the latter also assuming the office of Secretary General. Sister Louis Letourneau was re-elected Bursar General.

The next few days were devoted to discussion and explanation of articles and passages in the Constitutions as the final approval of these Constitutions was to be sought from Rome. The revised

---

[95] Statistics as reported in the 1947 edition of *Kenedy's Catholic Directory* show that during the previous year the Sisters of St. Joseph of Concordia instructed 3,726 grade school children; 695 high school students; 144 student nurses; and 487 college students, making a grand total of 5,052. During the same period the hospitals, sanatorium, and home for the aged ministered to 11,982 in-patients and 2,900 out-patients, making a grand total of 14,882. Hence, 20,934 persons came under the direct influence of the Sisters during that particular year. This number does not include music students, art students, and others who are not listed in the statistics.

[96] Letter of Mother Mary Chrysostom Wynn to the Sisters, Dec. 6. 1946.

[97] The only absent member was Mother Antoinette Cuff, who was a patient at St. John's Hospital.

Book of Observances and Customs also received deliberation.[98]

On July 27, 1947, the eve of her eighty-sixth birthday, Mother Antoinette Cuff was called to her eternal reward. Her death saddened her many friends among the clergy and laity. Upon hearing of her death, Bishop Thill remarked: "It is rather an extraordinary thing for a religious to live to celebrate the sixty-seventh anniversary of her profession in religion. It is not given to all men and to all women to live out a full life in so glorious a measure as has been given to Mother Antoinette. But then most of us are not called as she was to the pioneering work of helping to establish the Church in a new country; the pioneering work of establishing a religious community of Sisters; the pioneering work of building so magnificently as she has built. She was a religious who was able to command because she knew how to obey, a religious who always loved the Church."[99]

An editorial, dedicated to Mother Antoinette, written by the non-Catholic editor of the *Salina Journal,* was entitled "A Woman Builder":

That women are not to be discounted when the making of a country is at stake is demonstrated by the life of Mother M. Antoinette Cuff, who left this week for her heavenly home after eighty-six years of successful living. Born in Ireland, and without money, or friends, or position, she so impressed those with whom she came in contact that she was able to do things that bordered on the miraculous.

Without her, Marymount College would not have been born, at least not in Salina. Working with the late Senator Fred H. Quincy, we helped negotiate an option on the land on which Marymount stands, then owned by D. A. VanTrine. Because he was a devoted son of Salina, Mr. VanTrine put a reasonable price on land he did not want to sell.

It was about this time of year, and with Senator Quincy we scoured the business district most of a hot summer, taking pledges that would guarantee that the land could be purchased. When that was accomplished, we asked for and obtained an audience with Mother Antoinette, then living at Concordia. When the land was offered to her if she would locate Marymount in Salina, she looked over the subscriptions, and remarked:

"Salina really wants the school, doesn't she?"

When assured that the offer of a free site was the most tangible way Salina boosters could find to express their desire, a slow smile spread over her face, and with a twinkle she countered:

[98] Digest of Minutes for the General Chapter, June 13-17, 1947.
Northwestern Kansas Register, June 22, 1947.
[99] *Ibid.,* Aug. 3, 10, 1947.
Sister Evangeline Thomas, "A Woman Builder," *Marymount College Bulletin,* vol. XXIV, No. 3 (Oct., 1947), pp. 1-10.

"Well, money talks, especially when you are undertaking such an ambitious project as we have in mind. I can make no promises, but your proposal will be presented to our superiors and associates, and we may take you up. Many places have extended most gracious invitations to us, but Salina is the first to lay money on the barrel head. And I guess I'm Irish enough to appreciate the sentiment which prompts you to make an offer, and practical enough to realize that if you want us enough that citizens of all faiths will unite to provide a site, this must be the place for us to locate."

Later the site was accepted and Marymount was started. What happened is history; for the dream of Mother Antoinette was fulfilled almost from the beginning.

While this was but one of her achievements, it was one out of which she probably derived the greatest satisfaction. It was important to Salina, too, but the greatest value of the incident is the tangible proof that any individual— man or woman—given faith, energy, common sense, and dogged determination, can erect a monument more lasting than granite, and more valuable than rubies, or pearls, or gold. That Mother Antoinette did.[100]

The memory of Mother Antoinette Cuff will remain. Her monuments in granite and stone outlive her, but greatest of all, her example will serve as a beacon light to those with whom she labored in this life.

In August, 1947, the Sisters of Saint Joseph of Concordia opened a district consolidated school in the parish of Seguin, Kansas. Three district schools had been amalgamated to create the new school. Sisters Rose Gertrude Adams, Pius Bechard, and Mary Edwardine Flavim constituted the personnel of the school. The Reverend Michael Mulvihill, pastor of Seguin, was instrumental in securing the Sisters for the school.[101]

The most recent project undertaken by the Community is an expansion program for Marymount College, Salina. A second major building, costing over a half million dollars, will include a suitable auditorium for college and civic events, a fine arts wing, and a residence wing to accommodate approximately eighty additional resident students.[102]

Under the direction of Sister Etta Louise Knaup, superior of Marymount, a group of Salina business and professional leaders formed a civic committee to sponsor a drive to raise $150,000. In

100 *Salina Journal*, July 31, 1947.
101 *Northwestern Kansas Register*, Aug. 17, 24, 31, 1947.
102 *Salina Journal*, Jan. 19, 1948.
   Salina Advertiser-Sun, Jan. 22, 1948.
   Northwestern Kansas Register, Jan. 25, 1948.

charge of the campaign is an executive committee headed by W. H. Montgomery and including in its personnel Roy F. Bailey, Dan Bolen, Glenn Bramwell, C. E. Brock, Hugh Carlin, Jr., J. R. Epp, J. R. Geis, M. J. Kennedy, Richard King, R. J. Laubengayer, Dr. L. S. Nelson, Chester Peterson, Elmer Reed, Frank Roesner, R. W. Samuelson, T. W. Sanderson, Dr. Leo Schaefer, Albert Schwartz, Norb Skelley, A. W. Stedhan, John J. Vanier, and G. N. Waddell.

Mr. Don Sedgwick was chosen campaign chairman for the drive scheduled for May, 1948.[103] The same spirit, manifested a quarter of a century earlier when the Sisters of Saint Joseph built Marymount College, is evident in this promising and concerted campaign to enable the Community to enlarge the facilities of the college.

The cosmopolitan aspect of the Congregation has existed from its beginnings in Kansas when subjects of every nationality and from various parts of the United States were received. Through their common experiences on the frontier, their common rule, their Community tradition and spirit, they became an amalgamated group. This group early launched out on various national frontiers to work among the Germans, the French, the Irish, the Bohemians, the Russian-Germans, the Scandinavians, the Indians, and later among the Spanish-Americans in the Southwest. Invitations have recently come to the Community to open missions among the colored and to undertake foreign missionary work. These latter projects are still in embryo. Marymount College has pioneered among Catholic colleges in opening its doors to all races and creeds with members of the three races of the human family enrolled in the same classes.

The Sisters of Saint Joseph of Concordia have been active in the Religious Vacation School movement in the Dioceses of Salina, El Paso, Lincoln, Grand Island, Kansas City-in-Kansas, and Kansas City-in-Missouri.

The Diocese of Salina (formerly, of Concordia) made notable progress in this important phase of Catholic education. The work started in 1921, when Bishop Tief, Monsignor Luckey, and Father Edwin V. O'Hara[104] outlined plans for schools in the diocese. Father John G. Wolf was made diocesan director, and in 1927 the first schools were started in Greenleaf and Kimeo with an enrollment

[103] *Salina Journal*, Mar. 1, 1948.
[104] *Northwestern Kansas Register*, June 2, 1940.

of one hundred and five students. These schools were taught by four students from Marymount College, Salina. From this humble beginning, the splendid organization of Religious Vacation Schools in the diocese has emerged.[105]

Twenty years after the beginning of the Religious Vacation School movement, statistics show that approximately 45,000 children have come under the guiding influence of these schools.[106] This system together with the parochial school system enable over ninety percent of the Catholic children of the diocese to receive religious instruction.

The inspiration given by bishops of the diocese, by the diocesan directors, Father John G. Wolf and Father Emil Duchene, and by the pastors, lends encouragement to the work of the Sisters.

The work of the Sisters of Saint Joseph of Concordia is concentrated largely in rural sections of the United States. In an age when there is a steady shift of population from the rural areas to the more alluring life of the city, it is befitting to evaluate the contributions of rural life to the welfare of the nation and to its future stability. With this idea in mind, a Rural Life Institute was held at the Motherhouse in Concordia presided over by Monsignor Luigi G. Ligutti, executive secretary of the National Rural Life Conference, who explained the fundamental philosophy of rural life.

Since the object of the conference was to strengthen and develop Catholicity in the rural districts, and to promote the general welfare of the rural population, all phases of rural life were stressed. Two hundred Sisters attended the Institute.[107]

Annual educational conferences for members of the Community have been held each year for the past quarter-century. Outstanding speakers have appeared on these programs, and sectional meetings for the various interest groups have been conducted at each meeting.

In a Community which is working in several states of the Union, it is necessary to qualify the Sisters to teach in the various states and to meet other educational requirements. Marymount College

[105] Records of Religious Vacation Schools in the Diocese of Concordia, in the Archives of the Nazareth Motherhouse, Concordia, Kans.

Loc. cit.

[106] Northwestern Kansas Register, June 2, 1940; Nov. 20, 1938.

[107] Northwestern Kansas Register, June 11, 1944. The following day Monsignor Ligutti addressed the priests of the diocese on the same subject.

has assisted in this preparation of the Sisters during its summer sessions, and advanced degrees have been earned at most of the outstanding universities of the land.[108] Progress has been made in keeping abreast of the times in educational procedure and pedagogy.

And now at the end of almost three centuries since the first Sisters of Saint Joseph were invested with the habit of the Sisterhood in France, the Sisters of Saint Joseph of Concordia continue the noble work outlined for those first daughters. During sixty-five years they have worked on the frontiers of the Midwest from their Motherhouse in Concordia. They have met challenges and have conquered them. The frontier has vanished in these parts, but there will always be frontiers for noble souls to conquer. Wherever there is a challenge, there is a call to service.

It is fitting to close this book with the same challenge which was given to the original daughters of Saint Joseph in Le Puy, France, in 1650, when Bishop Henry de Maupas said: "Carry it [the profession cross] down the ways of pain into the homes of fever, into the warrens of the poor, and to far-off lands. Let it be your oriflame to light you on to victory, and, when in death you resign it, let other hands and hearts like yours in consecration take up the burden, preserving it in their and your society's keeping through the onrolling centuries."

---

[108] About 152 hold the degree of Bachelor of Arts, 49 that of Master of Arts, and 11 that of Doctor of Philosophy.

APPENDIXES

Archdioceses and Dioceses in the United States in Which the Sisters of Saint Joseph From the Various Motherhouses Labor*

Motherhouse	Archdiocese	Diocese
Augusta		Savannah - Atlanta
(Carondolet)		Altoona
Baden		Pittsburgh
		Hunan, China
Boston	Boston	
Brentwood		Brooklyn
		San Juan, Puerto Rico
		Ponce, Puerto Rico
Buffalo		Buffalo
Carondolet	Chicago	Green Bay
	Denver	Kansas City
	Indianapolis	Marquette
	Saint Louis	Mobile
		Oklahoma City - Tulsa
		Peoria
		Saint Joseph
		Honolulu, T. H.
Chestnut Hill	Baltimore	Camden
	Newark	Harrisburg
	Philadelphia	Raleigh
	Washington	Trenton
		Wilmington
Cleveland	Los Angeles	Cleveland
		Youngstown
Concordia	Chicago	El Paso
		Grand Island
		Kansas City
		Kansas City - in - Kansas
		Lincoln
		Marquette
		Rockford
		Salina
Crookston	Saint Paul	Crookston
	Saint Boniface	Fargo
	(Canada)	Superior
Erie		Erie

* Information supplied by various motherhouses early in 1948.

358

Motherhouse	Archdiocese	Diocese
Fall River		Fall River
Hartford	Baltimore	Hartford
		Springfield
La Grange	Chicago	
Los Angeles	Los Angeles	Boise
(Carondolet)	San Francisco	Gallup
		Monterey - Fresno
		San Diego
		Spokane
		Tucson
Nazareth	Detroit	Grand Rapids
		Lansing
		Saginaw
New Orleans	Cincinnati	Natchez
	New Orleans	
Orange	Los Angeles	Sacramento
	San Francisco	San Diego
	Amarillo	Honolulu, T. H.
		Vicariate N. Solomon
		Islands, T. N. G.
Rochester		Mobile
		Rochester
		Syracuse
Rutland		Burlington
Saint Augustine	Baltimore	Saint Augustine
Saint Paul	Saint Paul	Fargo
(Carondolet)		
South Berwick		Portland - in - Maine
Springfield		Springfield
Superior		Superior
Tipton		Baker City
		Fort Wayne
		Lafayette - in - Indiana
Troy		Albany
(Carondolet)		Syracuse
Watertown		Ogdensburg
Wheeling		Wheeling
Wichita		Kansas City - in - Kansas
		Oklahoma City - Tulsa
		Pueblo
		Wichita

Sisters of Saint Joseph in the United States: Date of Establishment, Parent Foundation, Diocese, Number in Community, and Status

Date	Motherhouse	Archdiocese or Diocese	Parent	Number	Status
1836	Carondolet	Saint Louis	Lyons, France	1,161	Pontifical 1877
1847	Chestnut Hill	Philadelphia	Carondolet	1,988	Pontifical 1895
1851	Saint Paul	Saint Paul	Carondolet	1,086	Pontifical 1877 Prov. Carondolet
1853	Wheeling	Wheeling	Carondolet	215	Diocesan
1854	Canandaigua (Buffalo)	Buffalo	Carondolet	430	Diocesan
1855	New Orleans	New Orleans	Bourg, France	192	Pontifical 1919 Prov. Bourg
1856	Brentwood	Brooklyn	Chestnut Hill	1,424	Diocesan
1858	Troy	Albany	Carondolet	821	Pontifical 1877 Prov. Carondolet
1860	Erie	Erie	Carondolet	348	Diocesan
1866	Saint Augustine	Saint Augustine	Le Puy, France	173	Diocesan
1867	Rochester	Rochester	Buffalo	802	Diocesan
1867	Augusta (adopted by Carondolet, 1922)	Savannah	Saint Augustine	82	Pontifical 1877 Prov. Carondolet
1869	Baden	Pittsburgh	Brentwood	502	Diocesan
1872	Cleveland	Cleveland	Saint Paul	322	Diocesan
1873	Rutland	Burlington	Brentwood	130	Diocesan
1873	Boston	Boston	Brentwood	1,581	Diocesan
1878	Los Angeles	Los Angeles	Carondolet	539	Pontifical 1877 Prov. Carondolet
1880	Watertown	Ogdensburg	Buffalo	115	Diocesan
1880	Springfield	Springfield	Brentwood	621	Diocesan
1883	Concordia	Salina	Rochester	553	Pontifical 1941
1885	Hartford	Hartford	Chambery, France	389	Pontifical 1875 Prov. Chambery
1888	Wichita	Wichita	Concordia	404	Diocesan
1888	Tipton	Lafayette-in-Indiana	Watertown	147	Diocesan
1889	Nazareth	Lansing	Watertown	628	Pontifical 1928
1899	La Grange	Chicago	Concordia	217	Diocesan
1902	Fall River	Fall River	LePuy, France	116	Pontifical 1902 Prov. Le Puy
1905	Crookston	Crookston	Bourg, France	99	Pontifical 1922 Prov. Bourg
1906	South Berwick	Portland	Lyons, France	38	Pontifical 1909 Prov. Lyons
1907	Superior	Superior	Crookston	45	Diocesan
1912	Orange	Sacramento	La Grange	326	Pontifical 1939

Sisters of Saint Joseph in the United States:
Parent Foundations and Geneological Connections

Bourg	New Orleans*
	Crookston*
Brentwood . . .	Rutland
	Boston
	Springfield
	Baden
	(Ebensburg)
Buffalo	Rochester
	Watertown
Canandaigua . .	Buffalo
	Rochester
Carondolet . . .	Philadelphia
	Wheeling
	Canandaigua
	(Buffalo and
	Rochester)
	Erie
	Cleveland
adopted . . .	Augusta
	Lewiston
Chambery . . .	Hartford*
Chestnut Hill . .	Brentwood
	Toronto, Canada
Concordia . . .	Wichita
	La Grange
adopted . . .	Silver City
LaGrange . . .	Orange
LePuy	St. Augustine
	Fall River
Lyons	Carondolet
	South Berwick*
Rochester	Concordia
Saint Augustine .	Savannah (adopted by Carondolet
	as Augusta)
Tipton	Silver City (adopted by Concordia)
	Lewiston (adopted by Carondolet)
Watertown . . .	Tipton
	Nazareth

* Starred motherhouses still maintain affiliation with European motherhouses.

Colleges Conducted by the Sisters of Saint Joseph: Date of Establishment, Place, Enrollment

Date	Name of College	Place	Motherhouse	Enrollment
1913	College of Saint Catherine	Saint Paul, Minnesota	Saint Paul	806
1916	St. Joseph's College for Women	Brooklyn, New York	Brentwood	520
1920	College of Saint Rose	Albany, New York	Troy	967
1922	Marymount College	Salina, Kansas	Concordia	501
1923	Fontbonne College	Saint, Louis, Missouri	Carondolet	537
1924	Chestnut Hill College	Philadelphia, Pennsylvania	Chestnut Hill	488
1924	Nazareth College	Nazareth, Michigan	Nazareth	273
1924	Nazareth College	Rochester, New York	Rochester	450
1925	Mount Saint Mary's College	Los Angeles, California	Los Angeles	465
1925	Villa Marie College	Erie, Pennsylvania	Erie	300
1927	Regis College	Weston, Massachusetts	Boston	624
1928	Our Lady of the Elms	Chicopee, Massachusetts	Springfield	243
1938	Mount Saint Joseph's Teachers College (Exclusively for Sisters)	Buffalo, New York	Buffalo	250
1941	College of Saint Teresa	Kansas City, Missouri	Carondolet	250
			Total	6,674

Communities of the Sisters of Saint Joseph in the United States: Statistical Data

Motherhouse	Number	C	HS	GS	H	NTS	O	HFA	S	FM
Baden	502	–	10	32	1	1	1	–	–	1
Boston	1,581	1	21	61	–	–	–	3	–	–
Brentwood . . .	1,424	1	10	58	2	1	–	–	–	3
Buffalo	430	1	3	35	1	1	3	1	–	–
Carondolet . . .										
St. Louis . . .	1,161	2	16	82	2	2	2	–	–	1
St. Paul . . .	1,086	1	10	46	5	2	3	–	–	–
Troy	821	1	22	44	2	2	2	–	–	–
Augusta . . .	82	–	2	7	–	–	1	–	–	–
Los Angeles . .	539	1	9	31	3	2	1	–	1	1
Chestnut Hill . .	1,988	1	27	113	–	–	4	1	–	–
Cleveland . . .	322	–	2	19	–	–	–	–	–	–
Concordia . . .	553	1	17	36	6	4	1	1	1	–
Crookston . . .	99	–	1	9	1	–	–	–	–	2
Erie	348	1	5	20	2	2	2	1	–	–
Fall River . . .	116	–	–	8	–	–	–	–	–	–
Hartford	389	–	2	17	3	2	1	–	–	–
LaGrange . . .	217	–	2	16	–	–	–	–	–	–
Nazareth . . .	628	1	13	30	4	1	1	–	–	–
New Orleans . .	192	–	5	13	–	–	1	–	–	–
Orange	326	–	2	16	7	1	–	–	–	3
Rochester . . .	802	1	5	51	2	1	1	1	1	1
Rutland . . .	130	–	3	9	–	–	1	–	–	–
Saint Augustine . .	173	–	9	16	–	–	2	–	–	–
South Berwick . .	38	–	2	4	1	1	–	1	–	–
Springfield . . .	621	1	14	32	–	–	–	–	–	–
Superior	45	–	–	2	1	–	–	–	–	–
Tipton	147	–	3	13	3	1	–	–	–	–
Watertown . . .	115	–	6	7	–	–	1	–	–	–
Wheeling . . .	215	–	6	19	4	4	2	–	–	–
Wichita	404	–	5	29	11	7	1	–	–	–
TOTAL . .	15,494	14	232	875	61	35	30	10	3	12

Key:	C	colleges
	HS	high schools
	GS	grade schools
	H	hospitals
	NTS	nurses training schools
	O	orphanages
	HFA	homes for aged
	S	sanatoriums
	FM	foreign missions

Missions Conducted by the Sisters of Saint Joseph of Concordia, 1883-1948

Mission	Diocese	Date of opening	Date if closed
Newton, Kansas	Leavenworth (Wichita)	1883	1896
Concordia, Kansas	Leavenworth (Salina)	1884	
Nazareth Academy,		1884	1922[1]
Concordia, Kansas	Leavenworth (Salina)		1942[2]
Saint Joseph, Kansas	Leavenworth (Salina)	1885	1925
Abilene, Kansas	Leavenworth (Salina)	1887	1888[3]
Clyde, Kansas	Concordia (Salina)	1889	
Beloit, Kansas	Concordia (Salina)	1889	
Saint George, Illinois	Chicago, Illinois	1889	
Zurich, Kansas	Concordia (Salina)	1889	1890
Tipton, Kansas	Concordia (Salina)	1889	
Danville, Kansas	Wichita	1890	1894
Chicago, Illinois (St. Joseph and Saint Anne Parish)	Chicago	1891	
Somerset, Wisconsin	La Crosse	1891	1903
Escanaba, Michigan	Marquette	1891	1922
North Platte, Nebraska	Omaha	1891	1902
St. Stephens, Wyoming	Cheyenne	1891	1892
Herndon, Kansas	Concordia (Salina)	1891	
New Richmond, Wisconsin	Winona	1892	1895
Grand Island, Nebraska	Grand Island	1893	
Saint Marks, Kansas	Wichita	1893	1897
Petersburg, Nebraska	Omaha	1893	1907
Hammond, Wisconsin	Superior	1893	1894
Monett, Missouri	Kansas City	1895	
Paris, Texas	Dallas	1895	1896
Gainesville, Texas	Dallas	1896	1897
Clay Center, Kansas	Concordia (Salina)	1896	1902
Norway, Michigan	Marquette	1896	1900
Lake Linden, Michigan	Marquette	1896	
Saint Libory, Nebraska	Omaha	1896	1898
Olyen, Nebraska	Omaha	1898	1899
L'Erable, Illinois	Chicago	1898	1901
Chicago, Illinois (Saint John Baptist)	Chicago	1899	1900

[1] Moved to Salina.
[2] Discontinued in 1942.
[3] Became Motherhouse of Wichita Community.

Mission	Diocese	Date of opening	Date if closed
Salina, Kansas			
(Sacred Heart School)	Concordia (Salina)	1900	
Concordia, Kansas			
(Nazareth Motherhouse)	Concordia (Salina)	1902	
Laramie, Wyoming	Cheyenne	1902	1903
Parkston, South Dakota	Sioux Falls	1902	1905
Concordia, Kansas			
(St. Joseph's Hospital)	Concordia (Salina)	1903	
Belvidere, Illinois			
(St. Joseph's Hospital)	Rockford	1904	
Aurora, Illinois	Rockford	1904	
Angelus, Kansas	Concordia (Salina)	1904	1912
Schoenchen, Kansas	Concordia (Salina)	1904	
Pfeifer, Kansas	Concordia (Salina)	1904	
Saint Peter, Kansas	Concordia (Salina)	1904	
Aurora, Kansas	Concordia (Salina)	1905	
Damar, Kansas	Concordia (Salina)	1905	
Gorham, Kansas	Concordia (Salina)	1905	
Junction City, Kansas	Concordia (Salina)	1906	
Walker, Kansas	Concordia (Salina)	1908	1923
Manhattan, Kansas			
(Sacred Heart Academy)	Concordia (Salina)	1908	
Rulo, Nebraska	Lincoln	1909	1910
Park, Kansas	Concordia (Salina)	1910	
Antonino, Kansas	Concordia (Salina)	1909	
Leoville, Kansas	Concordia (Salina)	1910	
Vincent, Kansas	Concordia (Salina)	1911	
Plainville, Kansas	Concordia (Salina)	1911	
Nevada, Missouri	Kansas City	1911	1917
Emmeram, Kansas	Concordia (Salina)	1912	1916
Clinton, Missouri	Kansas City	1912	1925
Gladstone, Michigan	Marquette	1912	
California, Missouri	Kansas City	1913	1917
Salina, Kansas			
(Saint John's Hospital)	Concordia (Salina)	1914	
Cawker City, Kansas	Concordia (Salina)	1915	
Abilene, Kansas			
(Saint Joseph's Home)	Concordia (Salina)	1915	
Sabetha, Kansas			
(Saint Anthony Murdock			
Memorial Hospital)	Leavenworth	1920	
Salina, Kansas			
(Marymount College)	Concordia (Salina)	1922	
New Almelo, Kansas	Concordia (Salina)	1922	
Boonville, Missouri	Kansas City	1923	
Concordia, Kansas			
(Home of the Little			
Flower)	Concordia (Salina)	1924	

Mission	Diocese	Date of opening	Date if closed
Silver City, New Mexico	El Paso	1926	
Collyer, Kansas	Concordia (Salina)	1926	
Herington, Kansas	Concordia (Salina)	1926	
El Paso, Texas (St. Joseph's Sanatorium)	El Paso	1927	
Abilene, Kansas (Villa Maria)	Concordia (Salina)	1927	
Manhattan, Kansas (The Saint Mary Hospital)	Concordia (Salina)	1936	
Fairbury, Nebraska	Lincoln	1939	
Seneca, Kansas	Leavenworth (Kansas City - in - Kansas)	1943	
Silver City, New Mexico (St. Vincent de Paul School)	El Paso	1944	
Concordia, Kansas (Concordia Catholic High School)	Concordia (Salina)	1944	
Concordia, Kansas (Fontbonne Hall)	Salina	1945	
Manhattan, Kansas (The Saint Mary-Parkview Annex)	Salina	1946	
Seguin, Kansas	Salina	1947	

BIBLIOGRAPHY

Bibliography

PART I. PRIMARY SOURCES

A. PRIMARY SOURCES BY LOCATION

Most of the material used in the writing of this history has been gathered from firsthand sources in scattered places. In brief it will be classified according to archival centers:

CONCORDIA, KANSAS — NAZARETH MOTHERHOUSE ARCHIVES

Correspondence of Bishops Fink, Scannell, Cunningham, Tief, Thill, Bona, Duffy, Johannes, Kucera, Lillis, O'Hara, Magner, Metzger, Hennessy, Nussbaum, Schuler, Winkelman; of Cardinals Mundelein, Stritch, Fumasoni-Biondi, and Cicognani; of the Sacred Congregation of Religious; of the Mothers General of the Congregation — Mothers Stanislaus Leary, Antoinette Cuff, Mary Rose Waller, Mary Chrysostom Wynn; of pastors of various missions negotiating for new missions.

Corporation charters; deeds; contracts; propositions; minutes of the corporation; minutes of the Councillors; minutes of the General Chapters of the Congregation; reception and profession books; incorporation papers for adoption of the Silver City, New Mexico, Community of the Sisters of Saint Joseph; by-laws of the corporation; Constitutions of the Sisters of Saint Joseph of Concordia in Latin and English versions; legal statement, 1885: ordinances; correspondence concerning Papal Approbation — Normae; petition for approbation; quinquennial reports; Relatio; Decree of Praise; Papal Approbation; decree of Sacred Congregation of Religious n. 4734/36, approving a third term upon postulation of the Congregation for same; diaries of Reverend Mother Stanislaus Leary; autobiographical sketch of Mother Stanislaus and day book; diaries of Reverend Joseph Conway, Mother Antoinette Cuff, and Mother Alexine Gosselin of the La Grange Community.

SALINA, KANSAS — DIOCESAN ARCHIVES OF SALINA OF KANSAS CITY-IN-KANSAS

Apostolic briefs concerning establishment of the Diocese; parish history material.

KANSAS CITY, KANSAS — DIOCESAN ARCHIVES OF KANSAS CITY-IN-KANSAS

Solemn Contract and Agreement between the Sisters of Saint Joseph, Newton, Kansas, and the Most Reverend Louis M. Fink, Bishop of Leavenworth, 1885; rare book on immigration written by the Reverend Felix Swemberg of Newton, Kansas.

YONKERS, NEW YORK — ARCHDIOCESAN ARCHIVES OF NEW YORK

McQuaid correspondence; some Fink letters concerning conditions in Kansas.

ROCHESTER, NEW YORK — NAZARETH MOTHERHOUSE ARCHIVES

Annals — a manuscript account of the administrations of the four Mothers General of the Community. Volume I was dedicated to Mother Stanislaus Leary and was of inestimable value in evaluating her activities in the Rochester Community before establishing the Sisters of Saint Joseph of Concordia; manuscript account of the Sisters of Saint Joseph of Rochester by Sister Teresina of that Community.

LA GRANGE, ILLINOIS — NAZARETH MOTHERHOUSE ARCHIVES

Two diaries of Mother Stanislaus Leary; notes on the Newton and Concordia foundations; tuition receipts; welcome address and silver jubilee account in manuscript; letters pasted in these diaries furnished splendid material for this book — letters from Bishops Salpointe and Fink; first negotiations for the Kansas foundation; letters from

Mother Katherine Drexel, negotiating for Indian mission in Wyoming, and with Fathers Ketcham and Panken regarding same; letters from Father Perrier of Concordia which were responsible for the location of the Motherhouse in that city.

ATCHISON, KANSAS — KANSAS CATHOLIC HISTORICAL ARCHIVES

Letters from and to Kansas governors Crawford and Glick; from immigration authorities such as Connolly, Fitzgerald, Onahan, and Father Swemberg; from Bishops Fink, Cunningham, and Ireland; correspondence from the Society for the Propagation of the Faith; from and to the Sisters of Saint Joseph in Newton and Concordia.

TOPEKA, KANSAS — KANSAS HISTORICAL LIBRARY

Packets of letters which had background bearing on this present work; scrapbook accounts of Catholic beginnings in Kansas, especially in Ellis County; extensive newspaper collections, most important of which is a complete file of the *Kansas Catholic* (for a time called the *Monthly Visitor*) covering the early period of the Sisters of Saint Joseph in Kansas.

B. PASTORAL LETTERS

Lettre Pastorale de Mgr. L'Évêque de St. Louis (Joseph Rosati), St. Louis, 1839.
Pastoral Letters of the Archbishop and the Bishops of the Province of New York, 1861.
Pastoral Letter of the Cardinal Archbishop and the Bishops of the Province of New York Assembled in Council, September 23-30, 1883.
Pastoral Letter of the Right Reverend Bishop of Rochester (Bernard J. McQuaid), Rochester, 1878.
Pastoral Letter of the Right Reverend John Joseph Hennessy, Bishop of Wichita and Administrator of Concordia, to the Clergy and Laity of These Dioceses, 1893.
Pastoral Letter of the Most Reverend Louis M. Fink, Bishop of Leavenworth, January 29, 1883.

C. INTERVIEWS

Anderson, Phil M. (Newton, Kansas), one of the original band of students taught by the Sisters of Saint Joseph in Newton in 1883.

Cuff, Mother Antoinette (Salina, Kansas), a member of the pioneer band of Sisters of Saint Joseph who came to Kansas in 1883 and settled in Newton.

Gosselin, Mother Alexine (La Grange, Illinois), one of the pioneer Sisters of Saint Joseph of Concordia, who later founded the La Grange Community and who was present at the death of Mother Stanislaus Leary.

Maher, Right Reverend John, Vicar General of the Diocese of Concordia, largely responsible for the location of two of the institutions of the Sisters of Saint Joseph in Salina, Kansas.

D. SERMONS

The Most Reverend Frank A. Thill, Bishop of Salina, on the occasion of the dedication of the scientific research unit of the Institutum Divi Thomae at Marymount College, Salina, Kansas, April 16, 1940.

The Most Reverend Frank A. Thill, Bishop of Salina, on the occasion of the diamond jubilee of Mother Antoinette Cuff, Marymount College, Salina, Kansas, June 18, 1940.

The Most Reverend Frank A. Thill, Bishop of Salina, at the funeral of Mother Mary Rose Waller, Nazareth Motherhouse, Concordia, Kansas, March 24, 1941.

E. QUESTIONNAIRES

The author prepared detailed questionnaires which were sent to the six hundred living members of her Community. These questionnaires and replies are in the files of the author.

F. NEWSPAPERS

Abilene (Kans.) *Reflector*
American Celt
Belvidere (Ill.) *Daily Republican*
Belvidere (Ill.) *Times*
Boston (Mass.) *Pilot*
Brooklyn (N. Y.) *Tablet*
Catholic Courier (Rochester, N. Y.)
Catholic Daily Tribune (Dubuque, Ia.)
Catholic Review (Baltimore, Md.)
Denver (Colo.) *Catholic Register*
Cincinnati (Ohio) *Times-Star*
Concordia (Kans.) *Blade*
Concordia (Kans.) *Blade-Empire*
Concordia (Kans.) *Empire*
Concordia (Kans.) *Kansas*
Concordia (Kans.) *Kansan*
Daily Courier (Buffalo, N. Y.)
Detroit (Mich.) *Free Press*
Eastern Kansas Register
El Paso (Tex.) *Times*
Ellis County (Kans.) *News*
Fairbury (Nebr.) *News*
Falls City (Nebr.) *Journal*
Grand Island (Nebr.) *Independent*
Hiawatha (Kans.) *World*
Holstein Friesian World
Home Missionary (New York), 1829-
    1909
Kansas Catholic, 1880-1890 (also known
    as *Monthly Visitor*)
Kansas City (Mo.) *Journal*
Kansas City (Mo.) *Catholic Register*
Kansas City (Mo.) *Star*
Kansas City (Mo.) *Times*
Kansas Knight
Manhattan (Kans.) *Chronicle*
Manhattan (Kans.) *Mercury*
Monett (Mo.) *Times*
Monthly Visitor (also known as *Kansas
    Catholic*)
Nashville (Tenn.) *Daily American*
Newton (Kans.) *Democrat*
Newton (Kans.) *Kansan*
New York (N. Y.) *Evening Mail*
New York (N. Y.) *Times*

Catholic Telegraph (Cincinnati, Ohio)
Catholic Times (Rochester, N. Y.)
Catholic Transcript (Hartford, Conn.)
Cayuga (N. Y.) *Republican*
Chicago (Ill.) *Tribune*
Cincinnati (Ohio) *Enquirer*
Cincinnati (Ohio) *Journal*
Cincinnati (Ohio) *Post*
Cincinnati (Ohio) *Telegraph-Register*
New York (N. Y.) *Weekly Register
    and Catholic Diary*
New World (Chicago, Ill.)
North Platte (Nebr.) *News*
Northwestern Chronicle (St. Paul,
    Minn.)
Northwestern Kansas Register
Oberlin (Kans.) *Herald*
Omaha (Nebr.) *Bee*
Omaha (Neb.) *World-Herald*
L'Osservatore Romano (Rome, Italy)
Presbyterian of the West
Rochester (N. Y.) *Courier*
Rochester (N. Y.) *Daily Advertiser*
Rochester (N. Y.) *Observer*
Rochester (N. Y.) *Republican*
Rochester. (N. Y.) *West End Journal*
    or *Orphan's Advocate*
Rochester (N. Y.) *Union and Adver-
    tiser*
Sabetha (Kans.) *Herald*
St. Louis (Mo.) *Catholic News*
Salina (Kans.) *Advertiser-Sun*
Salina (Kans.) *Daily Union*
Salina (Kans.) *Journal*
Seneca (Kans.) *Courier-Tribune*
Topeka (Kans.) *State Journal*
Truth Teller
United States Catholic Press
Western American (El Paso, Tex.)
Western Kansas World ..
Wichita (Kans.) *Catholic Advance*
Wichita (Kans.) *Catholic Advance-
    Register*
Wichita (Kans.) *Eagle*

PART II. SECONDARY SOURCES

A. BOOKS, PAMPHLETS, ETC.

Acta et Dicta: *Third Plenary Council, 1884*, Baltimore, 1884.
Adamson, Archibald R., *North Platte and Its Associations*, Lincoln, 1910.
Allison, John M. S., *Church and State in the Reign of Louis Philippe, 1830-1848*, tr. by
    Pablish and Byrne, Princeton, 1916.
Alzog, John B., *History of the Church*, 3 vols., New York, 1912.
American Catholic Historical Society, *Records*.
Anderson, Charles P., *Centennial of Illinois Statehood*, Springfield, 1918.
Andrews and Page, eds., *Picturesque Salina*, Salina, Kans., 1887.

Annales de la Propagation de la Foi, 1827-1899, Paris, 1899.
Atchison, Topeka and Santa Fe Railroad, *New Mexico Health Resorts,* Topeka, 1899.
Bachofer, Charles A., *A Commentary on the New Code of Canon Law,* 4 vols., St. Louis and London, 1922.
Baldwin, Sara A., *Illustriana Kansas,* Hebron, Nebr., 1933.
Barbara, Sister M., *A Covenant With Stones,* Nazareth, Mich., 1939.
Bare, Ira L., and McDonald, William H., eds., *An Illustrated History of Lincoln County, Nebraska, and Her People,* 2 vols., Chicago, 1920.
Barreul, Abbe, *The History of the Clergy During the French Revolution,* Dublin, 1794.
Beard, Frances B., *Wyoming from Territorial Days to the Present,* 3 vols., Cheyenne, 1933.
Becker, Carl Lotus, *Everyman His Own Historian: Essays on History and Politics,* New York, 1935.
Beckman, Peter, *The Catholic Church on the Kansas Frontier, 1850-1877,* Washington, 1943.
Bedford, Henry, *Life of St. Vincent de Paul,* New York, 1888.
Beecher, Lyman, *Autobiography,* 2 vols., Cincinnati, 1864.
———, *A Plea for the West,* Cincinnati, 1835.
Berichte der Leopoldinen Stiftung, 1831-1861, Vienna, 1861.
Bibliographie Universelle (M. Michaud), 54 vols., Paris, 1851.
Biggane, Cecil, ed., *Memoirs of the Marquise de la Rochejaquelin,* London, 1933.
Billington, R. A., *The Protestant Crusade,* New York, 1938.
Biographical and Historical Record of Kane County, Illinois, Chicago, 1898.
Biographical History of Central Kansas, 2 vols., Chicago, 1902.
Biographical Record of Houghton, Baraga, and Marquette Counties (Michigan), Chicago, 1903.
Bird, John Sterling, *Prairies and Pioneers,* Hays, Kans., 1931.
Blackmar, Frank W., ed., *Kansas: Encyclopedia of State History . . . Institutions . . . Counties . . . Cities . . . Prominent Persons,* 3 vols., Chicago, 1912.
Boehm, Mary Adeline (Mrs. A. G.), *History of the New Richmond, Wisconsin, Cyclone,* St. Paul, 1900.
Bogart, Ernest L., and Mathews, John M., *The Modern Commonwealth, 1893-1918; Centennial History of Illinois,* 5 vols., Springfield, 1920.
Bollig, Richard J., *History of Catholic Education in Kansas, 1836-1932,* Washington, 1933.
Bond, B., *The Civilization of the Old Northwest,* New York, 1934.
Bouchage, Leon, *Chroniques des Soeurs de St. Joseph de Chambery,* Chambery, 1911.
Bougaud, Louis-Victor-Emile, *History of St. Vincent de Paul, Founder of the Congregation of the Mission and of the Sisters of Charity,* London, 1899.
———, tr., *St. Chantal and the Foundation of the Visitation Order,* New York, 1895.
Boulenger, Jacques, *The Seventeenth Century* (National History of France, No. 3), New York, 1920.
Broglie, Prince Emmanuel de, *St. Vincent de Paul,* tr. by M. Partridge, London, 1898.
Brouwer, Desclée de, et Cie, eds., *Mère St. Jean Fontbonne: Fondatrice de la Congregation de St. Joseph de Lyon—Restoratrice de l'Institut,* Paris and Bruges, 1929.
Brown, R. S., *Western Gazetteer and Emigrants' Guide,* Chicago, 1817.
Bryne, Stephen, *Irish Immigration to the U. S.,* New York, 1873.
Buechler, August F., and Barr, Robert J., *History of Hall County, Nebraska,* Lincoln, 1920.
Burch, Lawrence D., *Kansas as It Is,* Chicago, 1878.
Burkhart, Peter L., *History of Sacred Heart Church, Park, Kansas,* Park, Kans., 1938.
Burns, James A., *Growth and Development of the Catholic School System in the U. S.,* New York, 1912.
———, and Kohlbrenner, Bernard J., *History of Catholic Education in the U. S.,* New York, 1937.
Burroughs, Burt E., *Legends and Tales of Homeland on the Kankakee,* Chicago, 1923.
Burroughs, George W., *Concordia—In Kansas, of Course.* Concordia, 1909.
Calvin, Ross, *Sky Determines,* New York, 1934.
Capuchin Fathers, *Some Early History of the Pioneer Catholic Settlers and Parishes of Northwestern Kansas,* Herndon, Kans., 1913.
Castaneda, Carlos, *Our Catholic Heritage in Texas, 1519-1936,* 5 vols., Austin, 1936-1942.

Catholic Almanac, New York, 1834-1857.
Catholic Directory (Dunigan's, 1858; Sadlier's, 1864-1891; Hoffman's, 1891-1899; Wiltzius', 1902-1912; Metropolitan, 1838-1842, 1844, 1845, 1848-1857, 1859-1861; Kenedy's, 1912-), New York.
Catholic Encyclopedia, 14 vols., New York, 1907-1914.
Catholic Encyclopedic Dictionary, New York, 1929.
Chaddock, Robert, *Ohio Before 1850: A Study of the Early Influence of Pennsylvania and Southern Populations in Ohio,* New York, 1908.
Cheap Homes for Everybody in Northwestern Kansas—Rooks County, Stockton, Kans., 1887.
Chiniquy, Charles P. T., *The Priest, the Woman and the Confessional,* Chicago, 1880.
Clark, Carroll D., and Roberts, Roy L., *People of Kansas: A Demographic and Sociological Study,* Topeka, 1936.
Clarke, Caroline C., *Village Life in America, 1852-1872,* New York, 1913.
Clarke, Richard H., *Lives of the Deceased Bishops of the Catholic Church in the United States,* 4 vols., New York, 1888.
Coan, Charles F., *History of New Mexico,* 3 vols., New York, 1925.
Cobb, Irvin S., *Kansas: Shall We Civilize Her or Let Her Civilize Us?,* New York, 1924.
Code, Joseph B., *Dictionary of the American Hierarchy,* New York, 1940.
Collet, M., *Life of St. Vincent de Paul,* Baltimore, 1805.
A Commemoration of the Seventy-fifth Anniversary of the First Foundation of the Sisters of St. Joseph in the Diocese of Buffalo, Buffalo, 1931.
Commemorative Biographical and Historical Record of Kane County, Illinois, Springfield, 1888.
Commons, J. R., *Report of the Industrial Commission,* Washington, 1915.
Congregation des Soeurs de St. Joseph de Lyon, Lyons, 1918.
Connelly, William E., *History of Kansas,* 5 vols., New York, 1928.
Conway, Joseph J., *Memoirs of Rev. Joseph J. Conway of St. Joseph's Home,* Abilene, Kans. (mss).
Creusen, Joseph, *Religious Men and Women in the Code,* tr. by Adam Ellis, S.J., Milwaukee, 1940.
Currier, Charles W., *History of Religious Orders,* New York, 1898.
Cutler, William G., *History of Kansas* (often referred to as Andreas edition), Chicago, 1883.
Dawson, Charles, *Pioneer Tales of the Oregon Trail and of Jefferson County, Nebraska,* Topeka, 1912.
Dehey, Elinor Tong, *Religious Orders of Women in the U. S.,* Cleveland, 1930.
Deuther, Charles B., *The Life and Times of the Rt. Rev. John Timon, D.D.,* Buffalo, 1890.
Dictionary of American Biography, 21 vols., New York, 1933.
Dictionnaire Universel (Pierre Larousse), Paris, 1873.
Diocese of El Paso, Texas, Centennial Celebration, 1536-1936, El Paso, 1936.
Dunigan's Catholic Directory, see *Catholic Directory.*
Dunne, Edward F., *Illinois, the Heart of the Nation,* 5 vols., Chicago, 1933.
Dunne, Sister M. of the Sacred Heart, *The Congregation of St. Joseph of the Diocese of Buffalo, 1854-1933,* Buffalo, 1933.
Elliott, L. R., ed., *Blue Valley in Kansas—Marshall, Nemaha, Riley, and Washington Counties,* Manhattan, Kans., 1888.
Elliott, R. S., *Report on Industrial Resources,* Chicago, 1883.
Ely, Elisha, *Directory of the Village of Rochester,* Rochester, N. Y., 1828.
Encyclopedia Americana, 14th ed., New York, 1946.
Encyclopedia Britannica, 14th ed., London, 1939.
Encyclopedia Catholique, 18 vols., Paris, 1847.
Epley, Anna P., *A Modern Herculaneum,* New Richmond, Wis., 1900.
Erskine, Marjory, *Mother Philippine Duchesne,* New York, 1926.
Facts About Kansas, Missouri Pacific Railroad Co., 1903.
Fitzgerald, Sister Mary Paul, *Beacon on the Plains,* Leavenworth, 1939.
Fitzpatrick, Edward A., *Wisconsin,* Milwaukee, 1931.
Foley, Albert S., *St. Regis: A Social Crusader,* Milwaukee, 1941.
Fox, D. R., ed., *Sources of Culture in the Middle West,* New York, 1934.
Franckieu, A. D. de, *Les Martyrs de l'Église de Grenoble,* Lyons, 1890.

Ford, James E., *A History of Moniteau County, Missouri*, California, Mo., 1936.
Freri, Joseph, *Society for the Propagation of the Faith and the Catholic Missions*, New York, 1912.
Fuller, C. N., *Economic and Social Beginnings of Michigan*, Lansing, 1916.
Garin, J., *Notices Biographiques sur Mgr. J. B. Miege, Premier Vicaire Apostolique du Kansas et sur les Prêtres de la Paroisse de Chevron (Savoie)*, Moutiers, 1886.
Garraghan, Gilbert J., *Catholic Beginnings in Kansas City*, Chicago, 1920.
———, *The Jesuits in the Middle United States*, 3 vols., New York, 1938.
———, *St. Ferdinand de Florrissant*, Chicago, 1923.
Garrison, George P., *Westward Expansion, 1841-1850*, New York, 1906.
Geser, Fintan, *The Canon Law Governing Communities of Sisters*, St. Louis, 1938.
Giobbio, Adolpho, *La Chiesa e la State im Francia durante la Riviouzione, 1789-1799*, Rome, 1905.
Gleanings in Historic Fields, 1650-1925, Philadelphia, 1925.
Golden Jubilee of St. Joseph and St. Anne Church, Chicago, Illinois, 1889-1939, Chicago, 1939.
Golden Jubilee of the German-Russian Settlements of Ellis and Rush Counties, Kansas, Aug. 21-Sept. 2, 1926, Hays, Kans., 1926.
Granger, J. Albert, *A History of Early Canandaigua (N. Y.)*, Canandaigua, 1905.
———, *The History of Canandaigua*, centennial ed., Canandaigua, 1876.
Grant County, New Mexico, Bureau of Immigration, 1901.
Great Northwest! Most Successful Farming Region in Kansas—Clay Center, Clay Center, Kans., 1888.
Griffin, Albert, ed., *An Illustrated Sketch of Riley County, Kansas—The Blue Grass County*, Manhattan, Kans., 1881.
Guilday, Peter K., *A History of the Councils of Baltimore, 1791-1884*, New York, 1932.
Guilhermy, Eleseban, *Menologue de la Compagnie de Jésus*, 2 vols., Poitiers, 1867-1868.
Hacker, L. M., and Kendrick, B. B., *The United States Since 1865*, New York, 1940.
Hafen, Leroy, and Young, Francis M., *Fort Laramie and the Pageant of the West*, Glendale, Cal., 1938.
Hall, J., *The Catholic Question to Which Are Annexed Critical Notices of a Plea for the West*, Cincinnati, 1838.
Hamon, Marie Jean, *Vie de St. François de Sales*, 2 vols., Paris, 1883.
Hassard, John R. G., *Life of the Most Rev. John Hughes*, New York, 1866.
Hebard, Frank R., *Washakie: An Account of the Indian Resistance to the Covered Wagon and the Union Pacific Invasions of Their Territory*, Chicago, 1885.
Heimbucher, Max, *Die Orden und Congregationen der Katholischen Kirche*, 3 vols., Paderdorn, 1939.
Helyot, Pierre, *Dictionnaire des Ordres Religieux*, 6 vols., Paris, 1847-1859.
Henthorne, Sister Evangela, *The Irish Catholic Colonization Association of the U. S.*, Champaign, Ill., 1932.
Hickey, Edward J., *The Society for the Propagation of the Faith: Its Foundation, Organization and Success, 1882-1922*, Washington, 1922.
Historical and Descriptive Review of Kansas, 2 vols., Topeka, 1890.
History of Henry and St. Clair Counties, Missouri, St. Joseph, 1883.
History of Howard and Cooper Counties, Missouri, St. Louis, 1883.
History of Newton, Lawrence, Barry . . . Counties, Missouri, Chicago, 1888.
Ho! For the Land of Sunshine! Santa Fe, 1909.
Ho! For the New Kansas! The Best Thing in the West! Atchison, Topeka, and Santa Fe Railroad Co., Topeka, 1876.
Hoffman's Catholic Directory, see *Catholic Directory*.
Hofman, Konrad, *Lexicon für Theologie und Kirche*, 10 vols., Freiburg, 1933.
Hollibaugh, Mrs. E. F., *Biographical History of Cloud County, Kansas*, Concordia, Kans., 1903.
Houck, Louis, *History of Missouri*, 3 vols., Chicago, 1908.
Illinois: A Guide, Federal Writers Project, New York, 1939.
Illinois State Historical Society, *Publications*, No. 10 (1905).
Illustrated Sketch of Riley County, Kansas, the Blue Ribbon County, Topeka, 1893.
Introduction to a Survey of Missouri Place Names, Kansas City, 1934.
James, George P. R., *The Life and Times of Louis the Fourteenth*, 2 vols., London, 1890-1891.
Jenkins, Thomas J., *Christian Schools*, Baltimore, 1889.

———, *The Judges of Faith: Christian vs. Godless Schools*, Baltimore, 1886.
Johannes, Sister Eloise, *A Study of the Russian-German Settlements in Ellis County, Kansas*, Washington, 1946.
Joslyn, Rudolphus W., and Joslyn, Frank W., *History of Kane County, Illinois*, 2 vols., Chicago, 1908.
Kankakee County, Illinois, Chicago, 1893.
Kansas: A Complete and Comprehensive Description, 4th ed., Union Pacific Railroad, St. Louis, 1893.
Kansas: Description, St. Louis, 1893.
Kansas Facts, 3 vols., Topeka, 1929-1931.
Kansas Farmer and Mail Breeze Directory of Saline County, Kansas, Salina, Kans., 1894.
Kansas: Go to Ellis and Rush Counties! Southwestern Agriculture and Migration Co., York, Pa., 1877.
Kansas: A Guide to the Sunflower State, Federal Writers Project, New York, 1939.
Kansas Souvenir, Kansas Immigration and Information Association, Topeka, 1896.
Kansas via Missouri Pacific Railroad, Missouri Pacific Railroad, St. Louis, 1893.
Kehoe, Lawrence, ed., *The Complete Works of Most Rev. John Hughes, D. D.*, New York, 1866.
Kelly, Sister Gilbert, *Catholic Immigrant Colonization Projects in the U. S., 1815-1860*, ed. by E. F. Prendergast, New York, 1939.
Kenedy's Catholic Directory, see *Catholic Directory*.
Kenrick, Francis Patrick, *Diary and Visitation Record*, Lancaster, 1916.
Kirkfleet, Cornelius J., *Life of Patrick Augustine Feehan, 1829-1902*, Chicago, 1922.
Koch, Ludwig, *Jesuiten Lexikon: Die Gesellschaft Jesu einst und jetzt*, Paderdorn, 1934.
La Congregation de St. Joseph de Lyon (vol. I of *Les Ordres Religieux*, Letouzey et Ane, eds.), Paris, 1927.
La Grande Encyclopedie (H. Lamirault, ed.), 31 vols., Paris, n.d.
Laing, Francis S., *German-Russian Settlements in Ellis County, Kansas*, Topeka (Kans.), 1908. (*Kansas Historical Collections*, vol. XI, 1907-1908), pp. 1-40.
Lake, Sister Victoria, *History of the Sisters of St. Joseph of Wichita, Kansas, 1888-1937*, unpublished M.S. thesis, Univ. of Wichita, 1937.
Lamott, John H., *History of the Archdiocese of Cincinnati, 1821-1921*, Cincinnati, 1921.
Lanman, James H., *History of Michigan*, New York, 1839.
Larousse, Pierre, *Dictionnaire Universel*, Paris, 1873.
Lebeurier, Pierre F., *Vie de la Révérende Mère St. Joseph*, Paris, 1869; tr. by a Sister of St. Joseph, New York, 1876.
Letham, John, *Historical and Descriptive Review of Kansas*, 2 vols., Topeka, 1890.
Lockard, Francis M., *The History of the Early Settlement of Norton, Kansas*, Norton, 1903.
Lyonnet, Jean Baptiste, *Le Cardinal Fesch, Archévêque de Lyon*, Lyons, 1841.
McCoy, Joseph G., *Historic Sketches of the Cattle Trade of the West and Southwest*, Chicago, 1874; reprint, Washington, 1932.
McEvoy, Sister Assisium, tr., *Life of Mother St. John Fontbonne* (from the French by Rivaux), New York, 1887.
McGee, Thomas D'Arcy, *A History of the Irish Settlers in North America From the Earliest Period to the Census of 1850*, Boston, 1852.
McGovern, James J., *The Catholic Church in Chicago*, Chicago, 1890.
Magaret, Helene, *Father de Smet, Pioneer Priest of the Rockies*, New York, 1940.
Maher, John, *Philosophic Musings*, Salina, Kans., 1921.
Martin Sister Aquinata, *The Catholic Church on the Nebraska Frontier, 1854-1885*, Washington, 1937.
Mather, Irwin F., *The Making of Michigan*, Chicago, 1935.
Matteson, Clark S., *History of Wisconsin from Prehistoric to Present Period*, Chicago, 1893.
Mau, Clayton, *The Development of Central and Western New York from the Arrival of the White Man to the Eve of the Civil War as Portrayed Chronologically in Contemporary Accounts*, Rochester, 1944.
Maxwell-Scott, Mary Monica, *The Life of Mme de la Rochejaquelin*, London and New York, 1911.
Maynard, Theodore, *Apostle of Charity: Life of St. Vincent de Paul*, New York, 1939.
———, *Story of American Catholicism*, New York, 1941.

Melton, Elston J., *History of Cooper County, Missouri*, Columbia, Mo., 1937.
Memorial Record of the Northern Peninsula of Michigan, Chicago, 1895.
Memorial Volume: The Centenary of the St. Louis Archdiocese, St. Louis, 1918.
Memorial Volume of the Third Plenary Council of Baltimore, Baltimore, 1884.
Méthode d'Enseignement pour les Classes des Soeurs de St. Joseph, Lyons, 1832.
Metropolitan Catholic Directory, see *Catholic Directory*.
Michigan Historical Collections.
Minogue, Anna C., *Loretto, Annals of the Century*, New York, 1912.
Moeder, John M., *Early Catholicity in Kansas and the History of the Diocese of Wichita*, Wichita, 1937.
Morse, C. and M., *Charter and Directory of the City of Rochester*, Rochester, 1834.
Mourret, Ferdinand, *A History of the Catholic Church*, tr. by Newton Thompson, 6 vols., St. Louis, 1946.
Mullany, John F., *Four Score Years, 1856-1916: St. Joseph's Church*, Rochester, 1916.
———, *The Pioneer Catholic Church in New York*, Syracuse, 1897.
Nebraska: A Guide, Federal Writers Project, New York, 1939.
Neustes von Kansas und seinen Hulfquellen, New York, 1887.
Noces d'Or de la Paroisse St. Joseph, Lake Linden, Michigan, 1871-1921, Lake Linden, 1921.
Norton, John T., *The Resources of Fremont County, Wyoming*, Lander, Wyo., 1891.
Nursery, Walter R., *The City of Escanaba, Michigan*, Escanaba, 1890.
O'Brien, Joseph D., *The Exemption of Religious in Church Law*, Milwaukee, 1943.
O'Hanlon, John P., *Life and Scenery in Missouri: Reminiscences of a Missionary*, Dublin, 1890.
Orange, California: A Brief History of the Sisters of St. Joseph, Eureka, Cal., 1922.
Origin of Nebraska Place Names, Federal Writers Project, New York, 1938.
Ornsby, Robert, *The Life of St. Francis de Sales, Bishop and Prince*, New York, 1860.
Pageant of Escanaba, Michigan, Escanaba, 1916.
Papi, Hector, *Government of Religious Communities*, New York, 1919.
———, *Religious in Church Law*, New York, 1924.
———, *Religious Profession*, New York, 1918.
Pardonnet, Georges de, *Émigration au Kansas—Conseils Pratiques aux Émigrants*, Mont-belierd, 1880.
Paxson, Frederick L., *History of the American Frontier, 1763-1893*, New York, 1924.
———, *The Last American Frontier*, New York, 1910.
Payne, R., *The Leopoldine Association and Its Work in Ohio*, M.A. thesis No. 10, Univ. of Illinois (Dept. of History), 1905.
Picturesque Canandaigua, Canandaigua, N. Y., 1899.
Picturesque Iron and Copper Mining in Northern Michigan, Lake Linden, 1891.
Polk, R. L., *Abilene City Directory*, Chicago, 1926.
———, *Directory of Junction City*, Chicago, 1905.
———, *Manhattan, Riley County, Kansas, Directory*, Chicago, 1938.
———, *Salina City Directory*, Chicago, 1909.
Portrait and Biographical Record of Dickinson, Saline, McPherson and Marion Counties, Kansas, Chicago, 1893.
Portrait and Biographical Record of Kankakee, Illinois, Chicago, 1893.
Powers, Perry I., *History of Northern Michigan*, Chicago, 1900.
Prat, Ferdinand, *Le Disciple de St. Jean François Regis, notes supplementaries*, Paris, 1856.
Prentis, Noble L., *A History of Kansas*, Topeka, 1899.
Prunel, Louis N., *La renaissance catholique en France au XVII siècle*, Paris, 1921.
Quaife, Milo M., *Wisconsin: Its History and Its People, 1634-1924*, 4 vols., Chicago, 1924.
Raney, William F., *Wisconsin: A Story of Progress*, New York, 1940.
Reiffert, Sister Bernadette, *Origins of Catholicity in Richardson County, Nebraska*, unpublished M.A. thesis, Creighton Univ., 1934.
Reynolds, John, *Illinois: My Own Times*, Belleville, Ill., 1855.
Rezek, Antoine I., *History of the Diocese of Sault Ste. Marie and Marquette*, 2 vols., Houghton, Mich., 1906-1907.
Rhodes, D. William, *Churches in the History of Cincinnati and Hamilton County, Ohio*, Cincinnati, 1895.
Ricard, Abbe J., *Le Cardinal Fesch*, Paris, 1893.

Ritch, William Gillett, *Illustrated New Mexico*, New York, 1883.
Rivaux, Abbe, *Vie de la Révérende Mère St. Jean Fontbonne*, Grenoble, 1885.
———, *Histoire de la Révérende Mère Sacre Coeur*, Lyons, 1878.
Robinson, Orrin W., *Early Days of the Lake Superior Copper Country*, Houghton, Mich., 1938.
Rochejaquelin, Marquise de la, *Memoirs*, Paris, 1823; reprint, New York, 1933.
Roemer, Theodore, *The Leopoldine Society*, unpublished M.A. thesis, Catholic Univ. of America, 1933.
———, *Ten Decades of Alms*, St. Louis, 1942.
Rothensteiner, John, *History of the Archdiocese of St. Louis*, 2 vols., St. Louis, 1928.
Russell, Joseph A., *A Geographic Study of Delta County, Michigan*, Chicago, 1939.
Sadlier's Catholic Directory, see *Catholic Directory*.
St. Pierre, Telesphore, *Histoire des Canadiens de Michigan et du comte d'Essex*, Chicago, 1895.
Salina and Saline County, Kansas, Directory, Salina, 1900.
Sanders, Ella K., *St. Francis de Sales, 1567-1662*, New York, 1928.
Santa Fe, New Mexico, Publicity Bureau, *A Guide to New Mexico for the Homeseeker, Investor, Tourist, Sportsman, Healthseeker*, Santa Fe, N. M., 1917.
Sargeant, Daniel, *Our Land and Our Lady*, New York, 1939.
Savage, Sister Lucida, comp., *The Century's Harvest, 1836-1936*, St. Louis, 1936.
———, *The Congregation of St. Joseph of Carondolet*, St. Louis, 1923.
Savage, I. O., *A History of Republic County, Kansas*, Topeka, 1883.
Sawyer, Alvah L., *A History of the Northern Peninsula of Michigan and Its Peoples*, 3 vols., Chicago, 1911.
Schaefer, P. Timotheus, *De Religiosis, ad norman Juris canonici*, Munster, 1931.
Schoensteiner, Ferdinand, *Grundriss des Ordensrecht*, Wien, 1930.
Schmucker, S. M., *Fremont's Life, His Explorations and Adventures*, New York, 1856.
Schumacher, Samuel M., *Memorable Scenes in French History*, New York, 1879.
Sciout, Ludovic, *Histoire de la Constitution Civile du Clerge, 1790-1802*, Paris, 1873.
Scudder, Horace E., ed., *American Commonwealths*, 2 vols. New York 1893.
Sempe, Louis, *St. Francis de Sales*, Milwaukee, 1933.
Seven Dolors Parish, Manhattan, Kansas, Manhattan, n.d.
Shea, John Gilmary, *History of the Catholic Church in the U. S.*, 4 vols., New York, 1888.
———, *Life and Times of the Most Rev. John Carroll*, New York, 1888.
Silver City and Southwest New Mexico—Home of the World's Finest Climate, New Mexico, n.d.
Sims, William, *Kansas: Information Concerning Agriculture . . . Churches . . .*, Topeka, 1884.
Sister of St. Joseph (Brentwood, L. I.), tr., *Mother St. John Fontbonne, a Biography*, New York, 1936.
Sisters of St. Joseph: A Brief History of an Apostolic Religious Order, La Grange, Ill., 1905.
Sisters of St. Joseph (Chambery, France), *The Chronicles of the Sisters of St. Joseph of Chambery*, tr. from the French by the Sisters of St. Joseph of Hartford, Altamont, Conn., 1938.
Sisters of St. Joseph (Toronto), *Diamond Jubilee, St. Joseph's Convent*, Toronto, 1926.
Sisters of St. Joseph, Wheeling, West Virginia: Harvestings in the Diocese of Virginia, 1853-1936, Wheeling, W. Va., 1936.
Sixtieth Anniversary of the Sisters of St. Joseph in Canandaigua, N. Y., 1854-1914, Canandaigua, N. Y., 1914.
Smith, R., *Guide to the Southwest along the Missouri, Kansas and Texas Railroad*, Kansas City, 1871.
Smythe, Bryan B., *The Heart of the New Kansas*, Topeka, 1880.
Sommervogel, P. Carlos, *Bibliothèque de la Compagnie de Jésus*, 10 vols., Paris, 1894.
Souvenir of the Golden Jubilee of the Rt. Rev. Joseph Perrier, V.G., of the Diocese of Concordia, Concordia, Kans., 1913.
Souvenir of the Silver Jubilee of the Most Rev. Patrick A. Feehan, Chicago, 1891.
Souvenir of the Silver Jubilee of the Rev. H. A. Spoorenberg, St. John the Baptist Church, Clyde, Kansas, Concordia, Kans. 1933.

Stolley, Wilhelm, *Geschichte der Ersten Anseidlung von Hall County im Nebraska con 1859 mit Anhang bis zum Jahre 1907,* Omaha, 1907.
Stritch, A., *Nativism in Cincinnati,* M.A. thesis, Catholic Univ., 1935.
Stuart, Henry, *Conquering Our Great American Plains,* New York, 1930.
Swemberg, Felix P., *Catholic Colonization in Kansas* (St. Dominic Colonization Society of the City of New York), New York, 1880.
Thomas, Sister Evangeline, *Nativism in the Old Northwest,* Washington, 1936.
Thwaites, Reuben G., *Wisconsin: The Americanization of a French Settlement,* Chicago, 1908.
Timon, Bishop John, *Missions in Western New York,* Buffalo, 1862.
Triggs, J. H., *History and Directory of Laramie City, Wyoming Territory,* Laramie, Wyo., 1875.
Turner, Frederick J., *Rise of the New West, 1819-1829* (vol. 14, American Nation Series), New York, 1906.
————, *The Significance of the Frontier in American History,* New York, 1894.
Turner, John, *Pioneers of the West,* Lincoln, Neb., 1903.
Twitchell, Ralph E., *Leading Facts of New Mexico History,* 5 vols., Cedar Rapids, Iowa, 1911-1917.
United States Catholic Almanac, 1833-1837, 1843-1847, 1853, 1859, 1860.
Venable, William H., *Beginnings of Literary Culture in the Ohio Valley,* Cincinnati, 1891.
Vine Clad City—Boonville, Missouri, St. Louis, 1900.
Waldron, Nell Blythe, *Colonization in Kansas, 1861-1890,* Ph.D. dissertation, Northwestern Univ., 1932, mss. in Kansas State Historical Society Library, Topeka, Kans.
Walker, F. A., *Discussion of Economics and Statistics,* 2 vols., New York, 1897.
Weston, K. W., *Guide to the Kansas Pacific Railroad for 1872,* Chicago, 1872.
Wetzer and Welte, *Kirchen Lexikon,* 2d ed., Freiburg, 1893.
Wheeler, Mabel Ranney, *The German Element and Development of Kansas,* unpublished M.A. thesis, Univ. of Kansas, 1920.
Wiltzius' Catholic Directory, see *Catholic Directory.*
Wittke, Carl, *We Who Built America,* New York, 1939.
Woods, Alfred E., ed., *Picturesque City—Clinton, Missouri,* Kansas City, Mo., 1896.
Young, A. A., *Report on Immigration,* New York 1872.
Zwierlein, Frederick J., *Life and Letters of Bishop McQuaid,* 3 vols., Rochester, 1925-1927.

B. ARTICLES

"American Civilization Comes to the Old Northwest," by B. Bond, *Mississippi Valley Historical Review,* vol. XIX (1932-1933).
"Archbishop Feehan," by Richard J. Purcell, *Catholic Historical Review,* vol. VIII (1923).
"Beloit's First Parochial School Opened by Germans in 1878," *Northwestern Kansas Register,* spec. ed., May 5, 1940.
"The Best Thing in Town," by Grace Alexandra Young, *Saturday Evening Post,* Sept. 14, 1946.
"Biographies of Bishops of Concordia Given," *Northwestern Kansas Register,* spec. ed., Nov. 20, 1938.
"Bishop McQuaid of Rochester," by Frederick J. Zweirlein, *Catholic Historical Review,* vol. V (1920).
"Bishop Thill Has Had Outstanding Career," *Northwestern Kansas Register,* souvenir ed. on installation of Most Rev. Frank A. Thill as Bishop of Concordia, Nov. 20, 1938.
"Bishop Tief Founded *Register,*" *Northwestern Kansas Register,* Nov. 20, 1938.
"Bohemians in Central Kansas," by Francis J. Swekla, *Kansas Historical Collections,* vol. XIII (1909-1910).
"Catholic Church and Schools of Saline County," by Prosper Maurer, Mar. 3, 1884, ISA 3, Clipping No. 1, Kansas State Historical Society Library, Topeka, Kans.
"Catholic Colonization as Actually Established," *Catholic World,* vol. XXIX (1879).
"The Celebration of a Century of Service of the Sisters of St. Joseph of Carondolet," *St. Louis News,* suppl., July 3, 1936.

"Centenary of St. Joseph Nuns in St. Louis Recalls Coming of First Nuns to Canandaigua," by Waldemer J. Isaac, *Catholic Courier*, Mar. 19, 1936.

"Colonization of the West," by Frederick J. Turner, *American Historical Review*, vol. XI (1906).

"Court House Scene of First Mass in Clinton, Mo.," by Sister Evangeline Thomas, *Kansas City Catholic Register*, Apr. 14, 1925.

"Diocesan Sodality Has Ninety-one Branches," *Northwestern Kansas Register*, Nov. 20, 1938.

"Dominant Forces in Western Life," by Frederick J. Turner, *Atlantic Monthly*, vol. LXXIX (1892).

"Early Catholicity in Chicago," by Gilbert J. Garraghan, *Illinois Catholic Historical Review*, vol. I (1919).

"Early Day Leoville Students Were Taught in Sod Building," *Northwestern Kansas Register*, May 5, 1940.

"Early Religious Methods and Leaders in Illinois," by W. F. Short, *Illinois State Historical Soc. Publications*, vol. VII (1902).

"Early Settlers of Victoria Worshiped at Wooden Crosses," *Northwestern Kansas Register*, Nov. 20, 1938; *Kansas City Times*, July 25, 1938.

"Educational Aims of the New College," by Sister Louise Cuff, *Salina Daily Union*, June 4, 1922; *Kansas City Catholic Register*, June 8, 1922.

"Emigration," by Felix P. Swemberg, *Catholic Review*, Mar. 15, 1879.

"The European Exodus," *Catholic World*, vol. XXV (1877).

"First Masses in Beloit Offered in Store Hall," *Northwestern Kansas Register*, spec. ed., Nov. 20, 1938.

"The First Parish School Begun in 1879," *Northwestern Kansas Register*, May 21, 1939.

"First Record of Beginning of Junction City Church, June 1861," *Northwestern Kansas Register*, spec. ed., Nov. 20, 1938.

"First School in Aurora District Was in Elm Creek on the Present Site of the Cemetery," *Northwestern Kansas Register*, spec. ed., May 5, 1940.

"The German Element in the U. S.," *Catholic World*, vol. XXV (1877).

"Golden Jubilee of the Wichita Diocese," *Catholic Advance*, golden jubilee suppl., 1937.

"Historical Sketch of the Sisters of St. Joseph of Wichita, Kansas," by Sister Victoria Lake, *Wichita Catholic Advance*, golden jubilee suppl., 1937; *Wichita Eagle*, Oct. 17, 1937.

"History of Cloud County, Kansas," by J. M. Hageman, *Concordia Blade Annual*, 1884.

"Home for the Aged Built in 1923," *Northwestern Kansas Register*, spec. ed., Nov. 20, 1938.

"The House of Silence," by Daniel A. Lord, *Queen's Work*, Apr., 1920.

"How the Germans Became Americans," by E. Bruncken, *Proceedings of the Wisconsin Historical Society*, 1898.

"Illinois Correspondence," *Home Missionary*, vol. XXVIII (Nov., 1854).

"Immigrants and Social Amelioration," by J. Schafer, *Norwegian-American Historical Assoc., Studies and Records*, vol. IV (1917).

"The Influence of the Frontier in American History," by Frederick J. Turner, *Proceedings of the Wisconsin Historical Society*, 1893.

"Jesuits First Served Needs of Faithful in Salina," *Northwestern Kansas Register*, spec. eds., Nov. 20, 1938; May 21, 1939.

"John Ireland," by John F. Carr, *The Outlook*, Apr. 24, 1908.

"Junction City School Teachers for Thirty-five Years Laywomen," *Northwestern Kansas Register*, May 5, 1940.

"Leopoldine Association," by Antoine I. Rezek, *Catholic Encyclopedia*, vol. XVI.

"Local Hospital Chaplain Founded Monett Parish," *Kansas City Catholic Register*, Aug. 6, 1925.

"Manhattan Founded as a Methodist Center," *Northwestern Kansas Register*, Nov. 20, 1938.

"Marymount is Distinctive Girls' Center," *Northwestern Kansas Register*, May 5, 1939.

"Monsignor Maher's Contribution to Growth of the Diocese Recalled," by Sister Evangeline Thomas, *Northwestern Kansas Register*, May 21, 1939.

"Monsignor Vornholt Served as Administrator," *Northwestern Kansas Register*, Nov. 20, 1938.

"Mother Mary Rose Waller Dies in Concordia," by Sister Evangeline Thomas, *Northwestern Kansas Register*, Mar. 27, 1941; *Eastern Kansas Register*, Mar. 30, 1941; *Fairbury News*, Mar. 27, 1941; *Salina Advertiser*, Mar. 27, 1941; *Salina Journal*, Mar. 22, 1941; *Western American*, Apr. 5, 1941.

"Nativism in the 'Forties and 'Fifties with Special Reference to the Mississippi Valley" by George M. Stevenson, *Mississippi Valley Historical Review*, vol. IX (1922).

"Nazareth Academy, Concordia, Kansas," *The Voice of St. Peter's Church, Aurora, Kansas*, 1920.

"Norwegians in the West in 1844: A Contemporary Account," by J. R. Reiersen, *Norwegian-American Historical Assoc., Studies and Records*, vol. I (1920-1921).

"Nuns Find Happiness in Cloistered Life Behind Convent Walls," by Bernice D. Burnett, *Concordia Kansan*, Dec. 12, 1935.

"Nursing School Conducted by the Sisters of St. Joseph," *Northwestern Kansas Register*, May 5, 1940.

"Original Catholics in Concordia Were French," *Northwestern Kansas Register*, spec. ed., Nov. 20, 1938.

"Pioneer Piety," by R. Payne, *Michigan Pioneer Collections*, vol. XIII (1888).

"Plenary Councils and Catholic Schools," by A. J. Emerick, *America*, vol. XXXIII (1925).

"The Problem of the West," by Frederick J. Turner, *Atlantic Monthly*, vol. LXXVIII (1891).

"Rev. Valentine Sommereisen, Pioneer Priest of the West," by John M. Lenhart, *Central-Blatt and Social Justice*, vol. XXIX (1936-1937).

"Rt. Rev. John B. Miege, S.J., First Catholic Bishop of Kansas," by James A. McGonigle, *Kansas State Historical Society Collections*, vol. IX (1905-1906).

"Rt. Rev. John Dubois," by C. G. Hebermann, *U. S. Catholic Historical Records and Studies*, vol. I, pt. II (Jan. 1900).

"Rt. Rev. Joseph Perrier, 1839-1917," *The Voice of St. Peter's Church, Aurora, Kans.*, 1917.

"Rosati's Elevation to the See of St. Louis," by Charles L. Souvay, *Catholic Historical Review*, vol. III (1917).

"Sacred Heart Academy, Manhattan, Was First Catholic High in Diocese," *Northwestern Kansas Register*, May 5, 1940.

"Sacred Heart Parish—Pioneers of Vision Established Salina," *Northwestern Kansas Register*, May 21, 1939.

"Sacred Heart School, Salina, First Had Classes in Tiny House," *Northwestern Kansas Register*, May 5, 1939.

"St. Joseph Nuns Mark Sixty Years in Diocese," by Sister Evangeline Thomas, *Northwestern Kansas Register*, Nov. 5, 1944.

"St. John's Hospital, Salina, Has Trained Nurses Since 1921," *Northwestern Kansas Register*, May 5, 1939.

"St. Joseph's Home Founded in 1887," *Northwestern Kansas Register*, spec. ed., Nov. 20, 1938.

"St. Joseph's Hospital in Concordia Offers Thorough Nurses Training," *Northwestern Register*, May 21, 1939.

Kansas Register, May 5, 1940.

"Salina Eighty Years Old," *Kansas City Star*, Mar. 13, 1938.

"Salina Founded by Colonel Phillips, New York Journalist, March, 1858," by Marion Klema, *Northwestern Kansas Register*, spec. ed., May 21, 1939.

"The Scandinavian Element in the American Population" by Kendric C. Babcock, *American Historical Review*, vol. XVI (1911).

"The Scandinavian Element in the United States," by Kendric C. Babcock, *Illinois Univ. Studies in Social Science*, vol. III (1914).

"Selection of Immigration," by P. F. Hall, *Annals of the Amer. Academy of Political and Social Science*, July, 1904.

"The Settlement of Illinois from 1830-1850," by W. V. Pooley, *Univ. of Wisconsin Bulletin, History Series*, vol. I (1909).

"Short Sketch of Salina, Kansas," *Northwestern Kansas Register*, May 21, 1939.

"Sister Recounts History of the St. Joseph Community," by Sister Evangeline Thomas, *Northwestern Kansas Register*, Nov. 20, 1938.

"The Sisters of St. Joseph," by Adam C. Ellis, *Queen's Work*, May, 1918.

"The Sisters of St. Joseph," *Catholic Chronologist*, vol. II (1914).

"The Sisters of St. Joseph in Minnesota," by Sister Ignatia Loyola Cox, *Acta et Dicta,* 1914.

"Sisters of St. Joseph, Rochester, New York," *Catholic Courier,* golden jubilee issue, 1939.

"Sisters of St. Joseph, Wichita, Kansas," *Wichita Catholic Advance,* suppl., May, 1937; Mar. 5, 1940, souvenir issue of installation of the Most Rev. C. H. Winkelmann.

"Speaking of Kansas," by Frederick Simplich, *Nat. Geographic Magazine,* vol. LXXII, No. 2 (Aug., 1937).

"Thousands Attended Marymount Dedication at Salina in 1922," *Northwestern Kansas*

"Vacation Schools Were Begun Early," *Northwestern Kansas Register,* Nov. 20, 1938.

"Very Rev. Louis Mollier," by Prosper Maurer, *The Voice of St. Peter's Church, Aurora, Kans.,* 1917.

"A Woman Builder," by Sister Evangeline Thomas, *Marymount College Bulletin,* vol. XXIV, No. 3 (Oct., 1947).

"Yankee and Teuton," by J. Schafer, *Wisconsin Magazine of History,* vol. VII (1908).

"Young People Don't Leave California, Missouri, Parish," *Kansas City Catholic Register,* Jan. 15, 1925.

INDEX

Index